Firm Foundations

Creation to Christ

By

Trevor McIlwain

with
Nancy Everson

New Tribes Mission, Sanford FL 32771-1487

© 1991 New Tribes Mission. All rights reserved.

Fourth printing, June 1993
Manufactured in Mexico

Dedication

This book is dedicated, with deep thanksgiving, to our Lord Jesus Christ and to His Church, with believing prayer that He will use His Word:

To bring men and women and children to Himself;

To build up and strengthen individual believers and His Church;

To raise up Bible teachers who will go and teach others, who will in turn teach others, who will also teach others...

"...that they may know thee the only true God, and Jesus Christ, whom thou hast sent"

(John 17:3).

IMPORTANT
NOTE TO TEACHERS:

To effectively use the lessons in this book,

READ AND STUDY PART 1 AND PART 2
before you begin
studying and teaching
the lessons themselves.

■

SUBSTITUTE TEACHERS:
Please see note on p. 72.

If you have time, also read and study
Part 1 and Part 2 of this book.

■

**PASTORS AND
SUNDAY SCHOOL SUPERINTENDENTS:**
Please see note on p. 72.

Even though you may not be the one teaching this material, please read Part 1 and Part 2 of this book, which explain the teaching rationale used in the lessons.

Firm Foundations—Creation to Christ
was adapted from the
Building on Firm Foundations Series
by Trevor McIlwain.

The original *Building on Firm Foundations* series by Trevor McIlwain was written primarily for church planters ministering among tribal people. Because of the great interest and demand for foundational, chronological teaching among a wide variety of people in modern societies, the evangelistic phase of these original lessons has been adapted into this course, *Firm Foundations—Creation to Christ*.

Part 1 of this book contains essentially the same material as Volume I of *Building on Firm Foundations*.

Part 2, "How to Use These Lessons," is changed substantially from the similar section in the beginning of Volume II of the original series. These changes reflect many considerations, such as teaching students who have their own Bibles, teaching in various environments—home, church, etc., and teaching different types of groups: large and small; believers, unbelievers, and mixed groups.

Part 3, the Lessons, have been adapted from the original lessons for tribal people in Volumes II and III, referred to as "Phase I" of the original Chronological Teaching Outline. (In this book, Phase I is referred to as the "evangelistic phase.") Many considerations were incorporated into these adaptations with the hope that the teacher will be adequately prepared to teach and respond to students who may have had varying degrees of exposure to the Scriptures.

The original *Building on Firm Foundations* series is still available from New Tribes Mission, Sanford FL 32771. Please see p. 70 for a more detailed explanation of the series.

Contents

Acknowledgements viii

Foreword ix

Part 1   Firm Foundations—
Building According to Plan   1

The Master Builder's Plan 3

Check the Foundations 7

People Unprepared for the Gospel 17

Foundations for the Gospel 23

Divine Building Principles 31

Building Chronologically in Evangelism . . . 39

Correct Foundations for Teaching Believers . 49

Part 2   How To Use This Bible Study   61

Practical Questions and Answers 65

Special Note 72

Guidelines for the Teacher 73

Specific Instructions About the Lessons . . . 85

Part 3   The Lessons   91

Lessons 1-50 97-582

Acknowledgements

This book is the result of a team effort, done with much prayer and dependence upon our Lord Jesus Christ.

The Research and Planning Department of New Tribes Mission has given direction, encouragement, and oversight since the inception of this project.

The following list includes some of the individuals who have made major contributions to this book:

Dick Sollis and Don Pederson — project direction and editing.

Ruth Bean — editing.

John R. Cross — special help in adapting these lessons for use with English-speaking audiences

Frances McIlwain, Lillian Sheffield, and Irene Lewis — proofreading

Gideon Bader — expediting and encouraging

Dave and Nita Zelenak, and Sharron Moseley — promotion

Phil Sutton and Doug Lotz — technical help with the computer

Dave Lewis — design consulting

Sharron Moseley and Dale Yap — cover design

Keith and Lin Higbee — cover photo

Special thanks to the Executive Committee of New Tribes Mission — Macon Hare, Dave Calderwoood, Dean VanVliet, Tom Bennett, Mel Wyma, Harold Jackson, Les Pederson, and Duane Stous.

Many, many others have had a part through their prayers, concern, good advice, and many other kinds of help. Thank you, all!

Foreword

You have in your hands a meticulously designed set of Bible lessons. The approach is unique. Each of the fifty lessons, while individually crafted, is part of the whole. Drafted from the Old and New Testaments, they join together—as beautiful pieces of a complex mosaic—to reveal God's marvelously conceived plan of salvation from Genesis to our Lord's ascension in the Gospels.

Beginning with God's miracles of creation in Genesis and continuing through select portions of the biblical narrative, the lessons reveal basic scriptural themes. These themes, used of the Holy Spirit, display the divine, incomparable logic of God's plan of salvation. The Gospel is powerfully presented within the revealed foundational context of His plan of the ages.

The lessons are well designed and the teaching approach is well tested. Adapted for other languages and cultures, Trevor McIlwain's original lesson materials have already been used in many countries by missionaries, pastors, teachers, and laymen.

The biblical foundation, so clearly defined and presented, is fundamental for all subsequent Christian life and ministry.

Richard D. Sollis
New Tribes Mission

Part 1

Firm Foundations — Building According to Plan

Part 1

Firm Foundations—

Building According to Plan

The Master Builder's Plan	3
Check the Foundations	7
People Unprepared for the Gospel	17
Foundations for the Gospel	23
Divine Building Principles	31
Building Chronologically in Evangelism	39
Correct Foundations for Teaching Believers	49

The Master Builder's Plan

With a thunderous sound, the walls cracked and crumbled. Timbers splintered. The roof buckled and fell into pieces. Floor after floor crashed one upon another, crushing, trapping, killing the tenants. In a few moments, the high-rise apartments were reduced to rubble.

How had the disaster happened? The building looked sturdy. Why would it suddenly collapse?

Subsequent investigations proved that the builder had not followed the proper building specifications and plans. Willing to gamble with the lives and the safety of human beings for the sake of money, he had cut corners and economized on every part of the building.

The depth of the concrete had been reduced, and not all of the steel reinforcements required for the foundations had been laid down. Thus, the foundations were inadequate for the height and the weight of the building. The walls and floors lacked the necessary steel rods to hold and strengthen the building.

The builder had disregarded the instructions which had been given to him. He had followed his own way because it was easier and quicker and brought him greater profit.

The results? Sorrow! Destruction! Death!

Just as this builder carelessly ignored construction standards and specifications, many Christians all over the world carelessly disregard the Master Builder's plans for building His Church.

In most instances, mass evangelism and personal evangelism, as well as the preaching and teaching of the Word of God, is not being done according to the biblical plans given to the Church by the Divine Architect. Many who are engaged in the work of building the Church are so engrossed in their own ideas and schemes that they do not stop to consider if they are working according to God's divine directions or whether their work will pass His final scrutiny.

God is the Builder of His Church (Matthew 16:18). But He has chosen His earthly children to be laborers together with Him (I Corinthians 3:9). The Christian's work in building the Church is similar to that of a building contractor. Just as a contractor is responsible to follow exactly the plans given to him by the owner of a building, so we are responsible to follow God's plans for building His Church.

> Many Christians disregard the Master Builder's plans for building His Church.

God is the true builder of all things. *"For every house is builded by some man; but he that built all things is God"* (Hebrews 3:4). God builds everything according to His eternal plans. He will not change. He will never accommodate man's ideas or go with the times. He will never permit any change in the specifications which He has laid down for all that He has planned to do in what we call "time." His work always has adequate foundations, and He builds carefully, patiently, and precisely. He refuses to take short cuts in anything He does, and He never uses inferior materials or methods which are contrary to His holy and perfect nature.

The first account in Scripture of God's building work is when He created the heavens and the earth. *"By the word of the LORD were the heavens made; and all the host of them by the breath of his mouth....For he spake, and it was done; he commanded, and it stood fast"* (Psalm 33:6,9). God was the Creator Builder of all things, seen and unseen. Satan's lie, the theory of evolution, foisted on foolish, unbelieving man, is contrary to the nature and character of God. Nothing is left to chance with God. He is always in full and complete control of all His works. Everything was created according to His perfect plan, and He declared that it was all good (Genesis 1:31).

Later in the Scriptures, we have the account of God's command to Noah to build an ark. But God did not command Noah to build the ark and then leave

Noah to formulate his own plans. God told Noah exactly what must be done; and Noah, God's faithful workman, did everything just as the Lord commanded him (Genesis 6:22).

When God chose to dwell with Israel, He commanded Moses to build the tabernacle. And how was Moses to build it? *"...See, saith he, that thou make all things according to the pattern shewed to thee in the mount"* (Hebrews 8:5). Every detail, from the silver sockets which were the foundations for the boards of the tabernacle to the outer coverings of badger skins, was to be made exactly according to the divine pattern shown to Moses on Mount Sinai. Scripture assures us that Moses was faithful to Him that appointed him (Hebrews 3:2). Only on one account is it recorded that Moses was careless and did not obey the clear command of the Lord. For striking, instead of speaking to the rock, he was banned from entering the promised land (Numbers 20:7-12). How important it is to do all things according to God's plan!

God's work of building the heavens and the earth was done by the power of His Word. Noah and Moses followed the Word of God in all that they built. God's present work of building His Church is also being accomplished through His mighty Word. *"For God, who commanded the light to shine out of darkness, hath shined in our hearts, to give the light of the knowledge of the glory of God in the face of Jesus Christ"* (II Corinthians 4:6).

The building of the universe was the work of God alone. He did not use any angelic or human agent. But the great work of building the Church, like the work of building the ark and the tabernacle, has been committed to His children. *"...we have this treasure in earthen vessels..."* (II Corinthians 4:7). *"...we are ambassadors for Christ..."* (II Corinthians 5:20). *"...ye shall be witnesses unto me...unto the uttermost part of the earth"* (Acts 1:8). God has chosen to bring His Church to completion through the teaching of His Word by the members of the Church.

If the ark and the tabernacle had to be built exactly according to God's plan, should not the Church also be built according to His plan? Surely the Bride of Christ is of even greater importance than the ark or the tabernacle. The use for the ark came to an end, and the tabernacle was superseded by the temple, but the Church is to last for eternity. Therefore, *"If any man defile the temple of God, him shall God destroy; for the temple of God is holy, which temple ye are"* (I Corinthians 3:17).

Every man's work, in relationship to the building of the Church, will be tried by fire. It will all come under the scrutinizing gaze of the Great Master Builder whose servants and co-laborers we are. *"For we are labourers together with God..."* and must therefore be wise, taking careful note to see if we are doing our work as He has commanded (I Corinthians 3:9-23).

Paul refers to himself as a wise masterbuilder (I Corinthians 3:10). He laid the foundations of the Gospel on which the Corinthians' faith and hope were built, and he warned the Bible teachers in Corinth to be careful what they built on those biblical foundations which he had laid (I Corinthians 15:1-4).

By what standard did Paul judge his own building methods and work and conclude that he was a wise masterbuilder? How can all subsequent builders be sure that they are proceeding in the correct way and that their work will meet with divine approval? Has God only told us what to teach in His Word, or has He also shown us how to teach? How can we be sure that the foundations we lay, on which others are to rest their faith, will see them safely into Heaven and stand firm in the great day of testing? How can we be certain that we have taught God's children everything that God wants them to know? What checklist shall we use to determine if we are making headway and whether the building is being brought to completion in accordance with the divine plan? How can church planters know if they have done all that they should have done? These questions gripped my mind and guided my search when, as a new missionary, I was responsible to lay the foundations of the Gospel and build up the individual members of the body of Christ in a remote island of the Philippines. Years passed before I understood the answers to these questions. Why did it take so long? Because my mind was captivated by traditional Bible teaching methods. The answers I needed were finally found through looking to God's Word alone.

After my prayers had been answered and the Lord had shown me the teaching principles which He has used and illustrated throughout His entire Word, He then opened opportunities for me to share these principles with others who were also searching. In 1980, I taught a seminar for missionaries in the Philippines. These biblical teaching principles excited and gripped the hearts of many missionaries who were struggling with problems identical to those I once faced in evangelism and church planting. These missionaries returned to their work with fresh enthusiasm, for they now had clearer guidelines and precise goals for their teaching ministry.

Seminars were also held in Bolivia, Indonesia, Papua New Guinea, Senegal, Thailand, and the United States. These initial seminars majored on evangelism, and as missionaries returned to their work and began to follow biblical guidelines for evangelism, there were immediate and lasting results. Firm foundations for saving faith were laid down by teaching a chronological overview of the Bible story, beginning in Genesis and concluding with the ascension of Christ. Many native people from various tribal groups have come to a clear understanding of God's nature and character, their own sinfulness, helplessness, and hopelessness, and Christ's all-sufficient saving work through His death, burial, and resurrection. Their understanding of God's plan of salvation and the certainty of their faith far surpassed that of many others who had professed conversion previously. Furthermore, through this chronological teaching, many sincere tribal people, who had previously professed Christianity, came to realize that they had misunderstood the missionaries' message when they were taught previously and are now trusting in a message which they clearly understand.

One of the first reports of great blessing came from Bob Kennell and George Walker. They had followed these scriptural methods when teaching the story of the Bible to the primitive and previously untouched Bisorio tribe in the Sepik region of Papua New Guinea. The Bisorio people responded to a message which they clearly understood from the Scriptures. Theirs is no blind faith, based merely on what the white man said. Instead, it is based on a clear understanding of the God of the Bible and the history of redemption.

Which is the clearest, most simple, and yet most comprehensive method of teaching the Word of God to prepare people for the Gospel and to teach them God's way of salvation? How should we teach in order to build up God's children and lead them into a knowledge of the whole counsel of God? These questions should be of great importance to us, whether we are seminary professors, pastors, missionaries, Bible class leaders, Sunday school teachers, youth workers, or concerned parents wishing to see our children taught the Word of God.

Christ and His Gospel are the only foundations which God has ordained as a basis for the faith of guilty sinners (I Corinthians 3:11, 15:1,2). But there is great confusion even among Christians regarding these foundations and the correct way to establish them through preaching God's Word.

In the construction of any building, the foundations are the first part of the structure to be prepared. The majority of Gospel preaching, however, is usually done with very little foundational preparation. This lack has contributed to a multitude of false professions and the uncertainty of many new Christians about the foundations of their faith.

Another obvious mistake in Christian education has been the failure to teach the Bible consistently as one book, just as God has prepared it for us through progressive revelation. Teaching outlines are carefully devised and prepared, but we rarely stop to consider that the Bible has already been prepared for us with an inbuilt teaching outline which, if followed, will give us a clear, uncomplicated, comprehensive coverage of the entire Word of God.

We usually approach the Bible as if it were a treasure chest full of beautiful, precious gems. We assume that these jewels have not been given any definite pattern or design and think that the responsibility is ours to arrange them in some order which will enhance their beauty and cause them to be better appreciated. While we recognize the value of the Scriptures, we presume that there is no definite, divinely-given teaching outline which runs through the entire Word of God. Having made this deduction, we then proceed to arrange the Scriptures into what we consider to be comprehensive and lucid outlines. This is a basic mistake made by many Bible teachers. Too much time is spent developing methods and theories for Bible teaching, and insufficient time is given to simply teaching the Scriptures as they have been written.

The majority of Christian teaching emphasizes individual doctrines of the Bible rather than presenting the Bible as one complete, interdependent revelation of God. Heresies, misinterpretation and overemphasis of certain Scriptures, and denominationalism can, in most cases, be traced to this lack of chronological and panoramic Bible teaching.

After many years of listening to non-sequential, topical, doctrinal sermons, most of which are based on

> Even a faithful Sunday school pupil is unlikely to graduate with an overall knowledge of the Bible.

isolated texts, many church members still do not know the Bible as one book. Often repeated verses and some doctrines may be known; but the Scriptures, according to their divinely-given historical structure, are seldom understood.

This is equally true in most Sunday schools. Children are usually taught stories from the Bible out of chronological order, and large portions of God's Word are never taught to them at all. Even a faithful Sunday school pupil is unlikely to graduate with an overall knowledge of the Bible.

Foreign missionaries have not usually been any wiser when teaching the Scriptures to people without any previous Bible knowledge. Few changes are made to the methods used in the homeland. Insufficient time is generally given to teach the Old Testament background and foundations for the Gospel. Syncretism of heathen and Christian beliefs is often the sad result. Many in foreign lands who have professed Christianity do not understand the Gospel and the Scriptures as one book. Many missionaries are so eager to preach the Gospel that they feel it is an unnecessary waste of time to teach tribal people too much of the historical portions of the Old Testament Scriptures. Nevertheless, these Old Testament historical sections form the basis for a clear understanding of the coming of Christ and the necessity of His death, burial, and resurrection. The Old Testament Scriptures, correctly taught, will prepare the heart of the believing sinner to receive the Gospel in true repentance and faith.

The following chapters record my frustrations, my search, and also my joy at discovering divine teaching principles and guidelines in the Word of God as well as a clear, simple, yet comprehensive way to teach the Scriptures to the unsaved and to the children of God.

Through my own experiences, but more importantly, on the basis of the truth of God's Word, I will endeavor to show that the Scriptures were progressively revealed by God within the context and framework of history; and, therefore, the best way to teach divine truth in any culture is God's way, within the chronological and historical framework of the Scriptures.

Check the Foundations

The Palawano tribe, living on the island of Palawan in the southwestern region of the Philippines, was downtrodden for centuries.

The proud, fierce Moslems who lived on the smaller islands lying off the coast of Palawan oppressed these timid, fearful jungle people for many years. Numerous stories, now part of Palawano folklore, tell of the massacres and molestations of the Palawano tribal people by the marauding Moslem sea warriors, called Moros.

Yet another oppression for the Palawanos came from some of the Filipino settlers who migrated from other islands of the Philippines. They came seeking land for rice fields and coconut plantations, and timber from the virgin forests for export. Many of these settlers took advantage of the native people of Palawan. They found that these unassuming, uneducated jungle people were easily intimidated. Through fear of these aggressive new settlers, many Palawanos left their ancestral lands and coconut plantations close to the sea for the less hospitable foothills and mountains of the island.

Then came a time of even greater sadness and testing. Their island home was invaded by the Japanese. This was a fearful era in the Palawanos' history. Women were molested, and children were brutally killed. Livestock was stolen and killed. Rice, their basic food, was often deliberately and maliciously scattered by the invaders as they knocked down the Palawanos' granaries. The suffering of these years surpassed all other segments of their inglorious history.

Then came an unexpected reprieve from their fear and degradation. The U.S.A. liberation forces landed in Palawan. In all my years with the Palawano people, I heard only praise and admiration for these soldiers, never one word of reproach. While visiting in the homes of the tribal people, many of the older Palawano men asked me if I knew some particular officer by whom they had been befriended. They spoke of them with great affection. They obviously enjoyed remembering incidents when the "Amirikans" had warned the national Filipinos not to ill-treat the Americans' "little Palawano brothers." The Palawanos saw it as a sad day when the U.S. forces withdrew from Palawan and their future became uncertain once again.

Years passed, and then, quite unexpectedly for the Palawanos, another American came to their part of the island. He was even more generous than all the other Americans they had known previously. Meanness and anger are frowned on in Palawano society. This missionary displayed love and kindness. Through his ministry and the ministry of the missionaries who followed him, several thousand Palawanos professed conversion, were baptized, and organized into indigenous churches.

When we arrived years later, we questioned the Palawanos as to why they had so readily submitted to baptism. One man answered, "We would have done anything for that first missionary. If he had asked us to cut our fingers off, we would have gladly done it for him."

The danger always exists that previously rejected and exploited people will respond to the Christian missionary's message, not because they see their real need as sinners and understand the Gospel, but because of genuine appreciation for the missionary and a longstanding desire to escape their difficult and degraded sociological conditions. This was the major reason for the "people movement" to Christianity which took place almost immediately when the first New Tribes missionary preached to the Palawanos.

Confusion regarding the Gospel

Following this major people movement to Christianity, more missionaries arrived to assist in the work. They faithfully taught the duties of believers to those who had professed conversion. Unbeknown to the missionaries, the majority of the Palawano church

> Obviously missing was praise to God for their salvation by Christ through His unmerited favor alone.

members were interpreting the responsibilities of believers in the only way that they could as unsaved people. They thought the duties of the believer were the things they must do so they could continue to be "in God." "In God" was the term they generally used to describe their conversion to Christianity. They had come "into God" by their acceptance of Christ through faith, baptism, church attendance, singing, prayer, not stealing, and not committing adultery. For the truly dedicated, abstinence from alcohol, betel nut, and tobacco were also understood as being necessary to guarantee their continued position "in God."

During their church meetings, they sometimes spoke of Christ and His death; but more frequently, they testified of their faithfulness to the Lord by abstaining from sinful works and by church attendance. Obviously missing was praise to God for their salvation by Christ through His unmerited favor alone. Even though salvation by faith through grace alone had been taught, the majority had not clearly understood. They were trusting in a mixture of grace and works.

In spite of the emphasis on Christian living, many failed to live according to biblical standards. Divorce, remarriage, and drunkenness were the normal practice in the Palawanos' old way of life and continued to be major problems in all of the churches. The missionaries and the church elders were very concerned about the condition of the churches and constantly exhorted the people to lay aside these old ways and follow the new way in Christ. The wayward church members would repent and function outwardly as Christians for a while; but often, they would fall back into their old ways until they were once again challenged and "revived," starting the cycle all over again.

Even though there were the faithful ones, the Palawano church was like a building lacking the correct foundations. Large cracks appeared continually in the upper walls. The missionaries and church leaders spent their time running from church to church, trying to patch up the gaping holes. The problem, however, was in the people's basic foundational understanding and acceptance of the Gospel.

Because they had never seen their own personal sinfulness and inability to please God, they had not realized that their only hope was to trust in God's provision for all sinners through the death, burial, and resurrection of Christ. If they had trusted only in Him for God's acceptance, then their faith would have produced godliness and obedience to the commands of Scripture, not in order to obtain salvation, but as the fruit of true saving faith.

My wife and I began our work as foreign missionaries with New Tribes Mission in 1965 in the Philippines. We worked with the Palawano tribe over a period of ten years. My responsibility was to see the elders and the churches brought to maturity through further instruction from the Scriptures.

Extensive hiking over the trails with the more zealous church elders was the only way I could reach and teach the more than forty small churches scattered among the mountains and jungle. Through these visits to the Palawano churches, it soon became evident that the majority of the professing believers were confused and uncertain about the basic foundations of the Christian faith. They agreed with the necessity of Christ's death for man's salvation, but Christ's death, in the understanding of many, only secured a part of salvation. They thought the remainder would be obtained through obedience to God.

The true spiritual condition of the people became apparent as I began to question them concerning their basis for salvation. I usually began by asking, "What must a person do to be saved?"

They were often reluctant to answer, but after some encouragement and direct questioning of individuals, they would begin to respond. Some answered, "Trust in God," and some said, "Believe on Christ."

To these answers, I replied, "What if a person truly believes and puts his faith in Christ as his Saviour, but he does not attend church? Could he truly be saved?"

Many answered emphatically, "No!"

Others said, "Yes, if a person truly believes, he is saved, even if he does not attend church."

"But," I added, "What if that person is not baptized?"

Only a few were persuaded that anyone could be saved without baptism.

I then added what seemed to many to be the deciding point, "But what if that person who truly trusts in Christ were to get drunk or commit adultery? Could he really be saved?" Only a few in each congregation believed that such a person could be saved, and even they had grave doubts.

In addition to questioning, I found another method to be effective in determining what the Palawano church elders and Bible teachers believed. I would first teach them the truth and then contradict the truth by teaching error. In the Palawano culture, it is improper to contradict a teacher, because this could cause the teacher to "lose face" and become embarrassed. This, in turn, would cause the person who had contradicted the teacher to also be embarrassed. Even so, these church leaders needed to be taught to stand for God's Word, regardless of the cultural discomposure caused by confronting a teacher with the truth. False cults were increasing on the island, and these Palawano church leaders were faced with the endeavors of these false teachers to lead them and their congregations into error. I needed to be sure that these Bible teachers really understood the Gospel, that they were personally trusting only in Christ, and that they would be able to stand firm against false teachers. Of course, I only used this method after months of teaching these men. This method would not have been effective if used in the beginning of my association with the Palawano leadership. They would have verbally agreed with me in spite of what they actually believed in their hearts.

Approximately one hundred Palawano elders and teachers had gathered on one occasion for our monthly conference. I had taught for many hours from the Scriptures on salvation by grace through faith alone. Then, without warning or explanation, I began to teach faith plus works as the way of salvation. Abruptly, I pointed to one of the men and asked him, "Is what I have just said correct? Is it true that sinners are saved, not only by faith, but by their good works?"

The tribal teacher hesitated and then finally answered, "No, it is wrong. We are saved by faith alone."

Feigning surprise, I continued to question him, "Do you mean to say you are telling me, the missionary, that I am wrong?"

Hesitatingly, he said, "Yes, you are wrong."

Still not giving them any clue to my real thoughts, I turned to another man and said, "He says that what I said was wrong. Do you agree or disagree?"

He answered, "What you said was wrong."

I then asked him, "How long have you been a Christian?" His answer indicated he was a much younger Christian than I. "Oh!" I said, "I have been a Christian for many years. I have also been to Bible college. Do you still think I could be wrong?"

Again, he answered that I was wrong.

Even then, I did not show agreement or disagreement but turned to a third man and asked him what he thought. Much to my surprise, he said, "You are right!"

Thinking he had misunderstood, I repeated what I had said previously, stating that we are saved not only by faith but also by our good works.

Again, he said that my statements were correct.

I then asked him, according to my usual procedure, to give scriptural proof for his statement. To my even greater surprise, he turned to Ephesians 2:8,9. Hoping he would understand his mistake once he read these verses, I asked him to read them to all present. He did so and concluded by saying, "There it is. We are saved, not only by faith, but by our good works also."

Many of the men listening were now smiling, but I was looking to the Lord for wisdom in what to say to avoid embarrassing him.

I, therefore, asked Perfecto, for that was his name, to read Ephesians 2:8,9 once again. He did but still maintained that these verses were teaching salvation through faith plus good works. I knew to simply tell him he was wrong would not establish the truth in his mind. It was important that he see for himself what these verses actually teach.

I said to Perfecto, "Those verses do not seem to be saying what you claim they do. Read them once again very slowly to yourself so you will understand what they really mean."

While we waited, Perfecto read the verses through slowly. Finally, he looked up at me with a look of great surprise and said, "No, I am wrong! We are not saved by faith and works, but by faith alone through God's grace."

The Palawano situation which I have described is not an isolated one. Multitudes throughout the world are members of evangelical churches but have no firm biblical foundations on which they build their hope for eternal life. Illustrations could be given from many areas of the world, including our own home churches, where confusion and syncretism have occurred through the sincere, but unwise or careless, ministry of Christian workers.

From South America, Dave Brown wrote about the Guajibo churches in Colombia:

"The Guajibos have a long history of missionary activity. As early as 1650, the Jesuits made missionary trips into this territory which covers almost the entire eastern plains of Colombia. They were particularly interested in the Guajibo tribe, as it was the largest in this area (today numbering about 15,000). When the Jesuits entered the area, the Guajibos were still nomadic; but with the progress of time, they have now settled in small permanent villages. About 1958, news of a new religion called the 'Evangelical Way' began to trickle into this area. It immediately attracted widespread attention; and before long, with the arrival of more information, many began to accept this new way of life. Today, almost thirty years later, this new influence from the outside world has made its mark on the Guajibo tribe. Many native-style, thatched-roof churches can be found throughout the region with religious meetings being held regularly.

"In each locality, a semi-annual evangelical conference is held. The first one I visited was attended by 700 Indians, some having traveled as far as a three days' walk. We were the first white missionaries to visit the area; and yet, here were 700 people gathered together to sing and preach to each other. Was there really any need for us as missionaries? Was this not a New Testament church in action? It was only the assurance that God had led us here that kept us.

"With the passing of time, serious problems have come to the surface in the Guajibo church. We are finding that they never really understood the message in the first place. Even those who seem keenest have hang-ups in the fundamentals of salvation. They quote catechismal answers to questions but do not understand the substitutionary work of Christ. 'Having a form of godliness, but denying the power thereof...' (II Timothy 3:5). And so, we have been forced to look back at the mistakes and failures of the past to try to determine where we are now and to look to God for divine direction for the future."

We can readily understand and accept that people are going to believe in faith plus works for salvation in places where the Gospel is not taught. But how is it possible that church attenders and members who have been taught the Gospel still do not understand that salvation is by the grace of God alone? What is the answer? Are we missing something in our preaching?

> It is unwise to instruct people in Christian living, merely hoping they have been born again.

Shepherds should know their flock

While it is true that the Gospel can be understood and refused, there are other reasons why people can continue in evangelical churches but not be truly saved. One is because many pastors, youth leaders, missionaries, and Christian workers do not check the spiritual foundations of those whom they are teaching. Or, even when Christian workers do make the effort to find out what people are really understanding and trusting in for their salvation, they are reluctant to confront people with their true condition before God.

It was only through persistent questioning that I found out that some of the Palawano church elders and many members were ignorant of basic biblical truths and had misunderstood the way of salvation. The majority of the people had been trusting in a false message for over ten years, but the missionaries who had taught them were unaware of the misunderstanding in the people's minds. Certainly, we must be wise in questioning people; but many Christian teachers are so cautious not to offend that they rarely, if ever, find out the truth about their congregations.

Some Christian teachers think that knowing a person's spiritual condition is not their responsibility because they believe it is something which should be totally between a person and the Lord alone. But the Lord has given His people not only the responsibility to preach the Gospel to the unsaved but also the responsibility to be shepherds of the flock of God. How can we protect, strengthen, and feed the flock of God if we do not even know who are the sheep and who are the goats?

I freely admit, as one who is a missionary and Bible teacher and has served as a pastor, that it is much more comfortable to teach from the pulpit than face people on an individual basis in order to meet their real needs. Nevertheless, if we are to have an effective ministry and follow in the steps of the Chief Shepherd, we must have one-to-one contact with the flock.

The Gospels contain many accounts of our Lord Jesus' personal contacts and ministry with individuals. Three well-known encounters are Nicodemus (John 3:1-12), the Samaritan woman (John 4:1-26), and the rich young ruler (Matthew 19:16-22). In each of these encounters, Jesus made clear their true spiritual condition, and then He applied the correct spiritual remedy from the Word of God. The Apostle Paul's ministry also involved personal contact and exhortation (Acts 20:20,31; Colossians 1:28).

Throughout the mission fields which I have visited, I have found a great reluctance on the part of many missionaries to seriously undertake this important task of knowing the true spiritual condition of each person under their care. Yet, it is unwise to instruct people in Christian living, merely hoping they have been born again. If we allow mere professors to act like God's children, even though they have no genuine faith in Christ, the result will be their everlasting damnation. This was the case in the Palawano churches. The great majority of professing Palawanos did not understand the Gospel. They had been instructed to live like Christians, but many were not children of God. Had they not been alerted to their grave danger, they would have gone on in this condition to a lost eternity.

One Sunday morning, after I had been teaching the Word of God in an evangelical church in Sydney, Australia, an elderly man said to me, "I am in deep trouble. I need to speak with you." Not knowing him personally, I did not understand what type of trouble he was referring to. The next day, I visited him in his home. As I sat talking with him, he said, "Your preaching has disturbed me. I have been a member of the church for forty years, but I do not know the Saviour." Later, I learned that, even though some fellow church members had wondered if he was saved, they had never questioned him. Most presumed he was a child of God. How sad if he had not finally faced up to his true condition before God!

An elderly Palawano man who had attended meetings for months came down to visit us from his little hut on the side of the hill. As we sat talking, I asked him, "Grandfather, what are you trusting in for your acceptance by God? What is your hope?"

He replied, "Grandchild, haven't I been coming to the meetings? When you pray, I close my eyes. I try to pray. I can't read, but I try to sing." And truly he did. He used to sit right at my feet and stare up into my face as I taught God's Word. He tried to do everything as I did it. But the old man had not understood the Gospel. He thought the things done in the meeting were a ceremony or ritual to please God, in order to be accepted by Him.

I said to him, "Grandfather, if that is your hope, if you are trusting in what you are doing, then God will not accept you. When you die, you will go to Hell. God will not receive you because of these things." We continued to talk for some time about these matters before he returned home. Later, some of the people came and told me that Grandfather was angry and he was not going to come to any more meetings.

I thought, "That's good. That's a beginning. At least he now knows that attending meetings will not save him."

I began visiting Grandfather in order to teach the foundational truths of the Gospel to him personally. He listened attentively, and he did eventually begin once more to attend the meetings. But even when my wife and I moved from that area to live and teach in another place without any Gospel witness, he still had not made a clear profession of faith in Christ.

Sometime later, we returned to visit the church in the area where this old man lived. Stepping out of the Mission plane, I asked the tribal people who had run down to the airstrip to welcome us, "Is Grandfather still living?"

They said, "Yes, he is. But he is blind and crippled."

Immediately, I made my way up the hill to his little old, rickety hut and sat down with him. He was pleased that I'd come. After visiting with him for a while, I said to him, "Grandfather, you are going to leave this world very soon. What is your hope? In what are you trusting for your acceptance by God?"

He answered, "Grandchild, it is like this. When I stand before God, I am not going to say to Him that I am not a sinner. God knows that I am."

I thought, "Well, praise the Lord! He has been taught that much of God."

He continued, "I am going to say this to God, 'God, you see your Son there at your right hand? He died for me!" And then turning to me, he said, "Grandchild, won't God accept me because of Him?"

I answered, "Grandfather, He certainly will!"

Cultures and people differ. Not all cultures respond to questioning, regardless of our persistence. Nevertheless, it is important to find out what they understand and what they believe. If there is a more appropriate and cultural way to get this information than by questioning, it should be followed. But, regardless of our methods, we must ascertain the true spiritual condition of the people, for only then will we know the correct spiritual medicine they need from the Word of God.

What is the Gospel?

Yet another reason why some people in evangelical churches remain unsaved is the way in which the Gospel is presented. Many dedicated Christians present the Gospel in such a way that unsaved, unprepared people do not understand that they deserve only God's judgment, that salvation is completely God's work, and that sinners are unable to contribute anything towards their own salvation.

Romans 1:3 tells us that the Gospel is God's good news concerning His Son, Jesus Christ our Lord. It is God's assurance *"...that Christ died for our sins according to the scriptures; and that he was buried, and that he rose again the third day according to the scriptures"* (I Corinthians 15:3,4).

The Gospel is first and foremost about Christ. It is the message of the finished historical work of God in Christ. The Gospel is a work of the Godhead alone. Christ was *"...smitten of God...." "...it pleased the LORD to bruise him; he hath put him to grief...."* The Lord made *"...his soul an offering for sin..."* (Isaiah 53:4,10).

Many confuse the Gospel, God's work FOR us in Christ, with God's work IN us by the Holy Spirit. The Gospel is entirely objective. The Gospel is completely outside of ourselves. The Gospel is not about the change which needs to be made in us, and it does not take place within us. It was completed in Christ, quite apart from us, almost two thousand years ago. The Gospel is not dependent on man in any way. The Gospel is distorted when we turn people's eyes to what is to be accomplished in them. We were not and cannot be involved in any part of Christ's historical, finished, redemptive work. The sinner must be taught to look completely away from himself and trust only in Christ and His work of salvation.

The following is a portion of an article written by missionaries who are truly saved and very sincere, but the way they presented the Gospel is incorrect. In this article, they are giving an account of a conversation which they had with a tribal person. They wrote, "Every Wednesday night, we visit Biaz' parents. We read a portion from Genesis and talk about it and ask questions. One night, Biaz said, 'I am so scared because the bad is in me, and I don't want God to throw me into the fire.'"

It is clear from this quote that Biaz was a soul prepared for the Gospel. There was an acknowledgement of personal sin and a fear of God's judgment. But what was the answer of the missionaries? They told Biaz, "If you ask Jesus to throw the bad out of your liver and give you His Spirit, then you belong to Him and you don't need to be frightened any more, and you will go to Him." Instead of the missionaries telling Biaz the historical, objective message of the Gospel as God's complete provision for her sin and God's coming judgment, they turned Biaz' attention to what needed to be accomplished within. What they taught Biaz was not the Gospel.

Unscriptural terminology

We distort and confuse the Gospel in people's understanding when we try to present the Gospel using terminology which turns people's attention to what they must DO rather than outward to what God has DONE on their behalf in Christ. We should use terminology which directs repentant sinners to trust in what has been done FOR THEM through Christ, rather than directing their attention to what must be done IN THEM. "Accept Jesus into your heart." "Give your heart to Jesus." "Give your life to Jesus." "Open the door of your heart to the Lord." "Ask Jesus to wash away your sins." "Make your decision for Christ." "Ask Jesus to give you eternal life." "Ask God to save you." These modern and commonly-used phrases confuse people's understanding of the Gospel.

In our preparation of people for the Gospel, we must bring them to the point where they realize they can do nothing. But even when people do understand their inability to do anything, many evangelists, missionaries, and preachers tell enquirers things such as, "Now, you must give your heart to Jesus." Having told them they are unable to do anything, they then tell them what they must do. The result? Confusion about the Gospel! People's interest and concern is turned inward to their own experience, instead of outward to trust only in Christ's death, burial, and resurrection on their behalf.

Methods and terminology used in evangelism all over the world have so distorted the Gospel that Christians need to be taught afresh the basic fundamentals of God's saving work in Christ, so their presentation of the Gospel will be according to the Word of God. Even though many people have been saved under present evangelistic methods, many others have not clearly understood the Gospel. The message they heard so emphasized man's part in conversion that God's perfect finished work and complete provision for helpless sinners in Christ was not understood and believed.

If people's attention is directed inward to their own doing, even those who are truly saved will often lack assurance of salvation. The question will constantly arise within their hearts, "Was I sincere enough? Did I do it correctly? Did I truly receive Christ? Did I really give my heart to Jesus?"

I have taught Bible students who were concerned and confused over these issues. One day, a student came to me deeply troubled. She talked with me about her conversion. She was concerned, "Did I do it in the right way? Was I really sincere? Did I really accept Jesus into my heart?" These questions plagued her. She had finally decided that, just in case she had not "done it in the correct way," she would check with me to see what she should do.

At her conversion, she had realized she could do nothing to save herself. But the evangelist told her she must ask Jesus into her heart and give her life to Christ. From that time on, she was constantly concerned as to whether or not she had done all that she should have done. As I talked with her, I explained that it wasn't a matter of whether SHE had "done it correctly" or not, but whether the LORD JESUS CHRIST had done everything correctly on her behalf. Did He satisfy God? If so, was she trusting, not in her own doing, but in Christ's finished work on her behalf?

The Gospel is not man accepting Jesus as his Saviour, but that God accepted the Lord Jesus as the perfect and only Saviour two thousand years ago. The Gospel is not man giving his heart or his life to Jesus, but that Christ gave His life, His whole being, in the place of sinners. The Gospel is not man receiving Christ into his heart, but that God received the Lord Jesus into Heaven as the mediator of sinners. The Gospel is not Christ enthroned in the human heart, but that God enthroned the Lord Jesus at His right hand in Heaven.

Do we see the great distinction between these two messages? One is subjective and puts the emphasis on what man must do. The other is objective and puts the emphasis on what Christ has already done. The sinner is only to trust in what has already been done on his behalf. The Lord Jesus cried, *"...It is finished...."* He did it all. He took upon Himself the load of sin, the full responsibility for the sin of mankind. Because Christ paid the complete debt, God raised Him from the dead and accepted Him into Heaven. The resurrection was God's sign to all that He accepted the Lord Jesus Christ forever as the perfect Saviour. God is satisfied. Is the convicted sinner? Will he rest the whole weight of his soul's salvation on Christ's acceptance by God as the perfect Saviour? Will the sinner cease once and for all trying to do anything to save himself? Will he trust only in God's Son for salvation?

> Multitudes of mere "professors" are resting their acceptance by God on their action of going forward in response to the appeal.

There are those who would call this type of Gospel presentation, "Easy Believism." When they present the Gospel, they consider it is necessary to place before sinners the need to take up the cross and follow Jesus and the necessity of crowning Jesus Lord of their lives. Some preachers believe that, by insisting on this, they prevent people from making false professions. The answer to false professions, however, is not found in adding to the Gospel by requiring the sinner to promise to follow, obey, and suffer for Christ. There aren't any strings attached to the Gospel. The answer to true conversion does not lie in these additions; it lies in the correct preparation of the sinner's mind and heart for the Gospel. This is accomplished by the Holy Spirit as the sinner hears and understands from the Scriptures that he is lost, helpless and hopeless, and stands condemned before God, who is his righteous, holy Creator and Judge.

Dependence on external, observable actions

There is yet another serious result of this confusion regarding the presentation of the Gospel. Multitudes, whose salvation is doubtful, assure themselves of their acceptance by God because, sometime in their life, they did what the preacher told them to do. They made their decision. They went forward and did what was required of them. Even though their lives have not been changed by the power of Christ and their way of life reveals an unconverted spirit, they still take refuge in what they did. They are trusting in what they did and not in what Christ has done. Multitudes of mere "professors" are resting their acceptance by

God on their action of going forward in response to the appeal. Because much evangelistic preaching is subjective and experience-oriented, the attention of the hearers is placed on themselves and their personal response to the preaching. Christians excitedly report the salvation of little children, teenagers, and adults, taking it for granted that they have understood the Gospel and are truly converted, simply because they have displayed an outward "decision for Christ."

In most evangelical circles, it is the norm to require people to publicly indicate their decision for Christ by raising their hand, standing, or walking to the front of the building, and praying a prayer of acceptance of Christ. The majority of Gospel preachers and Christians place so much emphasis on the "invitation" and people's outward response, that many Christians are now convinced that it is an integral and vital part of the ministry of the Church. On one occasion when a relative of mine clearly preached the Gospel but did not give a closing appeal, a Christian lady when leaving the meeting expressed her disapproval by the remark, "He didn't even give people the opportunity to be saved!" The great danger is probably not so much in giving people the opportunity to publicly express their faith in Christ, as in the emphasis before and after the "invitation" which causes people to rest their salvation on their own personal actions in response to God, rather than on the actions of Christ which are declared in the Gospel.

When addressing this subject during a seminar with missionaries in the Philippines, I made the statement that I had never "led" any of the Palawano believers to the Lord, and I carefully explained what I meant. I had not asked the Palawanos to pray and to verbally "accept Christ" in my presence, nor did I tell them that they needed to pray a prayer of acceptance in order to be saved. I simply preached the Gospel and then exhorted the Palawanos to place their faith completely in Christ and the Gospel. Where, how, and what they actually did at the time of their conversion was not the important thing.

One missionary in the seminar strongly disagreed with my statement, "A person does not need to pray in order to be saved." When she objected, I replied, "Then I have led many people astray. I told the Palawanos that if they simply believed the Gospel and trusted in Christ, they would be saved. But I did not tell them that they must pray. According to what you are saying, I must now ask the Palawano believers if they prayed when they believed. If they did not, then I must tell them that unless they do, they will be lost."

Some people use Romans 10:9,10 to substantiate their claim that a person must make a verbal acceptance if he is to be saved. But this would then mean that dumb people or those on their deathbeds who are beyond speaking would be unable to be saved. In addition, it would mean that unless a person was with someone else to whom he could *"...confess with his mouth the Lord Jesus...,"* he, too, would not be able to be born again. The first section of Mark 16:16 says, *"He that believeth and is baptized shall be saved...."* Does this mean that baptism is necessary for someone to be saved? Of course not! The first part of Mark 16:16 must be interpreted in the light of the rest of the verse, *"...but he that believeth not shall be damned."* All such Scriptures must be interpreted in the light of the unmistakable emphasis of the whole Bible—salvation in Christ is received through faith alone and is not dependent on any action of man.

On one occasion, during a conversation with another missionary, he told me how, many years earlier, he had come to assurance of salvation. His assurance came unexpectedly at the close of a meeting when the preacher asked everyone who was saved to raise his hand. Since, at that time, the man did not know if he was truly saved, he tried desperately to keep his hand down, but it was forced up by a power outside of himself. He related that, because of this experience, he never again doubted his salvation. Yet another Christian told me how she was assured of salvation through an unusual experience. When confronted by a wild, vicious bird, poised to attack her, she looked it in the eyes and said, "You can't touch me for I am a child of God." Because the bird did not peck her, she felt certain from that time that she was indeed in the family of God.

Experiences, regardless of their vivid and startling nature, should never be the grounds for believing that one is saved. The Word of God alone must be the foundation for assurance of salvation. John says of his Gospel, *"But these are written, that ye might believe that Jesus is the Christ, the Son of God; and that believing ye might have life through his name"* (John 20:31). Each Christian is responsible to make certain that his preaching and evangelistic methods focus on Christ and His death, burial, and resurrection as the only firm foundation for his hearers' assurance of salvation. Just as the physical eye does not behold itself but sees only the object on which it is focused, so true faith looks only to Christ. We should never accept any outward act of a professed convert as the basis for acceptance as a born again person. The only scriptural basis for receiving a person's claim to salvation is his understanding and faith in the foundational truths of the Gospel.

In Palawan, a wizened, almost toothless old Palawano lady, who had been sitting for more than an hour on the front porch of our house, finally got around to her reason for visiting. Smiling, she said, "Grandchild, I am trusting in Jesus."

Even before she spoke, it was evident that she had something to tell me because she had patiently waited until all of our other visitors had gone home. Even though I had guessed that her news was related to her faith in Christ, it did not lessen my excitement and joy when she declared her dependence on the Saviour. My natural reaction was to reach out and hug her, but Palawano decorum and culture, as well as a fear that such an action would seal her in a sincere but unfounded faith, restrained me. To immediately accept her testimony, without carefully questioning her, would not have been judicious. She might have been following the other members of her family who had already come in the preceding days to express their dependence on Christ and His redemptive work. For her own sake and for the fledgling church in that area of Palawan, I had to do whatever I could to ensure that her faith was resting on the foundations of Scripture which I had endeavored to lay down.

"Grandmother," I answered her, "it gives me great joy to hear that you are trusting in the Lord Jesus as your Saviour. But why did you trust in Him? Why do you need the Lord Jesus?"

"I am a sinner," was her immediate answer.

"But Grandmother, why do you say that? You love your family. You are kind and a very hard worker."

"Yes, but I am a sinner before God," she insisted.

"But Grandmother, even though you are a sinner, why is it that you need the Lord Jesus? Why did you trust in Him? What has He done for you?"

"Ah, Grandchild, He was the One who died for me. He died for my sins."

Tears of joy filled my eyes as I replied, "Grandmother, I am so very glad to hear what you have said, for God's Word says that all those who trust only in the Lord Jesus as their Saviour, believing that He died for them and then rose again, have all their sins forgiven by God and will never go to Hell. They have eternal life and will be received by God into Heaven."

How different was the testimony of this primitive, illiterate tribal woman compared to that of my wife's aunt, who went forward in response to an "altar call" at an evangelistic meeting in Australia. We were excited to think that this may be the first of Fran's relatives, outside of her immediate family, to be converted. So, while visiting with her, Fran began to question her regarding her profession. It soon became obvious that her aunt was taken up with her own personal feelings and experience rather than the historical accomplishments of Christ on her behalf. In an endeavor to determine her aunt's real grounds for assurance, Fran asked her, "Aunty, why did you go forward to the invitation of the preacher? Was it because you realized that you are a sinner?"

"Sinner? I'm not a sinner!" she exclaimed.

In spite of her lack of understanding of even the basic truths of Scripture, Christians had accepted her as having been saved simply because she had responded to the "invitation."

Regardless of how careful we may be in questioning professing converts, there will always be those, as portrayed in the parable of the sower, who will appear to be Christians but will fall away after a time. Being fully aware of this danger is all the more reason why we should do everything we can to retain the purity, simplicity, and objectivity of the Gospel message, so that people will rest in the rightness of Christ's actions, and not their own.

People Unprepared for the Gospel

We have already used the biblical analogy of "building" to illustrate the work of preaching the Gospel, but the Lord has also used "farming" in His Word to teach us the correct procedures for doing His work. Therefore, I would like to tell you a parable about a farmer and his sons.

A man, leaving home for a period, left his sons with instructions to plant good seed in every part of his farm. He provided them with the good seed and promised to return at harvest time.

Over the years, their father had written a book in which he recorded his experiences as a farmer. He explained how he had worked with each different type of soil. He recorded how he dealt with various weeds and conditions which hindered the growth of the good seed. Some of his accounts told of useless soil which produced only weeds and thorny bushes. Other soil, if properly prepared, had proven to be productive; but all of the soil, even the best, needed lots of preparation and constant care if it was to yield a good harvest.

The sons were glad to obey their father, so in accordance with his command, they set off for the fields. They took with them the book and the good seed.

Arriving in the fields, they found large trees and an undergrowth of tangled vines and thorny weeds. Even the fields where their father had worked previously were now filled with weeds, and the ground was rocky and hard.

Feeling despondent, the sons took up their father's book and reread his last command. Yes, it was clear, "Sow the good seed in every part of the farm." Therefore, they set about to do, as best they could, what their father had commanded. One son cut away some of the undergrowth; and removing some of the weeds, he began to plant the good seed. Another son chopped down some of the trees, while another tore away the undergrowth with his bare hands before he put in the good seed. Each tackled the job with enthusiasm and vigor but with little success. With great devotion, they tried many different ideas and methods. Although their ideas seemed to bring results for a little while, eventually, the weeds choked most of the new plants or they died because of the hard rocky ground. Only a little of the seed actually took root and grew.

Meanwhile, their father's book, containing the account of his experiences and farming methods, was cherished, but not applied to their own work.

Finally, in desperation, the sons took up their father's book and began to read how he had experienced problems which were exactly like their own. They carefully read his methods of preparation before he planted the good seed. Then, following his example, they chopped down the trees, dug up the weeds, ploughed, fertilized, and watered the ground. Once the ground was broken up and well prepared, they planted the good seed. As a result of following their father's recorded methods and principles, more and more seed took root and flourished.

> No person seeks God or can come to Christ by faith, unless God first seeks him out by His Spirit through His Word.

Unprepared ground

In Jeremiah 4:3, the Lord says, *"...Break up your fallow ground, and sow not among thorns."* This verse teaches a spiritual principle which is emphasized continually throughout the Scriptures, and it highlights one of the greatest failures in most evangelism. The majority of evangelists, preachers, and teachers at home and on the mission field do not spend sufficient time preparing the minds and hearts of people before they offer the Gospel to them. The Gospel seed is usually sown into hard, unploughed, poorly prepared, thorny ground. In many cases, the results are professions which last only for a short time. There is little permanent growth and fruit.

In the Parable of the Sower in Matthew 13:3-8, some seed fell on the wayside, some on shallow ground, and some among the thorns. This seed was soon taken away, withered, or choked. Some people believe this parable is teaching us that it is our responsibility to sow the seed of the Gospel, regardless of the condition of the hearts of our hearers. It is true that there will always be the types of people illustrated by the Parable of the Sower. Even some who claimed to believe and follow our Lord Jesus were false professors. But what is Jesus really teaching through this parable?

Was Jesus teaching that we should sow the seed on unprepared and rocky soil? Did the farmer plan to sow seed on the wayside? Was it his intention to sow seed among the thorns? Did he think he would receive a harvest from seed sown on shallow, rocky soil? Indeed not! This farmer had prepared the ground in order to plant it with good seed. His purpose was to plant the seed only in the ground which he had prepared. He did not intentionally throw good seed onto unprepared ground; but, as he sowed the seed on prepared ground, some of it fell on unprepared soil. None of the seed which fell on unprepared soil yielded a harvest. The main point Jesus is teaching through the Parable of the Sower is that good seed grows well and bears fruit only in prepared soil.

The human heart is not naturally good soil for Gospel seed. The history of man recorded in the Scriptures makes it clear that no descendant of Adam is naturally inclined towards God or His way of salvation. *"There is none that understandeth, there is none that seeketh after God." "...the way of peace have they not known: There is no fear of God before their eyes"* (Romans 3:11,17,18). *"...the carnal mind is enmity against God: for it is not subject to the law of God, neither indeed can be"* (Romans 8:7).

The natural person may follow false religions and serve man-made gods or even what he believes to be the true and living God. Some will even gladly accept a gospel which sounds like the true Gospel of Christ. According to the Scriptures, however, no person seeks the true and living God or can come to Christ by faith, unless God first seeks him out by His Spirit through His Word (John 6:44,45).

Felt needs

In recent years, in many missionary circles, an unscriptural emphasis has been placed on culturally felt needs as the basis for the presentation of the Gospel. Some teach emphatically that, if the Gospel is to be acceptable, meaningful, and relevant to our hearers, we must first find and understand their felt needs and then offer the Gospel as God's answer to these felt needs.

Those who stress culturally felt needs as the key for understanding and accepting the Gospel are confusing the results and blessings of the Gospel with the Gospel itself. The true Gospel is never culturally relevant. The Gospel was not given by God to satisfy the natural desires of any human being, regardless of his culture. Jesus Christ's prime mission in the world was not to make people happy, peaceful, secure, or even to provide them with a sense of belonging and feeling loved. These blessings are the fruit of the Gospel and should be experienced in the lives of those who believe the Gospel. The Gospel which we preach, however, is not sent by God as good news to those whose basic quest is to be happy, peaceful, secure, healthy, or who simply want to go to Heaven. These are natural desires and may also be the fruit of the evil, self-centered nature of man and are usually the desires of the most ardent atheist or depraved criminal.

Offering the Gospel on the basis of natural desires or culturally felt needs places man and his desires at the center of our message. Thus, man and his happiness are enthroned; and God's objective through the Gospel, when presented this way, is to satisfy man's needs, whatever man feels them to be. This is not scriptural. God does not exist for man. Man exists for God. *"Thou art worthy, O Lord, to receive glory and honour and power: for thou hast created all things, and for thy pleasure they are and were created"* (Revelation 4:11).

Did Jesus come into this world to meet felt needs? No! He came to settle the problem of sin. John wrote, *"And we have seen and do testify that the Father sent the Son to be the Saviour of the world"* (I John 4:14). The angel told Joseph, *"...thou shalt call his name JESUS: for he shall save his people from their sins"* (Matthew 1:21). *"...the Son of man is come to seek and to save that which was lost"* (Luke 19:10). The mission of our Lord was to deal, first and foremost, with the matter of man's lostness in sin, because sin is an affront to God and His position as sovereign creator and ruler. This is why the Son said to His Father, *"...Lo, I come to do thy will, O God..."* (Hebrews 10:9). Jesus fulfilled His mission by suffering the righteous judgment of a holy God.

Jesus did not try to meet the people of His day on the basis of their understanding of their needs. In Jesus' day, the natural desire of the average Jew was for a king or political figure who would deliver Israel from the yoke of their enemies. After Jesus had fed the five thousand, He realized that the people were going to try to take Him by force and make Him their king, so *"...he departed again into a mountain himself alone"* (John 6:15). The following day, the crowds looked for Jesus because they wanted to be fed. Jesus, however, did not respond to them on the basis of these felt needs. Instead, He told them their real needs as God saw them. He offended so many by His message that John tells us, *"From that time many of his disciples went back, and walked no more with him"* (John 6:66). Most Jews rejected Jesus' assessment of their needs, for they did not see their great need of a Saviour to release them from the bondage of sin (John 6).

Paul records that the Gentile world was more interested in human wisdom and philosophy than in salvation from the depravity and condemnation of its sins. To both the Jew and Gentile, unprepared by God, the preaching of the cross was irrelevant and foolish, but Paul did not accommodate the Gentiles' quest for wisdom or the Jews' desire for signs and miracles. Paul preached the Gospel, God's power which saves believing sinners. He said, *"But we preach Christ crucified, unto the Jews a stumblingblock, and unto the Greeks foolishness"* (I Corinthians 1:23).

"...when I came to you," Paul reminded the Corinthian believers, *"I came not with excellency of speech or of wisdom....my speech and my preaching was not with enticing words of man's wisdom..."* (I Corinthians 2:1,4). Paul knew the felt needs of the people in wicked Corinth were not sound foundations for the Gospel. Paul knew that *"...the natural man receiveth not the things of the Spirit of God: for they are foolishness unto him: neither can he know them, because they are spiritually discerned"* (I Corinthians 2:14).

The Holy Spirit came into the world to convince the world of sin, righteousness, and judgment (John 16:8). Jesus came to call sinners to repentance (Matthew 9:13). God *"...commandeth all men every where to repent"* (Acts 17:30). The biblical basis for the Gospel is a sense of our sinfulness before God and the recognition that only God's mercy and grace can provide us with forgiveness of our sins. No culture naturally recognizes this spiritual need.

When the majority of Palawanos first professed conversion, they had responded because of culturally felt needs and not because of spiritual needs taught by the Holy Spirit. They embraced Christianity for the wrong reasons. Being animists, they were convinced that their well-being, physically and materially, was dependent on their ability to keep the spirits happy and contented. Many who professed conversion took a similar attitude towards God. They tried to please God and gain His acceptance by being baptized, reading the Scriptures, and meeting together to sing and pray. They tried to keep what they understood to be the Christian rules so they would experience God's blessings on their lives.

Previously, when they believed the spirits healed them, they offered a thanksgiving feast. They believed this was necessary so the spirits would be satisfied and not do them any further harm. Later, when they attributed their healing to God, many believed it was obligatory to go to church and give a thanksgiving testimony telling all that had taken place during their sickness and healing. Such testimonies usually concluded with the words, "Therefore, God is really true." The Lord's healing seemed to be the greatest proof to the Palawanos that God was real, just as in previous years, they had trusted in the spirits and their power to heal. God's power and goodness in healing them and meeting their physical needs were extremely important to them and the basic reason for their faith in Him. But when it appeared that God failed to answer their prayers, many turned back to the spirits and the witch doctors to meet their felt needs. Their "Christianity" did not last because it was based on felt needs instead of spiritual needs revealed by God.

Having said this, I am not implying that the Lord does not care about people's feelings or their needs. He does, but He knows that no one's needs can ever be met unless he first allows God to meet his primary and greatest need—to be reconciled to God. Because God cares about his feelings and hurts, we should also. Even so, if we really want to be ministers of good to them, we must prepare sinners to see their real needs from God's perspective.

Although the presentation of the Gospel should not be based on felt needs, missionaries must have a good knowledge of the culture of the people whom they are teaching. Jesus and the Apostle Paul presented the Gospel within the cultural context of their hearers. In the same way, missionaries should use appropriate cultural illustrations and idiomatic expressions to communicate effectively within the cultural context of their hearers.

In addition, we need to be aware of the cultural felt needs of the people so we can, through corrective teaching, guard against misunderstanding and syncretism as we teach them the Scriptures.

Ignorance and misunderstanding

The heart must be prepared by God for the reception of the Gospel. Man's evil heart, with its natural, self-centered desires, is not fertile soil for the good seed of the Gospel. Furthermore, the preaching of the message of salvation through Christ will not bear fruit where people's minds remain in darkness, unenlightened to spiritual realities. Saving faith rests on the comprehended truth of God.

In the book, *Through the Looking Glass* by Lewis Carroll, the Queen tells Alice:

"'Now I'll give you something to believe. I'm just one hundred and one, five months, and a day.'

"'I can't believe that!' said Alice.

"'Can't you?' the Queen said in a pitying tone. 'Try again: draw a long breath, and shut your eyes.'

"Alice laughed. 'There's no use trying,' she said: 'one can't believe impossible things.'

"'I dare say you haven't had much practice,' said the Queen. 'When I was your age, I always did it for half an hour a day. Why, sometimes I've believed as many as six impossible things before breakfast.'"

One eminent Bible teacher quoted this dialogue and then pointed out that unregenerate people are mistakenly convinced that the meaning of faith is "Take a long breath; close your eyes to facts, to reality, and believe."

God always works within the realm of the mind. Truth is presented to the intellect to be received, understood, and believed. It is surprising that, in spite of the emphasis of the Scriptures on the need for truth to be understood, many Christians do not see it as a basic necessity for true saving faith.

The main reason for the confusion among the Palawano people was their ignorance of the Gospel as well as their ignorance of the truths which are given by God as the only preparation for the Gospel.

One day, I was hiking with a missionary who felt I expected the tribal people to understand too much biblical truth before I would accept them as true children of God. We were discussing the confusion in the minds of the Palawanos regarding the way of salvation. He made the statement, "When I was saved, I didn't know anything."

I replied, "If you didn't know anything, you didn't get saved. Tell me, what did you do when you got saved?"

"I trusted in Christ," he answered.

"But why did you trust in Christ and not Mohammed or Buddha?"

"I trusted in Christ because I knew that He died for me."

I questioned further, "But why did you need someone to die for you?"

"I knew I was a sinner going to Hell," he answered.

"Well, it appears you did know something after all," was my response.

In the parable of the sower, the Lord Jesus said, *"When any one heareth the word of the kingdom, and understandeth it not, then cometh the wicked one, and catcheth away that which was sown in his heart. This is he which received seed by the way side"* (Matthew 13:19).

When Philip met the Ethiopian eunuch and heard him reading from the Prophet Isaiah, Philip asked the eunuch, *"...Understandest thou what thou readest?"* (Acts 8:30). Philip recognized that this man could never exercise true saving faith unless he first understood what the Word of God teaches about salvation.

When a person is saved, there are scriptural truths he may not know, but there are certain facts he will know. He will know that God is the righteous, holy Judge of all. He will also know that he is a sinner before God and that he can do nothing to save himself. Furthermore, he will know that Christ died for him to pay the complete price for the forgiveness of his sins and that Christ rose from the dead. This is the Gospel which the Apostle Paul preached. *"...I declare unto you the gospel which I preached unto you, which also ye have received, and wherein ye stand; By which also ye are saved, if ye keep in memory what I preached unto you, unless ye have believed in vain"* (I Corinthians 15:1,2). This is the Gospel which must be heard,

> If the sinner is to exercise true saving faith, there must be enlightenment by the Holy Spirit through the Word of God.

understood, and believed if a person is to enter into God's salvation.

One day, two Palawano men who were teachers in their local church sent a message to me, asking me to come and baptize them. I was not aware that these men had not been baptized as almost everyone had been baptized many years earlier, when they first professed to believe.

A Filipino trainee missionary accompanied me to their village. We also sent a message to the leading elders from another, more established church, requesting they meet us in the village where these two men lived. My companion and I agreed not to raise the question of baptism but to teach on salvation by grace through faith alone.

We taught for two days both publicly and privately, focusing our teaching on the sinful, helpless condition of man, the Gospel, and justification by faith alone. The two men who had requested baptism were in the public meetings and also the group discussions. We purposely did not raise the matter of their desire to be baptized because we were not convinced they really were clear on salvation by grace alone. If through the teaching they realized they were unsaved, we wanted them to be able to decide not to be baptized without any embarrassment. If they raised the matter of their baptism, we would question them, in order to determine what they were trusting in for their salvation.

At the close of the final meeting, the men asked publicly if they could be baptized. Knowing the misunderstanding which most of the Palawanos had about baptism, I asked the men why they wished to be baptized.

Regardless of all the teaching we had given on salvation apart from works, one of them answered, "So that I will really know God."

I asked him to open his New Testament to John 14:6. "Ontoy," I asked, "does your Bible say, 'The river is the way, the truth, and the life. No man comes to the Father but by baptism?'"

He answered, "No."

I said, "Ontoy, if you die and you are trusting in baptism to get you to God, you will go to Hell. God will not accept you."

After some more teaching, we returned home. Several months later, Ontoy hiked from his village to our home for some medicine. As he stepped onto our verandah, I took his hand and, looking into his face, I asked, "Ontoy, how is it with you? Do you now know the truth?"

Ontoy replied, "Yes, I know the Lord!" He continued by saying, "Brother, when you told me that I would go to Hell if I was trusting in baptism, it was like a knife in my liver. I love you, and it hurt when you spoke to me like that. But I want to thank you for telling me the truth. I would have died and gone to Hell. Now I am trusting only in Christ."

Both of those men came to a clear understanding of the Gospel and trusted in the Lord Jesus as Saviour. Their testimonies were very clear when, at a later date, some of the Palawano church elders baptized them.

Faith is not some mystical feeling. It is not mere hoping or blind chance. Faith is not intellectual suicide. It is not contrary to reason. Saving faith is based on objective, historical, biblical facts. Saving faith is well grounded. True faith rests on the sure Word of God. The Gospel therefore must be understood if it is to be believed to the saving of the soul. If the sinner is to exercise true saving faith, there must be enlightenment by the Holy Spirit through the Word of God.

The salvation which God offers sinners rests on a simple understanding and faith in the Word of God concerning the death, burial, and resurrection of the Lord Jesus. God, in the person of Christ, stepped into history and acted on our behalf. He lived, died as our substitute, and rose again. A person exercises faith when he looks away from all self-effort to the saving history of Christ and depends only on Him and His work of salvation on the sinner's behalf.

Foundations for the Gospel

The Gospel is God's good news about His Son. But to whom does God offer this good news? Whom does God call to eat the bread of life? To whom does He offer the water of life?

It is clear from God's Word that He offers good news to those who know they are spiritually poor. He offers bread to the hungry, water to the thirsty, rest to the weary, and life to the dead. God's good news is meant for all, but the person unprepared by God will never accept God's Gospel of grace. God knows that, and He tells us not to cast the pearl of the Gospel before swine, that is, those who feel no need and have no appreciation of God's mercy.

Matthew says in his Gospel, *"And it came to pass, as Jesus sat at meat in the house, behold, many publicans and sinners came and sat down with him and his disciples. And when the Pharisees saw it, they said unto his disciples, Why eateth your Master with publicans and sinners? But when Jesus heard that, he said unto them, They that be whole need not a physician, but they that are sick. But go ye and learn what that meaneth, I will have mercy, and not sacrifice: for I am not come to call the righteous, but sinners to repentance"* (Matthew 9:10-13).

Because the Pharisees were self-righteous, Jesus did not invite them to come to Him. He told them to first, "Go and learn." What were they to learn? They needed to learn that they were unable to offer God anything which could satisfy His holy and righteous demands and were therefore in need of the mercy of the Lord. It is only to those who are heavily laden with the realization of their sinfulness before God that Jesus gives His gracious invitation, *"Come unto me, all ye that labour and are heavy laden, and I will give you rest"* (Matthew 11:28). God sent John the Baptist to do this necessary work of preparing Israel to receive their Messiah and His Gospel (Matthew 3:1-12). But the self-righteous religious leaders refused to accept John's message of condemnation. They remained hard and unbroken. Luke in his Gospel says, *"And all the people that heard him, and the publicans, justified God, being baptized with the baptism of John. But the Pharisees and lawyers rejected the counsel of God against themselves, being not baptized of him"* (Luke 7:29,30).

Jesus also said to the people of his day, *"...For judgment I am come into this world, that they which see not might see; and that they which see might be made blind"* (John 9:39). Those who realized they were spiritually blind would be given spiritual understanding through the truth which Jesus spoke, but those who, like the Pharisees, refused to acknowledge their ignorance would remain forever in spiritual darkness. When Jesus said this, *"...some of the Pharisees which were with him heard these words, and said unto him, Are we blind also? Jesus said unto them, If ye were blind, ye should have no sin: but now ye say, We see; therefore your sin remaineth"* (John 9:40,41). The proud Pharisees believed they were already enlightened and understood perfectly the will of God. They felt no need to receive spiritual sight, for in their own estimation, they could already see quite well. They claimed to be guides of the blind (Romans 2:17-20), so why, they felt, should they allow this man to teach them? Because they didn't see their great need and claimed they already had spiritual sight, they were left to perish in their blindness without an understanding of the grace of God available through the Gospel.

When addressing the same hardened Jewish leaders after Christ's resurrection and ascension, Stephen said, *"Ye stiffnecked and uncircumcised in heart and ears, ye do always resist the Holy Ghost: as your fathers did, so do ye"* (Acts 7:51).

Nicodemus came seeking Jesus, but Jesus did not immediately tell Nicodemus the good news of the Gospel (John 3:1-21). Instead, Jesus said to him, "Nicodemus, you must be born again." The teaching

> While people are filled with their own self-righteousness, it is useless to try to force the Gospel on them.

of the necessity of the new birth is not the Gospel. That was bad news for Nicodemus, who like his fellow Pharisees, depended largely on his birth as a son of Abraham for his acceptance by God. Jesus knew that Nicodemus wasn't ready for the Gospel. Nicodemus first had to face the impossibility of his entering God's kingdom by virtue of his Jewish birth or his own goodness.

While on a visit back to Palawan, I was asked to teach a seminar for some of our missionaries on the chronological approach to evangelism and church planting. During one of our sessions, I emphasized that, if a person's mind is filled with his own self-righteousness, he will not see any need or feel any hunger for the Gospel. A young Palawano man who was attending the seminar was unable to immediately grasp this particular point.

This young man had just finished eating breakfast with us, part of which was scrambled eggs. Turning to him, I asked if he was hungry and if he would like something to eat. He assured me he didn't feel like eating anything. Nevertheless, I continued to insist. I told him that my wife, Fran, would be only too glad to get him something to eat.

Realizing what I was aiming at, Fran also assured him that it wouldn't be any problem for her to cook some scrambled eggs. Again, he thanked us but declined our offer. Feigning sincerity and concern, I repeated the offer and tried to get him to let Fran cook some scrambled eggs for him.

By this time, he thought I was crazy. Emphatically, he said, "But I am not hungry."

"That's right," I answered, "You ate a good breakfast. You are not hungry. You have no appetite for food."

"Oh! Now I see!" he exclaimed.

As it is in the natural realm, so it is in the spiritual. While people are filled with their own self-righteousness, it is useless to try to force the Gospel on them. The Gospel is for the hungry, for the thirsty, and for the weary. It is for those broken before God through a realization of their own sinfulness.

But how is a person brought to this realization? How is the heart of man prepared for the Gospel? The Holy Spirit uses the Word of God to prepare the mind and heart of a person for the Gospel. But what particular part or message from God's Word accomplishes this preparatory work?

The knowledge of God

Years after missionary work had begun in a highland tribe in Papua New Guinea, some of the people announced that they were not going to tithe anymore. Why? Because they had decided that they had repaid God enough for giving Jesus to die for their sins. The judicial system of this tribe was based on a monetary "pay-back" arrangement, so it is easy to see why they thought they had to recompense God for giving Jesus to die for their sins. But why did they think it was possible to pay God back for the gift of His Son? What didn't they understand? These tribal people obviously had failed to comprehend the nature and character of God as revealed in the Old Testament and finally in the Gospel. They thought God was like the spirits and human beings. Because they demanded "pay-back," they thought God did also. To have told them that salvation is a gift would not be sufficient. They needed to see, through the Scriptures, the true nature and character of God. If they were to see God as He really is, they would have also seen themselves as helpless and hopeless sinners. In the light of God's majesty and their own depravity, they would have understood the futility of every endeavor to "pay God back."

Furthermore, through the teaching of the Old Testament, beginning with God's warning to Adam regarding the tree of the knowledge of good and evil, *"...in the day that thou eatest thereof thou shalt surely die"* (Genesis 2:17), they should have realized that death, eternal separation from God, is God's just judgment on sinners. This emphasis on death as the only payment for sin continues through the Old Testament historical accounts of God's judgment on sinners and ends with the New Testament account of Christ's death as the only satisfactory payment for sin. If the tribal people had understood the Old Testament emphasis on death, they would have also recognized that only the death of Christ could pay for sin and satisfy God who is holy and righteous.

The Aziana tribe in Papua New Guinea were sun worshippers. Missionaries claiming to preach Christianity preceded New Tribes missionaries into this area. But in spite of being "missionized," the Aziana tribesmen had no clear understanding of the God of the Bible. They thought He must be similar to their sun-god.

In their ceremonial worship of the sun, they killed a pig, cooked a mixture of its liver and blood in a piece of bamboo; and, as the sun set, they gathered together to worship and appease the sun. The priest first ate of the cooked blood and liver, after which all present partook. The priest also spat some of the mixture at the sun to blind it, so their sins would not be seen and avenged, for they believed this would appease the sun, a malicious and malevolent god, and make their souls invisible to it.

When the first missionaries to the Aziana people taught them to commemorate the Lord's supper, the people gave it the same name as this feast to the sun. They believed that, by partaking of the Lord's supper, they were appeasing God and blinding Him to their sins. But these people would never have misinterpreted the Lord's supper in this way if they had been taught and understood who and what God is. They would have realized that God is not malicious in His intents, that He cannot be appeased like their heathen deities, and that He, the omniscient, immutable God, can never be blinded to man's sinfulness. These people were not prepared for the Gospel because they did not have an understanding of the holiness and righteousness of God. Because they had never been exposed to the knowledge of God, they did not see themselves as incapable of doing anything which would please God.

Job, David, and Solomon all stated the truth: True wisdom begins with a solemn appreciation of who and what God is. *"The fear of the LORD is the beginning of wisdom..."* (Psalm 111:10). Only those whose senses have been tuned to know and accept something of God's nature, character, and sovereign position are prepared for the Gospel.

If God is not truly God, as revealed foundationally in the Old Testament and finally in the New Testament through Jesus Christ, then there is no need for the Gospel. Only those who are enlightened through this revelation of God as a righteous and holy God who hates and punishes sin will see their need for the Gospel.

Because God is man's sovereign Maker, He is also his Owner, Lawgiver, and Judge. If this is not true, then man is a free agent and cannot be called to give an account of himself to God. Man's great desire to be free to live only for himself and the satisfaction of his selfish, depraved, insatiable lusts has caused him to hate, flee from, and endeavor to destroy the knowledge of God, His rightful Master.

But even though people understand that God is their Owner, Lawgiver, and Judge, if God is not also seen as holy and righteous, then there is no need for the Gospel. God is not someone who will tolerate, overlook, or forgive sin without full retribution. God is perfectly righteous. His own holy character is the standard for goodness; therefore, anything which does not agree with, or is contrary to what He is, is sin. Anything less than what God is, is totally unacceptable to Him. God's holiness and righteousness are clearly revealed in history by His consistent hatred and judgment of the least departure from His holy standard. God will not overlook sin. All sin must be paid for. *"...the soul that sinneth, it shall die"* (Ezekiel 18:4). Because God is righteous, He will never lower His standard of holiness or accept anything less than the full, righteous payment for sin.

While people are ignorant of God's holiness and righteousness, they will never understand their desperate need for the grace of God in Christ. They may give lip service to the Gospel, speak about Christ, attend church, sing hymns, read the Bible, pray, and even seek to serve Christ, but they will still be unsaved. Man is by nature self-righteous and will never let go of his pride and self-confidence until he realizes God's infinite holiness and righteousness. The unsaved religionist does not understand this, for he is constantly trying, by his own good works and religious activities, to place God in a position where God will feel obligated to accept and bless him.

This knowledge of God, which man naturally hates and seeks to escape, is nevertheless man's greatest need for, apart from it, he will never truly repent, believe, and be saved. A revelation of God's nature and character is prerequisite to the realization of one's own unrighteousness and abject helplessness to escape the just judgment of God. It was only after Job received new, clearer awareness of God's character, that he said, *"I have heard of thee by the hearing of the ear: but now mine eye seeth thee. Wherefore I abhor myself, and repent in dust and ashes"* (Job 42:5,6).

Isaiah, when called to be God's prophet, needed a realistic assessment of himself and his people, for only then could he speak in true humility against the sinfulness of the nation. How then did the Lord show Isaiah his true self and the iniquity of his nation? Isaiah was given a vision of the Lord in all His sublime glory, sovereignty, and holiness. The immediate effect on Isaiah was to cry, *"...Woe is me! for I am undone; because I am a man of unclean lips, and I dwell in the midst of a people of unclean lips: for mine eyes have seen the King, the LORD of hosts"* (Isaiah 6:5).

All people, regardless of their religious or cultural background, must be led down this road of the revelation of God. Only an understanding of who God is will produce true self-knowledge, genuine repentance, and saving faith.

Jesus said, *"No man can come to me, except the Father which hath sent me draw him: and I will raise him up at the last day. It is written in the prophets, And they shall be all taught of God. Every man therefore that hath heard, and hath learned of the Father, cometh unto me"* (John 6:44,45). Every person who ever comes to Christ for salvation comes because he has been taught, through the revelation of God's character as revealed in the historical sections of the Scriptures, that God is holy and righteous and will not overlook sin.

The Law

The Law is yet another means which God uses to prepare the sinner for the Gospel and the realization that, without Christ, he will perish.

By the fall of man and through subsequent history, man has been made aware of his sinfulness through revelations of God's holy character and will. Why then was the Law given? *"...the law entered, that the offense might abound..."* (Romans 5:20). The Law was brought in to classify and clearly define sin. God gave the Law to fully expose man's sinfulness and, thus, prepare the human heart for the Gospel. *"...the law was our schoolmaster to bring us unto Christ, that we might be justified by faith"* (Galatians 3:24). God gave the Law to Israel, not to save them, but to show them the impossibility of salvation by human goodness. *"...by the deeds of the law there shall no flesh be justified in his sight; for by the law is the knowledge of sin"* (Romans 3:20). *"...the law worketh wrath..."* (Romans 4:15). The Law reveals God's wrath against sin and shows that man can only approach God if the complete, righteous demands of His Law are paid in full.

Jesus told the self-righteous Pharisees to go and learn that sinners are saved by God's mercy and not by their own sacrifices to God (Matthew 9:13). How were the Pharisees to learn this? Who or what was God's ordained teacher? How could they see their true condition before God as helpless sinners needing a Saviour? It was through a correct understanding of the Law!

The Jews had the written Law of God, but the scribes and Pharisees had given it such a carnal interpretation that it did not convict them of their inner heart attitudes. They did not understand the Law as God intended it to be understood. If they had, they would have realized the impossibility of anyone ever obeying it perfectly, and they would have seen their own unrighteousness. They would have then been prepared for Christ and the Gospel.

Jesus taught them the correct interpretation of the Law (Matthew 5:17-28). But even though Jesus taught them to understand what God's laws really meant, the Jewish leaders would not allow the Law to judge and condemn them. If they had, they would have been broken in heart and truly repentant.

John the Baptist also gave the right interpretation of the Law as preparation for the Gospel. But the religious leaders rejected both the ministry of John the Baptist and of Jesus because their correct interpretation of the Law exposed the true condition of the scribes' and Pharisees' hearts. They rejected this preparatory ministry of the Law; and, therefore, they rejected Christ and the Gospel of God's grace (Matthew 5:17-28).

> Did Jesus tell the young man, "Smile, God loves you?" No! Jesus used the Law to expose the covetousness which held him captive.

Jesus' conversation with the woman of Samaria is yet another example of the necessity of preparing a person for the Gospel by the correct use of the Law. After Jesus had gained her attention by speaking about her felt need for water, He brought her face to face with her real need. Jesus said to her, *"...Go, call thy husband..."* (John 4:16). Jesus knew this woman would never be prepared to trust only in the grace of God until she faced the truth that she was a transgressor of the Law which forbids adultery.

Jesus' method of dealing with the rich young ruler also shows that, unless a person faces the truth about his sin and condemnation before a holy God, he will not recognize his need for the Gospel.

The rich young ruler, secure in his own apparent goodness and ability to keep the Law, came to Jesus and asked Him what he had to do to inherit eternal life? Through this young man's greeting, Jesus recognized immediately that he was a soul unprepared for the Gospel. This young ruler greeted Jesus as a fellow human being, by saying, "Good Master." He had never been enlightened by the Law to realize that *"...there is none good but one, that is, God"* (Mark 10:17-22). He was unaware that all the goodness and righteousness of man, when judged in the light of the perfect goodness and righteousness of God, is nothing more than a bundle of filthy rags (Isaiah 64:6).

Jesus, recognizing this young man's lost condition as well as his unpreparedness for the Gospel, did not offer him the grace and forgiveness of the Gospel. Jesus had not come to call a self-righteous, rich young ruler to repentance; He came to call sinners to repentance. This young man must first be taught his sinfulness and unrighteousness in God's sight before he could understand that the Gospel of God's grace was the only way by which he could enter eternal life. What did Jesus use to reveal this man's true heart condition? Did Jesus use some cultural felt need to lead him into genuine repentance? Did Jesus tell the young man, "Smile, God loves you?" Did He ignore his lack of conviction and immediately introduce him to some easy steps to eternal life? No! Jesus used the Law to expose the covetousness which held him captive.

Because this man had asked what he must **do** to inherit eternal life, Jesus told him what God required him to **do**. Being self-righteous, this man believed he could be saved by **doing** and didn't need God's mercy as a sinner. Therefore, Jesus quoted some of the Law to him. The rich young ruler's response evidenced his lack of understanding of the perfection of God. He immediately claimed that he had kept these laws perfectly from childhood. Knowing this young man's true spiritual condition and his secret love of money, Jesus said, *"...go thy way, sell whatsoever thou hast, and give to the poor...."* Through this command, Jesus was confronting this young man with the practical realities of the second great commandment, *"...Thou shalt love thy neighbor as thyself..."* (Mark 12:31). Then Jesus said to this ruler, *"...come, take up the cross, and follow me."* This command was based on the first great commandment, *"...thou shalt love the Lord thy God with all thy heart, and with all thy soul, and with all thy mind, and with all thy strength..."* (Mark 12:30).

What was the young man's response? Did he turn and repent? Did he, like the publican in the temple, acknowledge that he was a sinner and needed God's mercy? No. He rejected the revealing, condemning ministry of the Law. He turned away, clutching his riches as his greatest treasure. He went away grieved but apparently unrepentant for his covetousness. Those who reject the message of the Law cannot receive the Gospel.

The majority of the Jews rejected the preparatory work of the Law given through Moses and also taught by John the Baptist, Jesus, and the apostles. Even though they had received the written Law of God, they were self-righteous and trusted in a mere outward conformity to the Law. Because of their self-righteousness, they were not prepared to come by faith alone and trust in the grace of God. In contrast, many of the Gentiles, who had been without the direct written message from God, accepted the condemnation of the Law and saw the reality of their spiritual bankruptcy. Therefore, they were ready to turn in faith to Christ and the Gospel as their only hope (Romans 3:19).

The hymn entitled "JEHOVAH TSIDKENU" was written by R. Murray M'Cheyne and is his testimony to the way the Lord taught and prepared him through the Law, to see his need of the Saviour. (Jehovah Tsidkenu means "Jehovah our Righteousness.")

> I once was a stranger to grace and to God;
> I knew not my danger, I felt not my load;
> Though friends spoke in rapture of Christ on the tree,
> JEHOVAH TSIDKENU was nothing to me.
>
> When free grace awoke me by light from on high,
> Then legal fears shook me, I trembled to die;
> No refuge, no safety in self could I see,
> JEHOVAH TSIDKENU my Saviour must be.
>
> My terrors all vanished before the sweet Name;
> My guilty fears banished, with boldness I came
> To drink at the fountain, life-giving and free;
> JEHOVAH TSIDKENU is all things to me.

The problem with many of the tribal professing believers to whom I first ministered in the Philippines was that they had never judged themselves according to the perfection and holiness of God as revealed in the Law. Because they had not been exposed to the correct ministry of the Law, they were trusting in a mixture of works and grace. They were offering God their own sacrifices of good works instead of accepting God's mercy in the Gospel of Christ.

Referring to the time in his life when he was one of the leading Pharisees, Paul said, *"...I was alive without the law once: but when the commandment came, sin revived, and I died"* (Romans 7:9). Paul was a self-righteous, self-dependent man. He did not see himself as being spiritually sick or needing a Saviour. But when God the Holy Spirit faced Paul with the holy and righteous claims of the Law, he realized he was unspiritual and a slave to sin (Philippians 3:4-9;

Romans 7:14). Paul wrote, *"Was then that which is good made death unto me? God forbid. But sin, that it might appear sin, working death in me by that which is good; that sin by the commandment might become exceeding sinful"* (Romans 7:13). Because Paul had been prepared by the Law, he was ready to trust only in Christ.

While people are ignorant of the perfect righteousness of God, they will endeavor to save themselves through their own imperfect righteousness. Paul said of his own countrymen, *"...For they being ignorant of God's righteousness, and going about to establish their own righteousness, have not submitted themselves unto the righteousness of God"* (Romans 10:3). If a person is ignorant of the righteousness of God, then he will go about trying to establish his own righteousness. Once he sees the holiness and righteousness of God as revealed by the Law, however, he will completely abandon any trust in his own goodness as a basis for acceptance by God. Once a person has been enlightened by the Holy Spirit through the Word of God, he will say, "If that is what God is like and if he demands perfection from me, then I give up. I will no longer try to merit His favor by what I do. I am unable to obey His holy commands and so please Him." Then, and only then, is a person's heart ready to receive the good news that, *"...when we were yet without strength, in due time Christ died for the ungodly"* (Romans 5:6).

Our responsibility

Today, in most evangelical circles, the usual practice is to present some verses and evidences of man's need and then swiftly turn to the Gospel. Following this quick presentation of man's need, a great deal of time is spent endeavoring to persuade the hearers to turn to Christ. Our great mistake is turning quickly to the remedy without spending sufficient time preparing people for the Gospel.

Because Western society has a facade of Christianity, most Christian workers presume that people already have the foundations for the Gospel. We assume they already have a basic understanding of God and His nature and character. However, the vast majority of people in so-called Christian countries have little biblical knowledge of God. Of the relatively few in our countries who do attend church, most have a humanistic and unscriptural concept of God. Regardless of this tremendous lack, the average preacher spends little time on this all-important, basic subject. It is small wonder that there is little respect for God and spiritual matters in our day. All true spiritual revivals and movements of the Spirit of God have been the result of the acknowledgment of who God really is. This alone brings true contrition of heart, genuine repentance, faith, worship, and holy living. If evangelists and preachers spent more time teaching about the true nature and character of God and less time trying to convince sinners of the advantages of coming to God, we would hear the question asked more often by repentant, anxious sinners, *"...Sirs, what must I do to be saved?"* (Acts 16:30).

While we may agree that there must be a preparatory work done in the heart of a sinner before he will trust only in Christ, some may be of the opinion that this is God's sovereign work in which we have no part. It is clear from the Scriptures that God prepares man's heart through His Word. *"Is not my word like as a fire, saith the LORD, and like a hammer that breaketh the rock in pieces?"* (Jeremiah 23:29). The Holy Spirit uses the Word of God to convict the world of sin, of righteousness, and of judgment (John 16:8). God has entrusted us with the proclamation of His message (II Corinthians 5:18-20).

We are responsible to prepare our hearers through the Scriptures before we offer the Gospel to them. I remember beginning to teach a new weekly home Bible study with a couple in Australia. Before I started teaching that first night, the husband interrupted me and said, "Now, just a moment. Before you say anything, I have something to say."

"OK, go ahead," I replied.

He said, "I reckon that if a person keeps the Law and does exactly what it says, he will be all right and will be accepted by God."

When I agreed with him, his head almost swelled visibly. Turning to his wife, he bragged, "There you are. I told you so. That woman at the City Mission didn't know what she was talking about. She told me I couldn't be saved by what I did."

I told him, "I agree with what you said so I want to write it down." So I wrote down, "Wim said that if we obey the Law and do exactly what it says, God will accept us and we will be OK." Of course, at that point, Wim didn't realize that he did not have the ability to obey the Law because he had been born a sinner. After I had written these words, I put the piece of paper in the front of my Bible. My plan was to produce it at an appropriate future date.

After a few months of weekly chronological Bible studies, beginning in the book of Genesis, we finally reached the story of the giving of the Law. It was obvious from Wim's questions and answers that the Lord was working in his life. As we continued studying the Law, giving the spiritual meaning and application of each of the commandments, Wim was listening carefully. Finally, one night, he interrupted my teaching and said, "I haven't got a hope. I break all of God's laws every day."

Praise God! Wim's spiritual eyes had been opened to see his own sinfulness and inability to please God by personal obedience to the Law. This knowledge had come to him through the study of the Old Testament stories and the Law which revealed the holy and righteous character of God. Later, during our Bible studies, Wim saw that Christ alone had kept the Law and, through His death, had provided a way of salvation for sinful, helpless sinners.

What would have been the result if I had given the Gospel at the beginning of our Bible study, without first exposing Wim to the demands of God's holy Law? Wim would not have clearly understood the absolute necessity of the Gospel. He was not prepared for the Gospel. He felt no need for the grace and mercy of God. He was self-righteous and therefore self-dependent. Possibly, he would have professed faith in Christ; but, in his heart, he would have still been dependent on his own efforts and self-righteousness.

Not only has the Gospel been committed to us, but the preparation of souls for the Gospel has also been committed to us. We need to take this seriously. Paul wrote to Timothy, *"...we know that the law is good, if a man use it lawfully; Knowing this, that the law is not made for a righteous man, but for the lawless and disobedient....According to the glorious gospel of the blessed God, which was committed to my trust"* (I Timothy 1:8,9,11). Paul knew that the Gospel would not be meaningful without the right application of the Law. The right use of the Law is the means to prepare sinners for the Gospel. The Law is God's appointed schoolmaster to lead the self-righteous to Christ.

We should, through the correct use of the Law, bring people to see that they need a righteousness equal to the righteousness of God, for only that will satisfy a holy God. The question then arises, "Where can I find this righteousness which will satisfy God? How can God be satisfied with me? I have broken His Law. I am condemned to everlasting punishment. How can my debt of sin be paid? How can I be justified and declared righteous before my perfect Judge?"

While some are of the opinion that this preparatory work is the sovereign responsibility of God, others believe that the Gospel should be immediately preached to all, regardless of their lack of preparation because the Gospel is the "power of God unto salvation." They believe the Gospel will prepare the sinner's heart and also save his soul. The Gospel is indeed the power of God unto salvation, but to whom? Romans 1:16 says it is the power of God unto salvation *"...to everyone that believeth...."* Who will trust only in the Gospel and be saved? Only those whose hearts have been prepared like the good soil—those who have been convicted and prepared by God and have been taught by the Holy Spirit to agree with God about their sin, Christ's righteousness, and God's coming judgment (John 16:8-11).

> I thought, "Maybe she is truly saved."

One Sunday morning, a Palawano woman came to our house for the first time. Many years earlier, she had heard some of the Word of God; but, for a long time, there hadn't been any missionaries in her area. We had just built a house and had started teaching God's Word in a location about a two or three hours' walk from her home. She came to see us and said excitedly, "I have been out of God for ten years, but now I want to come back into God." By this term "out of God," she meant that she hadn't been attending Christian meetings and doing all the things she associated with being a Christian. By the term "coming back into God," she indicated that she was going to attend the meetings once again, sing, pray, and listen to the teaching of God's Word.

I talked with this woman on several occasions about Christ and His death for sinners, and I asked her about her own personal faith in Christ and His death. She said, "Yes, I am trusting in Christ." Nevertheless, her emphasis was on the fact that she had at one time been "in God," that she had been baptized, and that she knew many hymns and prayed.

She no longer had a New Testament, but she wanted another one because she was coming back "into God." Unless specifically asked, however, she never spoke about the death of Christ for sinners.

I said to her, "All of the things you speak of are good in their place, but they will not save you. Only Christ can save you." Again and again when speaking to her, I emphasized Christ's death for sinners.

She answered, "Oh, yes, the previous missionary told me that Christ died. Yes, I believe that."

I thought, "Maybe she is truly saved."

When she returned a week or two later, she said, "I am so happy to be able to sing the hymns, pray, and attend meetings. I am so glad to be back in God."

Once again, I reminded her of Christ's death as the only way back to God.

She answered, "Yes, I remember that." But then she asked the new believers in the area if they had been baptized. When they said that they had not been baptized, she told them that they hadn't even started on the way.

Each time she visited and boasted of her good works, I reminded her about Christ's death as the only way to God. From her attitude, it was clear that Christ's death was not meaningful to her. It seemed as if she thought, I will be all right if I can only remember that part about Christ dying for sins and rising again.

On several occasions, my wife heard me reminding this woman of Christ's death for sinners. Finally, Fran said to me, "I can't understand you. You are doing the very thing you would tell other people not to do."

I questioned, "What's that?"

She replied, "You keep telling that woman the Gospel, but she is not prepared for the Gospel. She doesn't understand her need of the Gospel. She is not thirsty. She is not hungry. Her heart is not prepared for the Gospel."

My wife was right. I determined that, when this Palawano woman returned, I would not remind her again of the Gospel. She needed to be taught the Law, in order for her to comprehend her great need of Christ, and Christ alone, as her righteousness.

Shortly after this, she returned. I sat down to talk with her at about one o'clock in the afternoon. I began in Genesis and reminded her of the main stories in the Old Testament which provide the foundations for the doctrine of God, man, and sin. Because she had been attending the meetings, she needed only to be reminded of most of these stories.

Once again, I emphasized the holiness of God, His hatred of sin, man's sinfulness, and especially the fact that God's Law requires death as the payment for sin and that God would accept no compromise. I applied this truth to her personally by telling her that baptism, hymn singing, church attendance, reading the Scriptures, or any other thing that she could do would not pay for her sin.

About five o'clock that afternoon, she was frustrated and desperate and began to cry. Although Palawanos do not like to be seen crying publicly, she cried because she was so overcome by the hopelessness of her position before God.

While she was crying, I was silently praying, "Lord, give me wisdom. What should I say to her? I don't want her to mentally agree with what I have shared from your Word but not trust only in Your Son and the Gospel. Lord, save this woman! Bring her to that place where she sees her salvation is only in Christ, so she will put her faith in Him and never again in herself or anything that she can do."

Finally, I said to her, "God requires death, but isn't there somewhere you can find the payment instead of you dying? Isn't there someone who could pay it? I can't pay it for you because I, too, deserve to be separated from God because of my sins."

For a time, we sat there in silence. Finally, she looked up at me through her tears and answered, "Jesus."

Joyfully, I replied, "Yes, Jesus. He's the only One."

That woman's whole attitude was changed from that time. Gone was her boasting and trust in anything else except the Lord Jesus Christ. "How sweet the name of Jesus sounds to a believer's ear!" He is the answer. Christian, it will thrill your soul, if, through the correct teaching of the nature and character of God and the Law of God, you give the Holy Spirit the opportunity to prepare people for the Gospel, for then they will trust only in the Lord Jesus as the One who died for them and fully satisfied God on their behalf.

Divine Building Principles

During our first years with the Palawanos, many came to understand justification by faith through God's grace. Many who had previously been mere professors of salvation were saved, and others received assurance and clarity regarding their personal salvation. Not only was I teaching justification by faith, but other missionaries among the Palawanos had also realized the true condition of the Palawan churches and were endeavoring to strengthen the basic foundations of the people's faith. What a thrill to see the people trusting in Christ alone!

How could these babes in Christ best be nurtured and fed? With so many people to teach, I felt like a doctor dispensing vitamins to an undernourished and starving people. Our present itinerant teaching program was totally inadequate to meet the needs of these young believers and build them up in the faith. I decided to turn from a predominantly topical teaching approach to verse-by-verse exposition. I relocated my family in the middle of an area with six small churches and began to give these Palawano churches concentrated expositional teaching.

Because the congregations of these six churches were a mixture of saved, mere professors, and a few who didn't even claim to be children of God, I started teaching expositionally through the Gospel of John. Starting with great enthusiasm, it soon became apparent that my hearers were not ready for an expositional study of John. They could not understand any of the verses containing direct references or allusions to people or stories from the Old Testament because they had never been taught the basic Old Testament historical sequence of events as one complete story.

The following examples show a few of the problems I encountered:

John 1:1, *"In the beginning was the Word...."* Even though the people may have heard about "the beginning" from previous missionaries, it was vague and uncertain in their minds. So, I had to go back to Genesis 1 and teach about the beginning of time.

John 1:1, *"...and the Word was with God...."* After explaining that "the Word" is yet another title for the Lord Jesus, it was obvious that the Palawano people did not understand that Jesus was with the Father before the beginning.

John 1:3, *"All things were made by him...."* The people did not understand that God in Genesis 1 included the Son of God.

John 1:11, *"He came unto his own...."* This meant little to the Palawanos without the background of the call of Abraham, the Messianic promises, and the history of Israel.

John 1:14, *"And the Word was made flesh, and dwelt among us, (and we beheld His glory...)."* This alludes to the Old Testament tabernacle and the Shekinah glory wherein God lived in the midst of Israel. The Palawanos didn't know these stories.

John 1:17, *"...the law was given by Moses...."* The people had insufficient knowledge of the chronology of the Bible story, and they didn't know where the Old Testament and New Testament characters fit in the sequence of events. They questioned if Moses and John the Baptist were contemporaries and wondered if Jesus was on the earth at the same time as the people mentioned from the Old Testament.

As these few examples show, the Gospel of John is full of references to the Old Testament. Due to the Palawanos' sketchy understanding of the Old Testament, I had to intermittently break off the exposition of John's Gospel in order to teach the Old Testament story or truth to which John referred or alluded. This

> **The Old Testament is the logical introduction, foundation, and authority for the story of Christ.**

piecemeal form of teaching was frustrating for me as the teacher and confusing for my hearers. I was forced to conclude that a clearer and less complicated way to teach the Scriptures must exist. A major forward step had been made when I turned from predominantly teaching topically to direct verse-by-verse exposition of the New Testament books. Nevertheless, it was now apparent that choosing any book and teaching it expositionally was not the complete answer to teaching the Scriptures clearly. What was the answer?

One book

The Scriptures were written with a definite beginning and a definite ending. Between the beginning and ending are incidents which, when taught and understood in their historical sequence, form one complete, cohesive, intelligible story. If one were to teach the contents of any other book, he would naturally start at the beginning and follow the forward movement of the subject as the author develops and brings it to its logical conclusion. Little wonder we had difficulties when teaching the New Testament to the Palawanos!

Previously, I had approached the Bible as a book which contained the message of the Gospel. I now began to consider the Bible holistically—as God's complete unified message to all mankind. I realized the Old Testament is not a compilation of interesting stories to be used only as types and illustrations of New Testament truth. The Old Testament is the logical introduction, foundation, and authority for the story of Christ recorded in the New Testament. The Old Testament is by far the most important source of interpretive background material for the historical accounts of the New Testament. Just as God has given us two lips and both are necessary for clear verbal communication, even so both Old and New Testaments are indispensable for the communication of God's complete message to the world.

One story

The whole Bible is God's message about His Son, the Saviour. God's chief purpose in writing His Book was to reveal Christ. The Old Testament is the preparation for Christ. The New Testament is the manifestation of Christ. The Scriptures reveal Christ from Genesis to Revelation. Jesus said to the Jews of His day, *"Search the scriptures; for in them ye think ye have eternal life: and they are they which testify of me"* (John 5:39). The entire Scriptures find their meaning in the Lord Jesus Christ. Jesus Christ is the origin, the substance, and the object of all divine revelation.

His-story, that is, the story of Christ, begins in the first verse of Genesis, for He was there in the beginning. But it is not until the fall of man that the Son of the virgin is promised, One who will overcome Satan and deliver his captives. The story of Christ then continues through the entire Old Testament in numerous types and prophecies. The New Testament records the fulfillment of these prophecies through His birth, life, death, ascension, and present glory. The story of Christ as told in the Gospels is the sequel to the Old Testament.

The Gospel of Matthew opens with the story of the birth of Christ, not as the beginning of the story but as the fulfillment and consummation of all that was written previously. Matthew connects the story of Christ with Abraham to whom God had given the promise, *"...in thee shall all families of the earth be blessed"* (Genesis 12:3). This, and all the other promises given to Abraham, were to be fulfilled through his Seed, *"...which is Christ"* (Galatians 3:16).

The Gospel of Mark launches almost directly into the life of Christ, but Mark is nonetheless careful to remind his readers that this story is not the beginning but the fulfillment of that which was *"...written in the prophets..."* (Mark 1:2).

Luke traces the genealogy of Christ to Adam. By doing this, Luke shows us that the story which he wrote cannot be understood by reading only of Mary and Joseph or of Jesus born as a babe in Bethlehem. To clearly understand Luke's Gospel, we must also be aware of Adam's part as the first man in the historical drama of the Bible.

John's Gospel tells the ongoing story of the Word. The story of the Word begins in eternity. It continues in the Word's creation of all things and then in His incarnation (John 1:1-3). The future story of the Word is told in the Revelation, where He is described as being *"...clothed with a vesture dipped in blood..."* (Revelation 19:13).

When Jesus saw the need to put two sadly disillusioned men straight on the necessity of His death, He turned back to the Old Testament, *"And beginning at Moses"* (Genesis to Deuteronomy) *"and all the prophets"* (the remainder of the Scriptures), *"he expounded unto them in all the scriptures the things concerning himself"* (Luke 24:27).

Because the Christ-story cannot be clearly taught or understood apart from its God-given beginnings found only in the Old Testament, it is our responsibility to teach the beginnings in the Old Testament and then teach the fulfillment in the New Testament. In the Old Testament, God has given types and redemptive analogies to prepare people to understand the New Testament story of Christ. These Old Testament types and redemptive analogies point to and interpret the birth, life, death, burial, and resurrection of the Lord Jesus Christ.

Instead of emphasizing the Old Testament redemptive analogies as the basis for the understanding of the Christ story, some missionaries seem to depend more on redemptive analogies found in the cultures of various ethnic groups. A young missionary en route to his homeland for furlough passed through Australia. As I talked to him, it became obvious that he was discouraged with the lack of progress in his missionary work. When I asked if he had presented the Gospel to the people, he told me that he hadn't. My next inquiry was why he had been such a long time in the tribe but had not yet begun to evangelize. The reason he gave was that, in spite of all his searching, he had failed to find the cultural redemptive analogy or what he thought was the God-given key for their clear understanding and acceptance of the Gospel. Because he failed to find the key or redemptive analogy, he didn't have confidence to preach the Gospel to those lost tribal people. Since he was returning to the U.S.A., I asked him what the redemptive analogy or God-given key to open the door to understand salvation is in the American culture. Because he didn't know, I replied, "According to what you believe, it won't be of any use for you to tell your fellow Americans the Gospel until you find the key."

If God has placed such an effective medium of blessing within some cultures, then surely we can expect that the Lord has placed them in all. If God has indeed given redemptive analogies which are hidden within the cultures of primitive peoples to serve as the keys to open their understanding to accept the Bible, God, Christ, and salvation, then we must never cease in our search. But how will we know when we have found the right key? Who will be the judge? What will be our criterion or standard of judgment? If we come to the conclusion that we have found the key because we see tribal people understanding and accepting the Gospel, how do we know there is not yet another even more suitable key prepared by God and waiting to be used to unlock the cultural door for an even greater movement to God and the Gospel?

Cultural stories and rituals which resemble Bible stories and Old Testament rituals and ceremonies are not the God-given keys to open the people's understanding of the Gospel. These stories and rituals are remnants of the truth which the whole human race knew before the dispersion at the tower of Babel. They have been passed down orally in many primitive societies and have been greatly changed and grossly distorted. The truth of God once known has been deliberately set aside for the lies of Satan (Romans 1:18-32). One of the clearest illustrations of this would be the widespread use of blood as a way of appeasement and sacrifice. This knowledge originated with the blood sacrifices which God ordained after the fall of man. Blood sacrifices, once commanded by God as the only way of approach to Him, are now used in many tribal cultures as sacrifices to Satan and evil spirits.

Missionaries should know all they can about the culture, folklore, and beliefs of the people they are reaching for Christ, and they should use illustrations and cultural redemptive analogies when teaching God's Word. These, however, are not substitutes for the preparation of the hearts of sinners through the proclamation of the Scriptures. Cultural analogies and illustrations, regardless of their clarity, cogency, or incredible biblical parallelism, should never take precedence over the scriptural redemptive types and analogies. Cultural redemptive analogies are no substitute for the God-given redemptive analogies of the Old Testament which so graphically typify Christ and His work of redemption. Some secret significance or evil connotation may be hidden in cultural analogies of which the missionary may be totally unaware. If the missionary is dependent on cultural analogies, rather than biblical analogies, he may unwittingly guide the people into grievous misunderstanding, error, and syncretism.

Jesus told the Pharisees that the truth of God's Word sets Satan's captives free from sin's bondage, and He declared in His prayer to His Father, *"...thy word is truth"* (John 8:32, 17:17). Paul charged Timothy to *"Preach the word..."* (II Timothy 4:2). The living and enduring Word of God, the imperishable seed, when believed, results in souls being born again (I Peter 1:23). No evidence exists in the Scriptures to prove that God's Word is effectual for the release of tribal people from Satan's dominion only when interpreted by cultural redemptive analogies. God has provided us with spiritual weapons with which we are to fight Satan, demolish his strongholds, arguments, and pretensions which set themselves against the knowledge of God (II Corinthians 10:3-5).

The biblical redemptive analogies given by God to Israel were also for the whole world. *"For whatsoever things were written aforetime were written for our learning, that we through patience and comfort of the scriptures might have hope"* (Romans 15:4). God has not spoken directly to the Gentiles, but He has chosen to speak to the Gentiles through His Word given to Israel and the Church. All people must come to God's light shining from the Scriptures. By the infinitely wise and sovereign appointment of God, all of the redemptive story and the beginning of the Church of Jesus Christ is set within the cultural, geographical, and historical framework of the nation of Israel. Therefore, no one can understand the story of the New Testament without a basic knowledge of Israel's origin, development, and history from the Old Testament.

The Lord created the nation of Israel for Himself, so that He could use it as His witness and channel of blessing to all of mankind (Isaiah 43:1,10-12,21). The Lord's promises to Abraham, the progenitor of Israel, indicated that God's blessings through him and his seed would extend to *"...all families of the earth..."* (Genesis 12:1-3). This promise was fulfilled through Christ, the promised Seed, but also through the Scriptures, entrusted to Israel as the only revelation of God to the world. All other nations were left in ignorance, without God and without hope, unless they were willing to accept truth and wisdom which was given through God's chosen channel, Israel. The Lord said to Israel, *"You only have I known of all the families of the earth: therefore I will punish you for all your iniquities"* (Amos 3:2). In contrast, the Gentile nations, prior to Pentecost, are spoken of as *"...a people whom I have not known..."* (Psalm 18:43).

The Bible alone is God's revelation to the world. This is the foundational truth of Christianity. Buddhism, Hinduism, Mohammedanism, and many other false religions are gaining converts because liberal and modern writers, who claim to be Christians, teach that truth is not limited to the Hebrew-Christian Scriptures but is also found in the writings of other world religions. The animistic tribal people's claims to truth are based on folklore and revelations from the spirits. The Christian missionary's responsibility is to clearly establish, through teaching the Scriptures, that God's revelation of truth for all people was given through no other nation except Israel and that this revelation is only found in the Bible. Therefore, if the tribes and nations of the world are to know the truth and the blessings of God, they too must turn to the Bible as the only genuine and complete divine revelation. This revelation of God began with the Old Testament and was completed with the New Testament revelation in and through Israel's Messiah, Jesus of Nazareth. *"God, who at sundry times and in divers manners spake in time past unto the fathers by the prophets, Hath in these last days spoken unto us by his Son, whom he hath appointed heir of all things, by whom also he made the worlds"* (Hebrews 1:1,2).

The Bible then is one book. The Old Testament is the introduction and only sound basis for the understanding and interpretation of the New Testament story concerning Christ and His redemptive work. But has God only told us **what** to teach and left **how** we teach up to us? As my search continued, it became clear that the Lord wrote the Scriptures not only to tell us **what** to teach but also to demonstrate principles and guidelines as to **how** we should teach His message to the world. His methods of teaching are the best, and He means for us to study and be guided by them when we teach His Word to others.

The literary form of the Bible

God is the greatest teacher, and all intelligent beings are His pupils. No one can escape from His classroom, the universe. The angels, and even Satan and his demons, are subject to God's divine teaching process (Ephesians 3:10). The voice of God is heard in innumerable ways throughout all creation.

Man, created on earth by God and for God, was intended to be the willing pupil of God. God's voice of wisdom says, *"Unto you, O men, I call; and my voice is to the sons of man. O ye simple, understand wisdom: and, ye fools, be ye of an understanding heart"* (Proverbs 8:4,5).

The omniscient Teacher wrote a Book to teach and lead mankind into the full understanding of truth about Himself and His perfect will for all created beings. Because He created man, He understands perfectly the functions of man's mind. God knows how best to captivate the human imagination and lead people to a clear comprehension of truth.

The author of a book must decide what literary style he considers most suitable for his subject and his readers. The author of children's books must approach

---

> God actively revealed Himself within the context of the historical events recorded in the Scriptures.

his subject in a form suitable for his topic, considering the limitations of a child's mind; whereas a person writing for adults must choose a method of presentation suitable for the topic of his book and the intelligence of its prospective adult readers.

The divine Teacher, perfectly knowing His subject matter and human pupils, chose the most suitable literary style for His Book. This Book has been entrusted to the Church, the Body of Christ. The Church, God's representative on earth, was given the Bible to take God's message of reconciliation to the world (II Corinthians 5:18-20). Nevertheless, the Church has generally acted like a teacher who, having been given a well-prepared teaching manual, ignores the method and style of presentation chosen by the author and completely revamps and reorganizes the subject matter in his own teaching format. In most cases, teachers of the Scripture in every department of the church, from the Sunday School to the mission field, have failed to consider and follow God's form of teaching so clearly demonstrated in His teaching manual, the Bible.

History

That which God recorded in the Scriptures actually happened in time and space. God spoke. God acted. God interacted with real, historical human beings. The contents of the Bible are relevant to all people in every age, regardless of their culture, because the Bible is a book of case histories. We are able to identify with those people whose lives are recorded in the Bible. God interacted and spoke to real people, people like us.

God has revealed Himself through His acts in history. When God needed to remind Israel of His true identity, He pointed them back to His historical relationship with their forefathers. The Lord said to Moses, *"...Thus shalt thou say unto the children of Israel, The LORD God of your fathers, the God of Abraham, the God of Isaac, and the God of Jacob, hath sent me unto you: This is my name forever..."* (Exodus 3:15).

The Lord constantly reminded His chosen people, "If you wish to know who I am and what I am, then remember how I acted in relationship with your fathers Abraham, Isaac, and Jacob. Remember how I acted in my relationship with you as a nation. Recollect how I delivered you out of Egypt. Look what I did to the Egyptians through the plagues which I brought on that sinful nation. Remember how I delivered you at the Passover and at the Red Sea. Don't forget how I treated you in the wilderness. Did any of My promises fail? Call to mind how I brought you into this land which I promised you. Remember that I brought judgment upon you because of your idolatry and took you away into Assyria and Babylon but restored you to your own land in fulfillment of My promises." God revealed Himself as He walked through history with man. Cited in the Scriptures are numerous incidents relating to events in Israel's history through which God revealed His nature and character (Exodus 3:13-15; Deuteronomy 7:18-19, 8, 11:1-7; Psalms 105, 106, 111).

Because God actively revealed Himself within the context of the historical events recorded in the Scriptures, Israel's leaders and prophets constantly rehearsed and reminded the people of Israel of their history.

Israel's faith rested on God as revealed through His historical acts. This is seen in their continual remembrance of their deliverance by God out of Egypt at the time of the Passover. The faith of every generation was to be built on the firm foundation of the God of history who had revealed Himself as Israel's Redeemer on that memorable night in Egypt (Exodus 12:24-27). Each successive generation of Israelites was taught the historical facts regarding God's redemption of them as a people. Each individual Israelite had to personally exercise faith if he was to enter into the salvation of the Lord, but this faith was not in some personal subjective experience. It was faith in the Lord of history, the Redeemer of their nation. As the Israelites participated by faith in the Passover celebrations, they were signifying their faith in the God of Israel, the God of redemption, the God of history, the God of Abraham, Isaac, and Jacob. They looked to an historical event which had brought salvation to them as a nation. They knew and trusted in God as He had revealed Himself in history.

God has not only shown what He is like in action in the Old Testament, but also in the New Testament. When God planned to show us finally and completely what He is like, He stepped into history in the person of Jesus Christ His Son. What did Jesus answer when Philip said, *"...Lord, shew us the Father, and it sufficeth us"*? He said, *"...Have I been so long time with you, and yet hast thou not known me, Philip? he that hath seen me hath seen the Father..."* (John 14:8,9). The disciples needed to understand that Jesus was God in action. He was God—living, talking, walking, and speaking before them. If they wanted to see what God was like, they must look to, listen to, and believe on the Lord Jesus. *"No man hath seen God at any time; the only begotten Son, which is in the bosom of the Father, he hath declared him"* (John 1:18).

God was in action in the Old Testament as Jehovah. God was in action in the New Testament as

Jesus Christ. God was also in action in the Acts of the Apostles in the person of the Holy Spirit.

The apostles' emphasis

The apostles recognized the Old Testament as God's record of His involvement in the world and especially with His chosen people in preparation for the coming of the Saviour. The Old Testament was the Bible of the early Church. The apostolic preaching recorded in the Acts first emphasized God's historical acts in relationship to Abraham, Isaac, Jacob, Joseph, Moses, David, and the nation of Israel. The apostles then linked these acts of God in the Old Testament to the revelation of Himself in the history of His Son, Jesus of Nazareth. The apostles interpreted the whole of Christ's advent, life, death, resurrection, present glory, and all future revelations of His majesty on the basis of the historical accounts and prophecies of the Old Testament. They used the Old Testament to authenticate the claim of Jesus of Nazareth to be the Christ. For them, the story of Christ began long before they met Him beside the Sea of Galilee or at the River Jordan where John was baptizing. The faith of the apostles and those who believed the apostles' message rested on the basis of the testimony given concerning the Christ from the Old Testament. They taught the Old Testament and its history and the events which they had so recently experienced in the company of Jesus of Nazareth as one story.

This method of teaching is clearly evident, beginning with Peter's sermon on the day of Pentecost. Another classic example is the sermon of Stephen in which he gives an account of Old Testament history beginning with Abraham. Stephen climaxes his sermon with a brief account of the nation of Israel's attitude toward God's final messenger, the Lord Jesus. Acts 8 records the story of Philip who met the Ethiopian eunuch when the eunuch was reading Isaiah 53. Philip linked this Old Testament portion of Scripture to the events which had so recently taken place at Golgotha and brought this man to an understanding of the Gospel. (Note also Acts 2:22-36, 3:13-26, 7, 10:34-43, 13:16-41, 17:2,3.)

The Church's responsibility

The Old Testament Scriptures, which prepare the mind to see the need and purpose for the incarnation, have been badly neglected by the Church. Multitudes misinterpret the whole purpose of Christ's ministry and death because they have little, if any, understanding of the biblical reasons for His coming. If those who declare the Gospel in homes, churches, Bible studies, and Sunday Schools were to teach the beginnings of the redemptive story from the Old Testament before they teach its fulfillment in the New Testament, many more would clearly understand the advent of Christ as God's plan for their salvation. But, while Christians continue to ignore this divinely revealed order of teaching, the confusion in the minds of many concerning Christ and His mission will continue.

Missionaries who have taken the time to teach people the Old Testament beginnings of the Christ-story and who have carefully followed the unfolding historical drama to its consummation in the New Testament account have testified to the great clarity in their hearers' understanding of the Gospel. In contrast, many have launched almost immediately into the story of Christ with little preparation from the history of the Old Testament. Some, after many years, have found that their message was outwardly accepted but not truly understood.

Bob Goddard, Sr., wrote the following about the Ava tribal people of Paraguay:

"The Jesuit priests established colonies with many of these Indians over 400 years ago. The Jesuits were banished by the political leaders, and the Indian colonies were abandoned. In those days, the Mamelucos of Brazil made raids into Paraguay and carried off many Indians as slaves.

"The results of all this are reflected in the culture and religious beliefs of these Ava people. Religiously, they are willing to accept God and Jesus Christ, as they did from the Catholics years ago. They simply add them to their innumerable list of gods which is continually increasing. This was unknown to our missionaries when they first presented the Gospel to the Avas. Since there were those who were willing to accept their teaching and professed to be Christians, it seemed there was progress. However, as the years passed and very little sign of the reality of changed lives was observed, it was found that they did not understand the Gospel.

"A study of their culture and religion has brought us to the conclusion that we must begin with Genesis and lay a foundation upon which to build so that they can understand who God is, what sin is, how man fell through sin and can be saved only through faith in God's Son, Jesus Christ."

The God of Christianity is the God of history. The faith of Christians is based on God's great revelatory acts, beginning with God's acts of creation and culminating in the historic, redemptive acts of the Lord

Jesus Christ in His birth, life, death, resurrection, and ascension to glory. Therefore, just as it was the responsibility of Israel's teachers to keep the history of Israel, wherein God acted, forever alive in a real and meaningful way as the basis of the faith of all succeeding generations of Israelites, so it is our responsibility to teach, not only the New Testament history of God's redemptive acts in and through our Lord Jesus Christ, but also the Old Testament history wherein God revealed Himself as the God of creation, judgment, and salvation. Just as each individual Israelite was to look back to God's actions in history as the basis of his faith, so must we. For example, to remind us of God's central act of history on which we rest our faith, we have been given the Lord's Supper. *"...Christ our passover is sacrificed for us"* (I Corinthians 5:7).

The Church must teach the historical content of the Scriptures so that people will not look to some subjective personal experience as their hope of salvation but to the objective reality of the living God as He has revealed Himself in and through biblical history and to Christ's historical redemptive experiences on their behalf (II Corinthians 5:18-20). When the historical content of the Scriptures is ignored, people become absorbed with their own subjective experiences rather than with the objective historical saving experiences of Jesus Christ as their representative. What missionaries teach and emphasize to the tribal people will become the foundation and basis of their faith. If our emphasis is on personal experiences, the people will be looking to inner experience as the basis for their acceptance before God. But if our message is biblical history, culminating with God's historical saving work in Christ, their faith will depend on the reality of Christ's accomplishments for them completely, apart from themselves and their own experience. They will look to God's finished work in Christ on their behalf.

The message we are given in the Bible to take to the world is not a list of doctrines or topical points about God. What we declare is that which actually happened in time and space. It is real. It is factual. It is history. When we bypass or ignore the historical content of the Scriptures in which God has revealed Himself and divorce the words of God from their historical context, we are overlooking God's basic form of revelation. Furthermore, we are robbing the Bible of its strongest argument and reason to be recognized and accepted by the world as the only authentic revelation of God. God has stepped into the world's history, not once, not twice, but repeatedly. God has acted. God has spoken. God has not left man without a witness. He has revealed Himself to man as He has walked through history, not only as the Jehovah of the Old Testament but also as Jesus Christ of the New Testament. This marks the basic difference between the Hebrew-Christian faith and all other world religions, both past and present.

> God has revealed Himself to man—this marks the basic difference between the Hebrew-Christian faith and all other world religions.

When Christian theology is stripped of the historical acts of God and presented to the Moslem, the Buddhist, the animist, or adherents to other world religions as a list of doctrines, Christianity then appears to be a mere alternative—the white man's philosophy of God. Furthermore, Christian doctrines, taken apart from their historical revelatory content, can be easily adopted and added to the existing, established concept of God and religion. The result is adaptation and syncretism, a wedding of heathen and Christian doctrines.

The Bible proclaims that the God of history is the one and only Creator, almighty Judge, and Saviour of the world (Isaiah 43:9-17). There is only one true historical religion, that is, the religion of the Bible which was revealed and guided through history by God Himself. All other religions are false and are the deceiving work of Satan. The greatest safeguard against syncretism, misunderstanding, spurious converts, and an experience-oriented religion is the teaching of the Word of God as God has given it with all of its historical content. Therefore, we must not teach a set of doctrines divorced from their God-given historical setting, but rather, we must teach the story of the acts of God as He has chosen to reveal Himself in history. People may ignore our set of doctrines as our western philosophy of God, but the story of God's actions in history cannot be refuted.

God uses this biblical, historical presentation of Himself to convince people of the truth of the Scriptures. Through this, people understand and are convinced that the God of Christians was not created through the speculations and vivid imaginations of Hebrew or Christian philosophers but that He is indeed the living personal God who was and is involved in the history of the whole world. He is the God who is here. He is the God who knows them personally and knew their ancestors, even though they had never heard about Him (Acts 17:24-29). It is particularly important for tribal people to understand that the Christian God did not originate in the mind of some Western religious leader and is not the invented product of the Christian religion.

This then should be our message to the nations, for this has been entrusted to us by God. Through teaching, we are to make all men aware of God's acts in history wherein He has revealed himself. These historical revelations are for all people and have been recorded and preserved by God as the basis for saving faith.

Building Chronologically in Evangelism

As my understanding of biblical principles for teaching the Scriptures grew, so did my desire to put them into practice by evangelizing a new area of Palawan, yet untouched by the Gospel. In 1962, the Lord had used Paul's ambition, *"Yea, so have I strived to preach the gospel, not where Christ was named, lest I should build upon another man's foundation"* (Romans 15:20) to challenge me to leave full-time evangelism in Australia and go to unreached tribal people in the Philippines. Once again, the Lord used this verse to challenge me to go to an area in Palawan which was without a Gospel witness. As I prepared to begin this new work farther south, my greatest fear was lest, after a few years, I find that my methods and teaching had produced the same misunderstanding of the Gospel, syncretism, legalism, and inadequate Old Testament foundations for the understanding of the New Testament with which I had grappled for so many years among the Palawano churches. What needed to be included in my evangelistic teaching program to prevent such misunderstanding?

It was now clear to me that, when evangelizing, one should follow the teaching guidelines demonstrated in the Scriptures. These teaching principles have been discussed in the previous chapters. In order to consider the logical and biblical reason for the teaching program which I am about to introduce, a brief summary is in order.

1. The Scriptures taught in evangelism must expose our hearers to the revelation of God's nature and character in order to prepare them for the Gospel. When evangelizing, one should first teach the holiness, righteousness, and wrath of God against sinners so that people will judge themselves in the light of the biblical concept of God.

2. Because God chose to reveal Himself through His acts in history rather than by mere declarations and propositions, our evangelistic teaching must include the historical sections of Scripture wherein God has shown His true nature and character.

3. The Law must be part of our teaching as we prepare hearts to trust only in Christ, for *"...by the law is the knowledge of sin"* (Romans 3:20). If we want to avoid syncretism, legalism, and a mixture of works and grace, we must use the Law in the correct way so that the consciences of our hearers will be exposed to the Law's convicting and convincing power.

4. The goal of all true evangelism is to see people trusting only in the Lord Jesus Christ and His saving work on their behalf. If our hearers are to understand and correctly interpret the story of the Gospels concerning Christ, we should provide adequate Old Testament Christological background information.

5. During evangelism, our hearers should be taught the basic history and culture of Israel, for only then will they be able to understand the story of the Jewish Messiah, the Old Testament redemptive types which Christ fulfilled, Christ's position as the Son of David, King, and righteous Judge of Israel, His specific ministry to the lost sheep of Israel, and His final rejection by His own people.

These biblical teaching guidelines are essential when evangelizing. How then could I be sure that all of these necessary aspects would be included in my evangelistic teaching program? Where could I find a teaching format which included each biblical teaching principle?

> The best way to evangelize is to begin in the beginning and teach chronologically through the Scriptures.

Considering each principle brought me to the conclusion that the best way to evangelize is to begin in the beginning and teach chronologically through the Scriptures to ensure that people understand the story of Christ and are properly prepared for the Gospel.

This first section of the Chronological Teaching Outline, which is for evangelism and emphasizes **salvation**, begins in Genesis and concludes with the ascension of Christ, as recorded in the book of Acts. The fifty lessons in this course, *Firm Foundations— Creation to Christ,* cover this evangelistic segment of the Chronological Teaching outline.

The Old Testament provides the foundational revelation of God as man's sovereign, omnipotent, omniscient, omnipresent, holy, loving, righteous, merciful, and immutable Creator, Lawgiver, Judge, and Saviour. This revelation of God begins in Genesis 1 and continues through the historical development of the human race and through the lives of the patriarchs, beginning with Abraham. The revelation of God's nature and character is shown by His judgments on Pharaoh and Egypt, the deliverance of Israel from slavery, and God's care for the Israelites in their journey to Mount Sinai. The Lord's sovereign position as man's Creator, Lawgiver, and Judge is solemnly reinforced by the giving of the written Law. The disclosure of God's nature and character continues through His judgments on rebellious Israel, tempered by His mercy and ever-watchful preserving care. Through the ministries of Moses, Joshua, the judges, the kings, and the prophets, God fully manifested that it is His prerogative to condemn the guilty and forgive the repentant.

The Old Testament covers the dispensation of Law. This does not mean that the grace of God was not exhibited during the Old Testament era. The salvation of sinners, beginning with Adam and Eve, has ever and only been through the infinite grace of God. But even though the grace of God is evident in the Old Testament, the sovereignty, righteousness, holiness, and judgment of God are even more noticeable. Through the Law given to Israel, God revealed Himself as the Holy One who will not condone sin nor allow it to go unpunished. God's Law was given during the Old Testament era to expose the innate depravity of the human heart and God's holy anger against all who break His commandments. Therefore, there is no better nor more straightforward way to bring an unsaved person face to face with the demands of God's holy Law than to expose him to the Old Testament portions in which God used the Law to teach and prepare the Israelites to see their helplessness and need of a Saviour.

But is it necessary to teach all of the Old Testament to unsaved people before teaching them the life and saving work of Christ? No! It is quite unnecessary, for the greater part of the Old and New Testaments is addressed to believers. The main purpose of the Gospels, on the other hand, was to lead unsaved people into the knowledge of Christ's life and work of redemption. John said of His Gospel, *"...these are written, that ye might believe that Jesus is the Christ, the Son of God; and that believing ye might have life through his name"* (John 20:31). It logically follows that, when evangelizing, one need only teach those portions of the Old Testament which are the foundations for the story of Christ from His birth to His ascension. Sufficient of the Old Testament story should be taught so that when Old Testament historical and geographical data, prophecies, personalities, and illustrations are referred to or used as illustrations by the Gospel writers, the hearers will already know the stories and so be able to clearly understand the meaning of and reason for the reference.

Following the flow of biblical history

Because God has chosen to reveal Himself within the framework of history, the Scriptures will be most clearly taught if we follow the flow of history from Genesis to Revelation.

The Chronological Teaching Outline is based on the historical sections of the books of the Bible which record this forward movement of history. The chart on the following page illustrates the flow of biblical history.

It takes too long to teach

One of the most common complaints regarding the form of teaching suggested in this book is that it takes too long to teach.

This is the day of speed and easy ways to do everything. Precooked frozen meals, instant desserts, and microwave ovens help make sure everything is on the table in minutes. Every conceivable gadget to speed up the process of daily living is available.

The same type of thinking has made inroads into the Christian Church and is often applied to evangelism, church growth, and every other area of church life.

While Christians should be open to learn more efficient and effective ways to do their work, they must never forget that God's power is manifested and His work is accomplished by the declaration of God's truth in the power of the Holy Spirit. There is no other way.

The Flow of Biblical History

The Books of Historical Movement	Other Books Written During These Periods
Genesis	Job, Psalms
Exodus	Leviticus, Psalms
Numbers	Deuteronomy, Psalms
Joshua	Psalms
Judges	Ruth, Psalms
I and II Samuel	Psalms
I and II Kings	Proverbs, Ecclesiastes, Song of Solomon, I Chronicles, II Chronicles, Isaiah, Hosea, Joel, Amos, Obadiah, Jonah, Micah, Nahum, Habakkuk, Zephaniah, Psalms
Daniel	Jeremiah, Lamentations, Ezekiel
Ezra	Haggai, Zechariah
Nehemiah	Esther
Malachi	
Matthew, Mark, Luke, John	
Acts	James, I and II Thessalonians, Galatians, I and II Corinthians, Romans, Philemon, Ephesians, Colossians, Philippians, I Peter, I Timothy, Titus, II Timothy, Hebrews, II Peter, Jude, I, II, and III John
Revelation	

God does not change His methods to fit in with modern thought and so-called advancements. *"...I am the LORD, I change not..."* (Malachi 3:6). This is true of God's nature, and it is also true of His ways of working.

Man's greatest need is to hear, understand, and respond to the pure Word of God. God's power is inherent in His Word. It was through His Word that the Almighty God brought order out of chaos, light out of darkness, and life to a lifeless world. And it is by His Word that the Lord exposes the wickedness of the human heart, brings life to the dead spirit of man, delivers Satan's captives, and gives sight to the spiritually blind (Isaiah 55:10,11; Luke 4:18; John 8:32; I Peter 1:23-25).

The Christian's responsibility is to teach God's Word in total dependence upon the Holy Spirit. No amount of human wisdom, ingenuity, or high-pressure evangelistic methods can hasten the work of the Holy Spirit and the conversion of a soul. It is not our responsibility to determine or try to force the time of the new birth. We are to faithfully teach all that has been committed to us and leave the work of transformation to the Lord.

One of the greatest faults in the ministry of the Church worldwide is the unwillingness to take the time to teach unsaved people over a long period of time and allow God the Holy Spirit to do His work of enlightening, convicting, and leading people to the type of faith in the Lord Jesus Christ which will give them the assurance to say with Paul, *"...I know whom I have believed, and am persuaded that he is able to keep that which I have committed unto him against that day"* (II Timothy 1:12). Jack Douglas, missionary to the Pawaia tribe in Papua New Guinea, commented, "To teach right through from Genesis took a long time and much effort, but it was well worth it. The Pawaians know what they believe and why."

Most witnessing programs lead Christians into brief, face-to-face encounters with the unsaved. Insufficient effort is put into preparing the non-Christian to either understand the real reasons for or the meaning of the Gospel. Usually, just a few verses, such as Romans 3:23, are quoted to the unsaved and the person is then urged to make his or her decision for Christ.

The Scriptures make it clear that one person may be given the responsibility by God to sow the seed, another to water it, and yet another may reap the harvest (John 4:36-38; I Corinthians 3:6,7). In most methods of evangelism today, the person who sows is also expected to reap immediately. Truly the Lord is not limited. His Word is mighty to save, and He often does use the same person to both sow and reap. But our responsibility is to be sure that we are faithfully preaching all He has told us from His Word so that people are scripturally prepared for the Gospel. Then we can trust Him to give the increase.

The most effective witnessing programs are those which allow Christians to teach God's Word systematically and to depend upon the Holy Spirit to do the work in His time. God's children should get to know unsaved people, establish Bible studies in their homes and teach consistently, even over weeks or months, those things which God has recorded in His Word as the foundations for the Gospel.

Tell the Gospel to the prepared

I have already given the reasons why the basic structure of the Old Testament should be taught to unsaved people before they are taught the New Testament story of Christ and the Gospel. But it must not be inferred that I am suggesting that no person can be saved until he has heard and understood all of the Old Testament Outline presented in this teaching program. Nor am I saying that the teacher must not give the Gospel to a person prepared for the Gospel until he has been taught the proposed outline. We must not be bound by an outline, but we should be guided by biblical principles which are clearly taught throughout the entire Word of God.

If, at any point during the teaching of the Old Testament Outline, an individual in a group of people is spiritually enlightened to his lost condition before God, the teacher will need the spiritual discernment to know when he should give that awakened sinner further private teaching on the birth, life, death, and resurrection of the Lord Jesus Christ. Just as it is wrong to press the Gospel on those who have not been prepared by God, it is equally wrong to withhold the Gospel from those who have been taught by God, who are broken in spirit, and who are hungry for the mercy and forgiveness of the Saviour. Undoubtedly, some people will come to understand and will be well prepared by the Holy Spirit to receive the Gospel before the teaching of the Gospels is to begin. When I was faced with this situation, I took the individual aside from the group and questioned him carefully to see if he clearly understood the basic truths concerning God, His holiness, hatred and judgment on sin, and the person's own sinful condition in God's sight. Having determined that the person was truly under conviction and understood and accepted God's Word, I then briefly, but carefully, told him of God's complete provision for sinners through the holy birth, life, sacrificial death, burial, and victorious resurrection of Christ. If a person is truly prepared by God, faith in Christ will surely be the result of hearing and understanding the Gospel (John 6:44,45).

A young Palawano man named Kamlon was attending meetings where I had been teaching the Scriptures chronologically for about three months. One day, Kamlon came to me and said, "I am going to begin praying to your God." I had not prayed with the Palawano people during our teaching periods, but they knew the Roman Catholics prayed, and they had seen us giving thanks for our meals in our home.

I asked, "Kamlon, do you think that by praying you will be able to reach God? Don't you remember how God put Adam and Eve out of the garden and put His cherubim there with the flaming sword? Could praying remove the flaming sword? Could talking to God get them back into the garden?"

He answered, "No, it couldn't."

I asked, "Then why do you think that by praying you will be able to come to God? What is the punishment for sin?"

He replied, "Death."

We had already reached the story of the giving of the Law in our group meeting. So we talked together about the Old Testament stories which illustrate that death is God's righteous judgment on sin.

I said, "God requires death. It is a fixed price." This term, "fixed price," had been used during our teaching and is the term used in the Philippines when vendors indicate that they will not bargain for an article. In some larger stores, when a person begins to bargain, the sales assistant will often say, "Sorry, fixed price." They won't bargain because all the articles are at a fixed price. So I said to Kamlon, "God's price is fixed. God requires death. Prayer is not the price God requires. He will accept nothing less than death, which is separation from God."

Kamlon continued to attend the daily times of teaching; but, about one week later, he again came to speak to me. "Kalang Kayu," he addressed me. (This name, meaning "Big Tree," was the name given to me by the tribal people because of my height in comparison to theirs.) "I realize now," Kamlon said, "that praying will not get me back to God. But, what am I going to do? I know from God's Word that I am a sinner. I am sure of that. I know that I am going to Hell. What can I do?"

Praising God in my heart for what the Holy Spirit had taught this man, I replied, "Kamlon, you have asked me what you can do. Tell me, what is the price to be paid?"

He answered, "Death."

I said, "Kamlon, if you want to pay for your own sin, then you must go to Hell. You will be separated from God forever. The punishment for your sin will never end."

He stood there looking thoroughly miserable and finally said, "Then, I will have to go to Hell."

Immediately, I thought, No, you won't. I knew that Kamlon had been taught by God. Through the Old Testament Scriptures, he had seen the basic truths about God, himself, and his sin. He was prepared to understand the Gospel and to trust in Christ alone for salvation.

"Kamlon," I said, "Come up and we will sit on the veranda." We went up and sat down. Then I questioned him, "Do you remember how that in the garden, after man sinned, God promised to send One who would be the child of a virgin? God promised that He would destroy Satan because he had brought man under his control."

He answered, "Yes, I remember."

I then reminded him of the story of Abraham. I asked, "Do you remember how God promised the Saviour through Abraham?"

He replied, "Yes, I remember that."

I went over the key Old Testament stories which point forward to the coming Saviour. Then, on the basis of these Old Testament stories and God's promises concerning Christ, I said, "Kamlon, the Saviour has already come."

During the next hour or so, I briefly told him the story of Christ. When I finally came to the point where Christ died in our place, I told Kamlon, "God knew you would be born. God knew you would be a sinner. God knew you would deserve everlasting punishment because of your sinfulness. And God knew He could not save you unless that debt of sin was completely paid. The Lord Jesus, because of His great love, agreed to come and take the responsibility of paying for all of your sin."

When I spoke of Christ's death on the cross, Kamlon said with a great big smile on his face, "Then if He died for me, I don't have to die. He is my debt-payer."

Right there and then, his soul rested in the truth of the Scriptures. He trusted in Christ as his "debt-payer." He accepted the fact that what he could not do, God had done for him.

Dennis and Jeanie O'Keefe who are missionaries to the Molbog tribe in Southern Philippines wrote the following about a young tribal man to whom Dennis taught the Scriptures chronologically.

"Almost every day, either coming or going to his rice fields, Saya would stop by my office for a cup of coffee, and we would talk. Precious were those times. He was beginning to understand real biblical truth. Present in his conversation was an awakening realization that he could not meet God's requirements and would be punished eternally for his sins and his sin nature.

"After I had taught in other villages, it was time to continue with Saya. So, in one day, Saya and I went from the tabernacle to the Cross. What a joy! All the pieces of the puzzle came together in the man Christ Jesus. He was stunned. As his mind raced from Genesis 3:15 to John 19:30, '...It is finished...,' we sat in silence for a few moments. Then he said, 'Do you mean to say that He carried on Himself my sins?'

"God has done this, and it is beautiful in our sight. All of us can rejoice in the new horizons which have been made possible by God's grace demonstrated in this one man."

Brief encounters

I trust it is obvious all the way through this book that I have in mind situations where people can be ministered to over an extended period of time. This is possible in well-programmed missionary work, Sunday schools, Bible classes, and the ministry of the local church. But what does one do when he only has a short time to preach to people?

While we should never be bound to any teaching outline, we should always be guided, even in brief encounters, by biblical principles. One clear principle which we have already discussed is that only those prepared and drawn by God the Holy Spirit can and will come to Christ. God does not do what He commands us not to do. He does not "cast pearls before swine."

We should not press the Gospel on unprepared people. But there is a great difference between the general public declaration of God's historical work in Christ for the whole world and the personal application of that work to an individual. A preacher in a public gathering, speaking to a mixed group of people whose hearts' condition he does not and cannot know, may have complete liberty to present the Gospel and all of God's gracious invitations to repentant sinners. Even so, he should always be aware that only those taught, convicted, and broken by God through His Word and the work of the Holy Spirit, will believe and appropriate the saving message of the Gospel. Those who reject the foundations of the Gospel — that is, the holy and righteous, but merciful, character of God, and the sinful, lost, and helpless condition of every man outside of Christ — cannot trust in the saving historical work of God the Son and be born of the Spirit. Therefore, even in public Gospel meetings where the speaker may not have the opportunity to teach the same people again, the preacher should emphasize the nature and character of God and the demands of the holy and righteous Law of God before God's good news of the Gospel is offered.

In the book of Acts, when Paul entered a Jewish synagogue, he first reminded his hearers of the Old Testament foundational history wherein God revealed Himself and His promises regarding the coming Redeemer. Having done this, Paul then presented the claims of Jesus of Nazareth to be the long-promised Messiah and showed that Christ's death and resurrection authenticated Him as God's appointed Saviour for all who believe. Immediately, there was a division between Paul's hearers. The prepared ones longed to hear more; the hard-hearted and self-dependent rejected his message. Those who responded were taken aside and taught further by the Apostle, so that their faith would rest on a clear exposition of Old Testament Scriptures in the light of the new revelation in Christ.

In other situations where Christians have only a brief opportunity to witness to an individual — on a train, a bus, a plane, in a store, on the street, or at their home — the same biblical principles should be followed as much as possible in the limited time available. Rather than having a "hit and run" ministry in brief encounters, Christians should try to keep in contact with people and follow up with continued teaching, preferably in a Bible study. If that is impossible, then good literature may be used which will lead them through the Scriptures and bring them to a clear knowledge of Christ.

In one area where we worked as missionaries in Palawan, the local witch doctor was an elderly woman. Her husband was gravely ill and no longer able to walk. Day and night, he lay on his sleeping mat.

I passed their house daily on my way to teach a leper who was the brother of the witch doctor. In the beginning, I stopped to greet them, to inquire about the man's health, and to ask if we could be of any assistance. At first, they resisted our offers to give them medical help, but after some time, they relented. Following this, I took the opportunity to stay for a while to introduce the Bible as the Word of God and to speak of God, the only eternal supreme being. Very soon after this, they sent a message through their grandson saying that they did not want to hear anymore about God. Following this incident, they could barely bring themselves to bid me the time of day. Their antagonism to us and our message was obvious in their whole demeanor.

The Palawano custom for a married man requires him to leave his own locality and live with his wife in her home area. But if he becomes very ill or knows that he does not have long to live, he will generally ask to be taken back to his own people. When the witch doctor's husband realized his death was imminent, he was carried back to the home of his relatives.

Sometime later, we were greatly surprised when some of his relatives walked three hours to request me to come and tell the dying man about God. This invitation was certainly evidence of God's work in his life.

Rejoicing in the possibility that maybe the little seed previously sown in his mind had been used by the Holy Spirit, I went immediately with his relatives to the house where he was. He was close to death, but he was still able to whisper brief responses to my few questions.

Sitting close by his side, I leaned over him and began to explain, "What I am about to tell you are not my words or the thoughts of people, but the words of the only true and living God."

Inwardly, I have never felt more helpless than I did that day. I was calling on the Lord to give me wisdom and clarity and to give the dying man understanding, conviction, repentance, and faith.

I continued, "God tells us in His book that He created all things." I elaborated on this, adding, "God also created the first man, Adam, who was the father of the entire human race." I wanted this man to understand that this included the Palawanos and therefore him.

The old man appeared to be listening as I continued, "God placed Adam in a beautiful garden. In this garden, God had planted two very important trees, the Tree of Life and the Tree of the Knowledge of Good and Evil." After explaining in very simple terms the meaning of these two trees, I said, "God warned Adam that disobedience would bring death. Death not only means physical death but also everlasting separation from God in a place of punishment."

At this point, I suggested that he rest and think about what I had said. This also gave me an opportunity to teach his relatives who had gathered in the house.

Returning to him after a short while, I asked if he understood what I had told him so far. He assured me that he did, so from Genesis 3, I told of the temptation and fall of man. I then explained Genesis 3:15, "God promised that one day He would send a Saviour who would destroy Satan and deliver man from his power. God put Adam and Eve out of the garden. They were shut out, away from God, without any way to return, unless God Himself made a way for them."

I then related the story of Cain and Abel to this old man. I emphasized, "Both Cain and Abel were born outside of the garden and were sinners because of their father, Adam. They were separated from God and could not escape the judgment of God on sin, unless God Himself did something to save them."

The old man moved his position slightly in order to catch every word. I went on. "These truths apply to all people, and what is most important, they also apply to you. Because you, too, are a descendent of Adam, you were born away from God, cut off from the Tree of Life."

I paused and then explained how God instructed man that, if he wished to approach God, he must take a lamb and kill it. I stressed, "They had to come to God in the way which God had instructed them. They had to kill the lamb. Its blood had to be shed. Now, the blood of the animal could not pay for sin. But the blood had to be shed to remind the offerers that they deserved to die and that only God could save them. Their faith had to be in God, not in themselves or anything that they could do."

Then I briefly told the story of how Cain refused to come God's way and was therefore rejected, whereas Abel came God's way, trusting in God's mercy and promises and was accepted by Him. Having laid this groundwork, I applied all of these truths personally to my hearer.

"There is no way you can save yourself. Your sin must be paid for by everlasting separation from God. He will not accept anything less. Only God can save you. Like Abel, you must accept God's way if you want to be saved."

"Be warned. Don't be like Cain and think that you can come to God in your own way."

The old man looked thoughtful, and I said, "I will let you think about what you have heard, and then I will tell you what God has done so that you can be forgiven of all your sins and be saved from the punishment you deserve."

Returning a short while later to his side, I asked him a few questions, and he acknowledged, "Yes, I am a sinner." He then requested, "Tell me what God has done for me."

My heart was filled with joy as I unfolded, in the most uncomplicated way I could, the story of the Gospel.

"God sent His only Son into the world to be your Saviour. Christ was born of the virgin, just as God promised. He lived a perfect life. The majority of people rejected Him and crucified Him. He could have destroyed them all and returned to Heaven, but He allowed them to nail Him to the cross so that He could pay for the punishment for all of the sins of mankind."

I reminded this old man who was so close to eternal damnation, "God's punishment for sin is everlasting separation from Him in terrible punishment."

Then I said, "When Jesus was dying on the cross, He called out, 'My God, my God, why hast thou forsaken Me?' Why do you think the Lord Jesus was forsaken by God? The Lord Jesus was forsaken and died to be the Saviour of sinners. The Lord Jesus died for you to take your separation so that God could forgive all of your sins and give you everlasting life."

I quoted John 3:16 and shared with him the story of the resurrection.

Sitting close by his side and looking into his face which already had death etched on it, I told him, "The Lord Jesus can see you right now, just where you are lying on your sleeping mat. If you trust in Him and accept His payment on the cross for your sin, God will forgive you for all your sins."

There was a note of urgency in my voice as I continued, "If you accept him, you will not go to the place of everlasting punishment, but to Heaven to be with God forever."

"Don't be like Cain," I implored him. "Don't think that you can come to God in your own way. Your sin has to be paid for, and there is only one payment that God will accept; that is, the payment the Lord Jesus Christ made for you when He was forsaken by God because of your sins."

"Do you understand? Do you want to ask me any questions?" I inquired.

With barely a whisper, he answered, "Yes, I understand." He seemed to be deep in thought as he closed his eyes.

Hiking back through the jungle to our own home in the gathering darkness, my heart was calling on the Lord in His great mercy to save that man.

A short time later, we were visited by some of this old man's relatives who told us that the man had died in the early hours of the morning after my visit. But before he died, he had told them to tell the Big Tree (my tribal name) that there was no need to worry about him because he was trusting in the Lord Jesus who had taken the punishment for his sin. Praise God for His great mercy and the simplicity of the Gospel!

Situations vary greatly. Sometimes we may not have even as much time as I had with this dying man. We should do whatever we can in the time given to us by the Lord to make the Word of God clear and plain and trust the Lord to use whatever we are able to say in brief encounters. But whenever possible, it is our responsibility to teach in such a way so that people will know why they must come to Christ and so that they will trust only in Him and His death on their behalf.

Evangelism for mixed groups— unbelievers and believers

Many groups and churches, like those which we first taught in Palawan, are confused regarding the way of salvation. The evangelistic phase of the Chronological Teaching Outline has been effectively used to teach such churches and groups. Many individuals, who previously thought they were children of God, have been enlightened to their true condition through the Old Testament revelation of God's holiness, His demands for perfection as revealed through the Law, and His terrible judgments on rebellious sinners. Then, through the story of the Gospels, they have seen for the first time that they have no need to work for their salvation, for Christ has provided all that God righteously requires.

I wish I had understood this when I first began to teach the tribal churches in Palawan. I tried to straighten out their understanding by first teaching justification topically and then expositionally from the Epistle to the Romans even though they did not have solid Old Testament foundations. In spite of the difficulties I faced in teaching and they faced in understanding, many Palawano church members were eventually enlightened to their lost condition and came to trust in Christ. But how much more simple and clear the teaching and learning process would have been if I had followed the divinely revealed order and taught chronologically through the Old Testament as preparation for the Gospel of grace revealed in the New Testament!

Years later, after I had seen my mistakes and had taught the Scriptures chronologically in another area of Palawan, I returned to the area of our initial labors to teach chronologically from Genesis to the ascension of Christ. After teaching them for a short time, some of the elders came to me and asked, "Why didn't you teach us this way from the beginning? This way of teaching makes everything so much clearer!" They could now see how everything they had been taught previously from the New Testament fit together with the Old Testament and was one comprehensive whole. I readily agreed with them, because it was also obvious to me that those whom I had taught chronologically from the beginning had a clarity of understanding of the Scriptures and the Gospel far beyond those taught only topically or expositionally from the New Testament.

The following material was written by Tim Cain and Larry Richardson, concerning the Puinave Indian work in Colombia.

"When we went into the Puinave work, we went with the assumption that there was a legitimate New Testament Church which lacked good teaching. But the more we understood of the language and the people, the more we realized there were some real problems. We came to the conclusion that the majority of the Puinave who called themselves 'Christians' were, in fact, spiritually dead. Here are some of the things that we observed:

A. The 'elders' tried to force the younger generation to conform to 'Christianity.' Christianity to them meant (1) no smoking or drinking, (2) going to meetings daily, (3) going to conference, (4) giving a testimony by confessing a few sins or promising to live without sin from now on, and (5) getting baptized.

B. The people did not have an in-depth understanding of the Word of God. They knew a few Old Testament stories and a bit more from the New Testament, but they had no idea of the chronology of the stories or their significance.

C. There was no spiritual growth.

D. The people continued to practice witchcraft. The witch doctor was condemned, but his methods were not.

E. Genuine conviction of sin was not apparent.

F. The death of Jesus seemed to be something additional that God deemed necessary.

"We began to step back in our minds, trying to find where we should start teaching, and we found ourselves back at the beginning. The Chronological Approach was of great inspiration and help to us.

"As I (Tim) began to teach, I apologized to them for the confusion we had caused by not beginning at the beginning, and I promised that I would try my best to do it right this time.

"We taught up to the ascension of Christ, and all along, the people showed great interest. But nothing happened.

"What do you do but go over it all again?

"On the third time through, they began to spontaneously voice their understanding and acceptance.

"Alberto, one of the village leaders, told me he had come very close to going to Hell. He said he had 'played church' for thirty years and that his baptism was 'just a bath.' But now, he understood that it wasn't what he had done but what Jesus had done for him that made him right with God.

"One very old tribal man stood up at the end of one of our teaching sessions to testify. Standing there in all that noise and confusion, he said, 'I finally understand. I am a very bad sinner, but Jesus paid the price for my sin with his death.' The people around him tried to get him to sit down but he said, 'No, I want to say this!' He went on to share a clear testimony.

"Another man, who is a deacon in one of the Puinave churches, also testified, 'Up until now, I have always thought that God would accept me because of the things I have done for Him. I was baptized. I helped call the people together for meetings. I always got lots of food together so we could receive the people well when we hosted conferences. I always participated in the pre-dawn prayer meeting. I'm sure those are the things God saw upon my heart, because they are the things I was offering to Him in order to be able to approach Him. But now I understand that those things are just like the fruits Cain offered God, so I have removed them and replaced them with the blood of Christ. That's what God sees now upon my heart. That is what I am offering to God now, just like Abel slew the animal long ago.'

"In another Indian conference, we were also teaching from the first part of the Bible chronology. Alberto, who had been a believer for a year or so at the time, was helping teach, and he was also translating into Curipaco for those who did not understand Puinave. He and I both felt this particular group was not yet ready to apply what we had been teaching to salvation. Therefore, we closed the last meeting simply with an exhortation for the listeners to think carefully about what they had heard and to ask themselves what it was that they might be offering to God. Suddenly, without my even noticing it, an old lady stood up way back in the shadows and began to speak in Curipaco. In a moment, I became aware that something was going on and waited for an explanation. It was soon forthcoming. Alberto turned and told me, 'That old lady says she has found her offering—the blood of Jesus Christ, which He shed on the cross. That's what she will offer to God.'

"These people had previously received topical teaching from other missionaries and had read from the New Testament for many years, so this was not by any means their first exposure to Christianity."

Correct Foundations for Teaching Believers

Our emphasis thus far has been on Biblical guidelines for evangelism. At this point, I would like to turn our attention to biblical principles for teaching believers.

Because I had been schooled in traditional Bible teaching methods, the majority of my early teaching ministry to the tribal believers in Palawan was done topically. The practical difficulties I encountered in topical teaching impelled me to look to the Scriptures for more logical and practical methods of teaching the Word of God. In this chapter, I will share some of my experiences with tribal believers which prompted me to examine God's methods of teaching His children as recorded in the Bible. Even though many of the problems about which I will write are accentuated due to the primitive, poorly-educated people involved, the points are relevant and worthy of consideration by those teaching affluent and well-educated people.

Principally while teaching monthly Bible conferences for Palawano elders and Bible teachers, it became evident to me that topical teaching is not the best form of Bible teaching for those who are poorly-educated, slow in understanding, or easily distracted. Neither is it the best form of teaching for those not well conversant with the location of the individual books in the Bible or those who are lacking a simple but basic understanding of the overall progressive and historical biblical revelation.

These monthly conferences when the leaders from all of the scattered Palawano churches came together to be taught were of prime importance in my teaching program. The conferences were aimed at establishing the leaders and, through them, their churches in a basic understanding of the complete revelation of the Scriptures. Nevertheless, much valuable time was wasted during these sessions as over one hundred men, mostly poorly-educated and inexperienced in the Scriptures, searched in their New Testaments for the numerous references necessary to establish the doctrine being taught.

> The Scriptures were not prepared in an analytical, topical form.

Difficult to follow

When I gave a Scripture reference for the Palawanos to find, there would immediately be a great deal of mumbling and whispering. They could not easily remember the reference given, so they were continually inquiring what the reference was from whomever was sitting near them. The first ones to find the verse would often begin reading the section laboriously, audibly sounding out letters and words. Instead of paying attention to my teaching, they were absorbed in inquiring from one another or trying to read the passage which they were so pleased to have found. Instead of their minds being occupied with the subject being taught, they were repeatedly distracted because they had to find the portions from many parts of the Bible.

Difficult to record, review, and reteach

It was very important that these teachers be able to review all that they were taught during the conferences so that they would clearly understand and remember in order to teach the same truths to their congregations. In order to review the subject matter taught, all references had to be recorded, and notes made to indicate which part of the verse had to be emphasized.

The tribal people's attempts at taking notes were usually disastrous. The notes they made were of little use for review and too sketchy as a guide for them to use in teaching others. The notebooks which I provided for them were soon dirty and tattered and falling to pieces, especially after being tucked up between the palm-leaf roofing in their huts. Nevertheless, they struggled to do their best to take notes. They wrote down each reference, carefully and painstakingly forming the letters and figures with a stub of a pencil or their modern "bull-pin," as they called their ballpoint pens. Admittedly, after much practice, they did improve, and the younger men became quite proficient in note taking, but what an unnecessary and time-wasting exercise. Eventually, I typed and duplicated simple notes for them. These were a great help, but they caused other problems. If only I had taught them the Scriptures as they have been given by God! The teaching, learning, reviewing, and the passing on to others of that teaching would have been much less complicated.

Often, in topical teaching, only a phrase or a few words from a verse are needed to establish the doctrinal point being taught. This is a difficult concept for many people to comprehend. It was certainly troublesome for the Palawanos who tend to view subjects as a whole rather than in separate parts. This particular problem came to my attention when I had a book of doctrines prepared to be taught in the churches. I would teach a topic from this book to the church leaders, and they would return to their churches and teach the same subject to their own village congregations.

During one conference with these men, I taught from this book of doctrines on the nature and character of God. The following weekend, according to my custom, I hiked to a tribal church to give on-the-spot teaching to the whole church and to check how the elders were handling the teaching which had been assigned to them. On Sunday morning, I listened as one of the tribal elders began to teach. He turned to the point in the outline, "God is love." Under this heading, various references were listed, one being John 3:16. The elder read this verse, and then he began to teach. First, he emphasized that God is love from the words, *"For God so loved the world...."* According to the topical outline he had been given, that was as far as he was to go in John 3:16. But he continued. He went on to teach on the incarnation, basing his comments on the words, *"...that he gave his only begotten Son...."* And he didn't stop there. He continued reading, *"...that whosoever believeth in him should not perish...,"* and he emphasized the necessity of faith in Christ and the perishing condition of those who do not believe. He concluded his exposition of John 3:16 with some comments on the certainty of *"everlasting life"* and the bliss of Heaven for all believers.

While he and his hearers were enjoying God's Word, just as God had recorded it, I was frustrated and disappointed. I wanted him to teach as I had taught him at the conference from my book of topical, systematic theology. I wondered if they would ever be able to teach God's Word correctly. To teach it correctly, I reasoned, was to teach it analytically and topically.

As I sat there feeling I had failed and wondering what was the best way to train them to become able teachers of the Word, it suddenly occurred to me that the Holy Spirit wrote John 3:16 just the way the tribal elder had expounded it. Why then arrange it under subject headings? How much more straightforward and uncomplicated teaching and learning would be if all of the Scriptures were taught expositionally just as they have been revealed and recorded.

We make the teaching and learning of the Scriptures unnecessarily hard when we insist on topical teaching as our primary method of instruction. Western culture approaches most subjects analytically. We feel it necessary to dissect everything, examining and categorizing each portion. But many cultures do not approach the teaching and learning process in this way.

When the Lord prepared the Scriptures, He had all people in mind. If He had planned to speak only to us Westerners and had asked us what literary form His writing should take, our answer would probably have been, "A systematic theology." Wisely, the Lord did not do this. The Scriptures were not prepared in an analytical, topical form, for apparently this is not the preferable way to teach God's Word, even in Western culture.

While these things were going through my mind, the tribal elder proceeded to expound the next verse listed in the outline, and I began to observe the different people in the congregation. Across the aisle, a precious old lady who dearly loved the Word of God was holding her New Testament close to her face, trying to read it in the dim light. Other women were trying to follow the references and keep their attention on the speaker, in spite of the constant distractions caused by crying babies, wriggling and whispering children, and surly, growling dogs. The men and boys were all seated on my side of the palm-leaf and bamboo chapel. All ages were present. As I watched them, I wondered how much they really understood. Did they understand enough to be built up in true heart knowledge so their lives would reflect the character of the Lord? How much would they remember during the week? Would they be able to review the teaching in the quietness of their houses scattered through the jungle?

The Palawano believers were encouraged to pass God's message on to others during the week when they were working in their fields, washing clothes, pounding rice, visiting, or just sitting around the fire at night.

I also wondered if they understood clearly enough to be able to do this.

As I looked at this congregation with all ages and differing reading and writing abilities, I realized that our complex teaching methods hinder the spread of the Word of God by the ordinary people. We feel we have to arrange the Scriptures into individual topics and under, what we think, are suitable headings. How much more simple it would be if they were taught verse by verse and book by book! They would not need to turn to verses all over their Bibles or write down numerous references. At home, reviewing the section studied in the meeting would be greatly simplified. Discussing and sharing the portion with others would be much easier. Preparing for the coming meeting would be uncomplicated, for they would only have to read the next portion of Scripture instead of many scattered verses.

May cause division

Many missionaries find themselves dependent on younger men to teach and lead tribal churches because the difference between the young and the old, educated and uneducated, is unnecessarily accentuated by the analytical, topical approach which is taught to them as the primary method of teaching the Word of God. Younger men, however, lack the natural experiences of life which prepare one to be a wise instructor. In many cultures, the young men would not be granted the respect so necessary for a church teacher and leader. Many missionaries can testify to the heartache of seeing young, promising leaders ruined for the ministry through pride, adultery, and a host of other vices and inconsistencies.

Most of the young Palawano men had attended elementary school, but only a few of the older ones had any schooling. The young men's exposure to Western-style education enabled them to follow topical teaching more easily and to reteach, using the topical method. This meant that some of the younger men had to take the position of leading teachers in the churches. According to their culture, however, such leadership positions belonged to the older men.

Large sections of the Scriptures overlooked

We all have a tendency to "ride our own hobby-horse" and gravitate to the subject or doctrines which we feel are most important. The result is that large sections of the Scriptures are usually overlooked in many churches, while other parts of the Bible receive most of the attention.

In Palawan, the tribal teachers taught the same topics and passages over and over. Rather than teach unfamiliar, unexplored sections of God's Word, they returned frequently to the same verses or topics.

Misinterpretation of verses out of context

Due to topical and doctrinal sermons on isolated Scripture portions, many who have been Christians for a long time are not able to interpret even familiar verses in the context of the book or epistle of which they are a part. The reason for this is obvious. The majority have seldom, if ever, been taught the wider context of these well-known verses. Having never been introduced to the basic framework of biblical progressive revelation, they may understand verses, or even chapters or sections of Scripture which deal with some particular topic, but they do not understand the Bible as one book. They do not comprehend the great necessity to interpret all Scripture in the light of the whole of progressive revelation.

This was emphasized to me by the sermon of a sincere tribal man on Matthew 24:2, *"And Jesus said unto them, See ye not all these things? verily I say unto you, There shall not be left here one stone upon another, that shall not be thrown down."* After reading this verse, he pointed to the rocky hills surrounding the grass-roofed chapel where he was standing. He solemnly warned the people that when Jesus comes again to judge the world, all of the stones on the hills around them would be cast down. "Not one will remain upon the other," he emphasized.

While I sat there trying to still my inner turmoil at his incorrect interpretation, the truth dawned on me that he was not to blame. I was to blame. I had led him to scattered verses when teaching a doctrine or developing a topic, but I had not consistently taught the Scriptures in such a way that he could understand the need to interpret verses in context nor how to do it.

It was through such incidents that I was prompted to turn from using the topical teaching approach to the more simple and direct method of verse-by-verse exposition in order to help the people understand Scripture in its immediate context. But this, too, proved inadequate, for the believers had not been taught the Old Testament Scriptures which provide the background and foundation for the New Testament. They did not understand God's Word as one book.

God's teaching

God's fundamental form of teaching throughout all history is clearly progressive. God gradually unfolded the Bible's message over the ages. This God-controlled unfolding of truth has been likened to the growth of grain, *"...first the blade, then the ear, after that the full corn in the ear"* (Mark 4:28). God chose to make known His nature and character, His plan for the world, His purpose of redemption through Christ, and all other spiritual matters through progressive revelation.

God's basic method of teaching can be likened to the way an artist paints a picture. An artist does not begin painting in one corner of the canvas and immediately complete every detail. Instead, he will often do an initial, simple, light sketch of the whole picture. To an onlooker, the picture in the early stages will be indistinct. Even when studied, it may not be clear just what the artist intends to include in the final product. But, as the artist continues to work on the picture, here a little and there a little, the details begin to develop with greater clarity. This process continues until the final strokes are applied and the picture is complete.

This is how God painted His picture of the drama of redemption. He began the sketch in the early chapters of Genesis. Genesis 3:15 is a simple, undetailed sketch of the whole picture of the redemption story. Sharper, clearer details were then added by God in the call and life of Abraham. More color and features were put onto the canvas in the offering of Isaac and the perfect lamb substitute which God provided. Jacob's dream, the Passover, the manna from Heaven, the water from the smitten rock, the giving of the Law, the building of the Tabernacle, the brazen serpent, Joshua's victorious ministry, and other historical events are all strokes of the Artist's brush as He painted the background of the picture. The Master Painter continued adding details as He guided the events of Old Testament history toward the revelation of Christ, the main subject of the painting. Obscure images and lightly sketched areas suddenly emerged when Jesus came to live, die, and rise again. But even then, the canvas did not contain the whole picture. Through the apostles, the Holy Spirit continued the painting. The final strokes to God's picture were made when the revelation of Jesus Christ, given to John on the Isle of Patmos, was added.

> All doctrines begin in seed form in Genesis and are progressively revealed, little by little, throughout the Old and New Testaments.

God never taught all there was to know about any particular doctrine or subject at one specific time. He often revealed some new area of truth, but He never immediately gave the whole truth regarding any one subject. God's method of teaching can be compared to the way most people prefer their meals served. A man would be surprised if he went home to find his wife had prepared a meal consisting only of potatoes and if he heard her say, "Today, we are having potatoes. Tomorrow, we will have beans. The day after tomorrow, we will have just meat on the menu." Who would be happy with that type of menu? We usually like a meal to consist of different types of vegetables and some meat. This is how God wrote His Word. This is how God feeds us from His Word when we study it just as He has given it.

Turn anywhere in God's Word, and you will readily see that one verse can give information, either directly or indirectly, about many different subjects. Whole books could be written by carefully examining and expounding one verse. Just as there are many facets on a diamond, a verse, when scrutinized under the guidance of the Holy Spirit, will reveal many different points of truth relating to many different doctrines.

During some seminars with missionaries, I have asked an individual to turn in the Bible to the doctrine of the Holy Spirit. I have requested that another turn to the doctrine of Man, another to the doctrine of Satan, and another to the doctrine of the Church. Some people have started to open their Bibles, and then hesitated. They could not turn to a specific doctrine, because the teaching of doctrines is not grouped together in the Bible. All doctrines begin in seed form in Genesis and are progressively revealed, little by little, throughout the Old and New Testaments. It is impossible to turn to a complete doctrine by turning to one place in the Bible.

God's method of revelation and instruction is clearly progressive in the life of every individual He prepared for His service during the history of the Old Testament. When God created Adam, it was God's desire and purpose that Adam should be taught to know Him, in all His sovereignty, majesty, and glory. How then did God begin to teach Adam? What method did God use? Did He systematically and topically teach Adam all there was to know about Him, his Creator?

No! How mundane and limited God's first revelation to Adam appears to be! God said, *"...Be fruitful, and multiply, and replenish the earth, and subdue it: and have dominion over the fish of the sea, and over the fowl of the air, and over every living thing that moveth upon the earth"* (Genesis 1:28). The Lord then told Adam what he and Eve were to eat. In this initial revelation, God did not even speak directly of Himself. Yet, by what He said and commanded, God revealed basic and important truths about Himself. By commanding Adam to be fruitful and to multiply, the Lord clearly declared Himself to be Adam's lawgiver and master of every area of life. By authoritatively placing Adam as His vice-regent over the whole earth and by commanding Adam to have dominion over every living thing in the earth, He was showing Adam that He, the Lord, is the rightful owner of the earth and all things in it. After God had placed Adam in the garden of Eden, He again spoke to him and commanded him regarding the Tree of Life and the Tree of the Knowledge of Good and Evil. This was but a further revelation of God's role in His relationship to man, for by the solemn declaration that death would be the inevitable punishment for disobedience, He was showing Adam that He alone is God, the judge and executor of righteousness in the earth. These are the only accounts that we have of the words of God to Adam before Adam's disobedience. But, as God met with man, it would seem that He planned to teach Adam progressively, adding slowly to those initial revelations of His will and plan, according to Adam's ability to assimilate the information given to him.

How did God teach Abraham when He called him? Did God call Abraham and say, "Now, Abram, before you leave Chaldea, I want to tell you all of My plans for you and your descendents?" Is that what God did? No! Abraham went out, not knowing where the Lord was leading him. God revealed only what was necessary for each stage of Abraham's experience. Through progressive revelations, God taught Abraham, adding knowledge to knowledge, for Abraham was to walk by faith.

Further illustrations of God's progressive teaching method are evident in the stories of Jacob, Joseph, Moses, and the nation of Israel. Surely, even by these examples, it is obvious that God's basic way of teaching in the Old Testament was progressive – a slow, careful, building process.

The Lord Jesus Christ's teaching

The Lord Jesus did not teach His disciples everything there was to be known about any one subject at one particular time. He taught His disciples progressively. Look, for example, at John 14. The Lord began comforting and encouraging His disciples (verse 1). He then spoke of His future ministry of preparing dwelling places for His children (verses 2,3). This was followed by a discussion with Thomas and Philip about the way to see and know the Father (verses 4-11). After this, He spoke of the need for obedience and the coming Holy Spirit (verses 12-17).

The Lord Jesus usually included many relative subjects in His discussions with the disciples, but He dealt with none exhaustively. Having introduced a subject or some aspect of a subject, He would then leave His disciples to think about it. Often, a question by the disciples would raise the subject again at a later date. If expedient, the Lord would then give His disciples more information, but even then, He would not tell them all there was to be learned and understood about the matter. The Lord never gave out mere information. Rather, He presented transforming truth which needed to be understood and appropriated. Even at the close of His earthly life, He said, *"I have yet many things to say unto you, but ye cannot bear them now. Howbeit when he, the Spirit of truth, is come, he will guide you into all truth..."* (John 16:12,13).

The Holy Spirit's teaching

When the Holy Spirit came, how did He teach? Did He immediately reveal to the disciples all there was to be known about the New Testament Church and Christian living? Did He teach them topically and exhaustively on everything which God planned to reveal to the Church? No! Again, it was progressive teaching, for God was continuing His usual form of revelation. It was a building process. Foundational truths, partially revealed or hidden in the Old Testament, and truths introduced by the Lord Jesus but not fully revealed before His ascension, were slowly and carefully taught by adding knowledge to knowledge so the Church would be brought to *"...the stature of the fulness of Christ..."* (Ephesians 4:11-16).

The apostles' teachings

Because God has revealed all truth progressively, the apostles based their teaching and writings on God's previous revelations in the Old Testament and His more recent revelations through His Son, the Lord Jesus. Their writings cannot stand alone, for they are the continuation and culmination of God's progressive revelation which He first initiated through Moses. All that the apostles wrote and taught was on the basis of the Old Testament.

The following portions from Paul's writings will illustrate that the principle of progressive revelation continues on through Acts to the book of Revelation; and because of this, it is impossible to clearly teach believers the New Testament without first introducing them to the Old Testament.

Imagine a believer who has not been given Old Testament foundational teaching, trying to understand a portion such as I Corinthians 5:6-8, *"Your glorying is not good. Know ye not that a little leaven leaveneth the whole lump? Purge out therefore the old leaven, that ye may be a new lump, as ye are unleavened. For even Christ our passover is sacrificed for us: Therefore let us keep the feast, not with old leaven, neither with the leaven of malice and wickedness; but with the unleavened bread of sincerity and truth."* How could anyone possibly understand these verses without the necessary Old Testament foundational knowledge?

In II Corinthians 3, Paul contrasts the ministration of death through Moses and the ministration of life brought by Christ. He says, *"And not as Moses, which put a vail over his face, that the children of Israel could not stedfastly look to the end of that which is abolished: But their minds were blinded: for until this day remaineth the same vail untaken away in the reading of the old testament; which vail is done away in Christ"* (II Corinthians 3:13,14). This whole chapter, and particularly these verses, cannot be understood except in the light of the Old Testament.

What about the Epistle to the Galatians? How could anyone understand Paul's arguments about law and grace apart from a proper foundation in the Old Testament? The churches in Galatia, through the influence of the Judaizers, had turned away from interpreting the Scriptures according to the historical order of progressive revelation. When combating this error, Paul reminded them of the sequence of historical events recorded in the Old Testament through which God progressively revealed the doctrine of justification. In Galatians 3, we are told that the Judaizers were emphasizing obedience to Moses and the Law as necessary for salvation. They were saying, "Yes, Christ's death is necessary for salvation, but believers must also keep the Law." How does Paul meet their arguments? Paul takes his readers back into Old Testament history and shows that the doctrine of justification can only be understood according to progressive revelation. Paul wrote, *"And this I say, that the covenant, that was confirmed before of God in Christ, the law, which was four hundred and thirty years after, cannot disannul, that it should make the promise of none effect. For if the inheritance be of the law, it is no more of promise: but God gave it to Abraham by promise. Wherefore then serveth the law? It was added because of transgressions..."* (Galatians 3:17-19).

What is Paul doing? He is showing that the Law cannot supersede God's covenant of grace and faith as the way of justification, because grace and faith were revealed before the Law was given. Paul reminds the churches in Galatia of the order God used to progressively reveal these two doctrines.

The Gospel was first preached to Abraham; and, 430 years later, the Law was given through Moses to reveal sin as "exceedingly sinful." The full revelation of the Gospel was finally given through Christ. This same Gospel was preached to Abraham. All believers are the children of Abraham by faith and are not dependent upon the keeping of the Law for salvation. Therefore, Paul makes it clear that the sequence of historical events is vital in our interpretation and understanding of the Word of God.

Consider the doctrine of the Holy Spirit. In this present dispensation, we cannot appreciate what God has done for us through the indwelling of the Holy Spirit, unless we first understand the work and ministry of the Holy Spirit in the Old Testament. The joy and liberty which are rightfully ours as part of the body of Christ are only experienced if we first understand that, during the old dispensation, the Holy Spirit was only **with** believers. Now, He is **in** us. The doctrine of the Holy Spirit can only be comprehended on the basis of progressive revelation.

This is equally true of the doctrine of adoption. In Galatians 4, Paul taught that the Old Testament believers were like small children in the Father's household. Numerous laws and rituals controlled their every action. We, in contrast, have been placed into the family of God as adult sons. We share the Spirit of the Son, in contrast to the limited relationship which the Holy Spirit had with believers in the Old Testament. Our position through adoption can only be appreciated if we understand the historical and chronological development of God's relationship with believers as revealed in the Scriptures.

Consider Paul's letter to the Romans. As he introduced his main subject, the Gospel of God, he immediately reminds his readers that the Gospel was *"(...promised afore by his prophets in the holy scriptures,)"* and that it is *"Concerning his Son Jesus Christ our Lord, which was made of the seed of David according to the flesh"* (Romans 1:2,3).

In Romans 1:18, Paul begins to teach on the doctrine of man's sin. He does this on the basis of the beginnings of history when the true knowledge of God was common to all men (Genesis 1-11). From this original revelation, Paul affirms that man deliberately turned to gross idolatry and moral perversion.

In Romans 2, Paul proves the total depravity of all mankind by referring to the Law given to Israel at Mount Sinai and written in the heart of the Gentiles.

In Romans 3, Paul quotes extensively from the Old Testament and then points to what the Law says as the final proof that all the world is guilty before God (Romans 3:19). He then maintains that the doctrine of justification which he teaches is the same message to which the Law and the Prophets witnessed (Romans 3:21).

In Romans 4, Paul sites Abraham and David as examples of two sinners who were justified by faith.

In Romans 5, Paul lays the foundation for the doctrine of identification with Christ. Again, he points back to the Old Testament and shows that in Adam all sinned and all died. Death reigned as king over all because of the disobedience of the father and federal head of the human race. With these foundations, he then teaches that Jesus Christ our Lord was prefigured in Adam and that He is the second Man. Just as Adam represented us as the federal head of the human race, so Christ was appointed by God as the new beginning, the federal Head of sinners, whom He represented by complete obedience to His Father, both in life and in death. Note then that Paul did not try to teach this liberating truth of the believer's complete identification with Christ apart from its Old Testament foundations.

If Paul taught Old Testament foundations when teaching believers, why should we think we can teach believers successfully without first laying the substructure on which all New Testament doctrines rest. It is impossible to clearly and correctly teach the New Testament to believers without adequate Old Testament foundations.

The best way to teach God's Word is to follow His progressive form of revelation. We should first lay good foundations for the believer's faith and then build truth on truth, knowledge on knowledge. Bible doctrines can be most clearly understood if they are first seen in their beginnings in Genesis, then traced through the Old Testament historical accounts in which they were progressively developed, and then finally taught in their fullness in the New Testament.

God's progressive revelation of all truth has also been in conjunction with His historical acts in both Old and New Testaments. Therefore, all doctrines have an historical setting. New Testament doctrines are woven into the historical story of the Scriptures. The worldwide tendency to teach Christians the doctrines of the Bible, divorced from their God-given progressive, historical setting, has resulted in doctrinal confusion in many sections of the Church. Some interpret doctrine by personal experience, rather than according to its historical setting. The majority of doctrinal misinterpretations are due to the failure to understand the historical, progressive revelation of truth in the Bible. Because so many endeavor to teach Bible doctrines almost exclusively from the New Testament, bypassing their beginnings in the Old Testament, many believers have a clouded and unbalanced interpretation of Bible doctrines. Doctrines can only be clearly understood in the light of their historical revelation and development.

Foundations for the topical approach

Western culture and education use an analytical approach to almost every subject. Since most subjects are treated in this way, it seems to be automatically accepted by Christians that if one really wants to know his Bible, he must analyze and categorize every part of the Word of God.

While there is a definite need for analysis in our study, the first and greater need is for a holistic approach to God's Word. This method of studying and teaching the Scriptures holistically has been called the synthetical approach, in order to distinguish it from the analytical method. The synthetic begins with the general and looks at the whole rather than individual parts. Analysis begins with the specific and then moves to the general.

Imagine trying to instruct a primitive tribal man in watchmaking and repairing. If he had never seen a

> New Christians usually struggle for many years with a vague understanding of the Scriptures as one book.

watch nor understood its function as one instrument, he would find it impossible to understand the position and purpose of each separate part. The wisest procedure would be to first show him a complete watch. Following this, we could point out the minute parts and explain their individual contribution to the whole. This, too, is how we should approach and teach the Scriptures. The general, panoramic view provides the foundation for a more specific, analytical investigation.

The need for this holistic teaching of the Scriptures, before topical teaching is given, is clearly demonstrated by the experience of a missionary friend planning to go to the Philippines. When he returned to his home church to prepare his gear and await the time of departure, the pastor asked him to teach an adult Bible study. He decided to begin in Genesis and teach an overview of the Old Testament, leading into the New Testament. Later, when he met me in Manila, he said, "The more I taught, the greater the excitement and enthusiasm of my class. Even though these people had attended our church for many years, in all that time, they had never been taught the Scriptures chronologically and panoramically. At the close of one of the lessons, a lady asked, 'Why hasn't our pastor taught us like this? I have been hearing sermons all of my life but only now am I beginning to understand the Bible as one book!'"

New Christians usually struggle for many years with a vague understanding of the Scriptures as one book. The majority of preachers seldom, if ever, teach historically and chronologically through the entire Bible. Sermons on individual texts and topics limit one's understanding of the Word of God to certain sections and scattered verses. Through a panoramic study of the Old and New Testaments, however, the Bible can be seen as one volume.

Teaching Bible topics should have an important place in our program, but it should be used only with those who have already been taught the Scriptures as a whole. If this is our normal approach, then topical teaching, when needed, will be far more effective. The **part** we emphasize through topical teaching will be clearly understood and appreciated in the context of the **whole** of God's revelation.

Topical teaching in the Word of God is usually remedial. This is clearly evident in the ministry of the prophets whom God raised up to remind Israel of the righteous and holy laws which had been given to them in orderly progression through the ministry of Moses. The major part of the prophetic teachings are taken up with the topic of Israel's and Judah's rebellion and the warnings of God's coming judgments unless they returned in true heart repentance and obedience to the body of revelation already in their possession. The topical, remedial writings of the prophets are really interruptions in the straight line of God's progressive revelations pointing forward to Christ, the coming King and His kingdom.

Topical teaching then should be used when there is misinterpretation or disobedience to the Scriptures or when there is a need to emphasize or clarify some particular doctrine. If a problem arises in the church, the Bible teacher should temporarily change to topical, corrective teaching.

Paul's letter to the Corinthians is another example of topical, corrective teaching. Paul is basically reminding the Corinthians of what he had already delivered to them as the body of revelation which they must believe and obey. His initial teaching to the Corinthians was the same as in every place. His teaching was based on the Old Testament Scriptures (Acts 18:4,5; I Corinthians 10:1,11). To these, he added the teachings given by the Lord Jesus while He was here on earth (I Corinthians 11:23). His instructions to them were then completed by adding the revelations of the Holy Spirit, beginning on the day of Pentecost (I Corinthians 2:1-13). It was from this complete body of revelation that Paul drew his corrective, topical teaching in an effort to remedy the situation in the church at Corinth.

Thus we see that corrective topical teaching is much clearer when it follows this basic pattern of progressive revelation. Because God has revealed all doctrines progressively, the simplest and clearest method to emphasize a particular doctrine is to trace its development from Genesis through to the Revelation. If, for example, the need is to teach on marriage, there is no better way than to begin in Genesis, just as Jesus did when He answered questions regarding marriage (Matthew 19:3-6). After reminding our hearers of God's original purpose for marriage, as shown in Genesis 2, we can then turn to other Scriptures on marriage in their chronological order. We could teach on Deuteronomy 24:1, where Moses permitted the rebellious Israelites to deviate from God's ideal standard for marriage, and then Matthew 19, where Jesus comments on this portion from Deuteronomy. Finally, we should teach the apostles' instructions relating to marriage from the Epistles, where God's original plan and standard for marriage are reaffirmed.

Imagine a church where the basic teaching method is to consistently teach God's Word as one complete book. The teachers methodically cover all the Word of God so that the congregation will continually advance in their understanding of the whole revelation of God in both Old and New Testaments. But problems are bound to arise at some time within the church; so, at these times, it will be necessary to digress from the usual teaching program and give topical, corrective teaching. If the Word of God has been taught consistently as one whole, it will be relatively simple to draw the necessary corrective topical teaching from many parts of Scripture. The Bible teacher will be able to say to those who have been taught the overall plan of Scripture, "Do you remember what we learned previously in 'such and such a Scripture' about this particular subject?" Because they have been taught the Scriptures holistically, the teacher will be able to draw from the entire Word of God as the authority for his topical, corrective teaching.

Foundations to understand the Law and grace dilemma

Believers need to be taught the Old Testament so that they will be able to clearly distinguish the difference between the dispensation of Law and the dispensation of Grace. Old Testament foundations are necessary in order to understand the place of the Law during the Church age.

Believers will only be able to see the difference between Law and Grace if they are given a basic knowledge of Israel's position under the Law prior to the cross. Legalism, which is prominent in many churches and devastating to the believer's faith and walk, can only be avoided by teaching progressively from the Old Testament into the New Testament. If there is a clear understanding of the purpose of Law in the Old Testament, there will be little danger of the misuse or misinterpretation of the Law in the New Testament. It will be obvious that no one was ever justified or sanctified by the Law and that believers are fully dependent on God's grace alone for salvation and the Christian walk.

Furthermore, unless the Old Testament history of Israel is first taught, it is difficult to understand the Jews' attitude toward the Gentiles at the time of Christ and the time of the early Church, the anger of the Jewish leaders at the suggestion of the Lord Jesus that the Gentiles could also be recipients of the grace and blessings of God, the dilemmas of the Church in Acts regarding the matter of accepting uncircumcised believing Gentiles into full fellowship, why it was necessary for the Lord to give Peter a special and thrice-repeated vision before he would take the Gospel into the home of a Gentile, why Paul was hounded from city to city by the descendants of Abraham, and why it was necessary for Paul to constantly address the topics of Jew and Gentile, Law and Grace, and Circumcision and Uncircumcision.

Foundations for the Christian walk

Once people profess to be saved, most teachers are so zealous to see these new believers living and serving like Christians that they give them little time to grow in knowledge and experience. They are expected, in a very short period of time, to function in the Church alongside of those who have been Christians for many years.

Just as the unsaved must be prepared for the Gospel of God's grace in salvation by a revelation of God's nature and character, so believers need to be prepared to walk humbly with the Lord by deeper insights into God's nature and character.

The truth of the verse, *"The fear of the LORD is the beginning of wisdom..."* (Proverbs 9:10) should not only be applied to the unsaved but also to the believer and his growth in holiness. *"O fear the LORD, ye his saints: for there is no want to them that fear him"* (Psalm 34:9). The fear of the Lord in the life of the believer should not hold dread of condemnation or wrath, for there is *"...no condemnation to them which are in Christ Jesus..."* (Romans 8:1). However, through the knowledge of God in His holiness and glory as revealed in all the Scriptures, the Bible teacher should prepare foundations for the believer to respond to scriptural exhortations to godliness. The believer should continually advance in genuine awe and solemn appreciation of who and what God is. Only this will produce true biblical humility, brokenness of spirit, and meekness and contriteness of heart. The fear of the Lord is the preparation for the life of holiness and obedience to which the believer is called.

The scriptural truths necessary for a victorious and holy walk can only be understood, appreciated, and correctly appropriated if seen and interpreted in light of God's glorious nature, character, and eternal purposes as revealed in all the Scriptures. God must be seen by the child of God to be the supreme reason for everything he does. The believer should respond to the scriptural exhortations to holiness out of love and worship of God. The biblical basis for the believer to pursue holiness is epitomized in the words, *"...Be ye holy; for I am holy"* (I Peter 1:16). The Apostle Paul says to believers, *"Whether therefore ye eat, or drink, or whatsoever ye do, do all to the glory of God"*

(I Corinthians 10:31). The foundation for worshipful service to God is a Bible-oriented appreciation of God's supremacy, majesty, and holiness.

Believers need to come to know who God is before they are taught the things they must or must not do as believers. Anything less than this is an unscriptural and unstable foundation for the Christian life and can only produce counterfeit experiences which will lead people to glory in their own humility and dedication. Exhorting believers to holiness before they have these necessary foundations will lead them to mere outward conformity and perfunctory obedience based on the false foundations of human determination and fleshly dedication. Anything which the believer does for any reason other than genuine love and appreciation for who God is and what He has done is unacceptable to God and is idolatry, even when the believer's actions are based on some command from the Word of God.

Many sincere missionaries and Bible teachers lead believers into legalism because they fail to apply these biblical guidelines to their teaching methods. They immediately begin teaching new believers the "do's and don'ts" of the Christian life. They seem to think that, if they simply tell these new believers that they are indwelt by the Holy Spirit and some other positional truths, then this knowledge will bring the liberty and power to obey God's commands to holiness. Admittedly, these truths are vitally important and should be taught to believers, but the fact remains that spiritual growth is a process. Growth cannot be forced. It is the result of God's Word being understood and received in the heart. It is the result of God's Word dwelling in our lives (Colossians 3:16). The Word of God must be planted in the mind and heart in order for it to take root and grow (James 1:21). The growth of the believer comes not only through the knowledge of the written Word, but also through a deep and personal relationship with the Living Word, the Lord Jesus Christ. The believer must be *"Rooted and built up in him..."* (Colossians 2:7; II Peter 3:18).

The believer should grow spiritually through the teaching and appropriation of God's Word just as the human body develops and grows through eating and digesting good food (I Peter 2:2; Ephesians 4:11-16). The human body develops slowly from infinitesimal beginnings. At birth, a child has all the potential of the adult, but there must be development and growth before the latent potentiality of the child can be exhibited. Forcibly overfeeding a child or immediately giving it the food of an adult will not promote growth but, rather, will inhibit its progress. What is true in the natural is equally applicable in the spiritual realm.

The faithful servant of God must be careful and patient, just as God has shown Himself to be patient while teaching and preparing men for His service. Let us not forget how long the Lord took to teach and prepare Abraham before He finally gave Abraham the promised son, Isaac, and even then, there was more training for the patriarch. We need to contemplate God's patient work in preparing Joseph in an Egyptian prison, Moses in the Midian desert, Joshua as a servant to Moses, David in the wilderness constantly hounded by Saul, John the Baptist in the wilderness, Jesus as a Nazarene carpenter's son for thirty years, the disciples' three years of training, and Paul's three years of training in Arabia. These are but a few examples of God's faithful, patient, slow work of teaching and preparing His most useful instruments. Since the divine Teacher feels it necessary to take time to instruct and allow His students to grow, we, too, need to "take the time" to see people well taught, not only in the New Testament but also in the Old Testament. *"For whatsoever things were written aforetime were written for our learning, that we through patience and comfort of the scriptures might have hope"* (Romans 15:4).

Our understanding of God, if limited to the New Testament revelation, can easily become narrow and distorted. Liberal theologians who try to formulate a doctrine of God in the light of the Gospels alone, rejecting the revelation of Jehovah in the Old Testament, imagine that God will never judge and condemn sinners to everlasting punishment.

When Paul taught the truths for the Christian walk, he did so on the basis of the Old Testament Scriptures. To the Corinthians, he said, *"Moreover, brethren, I would not that ye should be ignorant, how that all our fathers were under the cloud, and all passed through the sea"* (I Corinthians 10:1). Paul did not want them to be ignorant of these Old Testament accounts. Why not? Because, he said, *"...these things were our examples, to the intent we should not lust*

> Let us not forget how long the Lord took to teach and prepare His servants.

after evil things, as they also lusted....Now all these things happened unto them for ensamples: and they are written for our admonition, upon whom the ends of the world are come" (I Corinthians 10:6,11). Paul's presentation of God included God's historical revelations to the nation of Israel. Paul reminded Timothy that, from a child, he had known the Holy Scriptures, which Paul assured Timothy, are able to make a person wise unto salvation through faith which is in Christ Jesus. Paul continued by saying, *"All scripture is given by inspiration of God, and is profitable for doctrine, for reproof, for correction, for instruction in righteousness: That the man of God may be perfect, throughly furnished unto all good works"* (II Timothy 3:16,17). It should be clear to all Bible teachers that Paul is speaking of the Old Testament Scriptures as well as the New Testament revelation.

What then is the best way to teach in order to give believers a knowledge of God as a basis for the Christian walk? We must teach all of the Scriptures according to the divinely provided pattern laid out in the Word of God. If we do not see and understand the teaching principles in the Scriptures, we will not be convinced of their importance to the spiritual development and growth of believers. The progressive, building approach to teaching will seem unnecessarily long and arduous. The quicker, more efficient way will seem to be, "Forget about the majority of the Old Testament and other introductory Scriptures. Just get on with the job and teach the Christian life." This attitude is akin to the one which says that the teaching of the Old Testament historical sections to unsaved people takes too long. In most cases, it is not the time factor which influences our thinking that way, but a lack in our understanding of scriptural teaching methods and our failure to appreciate the Lord's purpose for writing the Scriptures as He has.

Foundations for believers

There are many believers in churches who have not been taught the Scriptures holistically. Beginning from the time they were saved, these Christians have almost always been taught topically. Thus, their understanding of the Scriptures is fragmentary, for it is made up of isolated verses and portions of Scripture. They do not understand the Bible as one Book. In this type of situation, it is far more effective to begin in the evangelistic phase, laying the correct foundations, and, on this sound basis, continue building scripturally. The Old Testament section of this phase should be taught, uninterpreted by the New Testament, so that believers will see and understand the progressive development of God's revelation.

Believers who have been taught from the evangelistic phase of the the Chronological Teaching Outline, either as members of a mixed group of saved and unsaved or as a separate group of only believers, have greatly benefited by seeing the chronological and panoramic view of the history of redemption. Through it, they have been taught the basis of the faith and salvation of Old Testament saints. They have also received the Old Testament background necessary for a correct interpretation of the New Testament. Foundational evangelistic teaching has also demonstrated to believers how to evangelize others by first teaching the Old Testament to convince people that they are hopeless and helpless sinners, rather than trying to persuade them that they need a Saviour while they are still content in their sin or trusting in their own self-righteousness.

Don and Janet Schlatter, who have ministered to the Lawa tribal people in Northern Thailand for many years, have seen the Lord save a great number of the Lawa. The Schlatters taught these believers to function as members of indigenous church fellowships. Now, after many years, Don is teaching the evangelistic phase of the Chronological Outline to the Lawa churches. Don wrote,

"We praise God for the response in some of the older churches to the chronological presentation of Bible truth. We are going through the Old Testament passages which form a foundation to Christ's coming. One elder said it this way, 'Before, you taught us from the middle to the top of the tree. Now we are hearing about the bottom of the tree.' It brings into focus much which was confusing before. How we thank God for bringing this need to our attention. Lawa believers in sixteen villages are now hearing the Word, and we are trying to present it in a logical fashion in every place."

Mike Henderson, a missionary with the Aziana tribe in the highlands of Papua New Guinea, noted a change of emphasis in the ministry of the church elders and teachers and a change in the type of teaching illustrations they used after they had been taught foundationally through the evangelistic phase of the Chronological Outline.

Prior to being taught the Old Testament, the Aziana tribal teachers limited their illustrations of God's judgment on sin to local experiences within the tribe. They did not know the Old Testament accounts of the revelation of the character of God, so when they wanted to give historical proof of the scriptural picture of God, they looked for evidence and verification in the local happenings within the tribe. But local incidents which initially appeared to the tribal people to be God's judgment on individuals were dimmed through the passing of time. Different accounts and distortions of the incidents also undermined their usefulness as warnings to those who disregarded the Scriptures. All of this changed once the Aziana teachers had been taught the Old Testament. Now they had illustrations of actual written historical happenings with the accompanying interpretation in the Scriptures. Their teaching of the New Testament was now punctuated with Old Testament historical accounts of God's judgment and gracious provision which could not be discounted nor changed. They were now able to use the Old Testament writings for the purpose they were recorded by the Lord.

Foundations for future teachers

It is the responsibility of every Bible teacher to teach God's Word in such a way that the fellowship of believers will be able to interpret all doctrines in light of God's complete revelation. But does this mean that a Bible teacher or missionary who teaches believers in order to see them established as a New Testament church must teach every single verse of the Word of God, beginning in Genesis and concluding with the Revelation? No! That is not his responsibility.

The Bible teacher's primary responsibility is to lay the foundations. He should train and equip the local congregation and give them the responsibility to continue building on the foundations which he has laid down for them from the Word of God (I Corinthians 3:10-15; Ephesians 4:11-13; II Timothy 2:2). The one who lays the foundations is responsible to make sure that the foundations he lays are wide enough to support all that must be taught later by the other teachers. If the foundations are inadequate and lacking in some way, then the teachers who follow will not have the necessary basis for teaching the whole counsel of God.

The builder of the foundations must lay the theological, historical, dispensational, and doctrinal foundations which will support every part of God's revelation, so that the future teachers will be able to correctly expound and interpret the entire revelation of God and all doctrines in both Old and New Testaments.

Which then is the simplest way to do this? Should we have doctrinal check lists and check the doctrines off as we teach them? If we do, the future teachers will be as bound to our doctrinal outlines as they are to their Bibles. Every ambassador for Jesus Christ should determine that, when teaching believers, he will be guided by the divine principles exemplified in the Word of God. By closely following divine principles, the teacher will have done all in his power to bind his hearers' hearts and consciences to the complete Word of God and its glorious Author.

Part 2

How To Use This Bible Study

Part 2

How To Use This Bible Study

Practical Questions and Answers 65

    What is the purpose of this course? 65

    What's missing here? 65

    Why so much material? 66

    If you must teach this course in fewer sessions 67

    For whom was this study designed? 68

    How can I use this course in my church? 68

    How can I start a home Bible study? 68

    What does the teacher need for this course? 69

    What other materials are available? 69

    What about materials from other sources? 71

    What do the students need? 71

Special Note 72

    Pastors and Sunday school superintendents 72

    Substitute teachers 72

Guidelines for the Teacher 73

    Be prepared 73

    Teamwork 73

    Class format 73

    Authoritative evangelism 74

    Teach from the Bible, the sole authority 74

    It matters how you say it 74

    Know your students 75

    Accept unsaved students—as they are 75

    Teaching mixed groups—believers and unbelievers 76

    Large and small group dynamics 76

How To Use This Bible Study

Doctrinal themes	77
Keeping a balance	80
The Bible is "His story"	80
Asking questions	80
Handling students' questions	81
Avoid rabbit trails	82
Don't force verbal agreement	82
Make it interesting	83
Avoid unnecessary details	83
Build patiently	83
Revealing the Saviour to people who have already heard	84
When should I present the Gospel?	84

Specific Instructions About the Lessons . . . 85

General format	85
Lesson preparation section	85
Scripture references	85
Teacher's notes	85
Overview	86
Scriptures	86
Lesson goals; *This lesson should help the students*	86
Perspective for the teacher	86
Reference material	86
Visuals	86
Chronological chart	87
Chronological maps	87
Special notes	87

Part 2

How To Use This Bible Study

The Lesson	88
Lesson outline	88
Format	88
Introduction and conclusion	88
Themes	88
READ *Read*	88
Questions	89
Putting it all together	89
An encouragement to persevere	90

Practical Questions and Answers

What is the purpose of this course?

In John 17:3, Jesus said, *"And this is life eternal, that they might know thee the only true God, and Jesus Christ, whom thou hast sent."* That's what this course is all about.

Primarily, these Bible lessons are designed to bring unbelievers to a saving knowledge of Jesus Christ.

But this course is also very useful for helping believers to gain a deeper knowledge of God and to understand the Bible as a whole so they can grow in their faith and share God's Word with others.

The lesson outline follows a clear, chronological pattern, enabling your students to remember what they have been taught. Events and themes are placed on carefully built foundations.

An additional benefit is that, as you teach, you are passing on to your students a method of teaching which they may, in turn, use to teach others.

Keep the following goal in mind, and you will avoid getting sidetracked:

> **The purpose of this course is to clearly present the nature and character of God and His message of salvation as He has progressively revealed these truths to us through His Word, the Bible.**

What's missing here?

Works.

This study is limited to the theme of salvation by grace. It does not address the theme of sanctification—that is, the works that God desires to do in and through the believer.

Many of the Bible passages referred to are rich in examples of how believers were used of God to do His good works. But this course emphasizes **only those themes that are foundational to salvation.**

As mentioned in the previous chapters, teaching unbelievers how they should "act" has been a major source of confusion throughout the history of Christianity.

Even though you may have believers in your class, do not get sidetracked onto issues dealing with the works of the believer.

Your teaching will be a pattern for your students to follow, in turn, in teaching unbelievers. Don't cloud or clutter your teaching with messages for believers.

Practical Questions and Answers

Why so much material?

This is not an "instant" study
In a day of "instant everything," this is not an instant Bible study.

God planned a lifetime of learning. His design was that parents teach His Word to their children from infancy. Deuteronomy 6:6-9 says, *"And these words...shall be in thine heart: And thou shalt teach them diligently unto thy children, and shalt talk of them when thou sittest in thine house, and when thou walkest by the way, and when thou liest down, and when thou risest up....And thou shalt write them upon the posts of thy house, and on thy gates."* In II Timothy 3:14,15 Paul wrote to Timothy, *"But continue thou in the things which thou hast learned and hast been assured of, knowing of whom thou hast learned them; And that from a child thou hast known the holy scriptures, which are able to make thee wise unto salvation through faith which is in Christ Jesus."*

Surface knowledge isn't enough
Unfortunately, most people in our society have not had the privilege of growing up under this kind of godly teaching. They may have a surface knowledge of many Bible stories, but few people have an overall grasp of what the Bible is all about.

Facts can be learned quickly; foundational themes cannot. You may be able to acquaint a person with factual knowledge of the chronological order of the Bible in a short time, and this is certainly helpful. But this course is designed to give the basic thematic foundations that prepare the student for salvation, based upon a true understanding of God as He has revealed Himself in the Bible.

Building that foundation cannot be done overnight. **It takes time for abstract spiritual concepts to be firmly grasped.** Only clear, Scriptural teaching, done in the power of the Holy Spirit, can plant these truths firmly in the students' minds.

Dismantling misconceptions takes time
Misconceptions, too, are built over a lifetime. Remember, in addition to teaching truth, you are also dismantling any false teaching and misconceptions which are already established in your students' thinking.

A one-year program
These lessons are designed to be used over a one-year period, either as Sunday School curriculum or as a home or small-group Bible study which meets once a week. The schedule could be accelerated with more frequent or longer individual class sessions.

> The impact on lives is immeasurable.

Is it worth all that time? What could be more worthwhile? People who go through this material, teachers and students alike, gain foundational understanding that helps them see the Bible as a whole. Their understanding of God and His Word become the basis for their lives.

The pieces fit together
Once the foundation is built, all future understanding is built on that firm basis of truth. This invites continued personal Bible study because the pieces fall clearly into place. The impact on lives is immeasurable.

Yes, we live in an instant age. But not everything "instant" is worthwhile. Studying the foundations presented in God's Word is well worth all the time and effort it takes for both the teacher and the student.

Avoid shortcuts
"But I absolutely have to shorten the course if I'm going to reach this student." This may be true. However, a closer look may show that it's not really necessary to shorten. **Don't shortcut this material just for the sake of convenience.** Building the foundational themes that prepare the student for salvation is too important to shortcut. Use the following guidelines **only if absolutely necessary.**

Practical Questions and Answers

If you **must** teach this course in fewer sessions, follow these guidelines

If you must shorten the time it takes to go through this course, one of the best ways is to extend your class time for each session. The beginning of each class always takes extra time, so if you have a one-and-a-half-hour session instead of a one-hour session, you will actually gain more than a half an hour of teaching time. You will probably be able to teach two or three lessons during a one-and-a-half-hour session, effectively shortening the length of the course by one half or more.

Review carefully at the beginning of each session to be sure that your students are really absorbing the material. Adjust your teaching speed accordingly. You may find that your class may need more time with certain lessons while others lessons may be covered more quickly.

The material included in the fifty lessons has been carefully selected. If possible, cover all of it.

But if you absolutely must abbreviate the amount of material, use the following suggestions:

Lesson 8: God Made Eve
Use only points B, E, and G.

Lesson 19: Isaac's Sons, Esau and Jacob; Jacob's Son Joseph
This whole lesson can be omitted, but use the Chronological Chart to show Jacob's sons.

Lesson 20: God Promoted Joseph and Took Israel into Egypt
Note that Jacob's name was changed to Israel, and cover only point H. Omit the questions.

Lesson 28: Israel in the Promised Land Under Judges and Kings
Cover point B, Joshua led Israel into Canaan. Mention that after Joshua died, Israel turned away from God to idolatry, so God allowed Israel's enemies to defeat them. Then Israel turned back to God for help and God raised up men called judges to deliver and lead Israel. Point to the judges on the chronological chart.

Following this, Israel demanded a king, though God truly was their king. God granted their request, and Israel was under the rulership of kings for about 400 years. Show the kings on the Chronological Chart.

Cover points F, G, H, and I, and the appropriate questions that pertain to these sections. These sections must be covered, as they are referred to in the New Testatment lessons.

Lesson 29: God Sent His Messengers, the Prophets, to Israel; Israel Refused to Respond to Their Warnings
The following sections must be covered: C, D, H, and I, and the appropriate questions.

Lesson 34: Jesus, When Tempted, Resisted and Rebuked Satan
This lesson may be omitted.

Lesson 38: Jesus Calmed the Storm and Delivered the Demon-possessed Man of Gadara
This lesson may be omitted.

Lesson 41: Jesus Is the Christ, the Son of God; Jesus Was Transfigured
This lesson may be omitted.

Lesson 44: Jesus Loved the Children and Taught the Rich Young Ruler
This lesson may be omitted.

For whom was this study designed?

Large groups, small groups, Sunday school classes, home Bible study groups, one-on-one Bible studies, inner-city ministries, home schooling, family devotions, etc.— these lessons can fit many teaching situations.

Though written for adults, the lessons can be adapted for use with children. The teacher will have to evaluate his or her students and adapt the material to suit their particular needs.

(Please see comments regarding large and small groups under Sections 2 and 3.)

Note: This material is copyrighted and cannot be reproduced, with or without adaptations, without written permission.

How can I use this course in my church?

Familiarize yourself with the course

First of all, familiarize yourself with this material. Read the Teacher Preparation section and digest it. Be certain that you are willing to take the time necessary to study and to teach this course to others.

Offer to show "EE-TAOW!"

You may want to give your Pastor or Sunday school superintendant Volume I of the original *Building on Firm Foundations* series by Trevor McIlwain and suggest he read it. You might also offer to show the "EE-TAOW!" video (described on the following page).

Advertise

If your pastor and Sunday school department are willing to have you use this material, advertise the course. Offer to show the "EE-TAOW!" video to those you want to teach.

Be careful how you advertise

Be careful how you advertise this material! Most churches contain a mixture of believers and unbelievers. Remember that this course is evangelistic. You are not advertising a "Bible Survey" or "Old Testament Survey." This is a **foundational study, from Genesis to Christ, covering only those themes that pertain to salvation.** Here is a suggested course description:

> **Firm Foundations:**
> **Creation to Christ.**
> This unique Bible study systematically lays a solid foundation for both the Gospel and Christian growth. These lessons follow God's pattern of progressively revealing Himself and His plan of redemption within the context of history. Beginning with Genesis and progressing through the Old Testament and the life of Christ, you will learn the key themes of the Bible and get to know the character of God. This study answers the most significant of all questions: "How can I be accepted by God?"

How can I start a home Bible study?

Though people may not normally talk about the Bible, many are interested in a Bible study. A note on a bulletin board at work or school may be effective.

Talk to people about the study. You might say, "I think you'll enjoy it. It's a different type of approach. We'll be starting at the beginning, and we'll look at the basic things that tie the whole book together. We'll study the Bible in the order things really happened in history. "It's like putting together a puzzle, one piece at a time—when you get done, the whole picture is there. It makes a lot of sense."

Practical Questions and Answers

What does the teacher need for this course?

Basic items: your Bible, these lessons, the Chronological Chart, and the three Chronological Maps. The Chronological Pictures listed in the lessons are optional, as are other materials listed below.

What other materials are available to use with these lessons?

The following are optional materials that will help you in presenting these lessons:

Chronological pictures

Set of 105 12" x 16" laminated color pictures

(Note: All the pictures referred to in the lessons are included in this set, as well as additional pictures illustrating stories not covered in this course.) These laminated color pictures are very appropriate for small to medium-sized study groups, and are a great help in keeping students' attention and also in illustrating cultural details, as the pictures are well researched and accurate in historical detail. (See ordering information below.)

Black and white line drawings

These are outline drawings of the color pictures above, plus six additional Old Testament subjects not covered in this course. These black and white line drawings are available in two sizes:

111 6" x 8" black & white line drawings

111 3" x 4" black & white line drawings

The larger black and white drawings can be used effectively with a very small group or one-on-one study. They are also useful for children to color as a story reminder. The smaller drawings may be useful if you are making up any kind of review sheets for your class.

Note: All the materials including the pictures are copyrighted, but black and white line drawings can be copied for use in your Bible study or Sunday school class. (Reprinting or resale is prohibited, except by express written permission of New Tribes Mission, Sanford, FL 32771-1487.) (See ordering information below.)

"EE-TAOW!" video

This award-winning video is an excellent tool for presenting the foundational teaching methodology. Filmed in Papua New Guinea, "EE-TAOW!" presents the true story of how God worked among the Mouk tribal people to bring them to a clear knowledge of salvation through Jesus Christ. This is not only a strong missions challenge; it is a thrilling story of God's working in mighty ways to reach people through His Word. Highly acclaimed by both pastors and lay people, this video shows the value of preparing hearts by laying Old Testament foundations upon which the Gospel can be clearly presented. (See ordering information below.)

Building On Firm Foundations series

These books by Trevor McIlwain are the original series written for church planters working among tribal people.

Note: Volume I of this series is printed (with slight adaptation) in the front of the book you are reading, under Part 1, "Firm Foundations – Building According to Plan." Volumes II and III contain the teacher preparation and lesson material which have been extensively adapted for *Firm Foundations – Creation to Christ*. (This is the equivalent of "Phase I" of the Chronological Teaching Outline.)

On the following page is a brief explanation of each of the volumes of the original *Building on Firm Foundations* series.

The Building on Firm Foundations Series by Trevor McIlwain

Note: "Phases" are sections of the Chronological Teaching Outline.

Volume 1 Guidelines for Evangelism and Church Planting
In Volume 1, Trevor McIlwain presents the in-depth reasoning and framework for the chronological teaching approach.

Volume 2 Evangelism: The Old Testament.
Taken together, Volumes 2 and 3 cover Phase I. Volume 2 presents an introduction to cross-cultural evangelism (covering pre-evangelism, form of meetings, teaching aids, themes, etc.) along with 42 Old Testament lessons for evangelism.

Volume 3 Evangelism: The Life of Christ
Volume 3 concludes Phase I teaching with 26 lessons from the life of Christ. In addition, suggestions are given for presenting the Gospel using Old Testament lessons.

Volume 4 Teaching New Believers: Genesis through Acts
Volume 4 begins with a discussion about new believers meeting to form a local church. Trevor considers the missionary's role in helping establish the local church, including training the new believers in evangelism. He then presents a brief overview of Phase II along with 12 lessons for new believers, covering Genesis to the ascension, followed by a brief overview of Phase III along with 14 lessons covering the book of Acts.

Volume 5 Teaching New Believers: Romans and Ephesians
Volume 5 presents the order in which the Epistles should be taught and gives a brief overview of Phase IV. There are 14 lessons on Romans and 9 lessons on Ephesians, focusing on the believer's position of victory in Christ.

Volume 6 Teaching New Believers: I Corinthians, I Timothy, and Titus
Volume 6 considers the function of the local church, with 14 lessons from I Corinthians. The ministry of elders and deacons in the local church is presented with 6 lessons from I Timothy and 3 lessons from Titus.

Volume 7 Teaching New Believers: I & II Thessalonians and Revelation
Volume 7 focuses on eschatology with 7 lessons from I & II Thessalonians and 10 lessons from Revelation.

Volume 8 Teaching New Believers: Galatians and Colossians
Volume 8 discusses Paul's defense of two key doctrines, with 10 lessons from Galatians focusing on the doctrine of justification and 5 lessons from Colossians focusing on the doctrine of Christ.

Future Volumes:
Coming volumes in the *Building on Firm Foundations* series will present lessons on the remainder of the Epistles (Phase IV). The final volume in the series will be an overview of Phase V (Genesis through the ascension for maturing believers), Phase VI (Acts for maturing believers), and Phase VII (the Epistles for maturing believers).

The original Building on Firm Foundations series may be purchased as individual books or in sets.

Ordering information

All of these resources, including those on the previous page, may be ordered from:

Bookroom
New Tribes Mission Publications
1000 East First Street
Sanford, FL 32771-1487
Phone 407-323-3430

Practical Questions and Answers

What about materials from other sources?

Included in some of the lessons is a listing of suggested resource materials. **Before starting to teach, it would be wise to look through these suggested resource lists, particularly in Lessons 1, 4, and 14.** Since these lessons cover topics which have been the subject of much false teaching, it would be wise to have some extra resources on hand to help answer any questions your students may have.

You may also want to be alert to any appropriate books, pamphlets, videos, tapes, or other resources that would help to support the material taught in these lessons.

BE CAREFUL WHAT YOU RECOMMEND TO YOUR STUDENTS! The material recommended in these lessons has been carefully selected on the basis of doctrinal soundness and biblically accurate content. If you are using other material, be sure that, before recommending it to your students, you read it carefully (if possible, cover to cover) to be certain that it will not inject false teaching.

> Just because a book says that it is about the Bible is no guarantee that it is scriptural.

Just because a book says that it is about the Bible is no guarantee that it is scriptural. Sadly, much of the material available today is tainted by humanistic thinking. It is better to use only the Bible, which you know is true, than to use a colorful reference book, only to find that it has comments that cast doubt on God's Word. Good reference material **is** available. But be sure that it is, in fact, good before you share it with your students.

Whatever materials you use during class, no matter how scripturally sound they are, be sure that they are on the subject of the foundational truth you are covering. Don't get sidetracked unnecessarily.

Save your class time for Bible study. If at all possible, schedule another time for videos, etc. Keep your course moving; don't get bogged down with additional materials.

What do the students need?

The only material the student needs is a Bible. God's Word is the authority and the focus of the course.

The lesson outlines are for the teacher only, and are not intended to be used by the students.

You may want to provide Bibles for students who do not have them or who forget to bring theirs. If you are supplying Bibles, get something simple, without footnotes! It is very easy for a student to begin reading the footnotes while you are trying to teach; the student may miss what you are saying and also be sidetracked by whatever is contained in the footnotes. Some study Bibles contain footnotes that can be very misleading.

You do not need to spend a great deal of money for student Bibles; they can even be soft-cover editions. It is worth the investment to purchase enough Bibles so that each of your students can see the text for himself.

You may also want to keep paper and pencils handy for any students who want to take notes.

Special Note

Pastors and Sunday school superintendents

This material is different from traditional materials

This material is unlike traditional materials in that each lesson builds on the foundation laid in the previous lesson. For that reason it is extremely important that these lessons be taught consistently and thoroughly.

Probably the ideal method would be to have one teacher or a team of two teachers who would be committed to the task of finishing the course.

Prepare the teachers ahead of time. Give the teachers ample time to read the introductory material and to do preparatory study before offering this course. **It is essential that your teachers understand the nature and direction of this course before teaching it.**

Plan a training session

If you are considering using this material in your church or Sunday school and if you plan to involve more than one teacher, it would be well to consider having a teacher training session, covering the material in Parts 1 and 2 of this course (pp. 3-90).

Plan ahead

The teacher training session should be at least a month to six weeks before the Sunday school classes begin, so the teachers can become familiar with the course. Give your teachers the material a week ahead of the training session and instruct them to read the first section, "Laying Foundations—According to Plan."

Substitute teachers

If you are asked to substitute, use the following suggestions as guidelines:

- Read the overview of the lesson you are to teach, as well as the overview for the lessons immediately preceding and following that lesson. This will help you understand where the lesson is "heading."

- Stay within the lesson outline and the themes.

- Note the instructions to the teacher in the side columns and the large box preceding the lesson itself.

- Read through the preceding lesson and the questions that follow it, so you can do the review at the beginning of the lesson.

- Stay on the subject; remember this is a foundational course, designed to teach unbelievers. Don't get into issues concerning the behavior and works of the believer. The emphasis is on salvation by faith through God's grace.

- Remember that all of the material in the side columns is for the teacher only, not for the students.

Guidelines for the Teacher

Be prepared

Pray. Pray first. Pray as you study. Pray continually. God delights to answer believing prayer.

Read and digest Part 1, "Firm Foundations—Building According to Plan." Then read all of Part 2, "How To Use This Bible Study."

Briefly scan the "Overview" sections of all the lessons. It just takes a few minutes, and you will find that it will give you an overall perspective of the course. Thoroughly familiarize yourself with the first several lessons so you know where you are headed when you begin teaching.

As you go through the course, keep scanning the lessons ahead so you will keep your teaching on track.

Frequently review Parts 1 and 2. In addition to helping you stay on course, these sections address many practical issues that may arise as you teach.

Teamwork

Team teaching
If you work with a partner, be sure that both of you are familiar with all of the lesson material. A teaching partner can help keep the students' attention, and you can fill in for each other if one of you is unable to attend a session.

Helpers
Your students may not ask for help, but most will appreciate it, especially if they are unfamiliar with their Bibles.

A helper can be a significant benefit to the study. Explain at the outset that this person is there for the purpose of helping the students find the Bible passages. Let them know that you don't expect them to find the Scriptures on their own; that's why the helper is there. This way, the students won't feel embarrassed. If you have a large class, you may want to enlist several helpers and seat them strategically throughout the class.

Prayer warriors
Do you have Christian friends who will be willing to pray for you and for your students? Ask them to pray, and report back to them on the progress of your class.

Let your prayer warriors know what you are about to teach so they can pray intelligently.

Class format

The size of your class, who is in it, and your own personality will affect how you handle your teaching sessions. The lessons are designed to be adaptable to many different situations. You, the teacher, will have to decide what adaptations are needed. Some of the topics that follow may help you adapt the lessons to suit the needs of your class and your teaching style.

Guidelines for the Teacher

Authoritative evangelism

This is a directed Bible study, with the teacher taking the lead role in working through the outlined material and keeping any discussion on track. Though there is plenty of room for student comment, it is not a discussion format.

(A common form of Bible study is to have each person give his own ideas about the portion of Scripture under consideration. When all the opinions have been voiced, the leader summarizes the different thoughts and interpretations. This is not intended to be that kind of study.)

> In every case, **the Bible is the final authority.**

This study is designed to be directed along the themes given in the lessons, based upon the Scriptures read. In every case, **the Bible is the final authority.**

Of course, you do not want to squelch your students. You need to find out what they really believe, and their comments will help reveal that. But, in our society, "free speech" can quickly become a monopoly.

Be sure that you are continually directing your students toward the Bible as the authority.

Teach from the Bible, the sole authority

Always teach from your open Bible. It may be tempting to write down the lesson Scriptures all on one sheet so you don't have to keep turning to them in your Bible. Don't do it. Your students need to see that you are, indeed, teaching God's Word.

One way to make your task easier in lessons which have many Scriptures is to mark the Bible passages with stick-on, low-tack notes. You may even want to use a particular color of Bible highlighter to mark ahead of class time the exact verses from which you will teach.

Teaching directly from your Bible may take a little more time during class, but it will be worth it. This is a **Bible** study; make certain that your students know that what you are teaching is coming from God's Word.

It matters how you say it

Most people don't like to be preached at, but most people like to be talked to.

A humble attitude coupled with a well-prepared lesson can combine to make even a poor speaker very listenable.

Avoid religious terminology

You know the words — we hear them all the time in church circles: saved, born again, fellowship, testimony, salvation, sanctification, justification. All of these are **wonderful** words in the ears of the believer. But to the unbeliever, they are meaningless.

Think about what you are saying. If there is another way to say it without using religious terminology, use the other way. Your students will appreciate it, and you will find that it will force you to be clear and precise in your teaching.

Guidelines for the Teacher

Know your students

Jesus knew and cared about people. When He taught, He was able to communicate on a personal level. His well-chosen illustrations clearly related to His hearers. Jesus, the master teacher, is our pattern. Just as He knew those He taught, we should know our students.

Be on the alert for false teachings that have become a part of your students' thinking. Don't "attack" the student and don't immediately point out the false teaching. Just bear in mind what you learn about the student's areas of misunderstanding and be ready to teach the truth clearly and to dismantle the lie whenever that is appropriate in the lesson text. Whatever you do, avoid attacking the student's beliefs or any specific religion.

Some of the popular beliefs, such as humanism and New Age are quite subtle. Be on guard against unscriptural ideas. If you are not familiar with these false religions, do some research on your own. If you have a student who has been indoctrinated by a cult, you may need to do a brief study of what that particular cult believes so you can understand what the student perceives as truth.

Don't get off track; don't attack the cult directly. Just keep teaching God's Word, being alert to those areas which the student might misunderstand because of what he believes.

Above all, allow the Lord to love your students through you. Be concerned for each student as an individual. Pray for them. When you can, and when it is appropriate, interact with their lives outside of the study time. Help them however the Lord directs you to help them.

Your classroom should have an atmosphere of acceptance. You are teaching your students salvation by grace through faith in God. Don't try to reform them; lead them to understand God's way of salvation and regeneration through the new birth in Jesus Christ.

Accept unsaved students — as they are

The Holy Spirit only uses truth. The work and power of God are not dependent upon a man-made religious or spiritual climate. Jesus and the apostles spoke God's truth in normal everyday situations. Be willing to put up with the rough edges of the unsaved behavior. Do your students come in smelling like cigarette smoke? Don't mention it. Do they swear occasionally? Don't make a big issue of it. Accept them as they are.

The Lord has given them to you to teach them His Word. God's Word will work on the inside. When the inside is transformed, the outside will begin to change, too.

> They were willing to endure the smoke to give their friend the opportunity to join them in Heaven for all eternity.

A Christian couple with a beautiful home mentioned that they often entertained a friend who smoked. They would put out ashtrays for him so he would feel welcome. They never chided him about his smoking. They just taught him, little by little, about the Lord. Eventually they led their friend to Christ.

"But I could never allow that," you say! Maybe the Lord won't ask you to. This couple believed that God did ask them, and they were willing — willing to endure the smoke to give their friend the opportunity to join them in Heaven for all eternity.

Teaching mixed groups — believers and unbelievers

These lessons are designed to build firm foundations for presenting the Gospel to unbelievers. **Don't confuse and complicate the message.**

More than likely, you will have both unbelievers and believers in your class. You may not know at first which ones are which. Let God's Word do His work. **Stick to the themes presented in the lessons. Don't get sidetracked into issues relating to the believer, such as works, obedience, worship, etc.**

If your class includes some students who are believers, let them know from the beginning that you are only covering the theme of salvation. You may need to talk with them alone outside of class. Ask them for their help in limiting the discussion, so that unbelievers may have a clear understanding of salvation by grace.

In a church situation, the way you advertise this course can help to avoid misunderstandings. See the section entitled, "How can I use this course in my church?"

Encourage believers to learn the course material so they can go out and teach others clearly. If you realize that you have a keen believer in your class, you might even want to suggest that he purchase his own set of materials and study it on his own while he continues to attend the class. Keep your eyes open for someone whom you may be able to disciple to teach others.

Large group and small group dynamics

The overall tone of these lessons is directed toward a larger group. How much adjustment you need in that tone will depend upon the size of your group and your own individual teaching style.

If your group is very small, you will need to be very careful not to embarrass your students with personal applications of the lesson points. You will also need to be careful to ask only those questions to which you expect an answer. (If the group is very small, people will feel pressured to answer anything you ask.) Avoid the discussion questions; it's too easy to get sidetracked into personal preferences and arguments.

But the larger the group, the more personal you will be able to make your applications without embarrassing your students. You will also be able to ask rhetorical questions (no answer expected). And you will be able to move more easily to another student if one student begins to get involved too deeply in a discussion question.

As a teacher, you should be very sensitive to your students' needs. If you are teaching one-on-one, you will definitely not be able to press certain issues. On the other hand, you will be able to learn much more about that one student and know just where you need to teach with more emphasis.

Ask the Lord for wisdom. Your students need to be given respect and love, and spared embarrassment as much as possible. As mentioned before, the study should have an atmosphere where the earnest student senses that he is welcomed and accepted by you, the teacher, and, as much as possible, by the group.

Doctrinal themes

The doctrinal themes running through this course are those which will 1) show people they are sinful, condemned, and helpless before God, their holy and righteous Creator and Judge, and 2) generate faith and bring complete dependence on the Lord Jesus Christ as the all-sufficient Saviour.

Here are the specific doctrinal themes which will be emphasized:

The person and character of God

1. God is supreme and sovereign.

This truth is foundational to all other doctrines concerning God and to all spiritual matters.

> When God's sovereignty is clearly taught, other truths will begin to fall into place.

God's sovereign position is clearly evidenced throughout the Bible. He is the authority over all creation, over man, angels, and Satan. No one can question what He does. He is the great initiator, the Alpha and Omega, working all things according to the counsel of His will.

To a society that has exalted man to the throne, the concept of a sovereign God must be taught as a fresh thought—certainly not new, but one that has been obscured by humanism. In man's drive to be the center of everything, he has assigned to himself authority he cannot administer and has burdened himself with loads he cannot carry. The message of a sovereign God is good news to those who are seeking the truth, though it cuts against the grain of everything that has been taught by society. At first the message will seem strange and foreign, even irritating. But in the power of the Holy Spirit, the message of God's sovereignty provides the correct perspective for ruined lives and refocuses man's attention on his great Creator.

We need to clearly teach God's sovereignty. When that one truth is clear, other truths will begin to fall into place.

These lessons present God acting in and through history—always victorious, always overcoming all who oppose Him. He is the Creator of all and the eternal authority over all. He stands supreme and gloriously sovereign as Almighty God.

2. God communicates with man.

The Bible is not just a record of what God said to people in the past. It is also God's voice speaking to us in the present.

Sadly, this message has been ignored by millions who have had Bibles literally at their fingertips. Besides ignoring His Word, men have refused to acknowledge Him as their Creator, so they are deaf to the daily message of His creation which He so lovingly displays for everyone to see. God, in His grace, is still calling out a people for Himself. He is still giving us the opportunity to reach a generation of people whose parents have, for the most part, consistently rejected the truth that was available to them.

These lessons emphasize that God's Word is true—a true history and the living message of the living, active, sovereign God. Humanistic educational systems have attempted to smear lies across the face of God's Word. But His Word still stands—clear, righteous, and true, as it will for all eternity.

In these lessons we have the opportunity to present the truth, without apology. Our students need to know that the Bible is God's message to them personally. Everyone is without excuse (Romans 1:20).

3. God is everywhere all the time; He knows everything.

We have used this expression in place of the words "omnipresent" and "omniscient" so that the meaning will be very clear.

We need to be very careful as we teach these attributes of God. As noted in the lessons, New Age and other pantheistic religions teach that God is everything and everything is God. Be sure to make a clear distinction between the Creator God and His creation. He is everywhere, but He is not in everything; everything is not God.

4. God is all-powerful.
We are using this simple terminology instead of "omnipotent."

This attribute of God is particularly difficult to accept for people who are in the habit of "scientifically proving" everything. God's miracles seem like foolishness to many who simply explain them away with fabricated explanations they think to be more plausible.

Yet, as brought out in these lessons, God's miracles are really the only explanation that completely fits the evidence we see in creation and in the many historical accounts clearly recorded in His Word. God is dynamically shown to be the sovereign, almighty controller of all things.

5. God is holy and righteous. He demands death as the payment for sin.
God is the only standard for goodness. Anything less than God's perfect righteousness is unacceptable to Him. Anything which disagrees with or is contrary to God is sin.

Of all the truths about God, this one is most notably absent from today's "religious" thinking. Absent from most preaching are messages about God's holiness, man's sinfulness, the death penalty for sin, and the blood of Jesus Christ, poured out for sinners.

The message of the Bible is not, "Smile, God loves you"; it is, *"...the soul that sinneth, it shall die"* (Ezekiel 18:4). When this message is clear, then John 3:16 takes on its true meaning.

Many people in industrialized societies have no concept of blood sacrifice, though a distorted version of animal sacrifice is still widely practiced in many parts of the world. The Bible is full of this principle of substitutionary sacrifice, culminating in the one sacrifice that could effect remission of sins.

To many people, the idea of the death penalty for sin and the truth of a literal Hell are considered to be no longer relevant. But God hasn't changed His righteous standard. He will never allow any man to approach Him unless the complete and righteous demand of His Law is fully paid.

Even though the righteous demands of God's Law could only be met through the blood of Jesus Christ, God still accepted sinners who came to Him in faith during the time prior to the Cross, because Christ's death was, even then, a present reality to God (Revelation 13:8). Nevertheless, during the Old Testament dispensation, worshipers had to be reminded that their acceptance by God was not at the expense of justice. God demanded the death of the sinner. Animal blood could only act as a temporary covering for sin. There could be no complete satisfaction for the offerer prior to the Cross. There was always a consciousness of sin. Death, the wages of sin, was constantly portrayed by the death of innocent animals which had to be without blemish as a picture of God's unwillingness to accept anything less than a perfect payment for sin.

The first recorded example that we have of an animal sacrifice is the one Abel brought. Abel's sacrifice must have been on the basis of a divine revelation. The first time God gave man permission to kill and eat animals was after the flood. Abel would not have taken it on himself to take the life of one of God's creatures and give it as a sacrifice to God unless it had been ordered by God. Abel came by faith. Faith requires a revelation from God as its basis. It is mere human presumption, not faith, which acts apart from revelation, hoping that it will be satisfactory to God. This was the way that Cain tried to approach God.

Therefore, constant reference is made throughout these lessons to God's requirement of animal sacrifices because these emphasize God's holiness and righteous demands for the death of the sinner as the payment for sin. Animal blood could not be a replacement for the death of the sinner, but it was a constant reminder that nothing less than death could satisfy God's holy and just demands (Hebrews 10:1-12).

6. God is loving, merciful, and gracious.
God's love is unchanging, pure, and not dependent upon the merit or worthiness of the objects of that love. God *is* love (I John 4:8).

These lessons present God's love in that context; not in the man-oriented, self-serving context often presented today.

God's mercy is described in these lessons as His making a way for sinners to escape the punishment they deserve. His grace is described as His kindness toward undeserving sinners.

7. God is faithful; He never changes.
The theological word "immutable" is explained in the words "never changes."

This is another key concept for our society. Some "religious" scholars are engaged in rewriting the Bible to suit what they feel is appropriate for today. We must teach clearly that God does not change; neither does His Word.

These lessons also emphasize God's faithfulness—a thrilling message in a world of continual disappointment. God keeps His promises. This fact must be continually repeated because it is so unlike what men know of themselves and of each other.

Man

1. Man is a sinner. He needs God and is helpless to save himself.
Man cannot please God by his own efforts. Only the grace of God can save him.

Everything that man has—his life and all the things which sustain his life—is provided by God. Man's helplessness in the natural realm is used in the Scripture to illustrate man's spiritual helplessness and the need of God's gracious provision for deliverance.

2. Man can come to God only according to God's will and plan.
Because God is holy and supreme, He alone determines the way man can approach Him and be saved. It must be done God's way.

3. Man must have faith in order to please God and be saved.

Satan

1. Satan fights against God and His will. Satan is a liar and a deceiver. He hates man.
Satan (originally Lucifer) and his angels were created by God and, therefore, are dependent on, and finally subject to, His authority. They are the implacable foes of God and man. Satan uses his angels and sinful man in his efforts to establish his own kingdom and to try to destroy the kingdom of God.

Even though Satan and his demons are not often mentioned in the Old Testament text, it is good to remind our students of their continual presence and influence in the history of the world. We know from the New Testament that Satan is the *"god of this world"* (II Corinthians 4:4) so we know he is always present to tempt and guide men in their opposition to God and His will.

Even so, God is always triumphant over every endeavor of Satan to destroy God's plans to bless His people and bring salvation to mankind.

Jesus Christ (New Testament only)

1. Jesus Christ is God.

2. Jesus Christ is man.

3. Jesus Christ is holy and righteous.

4. Jesus Christ is the only Saviour.

Keeping a balance

We need to keep a balance between the doctrinal themes and the biblical, historical account. Both the historical stories and the doctrine taught by them are important. If the stories are presented as God's account of history, they will become a living, vibrant revelation of the doctrines which they contain, even though the doctrine is not specifically stated.

This is not to suggest that we should tell the stories uninterpreted, hoping that our students will understand from the biblical text what is so clear to us. As co-laborers together with God, we have been given the responsibility to expound and interpret the divine text and the recorded history. Like the Ethiopian eunuch, people need Spirit-controlled "Philips" to make the scriptural interpretation clear.

Keep a balance between storytelling and exposition so that one does not overshadow the other.

The Bible is "His story"

When the Bible is taught as a true history, it should come alive to the students. Unfortunately, many Bible stories have become very familiar apart from their historical context and their spiritual significance. To many, they are just "stories," nothing more. These lessons present the Bible as true history, with God as the author. He is the Creator of all things and the central figure of all history.

Asking questions

Tie every new segment of the story back to what has already been taught so that your students will see the Bible as one harmonious story.

You will notice that at the beginning of each lesson are the words, "REVIEW questions from Lesson...." This review will remind your students of the previous story and the doctrinal truths taught through it, providing a basis for the coming story. It will also give opportunity, before proceeding, to clear up any misunderstandings about what has already been taught.

In addition to review questions, questions asked throughout the lesson help to keep your students alert and give the teacher feedback regarding what is really being communicated. Asking questions also gives the students opportunity to express their views and gives the teacher opportunity to see what the students really believe.

Sometimes in the lessons, rhetorical questions are asked, and these are marked as such in the teachers' notes. (These are not appropriate for a very small group, as people feel pressured to answer.)

Once you have established the nature and character of each of the actors through clear interpretation of the early chapters of the Bible, you can rely more and more on questioning as a method of emphasizing the doctrines and the individual characteristics of each person and the significance of each event.

After giving a clear account of a particular incident, stop and ask a question designed to make your students think about the doctrine which is being stressed. You might ask, "Why do you think God did that?" "How did God know what they were thinking?" "Why was God able to do that?" "Do you think God forgot?" "How could Jesus do such a great miracle?"

Through questioning, you are teaching your students to look carefully at the story and the characters to learn what God wants them to know about Himself, themselves, Satan, and the Lord Jesus.

Guidelines for questioning:

1. Allow your students to answer in their own words.
2. Address some questions to the whole group and other questions directly to individuals. Try to involve every person.
3. Show respect by listening to whatever is said.
4. When someone answers, do not immediately agree or disagree with his answer. Ask one or two others or ask the whole group if they agree with the individual's answer.
5. Don't always correct them immediately if they are wrong.
6. Give them time to think and to discuss important points.
7. If they are unable to reply or if their answer is incorrect ask other questions which may remind them of the correct answer.
8. Do not grill them. The question time should not cause embarrassment.
9. Commend them for correct answers, the part they remembered, or anything else they say which is helpful.
10. Give the correct answer (written in the lessons).
11. Explain the answer in greater detail whenever necessary.

Handling students' questions

Many of your students may bring with them misunderstandings about the Scripture, about who God is, etc. Don't try to set them straight all at once! Faithfully teach them through the Word. Their knowledge of God will grow through the unfolding historical drama because this is the way God has chosen to make Himself known.

Continue to teach God's Word carefully and prayerfully, trusting the Lord to make Himself known in all His glory through the Scriptures.

Answer only those questions which relate to the subject at hand. If a student asks a question which will be answered in a future lesson, tell him so and leave the answer until then. If what you are teaching causes them to ask questions, good! They will be better listeners as you teach.

Handling difficult questions

People in our society have been bombarded with the media's passion for asking "the hard questions." It is a cultural sport to make a leader sweat under a barrage of difficult questions.

Don't allow yourself to be pressured into answering things that are off the subject. Don't feel you have to answer every question. Some questions truly have no answer; some are inappropriate; some have answers, but the answers are too high for us and belong to God alone.

When faced with a difficult question that is valid and really appropriate but seems unanswerable, always point the student to what has already been taught about the character of God and the truth of His Word. These truths do not change, even though we may not understand all that happens.

It is permissible to say, "I don't know." Your students will respect you for your honesty with them. If appropriate, you may want to add, "but I'll try to find out for you."

The reference materials listed in some of the lessons may be helpful to you and your students. As mentioned before, be sure to look ahead at the materials suggested for Lessons 1, 4, and 14, as these lessons cover subjects which may raise many questions in your students' minds.

> Always point the student to what has already been taught about the character of God.

Avoid rabbit trails

One of the most important jobs for the teacher is to keep the class on track. This is especially true in our culture where people have some knowledge (however faulty) of the Bible and a cultural penchant for discussion. It is your job to keep the lesson progressing and to avoid side trails.

There is a great deal of important material to cover in each session, and you want to focus the students' minds on the themes and main incidents of the story you are presenting from the Word. Some discussion is healthy. Don't end up being so authoritarian that your students are afraid to speak! But be sure to keep the class directed and moving along the course outlined in the lesson.

The three visuals shown in Lesson 1 are excellent tools for helping keep on track; the "clothesline," the graph of the peaks of the details, and the illustration of the foundational blocks can be used over and over again as a means to put the discussion back on track. Use these small visuals wisely, and you will save yourself a lot of frustration and even save your students unnecessary embarrassment. Simply direct a student to the appropriate visual to offer a sensible reason for returning the discussion to the main subject.

Don't force verbal agreement

At the beginning stages of the teaching, don't expect your students to agree with what you are teaching. When you ask questions, don't word them so that the students are forced to agree with you in their answers. Leave room for the Holy Spirit to work in hearts and minds. The job of the teacher is to clearly and faithfully present the Word. Allow time for it to take root and to grow under the direction of the Holy Spirit.

Note: It is best to wait until after the Law is taught to expect your students to acknowledge that they are sinners.

Human efforts to force the new birth result in mere professions of faith without true possession of the life of God. Only God can bring a soul to understanding and salvation (I Corinthians 3:7). This doesn't mean that we should not exhort people to accept the truth, to repent, and to believe the Gospel. This, too, is the responsibility of the faithful servant of Christ.

In most situations, however, it is unwise to force people to answer to a human being. The teacher's responsibility is to make people realize that they stand before God and must answer to God. If your students contradict what you teach them from God's Word, ask them what God says about the subject. The issue is between them and God, not between you and them.

Guidelines for the Teacher

Make it interesting

You cannot teach people unless you have their attention. Keep your students' minds active and receptive by using illustrations, questions, and even humor (as long as it does not make light of the Scriptures). Try to make sure that, at all times, the majority of the students are actively participating and are actually thinking along with you while you are teaching. Proceed with calculated precision, establishing each point firmly in their minds.

Faith comes through hearing the Word of God (Romans 10:17). "To hear" in the scriptural sense is also "to understand." As teachers, we are responsible for making sure that our students clearly understand what they are being taught. Questioning is the best way to know if they are really understanding and if you are communicating the message of the Bible. So in addition to the review questions and the final questions in each lesson, intersperse your teaching with pertinent questions which will cause your students to stop and think about what you have just said.

Use the suggested visuals. Some of them can be made into small posters which you can use again and again in reinforcing major points and themes. If your students **hear** what you are saying, **see** it, and then **say it themselves** in answer to your question, then the possibility of their remembering what you are teaching is significantly increased.

Avoid unnecessary details

Some people, in their zeal to be good teachers, crowd their lessons with many unnecessary details. While some interesting details should be included to give life and reality to the story, such details should never take center stage and so overshadow the more important aspects of the story or its spiritual message.

Build patiently

Some Bible teachers find it hard to follow the biblical principle of progressive teaching. In their eagerness for people to know all the truth, these teachers forget the necessity of first laying foundations and then building, step by step. They find it extremely difficult to leave people temporarily ignorant of important teachings which will come later.

Teaching is like building—both take time. A building is completed brick by brick, plank by plank, story by story, according to the plans of the building architect. Time must be given for concrete to harden, timber to dry, bonding to seal, and paints to dry before the builder can proceed with the next stage of construction.

The immediate goals for each lesson should contribute step by step toward reaching the long-term teaching goals. Therefore, it is important not to crowd all of the long-term goals into each lesson. Every story should move the students forward yet another step in their understanding of the complete story of the Bible and the body of doctrinal truth.

Guidelines for the Teacher

Revealing the Saviour to people who have already heard His name

Certainly your students have heard the name of Jesus. They may have even studied about Him. But many of them may not really know who He is or how He fits into the whole Bible.

These lessons are designed to progressively reveal God's nature and His plan of salvation. Don't rush ahead to the story of Christ. Follow the lesson outlines and cover the historical ground gradually.

You are building a foundation upon which the Gospel can later be presented clearly, in the light of Old Testament revelation.

When should I present the Gospel?

Any time a student has a heart prepared to hear it! There is no "rule" about when to present the Gospel.

These lessons follow the progressive revelation of scriptural truth, and it is good, during your class time, to follow this plan through to the completion of the course.

But individual students may be ready at any time to hear the Gospel. You do not know how much previous teaching they have had, nor do you know what the Holy Spirit has been doing in their hearts. The Lord alone knows these answers, and He is faithful to show us what we need to know as we ask Him in prayer, believing.

Always be ready to share the Gospel with anyone, anywhere. Just be careful to give the person opportunity to show that he really does understand his need for a Savior and that he understands that Jesus alone has met that need by what He did for him on the Cross.

Do not feel pushed to rush ahead and share the Gospel. But always be alert to the individual needs of your students.

Note: See "What is the Gospel?" on p.12.

Avoid religious terminology and jargon. We commonly hear the words, "ask Jesus to come into your heart," "receive Christ," "get saved," or even "go forward."

The person saying these things may or may not know exactly what he means by these words. It is much better to use scriptural terminology and to make sure that the student understands what the words mean.

How much more clear it is to say to your students, "Believe that Jesus shed His blood and died on the Cross to make full payment for your sins. He took on Himself the punishment you deserve. Therefore, put your faith in Him alone as your Saviour."

Specific Instructions About the Lessons

General format

These lessons are designed to be used by the teacher, along with your Bible. The students use only their Bibles; there is no "student lesson."

Each lesson is divided into two major sections: "Lesson Preparation" and "To Be Taught to the Students."

Material in the Lesson preparation section is in san serif type like this.

The lesson to be taught to the students is in serif type like this.

The side columns in both sections are for the teacher's reference and are not intended to be taught to the students.

Lesson preparation section

Take a look at Lesson 1. It begins with a box marked "LESSON PREPARATION." The box describes the function of the side column notes—they are for the teacher's own study, and not intended to be taught, as they may contain concepts that run ahead of the lesson. For the benefit of a possible substitute teacher, this Lesson Preparation note appears at the beginning of every lesson.

Scripture references

On each page, on the side toward the binding is a narrow column containing Scriptures just for the teacher's reference.

When Scriptures are listed in this column at the beginning of the lesson, beside the Lesson Preparation box, they are usually supplementary passages that give additional meaning or insight and help to prepare the teacher to teach the lesson.

When Scriptures are listed in other places, opposite the Perspective for Teachers and down through the lesson itself, they are usually "proof texts" for what is being said. Again, they are not intended to be used in the lesson, as they may be in a context that could confuse the student.

These Scriptures are important. The more you immerse yourself in the Word in preparation to teach, the more effective your teaching will be, because the Holy Spirit will work through God's Word to give you understanding about what you are trying to teach others.

Ask the Lord to apply the Word to your own heart so you can teach it clearly to others.

Teacher's notes

On the outside margin of every page is a wider column for teacher's notes. Some notes are already printed here, and space is provided for you to add your own. You will notice on the first page of Lesson 1 that the note at the bottom of the page has a number corresponding to a number in the text. Also, there is a small hollow box at the end of the note. The numbers and the boxes are there to help keep track of what the note refers to and where that note ends.

Specific Instructions About the Lessons

The notes are intended only for the teacher, not for the students. Some of these notes are practical; some are doctrinal; some refer to reference material. Many of the notes are in reference to handling students' questions. Some notes are warnings to avoid potential "rabbit trails."

All of the notes should be read ahead of class by the teacher.

The notes are included with the hope of making the teacher's job a little easier. They are a compilation of the comments of many teachers who have had experience using this material.

Overview

In the upper right hand corner of the first page of each lesson in the Teacher's Notes column is an overview which briefly describes the main thrust of the lesson, usually listing some of the major points. The main thought is in boldfaced type.

These overviews are a handy way to view the whole course in a few minutes. You can scan the overviews and get an idea of the overall direction of the entire course.

If you need to ask someone to substitute for you, suggest that they read the overviews of the lessons surrounding the one they will teach so they can place that lesson in its proper context.

Use the overviews to keep your own teaching on target. Remember that you are building one basic principle upon another. Don't leave any gaps in the foundations. The overviews will help you check the foundations as you lay them.

Scriptures

If you turn to Lesson 2, you will see that the Scripture is the first thing listed under the Lesson Preparation box. The Scripture listed is the main Scripture or Scriptures used in that particular lesson. Supplementary Scriptures used in the Lesson outline are not included in this listing. (Lessons 1 and 3 do not have this listing, because they are more general in nature and do not focus on a specific passage.) (See also READ under Lesson Outline.)

Lesson goals; This lesson should help the students

These two sections are to be used in conjunction with the overview to help you understand the major focus of the lesson and to keep your teaching on track.

Perspective for the teacher

Where does this lesson fit into today's thinking? How can I make this lesson meaningful to my students? What's really happening in this passage of Scripture?

These brief "perspectives" are designed to stir the teacher's thoughts to consider the Scriptures being covered, to focus on the lesson goals, and to be alert to the needs of their students. One teacher calls this type of material a "preheater" for the mind!

The Perspective is for the teacher only, and is not intended to be shared with the students.

Reference material

Several of the lessons contain a list of suggested reference materials. These are carefully selected and should be useful to the teacher and the student.

Please note: Read ahead the list of selected reference materials for Lessons 1, 4, and 14. These lessons cover topics which may stir up a lot of questions from your students. You may want to have some of these references on hand when you teach these particular lessons, so you can refer a student to them, or use them to help in your own preparation.

Visuals

Many of the lessons have suggested visuals incorporated into the lesson text. These visuals are listed in the Lesson Preparation section so the teacher can assemble ahead whatever may be needed.

Use of these visuals is optional but strongly recommended, as any illustrations will help keep your students' attention and will also help them understand and remember what you are teaching.

See p. 70 for ordering the Chronological Pictures.

Specific Instructions About the Lessons

The small posters and other charts and graphics are not available in printed form, but are intended to be prepared by the teacher. All of them are very simple and can be done on a blackboard or other visual surface.

Some of the visuals are used in more than one lesson and could be done more permanently on poster board so they could be reused. As noted in the lessons, some of the visuals could be displayed in your classroom, as you will refer to them often. This works well if you have a meeting room (like a Sunday school classroom) where you can keep things on the wall from week to week.

But even in a home setting, you could make up small posters which could be hand held and reused for later lessons.

Chronological chart

The three-section chart is designed specifically to be used with these lessons. It is not intended to be an exhaustive chronology (neither are the lessons). Rather, it highlights the characters and events covered in this course. Also displayed are supplementary lists, such as the judges, kings, and prophets. Although you will not mention each of these individually, it will give the student a better idea of the breadth of time and the depth of events you are spanning with the lessons.

The line of the Deliverer is shown in boxes outlined in red. Note: the genealogies are confusing; avoid getting entangled in a discussion on these. The note on the right hand genealogy is sufficient. If a student wants to do research, that is up to him. As noted, the genealogy in Luke is probably Mary's and the one in Matthew is probably Joseph's. Matthew traces the royal line from David; Luke probably traces the blood line through another son of David.

The chart is designed so that you can teach from Section 1 by itself until you reach the story of Abraham. Then tape Section 2 to section 1. Section 3 can be added when you reach the time of the kings of Israel and Judah. Doing it this way will give your students opportunity to learn each part of the chart as it is taught without being confused by what is ahead. Also, you will be avoiding the temptation to discuss events that you have not yet reached in the chronological order.

Chronological maps

The three Chronological Maps include the specific locations mentioned in these lessons.

You may want to mount these maps on heavy card or put them on a bulletin board.

Special notes

Special notes are included in some of the lessons at the end of the Lesson Preparation section. These notes cover a variety of subjects which may be a help in preparing for the lesson.

Specific Instructions About the Lessons

The lesson

The material to be taught to the students is clearly marked by a notation, "TO BE TAUGHT TO THE STUDENTS (Center Column Only).

Above this heading is a shaded gray bar and a note which appears in each lesson, "ON TEACHING THIS LESSON." The note is repeated for the benefit of substitute teachers. **This note is extremely important. If you are asking someone to teach in your place, be sure they read and understand this note.**

Lesson outline

The lesson follows this heading.

Format

The outline is an indented text format rather than the standard numbered style.

Note: The lettered, bold outline headings are not intended to be spoken by the teacher. The thoughts contained in them are incorporated into the lesson text that follows.

The outline text does not follow regimented outline style, as the material is more narrative than technical. The Bible itself is told in the oriental style of "weaving" a story, rather than the "straight line" method of direct logic. As the story unfolds, details build in a lifelike sequence rather than in an artificially regimented style.

Introduction and conclusion

Each lesson begins with an "Introduction" and closes with a "Conclusion." These sections should be carefully considered in case they need to be restructured for your particular students and class format. Avoid using personal applications with very small groups, as you do not want to embarrass your students.

> Take the time
> to be sure
> that your
> students find
> the Scripture
> passages.
> God's Word
> is
> the heart
> of this study.

Themes

Theme:

Keep your eye on these themes! As explained in the previous section, these themes are extremely important. Though you will not state the themes verbatim each time, they are written to show what underlies the text you are teaching. As you teach, keep the themes in mind and you will keep your lessons on course.

READ
Read

READ signifies the main Scriptures used as a basis for the lesson.

Read signifies additional Scriptures which are to be read but are in addition to the main text.

Whenever you see either of these two notations, these Scriptures are to be read aloud. You, the teacher, may read them aloud yourself, or you may want the student to read them aloud. Take the time to be sure that all of your students can find these passages and read along silently with whomever reads them aloud. God's Word is the heart of this study.

Occasionally, a Scripture is printed out alongside the instruction to READ, and part of the Scripture is in boldface type. This is done to show which part of the verse you are emphasizing. Usually, you will find a note, cautioning you not to get sidetracked with the rest of the verse. Stick to the subject!

Because your students have Bibles, many questions may be asked regarding some of the context surrounding the Scriptures you are reading. Use the three posters shown in Lesson 1 to help you

Specific Instructions About the Lessons

explain why you are going to stay on the main subject and not get involved in other passages. Always be gracious to your students and show appreciation for their interest, even though you cannot take the time to go into another area of discussion.

Questions

You may want to use these questions both at the end of the lesson you have just taught and as a review at the beginning of the next lesson.

You may prefer not to use them at the end of the lesson; but **don't skip the review at the beginning of the next lesson.** You will find that your students will need to be refreshed on the details of the previous lesson and reviewing will also give opportunity to clear up any misunderstandings before you go on with new material.

The questions are designed to help the teacher and the student ascertain if the message of the lesson has been clearly communicated. For the most part, these are not discussion questions. They are very objective. The idea is to keep the message uncluttered and to be sure that the main points of the lesson have been heard and understood by the student.

The student does not need to agree with what has been taught. But he needs to have heard the information clearly, and the questions will help the teacher evaluate how well the message has been transmitted and received.

There are a few discussion questions in some of the lessons. These are not intended for use with small groups, as the subjects could invite the expression of strong opinions and reactions. If you have a large group and have the time, you may want to add more discussion questions to suit the needs of your students. But first be sure that the basic message has been clearly understood.

Putting it all together

Paul wrote to Timothy, *"Study to shew thyself approved unto God, a workman that needeth not to be ashamed, rightly dividing the word of truth"* (II Timothy 2:15). That's clear instruction!

You may not be able to fulfill the following list each time you teach. But if you use it as a guide, and make it a habit, you won't need to "be ashamed" of your teaching.

1. Pray. Ask God to help you understand His Word and these lessons.

2. Read the lesson overview.

3. Read any Scripture passages which are listed in the "Scripture Reference" column on the left side of first page of the lesson (alongside the Lesson Goals, etc.)

4. Read the lesson Scriptures and read the lesson preparation section. Note and assemble any reference material or visuals you need.

5. Read through the lesson itself, making mental note of the themes, reading the Scriptures as they appear in the lesson, and also reading the suggested Scriptures for the teacher and the teacher's notes, as they appear alongside the lesson text. If you have any questions, note them in pencil in the teacher's note column.

6. Read the lesson again, perhaps once every night or as many times as you possibly can. Each time, read the Scriptures that are part of the lesson text. Carefully consider the themes listed for each passage. That is what you want to emphasize as you teach. Meditate on the Word, and ask the Lord to make His message clear to you so you can teach it.

Think of the possible responses of your students, and ask the Lord to help you to know how to best handle their comments and questions. Make note of answers to your own questions as the Lord shows you in His Word.

Specific Instructions About the Lessons

List any other Scriptures that help explain and reinforce the lesson. You need not share these with your students, but these will help you digest the lesson and prepare to teach based on full conviction of the truth of God's Word.

7. After you have read through the lesson several times, highlight words and phrases that will jog your mind. (It is best to wait to do this highlighting until after you have read through the lesson several times, because only then will you have an understanding of which are the key words and phrases to mark. If you do this at first, you may mark too much or the wrong things, and your highlighting will be wasted.)

8. Pray daily for your students. And pray for the Lord to help you to clearly understand and teach His Word.

9. Teach "on overflow." When you have read, reread, meditated on, and mentally taught through this lesson to the point that you believe what you are teaching and you can teach out of full conviction, then you are ready to teach "on overflow" of what God has already placed in your own mind and heart. No surface reading of the Word can compare with the deep joy that comes from study. Your students may not yet agree with God's Word, but they will see that you believe it. This is extremely important.

In short, make sure that you believe and understand the message before you try to teach it to someone else! Use the outline and your highlighting as a framework for your teaching to keep you on track.

If you have prepared in the way listed above, you will not be tempted to "just read the lesson." You have something to share which you personally believe, and it will come out in your own style and with your own sense of conviction. You will never have a dry lesson if you teach "on overflow"!

Sound like a lot of work? It is. But it's worth it. You will never regret the time you spend preparing your lessons. It will pay off in your own life, in the classroom, and in the lives of your students—for all eternity. Are you a teacher? **Study**! Then go and teach—"on overflow!"

An encouragement to persevere

"...God...hath given to us the ministry of reconciliation...Now then we are ambassadors for Christ..." (II Corinthians 5:18,20).

"Therefore, my beloved brethren, be ye stedfast, unmoveable, always abounding in the work of the Lord, forasmuch as ye know that your labour is not in vain in the Lord" (I Corinthians 15:58).

"For as the rain cometh down, and the snow from heaven, and returneth not thither, but watereth the earth, and maketh it bring forth and bud, that it may give seed to the sower, and bread to the eater: So shall my word be that goeth forth out of my mouth: it shall not return unto me void, but it shall accomplish that which I please, and it shall prosper in the thing whereto I sent it" (Isaiah 55:10,11).

"For I am not ashamed of the gospel of Christ: for it is the power of God unto salvation to every one that believeth..." (Romans 1:16).

"For God so loved the world, that He gave his only begotten Son, that whosoever believeth in him should not perish, but have everlasting life" (John 3:16).

Part 3

The Lessons

Part 3

The Lessons

1. Introducing the Bible	97
2. God Alone	109
3. God Created the Spirit Beings; Lucifer Rebelled	119
4. God Created the Heavens and the Earth — Part 1	129
5. God Created the Heavens and the Earth — Part 2	137
6. God Created Man	147
7. God Placed Adam in Eden	157
8. God Made Eve	169
9. Review of Lessons 1-8	175
10. Adam and Eve Disobeyed God	181
11. God's Promise and Curse	195
12. God's Provision and Judgment; The Birth of Cain and Abel	207
13. God Rejected Cain and His Offering, but Accepted Abel and His Offering	217
14. God Judged the Whole World and Delivered Noah and All in the Ark	231
15. God Remembered Noah and All in the Ark; God Scattered the Rebels at the Tower of Babel	245

Part 3

The Lessons

16. God Chose, Called, and Guided Abram; Lot Chose the Fertile Plains of Sodom and Gomorrah . . . 255

17. God Destroyed Sodom and Gomorrah; God Renewed His Promises to Abraham 265

18. God Gave Isaac; God Delivered Isaac from Death 275

19. Isaac's Sons, Esau and Jacob; Jacob's Son Joseph 283

20. God Promoted Joseph and Took Israel Into Egypt 291

21. God Preserved Israel Enslaved in Egypt; God Chose, Protected, and Called Moses to Deliver Israel. 297

22. God Sent Plagues on Egypt; God Passed Over Israel 307

23. God Delivered Israel at the Red Sea and Provided Them with Food and Water in the Desert . . . 319

24. Preparation for the Giving of the Ten Commandments 331

25. God Gave the Ten Commandments 341

26. The Tabernacle 353

27. Israel's Unbelief; God's Judgments and Deliverances 363

Part 3

The Lessons

28. Israel in the Promised Land Under Judges and Kings 373

29. God Sent His Messengers, the Prophets, to Israel; Israel Refused to Respond to Their Warnings . 383

30. God Foretold the Birth of John and Jesus. . . . 395

31 God Began to Fulfill His Promises Concerning John and Jesus 403

32. God Fulfilled His Promises by Giving Jesus, the Deliverer 413

33. God Sent John to Teach and Baptize; John Baptized Jesus 421

34. Jesus, When Tempted, Resisted and Rebuked Satan 431

35. Jesus Began His Ministry 439

36. You Must Be Born Again 447

37. Jesus Evidenced His Divinity, but the Religious Leaders Rejected Him; Jesus Chose Twelve Disciples 455

38. Jesus Calmed the Storm and Delivered the Demon-Possessed Man of Gadara 467

39. Jesus Fed Five Thousand People 477

Part 3

The Lessons

40. The Way of the Scribes and Pharisees Is Not God's Way 485

41. Jesus Is the Christ, the Son of God; Jesus Was Transfigured 493

42. Jesus Is the Only Doorway to Eternal Life . . . 501

43. Jesus Raised Lazarus from the Dead 509

44. Jesus Loved the Children and Taught the Rich Young Ruler 517

45. The Foolishness of Trusting in Riches 525

46. Jesus Rode into Jerusalem; Judas Planned to Betray Jesus; Jesus Instituted the Lord's Supper 533

47. Jesus Was Arrested by His Enemies 541

48. Jesus Was Crucified and Buried 551

49. The Meaning of Christ's Death from the Old Testament 562

50. Jesus Was Raised from the Dead, Appeared to His Disciples, Returned to Heaven, and Promised to Come Again 574

Scripture Reference

Joshua 1:8
Psalm 19; 119
Isaiah 40:8; 55:6-11
Luke 24:27,32, 44
John 1:1,2,17

LESSON 1 — Introducing the Bible

LESSON PREPARATION

This section is for you, the teacher.

The passages in the Scripture Reference column are for your own study in preparing for this lesson. Since they may contain concepts that run ahead of the lesson, they are not to be taught at this point.

Note: Please read carefully the note to teachers in the front of this book.

LESSON GOALS:

- To present the Bible as God's authoritative, inerrant, effective Word.

THIS LESSON SHOULD HELP THE STUDENTS:

- To understand where the Bible came from.
- To gain confidence in its authority.
- To gain respect for its uniqueness as God's written Word.

PERSPECTIVE FOR THE TEACHER:

Many of us live a society which was founded on biblical principles. Family structure, law and order, morality, social concerns, and many other basic elements of our culture were established by God and clearly recorded in His Word.

Though some people in our society have never set foot inside the door of a church, they have probably heard about the Bible; they may even own one. Other people may go to church week after week but never open their Bibles. Most people in our culture are not unaware of the Bible; but sadly, most people do not know what it says because they have never taken the time to read and study the Bible for themselves.

To many, the Bible may call to mind thoughts of "religion" and whatever religious experience they had as a child (regardless of whether or not it was based on God's true Word). Many presume its message to be out-of-date or irrelevant. Some people think that the Bible is a book from which men can pick and choose the ideas they like. Yet, deep within, most people realize that the Bible deserves respect, even if they do not really know or believe what it says.

God's Word is powerful. As you present His truth, God can give clear sight to confused, blinded minds and penetrate sin-stained hearts. Pray that God will open the minds and hearts of your students to learn and to believe this Book of all books, the Bible.[1]

REFERENCE MATERIAL:

Following is a list of books which may help you in preparing for this lesson:

From God to Us — How We Got Our Bible, by Norman L. Geisler and William E. Nix. Moody Press, Chicago, 1974.

What You Should Know About Inerrancy, by Charles C. Ryrie. Moody Press, Chicago, 1981.

Teacher's Notes

OVERVIEW

This lesson is designed to introduce the Bible to your students. Included are some interesting facts and general information about the Bible and how it came to us. The main point of this lesson is to establish the fact that the Bible is the Word of God.

This lesson also presents to the students the general guidelines for the entire study:
— God-centered
— chronological
— panoramic (rather than in depth of detail)
— dealing only with foundational issues.

[1] You will probably learn quite a bit about your students' knowledge of the Bible as you go through this lesson. Some may be students of the Bible themselves; others may have never opened a Bible with the purpose of studying it.

Don't assume that just because a student is a successful businessman or woman that he or she is familiar with the basic operations of finding books, chapters, and verses. And don't let a student know if you are surprised at how little he knows. They have come to study the Bible with you; try to find ways to encourage them in their progress. Consider even the most elementary question important. If their questions are off the subject, you may have to tell them that you must wait until a later lesson to fully answer. But let them know that you appreciate their interest. □

Lesson 1: Introducing the Bible

Teacher's Notes

Scripture Reference

Evidence that Demands a Verdict, by Josh McDowell, Here's Life Publishers, San Bernadino.

You may find additional reference materials such as these a great help in encouraging interested students. If a student asks questions which you don't have time to answer during class, you can refer him to the selected reference material so that he can research answers for himself. This will save class time and keep the discussion on track while still giving the student a thoughtful response to his questions.

VISUALS:

- Chronological Picture No. 1, "God's Word Written"
- Map or globe of the world
- Map of the Mideast
- Map of Israel

The maps could be from a current atlas so that the students may see that you are relating to present-day locations. (In future lessons you will use the Chronological Maps provided with these lessons. Chronological Map 1 may be used for this lesson.)

If possible, bring to class a few Bibles translated into other languages.

LOOKING AHEAD:

Suggestion: Read through Lesson 4, "God Created the Heavens and the Earth," and consider which reference materials you may want to locate or order and study ahead of time. Though you will **not** be debating creation versus evolution, you will find it helpful to be prepared to handle the discussion which may arise as you teach Lesson 4. By making available selected books, tapes, and/or videos, you will be able to concentrate on the primary goals of the lesson during class time and still provide the students opportunity to seek out answers to their questions as they study the additional materials on their own.

NOTES REGARDING THE INERRANCY OF SCRIPTURE:

The inerrancy of the Scriptures is an extremely important fact. It can be shown to be true through many avenues of proof, some of which are explored more fully in the resource materials listed above.

For us who teach, it is **vital** that we believe in the inerrancy of the Bible. If you are not clear on this issue yourself, it would be wise to study some of these resources so that your faith can rest more firmly in God's true Word.

But for your students, some of whom may not even be believers, it is **not** essential that you "prove" or force the issue of inerrancy at this point.

The Bible itself is its own strongest proof. As stated in Hebrews 4:12, *"For the word of God is quick, and powerful, and sharper than any twoedged sword...."* As you teach God's Word, His Spirit will be working on blinded minds and hardened hearts.

The need at this early stage of your teaching is to make sure that you are communicating the facts in such a way that the students are hearing what you intend to say to them. Don't be upset if they don't believe you. Just be sure you are delivering the truth. God will do the rest.

You may be amazed at how, after you have taught many lessons, the person who scoffed at the Bible will become a more open-minded, interested listener, thirsty to learn more about our wonderful God from His matchless Word!

Lesson 1: Introducing the Bible

Scripture Reference | **Teacher's Notes**

ON TEACHING THIS LESSON:

These lessons are designed to **teach unbelievers**. You are carefully laying a scriptural foundation on which the Gospel will later be presented. If your class contains believers, teach with the goal of giving them an understanding of the basis for their faith and **with the goal of enabling them to teach the same material to unbelievers**.

DON'T COMPLICATE THE MESSAGE!

As you teach, keep in mind that this is a directed study—not an exhaustive survey of the Bible and not an unlimited group discussion. Keep your lesson on track and moving ahead by limiting and directing any discussion.

Carefully follow the outline. Emphasize the doctrinal themes.

LESSON FORMAT: The **center column** below contains the lesson material to be taught to the students. The **bold outline headings** are only for reference and need not be spoken, as they are incorporated into the outlined material that follows. The material in the **side columns** is for the teacher's own reference and is not intended to be included in the lesson.

TO BE TAUGHT TO THE STUDENTS
(Center Column Only)

LESSON OUTLINE:

A. Introduction

We have met for one purpose: to study the Bible.

Many people have Bibles in their homes, but most people know very little of what is in the Bible.

- It IS a big book.
- Many people start to read it and get "bogged down."

We want to help you understand the Bible because it is God's personal message to each one of us.

- A person can spend a lifetime enjoying the study of this book.
- But in our study we are going to examine some of the **basic** things the Bible teaches. Once you understand these basic truths, the rest of the Bible will begin to make more sense.

B. God is the focus of our study.*

We are going to study who God is and what He does.

- God really wants us to get to know Him; that's why He gave us the Bible.
- God is the central character of the Bible.
- As we study, you will learn what He is really like:

    Who He is

    What He does

    What He is like—His personality.

God will be the main focus of our study because He is the main focus of the Bible.

*Remember that these lettered, bold outline headings are not to be spoken; the thought is included in the lesson text.

Lesson 1: Introducing the Bible

Teacher's Notes

Scripture Reference

C. We will study the Bible chronologically.

The Bible is not just a book of doctrines, or teachings, about God; it is the story of history as seen from God's perspective.

It is God's recounting of history from its very beginning.

Therefore, in our study of the Bible we are going to walk through history, so to speak, seeing little by little what God reveals about His own character, about Satan, and about mankind.

We are going to study the Bible chronologically; that is, in the order in which events took place.

Suggested Visual:

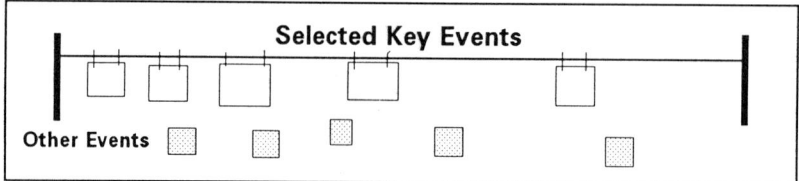

- Explain:

Studying this way is a little like stretching out a clothesline and then hanging clothes on it.

We will be stretching out the Biblical time line and placing selected events on that line.

You may already know about certain details of the Bible but not yet have a clear understanding of where they fit into the overall picture.

But when the events we study are securely "hung in place," the details you may have wondered about will begin to fit into their proper position among the things already on the line.

We will concentrate on "setting up the clothesline," that is, establishing the basic time line of Bible history; and we will be placing some key events on that line. But we will not have time, so to speak, to put everything on the line.

We are going to begin our next lesson in Genesis, which is where God's story of history begins.

Genesis is the foundational book of the Bible.

- You might make a comparison to the way that a house is built:

    Foundations are laid first.

    Then structures can be added on top of firm foundations, one piece at a time.

    If the foundations aren't first built properly, the rest of the house is structurally weak.

For this reason, it is very important that you attend every lesson.

- Everything we study will be important and will become part of the "foundation" for our future studies.

- If you miss a session, you will find it more difficult to understand later lessons.[2]

D. We will be skimming the surface of events but laying firm foundations for understanding the Bible.

The Bible is rich and deep in content and themes.

We are only going to skim the surface of the vast wealth contained in it.

[2] You may want to tape your lessons and offer a tape to any student who can't attend a particular session. ☐

Lesson 1: Introducing the Bible

Suggested Visual: ³

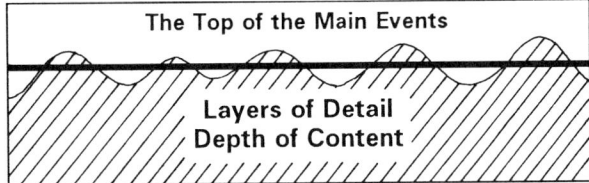

- Explain:

   Just like this visual shows, there are many layers and depths of details and content in the Bible. We are not going down deeply into these layers. Rather, we are going to skim the top of some of the main events.

Suggested Visual:

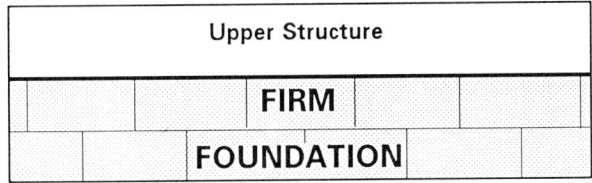

- Explain:

   As we mentioned, we are going to be laying blocks for a firm foundation. We are going to study the basic things that will help you later to understand some of those depths and details of the Bible.

   If a building is to stand, it needs a firm foundation. That is the purpose of this study. We are going to concentrate on the foundation and will not work on the upper structure until the foundation is firmly built.

   So when you ask a question that goes down deeply into the details or pertains to the upper structure, I will have to hold off on answering you.

   We are laying a solid foundation upon which we can later build more understanding.

E. We want to avoid sidetracks and the confusion that comes from mixing the themes of the Bible.

We will try to stay on target with our lesson outline and not get sidetracked.

We want you to be able to learn these foundational truths of the Bible and not be distracted.

The Bible is basically written in a chronological order, but we will reach certain events in the time line that are expanded upon in greater detail in later portions of the Bible.

Suggested Visual:

- As we study chronologically, we may draw certain details from these later portions to enhance our understanding.

Scripture Reference

Teacher's Notes

³If wisely used, these two simple illustrations and the one on the previous page will be a help throughout the entire chronological study. If possible, keep these three illustrations on the wall or have them handy so that you may point to them as needed to pull a discussion back on track.

Using simple visuals takes the attention away from the student (who is pulling the discussion away from the main subject) and puts the focus on the direction of the course. It is a polite, non-threatening way to stay on track and to avoid arguments and confusion.

For example, if a student wants to go into details that are not covered in the outline, you could thank them for their question but say, "Just like our illustration here shows, we're only going to skim along the top of the main events. We don't want to get bogged down in details."

Or, if a student starts to discuss one of the themes, such as sanctification, which is not covered in the course, you might say, "That is an interesting thought, but, like our illustration, the issue you're talking about pertains to the upper structure. We want to stick to building the foundations right now."

Or, if a student wants to ask a question about an event that runs ahead, chronologically, of the current lesson (but an event you will not be covering later), you might say, "Just like our clothesline illustration shows, that's one of the details we won't be covering in this course. But later in our studies we will be filling in some events of that time period that will help you see how what you're talking about fits into the overall picture." ☐

Lesson 1: Introducing the Bible

Teacher's Notes

4The three issues we are speaking of are:

1. Salvation from the penalty of sin
2. Salvation from the power of sin (sanctification)
3. Salvation from the presence of sin (glorification).

Don't discuss these issues; just go on with the lesson. (For your own reference, see the discussion of foundational themes in "How To Use These Lessons" in Part I of this course.)

In reference to the first issue a student may ask, "What is the problem sin has caused?" Assure him that the answer to this question will be covered in a later lesson. ☐

5Don't get into a discussion of the various religions, denominations, cults, etc.!

This point is made here because it addresses one of the major issues in the minds of many students; that is, "Where did all of the different religions come from? Why are there so many denominations?"

If someone wants to venture into this subject, tell them that this is not the purpose of this study. We are, instead, looking at what the Bible has to say.

You might tell them that when a person knows what the Bible really says, then he has a basis for evaluating the various religions and denominations. ☐

6Some of your students may not be familiar at all with the Bible. They may not know how to find books, chapters, verses, etc. Take time to give whatever help they need. ☐

7Some Bibles have extensive footnotes which can be very misleading. If you are providing Bibles for your students, use Bibles which have only the Bible text without commentary.

If your students have brought their own Bibles, take the time to point out for the students, in their Bibles, which part is God's Word and which part is not. ☐

Scripture Reference

- When we do this, we need to be very careful to stick to the original topic of our study.

We need to understand that the Bible deals with many different issues, questions, and themes.

- Some of these themes and questions and answers begin in the earliest parts of the Bible and continue through to its closing pages.
- Often you will find two or more themes or questions being addressed in one portion.
- This could be confusing—indeed it has been to many people.

One example of this confusion is that the Bible addresses three major issues about the topic of sin:**4**

1. What God has done so people can be saved from the first great problem sin has caused.**4**
2. What God has done to set people free from sin that is controling their lives.
3. What God will do so people will be completely free from all the problems sin causes.

The mixing of these three issues has been one of the major contributing factors to the existence and increase of the many different cults, religions, and denominations.**5**

We, too, will get confused unless we tenaciously stick to the first issue: **What God has done so people can be saved from the first great problem sin has caused.**

- Therefore, as we study chronologically, there will be times when you may ask questions or we may look at verses which include other issues or themes that are not part of this foundation.
- When this happens, my job as a teacher is to make sure that we stick to the subject at hand.
- We, too, will become confused unless we build our understanding one step at a time.

Indeed, **the other themes in the Bible cannot be clearly understood unless we first understand the foundational themes.**

- Therefore we are going to limit our discussion to the foundations; that is what this study is all about!
- So you might say, in light of our illustrations, that we will be building a firm foundation, skimming the peaks of the details, and stretching a line upon which we can place the events in time.

F. A look at the Bible

Now open your Bible.

Let's take a look at the many things the Book contains:**6**

- Table of Contents
- Old Testament
- New Testament
- Chapters, verse numbers
- Footnotes, various helps.

The Bible is God's Word.

- When we talk about the Bible being God's Word, we are referring to the text of the Bible, not the various notes that men have added.**7**

The Bible means a lot to me.

Lesson 1: Introducing the Bible

- Example:

    "The Bible is my favorite book. I know that when I read God's Word, I'll find the help I need for every day. The Bible tells me what God is like. He's wonderful! The more I read, the more I want to read and to know Him better." **8**

G. The Bible is the most important and unique book in the whole world because it is the Word of GOD.

 Theme: God is supreme and sovereign.

 Theme: God communicates with man.

 READ II Timothy 3:16: "**All scripture is given by inspiration of God,** *and is profitable for doctrine, for reproof, for correction, for instruction in righteousness.*" **9**

God spoke to men called "prophets" the exact messages He wanted written down.

- Sometimes He spoke audibly.
- Sometimes He spoke to them in visions.
- Sometimes He just put the message directly into their minds.
- God caused the prophets to write exactly what He spoke to them.

 READ II Peter 1:20,21.

The Bible is not men's ideas, but God's own Word.

Suggested Visual:

This picture portrays a prophet writing down on a scroll the message given him by God.

CHRONOLOGICAL PICTURE NO 1, "GOD'S WORD WRITTEN"

The Bible is the only book in the world authored by God.

God wrote the Bible over the course of 1,600 years, using over 40 men.

 Theme: God does not change.

But the Bible has absolute unity, from beginning to end, because **God is its one Author.**

- Illustrate:

    If several people standing together witnessed the same incident, they would have different stories about what actually happened.

    But the Bible, written in vastly different cultures and different times by different men is one unit.

- The only answer for the unity of the Bible is **one author – God!**

Scripture Reference

Teacher's Notes

8This is not a salvation testimony; rather, it is a simple testimony of your appreciation for the Bible. ☐

9Remember that when the verse is printed in the lesson like this, the highlighted portion is the part you want to talk about.

The other part of the verse contains themes that you do not want to cover at this point. Stick tenaciously to the subject!

Also, you may want to tell your students how to find II Timothy. You could tell them that this book is almost to the end of the Bible; that is, if they open their Bibles in the middle, II Timothy is almost all the way to the right...etc. ☐

Lesson 1: Introducing the Bible

| Teacher's Notes | | Scripture Reference |

H. The Bible is God's message to the world which He gave through the Jewish people.

 Theme: God communicates with man.

 Theme: God is supreme and sovereign.

All but one of the men whom God used to write His Word were Jewish. (Luke was apparently a Gentile—a Gentile is anyone who is not Jewish.)

In Isaiah 43:10, God says of Israel (that is, the Jewish people), *"Ye are my witnesses, saith the LORD...."*

SHOW MAP OF WORLD, MIDEAST, ISRAEL.

God used one group of people through whom He expressed His message to and for the whole world.

Romans 3:1,2

In Isaiah 45:22 God says, *"Look unto me...all the ends of the earth: for I am God and there is none else."* **10**

Suggested Visual:

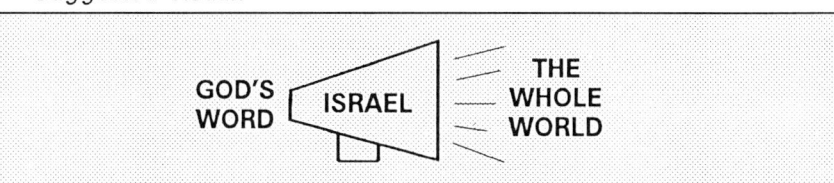

- *Explain:*

  You might say that Israel was like God's megaphone, broadcasting God's message to the whole world.

I. The Bible has been passed down to us intact and with extreme accuracy.

 Theme: God does not change.

Originally, God's prophets wrote down God's message.

As the original documents wore out from use and age, new copies had to be made.

Copying was done with extreme care. **11**

- In the *Illustrated Bible Dictionary,* **12** we read the following statement regarding the men who made handwritten copies of the Bible:

  "They used every imaginable safeguard, no matter how cumbersome or laborious, to ensure the accurate transmission of the text. The number of letters in a book was counted and its middle letter was given. Similarly with the words, and again the middle word of the book was noted...."

- Though every word was hand copied, there are more ancient manuscripts of the Bible than of any other ancient document.

- All of the ancient manuscripts that have been found are extremely close in content, differing only in minute details that do not affect the meaning.

  Example:

  In 1947, about 15 miles from Jerusalem, a shepherd boy threw a rock into a cave, hoping to scare out one of his animals that

---

10 This verse contains themes that you should not cover at this point. That is why you are only quoting part of the verse. Don't get sidetracked! ☐

11 See "Notes Regarding the Inerrancy of Scripture" in the Lesson Preparation section at the beginning of this lesson.

The issue of inerrancy is hotly contested by many scholars, and you do not want to set the stage for a debate. However, you do want to make it clear that **the Bible is true.**

If the discussion seems to be getting out of hand, simply refer the student to the suggested reference books, thank him for his questions, and tell him that you must go on with the lesson. ☐

12 *The Illustrated Bible Dictionary,* Part 3, J. D. Douglas, Editor, p. 1538, Inter-Varsity Press, Tyndale House Publishers, Wheaton, IL, 1980. ☐

Lesson 1: Introducing the Bible

had strayed into the cave. He heard the sound of pottery breaking and went inside the cave to investigate. To his amazement, he beheld pottery urns holding ancient scrolls. He reported his find, and when scholars investigated, they found hundreds of scrolls. These "Dead Sea Scrolls" had been hidden in area caves by a religious sect sometime during the first century before Christ.

At the time of this discovery, translators were using manuscripts which had been copied in about 900 A.D. When scholars compared the Dead Sea Scrolls with the manuscripts which they had been using, there were no significant differences in text! Though separated by 1,000 years, these ancient manuscripts said the same thing. God preserves His Word.

- The *Illustrated Bible Dictionary* [13] gives us more insight regarding the Old Testament texts:

    "...it is important to recall the attitude of the Jews toward their Scriptures. It can best be summed up in the statement by Josephus [a Jewish writer of the 1st century A.D.]. 'We have given practical proof of our reverence for our own Scriptures. For, although such long ages have now passed, no one has ventured either to add, or to remove, or to alter a syllable; and it is an instinct with every Jew...to regard them as the decrees of God....'

How did we get the Bible in our language?

- For many centuries, only a few people were able to have copies of the Bible.

    In the time of Christ, the scribes kept the scrolls (rolls of parchment or leather on which text was written in ink) in the temple.

    Many of the New Testament books were originally written as letters which were circulated from one church to another.

- The original texts of the Bible were written in one of three languages: Hebrew, Aramaic, or Greek.

    Down through the ages, God enabled men to translate the Bible into different languages.

    Many copies of the ancient Hebrew, Aramaic, and Greek texts are still in existence. Translators have been able to study these as they translate the Bible.

    Today, we have a variety of printed Bibles readily available in our language.

- The Bible has been translated into more languages than any other book.[14]

J. The Bible is an accurate historical record.

Archeological discoveries in recent years have revealed many pieces of ancient information that agree in minute detail with the Bible.

- Places
- Cultural details
- Names
- Dates.

Writings contemporary with the Bible agree in historical detail, cultural information, writing style, etc.

Over the years, thousands upon thousands of archeological and historical evidences relating to the Bible have been uncovered, and ALL of these support the accuracy of the Bible.

[13] J. D. Douglas, Editor, p. 1537. ☐

[14] If you have brought Bible translations, show them to your students. ☐

Lesson 1: Introducing the Bible

Teacher's Notes

Scripture Reference

[15] Quoted from *More Evidence That Demands a Verdict,* by Josh McDowell, p. 21. ☐

In *Archeology and Bible History*, Joseph Free wrote that "...numerous passages of the Bible which long puzzled the commentators have readily yielded up their meaning when new light from archeological discoveries has been focused on them....archeology has confirmed countless passages...." [15]

As we study future lessons, we will discuss some of these archeological and historical discoveries.

Many of the cultures, places, and names mentioned in the Bible are visible today, having remained almost unchanged over the centuries.

The Bible has withstood the test of time.

 Theme: God does not change.

- New discoveries only serve to echo and reinforce the absolute accuracy, authority, and authenticity of every word God has given us in His Book.
- By contrast, books written by men, such as school textbooks, reference books, and scientific texts, all must be drastically changed every few years as more is learned and old theories are replaced.
- The Bible has not and will not change because God is its author.

 READ Psalm 119:89.

K. The Bible has the answers for the most important questions of life.

The Bible is not just another "religious" book.
- Many men have written books, trying to tell men about God.
- God is the author of the Bible, and in it He reveals Himself to us. In the Bible God tells us who He is: what He wants us to know about Him—what He is like.

In the Bible, God tells us about ourselves: our relationship to Him, to the world around us, to one another, for now and for all eternity.

Only the Bible addresses these issues with absolute authority.

 Theme: God is supreme and sovereign.

 Theme: God communicates with man.

 READ Hebrews 4:12.

The Bible is God's voice speaking to us.

Through His Word He shows us what we really are inside.

L. The Bible is God's personal message to each of us; it is the most important message we will ever be given.

Why is it so important for you and me to study the Bible?

Why should we take the time to study the Bible?
- A lot of other things call for our attention: [16]

  Our work

  Our home

  Recreation

  Studies.

[16] The tone here should be objective. You are hoping to encourage your students to come back and study the Bible. The Word itself will, in time, bring conviction. ☐

Lesson 1: Introducing the Bible

- Lots of other material is available:

    Books and magazines

    Television, movies, and videos.

The Bible is unique.

- The Bible alone has God's message for our lives today.
- The Bible alone tells us what God thinks of us and what He sees as our greatest need.

The Bible is important because it is God's personal message to each one of us!

- Young, old, man, woman, or child — God wrote the Bible to each one of us personally.
- God wants you and He wants me to know what is in this Book; that's why He wrote it.

M. Conclusion:

It will take time to go through these lessons, but you will find it to be one of the most worthwhile investments you will ever make.

- You will be learning about God.
- And you will be learning what He has written for you in His Book, the Bible.

In the book, *From God to Us, How We Got Our Bible,* the authors open by saying that the Bible is "the most quoted, the most published, the most translated, and the most influential book in the history of mankind." [17]

The Bible is also God's personal message to us. He wrote it to communicate with people — with you and with me. If someone writes us a letter, we want to read it. This Bible is God's letter to us. Let's study God's Word together and find out what it says!

[17] *From God to Us — How We Got Our Bible*, by Norman L. Geisler and William E. Nix. Moody Press, Chicago, 1974, p. 7.

QUESTIONS:

1. When God wanted His words written down, did He get just anyone to do it? *No, He chose special men.*

2. What are these men called? *Prophets.*

3. Did these men all live during the same time in history? *No, many of them lived at different times. It took about 1,600 years before all of God's words were written.*

4. How many men were there? *Approximately forty.*

5. What nationality were they? *They were all Jewish, except one man. (Luke was a Gentile.)*

6. Did they write God's words in English? *No. (They were written in Hebrew, Greek, and Aramaic.)*

7. Who is the author of the Bible? *God.*

8. Why should a person study the Bible? *The Bible is God's personal message to every individual.*

Scripture Reference

Job 38:4
Psalm 50:21; 90:2
Isaiah 43:10; 46:9,10; 55:8,9
Colossians 1:17
Hebrews 1:10-12
Revelation 1:8

Daniel 11:36; 12:4

The Trinity:
Genesis 1:1,2; 1:26; 3:22
Matthew 28:17-19
Romans 8:26,34
II Corinthians 13:14
Ephesians 1:17; 2:13,18
Hebrews 9:14

LESSON 2

God Alone

LESSON PREPARATION

This section is for you, the teacher.

The passages in the Scripture Reference column are for your own study in preparing for this lesson. Since they may contain concepts that run ahead of the lesson, they are not to be taught at this point.

Note: If you have not taught previously from this series of lessons, please read carefully the note to teachers in the front of this book.

SCRIPTURE: Genesis 1:1

LESSON GOALS:

- To present the fact of God's existence before all things.
- To establish the fact of God's sovereignty.[1]

THIS LESSON SHOULD HELP THE STUDENTS:

- To have an increased awe of God as the sovereign and eternal Lord.
- To consider God's account of the beginning.

PERSPECTIVE FOR THE TEACHER:

In our culture, self is exalted and assigned that place of control and supremacy that belongs to God alone.[2] Here are just a few of the evidences of this self-centered thinking: People in our country spend millions of dollars every year to improve their self-image and to try to exert more control over their lives and over the world around them. Our schools are being swiftly and subtly taken over by humanistic philosophies that put man in the place of God. At every turn, men are seeking knowledge and boasting of their discoveries as if they had originated life and the laws that control the universe. To be anything but the best and the one in control of one's own destiny seems unthinkable in our culture.

These lessons will cut against the grain of this type of thinking. To some who have been accustomed to putting self on the throne, it may seem that they are showing weakness if they allow God His rightful place. But God says that this is the beginning of wisdom. (Note Proverbs 1:7.)

God's Word, taught in the power of the Holy Spirit and with prayer, is able to transform minds and hearts.

INTRODUCING THE TRINITY:

Point "D" of the lesson outline introduces that God is a Trinity. The word "Trinity" does not appear in Scripture, but the fact of the Trinity is evident from Genesis to Revelation. (The Scripture Reference column gives some examples.)

The Trinity is introduced at this point in the lessons because:

1. The Trinity is eternal and, chronologically, existed before the beginning.
2. The word "God" in Genesis 1:1 is the Hebrew word *Elohim*. Because of its ending, *Elohim* is a plural name with a singular meaning (indicated

Teacher's Notes

OVERVIEW

This lesson begins to lay the foundational truth of God's sovereignty by showing that God existed alone before the beginning and that He exists independently of all else and needs nothing. It gives a very brief introduction to the Trinity.

It also establishes the fact that because God was the only one there before the beginning, He alone can tell us what happened in the beginning.

---

[1] In presenting His sovereignty, we will be introducing several characteristics and attributes of God: His eternality, His omnipresence, the fact that He is Spirit; the fact that He is a Trinity.

We will use a few selected proof texts to establish these points. But remember, this study is **foundational**. Do not turn this lesson into a topical study with many proof texts. **Keep it simple.** Let the Word do its work in hearts by carefully planting selected portions, a little at a time. ☐

[2] Be alert to your students' comments and questions. Their responses to the lesson will begin to reveal their understanding of God.

Some of your students may be deeply involved in humanistic thinking. Avoid debating with them. Rather, try to show them that the difference is not between what they think and what you think, but between what they think and what God's Word says. ☐

Teacher's Notes — *Lesson 2: God Alone* — Scripture Reference

    by the fact that it is used with singular verbs). This suggests the uni-plurality of the Godhead.

3. God the Son was there in the beginning. He is included with God the Father and God the Holy Spirit in the words, *"In the beginning God created the heaven and the earth."* — John 1:1-3

4. If we fail to teach the Trinity in the beginning and throughout the Old Testament, it will be more difficult to teach the deity of Jesus when we come to the story of His birth. It is much easier for us to teach and for our students to understand if we have taught—from the beginning—that Jesus was forever co-equal with the Father, active in creation, and in the entire Old Testament story. A statement such as, *"...Before Abraham was, I am"* (John 8:58), will be less difficult for people to understand if we have taught them that God the Son was there, even before the beginning.

   NOTE: We will not use His name, Jesus, or His title, Christ, while teaching the Old Testament. Both are connected with His earthly ministry. Refer to Him only as God the Son during the Old Testament teaching.

5. Since the Holy Spirit is mentioned in the Old Testament, the subject of the Trinity cannot be avoided (Genesis 1:2, cf. 6:3).

6. Genesis 1:26 uses the plurals "us" and "our."

   Do not try to explain the Trinity. It is impossible, and all illustrations (e.g., water, egg, triangle) fall far short of the truth. It is better to admit that we cannot understand the Trinity.

A WORD OF CAUTION:

If you have a student who is a Jehovah's Witness or who has been exposed to their teachings, you may find that he will try to argue the fact of the Trinity.

If this situation arises, graciously tell the student that the purpose of this class is to study the Bible. You will be presenting foundational truth, a little at a time. If he is interested and wants to listen with an open mind, he is welcome. Tell him that if he really wants to get to know God, you are really interested in helping him.

Tell them that honest questions relating to the subject are always welcome, even though you may hold off on answering until a later lesson. But arguments and debates just aren't appropriate here. (See II Timothy 2:24-26.)

Talk with him after class if needed. But if he still won't comply, you may have to ask him not to continue the study with the group. You may want to offer to study with him alone. But in some instances, you may need to refrain. (See Titus 3:10.)

VISUALS:

- "The Bible Is HIS STORY"—This can just be written on a board as you teach, or, it could be a small poster that you keep on the wall in your class throughout the course. Small posters like this can brighten your classroom and are excellent reminders of the truths you are teaching.
- Chronological Chart
- Chart comparing GOD and man (see below)

For this lesson, you may want to make a chart comparing God and man. This could be done beforehand on a sheet of poster board; or it could be done as you teach, using a chalkboard or other visual surface; or you may want to prepare the chart for use on an overhead projector. Notes for adding to the chart as you teach are included in the lesson.

Write in man's characteristics, but do not comment on them. The purpose of the chart is to exalt God as sovereign and to help the students to think about God's greatness. The comments on man are just visual "seeds" to plant in your students' minds.

The completed chart will look like this:

Lesson 2: God Alone

GOD	MAN
GOD had no beginning, will have no end.	MAN is born and dies.
GOD is a Trinity of three persons.	MAN is only one person.
GOD needs nothing.	MAN needs food, water, air, sleep, light, protection, etc.
GOD knows everything.	MAN needs to be taught.
GOD is Spirit and has no material body.	MAN has a material body.
GOD is everywhere all the time.	MAN is only in one place at a time.
GOD is greater than all and more important than all; He is the highest authority.	MAN should be under God's authority and listen to everything God says.
GOD was there before the beginning of everything.	MAN was not there before the beginning.

ON TEACHING THIS LESSON:

These lessons are designed to **teach unbelievers.** You are carefully laying a scriptural foundation on which the Gospel will later be presented. If your class contains believers, teach with the goal of giving them an understanding of the basis for their faith and **with the goal of enabling them to teach the same material to unbelievers.**

DON'T COMPLICATE THE MESSAGE!

As you teach, keep in mind that this is a directed study—not an exhaustive survey of the Bible and not an unlimited group discussion. Keep your lesson on track and moving ahead by limiting and directing any discussion.

Carefully follow the outline. Emphasize the doctrinal themes.

LESSON FORMAT: The **center column** below contains the lesson material to be taught to the students. The **bold outline headings** are only for reference and need not be spoken, as they are incorporated into the outlined material that follows. The material in the **side columns** is for the teacher's own reference and is not intended to be included in the lesson.

TO BE TAUGHT TO THE STUDENTS
(Center Column Only)

LESSON OUTLINE:

REVIEW questions from Lesson 1.

A. Introduction

Who is God?

What is He like?

How can we know Him?

In our first lesson we said that God is the main character, the central focus, of the Bible.

- He is the one who gave this message to us.

Teacher's Notes

Lesson 2: God Alone

Scripture Reference

- The Bible is a book of true history—history from God's perspective.
- It is God's story, or, as someone has so correctly said, the Bible is "HIS STORY."

Suggested Visual:

> The Bible is
> # HIS STORY

We are going to learn about God from God Himself.

We will study what He has said about Himself in His Word.

- Sometimes, as in today's lesson, we will study specific statements He has made about Himself.
- Other times we will learn about Him by studying **what He does**.
- His nature and character are revealed through what He has done in and through events He recorded for us in His Word.

God has given us a wealth of knowledge about Himself.

- Why would He do this?
- Why? Because He wants us to know Him!
- In Jeremiah 9:23,24 God says, *"Thus saith the LORD, Let not the wise man glory in his wisdom, neither let the mighty man glory in his might, let not the rich man glory in his riches:* **But let him that glorieth glory in this, that he understandeth and knoweth me, that I am the LORD....**" ³

How great is God? ⁴

- How important is He?
- Did He have a beginning?
- Will He have an end?
- Where did He come from?
- What does God need?

Let's see how God answers these questions in His Word, the Bible.

B. Only God is eternal. All else has a beginning.

 READ Genesis 1:1.

The first words God wrote for us in the Bible are, *"In the beginning..."* (Genesis 1:1). ⁵

- God gave us these words so that we would know there was a beginning to all things.
- Everything that we can see and everything that we know about but can't see had a beginning, except God Himself.
- Before the beginning, there was:

    No universe

    No earth

    No angels

    No Devil

    No plants

    No animals

    No people.

- All these had specific beginnings.

---

³The teacher reads this verse in part because the rest of it (not printed here) contains themes that run ahead of the lesson. The words in bold type are what you want to emphasize. ☐

⁴Do not pause long enough for discussion to begin on these questions. They are not intended to evoke answers; they are posed to cause the students to think. ☐

⁵Genesis is the foundation for all the Scriptures and Genesis 1 is the foundation for Genesis. Do not rush through Genesis 1 because the basic revelations of the nature and character of God are presented in it. ☐

Lesson 2: God Alone

| Scripture Reference | | Teacher's Notes |

C. God alone had no beginning; God will have no end; God is ETERNAL.

 Theme: God is supreme and sovereign.

Before anything came to be, God existed as He does now and will forever.

We're going to make a chart listing some things about God and about man. We'll begin with this: **6**

BEGIN CHART:

GOD	MAN
GOD had no beginning, will have no end.	MAN is born and dies.

 Read Psalm 90:2.

- There never was a time when God did not exist.

    He did not have a beginning.

    He was not created.

    He has always been alive.

    He has always been and will always be the same.

    There never will be a time when God does not exist.

    God can never die.

D. God is a Trinity. **7**

SHOW CHRONOLOGICAL CHART DISPLAYING THE WORDS: GOD—FATHER, SON, HOLY SPIRIT.

God is eternally one God.

But look at Genesis 1:26: "And God said, Let **us** make man in **our** image, after **our** likeness...." **8**

We aren't going to study this verse right now; we just want to look at the pronouns "us" and "our."

Even in Genesis 1:1 the Hebrew word for God is a plural word.

As we study God's Word, we will discover that, although there is only one God, there are three persons who are equally God:

Who are these three persons?

All of the three are named in Matthew 28:19: **8**

- God the Father
- God the Son
- God the Holy Spirit ("Holy Ghost" means "Holy Spirit")

We use the word "Trinity" to describe these three persons who are the one Eternal God.

ADD TO CHART:

GOD is a Trinity of three persons.	MAN is only one person.

As we study the Bible, we will see these three persons at work and we will learn much more about them.

Teacher's Notes:

6 Remember that the statements about man are written without comment. They are just there to make your students consider God's greatness and to prepare their minds for later studies.

If a student starts discussing man, remind him that in this lesson we are just focusing on God. ☐

7 As mentioned in the introduction, do not try to explain the Trinity.

This subject will probably stir up many questions, and some students will have a hard time waiting until later lessons for answers. As tactfully as you can, try to assure them that their questions are good, but that you must wait to answer them. Unless you hold your ground in this, you may find yourself on a "rabbit trail" that detracts from the lesson and confuses those who haven't enough knowledge to understand the answer. How much you can answer will depend upon the level of understanding of your students. Always keep in mind that those who do not have a background in Scripture may be easily confused. If you have students at several levels of understanding, it may be necessary to spend time separately with those who have some previous knowledge and understanding of the Word.

If you encounter a student who wants to debate the fact of the Trinity, please note the suggestion under "Introducing the Trinity," in the Lesson Preparation section of this lesson ☐

8 Be careful to stick to the subject here. Both of these verses, Genesis 1:26 and Matthew 28:19 are used only to show specific words. Don't get sidetracked into the subject of the verses themselves. ☐

113

Lesson 2: God Alone

Teacher's Notes

But for now we will just establish that these three persons are **one God** who is eternal and that God the Father, God the Son, and God the Holy Spirit are all equally God.

There is the Father who is God, the Son who is God, and the Holy Spirit who is God.

Confusing? Yes, to us it certainly is!

God is so much greater than we can imagine.

- The Trinity is beyond our understanding.
- We can only describe what we understand from God's Word.

The amazing fact of the Trinity is just one of the things that shows us the greatness of God—greatness that is beyond our ability to comprehend.

E. Because God alone existed before all things, God is completely independent of everything and everyone.

 Theme: God is supreme and sovereign.

Because God existed before all things, we know that He had need of nothing to sustain Him. **9**

- God was there alone, before the earth, the sun, the moon, the stars, the galaxies.

    He does not need the earth nor anything on it.
    - He doesn't need air to breathe.
    - He doesn't need food to eat.
    - He doesn't need water to drink.

    God does not need the sun.
    - He can see perfectly without any light.
    - He doesn't need to sleep; He has no need of day or night.

    God doesn't need any source of energy.
    - He never gets tired, thirsty, or hungry.

ADD TO CHART:

GOD needs nothing.

Read Isaiah 40:28: *"Hast thou not known? hast thou not heard, that* **the everlasting God, the LORD,** *the Creator of the ends of the earth,* **fainteth not, neither is weary? there is no searching of his understanding."** **10**

God doesn't need anyone to teach Him.
- He knows everything; He possesses all knowledge.
- He is aware of everything.

Read Psalm 147:5: *"Great is our Lord, and of great power:* **his understanding is infinite."**

---

9 To support this point, you may want to use God's name, "I Am," (Exodus 3:14), which implies that God is the self-existent one. (See further treatment of this name in Lesson 21, Point I.)

10 Be sure to keep on the subject, indicated by the boldface type. ☐

Scripture Reference

Psalm 121:3

Isaiah 40:28

Lesson 2: God Alone

 Read Romans 11:33,34.

ADD TO CHART:

GOD knows everything.

What about us? **11**

- Could we have been born into the world without parents?
    - Could we have survived as infants without care?
    - Could we have learned to be productive adults without someone to teach us?
- What about our bodies?
    - How long could we live without food and water?
    - How long could we live without oxygen?
    - How many days could we function rationally without sleep?
    - How long could we survive without protection against the sun's ultraviolet rays?
- We are totally dependent in these areas; but God does not need anything or any person.

11Again, these are not discussion questions; they are simply intended to make your students think. ☐

ADD TO CHART:

	MAN needs food, water, air, sleep, light, protection, etc.
	MAN needs to be taught.

F. God is Spirit.

God does not need the earth to live on and the many other things which we humans need because God does not have a body as we do. John 4:24 says that *"God is a Spirit."* **12**

- God does not have flesh and bones like humans, animals, birds, or reptiles.
- Because He does not have a material body, He does not have bodily needs.

ADD TO CHART:

GOD is Spirit and has no material body.	MAN has a material body.

12The teacher reads this verse only in part because the rest of the verse (not printed here) contains themes not covered in these lessons. Be sure to keep the lesson on track. Stick to the main themes. ☐

We cannot comprehend one who has such ability, yet has no material body.

But it is important for us to take note of the fact that God is Spirit.

He is not just a "force," as some would describe Him.

No, God is Spirit, a Trinity of three persons, all with mind, personality, and will.

He is the God who has personally given us His Word so we can know Him.

We are very limited in our understanding.

We are very limited by our bodily needs.

But God has none of these limitations.

Lesson 2: God Alone

Teacher's Notes

Scripture Reference

G. God is in all places at the same time.

 Theme: God is everywhere all the time.

 Theme: God is supreme and sovereign.

Where is God?

Where was He before everything else existed?

We cannot see God, and we cannot know where He is unless He tells us.

- Through our study of the Bible, you will see repeatedly that God is everywhere.
- God made everything, and He is present everywhere.
- He is **not** "in everything." ¹³

[13] Be certain that you make a clear distinction between God the Creator and His creation. Pantheistic religions (such as New Age) believe that god is everything and everything is god.

(Do not get into a discussion on creation here; it is simply mentioned to clarify the point of God's sovereignty.) ☐

- He is the Creator, distinct from His creation.
   God is higher than all.
   God is greater than all He has made.
- God fills the universe.

 Read Jeremiah 23:23,24.

- He is in all places on the earth.
- God is here right now and can see us all.
- Illustration:

Sometimes when we are especially busy, it might seem to us that we would like to be in more than one place at a time! But, obviously, as much as it might seem to help to be able to be "everywhere" at once, we are limited to being in one place at a time.

- Note:

One little boy, when hearing this teaching said, "God is so big He doesn't have to go anywhere!"

ADD TO CHART:

GOD is everywhere all the time.	MAN is only in one place at a time.

[14] Some of your students may think that Satan can be everywhere, all the time. He cannot, though he has many demons spread over the earth. Each demon, also, can only be in one place at one time.

At this time, avoid getting into a discussion on Satan and his demons, as this will be addressed in the next lesson. ☐

- God and God alone is able to be everywhere all the time. Since God is everywhere all the time, is there any place you can be or go where He is not? ¹⁴

   Is there any place you can "hide" from God?

Proverbs 15:3

 Read Psalm 139:7-12.

H. God alone was before all things; He alone is greater than all; God is SOVEREIGN.

God is beyond our comprehension:

AS YOU TEACH, POINT TO THE CHART YOU HAVE MADE.

- We cannot comprehend one who had no beginning and will have no end.
- We cannot imagine one who is three persons in one.

Romans 11:33-36

Lesson 2: God Alone

- We cannot understand one who is never in need of anything.
- We cannot fathom one who knows everything.
- We cannot see one who is Spirit.
- We are unable to know what it is like to be everywhere at the same time.

 Read Jeremiah 10:6.

We must simply admit that there is one who is infinitely greater than all—who is in every way superior to us.

The way we describe God's infinite superiority is to say that God is SOVEREIGN.

- Webster's Dictionary says that "sovereign" means "ruler, supreme in power, chief, efficacious [effective] in highest degree...."
- The Bible often refers to God as "The Most High."
- Psalm 83:18 calls God *"the most high over all the earth."*
- In Isaiah 45:5, God says, *"I am the LORD, and there is none else, there is no God beside me...."*

ADD TO CHART: [15]

| GOD is greater than all and more important than all; He is the highest authority. | MAN should be under God's authority and listen to everything God says. |

[15] Again, it is not necessary to comment on the note about man. ☐

I. God alone can tell us about the beginning.

 Theme: God is supreme and sovereign.

Only God was there in the beginning!

ADD TO CHART:

| GOD was there before the beginning of everything. | MAN was not there before the beginning. |

He who had no beginning knows all that came to be and how it came to be.

And in the Bible He has given us the record of all beginnings.

J. Conclusion

God is great beyond our imagination:
- He is truly greater than all.
- He is sovereign.

    He alone had no beginning.
    He will have no end.
    He is a Trinity, the great God who is three in one: God the Father, God the Son, and God the Holy Spirit.
    He has need of nothing.
    He has no bodily needs because He is Spirit.
    He is in all places at the same time.

God is greater than all and more important than all; He is the Most High. He is sovereign.

Lesson 2: God Alone

He alone can tell us about the beginning, and we will study in the weeks ahead what God, the only one who was there, has told us about the beginning.

QUESTIONS

1. Was there ever a time when God was not living? *No.*

2. What does God need in order to exist? *God doesn't need anything.*

3. Does God have a body? *No.*

4. How many Gods are there? *There is only one God.*

5. Who are the three living beings who are the one God? *God the Father, God the Son, and God the Holy Spirit.*

6. Is there some remote place you could go on this earth or in this galaxy or this universe or anywhere that God would not be? *No.*

7. What do we mean when we say that God is sovereign? *He alone is ruler, supreme in power, chief, and efficacious [effective] in highest degree; He is the Most High.*

Scripture Reference

Isaiah 14:12-20
Ezekiel 28:11-18
Romans 8:37-39
Ephesians 6:10-18

Revelation 20:10-15

Jeremiah 32:27
Matthew 16:18
Revelation 1:8

LESSON 3

God Created the Spirit Beings; Lucifer Rebelled

Teacher's Notes

OVERVIEW

This lesson establishes that God created all the spirit beings. It presents God who is sovereign and holy, greater than all created beings, creating all things perfect. It also shows God's sovereignty and holiness in dealing with Lucifer's willful rebellion against God.

LESSON PREPARATION

This section is for you, the teacher.

The passages in the Scripture Reference column are for your own study in preparing for this lesson. Since they may contain concepts that run ahead of the lesson, they are not to be taught at this point.

Note: If you have not taught previously from this series of lessons, please read carefully the note to teachers in the front of this book.

LESSON GOALS:

- To show the sovereignty and holiness of God in His creation of the spirits and in His dealing with Lucifer and the other spirits who rebelled against God.

THIS LESSON SHOULD HELP THE STUDENTS:

- To see the sovereignty and omnipotence of God.
- To see the seriousness of rebellion against God.

PERSPECTIVE FOR THE TEACHER:

In our society, Satan has been given increasing attention in films, books, music, games, and even as a focus for worship. People from all economic levels and backgrounds have become involved in satanic-oriented practices. II Corinthians 11:14 says that Satan masquerades as an angel of light. The Enemy's subtlety has fooled some (like Eve), while others have simply made knowing steps of rebellion (like Adam).

Anything that causes people to search for answers or "power" from any source other than God is of Satan. Satan is a liar, a thief, a deceiver, an accuser, and a murderer. He wants to fill the Lake of Fire with as many people as he can draw away from God.

As this lesson is studied, you may find that your students have many questions. You may even find that some are involved in satanic things, such as (to name only a few), horoscopes, ouija boards, mediums, seances, satanic games, or rock music with filthy words.

But remember: no matter what opposition we face to the message of the Bible; no matter what difficulties, entanglements, and sins may be manifest in our students, we have assurance in God's Word that He is stronger than all. Nothing is too hard for Him. In Jesus Christ, we have victory.

God will use His Word in hearts and will give you wisdom in dealing with your students. Our Enemy is strong, but OUR GOD IS STRONGER THAN ALL!

NOTE:

Before we teach how God created all the material things which can be seen, we will first teach that God created the spirit world which generally cannot be seen. It is best to teach about the spirits and Satan at this stage because:

1. All spirits—that is, all angels—witnessed the creation of the earth (Job 38:4-7).

119

Lesson 3: God Created the Spirit Beings; Lucifer Rebelled

Teacher's Notes

2. It is much easier for both teacher and learner if each actor is introduced into the story at the time of its creation or birth, rather than the teacher having to return to an earlier point in the story to fill in the gaps.
3. The story of Genesis 3 is complicated enough in itself, without adding the teaching of the creation and fall of Satan and his hosts.

The Bible does not give a clear chronology of the fall of Satan. For this reason, theologians have often come to differing conclusions regarding whether this took place before, after, or during the creation of the world. (Many point to Genesis 1:31, *"And God saw everything that he had made, and, behold, it was very good..."* to support the view that all the spirit beings were still in their original, perfect state at this point.) In these lessons we will not deal with this issue, as it is not critical to a foundational understanding of the Word.

CAUTION: Two of the key Old Testament passages relating to the doctrine of Satan are Isaiah 14:12-20 and Ezekiel 28:11-18. These are used carefully in the outline because they are difficult passages to interpret, since they also contain prophecy pertaining to men. **Be very careful to limit any discussion to the subject at hand.**

A good source of Scriptures relating to angels and to Satan and demons is Vine's *Expository Dictionary of New Testament Words*.[1] This is just a quick reference; obviously, more comprehensive studies and books are available.

[1] *An Expository Dictionary of New Testament Words,* W. E. Vine, M.A. Fleming H. Revell Co., 1966.

VISUALS:

- Chronological Chart

ON TEACHING THIS LESSON:

These lessons are designed to **teach unbelievers.** You are carefully laying a scriptural foundation on which the Gospel will later be presented. If your class contains believers, teach with the goal of giving them an understanding of the basis for their faith and **with the goal of enabling them to teach the same material to unbelievers.**

DON'T COMPLICATE THE MESSAGE!

As you teach, keep in mind that this is a directed study—not an exhaustive survey of the Bible and not an unlimited group discussion. Keep your lesson on track and moving ahead by limiting and directing any discussion.

Carefully follow the outline. Emphasize the doctrinal themes.

LESSON FORMAT: The **center column** below contains the lesson material to be taught to the students. The **bold outline headings** are only for reference and need not be spoken, as they are incorporated into the outlined material that follows. The material in the **side columns** is for the teacher's own reference and is not intended to be included in the lesson.

TO BE TAUGHT TO THE STUDENTS
(Center Column Only)

LESSON OUTLINE:

REVIEW questions from Lesson 2.

A. Introduction

Have you ever wondered:

- Where did the angels come from?

Lesson 3: God Created the Spirit Beings; Lucifer Rebelled

- What about Satan?
- What about demons?

In this lesson we are going to briefly study the creation of all of the spirit beings.

To gain an understanding of the spirit beings requires knowledge of many Scriptures throughout the Bible.

- For our study we will simply present a summary of the basic truths (doctrine) about the spirits.
- We will not go through a lot of Scripture references because to do so would require considerable study and background understanding of each text.
- Many questions may come to your mind as we study.
- This lesson may not answer all your questions, but future lessons may help clear up some issues.

God's Word tells us what we need to know about the spirit beings.

Let's look at some basic truths as they are taught in the Bible.

B. God created all of the spirits.

SHOW CHRONOLOGICAL CHART DISPLAYING THE WORDS: GOD'S ANGELS, LUCIFER.

 Theme: God is supreme and sovereign.

John 1:3
Colossians 1:16

In the beginning, God created all of the spirit beings.

- The Bible refers to these spirit beings with many different terms:

    Spirits

    Angels

    Cherubim

    Seraphim

    The host of the Lord or host of Heaven

    Powers

    Principalities

    Rulers in high places

    Stars or morning stars.

- The context of each passage must be used to clarify its meaning.

All of the spirits were created at this time.

- Before the beginning, none of them were alive.
- It was God who gave them life.
- They wouldn't have life if God had not given it to them.

 Read John 1:3. **2**

- Nehemiah 9:6 says, *"Thou, even thou, art LORD alone; thou hast made heaven, the heaven of heavens, with all their host...and the host of heaven worshippeth thee."*

God is greater than the spirits.

- He lived before them eternally.
- He is the one who made them.
- He gave them life.

God did not give the spirits material bodies when He created them.

2Be sure to keep on the subject. Don't go into the surrounding context of this verse at this time. ☐

Lesson 3: God Created the Spirit Beings; Lucifer Rebelled

- Because they are spirits and do not have flesh and blood, they can move about wherever they want to.
- The spirits are **not** everywhere at the same time like God is. The spirits can only be in one place at one time.
- Even though the spirits do not have material bodies like we do, they sometimes show themselves to people as human beings and may also appear in other forms.

C. The spirits were created to serve God.

 Theme: God is supreme and sovereign.

The spirits were all created by God to love and serve Him.

- In the beginning, all of the spirits were God's angels.
- The word "angels" means "messengers" or "servants."
- Because God created them, they belonged to Him.
- They were created to do whatever God wanted them to do.
- Illustrate:

  If you build a house, to whom does that house belong? If you take your own materials and assemble something, then you are the rightful owner of what you have made.

  Just as you are the owner of what you have made, in the same way everything that God created rightfully belongs to Him. God was the one who made all of the spirits. He gave them life. He made them to serve and obey Him. Therefore, all of the spirits rightfully belong to God.

Scripture Reference: Psalm 103:20; Hebrews 1:14

D. The spirits were created perfect by God.

 Theme: God is holy.

God created all the spirits perfect; not one of them was evil or unkind.

- God cannot create anything evil because God is holy.
- Everything He thinks, says, and does is perfect.

Scripture Reference: Genesis 1:31; Ezekiel 28:15

E. The spirits were created with great wisdom and strength.

God created the spirits with great wisdom and strength.

 Read Psalm 103:20.

- Angels are very intelligent, but they are not all-knowing like God is.
- Angels are stronger than we are, and the Bible records that God has given them the ability to do amazing things, but they are not all-powerful like God.

God is wiser and stronger than all of the spirits.

- This is an important truth for us to remember.
- No matter what you may have heard or seen presented in movies or books or anywhere else, the Bible tells us that God is greater than all.

Lesson 3: God Created the Spirit Beings; Lucifer Rebelled

F. The spirits are innumerable.

 Theme: God is all-powerful.

God created so many spirit beings that it is impossible for us to count them.

Revelation 5:11 says, *"...the number of them was ten thousand times ten thousand, and thousands of thousands...."*

How could God create so many good, strong, wise spirits?
- He is almighty.
- He can do anything and everything He wants to do.

G. The spirits lived in Heaven.

All of the spirits lived in Heaven with God in the beginning.
- Where is Heaven?
  - We don't know where it is.
  - It certainly isn't here on earth!
  - But it is a real place, mentioned many times in the Bible.
- Heaven is God's dwelling place.
  - Though He is everywhere, all the time, Heaven is His home. ³
  - Psalm 11:4 says that *"the LORD'S throne is in heaven."*
  - The Bible tells us that Heaven is a wonderful place, far better than any place we have ever known or could ever imagine.

³As mentioned in Lesson 2, be careful to clearly present the fact that God the Creator is distinct from His creation: He is everywhere, but everything is **not** God. ☐

H. Lucifer's original position before God in Heaven

Ezekiel 28:14

God didn't create all of the angels exactly the same; some were more beautiful, intelligent, and wise than others.

The greatest angel was called Lucifer.

The name Lucifer means "morning star."

God gave Lucifer a very important position in Heaven.
- He was given a place of great authority and power over the other angels.
- Ezekiel 28:14 calls him *"the anointed cherub."*

He, like all of God's creation, was created perfect.
- Ezekiel 28:15 says, **"Thou wast perfect in thy ways from the day that thou wast created,** *till iniquity [evil, wickedness] was found in thee."* ⁴

⁴The boldfaced part of the verse is what you are teaching here. Do not get sidetracked on the rest of the verse. ☐

I. Lucifer's rebellion

Because Lucifer was created by God and given the highest position over all of the other angels, he should have loved, obeyed, and served God.

But after a time, Lucifer became very proud of his beauty, intelligence, and position.

Ezekiel 28:17 says, *"Thine heart was lifted up because of thy beauty, thou hast corrupted thy wisdom by reason of thy brightness...."*

Another passage of Scripture gives us insight into Lucifer's attitude.

 Read Isaiah 14:13,14. ⁵

Lucifer wanted to be like *"the most High."*

⁵As mentioned in the note in the Teacher Preparation section, be careful to avoid discussion on the surrounding verses, as they will be very confusing and will sidetrack away from the lesson goals and themes. ☐

Lesson 3: God Created the Spirit Beings; Lucifer Rebelled

Teacher's Notes

- He decided that he wanted to take over God's position as the ruler of all things.
- Lucifer was the first one to do evil. (Evil is anything that is different from what God wants or agrees with.)

You may ask, "If Lucifer was created perfect, how could he rebel?"

- The Bible does not give a clear answer for this, but it does show many examples of the fact that God allows choices to be made regarding obedience and disobedience.
- Look at the passage we just read in Isaiah 14:13,14.
- Note, Lucifer said, "**I will** *ascend*," "**I will** *exalt*," "**I will** *sit*," "**I will** *ascend*," "**I will** *be like the most High*."
- Lucifer's rebellion was an act of the will, a conscious choice.
- An illustration from a human perspective may help:

Suppose that someone was very kind and helpful to you and told you that he loved you. This might be a very pleasant situation. But what if you learned that this person was under someone's strict control and had been forced to act this way and to say that he loved you. His words and actions would not be meaningful or pleasant; in fact, they would be offensive.

God does not "program" His created beings like robots. He allows them to make meaningful choices—to obey or to disobey.

J. Other angels followed Lucifer in his rebellion.

Many of God's angels followed Lucifer, their leader. [6]

They, too, rebelled against God.

We will not discuss this in depth, but a good reference to show that other angels participated in Lucifer's rebellion is Matthew 25:41, which mentions "the devil and his angels."

K. God knew what Lucifer and the other spirits were thinking and planning.

 Theme: God is everywhere all the time; He knows everything.

Isaiah 14:13,14 says of Lucifer, "...**thou hast said in thine heart,** *I will ascend...I will exalt...I will be like the most High.*"

God created all of the spirits, and He knew what they were thinking and planning.

- He knew that Lucifer had become proud and wanted to take the place of his Maker.
- God knew Lucifer's thoughts and the thoughts of each of the rebellious spirits.

Nothing can be kept secret from God.

- Nothing can surprise God.
- He knows everything before it ever happens.
- He knows what we are going to think before the thought even comes into our minds.
- He is everywhere.
- He sees everything.
- He knows everything.

---

[6] This point is a deduction made from several Scriptures, including those listed in the reference column at the right.

If a student questions you on this, you may want to use these Scriptures briefly to support your statements; but be very careful not to get sidetracked. ☐

Scripture Reference

Matthew 25:41
Luke 8:30
Ephesians 6:12
II Peter 2:4

Lesson 3: God Created the Spirit Beings; Lucifer Rebelled

- Hebrews 4:13 says, *"Neither is there any creature that is not manifest [made known] in his sight: but all things are naked and opened unto the eyes of him...."*

L. God removed Lucifer and his followers from their position as God's servants. [7]

 Theme: God is holy and righteous. He demands death as the payment for sin.

- Consider:

Do you think God would let Lucifer take His position? What do you think God's reaction was to Lucifer's selfish ambition?

If someone suddenly tried to take over our government, strong defense measures would be taken immediately. Our government is important and powerful, but think how supremely important and powerful God is!

Who is wiser than God? Who is stronger than God? He has always lived. He lives by His own power. He doesn't need anything to live. He lived before the beginning. He gave life to all of the spirits.

God would not allow Lucifer to take His position.

- No one can take God's place, because
- He is the only true God.

God, in great anger, removed Lucifer from his important position of leadership over the angels.

God also removed the other angels who followed Lucifer from their place of service in Heaven.

God is perfect and right in everything He thinks and does.

- Anyone who doesn't think and act like God is totally unacceptable to Him and cannot be His friend.
- God would not allow Lucifer and his spirit followers to continue in their former positions in Heaven.

As we mentioned in the beginning of this lesson, some of these details must be understood in the light of many passages of Scripture which we aren't going to take the time to study in these lessons.

But in numerous instances, the Bible records the activity of Satan and his demons here on earth.

They are no longer recorded as God's servants; they are always in opposition to Him.

Job 1:6,7 and 2:1,2 show us that Satan still had access to God in Heaven but no longer resided there.

Matthew 25:41 refers to the eventual punishment of *"the devil and his angels."*

M. God prepared the Lake of Fire for Lucifer and his spirit followers.

 Theme: God is holy and righteous. He demands death as the payment for sin.

God prepared a terrible place of everlasting punishment called the Lake of Fire. [8]

Scripture Reference

Isaiah 14:12-15
Ezekiel 28:16,17
Matthew 25:41
II Peter 2:4
Jude 6

Teacher's Notes

[7] Point L. of this outline must be deduced from several Scriptures, including those listed at the left.

Note the general deductions in the last four statements in Point L.

Again, do not get sidetracked. ☐

[8] At this point, teach about the Lake of Fire in relationship to Satan only. Don't teach that people are going to the Lake of Fire. Remember, you have not yet taught the creation of man and his sin. ☐

Lesson 3: God Created the Spirit Beings; Lucifer Rebelled

- He is going to send Lucifer, and the other spirits which followed him, to the Lake of Fire to be punished forever.
- God will not tolerate disobedience to Him; God always punishes those who fight against Him.
- Matthew 25:41 speaks of *"everlasting fire, prepared for the devil and his angels."*
- Revelation 20:10 tells us that at the end of the world, the Devil will be *"...cast into the lake of fire...and shall be tormented day and night for ever and ever."*

N. Lucifer and his angels hate God.

 Theme: Satan fights against God and His will. Satan is a liar and a deceiver. He hates man.

Lucifer and his followers hate God and every good thing that God loves.

Right from the time when God removed them from His service until today, Lucifer and these other spirits have been fighting against God and everything He does.

Lucifer is now called Satan, which means "enemy, adversary, opponent, or accuser."

His spirit followers are called demons.

Satan is God's great enemy.

- Satan fights against God day and night to try to stop the things God does.
- Satan's demons help Satan in opposing God.

SHOW CHRONOLOGICAL CHART DISPLAYING THE NAMES: SATAN AND HIS DEMONS.

O. Satan and his spirit servants no longer live in Heaven.

Satan and his demons are now active all over the earth.

The passages we mentioned earlier in Job 1 and 2 record conversations between God and Satan in which Satan says he has been *"going to and fro in the earth, and...walking up and down in it."*

And, as also mentioned before, many passages record demon activity on the earth.

We will talk about this more in coming lessons.

Scripture Reference: Job 1:7, 2:2 (Numerous N.T. passages also refer to demon activity on earth.)

P. Closing

 Theme: God is supreme and sovereign.

 Theme: God is holy and righteous. He demands death as the payment for sin.

God is the supreme God and the Creator of everything, seen and unseen.

God is greater than all.

Everything He does is perfect and holy.

He is greater than all created beings:

- God is greater than the angels.

Lesson 3: God Created the Spirit Beings; Lucifer Rebelled

- God is greater than Satan and the demons.
- How important that is for us to know and remember!

God alone can tell us what happened in the beginning.

In our next lesson we will examine what the Bible says about the beginnings of the physical world:

- The heavens
- The earth.

It's extremely important for us to consider what He says about creation.

Remember, God was the only one there before the beginning.

QUESTIONS:

1. Who is the only one who lived before the beginning? *God.*
2. Where did all the spirits come from? *They were all created by God.*
3. Did God create the spirits with bodies of flesh and bones? *No.*
4. Did God create all of the spirits good, or did He create some good and some bad? *God created them all good.*
5. Why did God create the spirits? *To be His servants.*
6. How many spirits are there? *More than can be numbered.*
7. Where did they all live in the beginning when God first created them? *With God in Heaven.*
8. Who was the most intelligent and beautiful angel created by God? *Lucifer.*
9. What position did God give Lucifer? *Leadership over all of the other angels.*
10. What did Lucifer do? *He planned to be like God and to take God's position.*
11. Who else followed Lucifer in His rebellion against God? *Many of God's angels.*
12. Did God know what Lucifer and his followers were planning? *Yes.*
13. What did God do? *He removed Lucifer and the angels who joined him in rebellion from their position as God's servants.*
14. Is there anything that God doesn't see, hear, and know? *No! God sees, hears, and knows everything.*
15. What place did God prepare as a punishment for Lucifer and his angels? *The Lake of Fire.*
16. What is Lucifer's name now and what does it mean? *Satan, which means "enemy, adversary, opponent, or accuser."*
17. Whom is Satan against? *He is against God.*

Scripture Reference

Job 38-41

Psalms 19:1-4; 24:1,2; 33:6-9; 95:3-5; 104

Isaiah 40:28; 44:24; 45:7-12; 48:12,13

Jeremiah 10:12,13; 32:17

Colossians 1:16

Hebrews 1:10-12; 11:3

God Created the Heavens and the Earth — Part 1

LESSON PREPARATION
This section is for you, the teacher.

The passages in the Scripture Reference column are for your own study in preparing for this lesson. Since they may contain concepts that run ahead of the lesson, they are not to be taught at this point.

Note: If you have not taught previously from this series of lessons, please read carefully the note to teachers in the front of this book.

SCRIPTURE: Genesis 1:1-8

LESSON GOALS:

- To show that God created the heavens and the earth and that He created from nothing.
- To show God's character and attributes as revealed through His creative acts.[1]

THIS LESSON SHOULD HELP THE STUDENTS:

- To give consideration to the biblical account of creation.
- To have an increased awareness of God's sovereignty, His holiness, and His power.

PERSPECTIVE FOR THE TEACHER:

We live in a society that has forgotten its Maker. Theories of evolution are taught as if they were fact; yet the biblical account, given by the one who designed and made everything, is usually totally disregarded.

Unless a person has studied the Bible and drawn his convictions from it, he will almost certainly have been affected by man's incorrect ideas about creation. Virtually everyone in our society has been told by the educational system, television programs, and the print media that evolution is an established fact and that only the naive or uneducated question it. For the most part, evolution is assumed to be fact, not theory.

This lesson will present the true, biblical facts of creation. It should not be a "debate" of creation versus evolution. However, due to the pervasive influence of evolutionary thinking, you will need to be prepared to deal with the issue to some extent. For some people, you will have to give enough information to bring them to the point where they will acknowledge the possibility that the scriptural account is valid. (See "HINTS FOR TEACHING" on the next page.) The resources section that follows lists some good sources of information.

Prepare for this lesson by meditating on God's Word. As you teach, share the wonder, awe, and praise that you have for our Creator. Let your students know that you believe God!

RESOURCE MATERIAL:

If you wish to study the evidences for creation to help you in answering students' questions, or if you wish to refer those with questions to some materials that may help them, the following books may be useful:

Teacher's Notes

OVERVIEW

This is more than a lesson on the biblical facts of creation. God's nature and attributes are clearly displayed in His creative acts. Your primary goal in teaching on creation is to point out the attributes of God through His creative acts.

Note: This is the first of two lessons on God's creation of the heavens and the earth, followed by a lesson on God's creation of man.

[1] Carefully lay the foundations regarding the nature and character of God. For example, you will be teaching that God knew how to create. You will stress that God knows everything. With these foundations, you will later be able to teach that God knows everything about every person. God knows about our sin. God even knows our thoughts. God knows everything. (Note Hebrews 4:13.)

If you don't lay these foundations of truth deeply in the minds of your students now, you are not going to be able to use them later on. The Holy Spirit will not be able to use them to bring conviction of sin.

The doctrine of creation runs throughout the entire Bible, from Genesis to Revelation. Even where creation is not stated in words, it is still an underlying truth — God is sovereign; all things began in Him (Colossians 1:16,17).

Keep in mind, however, that most Scriptures which refer to creation also include concepts and truths that have not yet been introduced in your chronological teaching program; therefore, it would be inappropriate at this time for students to do a topical study using many proof texts. The verses used in the outline provide texts that do not jump ahead chronologically. ☐

Lesson 4: God Created the Heavens and the Earth — Part 1

Teacher's Notes

The Twilight of Evolution, Morris, Henry M., Baker Book House, Grand Rapids, MI, 1963.

Biblical Cosmology and Modern Science, Morris, Henry M., Baker Book House, Grand Rapids, MI, 1970.

The Collapse of Evolution, Huse, Scott M., Baker Book House, Grand Rapids, MI., 1983.

Evolution: A Theory in Crisis, Denton, Michael, Adler and Adler, Bethesda, MD.,1986.

The best source for material presenting scientific evidence for creation is:

Institute for Creation Research
P.O. Box 2667, El Cajon, CA 92021

Australian address:

Creation Science Foundation Ltd.
P.O. Box 302, Sunnybank, Qld. 4109, AUSTRALIA

British Address:

Creation Science Foundation
c/- P.O. Box 770 Highworth, Swindon, Wilts, SN6 7TU, UK

They publish a wide variety of material and will send a catalog of available material on request.

As noted in Lesson 1, you can offer to let the students research answers to their questions outside of class, using these selected materials. This will allow you to keep the class time directed to Bible study. It is important that the Bible study time does not become a forum for debate. The reference materials, wisely used, may help answer some of the students' questions without distracting from the purpose of the lesson.

You might even want to set up a time (other than class time) to show a video about the biblical record of creation.

HINTS FOR TEACHING:

Be very careful, especially on these lessons about creation, that you keep the discussion under control. You are presenting what God says about creation. You may very possibly find that one or more students want to go into a discussion on evolution. This is where you will have to use discernment as to how much information to share verbally in class and how much information you should offer them to read on their own. As much as possible, keep them on the subject of what the Bible says. Remember, again, this lesson is not a debate. You are presenting what has probably not been taught previously to many of your students.

Take your time in teaching. Be sure your students are logically thinking through your points with you. Appeal to their minds and natural logic. Remember, however, I Corinthians 2:14: *"...the natural man receiveth not the things of the Spirit of God: for they are foolishness unto him: neither can he know them, because they are spiritually discerned."* Don't expect them to agree with what you are teaching. Just be sure you are clearly presenting what the Bible says. Expect the Word itself to do the work in their hearts. This may take time. Be gracious with your students, even though they may be wrong and even offensive in their comments. It might be an encouragement for us who teach to remember that some of the most effective and well-known spokesmen for the Word were once outspoken critics of it.

If your students contradict what you have already taught them from God's Word, ask them what God says about that subject. Help them realize that God is the final authority, not you. The issue should be a difference of opinion between them and God, not between them and you.

Don't let them draw you into subjects or details which you should not teach yet. If they ask you a question that will be answered later in the chronological lessons, answer, "That is a very good question. We will find the answer to that question later on as we study further in the Bible."

Don't always correct them if they are wrong.

Scripture Reference

Lesson 4: God Created the Heavens and the Earth— Part 1

Scripture Reference

Teacher's Notes

ON TEACHING THIS LESSON:

These lessons are designed to **teach unbelievers**. You are carefully laying a scriptural foundation on which the Gospel will later be presented. If your class contains believers, teach with the goal of giving them an understanding of the basis for their faith and **with the goal of enabling them to teach the same material to unbelievers.**

DON'T COMPLICATE THE MESSAGE!

As you teach, keep in mind that this is a directed study—not an exhaustive survey of the Bible and not an unlimited group discussion. Keep your lesson on track and moving ahead by limiting and directing any discussion.

Carefully follow the outline. Emphasize the doctrinal themes.

LESSON FORMAT: The **center column** below contains the lesson material to be taught to the students. The **bold outline headings** are only for reference and need not be spoken, as they are incorporated into the outlined material that follows. The material in the **side columns** is for the teacher's own reference and is not intended to be included in the lesson.

TO BE TAUGHT TO THE STUDENTS
(Center Column Only)

LESSON OUTLINE:

REVIEW questions from Lesson 3.

A. Introduction

Many theories exist about what happened in the beginning.[2]
- There are many theories about how the earth was formed.
- There are many theories about how life started.

As we mentioned in our last lesson, questions may come to your mind as we study.
- We won't be able to take time to discuss the various theories that men are teaching.
- We do have some reference materials to recommend to you after class.

What we are going to do in this lesson is examine what God has told us in the Bible about creation.

Keep in mind that the things taught in Genesis are upheld throughout the rest of Scripture.
- God never changed His mind about His record of creation (or about any other part of the Bible!).
- Genesis is an ancient book, but even the New Testament writings affirm the Genesis account of creation.

Genesis has often been criticized as being a book of myths.
- But recent archeology has confirmed many exact details, including names of people and cities back as far as the early chapters of Genesis.
- We will refer to some of those discoveries in later lessons.

[2] Keep careful control of any discussion which comes up in response to these points. Some students may be content if you simply say that, although many theories exist, you will be presenting what Scripture clearly states. Others may need more detailed information to even consider the biblical account as valid. You will need to discern how much discussion is necessary while at the same time keeping your goal of presenting God's account of creation clearly in mind.

If the students wish to study this further, offer to recommend tapes and books after the class. ☐

Lesson 4: God Created the Heavens and the Earth— Part 1

We need to listen to what God says in the Bible.
- It is not a book of "myths."
- It is a true history.

This lesson will cover what God says happened at the beginning.
- We have already learned that God created the spirits.
- Now we will study God's creation of the physical universe.

B. "In the beginning, God created the heaven and the earth" (Genesis 1:1).

 READ Genesis 1:1

 Theme: God is supreme and sovereign.

The word "genesis" means "beginnings" or "origins."
- All things had a beginning.
- Nothing/no one (except God) existed before the beginning.
- What then did God use to make the heavens and the earth?

"Created" means "to make out of nothing."
- "To make something out of nothing" is an idiom in our society.
- Discuss:

  If we want to build a house, what do we need?

  If we want to bake a cake, what do we need?

  Can you think of anything you can make without first having materials to use?[3]

 Read Hebrews 11:3

- God literally made the heavens and the earth out of nothing!
- God alone can make something out of nothing.

 Theme: God is all-powerful.

How was it possible for God to make the heavens and the earth out of nothing?
- The Bible tells us that nothing is too hard for God.

 Read Jeremiah 32:17

- God's power is beyond our comprehension.
- Is anyone stronger than God?

  Angels?

  Satan?

  Demons?
- No! God alone is all-powerful.

 Theme: God is all-knowing.

How did God know how to make the heavens and the earth?
- Compare:

  We had to learn how to do all the things that we do.
  - We are not born with knowledge and understanding.

---

[3] Give the students a moment to think this over and let it "soak in." □

Psalm 147:5

Jeremiah 51:15

Lesson 4: God Created the Heavens and the Earth— Part 1

- Most of us have gone to school to learn.
- We continue to learn throughout life.
    - By trial and error
    - The school of hard knocks
- Some things require highly specialized training which we have not had.
- There are still many things we don't know.

Did God need someone to teach Him?
- Was anyone else living in the beginning who could teach God?
- God did not need someone to teach Him how to make the heavens and the earth.
- There is nothing that God doesn't know and completely understand. **4**

 Read Romans 11:33,34.

C. The earth, when first created (Genesis 1:2)

 READ Genesis 1:2

The earth was formless and empty.
- We will see God form it.
- We will see God fill it.

The earth was covered by darkness.
- Illustrate:

    Try to imagine what it would be like if there were no light anywhere. Have you ever been in a cave with no lights? The darkness is so absolute that you can "feel" it. Imagine this kind of darkness everywhere.

The earth was covered with water.
- There was no dry land.
- Water covered the entire world.
- There was no life anywhere on earth.

D. God was ready to create everything.

 Theme: God is all-powerful.

God is all-powerful, and He was about to unleash His mighty power to create.

- The Bible says that the Spirit of God *"moved upon the face of the waters."*

    In Henry Morris' book, *The Genesis Record,* he notes that the word "move" used here is also translated as shake, flutter, or hover.

    The word suggests the tremendous creative power of God, the Prime Mover of all things.
    - He alone sets things into motion.
    - He alone is the source of all energy.

    God the Holy Spirit was moving, hovering, fluttering over the waters, vibrating with dynamic energy to create all things.

4You may have students who ask **why** God created the heavens and the earth. Though you do not want to get sidetracked into a discussion like this, you might want to give the student the answer that God does give us insights in His Word regarding that question, and tell them that some of these things will be covered in later lessons.

Use discretion as to how much to share. But it may be a help to the student who is sincerely seeking to know God to see that He truly does have answers in His Word.

Some excellent passages are:

Isaiah 45:18 (God prepared the earth to be inhabited.)

Isaiah 43:7 (He created man to glorify God.)

Psalm 19:1-3 (He created the heavens for His glory.)

Romans 1:20a (All creation shows forth His existence and His character.)

Revelation 4:11 (God did it as an act of His sovereign will [KJV "for thy pleasure"].) ☐

Lesson 4: God Created the Heavens and the Earth — Part 1

Teacher's Notes

⁵Again, do not try to explain the Trinity. See teacher note, "Introducing the Trinity," in the introduction to Lesson 2. ☐

- God the Father, God the Son, and God the Holy Spirit all participated in the mighty act of creation.⁵
- God is one, yet God is three in one, the Almighty God, the Creator of everything.
- We cannot comprehend the Trinity; we cannot comprehend God's awesome power.

E. The first day: Light created (Genesis 1:3-5)

 READ Genesis 1:3.

 Theme: God is all-powerful.

 Theme: God is all-knowing.

Only God could create light by simply speaking!

- Discuss:

    Wouldn't it be something if we could simply speak and have light appear? But it doesn't work that way. No, we are totally dependent on light that was created by God from the beginning of time.

    Whenever we see the light of the sun, the moon, or the stars; flip on a light switch; or light a match or a candle; let's remember that it was God who in the beginning created light. He alone could do that because He alone is all-powerful and all-knowing. He created light out of absolutely nothing.

    Scientists can evaluate some of the characteristics of light. All of us experience and use some of the effects of light. But God alone understands light, for He created it.

 Theme: God is holy.

 READ Genesis 1:4.

The light God made was very good.

- You will notice that each time God created, He said, "It is good."
- Compare:

    We are not able to make anything perfect.
    - Even though things are usable, they still:

        Need repair

        Wear out

        Are replaced because someone designed something better.
    - What we make can always be improved upon.
    - Example:

        Even the best state-of-the-art stereo equipment is labeled to indicate the amount of sound distortion it will produce. Everything man produces is flawed.

⁶Both of these Scripture portions are read by the teacher (rather than the whole class) because they are part of passages containing material that could lead to discussion which would side-track from the lesson. ☐

But everything God made was perfect because:
- God is perfect.
- God is flawless.

In other words, God is holy.

Psalm 18:30 says, *"As for God, his way is perfect...."* ⁶

Scripture Reference

Father—
James 1:17,18

Son—
Colossians 1:16

Holy Spirit—
Genesis 1:2

God is perfect, holy:
Psalm 18:30; 93:5; 99:3,5,9

Isaiah 6:3

James 1:17

Revelation 4:8

Lesson 4: God Created the Heavens and the Earth— Part 1

Isaiah 6:3 says, *"...Holy, holy, holy, is the LORD...."*

 READ Genesis 1:5.

God divided the light from the darkness.**7**
- He called the light "day."
- He called the darkness "night."
- This was the first day in the beginning of the world.

7God created light at that time, not the sun. ☐

F. The second day: Firmament created (Genesis 1:6-8)

 READ Genesis 1:6-8.

On the second day, God created the air and the sky.
- Above this "firmament" or "thin, stretched-out space" that we call the atmosphere, God placed some of the water from the world He had created.
- It is important to remember this point in God's account of creation because it will be an important factor in a later story.**8**

 Theme: God is all-powerful.

 Theme: God is all-knowing.

 Theme: God is holy.

- Again God merely spoke, and the firmament was created.
- Discuss:

Look at the vastness of the sky. We can only see a tiny portion of what encircles the earth. Yet God spoke and created all of the earth's atmosphere, and it was perfect.

8Although we are not told specifically in Scripture what God actually did when He placed the water above the firmament, many dependable scientists believe that these waters are not the clouds but water which God turned into mist or vapor and placed as a canopy surrounding the earth, high above the atmosphere. (Reference: *The Genesis Record,* by Henry M. Morris, Baker Book House, Grand Rapids, Michigan, pages 58,59.)

It is important to establish that God placed water above the earth so that, when you teach the story of the flood, it will be simple to explain how God reversed the process and returned to the earth the water which He had placed above the firmament. ☐

G. Conclusion:

Unlike man's theories, God's written account of creation has not changed.
- He was there before the beginning.
- He is the Sovereign Creator, and He alone knows how all things came to be.
- God has told us throughout His Word that He created everything.

As we study the Bible, we see that God is absolutely sovereign, greater than all and more powerful than all.

Nothing is too hard for Him.
- He is the source of all energy and the Creator of all matter.
- He made everything from nothing.

We have covered the first two days of creation.

We will explore the rest of creation week in our coming lessons.
- As you go about your duties in the days ahead, think about what we have studied thus far about God.
- He is infinitely greater than we can imagine, but He has given us the Bible, His Word, so we can know Him.

Teacher's Notes

Lesson 4: God Created the Heavens and the Earth— Part 1

Scripture Reference

QUESTIONS:

1. Who, in the beginning, created the heavens and the earth? *God.*

2. **What** did God use to make the heavens and the earth? *God didn't use anything. He made everything out of nothing.*

3. Why was God able to make the heavens and the earth? *God is almighty. There is nothing He cannot do.*

4. **How** did God know how to make the heavens and the earth? *God knows everything.*

5. Who taught God how to make everything? *No one taught God.*

6. Is there any person or any spirit who knows everything like God does? *No. Only God knows everything.*

7. What was the condition of the earth before God began to prepare it for people to live in? *It was without form and in total darkness; no land and no life.*

8. What did God **do** in order to create everything? *He spoke and commanded that things appear.*

Scripture Reference

Job 38-41
Psalms 19:1-4; 24:1,2; 33:6-9; 95:3-5; 104
Isaiah 40:28; 44:24; 45:7-12; 48:12,13
Jeremiah 10:12,13; 32:17
Colossians 1:16
Hebrews 1:10-12; 11:3

Psalm 119:89

LESSON 5

God Created the Heavens and the Earth— Part 2

LESSON PREPARATION
This section is for you, the teacher.

The passages in the Scripture Reference column are for your own study in preparing for this lesson. Since they may contain concepts that run ahead of the lesson, they are not to be taught at this point.

Note: If you have not taught previously from this series of lessons, please read carefully the note to teachers in the front of this book.

SCRIPTURE: Genesis 1:9-25

LESSON GOALS:

- To show that God created the heavens and the earth and that He created from nothing.
- To show God's character and attributes as revealed through creation.

THIS LESSON SHOULD HELP THE STUDENTS:

- To give consideration to the biblical account of creation.
- To have increased awareness of God's sovereignty, holiness, and power.

PERSPECTIVE FOR THE TEACHER:

God's Word is eternal and unchanging. Yet, over the span of a few decades, our society has allowed evolutionary theories to be widely published, taught, and accepted as fact. What is not widely published is the fact that much of the data on which evolutionists once based their theories is now being proven false. Many of the so-called links in the evolution of man have been revealed to be nothing but cruel hoaxes. Other "data" once viewed as evidence for the theory of evolution is being overruled by new scientific discoveries which confirm instead the FACT of creation.

One of the outstanding spokesmen for biblical creationism, Dr. John Whitcomb, has often said that evolutionism is a religion which puts faith in time and chance. All the questions about life and its infinite complexity and order are answered by the evolutionists in terms of millions of years and chance.

Satan has blinded the minds of men, but God's Word is powerful to penetrate that blindness. What good news we can share: God, the sovereign Creator made all things by His power. His Word, the Bible, is the greatest of all texts and the basis for all science. We can teach with confidence—not in time and chance, but in the Living God and His unchanging Word.

REFERENCE MATERIAL:

Lesson 4 lists several kinds of reference materials that may help your students who have questions about creation. Encourage them to use materials like this. Even if you do not have anything available at the time you teach this lesson, you may want to make these resources available to your students whenever possible. Creation is not taught in most schools, so your students probably have not been exposed to books that teach it.

Teacher's Notes

OVERVIEW

This is more than a lesson on the biblical facts of creation. God's nature and attributes are clearly displayed in His creative acts. Your primary goal in teaching on creation is to point out the attributes of God through His creative acts.

Note: This is the second lesson on God's creation of the heavens and the earth. If you are substituting for another teacher and have not yet studied Lesson 4, take the time to thoroughly study that lesson and the preparatory notes and Scriptures before teaching Lesson 5.

Lesson 5: God Created the Heavens and the Earth— Part 2

Teacher's Notes

Scripture Reference

ON TEACHING THIS LESSON:

These lessons are designed to **teach unbelievers**. You are carefully laying a scriptural foundation on which the Gospel will later be presented. If your class contains believers, teach with the goal of giving them an understanding of the basis for their faith and **with the goal of enabling them to teach the same material to unbelievers.**

DON'T COMPLICATE THE MESSAGE!

As you teach, keep in mind that this is a directed study—not an exhaustive survey of the Bible and not an unlimited group discussion. Keep your lesson on track and moving ahead by limiting and directing any discussion.

Carefully follow the outline. Emphasize the doctrinal themes.

LESSON FORMAT: The **center column** below contains the lesson material to be taught to the students. The **bold outline headings** are only for reference and need not be spoken, as they are incorporated into the outlined material that follows. The material in the **side columns** is for the teacher's own reference and is not intended to be included in the lesson.

TO BE TAUGHT TO THE STUDENTS

(Center Column Only)

LESSON OUTLINE:

REVIEW questions from Lesson 4.

A. Introduction

In our last lesson, we began to study what the Bible says about God in His mighty acts of creation.

- We discussed the fact that the Bible presents God's true record of creation.

    It is not a theory.

    It is the truth.

    It has not and will not change.

- We discussed the fact that the account of creation helps us see who God is:

    The sovereign Creator

    The all-powerful God

    The all-knowing one

    The God who exists by his own power

    The holy and perfect God.

- And we discussed the events of the first two days of creation.

    We read that God created light just by speaking.

    He created the air and the sky and placed some water above the sky.

Now we will read how God made the land and the seas and filled them with living creatures.

Lesson 5: God Created the Heavens and the Earth— Part 2

Scripture Reference | Teacher's Notes

B. The third day: Dry land, ocean, and all flora created (Genesis 1:9-13)

 Theme : God is all-powerful.

 READ Genesis 1:9,10.

Job 38:8-11

God gathered the waters into seas and made the dry ground appear.

- Consider:

  Have you ever witnessed the devastation caused by a flood or a tidal wave? [1] *What man can think of standing against such forces, much less commanding them? Imagine the power involved in shaping the seas—all in a day! Only Almighty God could command the waters encircling the earth to move and make the dry ground appear.*

 Read Psalm 95:5.

- God alone, who made the waters of the earth, can control them.

 READ Genesis 1:11-13.

 Theme: God is all-powerful.

 Theme: God is all-knowing.

God made all of the plants and trees.

- God alone has the knowledge and power to create plant life.

  The more scientists study plant life, the more complexities they discover.

  God, in His infinite wisdom, was able to create all plant life and to perfectly suit every kind to the rest of the earth's systems that He was creating.

- God made the plants to produce seeds which would produce more plants like the originals.

- Consider:

  A fir tree doesn't produce petunia seeds!

- Discuss:

  Have you ever made something you liked, only to have it wear out? If you want another like it, you have to start over. But when God created plant life, He put within each plant the capability to bear seeds which could sprout into new plants like the first. God is the giver and sustainer of life.

  The plants we have today came from those God created in the beginning.

 Theme: God is love.

- Why did God make flowers, trees, and plants?

  Did God need them?

  - God is independent of all things.
  - God doesn't need anything.

[1] A student may ask, "Why does God allow things like floods and tidal waves? You might reply that disasters like these were not part of man's original environment. As we study later lessons, we will discuss what brought these and other terrible changes to a perfect earth. □

Teacher's Notes

Lesson 5: God Created the Heavens and the Earth— Part 2

Scripture Reference

God made the plants and trees for man, whom He was going to create next.

- God made the plants to meet our physical needs:

    To provide food for us to eat

    To give off oxygen for the air we breathe

    To provide wood for building

    And to provide many other things which are essential to our lives.

- God made the plants to delight us with His love for us:

    He didn't have to make such a variety of colors, sizes, shapes, flavors, and fragrances.

    A few kinds would have met our needs.

- Consider:

    God could have made everything black and white. But instead, He created colors—colors that could be seen by the eyes of the man he would soon create.

    Everything could have been tasteless. But God created flavor (and taste buds to taste it.)

    He did the same thing with fragrances.

- The variety He made was to be a daily reminder of His great love and care for man.

- He made the earth not just liveable, but truly beautiful.

- In plants we can see that God is a God of order—the Master Designer.

- Illustrate:

    Look at a flower. Each flower of a certain kind has an identifying pattern that makes it recognizable as that kind of flower. The tiny seed from which it grew contained certain characteristics which always produce that kind of flower with that kind of orderly petal and stem arrangement, fragrance, etc.

    If you were to look at that flower under a magnifying glass, you would see other patterns characteristic of that kind of flower.

    If you took a tiny slice of the petal or stem and put it under a microscope, you would see still more orderly arrangements of minute cells characteristic of that kind of flower.

    All these things show that there is a Master Designer.

- Illustrate:

    What if you took a handful of marbles and dropped them on the floor? Would they fall into a beautiful pattern?

    What if they did happen to land in some pattern? Could you repeat the pattern over and over again?

    Now, what if you took the marbles one by one and placed them into a pattern of your choosing? You could do this over and over, because you designed the pattern and insured its repetition. Your design would not be a product of chance; rather, it would reflect the work of a designer—you.

    What God has created endlessly reflects His work as Master Designer of everything.

    When you see a design, bear in mind that there was also a designer. And when you see a design in plants or flowers or any other part

Isaiah 45:18

I Timothy 6:17b

Psalm 19:1-3

Romans 1:20

Lesson 5: God Created the Heavens and the Earth— Part 2

Scripture Reference		Teacher's Notes

Genesis 1:31
Psalm 18:30
Psalm 93:5
Psalm 99:3,5,9
Isaiah 6:3
James 1:17
Revelation 4:8

of creation, remember that God is the one who is being reflected in that design. It didn't just happen that way. God designed it all.

- Everything that God created on this day was good.

 All the plants were beneficial, lovely—created perfect.²

 - Thorns and weeds did not exist.
 - No fruit was poisonous.
 - Vegetables and fruit did not get diseases or spoil.

 Everything was perfect in the beginning, because God is perfect, and everything He does is perfect.

²If a student asks why things are so different now, tell them that in later lessons we will see the answer to that question. ☐

C. The fourth day: Sun, moon, and stars created (Genesis 1:14-19)

Discuss the vastness of the universe.

- Suggested illustration:

 In the last few decades, man has learned more about the universe than he knew in all previous generations. Powerful telescopes, controlled radio beams, electronic devices, space travel—all of these are products of this century. Men have set foot on the moon; space probes orbit the earth and travel outward through our solar system, gathering amazing new data.

 But what we are really learning is that we know very little about this solar system that includes planet Earth; and we know even less about our galaxy, the Milky Way; and we know still less about the endless reaches of the universe.

 We have assembled many facts and figures about distance, yet none of us can begin to fathom the immensity of the universe. For instance: light, traveling at 186,000 miles per second, takes several years to reach us from the nearest stars outside our solar system. And we are told that there are literally billions of stars beyond what we can see.

Now let's read what God says about this.

 READ Genesis 1:14-19.

 Theme: God is all-powerful.

Psalm 33:6

God spoke, and the sun, moon, and stars came into being.

- Only God has the power to create such vastness!
- In Isaiah 44:24, God says, *"...I am the LORD that maketh all things; that stretcheth forth the heavens alone; that spreadeth abroad the earth by myself."*

Isaiah 40:26

- As in the plants He created, the whole universe reflects the work of the Master Designer.
- Illustrate:

 Centuries ago, men discovered that our planet Earth revolves around the sun. Then they realized that we are part of a solar system, that is, a group of planets which revolve around the sun. Then, as more powerful telescopes were developed, other galaxies were discovered.

 But in the twentieth century, men were able to take a look inward at another system, so similar in design that it overwhelms the mind to consider it. Powerful microscopes revealed that the atom, once thought to be the smallest part of matter, appears to consist of tiny

Lesson 5: God Created the Heavens and the Earth— Part 2

parts, revolving around a center called the nucleus. The pattern in what was thought to be the smallest part of matter closely resembles the pattern of our vast solar system.

How could this be? There is only one answer: one Designer created everything, from the smallest to the largest. God and God alone created the universe and everything in it, and the stamp of His design is deeply imprinted in every part.

 Theme: God is everywhere all the time.

We can see only a tiny part of the endless reaches of the universe.

Yet God created even the most remote galaxies and stars—He created everything.

How could God have gotten to all those places that are countless light years apart?

- Jeremiah 23:23,24 says *"Am I a God at hand...and not a God afar off?...Do not I fill heaven and earth?..."*
- Distance is no problem for God.
- God is everywhere.
- We cannot imagine the immensity of the universe; much less can we comprehend the greatness of God!

Although God is everywhere present in the universe, He is distinct from it. **3**

- The idea that God is everything and everything is God is a concept totally foreign to Scripture.
- There is one true God, not many "gods."
- The Bible refers to the universe and everything in it as God's creation, not as part of His being.

 Theme: God is all-knowing.

 Read Jeremiah 10:12.

- God's infinite wisdom and knowledge are displayed in the universe He created.
- Suggested illustration:

As scientists have studied and experimented, they have discovered physical laws that apply consistently throughout the known universe. These laws govern the physical behavior of all matter. Knowing these laws, men have been able to do amazing things, such as travel in space. Yet these "discoveries" are actually laws established by God and put into effect in the beginning when He created the universe.

 Theme: God never changes.

- God never changes, nor do the laws of His creation.
- Consider:

Imagine! One system of physical laws regulates the behavior of every part we know of the universe! And it is only as scientists and engineers operate in strict adherence and dependence upon these predictable laws that they are able to design a reliable spacecraft or family automobile or anything else.

Teacher's Notes

3 As mentioned before, this is an important distinction. New Age and other pantheistic religions teach that God is everything and everything is God. ☐

Scripture Reference

Proverbs 3:19

Lesson 5: God Created the Heavens and the Earth— Part 2

You don't have to be an engineer or scientist to see God's laws at work. All of us depend on these laws every day, just to keep our feet on the ground.

Has there ever been a day in your life when the sun didn't rise and set? Granted, it may have been hidden by clouds, but it did just what it always does, day after day. How about the moon? Did you know that calendars and tidal charts can be made years in advance because the movement and position of the moon and earth and sun are completely predictable?

This certainly isn't happening by chance; it was designed that way by God Himself.

 Read Psalm 104:19.

He wanted us to have an orderly world with dependable days, nights, seasons, and tides.

- Compare:

We get very excited about seeing one vehicle thrust into a tiny path in space; and we certainly should, for it has taken an unbelievable amount of research and effort to achieve this feat.

But imagine God's knowledge! Imagine God's creativity and skill as a Master Designer! Imagine His power! God spoke, and the entire universe was created!

 Read Psalm 19:1-3.

- We need to watch this display and listen to the message God is sending us!

 Theme: God is holy.

Everything God made on the fourth day was good.

- God is perfect, and everything He does is perfect.
- God was very pleased with His creation.

Psalm 18:30; 93:5; 99:3,5,9
Isaiah 6:3
James 1:17
Revelation 4:8

D. The fifth day: All sea life and birds created

 Read Genesis 1:20-23.

 Theme: God is love.

Imagine the beauty that suddenly filled the water and the skies!

- Just as He had done in His creation of plant life, God made numerous kinds of water creatures and birds with countless, colorful designs and shapes.
- The more we search the ocean depths and the remote places of the earth, the more kinds of fish and birds we discover!
- Why did God create such variety and beauty?

    He did it to show His love to us.

    He did it to show us His creative power and understanding.

 Theme: God is all-powerful.

Psalm 104:24

God made these wonderful things by His great power and understanding.

Lesson 5: God Created the Heavens and the Earth— Part 2

Teacher's Notes

Scripture Reference

- Compare:

  Could we make even one common sparrow?
  - We might make a model or an "imitation."
  - But we will never make a living sparrow.

  But God can; He made sparrows and every other creature.
- Even the tiniest, most ordinary creatures are God's creation and are incredibly complex.
- Suggested illustration:

"Molecular biology has shown that even the simplest of all living systems on earth today, bacterial cells, are exceedingly complex objects. Although the tiniest bacterial cells are incredibly small, weighing less than 10^{-12} gms, each is in effect a veritable micro-miniaturized factory containing thousands of exquisitely designed pieces of intricate molecular machinery, made up altogether of one hundred thousand million atoms, far more complicated than any machine built by man and absolutely without parallel in the nonliving world." [4]

[4]*Evolution: A Theory in Crisis,* by Michael Denton, p. 250.

E. Sixth day: The creation of the animal world

 Theme: God is all-powerful.

 Theme: God is all-knowing.

 READ Genesis 1:24,25.

God created an unbelievable number and variety of animals.
- Some animals are very familiar to us as a part of our daily lives.
- Some can be seen at a zoo.
- Through television and books, we learn about many more.

God created each kind of animal with unique characteristics, and each kind of animal is capable of reproducing only other animals like itself.
- Dogs have puppies.
- Cats have kittens, etc.
- Even in the smallest animal we can see the stamp of the Master Designer.

Only God has the power to create animals.

Man has never created nor will he ever be able to create an animal.

 Theme: God is holy.

All of the living things that God made on the fifth and sixth days were good.

Everything He made was good.

Because God is perfect, everything He made was perfect.

F. Conclusion

We are daily surrounded by evidences of:
- God's existence
- God's infinite power and knowledge

Psalm 18:30
Psalm 93:5
Psalm 99:3,5,9
Isaiah 6:3
James 1:17
Revelation 4:8

Lesson 5: God Created the Heavens and the Earth— Part 2

- God's love
- God's orderliness
- God's holiness.
- We are surrounded by reminders of a Master Designer who created with skill and purpose.

We can learn a great deal about God by observing the things He has made, but our true understanding of Him and how He created everything must be based on what God has told us in His Word.

- Hebrews 11:3 says, *"Through faith we understand that the worlds were framed by the word of God, so that things which are seen were not made of things which do appear."*
- God, the Creator, the one who was there before the beginning, has given us His record of creation in His Word.

This week:

- Look for evidences of the Designer, the Creator of all things.
- And think about what we have studied in His Word.
- In our next lesson we will continue to study God's account of creation.

QUESTIONS:

1. Why was God able to command the ocean to go back and stay where He wanted it? *Because He is all-powerful and He created the ocean.*

2. Why did God create everything beautiful, and why did He create water and all different kinds of fruit and vegetables to eat? *He made them because He is loving and kind. He prepared everything on earth for us.*

3. What did God say about all of the things which He created? *God said that they were good.*

4. Why was God able to create all things perfect? *Because He is perfect.*

5. How was God able to create such a vast universe, with so many stars, so far apart? *God is all-powerful and He is everywhere, all the time.*

6. Why did God create the sun to rise and set each day and the moon and the stars to follow the same path every year? *God did it because He is a God of order. He placed the sun, moon, and stars in the sky to show us the days, the months, the seasons, and the years and to give order to our lives.*

7. Upon what principles do scientists and engineers depend for everything they study and design? *God's laws, set forth in the creation of the world.*

Scripture Reference

Job 12:10
Psalm 95:6; 100:1-3; 139
Psalm 144:3
Isaiah 45:5-12
Acts 17:24-28

LESSON 6

God Created Man

LESSON PREPARATION

This section is for you, the teacher.

The passages in the Scripture Reference column are for your own study in preparing for this lesson. Since they may contain concepts that run ahead of the lesson, they are not to be taught at this point.

Note: If you have not taught previously from this series of lessons, please read carefully the note to teachers in the front of this book.

SCRIPTURE: Genesis 1:26-31; 2:7

LESSON GOALS:

- To show God's sovereignty.
- To show the uniqueness of man in all of God's creation.
- To show God's original plan for man to be God's chosen manager over all of the earth.

THIS LESSON SHOULD HELP THE STUDENTS:

- To see man's unique creation (distinct from all the animals) and man's unique relationship to God.
- To see God's ownership of man.

PERSPECTIVE FOR THE TEACHER:

Like the first part of the creation story, this part also cannot be scientifically proven; it must be accepted by faith. God's Word is very clear in showing forth the uniqueness of man in God's creation. The Bible does not leave an option for man to be any less than the **only** being created in the image of God. This unique creation includes man's unique **relationship** to God. Man is not only God's creation, made in God's image; man is also God's cherished possession— **accountable** to his Creator.

Believing and understanding this relationship between God, the Creator, and man, the one created in God's image, is essential to the student's understanding of all other biblical truth. If this part of the foundation is lacking, nothing else will be stable. The person who is blind to the fact that he was created is also blind to the fact that he is accountable to his Creator. If a man thinks that he evolved, why should he worry about what God has to say?

Isaiah 45:5,21,22
Isaiah 46:9
Acts 17:28

The subtlety of the lie of evolution is that it deceives man about the existence and character of God and makes man think that he has no need of God. Strangely, this kind of thinking produces tremendous insecurities because man was never designed to be his own god. We were created to be in submission to one who is almighty, sovereign, all-knowing, all-powerful, eternal; one who can supply **all** our needs. Little wonder that without faith in our almighty Creator, men live lives of utter frustration, for man **cannot** find in himself the supply for all that he needs.[1] The only one who can truly meet our needs is God.

Teacher's Notes

OVERVIEW

This lesson presents God as the sovereign Creator and owner of man and presents man as God's unique creation, made in the image of God.

Also considered:

"The image of God," with regard to mind, emotions, and will

Adam, the first and only man created from the ground—the ancestor of all people

God's choice of Adam as manager of the earth.

[1] The Bible exalts God as the Creator and owner of man. Humanistic thinking seeks to exalt man as the one in control. Like the lie of evolution, the lie of humanism has permeated our society and deceived many. Even though your students might not call themselves "humanists," they may have been deeply affected by humanistic teachings. The truths of this lesson may seem both fresh and yet irritating to those who have never heard them. Make your presentation very positive and objective and try to avoid arguments. Be patient to allow the truth of God's Word to gradually penetrate their thoughts and their hearts. Today they may be hearing and resisting; later on, the same student may fully embrace the truth of God's Word. ☐

Teacher's Notes

Lesson 6: God Created Man

Scripture Reference

VISUALS:

- Chronological Picture No. 3, "Creation"
- Chronological Chart

ON TEACHING THIS LESSON:

These lessons are designed to **teach unbelievers.** You are carefully laying a scriptural foundation on which the Gospel will later be presented. If your class contains believers, teach with the goal of giving them an understanding of the basis for their faith and **with the goal of enabling them to teach the same material to unbelievers.**

DON'T COMPLICATE THE MESSAGE!

As you teach, keep in mind that this is a directed study—not an exhaustive survey of the Bible and not an unlimited group discussion. Keep your lesson on track and moving ahead by limiting and directing any discussion.

Carefully follow the outline. Emphasize the doctrinal themes.

LESSON FORMAT: The **center column** below contains the lesson material to be taught to the students. The **bold outline headings** are only for reference and need not be spoken, as they are incorporated into the outlined material that follows. The material in the **side columns** is for the teacher's own reference and is not intended to be included in the lesson.

TO BE TAUGHT TO THE STUDENTS
(Center Column Only)

LESSON OUTLINE:

REVIEW questions from Lesson 5.

A. Introduction

We have come to the climax of the creation story.

- God spoke into being the heavens and the earth.

　He created light.

　He created the waters above the earth, the expanse in between, the dry land, and the oceans.

　He created the plants, the trees, and the flowers.

　He created the sun, the moon, and the stars.

　He filled the sea with creatures and the air with birds.

　He created all the animals.

Lesson 6: God Created Man

Suggested Visual:

CHRONOLOGICAL PICTURE NO. 3, "CREATION"

- God had not done all this for Himself; God doesn't need anything!
- Why, then, had God created all these things?

B. The earth finally prepared for man

 Theme: God is supreme and sovereign.

God had done all of this marvelous work of creation because He is sovereign and chose to do it for His glory.

 Theme: God is loving.

And He did it because He is loving and kind and caring.

God had lovingly, carefully, perfectly created everything in preparation for His final creation: man.

 Read Isaiah 45:18.

- All that man would ever need was waiting and ready.

Compare:

Think of how it is when a family is expecting their first child. They usually find much pleasure in fixing up a room for that new little baby. The mother wants to have everything ready ahead of time so she can bring the baby home to a place where all his needs can be met in a special, loving place prepared just for him.

In the same way, God had prepared a place for man.

C. God's plan to create man in the image of God

 READ Genesis 1:26.

To whom do you think God was speaking when He said, *"...Let us make man in our image..."*?[2]

- It was God the Father, God the Son, and God the Holy Spirit who were talking together.
- They were discussing their plan to make man in the image of God.

 Theme: God is supreme and sovereign.

- Compare:

When you are going to make something which is very important, for example a new home, you first think about it and plan how you want it to be.

Scripture Reference: Revelation 4:11

Teacher's Notes:

[2] See notes in Lesson 2 regarding the Trinity, especially the note with point D. of Lesson 2. ☐

Lesson 6: God Created Man

Teacher's Notes | **Scripture Reference**

That's what God did. God planned how He would make the first man.

God is sovereign; He alone decided how all things would be made.

- God decided how man would be made, just like He previously decided how the spirits, the sun, moon, stars, the earth, and all things on the earth were to be made.
- God alone decided; He didn't ask anyone's advice.
- God is greater than all and more important than all.
- Man was the most important thing God created on the earth, so God decided to make him in the "image of God."

God made man in His image so that:

- Man would be able to know God and communicate with Him.
- Others would see God's likeness reflected in man and praise and glorify God.

Job 38-41

Matthew 5:16

D. What does it mean that man was made in the image of God?[3]

³The Bible does not give us a direct answer to this question. The lesson outline covers the answer from a viewpoint of what can be deduced from Scripture.

This discussion is not intended to be the only possible interpretation of "the image of God." ☐

What does it mean when God tells us here in His Word that the first man was made in God's image?[4]

- We know it is not talking about our bodies.

    God is Spirit.

    God doesn't have a body of flesh and bones like we do.

- Rather, God was referring to the part which cannot be seen.

    The Bible calls this part of us which cannot be seen our soul and our spirit.

    Man's body was created to be the "house" of this unseen part, the soul and the spirit.

God planned that the unseen part of man would have a **mind, emotions, and a will, created in the image of God.**

 Theme: God communicates with man.

⁴Man was created a rational, moral, and spiritual being, for he was created in the image of God. In other words, man was created so that he could respond to God. He was endowed with intellect so he could know God. He was given emotions so he could love God. He was created with a will so he could obey God.

Make it clear that, when it says man was created in God's image, it was not in the physical image of God. ☐

- Man's mind—his intellect:

    Because God has a mind, He planned to make people with a mind which had the ability to know God, think like God, and reason like God.

    - God wanted to talk to man, and He wanted man to talk to Him.
    - He wanted to be able to communicate with man, not only by spoken word, but also by written word, as He does through His Word, the Bible.
    - God wanted to enable and equip man to do His work here on earth.
    - Note:

        We realize that God has given animals minds, too. But an animal does not have the same kind of mind that man has. Animals can be very good company as pets; they can also be a great help to us in certain kinds of work, such as the work done by horses, mules, oxen, and even dogs. But an animal does not have the ability to converse with us; it does not have the ability to share our thoughts and make the kind of decisions we make. An animal cannot reason in the way we

John 4:24

Psalm 86:11; 119:73

Proverbs 2:1-6

Jeremiah 33:3

John 17:3

Philippians 3:10

I John 3:1,2

Lesson 6: God Created Man

Scripture Reference

Romans 11:33,34

reason; it cannot communicate with us by speech and by writing.

God decided that He would give man a mind so man could think and reason like God does, but that doesn't mean that any man could ever think and reason exactly as God thinks and reasons.

- Compare:

  Think about children. Do they know all the things that you do? No, they don't. But because they have a mind like you, you are able to teach them.

  Even the wisest man in this world is like a little child compared to God. But because God chose to make man with a mind, he would be able to listen to God's Word, understand it, and then do what God said. That is what God planned for man. God decided to give man a mind so He could talk with man, enjoy man's company, and teach man to do God's work.

- **Man's emotions** — his feelings:

  - Consider:

    People often think that emotions have a bad connotation. They may just think of being "emotional." But emotions are very necessary and helpful.

  The Bible shows us that God has emotions: He is compassionate and tender and is angry at injustice.

  We can readily see in God that emotions are good.

  God loves, hates, feels sadness, and also feels joy and happiness.

  Because God has feelings (emotions), He decided that He would also create man with feelings.

A few of countless examples:
Love:
Jeremiah 31:3
John 3:16
I John 4:7-10
Hate:
Proverbs 6:16-19
Malachi 2:16
Sadness:
Matthew 23:37
Luke 19:41
Joy, Delight:
Jeremiah 9:24
Zephaniah 3:17

  - Compare:

    You who have children all love your children, don't you? But do you also want your children to love you? Of course, you do! Every parent wants his children to love him.

    God is like that, too. God planned to love man, but God also wanted man to be able to love Him. This is the reason God planned to create man with emotions.

- **Man's will** — his ability to choose:

  Besides having a mind and feelings, God also has a will; He is able to decide that He will do something or that He will not do it.[5]

  Therefore, God decided to make man so that he would be able to make decisions for himself.

  - Compare:

    When you get up in the morning, you decide what you are going to wear. You decide what you will have to drink and eat for breakfast; you decide where you are going to drive your car.

    When you get dressed, do your clothes have any say in what you wear? Does your food have any opportunity to say when it will be eaten? Does your car have any choice where you will drive it? No. You are the one who makes the choices about all of these and countless other things.

    God could have made the first man so he would have had no choice (just like your clothes and your food and your car). God could have made man so he would have to do everything that God made him to do, without any choice.

Teacher's Notes

[5]The story of creation and the entire Bible resound with God's Sovereign will.

Don't get sidetracked in a discussion of God's sovereign will and man's free choice. If you need a way to avert a discussion, you may always remind your students that you want to keep the studies on course so that you will be able to cover each lesson in the time allowed and be able to move ahead. Tell them that each succeeding lesson will help build understanding.

You may also remind them that many things in the Bible are beyond our comprehension. We want to take the time to study those things that God has clearly revealed to us. If then, on their own they wish to do more study, they can do that.

Thank them for their questions and interest. ☐

Lesson 6: God Created Man

Teacher's Notes

That is how God made the sun, the moon, and the stars. God made them so they have to do the same thing every day, every month, and every year. But God didn't plan to make man like that. God has a will. God decides what He will do, and God wanted man to be able to make choices just as God makes choices.

God planned to make man so he could **choose** to love and obey God — a choice man could make intelligently because by his mind he would know that God is his loving, kind, and all-wise Creator.

- Compare:

  If children know and are convinced that their parents are wise and kind, then it is much easier for them to obey their parents.

  God's plan was to make man so he could talk with God and come to know what a wise and loving God He is. Then man should choose to obey such a wonderful God who made him.

- Summary:

  Man was given a mind to hear and understand God's communication with him, to think through what God had told him, to learn the true character of God, and to communicate with God in return.

  Man was given emotions to respond to God out of love and devotion.

  Man was given a will so he could choose to carry out God's plans, not as a "robot," but as one who has listened to God, loved God, and has chosen to obey God.

  Scripture Reference: John 14:21

- God planned for man to be made in God's image so he could do God's work on earth.
- God was giving man a unique role in His creation.

  Man was to be God's representative on the earth.[6]

  Man was to look after God's things here on the earth and to be the leader over the animals, the birds, and the fish.

  God gave man a mind and emotions and a will so that man could do God's work in just the way God wanted it to be done, which would bring joy to both God and man.

  Psalm 97:11, 12

E. The creation of Adam

 Theme: God is all-powerful.

 Theme: God is supreme and sovereign.

CHRONOLOGICAL CHART: DISPLAY THE NAMES "ADAM AND EVE."

READ Genesis 1:27, 2:7.

God created the first man and woman.[7]

- God created the man first, and then, after the man was living, God made a wife for the man on the same day.

  Since the Bible tells us in the following chapter about God's creation of woman, we will wait for a later lesson to read about that.

  Today, we will just study what the Bible says about how God made the first man.

---

[6] The creation of man was unique. Just as it is important to give God His rightful position, so we should stress the original, unique position which God gave man over creation.

We see our true value and self-worth in the light of God's estimation of us. As a person sees the value God has placed in him, he can better understand the necessity of having a right relationship with God. It is important then for us to emphasize man's unique creation and place of authority on the earth. God placed man as lord or master over the earth to take care of it. ☐

[7] In your attempts to give imaginative descriptions of biblical events, avoid literal terminology or explanations which may give an incorrect picture of God. One man was heard teaching that God put out His hand and picked up the dust to make man. The teacher even asked his listeners if they thought God may have gotten dirt under His fingernails. This type of literalism which presents God as a superhuman must be avoided. Teach just what His Word says, and give it neither a literal nor spiritual meaning beyond what is written. God did not take the dust in His hands to form man. God does not have material hands as we do. God is Spirit. ☐

Lesson 6: God Created Man

Scripture Reference		Teacher's Notes
	- God named the man "Adam," which means "man."	
	- But after God had made every part of man's body, the man still didn't have life.	
	Every part of his body was there, but he was like a dead man.	
	His body was not breathing because the part which was to be in God's image was not yet living in his body.	
	It was only after God breathed into man's body that he became a living person who could know, love, and obey God.	
Deuteronomy 30:20 Job 12:10 Acts 17:25	- God alone could put life into Adam.	
	Neither the sun, moon, earth, birds, animals, fish, God's angels, any man, Satan, nor his spirit followers can give life.	
	All things received their life from God and are unable to give life to anything or anyone else.	
	God is distinct from all created things and greater than all the things He created.[8]	[8]Again, make this distinction clear. (New Age and other pantheistic religions teach that God is everything and everything is God. ☐
	- Compare:	
	We all depend upon electrical power. A light bulb that is not screwed into the socket doesn't give any light. Until the switch is turned on, our homes don't receive any power. Not only our homes, but commerce and industry are very dependent upon that flow of electrical power. When it is interrupted, many things we are accustomed to using simply won't work. Without power to run them, very complex, useful machines are absolutely useless.	
	Just as the power company is our source of electricity, so also God is our source of life. All things received their life from God and are utterly dependent upon Him.	
	- When God breathed into the first man's nostrils, the man was immediately alive.	
	He was breathing, and he was a strong, healthy man.	
	There wasn't any sickness or death in the world.	

F. Adam was the first and only man God created from the ground.

 READ Genesis 2:7.

	Adam was the first and only man God created from the ground.[9]	[9]This is very important. Satan does not want people to know that we all came from one source. We will apply this truth personally again and again as we teach these first 10 chapters of Genesis. It is absolutely necessary that your students come to understand that they, too, had their beginnings "in Adam." They will never be able to understand their salvation "in Christ" unless they understand that they died "in Adam" (Romans 5:12-21; I Corinthians 15:22). ☐
Acts 17:26	God only made one man from the ground and one woman from him, and God told them to have children so all the world would eventually be filled with people.	
	Adam is the ancestor of all people.	
	- He is the ancestor of all people, regardless of race, culture, or country.	
	Adam is your ancestor.	
	Adam is also my ancestor.	
	He is the ancestor of all people.	
	We all came from this first man.	
	- He is the beginning and the father of the entire human race.	

Lesson 6: God Created Man

Teacher's Notes | Scripture Reference

G. Man placed as manager over the earth

 Theme: God is supreme and sovereign.

 Theme: God communicates with man.

 READ Genesis 1:28-30.

God put man in charge of the earth and everything in it.

God desired to help man learn to take care of all the responsibilities God had given him.

- Compare:

    Consider a wealthy man who owns many properties and businesses. He loves his son and is very pleased with him. The day comes when he decides to give to his son the management of all of the father's assets. The father knows that his son will need guidance in this huge responsibility, and he is delighted and willing to help his son to learn all that is necessary. He is glad to entrust the work to his son; he is also glad to sit down and talk with him about each decision and to tell him all that he would like to see done in the work he has given his son to oversee.

    God, too, was very pleased with the first man He made. God spoke to Adam, the first man, and God told him what he was to do as God's representative on earth.

Psalm 32:8

Isaiah 48:17

Matthew 11:29

God had the right to decide to whom He would give the earth.

- He didn't give the earth to His angels.
- He didn't give it to Satan and his demons.

Why was God the only one who had the authority to give man control over the earth and everything in it?

God created everything.

 Read Psalm 24:1.

Therefore, God could give it to whom He pleased.

Read I Chronicles 29:11: "**Thine, O LORD, is the greatness, and the power,** *and the glory, and the victory,* **and the majesty: for all that is in the heaven and in the earth is thine;** *thine is the kingdom,* **O LORD, and thou art exalted as head above all.**" [10]

- Compare:

    The wealthy man chose to make his son manager. It was the father's right to make that choice, and he did not give that responsibility to anyone else but to his son. No one else would have the right to oversee that man's assets except the son.

    God is the Creator of all things, so this world and everything in it belongs to God. He had the right to decide to whom He would give the earth, and He gave it to man. God is supreme and sovereign.

What a special place God gave to man!

By giving man that responsibility, God gave man a great honor and privilege.

[10]This Scripture contains themes that run ahead of the chronological order. The parts that are boldfaced here are what you want to emphasize. Do not get into discussion about other themes. ☐

Lesson 6: God Created Man

| Scripture Reference | | Teacher's Notes |

 Read Psalm 8:3-9.

H. Everything God made was good.

 Theme: God is holy.

 READ Genesis 1:31.

God is perfect, holy:
Psalm 18:30; 93:5; 99:3,5,9
Isaiah 6:3
James 1:17
Revelation 4:8

Because God is perfect and good, everything He created was absolutely right and beautiful.[11]

- In the beginning, nothing in the animal world would hurt or harm man.
- Neither man nor animal had to kill in order to eat.
- Thorns, thistles, and weeds didn't grow as they do now.

I. Conclusion

God is sovereign.

He is the great and only **Creator** of all things; therefore, He is the **owner** of all things.

He made the first man from the dust of the earth.

He created man in His own image, giving man:

- A mind so he could know God
- Emotions so he could love God
- A will so he could choose to obey God

Adam, the first man, is the ancestor of all men everywhere.

As Creator and owner of man, God gave man the responsibility of being manager over the earth.

In our next lesson we will study more about God and His sovereign, loving dealings with Adam.

[11] When you mention God's perfect creation, someone may ask why things are so different now. Don't answer at this point, but tell them that you will be studying the answer to that question in future lessons. ☐

QUESTIONS:

1. For whom did God prepare the earth? *For man.*

2. What great difference was there between the creation of man and that of the animals? *God created man in His image.*

3. What does it mean that God made man in His image? *God is Spirit, so it was not man's body that was created in God's image. God made Adam and Eve so they could know, love, and obey God.*

4. How many men and women did God make in the beginning? *God created only one man and one woman.*

5. Who is your very first forefather and my first forefather? *Adam.*

6. After the creation of Adam, the first man, over what did God give him control? *The earth and everything in it.*

7. Why don't Satan and his demons have the right to control the earth and the things on the earth? *Because God never gave them the right to control anything on the earth. God gave the earth to man.*

8. What was everything in the world like in the beginning? *Very good. Everything was perfect.*

LESSON 7: God Placed Adam in Eden

OVERVIEW

This lesson continues to present God's sovereignty as Creator and owner of man. It also establishes the fact that the penalty for sin is death.

Also presented:

- God's rest on the 7th day: not a physical rest, but a ceasing from work that was completed
- God's placing Adam in the garden: an act of God's sovereignty as the creator/owner of man
- God's care for Adam
- The tree of life: God wanted Adam to choose to eat of it and live forever
- The tree of knowledge of good and evil: God instructed Adam clearly that he would die if he disobeyed God and ate of this tree
- Death penalty for sin: separation from God, separation from the body, separation forever in the Lake of Fire.

LESSON PREPARATION
This section is for you, the teacher.

The passages in the Scripture Reference column are for your own study in preparing for this lesson. Since they may contain concepts that run ahead of the lesson, they are not to be taught at this point.

Note: If you have not taught previously from this series of lessons, please read carefully the note to teachers in the front of this book.

SCRIPTURE: Genesis 2:1-9,16,17

LESSON GOALS:

- To present God as the sovereign, loving, wise Creator and owner of man.
- To establish that the penalty for sin is death.

THIS LESSON SHOULD HELP THE STUDENTS:

- To see their need to get to know God.
- To see their need to be in submission to God.
- To value God's care for them.
- To see that the penalty for sin is death.

PERSPECTIVE FOR THE TEACHER:

This is a lesson about God's sovereignty and holiness and man's relationship to his God. Our society teaches us to be independent and to do "our own thing"; God's Word teaches us to be in confident submission to our holy, righteous Creator. Our society teaches us to stand up for our rights; the Bible teaches us the privilege of receiving what is given to us by our sovereign, loving, all-knowing God. Our society teaches us to go as far as we dare and to get away with whatever we can; God's Word teaches us that God is holy and that the punishment for sin is death. Our society tells us to find out who we are so that we can have more self-esteem; God's Word says we should first know Him and then understand who we are in Him!

SPECIAL NOTE:

This lesson presents some concepts which are seldom taught in our culture: God's ownership of man and man's need to fear God. To prepare your own heart for teaching and for handling any discussion on these issues, be sure to study ahead the Scriptures in the side columns adjacent to the lesson outline.

VISUALS:

- Bring to class a tree branch with green leaves. You will use this same branch in several future lessons to illustrate the effect of sin in separating man from God, man's source of life.
- The visual, "The Penalty of Sin is Death," can be done as you teach or made ahead as a small poster to keep on the wall in your classroom.

Lesson 7: God Placed Adam in Eden

Teacher's Notes | Scripture Reference

ON TEACHING THIS LESSON:

These lessons are designed to **teach unbelievers.** You are carefully laying a scriptural foundation on which the Gospel will later be presented. If your class contains believers, teach with the goal of giving them an understanding of the basis for their faith and **with the goal of enabling them to teach the same material to unbelievers.**

DON'T COMPLICATE THE MESSAGE!

As you teach, keep in mind that this is a directed study—not an exhaustive survey of the Bible and not an unlimited group discussion. Keep your lesson on track and moving ahead by limiting and directing any discussion.

Carefully follow the outline. Emphasize the doctrinal themes.

LESSON FORMAT: The **center column** below contains the lesson material to be taught to the students. The **bold outline headings** are only for reference and need not be spoken, as they are incorporated into the outlined material that follows. The material in the **side columns** is for the teacher's own reference and is not intended to be included in the lesson.

TO BE TAUGHT TO THE STUDENTS
(Center Column Only)

LESSON OUTLINE:

REVIEW questions from Lesson 6.

A. Introduction

Have you ever started something and not finished it?

All of us can probably remember something which we started to do and, for some reason, weren't able to finish.

- Can you think of something you started recently and didn't finish?

   Why didn't you finish what you started? [1]

   - You changed your mind.
   - You lost interest.
   - It turned out to be too hard for you to do.
   - It was a bigger job than you had thought.
   - You were interrupted.
   - You ran out of time.
   - You ran out of money.
   - Etc.

God is not like us.

- He never gives up on what He plans to do.

   When He begins a work, He always finishes it.

   He does not change His mind and then decide He will do something different.

B. God finished making all He had planned.

 Theme: God is supreme and sovereign.

---

[1] Give your students a brief opportunity to name some of their reasons for not finishing what they started. ☐

Lesson 7: God Placed Adam in Eden

Scripture Reference

Teacher's Notes

 Theme: God is faithful; He never changes.

READ Genesis 2:1.

God finished all that He planned to do.
- Compare:
    We change our minds and we change our plans.
    But it is never that way with God.

Isaiah 46:10,11; 55:8-11

God never changes His mind about something that He plans to do.
Nothing and no one can hinder God from doing all He plans to do.
- No human can hinder God.
- Satan cannot stop God.
- God is greater than all.

He always does whatever He plans to do.

Therefore, when God promises to do something, we can be confident that He will do it.

Read Psalm 33:11.

C. God rested from His work of creation on the seventh day.

 Theme: God is all-powerful.

 READ Genesis 2:2,3.

How many days did it take for God to make everything? Only six days! **2**

- Compare:

    How many days does it take to build a house? It takes a long time, doesn't it, even for a building contractor. He has to assemble the needed materials and have all the workers ready for the various building tasks, and then all the labor must be done and inspected before the house is completed.

    But look at all the things God created in just six days. There is none other as great as God. He is almighty. He can do anything He wants.

God finished in six days all He planned to do, so on the seventh day, He rested from His work of creating. **3**

- Did God rest from His work because He became tired after all the work He had done?

- Compare:

    After a hard day's work, we want to come home and rest. Sometimes we get involved in some pretty exhausting tasks. Just think of all that God had done that week!

    Do you think that God rested because He was tired? He had made millions of stars, the sun, and the moon. Look at all the things He created on the earth. Do you think He lay down and said, "I'm tired. I am going to have a good rest today"?

    No, God doesn't get weary or sleepy like we do. He doesn't have a physical body that needs rest or sleep. God is Spirit. He is always

2 A student may ask if these are six 24-hour days.

Beware. This is a sensitive issue — one that has been debated many times. (Don't raise this point unnecessarily.)

Probably the clearest answer we have from Scripture is the words, *"the evening and the morning were the first [second, third, fourth, etc.] day"* (Genesis 1:5,8,13,19,23,31). This would indicate 24-hour days.

Many people view these days as ages of time in which everything evolved.

But nowhere in the Bible does God say anything like this. II Peter 3:8 says that *"one day is with the Lord as a thousand years,"* but the context is very different from the Genesis 1 context which mentions morning and evening and a clear succession of numbered days. ☐

3 Someone may raise the question of sabbath days or going to church on Sunday. Avoid this discussion at this point.

You might want to say that in this lesson we are just going to focus on what God is saying about His rest from creating all things. ☐

Teacher's Notes

Lesson 7: God Placed Adam in Eden

Scripture Reference

the same. He is still the same today as He was when He first made the earth. God will never change.

 Read Isaiah 40:28.

- Compare:

When you have finished an important project, haven't you sometimes just stood back and taken a look at all that was accomplished? Even if you had the energy to do more, you wouldn't, because everything that needed to be done on that project was completed. Nothing more could be added to it.

That's how it was with God and all He had created. God was very pleased with everything that He had made.

God created everything in six days, and so He rested on the seventh day.

God rested from creating because He saw that all His work which He had planned to do was finished.

D. Mist, not rain, watered the earth.

 READ Genesis 2:4-6.

Before we consider what these verses are teaching, notice that God now uses another name for Himself.

- In the first chapter, He called Himself "God" which means that He is the great and mighty God who created the heavens and the earth and all things that are in them.
- But the name He now uses in these verses is "the LORD," which means that God is the eternal one who is totally independent of all things and who will never change.
- From this point onward, the Bible sometimes uses the name "God," but at other times, it uses the name "the LORD God" or just "the LORD."

These verses teach us something very interesting about the beginning.

- When God first created everything, He did not water the earth by giving rain.
- Instead, He watered it by mist which came up from the earth. **4**

E. God planted a garden.

 Theme: God is love.

 READ Genesis 2:7,8.

Because God loved Adam very much, God planted a beautiful garden especially for Adam. **5**

God included in that garden all the vegetables and fruit trees that Adam needed to keep him happy, strong, and healthy.

- Compare:

For whom do you make something lovely? A lady will prepare a special meal for her family—because she loves them. A man will work hours on a carpentry project for his wife—because he loves her. Even a little child will spend a great deal of time making a pretty gift for dad or mom—because that child loves his parents.

4 This explanation is necessary preparation for the story of the flood and the first rain seen by men. *"By faith Noah, being warned of God of things not seen as yet..."* (Hebrews 11:7). ☐

5 Note to substitute teacher: The creation of man was covered in Lesson 6.

Lesson 7: God Placed Adam in Eden

God planted a beautiful garden for Adam—because God loved him!

All of the gardens and zoos in the world could not begin to compare with God's garden.

F. God put Adam in the garden.

 Theme: God is supreme and sovereign.

 READ Genesis 2:8.

When God had the garden ready, He took Adam and put him there.

- God didn't ask Adam if he wanted to live there.
- God just took Adam and put him in the garden called Eden.[6]
- Explain:

  God didn't say to the man, "Adam, I have planted a garden. It is a really beautiful place. Would you like to live there?" God didn't offer it to Adam as a place in which to live. God took the man whom He had formed, and He put him in the garden.

- Why could God do this?
- Because God created man, He had the right to put him where He wanted him and to tell him what to do.
- Illustrate:

  In some areas of the world, the relationship between the maker and the owner of things is easily understood, because people have to make for themselves everything they use.

  For example, if a man said, "Who owns that paddle?" the answer would be the name of whoever made it. He made it; therefore, he owns it, and it's his to do with as he wants.

- Compare:

  The distinction in our culture might not be as obvious, but the relationship between the maker and the owner still applies.

  For instance, if you planted a vegetable garden, would your neighbor be right in coming over without asking you and harvesting all your vegetables and taking them home for himself? Of course not! You planted and own the garden; it is yours to do with as you want.

  Does anyone have the right to come into your house and take the things you own? No. Those things belong to you.

  Or, from a different perspective, could a man say to some other man, "I have built a house, so you must live there and take care of the house and the yard." A man could say that to his own wife and to his own children because they are his family. But he does not have the right to say that to others.

  Well, what about Adam? Did God have the right to take Adam and put him in the garden?

  Who owned Adam? God did, because God made him.

- God is the owner of all things.

  He has the right to do what He wishes with us and with all the other things that He has made.

  He has the right to tell us what to do.

  God created Adam, so Adam belonged to God.[7]

Scripture Reference

I Chronicles 29:11,12
Psalm 24:1; 97:9; 100:3
Jeremiah 10:10,23

Teacher's Notes

[6]Some students may ask where the Garden of Eden was located. Bible scholars take different views about this. Some believe it was located in the area of present-day Iraq, as the rivers there bear the same ancient names given in Genesis 2.

Others believe that those who survived the flood of Genesis 6 and 7 gave these pre-flood names to new rivers in a landscape totally transformed by the destructive deluge. They believe that the location of the Garden of Eden is impossible to ascertain. (See *The Genesis Record*, by Henry Morris, p. 90.) ☐

[7]The truth of God's ownership of us is very important to establish. It is a foundational truth which is often missing, even among believers.

One lady who had been a Christian for many years heard this lesson being taught to others. Within a short time, she found out that she needed to go into the hospital for a biopsy. The surgeon's plan was to go ahead and operate if he found cancer. Surgeries had always caused her great fear, but when she meditated on the truth that she and her body belonged to God, she was able to find peace and even joy in trusting Him to do whatever He wanted to with His possession. The night before the biopsy surgery, she was actually excited just to look forward to whatever God had planned for her. The biopsy proved to be benign, but the lady's real joy came from the awesome peace that God had given her beforehand. ☐

Lesson 7: God Placed Adam in Eden

God is the greatest authority; there is none who is higher than God.

 Theme: God is love.

 Theme: God is holy and righteous.

 Theme: God never changes.

God told Adam to take care of the garden, but Adam didn't need to work hard because everything was perfect.

- The weeds didn't grow.
- Snails, grubs, and insects did not eat the fruit or vegetables.
- Consider:

It is impossible for us to picture how things really were in the Garden of Eden. Can you imagine a garden with no weeds or pests? Can you imagine getting all your orders directly from God, knowing that He had entrusted to you the care of all of His wonderful creation? Can you imagine the tremendous love that He had already displayed to Adam?

God had made the earth beautiful; He had set it amidst a backdrop of the sun, moon, and stars; He had filled it with an amazing variety of plant and animal life—not just enough to "live on," but an abundance of everything, all done as an outpouring of God's love. A few plants and a few animals surely would have been enough, but God poured out colors, textures, sounds, tastes, fragrances, varieties, beyond what can be imagined. Adam's situation was perfect and lovely in every way.

How different, you may say, from the world we live in! Different, indeed; and the Bible tells us exactly what has caused the awful changes. Future lessons will deal with these things.

But for now, we will do well to learn this lesson about God, who has not changed one bit: "As for God, his way is perfect..." (Psalm 18:30). God does everything perfectly and in love; He can be trusted to do that which is good and right. "The Lord is righteous in all his ways, and holy in all his works" (Psalm 145:17).

G. The tree of life and the tree of the knowledge of good and evil

 Theme: Man needs God.

 READ Genesis 2:9.

God planted two very important trees in the middle of the garden: the tree of life and the tree of the knowledge of good and evil.

God was Adam's source of life.

- God wanted Adam to have what was good.
- Adam was dependent upon God for everything.
- God wanted to guide Adam in every choice and decision.

 READ Genesis 2:16,17.

Lesson 7: God Placed Adam in Eden

Scripture Reference

Teacher's Notes

 Theme: God communicates with man.

God clearly instructed Adam:

- When God put Adam in the garden, God did not leave it up to Adam to decide which things were right and which things were wrong to do.
- God spoke to Adam and told him what he **must not do** or he would surely die.

God clearly instructs us:

- God is still the same today.
- He has not left us to decide for ourselves what is right and what is wrong.
- God has given the Bible so we can know what pleases and displeases Him.

Psalm 119:105, 128

God instructed Adam:

- God planted an endless variety of trees—trees which supplied food for man and gave beauty to the garden.
- Only **one** tree was denied to Adam.
- He must not eat of the fruit from this tree which was called the tree of the knowledge of good and evil.[8]

[8]Some students may question why God put the tree of the knowledge of good and evil in the garden. Was God trying to "tempt" the man he had made? For the teacher, James 1:13-15 is a good text to consider. It is not yet totally appropriate in the chronological order, so had best not be introduced to the student. But the point can be stated that God is not the one to blame when we disobey. ☐

God knew what was best for Adam.

- From the time God created Adam, God had decided what was good for him.
- God had decided what Adam needed, and God put Adam in the Garden of Eden.
- Adam didn't know anything that was evil or bad because God had given him everything that was good.

Adam had a choice about whether or not to obey God.

Deuteronomy 30:19, 20

- Adam could choose to obey God and eat only what God had said was good, knowing that God's choice was the best for him.
- He could eat of the tree of life and live forever.
- But if Adam disobeyed God and ate the fruit from the tree of the knowledge of good and evil, it would be because Adam had decided that he wanted to be independent of God.
- From the time he ate, he would not only know what was good but he would also know what was evil.
- Instead of God telling him what was good and what was evil, he would have decided to choose for himself.

The result of disobedience:

Romans 6:23a

- If he disobeyed God and wanted to be independent of God, then the result would be death, separation from God.

H. Death is the punishment for disobedience to God.

 Theme: God is holy and righteous. He demands death as the payment for sin.

 READ Genesis 2:17.

God warned Adam: "If you eat the fruit of this tree, you will die immediately."

Teacher's Notes

Lesson 7: God Placed Adam in Eden

Scripture Reference

- Until this time, Adam had only experienced good things because it was God who had provided everything for Adam.
- But now, God warned him very clearly that, if he wanted to be independent of God and disobey Him by eating the forbidden fruit, then he would also come to know what is evil.
- Adam would die.
- Compare:

We may be very vague when we issue a warning, but God's warning was direct. Adam could not miss what God had said: "...in the day that thou eatest thereof thou shalt surely die" (Genesis 2:17).

What did God mean when He told Adam that he would die?

1. **Separation from God**—death of a relationship.
   - Adam would be separated from God.
     - Compare:

     Do you remember what happened to Satan and the angels when they sinned?

     They were cut off from God's love and friendship.
       - Because Satan and the angels who followed him rebelled against God, they were no longer the friends of God.
       - They were separated from God.
       - They were put out of their positions in Heaven, and God prepared a place of terrible punishment where He is going to put them forever.
     - Compare:

     If two friends have a big dispute or an argument which they refuse to forget, do they continue spending time together—just to chat, or to go shopping, or go fishing, or whatever they have previously enjoyed together? No! Disagreement causes separation. People don't want to be with those with whom they disagree.
   - God warned Adam that, if he disobeyed His command, he would no longer be God's friend.

     Adam would become God's enemy as Satan had.

     Adam would be separated from God's love and friendship.

     Adam would die.

     Adam would be separated from God, the source of life and all that is good.

     That part of Adam which was created in God's image so Adam could know, love, and obey God would be separated from Him if Adam ate the forbidden fruit.

2. **Separation from the body**—death of the physical body.
   - God didn't mean that Adam would die physically the same day he ate the fruit.
   - God meant that on that day, Adam would be cut off from God who was the source of his life.
   - Because of this, he would also have to die physically.

   DISPLAY BRANCH BROKEN OFF FROM A TREE

   What happens when a branch is cut off from a tree? The branch doesn't die immediately, does it? The leaves are still green for a few days, and it looks just like it did before it was cut. But because it has been separated from the tree, it cannot receive what it needs

Isaiah 14:13-15

Ezekiel 28:14-17

II Peter 2:4

Revelation 20:10

Lesson 7: God Placed Adam in Eden

to keep it alive. It has been cut off from its source of life. Very soon, it will wither and dry up.

That's what God meant would happen to Adam. If Adam ate of this fruit, he would be immediately cut off from God, the source, giver, and sustainer of his life. The result would be that he would also have to die physically.

- Explain:

When a person dies, he is separated from his body. A person's spirit and soul, that is, the part of him which cannot be seen, leave his body and so he dies.

When God first created Adam's body, Adam didn't have any life. His body was like a dead person's body. Then God breathed life into Adam's nostrils. When God breathed into Adam's body, God gave him his soul and spirit. Our bodies are the houses of our souls and spirits. Every person has his own soul and spirit in his body.

- Compare:

When you go to visit your neighbors, you go to their house. But if they have moved away to another town, they have left their house and are no longer living in it. They are separated from their house. If someone asks where they are living, you would say, "They have moved away to another town. They are not living here in their house anymore."

That is what happens when a person dies. He leaves his body which is the house of his spirit and his soul.

- More clarification:

God told Adam that, if he disobeyed Him and ate the fruit from the tree of the knowledge of good and evil, he would be separated from God who gave him his life.

Adam would no longer enjoy God's love and friendship.

Eventually, Adam's body would also have to die. (His soul and spirit would leave his body and he would die.)

3. Separation forever in the Lake of Fire — death of future joys which God had planned for Adam.

– Finally, if Adam disobeyed God, then not only would his body die, but he would also go eventually to the Lake of Fire.

This is the same place of terrible punishment which God prepared for Satan and his spirit followers.

If Adam chose to disobey, he would be choosing Satan's "reward" instead of enjoying the wonderful things God had in store for him.

– There is no way of escape; no one can escape from God.

– Adam's punishment would be forever and ever.

TO SUMMARIZE, SHOW VISUAL:

THE PENALTY FOR SIN IS DEATH.
1. Separation from God.
2. Separation from the body.
3. Separation from God forever in the Lake of Fire.

Scripture Reference

Matthew 27:50
John 19:30
Acts 7:59

Teacher's Notes

Teacher's Notes

Lesson 7: God Placed Adam in Eden

Scripture Reference

I. God's position of authority over Adam

 Theme: God is supreme and sovereign.

God is sovereign; He had the right to tell Adam what to do.
- God made Adam and gave him his life.
- Adam belonged to God.
- Compare:

  Whatever a person makes belongs to him. If you bake a cake or build a bookshelf, it is yours, and you have the right to do with it as you wish.

  God had the right to tell Adam what to do because Adam belonged to God.

Psalm 24:1

Jeremiah 10:23

 Theme: God is love.

God told Adam what to do because God is loving.
- God wanted to enjoy Adam's love and friendship.
- God only wanted what was best for Adam.

Psalm 32:8-10

 Theme: God knows everything.

God had the right to tell Adam what to do because God knows everything.
- God knew what was best for Adam.
- God was wiser than Adam; God is wiser than all.
- God knew that, if Adam ate the fruit of the tree of the knowledge of good and evil, he would be separated from God, his Creator.
- Compare:

  God still knows what is best. He knows the truth. He has given us the Bible so that we, too, can know the truth. We should listen carefully to God's Word, for He is our all-wise Creator.

Psalm 19:7-11

J. Conclusion:

 Read Psalm 119:73.

 Read Proverbs 1:7.

This kind of fear is not the same kind of fear with which we fear evil; rather it is the sense of awe and overwhelming respect that comes from realizing who God is. **9**
- God is sovereign over all.
- God is our Creator.
- God is our owner.
- God is the all-knowing and all-powerful one.
- God is the holy and righteous one who demands death as the payment for sin.

Think of the things we have already learned about God!
- He alone existed in eternity past before anything was created.
- He created all things from nothing.

Psalm 90:1,2

Proverbs 2:1-5

Isaiah 43:7

Hebrews 1:10-12; 11:3

---

9 These truths which are so foundational to spiritual knowledge are exactly 180 degrees away from what our society is teaching. Do not be surprised if your students have some problems with God's ownership of us and our need to fear God. Your students may disagree with the Bible, but the Word will still be doing its work, piercing deeply into their hearts. Just be sure to present these truths clearly. Do not "argue" them—just establish them as what God says! ☐

Lesson 7: God Placed Adam in Eden

Scripture Reference		Teacher's Notes

- He has all power and all knowledge, is everywhere all the time, and is unchanging.
- He created man and designed man to be under God's sovereign authority.

We would be very foolish not to have a fear of and a high regard for one with such awesome power!

Yet this same God wants to communicate with us and has given us His Word.

In our next lesson we will study God's creation of the first woman, Eve.

Only as we consider who God is can we begin to have true knowledge about life, for God is the one who created life.

And He loves us enough to communicate these answers to us as we seek to know Him through His Word, the Bible!

QUESTIONS:

1. Does God ever begin a thing and then not finish it? *No.*

2. Why doesn't God begin things and then leave them unfinished? *Because God never changes. Nothing can hinder Him from doing what He plans to do.*

3. Why did God rest on the seventh day? *Because all His work of creating things was finished.*

4. Did God send rain to water the plants when the earth was first created? *No, God watered the plants by mist which rose up from the earth.*

5. For whom did God plant the garden of Eden? *For Adam.*

6. Why was it right for God to put Adam in the garden even though God didn't ask him if he wanted to live there? *God created Adam, so he rightfully belonged to God.*

7. To whom do all things, spirits, and people belong? *To God, their Creator.*

8. Of how many trees in the garden was Adam allowed to eat the fruit? *All of them except one.*

9. Who put the tree of life in the garden for Adam? *God.*

10. What was the name of the tree, the fruit of which God did not want Adam to eat? *The tree of the knowledge of good and evil.*

11. What did God say would happen to Adam if he ate of the fruit from the tree of the knowledge of good and evil? *Adam would die.*

12. What did God mean when He said that man would die?

    a. *Man would be immediately separated from God, the source of his life.*

    b. *His body would die when his soul and spirit were separated from his body.*

    c. *Man's body, soul, and spirit would be separated from God forever in the place which God prepared for Satan and his demons.*

Scripture Reference		Teacher's Notes

LESSON 8: God Made Eve

OVERVIEW

This lesson shows God's sovereign creation of woman as a gift to man.

Some points:
- God knew Adam's need for a wife.
- Adam named all the animals but found no suitable companion among them.
- God created the woman from Adam's rib.
- God created the woman perfect because God is perfect.
- God ordained marriage.

LESSON PREPARATION
This section is for you, the teacher.

The passages in the Scripture Reference column are for your own study in preparing for this lesson. Since they may contain concepts that run ahead of the lesson, they are not to be taught at this point.

Note: If you have not taught previously from this series of lessons, please read carefully the note to teachers in the front of this book.

SCRIPTURE: Genesis 2:18-25

LESSON GOALS:

- To show that God in His sovereignty and love and holiness and wisdom and power provided a wife for Adam.

THIS LESSON SHOULD HELP THE STUDENTS:

- To see God's wisdom and love in providing exactly what we need.
- To see that God values both man and woman very highly and wants us to value one another.
- To see that marriage was ordained by God.

PERSPECTIVE:

In our culture, the sanctity of marriage has been almost obscured by the popular desire to control one's own life and to submit to no one. Sanctity is an appropriate word to describe marriage; "sanctity" means "holiness of life and character...inviolability, sacredness...." (Webster's Dictionary).

A thoughtful look at Scripture is the best way to renew our correct perspective on marriage. This lesson "lays the first block" in understanding God's plan for marriage. If we see that marriage is a union ordained (officially decreed) by God, we cannot consider it outdated (God has not changed His decree regarding marriage), nor can we consider it something just to be tried out to see if it works.

God designed man and woman in His image and gave them sacred responsibilities toward Him and toward each other. If we see ourselves in the light of God's original design for mankind, we will also see ourselves accountable to Him and loved by Him. The self-esteem so earnestly sought by many in our society can only be found in seeing ourselves as related to our Creator.

VISUALS:

- Chronological Picture No. 4, "Adam and Eve in the Garden"

NOTE:

This lesson is short. If you have time remaining at the end of this lesson, you may want to begin Lesson 9, which is a review of all that has been taught thus far.

Lesson 8: God Made Eve

Teacher's Notes | **Scripture Reference**

ON TEACHING THIS LESSON:

These lessons are designed to **teach unbelievers**. You are carefully laying a scriptural foundation on which the Gospel will later be presented. If your class contains believers, teach with the goal of giving them an understanding of the basis for their faith and **with the goal of enabling them to teach the same material to unbelievers**.

DON'T COMPLICATE THE MESSAGE!

As you teach, keep in mind that this is a directed study—not an exhaustive survey of the Bible and not an unlimited group discussion. Keep your lesson on track and moving ahead by limiting and directing any discussion.

Carefully follow the outline. Emphasize the doctrinal themes.

LESSON FORMAT: The **center column** below contains the lesson material to be taught to the students. The **bold outline headings** are only for reference and need not be spoken, as they are incorporated into the outlined material that follows. The material in the **side columns** is for the teacher's own reference and is not intended to be included in the lesson.

TO BE TAUGHT TO THE STUDENTS
(Center Column Only)

LESSON OUTLINE:

REVIEW questions from Lesson 7.

A. INTRODUCTION:

We continually hear conversations about marriage.[1]

- Some say that marriage is something to be tried out to see if it will work—sort of an option, depending on how you feel about it.
- Many people are even suggesting that the idea of marriage is outdated.

But what does the Bible say about marriage?

- Did you know that God instituted marriage in the beginning?
- Right here in Genesis 2 we find part of the wedding service spoken in many ceremonies even today.

Let's take a look at the roles God gave the first man and woman.

B. God decided that Adam needed a wife to help him and to be his companion.

 Theme: God is supreme and sovereign.

 READ Genesis 2:18.

God decided that Adam should not live alone.

- God was his Creator and knew what was best for him.
- God didn't ask Adam what he wanted or thought best.
- God made the decision to make a wife for Adam.

 Theme: God is love.

---

[1] In this lesson you will **not** be discussing marriage relationships. You will simply be presenting the fact that God originally ordained marriage, and He has not changed.

(See also note 4 with outline point F.) ☐

170

Lesson 8: God Made Eve

Scripture Reference		Teacher's Notes
	God loved Adam and wanted him to be complete.	
	- God knew that Adam wouldn't continue to be happy if he remained alone.	
	- Because God loved Adam and wanted the best for him, He decided to make a wife for him.	
Matthew 6:8b Philippians 4:19	God knows ahead of time just what our needs will be, and He also knows the best way to meet those needs.	
	- You will see that He didn't create Adam's wife at the same moment or in the same way He created Adam.	
	- He created her at just the right time and in just the right way to meet Adam's needs.	

C. God brought all of the animals before Adam to be named by him.

 READ Genesis 2:19,20.

God had placed Adam as master over all the animals, so God also gave Adam the responsibility of giving them all their names.[2]

God brought to Adam every creature He had made, and Adam named them all.

[2]Dr. John Whitcomb, a spokesman for biblical creation, has said that Adam's ability to name all the animals gives insight into his perfect intelligence. At this point, Adam had not sinned, so his mind was still in the perfect state in which God had created it. ☐

D. There was no suitable companion for Adam among the animals.

 Theme: Man needs God.

 READ Genesis 2:20.[3]

God created man very different from the animals.
- Man was made in God's image so he could know, love, and obey God.
- The animals could not know, love, and obey God like man could.
- Animals are not interested in the things in which people are interested.
- They cannot do many of the things that people do.

Adam needed someone to whom he could talk and who could do the same things that he could do.
- No animal could be a suitable companion for man.
- He needed someone more like himself.

Man couldn't do anything to provide himself with a companion and wife.
- Neither the angels nor Satan, or his demons, could make a wife for Adam.
- God alone could make a wife for Adam.

Acts 17:24,25

God knew that Adam would need a wife; God loved man and did not want him to be alone.

[3]Note: the KJV words "help meet" mean "suitable helper." ☐

E. God created Eve from Adam's rib.

 Theme: God is all-powerful.

 READ Genesis 2:21,22.

Lesson 8: God Made Eve

Teacher's Notes

Scripture Reference

Only God could do this.
- He knows everything.
- He can do anything He wants to do.

Jeremiah 32:27

God made the first woman as a gift for man.

- Compare:

  If someone who loves you were to give you a very special gift, would you take good care of it? Of course you would! It would be valuable to you because of the care and concern and love expressed by the one who gave it to you.

  God gave a wife to Adam, and God expected Adam to take good care of her and to love her.

- Consider:

  Even though all of the animals must have seemed very interesting (and Adam had seen them all as he named them), imagine Adam's delight in seeing this lovely woman whom God had made for him! She, like Adam, was created by God, but God had not made her from the dust of the ground as he had made Adam. God had actually made her from part of Adam's own body, Adam's rib. How precious and close she must have been to Adam! And God had given her a mind and emotions and a will, so she also was able to communicate with God and with Adam.

F. Marriage was ordained by God.

 Theme: God is holy and righteous.

 READ Genesis 2:23,24.

God made woman for man so they could be married, live together, and have children. **4**

- *"...Be fruitful, and multiply, and replenish the earth..."* (Genesis 1:28).
- This was God's command to Adam.

  Consider:

  Because God created everything perfect, we can only imagine just how lovely this woman really was! And God had made her to be that perfect "suitable helper" (Genesis 2:20, KJV "help meet") that Adam needed.

  How satisfied Adam must have been with this dear wife who was given him by God, suited perfectly for his needs, made from part of his own body, endowed with the ability to communicate with him and with God, and commanded, with Adam, to fill the earth and to rule over it. To Adam, uniting with his wife in marriage must have seemed very good indeed.

Marriage was God's perfect plan for Adam and Eve.

- Eve was Adam's gift from God, perfectly suited to Adam's needs.
- Everything that God does and says is good because He is perfect.

  He cannot think, say, or do anything evil.

 Read James 1:17.

Marriage is good because God gave marriage to man.

---

4 At this point, do not begin teaching on husband and wife relationships, adultery, or sexual immorality. Do not teach reformation or sanctification before you have discussed the need of and God's provision for salvation. You are laying foundations on which you will build later.

Our teaching must begin with the root of sin before we point to the fruit of sin. In Genesis 3, we will teach about the root of sin. Man, through disobedience, was separated from God and so became a sinner by nature. In Genesis 4, we begin to see the fruit of man's sin nature clearly evidenced in the life of Cain. If you emphasize the fruit of sin (e.g., adultery, stealing, lying, etc.) before your students realize that what they do only shows what they are, they may turn to self-reformation in an effort to clean up their lives before God. Do not run ahead of the chronological story in either its historical or doctrinal development. ☐

Lesson 8: God Made Eve

Scripture Reference | Teacher's Notes

G. Adam and Eve were unaware that they were naked, and they were totally unembarrassed.

 READ Genesis 2:25.

Suggested Visual:

 CHRONOLOGICAL PICTURE NO. 4, "ADAM AND EVE IN THE GARDEN"

H. Conclusion

Life was perfect for Adam and Eve.
- God had given them everything they needed.
- And He had surrounded them with beauty and abundance far beyond their physical needs.
- They were able to communicate with God and with each other.
- He had made them rulers over His creation.
- He was present with them to guide them in every decision.
- Their work wasn't hard.
- They had no sickness.

What happened?
- We will study later about the drastic events that changed all this peace and beauty.

But God's Word hasn't changed.
- Thousands of years have passed since Adam and Eve became man and wife, but God has never altered what He first wrote about marriage.
- God has not changed His mind about marriage.

Hebrews 13:4

Next we are going to review what we have learned so far.
- Review gives you a good opportunity:
    To "firm up" what you have learned
    To clear up misunderstandings
    To learn things you might have missed the first time through.
- Be sure to come.

QUESTIONS:

1. Who decided that Adam needed a wife as a companion? *God did.*

2. Why did God decide to make a wife for Adam? *Because God loved Adam and did not think it was good for Adam to be alone.*

3. Was it right for God to decide to do this without asking Adam? *Yes, God created Adam. God is over everything, every spirit, and every person.*

173

Lesson 8: God Made Eve

Teacher's Notes

Scripture Reference

4. How did God make the first woman? *God put Adam to sleep. He took out one of Adam's ribs. God then made the first woman from Adam's rib.*

5. How was it possible for God to make Eve from one of Adam's ribs? *Nothing is impossible to God. He can do anything He wants to do.*

6. Who told Adam and Eve to marry and to have children? *God, their Creator.*

Scripture Reference

Teacher's Notes

LESSON 9

Review of Lessons 1-8

LESSON PREPARATION
This section is for you, the teacher.

Note: If you have not taught previously from this series of lessons, please read carefully the note to teachers in the front of this book.

SCRIPTURE: Genesis 1, 2

GENERAL TOPIC:

- Review of what has been taught so far about the Bible, God, Satan, and man.

REVIEWING WHAT HAS BEEN TAUGHT—
Some Special Considerations:

As we have taught through Genesis 1 and 2, we have introduced God, Satan, and man, the three main characters in the whole historical drama recorded in the Scriptures. We are now ready to teach Genesis 3, one of the most important chapters in the whole Bible. The origins of man's sinfulness, death, and all earth's miseries, along with the first promise of a Saviour are revealed in Genesis 3. However, the historical and the doctrinal foundational truths of Genesis 3 cannot be grasped apart from a basic understanding of the character of God, Satan, and man. In order to ensure that your students really do comprehend, Lesson 9 is a review of the main points already taught about these three persons. Also included are some questions concerning the authority of God's Word, the Bible.

Review by asking questions.

1. If you ask a question and they cannot answer or give a wrong answer, ask some other relevant question or give them some clues. If they cannot answer after a little help, go ahead and tell them. Do not rebuke them if they do not know the answer, and be careful not to embarrass anyone by belaboring the question.

2. If you have several students, direct some questions to the whole group and others to individuals.

3. If one or two people are answering most of the questions, you may want to go around the group, one by one, giving each person the opportunity to answer. Be careful not to embarrass anyone by pressing for answers.

4. If your class is very small, you may want to give each student a question sheet and talk through the questions less formally. You still need their feedback, and this will keep you from having to do all the asking if they can look at the sheet with you.

5. Some of these questions involve controversial issues. You may have some students who want to debate these issues. Let them know that you appreciate their interest, but let them know, too, that the purpose of the class is not debate. Many of these issues have been debated in the past and undoubtedly will be in the future. But the purpose of the class is to show what the Bible says and to learn the Word of God accurately. Whatever you do, be sure to limit discussion of these controversial sub-

OVERVIEW

This lesson is a review of what has been taught thus far regarding the Bible, God, Satan, and man.

This review is important preparation for Genesis 3, the story of the fall of man, which is covered in following lessons.

Lesson 9: Review of Lessons 1-8

jects. Winning an argument will not help convince a heart. Just allow the Holy Spirit to use the truth and be firm but loving and patient with those who disagree.

Remember to use the graphics described and illustrated in Lesson 1: the "clothesline" showing key events; the visual showing that we are studying the top of the main events, not the layers of detail; and the visual showing that we are studying the firm foundation, not the "upper structure."

Review is extremely important; don't skip it just to save time. Reviewing will help to solidify information in the students' minds and will help you as a teacher to know how well you are communicating and what areas need extra attention as you continue to teach. No matter how well you may have said it, the proof of the teaching will lie in what your students have learned! And an excellent way to know what's been learned is to ask questions.

ON TEACHING THIS LESSON:

These lessons are designed to **teach unbelievers.** You are carefully laying a scriptural foundation on which the Gospel will later be presented. If your class contains believers, teach with the goal of giving them an understanding of the basis for their faith and **with the goal of enabling them to teach the same material to unbelievers.**

DON'T COMPLICATE THE MESSAGE!

As you teach, keep in mind that this is a directed study—not an exhaustive survey of the Bible and not an unlimited group discussion. Keep your lesson on track and moving ahead by limiting and directing any discussion.

Emphasize the doctrinal themes.

The center column below contains the questions to be asked of the students. The material in the side columns is for the teacher's own reference and is not intended to be included in the lesson.

TO BE TAUGHT TO THE STUDENTS
(Center Column Only)

LESSON OUTLINE:

A. The Bible

Before we learn any more about the story of Adam and Eve, we are going to review what we have already learned about the Bible, God, Satan, and the first man and woman God created. We will begin by asking you some questions about God's Word, the Bible.

1. Who is the author of the Bible? *God.*

2. Whom did God use to write down the Bible? *He used over 40 men, all of whom were Jewish except one.*

3. To whom is the Bible written? *To everyone in the whole world.*

4. Has the Bible changed over the years since it was first written? *No. The Bible has not and will not change.*

5. God's Word was written down over a period of how many years? *1,600 years.*

Lesson 9: Review of Lessons 1-8

Scripture Reference

Teacher's Notes

OPTIONAL DISCUSSION QUESTION:

6. Why has God given us the Bible? *He wants to communicate with us—He wants us to know Him, and He wants us to know how to live.*

B. God

1. In your own words, define what we mean when we say God is sovereign. *Sovereign means the highest power; supreme; ruler.*

2. Does God have a material body? *No, He is Spirit, and does not have flesh and bones as we do.*

3. Was there ever a time when God wasn't living? *No.*

4. Does God change or could God die? *No, God is always the same. He can never die, for He is eternal.*

5. We need food, water, air, the earth to walk on, and the sun to warm us, but what does God need? *God doesn't need anything.*

6. How then does God live? *He lives by His own power.*

7. Where is God? *God is everywhere at the same time.*

8. How many Gods are there? *There is only one God.*

9. Who are the three persons who are this one God? *God the Father, God the Son, and God the Holy Spirit.*

10. What did God use to make the heavens and the earth? *God didn't use anything. He made everything out of nothing.*

11. How did God create everything? *By speaking and commanding them to appear.*

12. How could God make the heavens and the earth? *God is almighty. There is nothing He cannot do. He knows everything and has the power to do anything.*

13. What did God say about everything that He made? *He said that everything was very good.*

14. Why could God make everything perfect? *Because He is perfect.*

15. Why did God prepare such variety and beauty and make so many good things on the earth for man? *Because God is loving and kind.*

16. God created the sun, the moon, and the stars to always follow the same course. What does this teach us about God? *God is a God of law and order.*

17. When scientists and engineers speak of physical laws, whose laws are these? *God established all the physical laws of the universe. Man is only using what God made.*

18. Why is God the rightful owner of everything? *He created all things, and He gave everything life.*

19. Why does God have the right to demand obedience from us? *Because He is our Creator and owner.*

THE FOLLOWING ARE OPTIONAL DISCUSSION QUESTIONS. **1**

20. Considering what you have already learned about God, what do you think of statements like these:

    a. "The Man Upstairs"

[1] If you use this type of discussion question, be careful to keep the discussion under control. Students should be given opportunity to briefly express their opinion and not be put down for what they think. But do not let someone dominate the discussion, especially with wrong answers.

You are trying to make your students evaluate their own ideas from the past in light of what they are learning.

Be patient with them.

If someone says of another student's answer, "That's wrong!" you might reply, "Well, we are just asking for opinions now. What do **you** think?" ☐

Teacher's Notes

Lesson 9: Review of Lessons 1-8

Scripture Reference

b. "Everyone has to find a 'higher power.'"

c. "Religion is a personal thing; everyone is entitled to his own opinion about God."

21. How do Genesis 1 and 2 counter the common belief that everything came into being by chance? *The Bible says God created everything, and that He did it in a very systematic way. Chance was not involved in creation.*

22. How do Genesis 1 and 2 counter the common belief that man evolved? *The creation of man is specifically detailed as being unique from all the rest of creation: man was created in God's image and God breathed into man the breath of life; Eve was created from Adam's rib. No "evolutionary process" is mentioned or hinted at.*

23. Give some evidences from things you can see around you and from what you know about the Bible that show that life was created rather than evolved. *Animals, plants, man all have complex systems that could not have happened by chance. The Bible is a historical document, not a book of theories. The Bible says God created everything. The Bible has not changed through the centuries; man's theories are constantly changing.*

24. God has shown us a great deal about Himself by what He has made — every day we see His creation and should know that one greater than us has done these things. You have also learned many things about God's character in what we have studied so far in His Word. What things in particular stand out to you about God's character?

C. Satan

1. Where did all the spirits come from? *They were all created by God.*

2. Did God create the spirits with bodies of flesh and bones? *No.*

3. Did God create all of the spirits good, or did He create some good and some bad? *God created them all good.*

4. Why did God create the spirits? *To be His servants.*

5. Where did they all live in the beginning when God first created them? *With God in Heaven.*

6. Are each of the spirits everywhere at the same time like God is? *No. There are spirits all over the world, but they cannot be in all places at the same time like God.*

7. Who was the most intelligent and beautiful angel created by God? *Lucifer.*

8. What position did God give Lucifer? *Leadership over all of the other angels.*

9. Whom was Lucifer to serve and obey? *God, his Creator.*

10. What did Lucifer plan to do? *He planned to be like God and to take God's position.*

11. Who else followed Lucifer in His rebellion against God? *Many of God's angels.*

12. What did God do? *God removed Lucifer and the angels who joined him in rebellion from their position as God's servants.*

Lesson 9: Review of Lessons 1-8

Scripture Reference

Teacher's Notes

13. What is Lucifer's name now and what does it mean? *Satan, which means adversary, enemy, opponent, accuser.*

14. What place of punishment did God prepare for Satan and his demons? *The Lake of Fire as their future place of punishment.*

15. Whom is Satan against? *He is against God and everything which God loves.*

D. Man

1. What great difference was there between the creation of man and the creation of animals? *God made man in His image.*

2. What does it mean that God made man in His image? *God made man like Himself with a mind so man could know God, emotions so man could love God, and a will so man could choose to obey God.*

3. Was man good or bad when God created him? *Man was good.*

4. After the first man Adam was created, over what did God give him control? *The earth and everything in it.*

5. Where did God place Adam after He created him? *In a beautiful garden called Eden which God Himself prepared for Adam.*

7. What two very important trees did God also place in the garden of Eden? *The tree of life and the tree of the knowledge of good and evil.*

8. God told Adam that he must not eat of the fruit of which tree? *The tree of the knowledge of good and evil.*

9. What did God say would happen to man if he disobeyed and ate the fruit of the tree of the knowledge of good and evil? *God said that man would die.*

10. What did God mean when He said that man would die?

    a. *Man would be separated immediately from God, the source of his life. He would no longer be in friendship with God.*

    b. *His body would die when his soul and spirit were separated from his body.*

    c. *Man's body, soul, and spirit would be separated from God forever in the place which God prepared for Satan and his demons.*

11. Whom did God create for Adam after He placed Adam in the garden of Eden? *God created Eve to be Adam's wife.*

12. Why did God create Eve? *Because there was no animal that was a suitable companion for Adam and because God loved him, He did not want Adam to be alone. God wanted man to have children.*

13. Describe Eve's God-given role at the time God created her. *She was to be Adam's helper, a companion for him so he would not be lonesome. She was also commanded, with Adam, to rule over all of the other creatures God had made and to be fruitful and fill the earth and subdue it.*

14. Was Adam the only one who could communicate with God? *No, Eve was also created in God's image and given a mind and emotions and will so she could communicate with God and with Adam.*

179

Lesson 9: Review of Lessons 1-8

Teacher's Notes

Scripture Reference

OPTIONAL DISCUSSION QUESTION:

15. In light of what we've learned about God and man, what do you think about these statements:

　　a. "Do your own thing!"
　　b. "I don't answer to anybody!"
　　c. "I can do whatever I want with my life, because it belongs to me."

Scripture Reference

Teacher's Notes

Lesson 10: Adam and Eve Disobeyed God

LESSON PREPARATION
This section is for you, the teacher.

The passages in the Scripture Reference column are for your own study in preparing for this lesson. Since they may contain concepts that run ahead of the lesson, they are not to be taught at this point.

Note: If you have not taught previously from this series of lessons, please read carefully the note to teachers in the front of this book.

SCRIPTURE: Genesis 3:1-8

LESSON GOALS:

- To show Satan's hatred for God and for man, and Satan's character as a liar, deceiver, accuser, and murderer.
- To show man's choice to willfully disobey God and the immediate results of that sin.

THIS LESSON SHOULD HELP THE STUDENTS:

- To see that Satan is God's enemy and the student's enemy.
- To recognize some of Satan's schemes.
- To realize the need to know and believe God's Word.
- To see the terrible consequences of sin.

PERSPECTIVE FOR THE TEACHER:

Many people in our society think that they know a great deal about the Bible. They have heard about God; they have heard about Adam and Eve and the garden; they have heard about Adam and Eve's sin; they have heard about Satan.

But to many people, these things they have heard are only a story or a myth. They may have been taught to view the story of Adam and Eve as an allegory or a myth. Or they might even tell you that they believe the Bible, but in actuality, they have not taken the time to read or study God's Word nor have they allowed what little they have heard to have any application in their own lives.

What a tragedy and shame this is when we have the Bible so readily available to us! How accountable we are to God for what we have decided to ignore or reject!

Reading these passages of Scripture should begin to open the eyes of your students who have merely "heard of" the story. Discussing the truths presented here should allow your students to realize that this is no simple story of an "apple" and a snake and a woman. Instead, this is the critical point of all human history before the coming of Christ.

VISUALS:

- Chronological Picture No. 4, "Adam and Eve in the Garden"
- Chronological Picture No. 5, "The Fall of Man"

OVERVIEW

This lesson presents Satan's deception of Eve and Adam's disobedience of God's command.

Considered in this lesson:
- Satan's characteristics and tactics
- The immediate results of Adam and Eve's sin—separation from God.

Teacher's Notes

Lesson 10: Adam and Eve Disobeyed God

Scripture Reference

- Chronological Picture No. 6, "Fig Leaf Coverings"
- This lesson contains visuals which may be prepared ahead of class or done as you teach.
- Bring the tree branch that was used with Lesson 7. (This branch will be used again in Lesson 13.)

ON TEACHING THIS LESSON:

These lessons are designed to **teach unbelievers.** You are carefully laying a scriptural foundation on which the Gospel will later be presented. If your class contains believers, teach with the goal of giving them an understanding of the basis for their faith and **with the goal of enabling them to teach the same material to unbelievers.**

DON'T COMPLICATE THE MESSAGE!

As you teach, keep in mind that this is a directed study—not an exhaustive survey of the Bible and not an unlimited group discussion. Keep your lesson on track and moving ahead by limiting and directing any discussion.

Carefully follow the outline. Emphasize the doctrinal themes.

LESSON FORMAT: The **center column** below contains the lesson material to be taught to the students. The **bold outline headings** are only for reference and need not be spoken, as they are incorporated into the outlined material that follows. The material in the **side columns** is for the teacher's own reference and is not intended to be included in the lesson.

TO BE TAUGHT TO THE STUDENTS
(Center Column Only)

LESSON OUTLINE:

A. Introduction

The portion of the Bible we're going to study today relates one of the most critical events in all history.

We need to understand the background of what took place; that's why we took time last week to review.

Now we're going to do another brief review which will lead us into today's lesson.

1. Where did God place Adam after He created him? *In a beautiful garden called Eden which God Himself prepared for Adam.*

2. What two very important trees did God also place in the garden of Eden? *The tree of life and the tree of the knowledge of good and evil.*

3. God told Adam that he must not eat of the fruit of which tree? *The tree of the knowledge of good and evil.*

4. What did God say would happen to man if he disobeyed and ate the fruit of the tree of the knowledge of good and evil? *God said that man would die.*

5. What did God mean when He said that man would die?

182

Lesson 10: Adam and Eve Disobeyed God

a. *Man would be separated immediately from God, the source of his life. He would no longer be in friendship with God.*

b. *His body would die when his soul and spirit were separated from his body.*

c. *Man's body, soul, and spirit would be separated from God forever in the place which God prepared for Satan and his demons.*

6. Whom did God create for Adam after He placed Adam in the garden of Eden? *God created Eve to be Adam's wife.*

7. Why did God create Eve? *Because there was no animal that was a suitable companion for Adam and because God loved him, He did not want Adam to be alone. God wanted man to have children.*

B. Life in the Garden of Eden

Life in the garden was pleasant for Adam and Eve; everything was perfect.

Suggested Visual:

CHRONOLOGICAL PICTURE NO. 4, "ADAM AND EVE IN THE GARDEN"

- They had everything that they needed.
- God was their friend; He loved them, and they were very happy.
- God had put Adam in the position of manager over all of God's beautiful creation.

    Since there was no disease or sickness or pests or weeds or thorns, Adam's job was pleasant.

    He only needed to go to God for direction, and God would tell him exactly what was best to do.

- God had given Adam and Eve a variety of plants and fruits and vegetables to eat.
- Financial worries were unknown because finances were unknown—everything they needed was already provided!
- Adam and Eve were able to communicate with God and with each other.

    They had not sinned, so there was no hindrance to their communication with God or with each other.

    They had never argued or hurt each other with words, nor had they done anything wrong.

- They had perfect friendship and fellowship with God and with each other.

Suggested Visual:

Lesson 10: Adam and Eve Disobeyed God

Teacher's Notes

Scripture Reference

[1] We know that Satan was aware of this warning because he falsely restated it to Eve (Genesis 3:1). ☐

But what about God's great enemy, Satan?
- Satan knew about God's warning to Adam concerning the tree of the knowledge of good and evil.[1]
- Because Satan hates God, he wanted to destroy the man and woman that God had made.
- Therefore, Satan planned to deceive Eve.

C. Satan used the serpent to disguise himself and deceive Eve.

 Theme: Satan fights against God and His will. Satan is a liar and a deceiver. He hates man.

 READ Genesis 3:1.

This wasn't just a snake talking to Eve.
- Satan himself had entered into the snake.
- He disguised himself as a snake so he could deceive Eve.
- The serpent was more clever than any other animal which God had made.

Satan is a deceiver.
- He didn't allow Eve to know that he was the one talking through the snake.
- The more you learn from God's Word, the more you realize how deceitful and wicked Satan is.

  He knows that he is lying.

  John 8:44 says that Satan is a liar and a murderer.

  His name means "deceiver" or "accuser."

  That's exactly what he tries to do.
  - He tries to make what is good appear useless or evil.
  - He tries to make what is evil appear good.
  - He tries to infer that God is lying, but he knows only too well that what God says is absolutely true.

 Read II Corinthians 11:14.

  This is what Satan did to Eve: he deceived her by coming to her in the form of a snake.

  Up until that time, the animals had not been harmful in any way to Adam and Eve or to each other, so Eve was not afraid.

D. Satan still deceives people.

Satan's motives and his deceitful tactics haven't changed; he's still trying to deceive and destroy people.

He doesn't use a serpent like he did with Eve, but he uses whatever means and tactics people will accept.
- Many times Satan deceives people by speaking lies right into their minds.

  When Satan comes to speak to people, he doesn't let them know that he is the one who is speaking to them.

  They think that the thoughts in their minds are their own.

Lesson 10: Adam and Eve Disobeyed God

Scripture Reference		Teacher's Notes
Acts 5:3	But it is really Satan who is putting the thoughts into their minds.	

- Explain:
  - *Actually, Satan himself can only be in one place at one time. But, you may remember that many of the angels followed Satan in his rebellion against God. God removed Satan and his rebellious followers from their positions of service to God in Heaven. These rebellious angels, or spirits, now roam the earth unseen and work with Satan against God and against men. These spirits are the ones whom Satan uses to tell us lies in our minds.*

Satan will speak to you even when you are listening to God's Word.
  - He may put a question into your mind such as, "Why should I believe the Bible?"

II Corinthians 4:4
  - Satan doesn't want anyone to know or to believe God.
  - He hates God and he hates God's Word, the Bible, even though Satan knows that it is true!

Sometimes Satan uses other people through whom he speaks his lies to us.
  - These people may be knowingly following Satan, or they may just be deceived, like Eve.
  - Satan tries to make following these people look very attractive to us, even though it is the way of eventual death.

    He tries to make us feel:
    - That we will miss out on something if we don't follow along.
    - That it is more important for us to follow a wrong leader or a wrong crowd rather than to risk losing our friends by doing what we know is right.

- Or Satan may reach us through another area of our own pride.

    We may not want to identify with the crowd but instead we want to be more wise than everyone else and to be very self-sufficient.

    Satan has brought many people to destruction through the lie that says man can be independent of God and do as he pleases because he is so intelligent and capable.[2]

- In recent days, we are hearing a great deal about Satan worship and similar practices.

    Most people have no desire to follow these things that are obviously satanic.

    But many people are becoming involved in more subtle things that actually have Satan as their focus.

Beware of:
- Anything that makes you look to a power other than God for answers to life.
- Anything that exalts or gives a good, pleasant, or attractive connotation to anything that is really evil.
- Games or music or other entertainment that exalt killing or lying or stealing or filthy language or immorality.
- Anything that denies God's existence or even "waters down" the Bible.

All of these kinds of things are really authored by Satan.

He is the one behind them, no matter how innocent or popular or harmless they might seem.

[2]With these words you are describing humanism. It is not necessary to mention the name, just to identify the characteristics. ☐

Lesson 10: Adam and Eve Disobeyed God

E. Satan tempted and deceived Eve.

 Theme: Satan fights against God and His will. Satan is a liar and a deceiver. He hates man.

 READ Genesis 3:1.

Why did Satan ask Eve this question?
- He already knew the correct answer.
- He didn't care what God had said.
- He was testing Eve so he could trick her.
- He was attempting **to cast doubt on God's Word** — this is one of Satan's favorite tactics.

 Theme: God communicates with man.

 READ Genesis 3:2,3.

Satan had already succeeded in confusing Eve.

Her answer was not what God had said.
- God didn't say they could not touch the fruit.
- He had said they must not eat it.

God's command was for both Adam and Eve.
- God first gave this command to Adam.
- Adam apparently told Eve what God had said.
- But, even though God did not give the command directly to Eve, the command included Eve.
- Whatever God said to Adam included Eve.
- Consider:

  The words in the Bible were spoken to people many years ago, but they are still God's words to each one of us today. God doesn't have different messages for different people. His message is the same to everyone — to all races and nationalities; to men, women, and children. Whatever He says to me in His Word, He also says to you.

 READ Genesis 3:4,5.

Now Satan was calling God a liar.

He was no longer casting doubt; he was **denying the truth** — another of his favorite tactics.

Satan himself is really the liar.
- He said the opposite of what God had told Adam.
- He was saying that what God said was not true.
- Consider:

  God had said: "If you eat the fruit from the tree of the knowledge of good and evil, you will die that same day." God meant that Adam and Eve would be cut off from God, the one who gave them life. God said, "You will die." Satan said, "You will not die." Satan was lying.

What was really behind Satan's lie?
- Satan had rebelled against God's authority.

Lesson 10: Adam and Eve Disobeyed God

Scripture Reference

Teacher's Notes

He sinned when he wanted to take God's place.

He didn't want to obey God any more.

He wanted to be independent of God and rule his own life.

- Now Satan was suggesting to Eve that she should rebel against God.

Satan was suggesting that she should eat the fruit so that she could be like God in knowing what was good and what was evil.

Satan wanted Eve to believe that she wouldn't need God to tell her what was right and what was wrong.

But here is the truth:

Psalm 19:7-12; 119
Proverbs 2; 3:5,6
II Timothy 3:16,17

- God didn't make people to live by their own ideas and thoughts.
- God made us to be guided by His own Word.
- It doesn't matter what I think, what you think, what other people think, or what Satan and his demons say.
- The important thing is what God says.

F. Eve ate and also gave the fruit to Adam.

 Theme: Man is a sinner. He needs God and is helpless to save himself.

 READ Genesis 3:6.

Suggested Visual:

CHRONOLOGICAL PICTURE NO. 5, "THE FALL OF MAN"

I Timothy 2:14

Satan deceived Eve, and she believed him.

- She believed that Satan was telling the truth.
- She believed that she would be wise like God.

Even though Adam knew that God had said not to eat, he deliberately disobeyed God's command.

- Adam turned away from depending on God.

He wanted to be independent of God.

He wanted to decide for himself what was good and what was evil.

Instead of God being first in Adam's heart, Adam now made himself first.

He wanted to be his own boss and do whatever he wanted to do.

Adam didn't want God to rule over him anymore.

Did God have the right to rule over Adam?

I Chronicles 29:11,12
Psalm 24:1

- Yes, God was his Creator.
- Everything he had came from God.

Does God have the right to tell us what to do?

Yes, all that we have comes from God; He gave us our life.

Teacher's Notes

Lesson 10: Adam and Eve Disobeyed God

Scripture Reference

G. Adam and Eve's sin separated them from God.

 Theme: God is faithful; He never changes.

 READ Genesis 3:7,8.

What did God say would happen to them if they ate of the tree of the knowledge of good and evil?

What did God mean by "die"?

- They didn't drop dead immediately when they ate the fruit.
- They were still walking around.
- They were making themselves coverings out of leaves.
- Does this mean that God's Word didn't come true?
- Was Satan right after all?

No! They were separated from God immediately when they ate the fruit.

- God always does what He says.
- He never changes.
- He doesn't forget His threats to punish disobedience of His commands.

 Theme: God is holy and righteous. He demands death as the payment for sin.

Why did their sin separate them from God?

 Read Isaiah 59:2: *"But **your iniquities [sins] have separated between you and your God**, and your sins have hid his face from you, that he will not hear."* ³

[3] The boldfaced portion of the verse is the part you are to emphasize. Don't get sidetracked. ☐

- Because God is holy and righteous, He will not continue in friendship with those who disobey His commands.
- He hates everything that is wrong and punishes all disobedience of His commands by death.
- Romans 6:23 says, *"...the wages of sin is death...."*

Because Adam and Eve disobeyed God, they were cut off from their friendship with God.

- Their relationship with God was dead.

Suggested Visual:

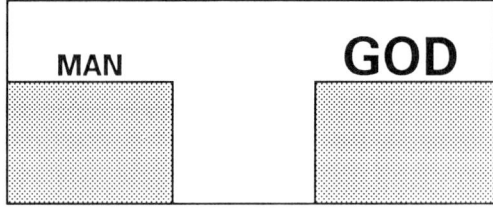

- They were no longer in oneness with God.
- They had taken sides with God's great enemy, Satan, and they, too, were now the enemies of God.
- Illustrate:

Imagine how horrible it would be if a friend of yours turned away from you and began to follow an enemy who hated you and even

Matthew 12:30
Luke 11:23

Lesson 10: Adam and Eve Disobeyed God

wanted to kill you. How heartbreaking it would be to realize that the one who was your friend had become your enemy!

- Compare:

This is what happened when Adam and Eve turned away from their friendship with God and began to follow Satan. Satan is God's great enemy, so when Adam and Eve turned away from God and followed Satan, they, too, became the enemies of God.

DISPLAY BRANCH BROKEN OFF FROM A TREE.

A branch doesn't die immediately when it's broken off from the tree that was its source of life. The process of dying may take many days. But in time the once-green leaves become dry and brown — they are completely dead.

The same thing happened to Adam and Eve. Death wasn't evident in their bodies on the day they disobeyed God. They were still breathing and walking around. But they had died to God. That part of them which was made in God's image so they could know, love, and obey Him was immediately separated from God when they disobeyed His command. They were now separated from Him and had become the enemies of God. Their bodies would also eventually die, and they would go to the place of everlasting punishment which God prepared for Satan and the evil spirits.

H. Signs of separation from God

These were the signs that they were now separated from God:

- First, their attitude toward their bodies changed immediately.

    Before they disobeyed God, they were naked but unembarrassed.

    Now they were separated from God, and their minds were no longer under God's control.

    - Their minds became evil, and their attitude toward their bodies changed.
    - They were embarrassed by their naked bodies.

- Secondly, they tried to provide their own needs.

    Before they were separated from God, they looked to God to provide everything they needed.

    But now they tried to do things for themselves.

    - They clothed themselves with fig leaves.
    - They no longer trusted God to give them what they needed.
    - They were trying to live independently of God.
    - Perhaps they reasoned that if they clothed themselves, God wouldn't notice that anything had happened.

Suggested Visual:

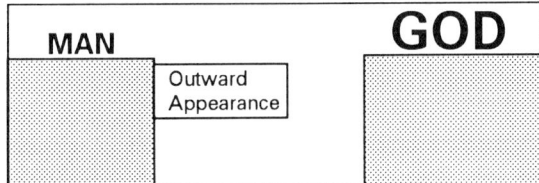

- But God does not accept us based upon our outward appearance.
- Consider:

Just as Adam and Eve tried to make themselves acceptable to God by putting on clothes, many people today think they can

Lesson 10: Adam and Eve Disobeyed God

make themselves acceptable to God by the outward appearances of respectability. Here are some examples:

- *Becoming church members*
- *Being good parents*
- *Endeavoring to be law-abiding citizens*
- *Holding membership in civic and charitable organizations.*

- I Samuel 16:7 says, *"...man looketh on the outward appearance, but the LORD looketh on the heart."*

- Adam and Eve not only tried to cover their nakedness, but when God came to visit Adam and Eve, they also tried to hide from Him.

Suggested Visual:

CHRONOLOGICAL PICTURE NO. 6, "FIG LEAF COVERINGS"

Theme: God is loving, merciful, and gracious.

- Compare:

  Do you have friends whom you enjoy visiting? God loved Adam and Eve, and so He came at the close of the day to talk with them.

  Before they were separated from God, they loved Him and wanted to talk with Him. But when God came after they had disobeyed Him, Adam and Eve hid. Their attitude toward God had changed. Because of their disobedience to God, they were no longer His friends. When God first made Adam and Eve, they were of one mind with God. But this was no longer true. They were now of one mind with Satan. They could no longer know and understand God. They didn't love God anymore, and they were under Satan's control. Now they were on Satan's side.

  Because they had disobeyed God's command, they were ashamed, and they were afraid of God.

- Compare:

  When children deliberately disobey their parents, do they want to be near the parent they have disobeyed? Can they look their parent in the eye? Are they happy to be with the one they've disobeyed?

- Sin—disobedience to God—brings fear and causes people to turn away from God.

- When God created Adam and Eve, they didn't fear anything.

   There was nothing in the world to fear.

   God was their friend.

   No animals would hurt them.

   All the world was good and beautiful.

   Sickness and death did not exist.

- Disobedience to God is the reason that we have fear in the world today.

Hebrews 2:15

Lesson 10: Adam and Eve Disobeyed God

Ever since Adam and Eve disobeyed God, there has been terrible fear in the hearts of men and women.

We may not like to talk about our fears, but each of us has them.

- A few examples:

  Sickness

  Death

  Financial ruin

  Enemy attack

  War.

- Read the paper or listen to the news; we are a society full of fears.

  Is the water really drinkable?

  Is the food safe to eat?

  What will be the outcome of the arms talks?

  What's going to happen in the stock market?

  Or, more personally, will I be able to pay next month's bills?

  Will cancer strike in our home?

  Is it safe for the children to go to the playground?

Do you realize that Adam and Eve did not have to fear any of these things or anything else when God first created them?

Theme: God is faithful; He never changes.

- Do you think that Adam and Eve should have been afraid of God?

  Would God really punish them for their disobedience?

  Or is God like many people who only make idle threats?

  - Compare:

    How often we hear in the news of some terrible threat that comes to nothing. Political leaders threaten war but are not ready to follow through with what they have announced they will do.

  - Compare:

    Or, on a much more personal level, we have known parents who threaten to punish their children for the next episode of wrong behavior. But when the next time comes, the offense is overlooked because the parent is too busy or too tired to carry out the threatened punishment.

    Do you think God is like that? Did God merely threaten Lucifer and the angels when they rebelled? No! God always does exactly as He has promised to do. He is not like us who often fail to do what we have said we would do. God is faithful and does not change or waver or neglect to do what He has promised.

Had Adam and Eve been warned of the consequences of sin?

- Yes! God had clearly warned them.
- He had shown them His lovingkindness, but He had plainly told them the terrible thing that would happen if they disobeyed Him.

- The Devil did not "make them do it;" they themselves chose to sin.

Teacher's Notes

Lesson 10: Adam and Eve Disobeyed God

Scripture Reference

What should Adam and Eve have done in response to God's command?
- They should have obeyed Him out of love.
- And they should have obeyed Him because He had clearly warned them of the punishment for disobedience.
- But Adam and Eve went ahead and disobeyed God in spite of all of His kindness and His stern warning to them.

Now Adam and Eve had good reason to be afraid of God.

Why? Because they had disobeyed Him and He was their Creator.
- They depended upon God for everything.
- The very breath that they had in their bodies was given by God.
- All that they had came from God, and yet Adam had deliberately disobeyed God's command.
- God always punishes those who disobey any of His commands.

John 14:21

Genesis 2:7
Acts 17:25

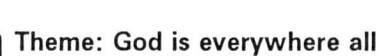 **Theme: God is everywhere all the time; He knows everything.**

Were Adam and Eve able to hide from God?

No! God saw Adam and Eve when they were trying to hide among the trees.

Can anyone hide from God?

Is there anywhere we can go where God is not already there?

No! God is everywhere.
- No one can hide from Him.
- The darkness and the light are all the same to Him.

Psalm 139

 Read Jeremiah 23:23,24.

- Illustrate:

When people do things that they know are wrong, they usually try to do them when other people cannot see them. People do evil things in the dark. But God always sees and hears everything. Nothing can be hidden from God.

God has heard and seen everything that we have said and done from the day that we were born.

H. Conclusion

What you have just heard is no simple tale about a man and a woman and a snake.
- It is the tragic event of man's separation from God.
- Adam and Eve were separated from God because of their sin.
- They were separated from Him immediately, just as He said they would be.

This is one important thing we can learn from this story: God always tells the truth.
- His Word is true.
- He always does exactly what He says.

But in contrast to God who always speaks the truth, Satan is a liar and a murderer.

Lesson 10: Adam and Eve Disobeyed God

- He said Adam and Eve would not die if they disobeyed God, but he knew that they would.
- He deceived, lied, and tempted Adam and Eve because he wanted them to die.

Beware! Satan is still the same today.

- He is not the character with the pitchfork and red suit who is easy to identify.
- He is the Deceiver, the enemy of our souls.
- He will use any method to keep us from listening to God's Word.
- He doesn't want us to listen to God's Word because He wants us to be separated from God forever.

QUESTIONS:

1. When Satan came to deceive Eve, did he come and talk to her face to face so she could see him and know who he was? *No.*

2. What did Satan use to disguise himself when he spoke to Eve? *A snake.*

3. God told Adam that, if they ate the fruit from the tree of the knowledge of good and evil, they would definitely die, but Satan told Eve they would not. What was Satan suggesting God to be? *A liar.*

4. What did Satan tell Eve would happen to them? *Satan said that they would not die but that they would become like God and be able to decide for themselves what is good and what is evil.*

5. Does Satan still try to deceive and trick people? *Yes.*

6. How does Satan speak to people today (not specific instances, but what channels does he use)?

    a. He and his demons can speak directly to people's minds.

    b. He speaks through other people.

7. Does Satan want you to listen to and believe God's words? *No.*

8. Why doesn't Satan want people to hear and believe God's words?

    a. He hates God.

    b. He hates every person and wants them all to go to the everlasting fire.

9. God said that Adam and Eve would die if they ate of the fruit of the tree of the knowledge of good and evil. Satan said they would not die. Who spoke the truth? *God did.*

10. Satan is very strong. Was it all his fault that Adam and Eve sinned? *No. Adam and Eve chose to sin. God had made His instructions clear to them; He had been very loving to them. He gave them a will to make choices; they chose to disobey.*

11. Adam and Eve didn't fall dead immediately when they ate the fruit of the tree of the knowledge of good and evil. God had said they would die for their disobedience. What did He mean?

    a. They would immediately be separated from God, the source of their life—their relationship with God would die right then.

    b. Their bodies would eventually die because of their disobedience.

Teacher's Notes

Lesson 10: Adam and Eve Disobeyed God

Scripture Reference

    c. They would eventually be separated from God forever—body, soul, and spirit—in the Lake of Fire.

12. What did Adam and Eve do when they realized they were naked? Why did they do this? *They made clothes of leaves because their attitudes toward their bodies had changed. They tried to take care of their own needs instead of asking God to help them.*

13. What did Adam and Eve do when they heard God coming to see them? Why did they do this? *They hid because they no longer felt comfortable in God's presence. Their attitude toward Him had changed because of their sin, and they were no longer His friends. They were ashamed and afraid.*

14. Is it possible to hide from God? *No, God is everywhere.*

Scripture Reference		Teacher's Notes

LESSON 11: God's Promise and Curse

LESSON PREPARATION

This section is for you, the teacher.

The passages in the Scripture Reference column are for your own study in preparing for this lesson. Since they may contain concepts that run ahead of the lesson, they are not to be taught at this point.

Note: If you have not taught previously from this series of lessons, please read carefully the note to teachers in the front of this book.

Romans 5:12-21; 8:20-22
I Corinthians 15:21,22

SCRIPTURE: Genesis 3:9-20

LESSON GOALS:

- To show that God knows everything and will punish all sin.
- To show that God would not allow Satan to have a permanent victory in leading man to sin, but that God would send a Deliverer who would overcome Satan and deliver mankind from Satan's power.
- To show the horrible, lasting results of sin.
- To show that man cannot save himself from sin.

THIS LESSON SHOULD HELP THE STUDENTS:

- To realize that no one can get away with sin.
- To realize that God has made a way to overcome Satan.
- To realize that all the problems in the world have come as a result of sin.

PERSPECTIVE FOR THE TEACHER:

You might say that this lesson explains the "mess we are in." We often hear men and women blaming God for their problems and for the problems of the world around them. But Genesis 3 states the truth of the matter very clearly: <u>man's own sin is the cause of man's problems</u>.

Attitudes have not changed since Adam and Eve; if men do not blame God, they blame other men and women for their sins. Reading this passage of Scripture should strike a familiar chord in even the hardest heart. It is like a mirror of what we are inside apart from the new birth in Christ.

Hopefully, your students will not only begin to realize their responsibility for their conduct but also will begin to see their helplessness to hide from God. Remember that men who disobey do have reason to fear God's wrath, so in your teaching do not diminish the awful consequences of sin.

The introduction of God's grace and His promise to send a Deliverer will be meaningful only if you have clearly taught: (1) man's original position of friendship with his loving Creator and owner, God, (2) the awfulness of man's rebellion and disobedience to God, and (3) the horrible and sure consequences of that sin.

Many people in our society feel that they deserve forgiveness. They have a terribly twisted view of God and do not know Him as He is. God is holy and righteous and has decreed that the punishment for sin is death. His provision of a Saviour is the supreme act of His grace—totally unmerited favor.

OVERVIEW

This lesson presents the events that took place immediately following Adam and Eve's sin.

Here in this passage is the first promise of God's plan to send a Deliverer.

Considered in this lesson

- God's omniscience:
  He saw Adam and Eve.
- God's love:
  He called Adam.
- God's holiness:
  He cursed the serpent, Adam and Eve, and the ground.
- Man's sin:
  All men are descendants of Adam; therefore, all die.
- God's grace:
  He promised to send a Deliverer.

Teacher's Notes — Lesson 11: God's Promise and Curse — Scripture Reference

VISUAL:

- Small visual (see illustration in the lesson) showing that Adam and all of Adam's descendants would die

ON TEACHING THIS LESSON:

These lessons are designed to **teach unbelievers.** You are carefully laying a scriptural foundation on which the Gospel will later be presented. If your class contains believers, teach with the goal of giving them an understanding of the basis for their faith and **with the goal of enabling them to teach the same material to unbelievers.**

DON'T COMPLICATE THE MESSAGE!

As you teach, keep in mind that this is a directed study—not an exhaustive survey of the Bible and not an unlimited group discussion. Keep your lesson on track and moving ahead by limiting and directing any discussion.

Carefully follow the outline. Emphasize the doctrinal themes.

LESSON FORMAT: The **center column** below contains the lesson material to be taught to the students. The **bold outline headings** are only for reference and need not be spoken, as they are incorporated into the outlined material that follows. The material in the **side columns** is for the teacher's own reference and is not intended to be included in the lesson.

TO BE TAUGHT TO THE STUDENTS
(Center Column Only)

LESSON OUTLINE

REVIEW questions from Lesson 10.

A. Introduction

Genesis teaches us a great deal about God.

- As we mentioned in our first lesson about the Bible, we are not just reading stories; we are learning about God:

    We are learning what He is like.

    We are learning what He does.

    We are learning how He deals with man.

- Let's listen carefully as we study God's response to Adam and Eve's sin.

    Keep in mind:

    - God had created them—in His own image and for His glory.
    - They belonged to Him.
    - He loved them.
    - He had given them everything they could ever need.
    - He had warned them of the consequences of disobedience.
    - They had **chosen** to disobey Him.

Lesson 11: God's Promise and Curse

B. God called Adam.

 Theme: God communicates with man.

 READ Genesis 3:9.

Because Adam and Eve didn't come to talk with God, God called out, "Adam, where are you?"

- Why did God call out?

    Didn't He know where they were hiding?

    Isn't He everywhere?

    Wasn't He there beside them among the trees?

    Couldn't He see them all of the time?

- Yes, God could see Adam and Eve where they were hiding.
- Why then did He call Adam?

    God called Adam because, although God intended to punish Adam and Eve for their sin, He still loved them.

    God was giving them the opportunity to agree with Him that they were wrong in believing Satan instead of Him.

    God was giving them the opportunity to agree that all He had said to them was the truth.

God has not changed; He still calls today even though we cannot hear His voice like Adam did.

- How does God call to us today?

    God calls us through all the things we can see around us.

    - Illustrate:

    Every day, God's voice is saying to us, "Listen to Me. I am the Creator of all things. I am the true God. I know everything. I am almighty. Look at all the things I have created for you. I love you. Look at all of the food I have made for you. I love you. Look at the life I have given to you. I love you. Listen to Me and seek Me."

    As we look at all the things on the earth and as we look above and see the vastness of the sky and all of the stars and think about the universe that reaches beyond our sight, remember that God is calling out to us, and He wants us to listen to Him.

 Read Psalm 19:1-3.

- God calls to us because He wants us to know Him.

    The great variety and beauty and expanse of His creation should make us stop and think:

    - There is someone greater, wiser, more powerful than man.
    - We need to know Him!

- But God is not only speaking to us through the things He has made; He is also calling us through His Word.

    The Bible is God's message to each one of us.

    - Do you remember learning what a privilege it is for us to have God's Word readily available to us?

        What a horrible thing it would be for us to ignore God's Word!

Scripture Reference:
II Peter 3:9
Romans 1:16,17
Hebrews 2:3

Teacher's Notes

Lesson 11: God's Promise and Curse

Scripture Reference

How important it is for each of us, for me and for you, to know, understand, and believe God's message!

Remember that we discussed how, down through the ages, God has brought His Word to us with extreme accuracy?

He has preserved His message carefully:
- So that we, of this century, may know Him.
- So that you may know Him.
- So that I may know Him.

John 17:3

Philippians 3:10

C. Adam and Eve tried to hide from God.

 Theme: God knows everything.

 READ Genesis 3:10.

Adam and Eve were afraid of God because they had disobeyed His command.
- Compare:

  If children decide to do something their parents have forbidden them to do, they will wait and do it when they think their parents aren't around. But if they hear their parents coming, they will try to hide because they are afraid of being caught and punished. And when a child knows he has disobeyed, he is ashamed and doesn't want to come close to his parents at that moment. Just as children hide because they are afraid and ashamed, so Adam and Eve hid from God.

Adam and Eve had reason to fear.
- They knew what they had done.
- They knew what God had told them would happen because of their sin.

D. God questioned Adam.

 READ Genesis 3:11.

God questioned Adam and Eve in order to give them an opportunity to repent, that is, to change their minds and agree with God that they had done the wrong thing.
- God had the authority and power to question Adam because He created him.

  God created Adam and then made Eve from Adam's rib.

  They both belonged to God.

  He made them to love and obey Him so they would bring glory to His name.

  Isaiah 43:7 says, "...*for I have created him for my glory, I have formed him; yea, I have made him.*"[1]
- God also gives life to us and all people.
- Acts 17:25 says, "...*he giveth to all life, and breath, and all things....*"

  He is our rightful owner.

  Adam and Eve had to answer to God for what they did, and we, too, will all have to answer to Him for everything we have thought and done during our lives.

---

[1] The teacher should quote only the suggested part of Isaiah 43:7 and Acts 17:25 because these verses are both in contexts that would be confusing to the students if the whole verses were read at this time. ☐

Lesson 11: God's Promise and Curse

 Read Hebrews 4:13.

- This verse expresses Adam and Eve's situation, and it also expresses our situation right now.

   God sees everything.

   We must give account to Him for everything we have done.

E. Adam and Eve tried to pass the blame.

 Theme: Man is a sinner. He needs God and is helpless to save himself.

 Theme: God is holy and righteous. He demands death as the payment for sin.

 READ Genesis 3:12,13.

Adam put the blame on Eve.

Eve blamed the serpent.

But God already knew everything that had happened; nothing is hidden from Him.

- Compare:

   When a person gets caught for something he does wrong, he usually tries to blame someone else. Sometimes an innocent person is punished because the one who did wrong puts the blame on him.

   We may try to pass the blame onto someone else, as Adam and Eve tried to do; but God knows everything and will not allow us to escape punishment by blaming someone else.

   Young and old, men and women, will go to great lengths to try to avoid taking responsibility for their own sins. In our society, people often spend large sums of money to buy their way out of punishment for crimes they have actually committed. Unfortunately, clever lawyers, judges who do not uphold justice, and a twisted system of laws all contribute to a legal system in which we see less and less just punishment for crime. Often it is the victim who suffers the worst abuse, even at the hands of the courts.

   This is a sad picture and does not reflect in any way what God intended for justice to be. Some lawyers may be "bought;" some judges may be unwise or easily swayed or even dishonest; some of our laws may be very unjust. But God has not changed. Whatever has slipped past man's justice will not slip past God's justice. God's judgments are firm and unchanging. He is holy and righteous and knows everything and will always do exactly what He has said He will do.

F. God's curse on the serpent

 Theme: God is holy and righteous. He demands death as the payment for sin.

 READ Genesis 3:14.

God cursed the serpent because it had been used by Satan.

Teacher's Notes

Lesson 11: God's Promise and Curse

Scripture Reference

- God does not tell us what the serpent was like before Satan used it to deceive Eve, but we know it did not slide on its belly when God first created it.
- But now God said it must slide on its belly and eat dust.

God knew it was Satan who spoke through the serpent to tempt Eve.

- God knows everything that Satan and his evil spirits think and plan to do.
- They can't hide anything from God.

God will punish Satan and all of his followers for all of their evil deeds and their horrible disobedience to God.

G. The promised Seed of the woman

Once Adam and Eve disobeyed God and followed the advice of Satan, they were separated from God and controlled by Satan.

Ephesians 2:1,2

- They were no longer the children of God.
- They were Satan's children.

Satan had become the god of this world.

John 12:31
II Corinthians 4:4

- At this point, Satan probably thought that he had beaten God and that he would now have complete control of the world and all people.
- This was what Satan had wanted.

But no one can win against God.

- God is the almighty Creator.

God promised that He would send a Deliverer who would overcome Satan and deliver mankind from his power. **2**

READ Genesis 3:15.

- God planned that the promised Deliverer would be the child of a virgin woman.

Isaiah 7:14
Luke 1:27

  Notice that it does not say "their" offspring.

  The man is not even mentioned in this verse.

- When we read of crushing the "head," this is a picture of crushing the leadership or authority of a great power.

  When the "head" is crushed, the rest of the body cannot survive.

  But the one whose "heel" is crushed survives, even though wounded.

  - Explain:

  The Deliverer would fight against Satan, the god of this world and the ruler of evil powers, and the Deliverer would overcome him. Satan would fight against the Deliverer and wound Him, but Satan would not be able to overpower Him. This promised one would destroy Satan and deliver mankind from Satan's power so man would again be in oneness with God.

Theme: God is loving, merciful, and gracious.

We have already learned many things about God through studying Genesis 1 and 2.

- We learned that:

  He was already there when all things began.

---

2 The introduction of the Deliverer opens up the possibility of many comments from your students.

First of all, they may have some knowledge of Christ, so they may want to talk about Him at this point. If your class includes any whom you know are not or who may not be believers, try to encourage all the students to discuss only what has already been presented chronologically to this point. Let them know that you are eager to talk about Jesus Christ, too, and you will be glad to talk with any who are interested after class. But during our class, we will just talk about things as they are introduced in the Bible. Let them know that for now, they need to concentrate on learning these foundational truths.

You may have some students that you will want to talk with alone after class. If they have understanding of the Scriptures, you can go over their comments and questions then. Let them know that you appreciate their interest during class, but remind them that the purpose of the class is to study the Bible chronologically. You might want to mention to them that there are those in the class who do not yet know the whole story, and that during class you will have to be sure to stay with the text so those students can learn without extra confusion. (Continued on next page)

Lesson 11: God's Promise and Curse

|Scripture Reference| |Teacher's Notes|

He is eternal.

He never had a beginning.

- We also learned through observing His acts of creation that:

  He is all-powerful.

  He is everywhere all the time.

  He knows everything.

  He is loving and kind.

- We have also learned that He is holy and righteous; He punishes those who fight against Him and disobey His commands.

- Now we also see that God is gracious and merciful.

 Read Psalm 145:8.

Grace and mercy are two wonderful words.

Someone has said that:

- "Grace" is giving us the good things we need but do not deserve to have.
- "Grace" is God's kindness poured out on undeserving people.
- "Mercy" is not giving us any of the punishment we deserve!
- Explain:

  We know from what we have learned about God that He always punishes sin. But in His great love, God promised to make a special way out by sending a Deliverer so that man could be saved from the punishment he deserved.

  He could have just left Adam and Eve to die and go to everlasting punishment. That is what they deserved, but God promised a Saviour who would deliver them and all mankind from Satan's control and bring them back to God. God is gracious and merciful.

- Illustrate:

  Think about a young man who has gone against his father's instructions and has taken the family car out for a drive. The young man loses control of the car and is seriously hurt. When the father hears of his son's accident, he immediately comes to the hospital to be with his son. The son is very ashamed and fearful to even look at his father. The son knows he is fully deserving of an outpouring of his father's anger.

  But instead of displaying his anger, the father shows his concern for his son's needs. He is kind to his son. Though he knows there must be serious penalties for his son's disobedience, the father concentrates on helping his son recover from his injuries.

  The father has displayed grace by giving his son what he needs instead of what he deserves.

- Compare:

  But God is more loving and gracious than any earthly father could ever be. God gave Adam and Eve everything they needed when He created them. God did not have to give so many good things to them; but He did, because He is loving and kind. When Adam and Eve rebelled against God, they deserved the wrath of God. But what did God do? Did He immediately send them to everlasting punishment? No! Because He is

2(Continued from previous page)

Another problem that you may have is that some students may want to know why God didn't send the Deliverer immediately when Adam and Eve sinned.

This is another of those areas that God does not tell us directly in His Word; we must simply believe that He does all things well and in the proper time. This will probably not satisfy the person who will ask this question. Encourage them to think about what they have already learned about God and His position of sovereignty and His knowledge of all things. Remind them that He is infinitely wiser than we are. Encourage them to direct their thoughts and energies toward learning what the Bible actually tells us. (Few people have really done that!) You might suggest that they concentrate on learning what God is like and what He has done according to His Word, rather than questioning the things which they cannot understand or would have done differently had it been up to them. Be gracious and let them know that you appreciate their questions and their interest. ☐

merciful and gracious, He promised to send a Deliverer to save them from the punishment they deserved.

- When we speak of God's grace and God's mercy, we are usually contrasting it against the background of man's sin.

  God's love is shown throughout creation.

  But we see God's grace and mercy after man has rebelled against the God who loves him.

H. God's curse on the woman

 READ Genesis 3:16.

God spoke to Eve and told her that because she had disobeyed the Lord:

- She and all future mothers would suffer in childbirth.
- Her husband would have authority over her.

I. God's curse on the man and on the earth

 READ Genesis 3:17-19.

Adam had foolishly listened to Eve instead of obeying what God had said to him.

- Adam knew what God had said.
- But he was willing to follow Eve's suggestion rather than to do what he knew to be God's will.
- How subtly Satan works to cause us to believe him instead of God!
- Compare:

Even our own families can hinder us and make us think that we don't need to believe God. Satan used the snake to deceive Eve. But he used Eve to cause Adam to disobey God. Neither Adam nor Eve made right choices, and both of them knew what God had said.

We need to be sure that we are believing God instead of believing men. As we learned before, Satan often speaks his lies to us through people; and he tries to make those lies seem very attractive.

You may remember that our first lesson was on the authority of the Bible. We must keep continually in our minds that God's Word was written to us so that we could know Him and know what is right. God is the supreme authority for all truth; no one is as wise as He is. Eve decided to find out if Satan was wiser than God. And Adam decided he would like to make his own choices about life. The story of the results of Adam and Eve's sin should be enough to warn us to take a good, long look at the Bible, to learn what it really says, and to believe what God tells us in His Word.

Because Adam and Eve listened to Satan, they fell into his trap and disobeyed God; therefore, God said that, from that time, the ground would be cursed.

- Compare:
- Before Adam sinned, he took care of the garden.

  Everything grew without Adam doing any hard work.

  Weeds didn't grow; there were no pests.

- But when Adam sinned, God cursed the earth.

  Many weeds began to grow.

Lesson 11: God's Promise and Curse

This made Adam's work difficult.

The results of sin impacted not only Adam and Eve but also the lovely garden God had given them.

In fact, all of the bad things in the world exist because of disobedience to God.

- Satan and his followers disobeyed God and now roam the earth.
- When man disobeyed, man's sin affected all of God's creation.

Why should man's sin have affected all creation?

- God had made the earth for man.

    Because He loved man, God had given man everything he needed.

    Because He loved man, God had made things not just adequate, but also very beautiful and abundant.

- Now man had rejected God's love for him.
- Part of the consequence was that man would no longer live in a perfect environment.

We live in a world that still suffers from that curse.

- We constantly struggle against sickness, pain, weakness, pain in childbearing, hard work, difficult weather conditions, animal and insect pests, weeds, sorrow, grief, and death.
- None of these things were in the world before Adam and Eve sinned.

    God had given them a perfect place to live and wanted them to live in perfect harmony with Him forever.

    But man chose to rebel against God, and that rebellion brought disastrous consequences which we still suffer under to this day.

Adam's body must die, just as God had said.

- God had made Adam from the dust of the ground.
- Because Adam sinned, God told Adam that his body must die and go back again to the earth.

When He created Adam and Eve, God did not intend for them to die.

- But now Adam and Eve must die because of their disobedience to God.
- The punishment for sin is death—

    Not just physical death

    But separation from God now and forever and eternal punishment in the Lake of Fire.

J. Adam and Eve are the parents of all people.

 READ Genesis 3:20.

Even though people have different colors of skin, we all originally came from the same parents, Adam and Eve.³

Acts 17:26 says that God *"hath made of one blood all nations of men."*

- Eve is the first woman and the mother of every human being.
- Adam is the father of us all.

Adam was separated from God because he turned away from obeying Him.

- Adam's sin ruined his perfect relationship with God and also the perfection of the earth that God had given him to live in.

³This point is very important. Some students may try to argue this fact. Do not argue with them; simply point them to the truth stated in Acts 17:26. ☐

Lesson 11: God's Promise and Curse

- His sin set off a chain of sorrows.

Because of Adam's sin, he would die, and all of his children would also die.

Suggested Graphic:

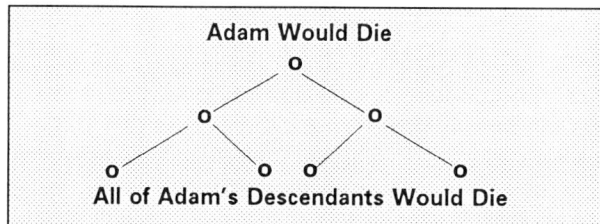

 Read Romans 5:12.

All people in every country die because we are all the descendants of Adam.

K. Conclusion

The Devil did not "make them do it."
- Adam and Eve knew what God had said.
- But they disobeyed Him anyway.

Think about the tremendous love that God had poured out upon Adam and Eve.
- He had created everything good and beautiful and useful for them.
- He created them and gave them life.
- He was their loving Creator, and He communicated with them, telling them everything they needed to know.

Think of the horribleness of their sin and our sin in the face of our loving, holy God.

But think of the grace that God displayed in His promise to send a Deliverer!

God's love is absolutely amazing.

How sad sin appears in light of His love!

Sin brought terrible consequences.
- We live with those consequences every day.
- In the Bible we have seen how all the sorrows of life began.
- And we can see a holy, righteous God—just and true and perfect in all He does.

In our next lesson we will see what God did to graciously provide for Adam and Eve.

QUESTIONS:

1. Did God call Adam because God didn't know where Adam and Eve were? *No, God knew where they were. God wanted them to voluntarily come to Him and admit their sin.*

2. Can anyone hide from God? *No, God sees us at all times, no matter where we are.*

3. Why did God have the right to call Adam and question him?

Lesson 11: God's Promise and Curse

a. God was Adam's Creator.

b. Adam and Eve belonged to God.

c. God made Adam to love and obey Him.

4. Why does God have the right to demand obedience? *Because He gave life to everyone.*

5. What was God's curse on the snake? *From that time, it was to move by crawling on its belly.*

6. What can Satan and the spirits hide from God? *They cannot hide anything from God. He knows their every thought.*

7. Whom did God promise to send? *God promised to send a Deliverer.*

8. How was this Deliverer to come? *Through the seed of the woman.*

9. What did God say that the virgin's Son would do? *He would overcome Satan and deliver man from death and Satan's power.*

10. Why did God promise to send a Deliverer for man? *Because God loves all people.*

11. Did Adam and Eve deserve God's love and His promise of a Deliverer? *No, they deserved to go to everlasting punishment.*

12. How would you describe to someone else the meaning of grace? *Grace is giving what is needed rather than what is deserved.*

13. Why didn't we talk about God's grace and mercy during the first lessons on creation? *Grace and mercy are God's responses to man's sin and were not needed by man before he sinned.*

14. In each of the areas listed, contrast Adam and Eve's situation before they had sinned with their situation after they had sinned and had been put under God's curse for their sin.

    a. Their relationship with God. *They had been friends with God; now they were enemies. They had been under God's control; now they were under Satan's control. They had had the opportunity to live forever with God; now they faced eternity in the Lake of Fire away from God's presence.*

    b. Their relationship to each other. *Eve had been given to Adam as a helper to be co-ruler with Adam over the earth; now Adam was to rule over her.*

    c. Their daily life and health. *Adam's work had been pleasant; now it would be hard because weeds and pests would make gardening difficult. Neither Adam nor Eve had known pain; now Eve was to experience much pain in childbirth, and both of them would be subject to suffering and disease and death.*

15. What evidence is there in the world today of God's curse on Adam and Eve? *Sickness, sorrow, birth pains, death, hard work, thorns and weeds, droughts, devastating storms, poisonous plants, animal and insect pests. These are all signs of God's curse.*

16. Who were the first parents of all people? *Adam and Eve.*

17. Why do all people die? *Because Adam disobeyed God, all Adam's descendants die.*

LESSON 12

God's Provision and Judgment; The Birth of Cain and Abel

LESSON PREPARATION

This section is for you, the teacher.

The passages in the Scripture Reference column are for your own study in preparing for this lesson. Since they may contain concepts that run ahead of the lesson, they are not to be taught at this point.

Note: If you have not taught previously from this series of lessons, please read carefully the note to teachers in the front of this book.

SCRIPTURE: Genesis 3:21-24; 4:1,2

LESSON GOALS:

- To show that God knows everything and will punish all sin.
- To show that man cannot save himself from sin.
- To show that only God can make man acceptable in His sight.
- To show that the sin of Adam has been passed on to all men.

THIS LESSON SHOULD HELP THE STUDENTS:

- To realize that they are sinners.
- To realize that no one can "get away with" sin.
- To realize that there is nothing they can do to make themselves acceptable to God.

PERSPECTIVE FOR THE TEACHER:

This lesson introduces some basic principles that much of our society has chosen to blur or even totally reject. Sadly, among those who reject these truths are many so-called Christian groups, who have chosen, as Paul said, *"another gospel"* (Galatians 1:6).

First of all, the Word is very clear in stating that God killed animals in order to make acceptable coverings for Adam and Eve. Although the blood of animals could never pay for sin, from this time until the death of Christ, God accepted the blood of animals as a type, or picture, of the punishment that all sin deserves. Romans 6:23 says, *"For the wages of sin is death...."* Hebrews 9:22 says, *"...without shedding of blood is no remission."*

Secondly, the Word shows us that man cannot come to God on man's terms; man must come to God in the way that God has provided as His acceptable way. Adam and Eve's clothing of leaves was not acceptable to God; neither is anything that we might do to try to make ourselves acceptable to God.

Refusal or distortion of these two principles has given rise to many false religions. How tempted man is to follow a religion that overlooks the heavy penalty for sin! How tempted man is to try to find his own way to take care of his sin problem! How deceitful sin is! How deceitful man's heart is! And how deceitful the Enemy is!

If Satan can get us to "feel religious" and still miss the truth of God's Word, he has subtly cut us off from God and from eternal life. As long as a man feels adequately religious, he is not going to seek to know more about God. John

---

OVERVIEW

This passage of Scripture emphasizes God's holiness and His grace. Here we see the first blood sacrifice for sin and God's gracious act of clothing Adam and Eve. God is establishing the fact of man's helplessness to save himself and providing an analogy regarding the coming Deliverer.

Some points:

- The clothing Adam and Eve had made for themselves was not acceptable to God.
- God made clothing of skins for them.
- God put Adam and Eve out of the garden and guarded the entrance so they could never return.
- God is the giver of all life.
- Cain and Abel were born outside of the garden; they were born sinners.
- All of Adam's descendents were and are born sinners, separated from God.

Lesson 12: God's Provision and Judgment

Teacher's Notes

9:41 records Jesus' words to the Pharisees: *"...If ye were blind, ye should have no sin: but now ye say, We see; therefore your sin remaineth."*

This is the story of the first blood sacrifice for sin, and shows us that God will only accept those who come to Him in the way He prescribes.

Many religious groups would call this teaching "narrow." Jesus did, too! Matthew 7:13,14 quotes His words: *"Enter ye in at the strait [narrow] gate: for wide is the gate, and broad is the way, that leadeth to destruction, and many there be which go in thereat: Because strait [narrow] is the gate, and narrow is the way, which leadeth unto life, and few there be that find it."*

May we be faithful to help our students to see and to choose the narrow way! The truths in this lesson are an essential part of the foundation upon which the rest of the truths of that narrow way can be firmly established.

VISUALS:

- Chronological Picture No. 7, "Adam and Eve Driven from the Garden"
- Chronological Chart
- Visuals (illustrated in lesson) showing that Adam and all his descendants are sinners and showing the separation between God and Adam and all of Adam's descendants (these can be done as you teach)

ON TEACHING THIS LESSON:

These lessons are designed to **teach unbelievers.** You are carefully laying a scriptural foundation on which the Gospel will later be presented. If your class contains believers, teach with the goal of giving them an understanding of the basis for their faith and **with the goal of enabling them to teach the same material to unbelievers.**

DON'T COMPLICATE THE MESSAGE!

As you teach, keep in mind that this is a directed study—not an exhaustive survey of the Bible and not an unlimited group discussion. Keep your lesson on track and moving ahead by limiting and directing any discussion.

Carefully follow the outline. Emphasize the doctrinal themes.

LESSON FORMAT: The **center column** below contains the lesson material to be taught to the students. The **bold outline headings** are only for reference and need not be spoken, as they are incorporated into the outlined material that follows. The material in the **side columns** is for the teacher's own reference and is not intended to be included in the lesson.

TO BE TAUGHT TO THE STUDENTS
(Center Column Only)

LESSON OUTLINE:

REVIEW questions from Lesson 11.

A. Introduction

Students of history tell us that knowing what happened in the past gives us insight and understanding into what's going on today.

The Bible is true history.

Lesson 12: God's Provision and Judgment

The events recorded in Genesis 3 affected **all** mankind — every person today — you and me.

God had these things recorded in His Word so we could read them and gain understanding.

God communicated these things to us because He wants us to know Him.

As we continue to read, let's give special consideration to what **God** was doing in this critical passage of the history of mankind.

B. God refused the clothing which Adam and Eve had made.

 Theme: Man is a sinner. He needs God and is helpless to save himself.

 Theme: Man can come to God only according to God's will and plan.

 READ Genesis 3:21.

Let's read again what Adam and Eve had done to try to cover their nakedness.

 READ Genesis 3:7.

- They made themselves coverings of leaves.
- Because they had disobeyed God, they were embarrassed to have God see them naked.

But God refused to accept the clothes which Adam and Eve had made.

- Why?

   Isaiah 64:6
   Ephesians 2:8,9

   He wanted to teach them that they couldn't do **anything** to make themselves acceptable to God.

   God will not accept anything that is done according to man's ideas.

   God only accepts whatever is done according to His way.

   No one can make himself acceptable to God by what he does.

People today still do many things to try to make themselves acceptable to God; they try to "cover" for their sins, just as Adam and Eve did.

- Example:

   Some people think that if they go to church or do a lot of good deeds, it will help to make up for the wrongs they have done.

   You can probably think of lots of other examples of this kind of "do-it-yourself" covering for sin. God sees right through it, and it is completely unacceptable to Him. We must instead come to God and find His way to make us acceptable to Him. He simply won't accept anything we could ever do. No matter how thoughtful or religious or costly our efforts might seem to us, they will never cover our sins in such a way that God will not see them and require the death payment.

209

Lesson 12: God's Provision and Judgment

Teacher's Notes

Scripture Reference

C. God killed animals.

 Theme: **God is holy and righteous. He demands death as the payment for sin.**

The first death in the world was brought about by sin.
- God killed animals.
    - The animals' blood was shed.
    - God then took the skins off the animals.
- Adam and Eve did not do this; God killed the animals, and He took the skins off.
- God was reminding Adam and Eve that disobedience to Him brought death into the world.[1]

[1] Here God is preparing a redemptive analogy of the truth presented in Isaiah 61:10, *"...he hath clothed me with the garments of salvation, he hath covered me with the robe of righteousness...."* Later, we will draw on this analogy to reveal the truth of substitution and the covering of the righteousness of Christ received through faith. Do not apply this truth to your students yet by telling them the Gospel. Just make it clear that God would not accept what Adam and Eve had made but that God provided them with clothing, and that what we do outwardly cannot make us pleasing to God. This is all you need to say at this point. You are laying foundations and establishing spiritual principles. Later on, when teaching the Gospel, you will point back to this illustration. □

D. God provided clothing for Adam and Eve.

 Theme: **God is loving, merciful, and gracious.**

Why did God kill the animals?

To provide clothing for guilty Adam and Eve.
- God provided them with clothing made from the skins of the animals which He had killed.
- God did this for Adam and Eve, even though they did not deserve it.

Only God could supply them with clothing which would make them acceptable to Him.

E. God put coats of skin on Adam and Eve.

God put coats of skin on Adam and Eve.
- He didn't just give them clothing and tell them to put it on.
- God put the clothing, which He made, on Adam and Eve.

F. God put Adam and Eve out of the garden, away from the tree of life.

 Theme: **God is holy and righteous. He demands death as the payment for sin.**

 READ Genesis 3:22,23.

God the Father, God the Son, and God the Holy Spirit said this.
- They were talking about Adam and Eve.
- When God first made Adam and Eve, they didn't know anything evil or bad.
- They only knew what was good.
    - Everything God made and gave to them was good.
    - Everything God told them to do was good.
- But when they disobeyed God their Creator, they found that not everything was good.[2]

Satan had deceived Eve so she thought the fruit from the tree of the knowledge of good and evil would be good for food.

But as soon as Adam and Eve ate that fruit:

[2] Someone may ask, "If God created everything perfect, how could anything be bad?" You might remind them that Satan had chosen to disobey God. He was evil. □

210

Lesson 12: God's Provision and Judgment

- They were filled with shame and fear.
- They now knew that not everything was good but that some things were evil.

Adam and Eve should have trusted God.

- God knew what was good and what was evil.
- Adam and Eve should have trusted Him to tell them instead of finding out for themselves.

God had given them every good thing to eat—He had even offered to them the opportunity to eat from the tree of life.

But they had chosen to disobey God and to eat, instead, from the tree of the knowledge of good and evil—the one tree from which God had forbidden them to eat.

Now, because they had disobeyed God, He would not allow them to eat of the tree of life.

- Consider:

  Genesis 3:22 says that the reason God put them out of the garden was so that they would not eat of the tree of life and live forever.

  This was actually an act of God's mercy.

   - *God did not want men to physically live forever as sinners. (Can you imagine what the world would be like if all the evil men that ever lived were still alive now?)*
   - *By putting man outside of the garden, God allowed the consequence of sin to take its eventual toll—that is, death.*

Because they were separated from God, they would also have to die physically.

Therefore, God put Adam and Eve, the father and mother of us all, out of the garden, away from the tree of life.

 Theme: God is supreme and sovereign.

- God had put them in the garden and told them they could eat of the tree of life.
- Now that they were sinful before Him, God put them out of the garden, away from the tree of life so they would die.
- Compare:

  When Satan sinned, God put him out of his wonderful position in Heaven. Now, because of God's hatred for sin, He also put Adam and Eve out of the garden.

God doesn't ask anyone what He should do; He is the supreme one in the whole universe.

- No one can fight against God and win.
- We cannot trick or deceive Him.

God hates disobedience to His commands and will not allow any disobedient person to live with Him.

G. God put cherubim and a flaming sword to guard the way to the tree of life.

 Theme: Man is a sinner. He needs God and is helpless to save himself.

 READ Genesis 3:24.

Lesson 12: God's Provision and Judgment

Teacher's Notes | **Scripture Reference**

Suggested Visual:

CHRONOLOGICAL PICTURE NO. 7, "ADAM AND EVE DRIVEN FROM THE GARDEN"

At the east of the garden of Eden, God put some of His good angels called cherubim and a sword of fire which turned every way to make sure that Adam and Eve could not return and eat the fruit from the tree of life.
- If they had tried to go back, the good angels of God would have seen them, and they would have been killed by the sword of fire.
- There was nothing they could do.[3]
- When God put them out of the garden, that was the end.
- There was absolutely no way they could get back to the tree of life.

They would now grow old and die.

H. God is the giver of life.

 Theme: God is supreme and sovereign.

 READ Genesis 4:1.

Eve said this because she knew that God is the giver of all life.
- God made Adam from the dust of the ground and breathed into him to give him life.
- God made Eve from Adam's rib.
- Every person is given life by God.
- Your life was given to you by God.
- Psalm 100:3 says, *"Know ye that the LORD he is God: it is he that hath made us, and not we ourselves...."*

CHRONOLOGICAL CHART: Point to the names "Cain and Abel."

I. Cain and Abel were both born outside of the garden.

 Theme: Man is a sinner. He needs God and is helpless to save himself.

 READ Genesis 4:2.

Because Adam and Eve had sinned against God, they were put outside of the garden, away from the tree of life.
- Cain and Abel were born outside of the garden, away from the tree of life, because Adam their father was outside of the garden.
- Cain and Abel were born sinners because their father Adam was a sinner.

---

[3] When teaching that man was put out of the garden, we must stress that there was no way back. Through the teaching of God's Word, we are laying the foundations for our students to realize that, if God doesn't make a way back to Him, they are destined for eternal punishment. ☐

Psalm 100:3

Acts 17:25

Lesson 12: God's Provision and Judgment

Had Adam not sinned, Cain and Abel would have been born with the ability to know, love, and obey God.

Instead, they were born under Satan's control.

When God created Adam and Eve, they were perfect before God, and He loved and accepted them.

- If they had obeyed Him, then they would have continued to live in the garden and eat of the tree of life.
- Their children would have been born perfect and would also have lived in the garden.
- They, too, would have loved God and been fully accepted by Him.

But because of Adam's sin in eating the forbidden fruit, Cain and Abel were born sinners, separated from God, outside of the garden, and away from the tree of life.

Not only was Adam the father of Cain and Abel, but he was also the father of the whole human race.

- Adam was your forefather.
- He was my forefather.
- He was everyone's forefather.

Romans 5:12

Therefore, because Adam disobeyed God and was separated from Him, all people in this world are born sinners, cut off from God and with Satan as their father.

Suggested Visual:

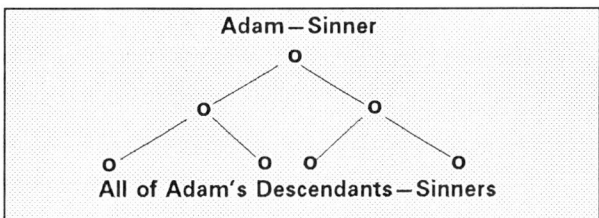

- Explain:

We do not like to think of being born with a disposition to sin. But think for a moment about children. Have you ever seen a little child who is totally unselfish? No. Children must be taught to share and to care about others. Children are not born with a nature to obey; they must be taught. Have you ever heard a tiny child learn to say "yes" before he learned to say "no"? Have you ever seen a little child who wanted to do everything that his parents asked him to do, just when his parents asked him to do it? No. Children are self-willed (some more than others) and must be taught to submit themselves to their parents' authority and to God's authority.

Both our heredity and our environment strongly influence our development. We are, in many ways, a product of our parents, and of their parents, and of their parents' parents, and so on, all the way back to Adam. We have inherited not only genetic characteristics and behavioral and cultural patterns from our forebears; we have also inherited the disposition to sin. We are the product of sinners; and the line of sin can be traced through every generation right back to Adam, the father of the human race.

Acts 17:26

God is the one who gives life to all people, but we are not born in friendship or oneness with God.

Teacher's Notes

Lesson 12: God's Provision and Judgment

Scripture Reference

Suggested Visual:

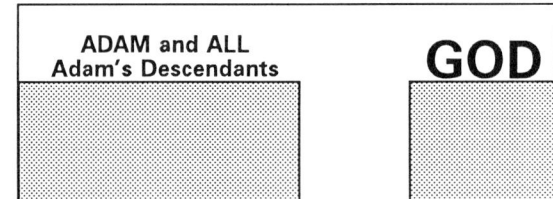

- Satan has taken God's place as our spiritual father.
    - What does this mean?
    - It means that we, too, just like Cain and Abel, were born unable to know, love, and obey God.
    - From birth we are under Satan's control.
- It is important that we realize we were born sinners.
- We were born separated from God, with Satan as our father, just as every other human being was born separated from God.

We must also remember that, even though we are born sinners, it is God who has given us life.

- All life comes from God.
- All life is owned by God.
- He created everyone and everything.
- Contrast:

Some people like to think that we are "all God's children." This is a very comforting thought and sounds very loving and religious. In a very subtle way, people are using this idea to relieve their minds of considering the possibility that God would ever reject them.

But this kind of thinking is totally unscriptural. Yes, God created us. But as we have just discussed, Adam's sin put all men into Satan's family. So we are not born "God's children," but Satan's children, cut off from God.

I Chronicles 29:11

Job 41:11

Psalm

J. Conclusion

What we are reading from the Bible is true history.

- Adam and Eve were real people, and we are their descendants.
- God mentions their story and their names even in the New Testament.
- Adam and Eve's sin affected all of us.

God has written these things for us so we can know Him.

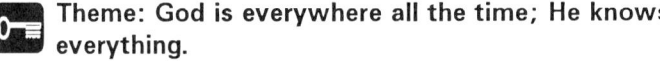 **Theme: God is everywhere all the time; He knows everything.**

God has not changed; He sees and knows everything we do.

- There is no place where we can hide from Him.
- It is impossible to deceive or trick God.
- Darkness and light are the same to God.
- There is never a time when we are out of His sight.
- He even knows our every thought.

Lesson 12: God's Provision and Judgment

Scripture Reference

Teacher's Notes

In our next lesson we will study about God's dealings with the children of Adam and Eve.

QUESTIONS:

1. Why did God refuse the clothes which Adam and Eve made? *Because God wanted to teach Adam and Eve that they couldn't do anything to make themselves acceptable to God.*

2. Can a person make himself acceptable to God by anything that he does? *No.*

3. What are some of the things you can think of that men do to try to make themselves acceptable to God?

4. Will God accept any of these things? *No.*

5. Who is the only one who could make Adam and Eve acceptable to God? *God.*

6. Why did God kill animals to make clothing for Adam and Eve? *Because God was reminding Adam and Eve that the punishment for sin is death.*

7. Why did God make them clothes? *Because, even though they had sinned, He still loved them, and He wanted to show them that He was the only one who could make them acceptable to Him.*

8. In what way did Adam and Eve become like God after they ate the fruit of the tree of the knowledge of good and evil? *They now knew that there was evil as well as good.*

9. Why did God put Adam and Eve out of the garden of Eden? *So that they wouldn't be able to eat the fruit from the tree of life and live forever in sin.*

10. How did God make sure they wouldn't be able to return? *He placed angels called cherubim and a sword of fire flashing every direction to keep them away.*

11. Can anyone trick or deceive God? *No.*

12. Who gives every person his life? *God.*

13. Where were Cain and Abel born? *Outside of the garden of Eden.*

14. Why were Cain and Abel born sinners and separated from God? *Because of their father, Adam.*

15. Why were we all born sinners and separated from God? *Because Adam is also our father.*

| Scripture Reference | | Teacher's Notes |

LESSON 13

God Rejected Cain and His Offering, but Accepted Abel and His Offering

OVERVIEW

This lesson presents God's acceptance of Abel, who came to God by faith in the way that God prescribed, and God's rejection of Cain, who tried to approach God in his own way.

God's holiness is shown by His requiring the death penalty for sin.

God's grace and mercy are shown by His provision of a way for sinners to come to Him and by His reasoning with angry Cain.

God judged Cain for killing his brother.

All of Cain's descendants were worldly-minded.

God continued the line of the Deliverer by raising up Seth to replace Abel.

LESSON PREPARATION

This section is for you, the teacher.

The passages in the Scripture Reference column are for your own study in preparing for this lesson. Since they may contain concepts that run ahead of the lesson, they are not to be taught at this point.

Note: If you have not taught previously from this series of lessons, please read carefully the note to teachers in the front of this book.

SCRIPTURE: Genesis 4:3-16,25

LESSON GOALS:

- To show that the sin of Adam has been passed on to all men.
- To show that man can come to God only according to God's will and plan.
- To show that man must have faith in order to please God and be saved.
- To show that God started a new line with Seth to replace the line of Abel. God was keeping His promise to send a Deliverer.

THIS LESSON SHOULD HELP THE STUDENTS:

- To realize that we are all sinners.
- To see that we are helpless to save ourselves.
- To see their need to come to God His way by faith.
- To see that the penalty of sin is death.

PERSPECTIVE FOR THE TEACHER:

Historically, man has continually refused to acknowledge God and the seriousness of sin. But our present society has plunged itself into a period of particular decline and degradation. Moral values used to be clearly defined, even among non-Christians. But now values have eroded into a blur of gray areas that seem to allow the sinner to roam freely even into areas of gross sin. The prevailing morality seems to be "If it feels good to me, I'll do it."

But God has not changed. His values are still the same; sin still requires the death penalty. God is eternally holy.

The life of Cain is a stinging example of the horrible results of rebellion against God. Cain refused God's loving call to repentance, turned and killed his brother, and spent the rest of his life on earth and all eternity away from the presence of God.

The story of Cain and Abel is a classic for all times but especially for our times. Many in our society are rushing away from God. In the process, they are hurting, lying against, stealing from, and killing fellow men and women.

Yet when someone is the victim of a crime, or hears of a crime, often the first question asked is, "Why did God let that happen?" This may be the first question, but it is the wrong question.

It is a little like a mother telling her six-year-old son not to hit his baby sister. The six-year-old turns right around and hits his sister anyway. Now, would you ask, "Why did the mother let the boy hit his sister?" No, the question is, "Why didn't the boy obey his mother?"

Lesson 13: God Rejected Cain but Accepted Abel

Teacher's Notes

Scripture Reference

God had told Cain what was right and was even gracious to tell Cain why He did not accept him when Cain disobeyed. But Cain turned against all that God had told him to do and went out and killed his brother.

This is the problem that we are faced with continually; our news is full of every kind of crime and evil—not because God should have stopped it, but because man should have believed God and obeyed Him.

The spread of sin is horrible. Romans 5:12 says, *"...by one man sin entered into the world, and death by sin; and so death passed upon all men, for that all have sinned."* But men, not God, are responsible for their conduct.

God hates sin. Man is given the choice to believe and obey God. Man is responsible for his choices. Sin is not God's fault. Sin cannot be paid for by man's earthly efforts. Teach these truths clearly; many people today have lost sight of them. God promises that His Word will *"prosper in the thing whereto [He] sent it."* (Isaiah 55:11).

VISUALS:

- Chronological Picture No. 8, "Cain and Abel Bring Offerings to God"
- Chronological Picture No. 9, "Cain Kills Abel"
- Bring the branch used in Lessons 7 and 10.
- Chronological Chart

ON TEACHING THIS LESSON:

These lessons are designed to **teach unbelievers.** You are carefully laying a scriptural foundation on which the Gospel will later be presented. If your class contains believers, teach with the goal of giving them an understanding of the basis for their faith and **with the goal of enabling them to teach the same material to unbelievers.**

DON'T COMPLICATE THE MESSAGE!

As you teach, keep in mind that this is a directed study—not an exhaustive survey of the Bible and not an unlimited group discussion. Keep your lesson on track and moving ahead by limiting and directing any discussion.

Carefully follow the outline. Emphasize the doctrinal themes.

LESSON FORMAT: The **center column** below contains the lesson material to be taught to the students. The **bold outline headings** are only for reference and need not be spoken, as they are incorporated into the outlined material that follows. The material in the **side columns** is for the teacher's own reference and is not intended to be included in the lesson.

TO BE TAUGHT TO THE STUDENTS
(Center Column Only)

LESSON OUTLINE:

REVIEW questions from Lesson 12.

A. Introduction

How serious is sin?[1]

What if someone refuses to believe God and chooses to disobey Him?

---

[1] Don't give time for discussion of these questions; just go on with the lesson. These are asked only for the purpose of causing the students to think about the subject of sin.

Note: These questions are not appropriate for a very small group, because a student might feel pressured to answer. ☐

Lesson 13: God Rejected Cain but Accepted Abel

- Could you say, "Well, that's his own business, if he wants to do that"?
- Does a man's sin affect other people?

Can a man work out some way to take care of his sins?

Is it true that each man can choose his own way to come to God?

Won't God accept any sincere effort we make?

Let's see what answers God gives us to these questions as we study the story of Adam and Eve's sons, Cain and Abel, and their descendants.

B. God told them what they must do when they came to worship Him.

 Theme: Man is a sinner. He needs God and is helpless to save himself.

There was no way that Adam and Eve or Cain and Abel could come to God.
- They were all sinners, and God hates sin.
- They were separated from God.
- The punishment for sin is death.
- They could not give anything to God to pay for their sins.

 Theme: God is supreme and sovereign.

 Theme: God is loving, merciful, and gracious.

 Theme: Man can come to God only according to God's will and plan.

But God planned a way so they could come to Him.
- It was not man's way.
- It was God who decided on this way.
- No one else could make a way for them.

John 3:16

God made a way for them because He loved them.

 Theme: God communicates with man.

God must have told Adam and Eve what they must do if they wanted to come to Him.

Adam and Eve probably told Cain and Abel what God said they must do if they wished to come to God.

The Bible gives us good reason to believe that God communicated these things to Adam and Eve and that Abel and Cain knew, too.

Later in this lesson, we plan to talk about this subject in more detail.

 Theme: God is holy and righteous. He demands death as the payment for sin.

Here is what God must have told them:
- When they came to Him, they had to bring a sheep as an offering to Him.

Lesson 13: God Rejected Cain but Accepted Abel

Teacher's Notes

Scripture Reference

Leviticus 17:11
Hebrews 9:22b
Hebrews 9:24
Ezekiel 18:4
Romans 6:23a

- They had to kill the animal in such a way that the animal's blood would flow out.

The blood of the animals could not pay for their sin; why then would God tell them to kill a sheep?

- Because God wanted them to remember that the punishment for sin is death.
- He wanted them to remember that they would die and go to everlasting punishment unless He saved them.
- If they agreed with God that they were sinners and that only He could save them from everlasting punishment, then they were to bring a sheep and kill it, as God had told them to.

 God never changes.

- Explain:

At the beginning of this course, we said that we would be studying the foundational issues and the main themes of the Bible. This is one of the wonderful things about God's Word: these main themes are consistent all the way through the Bible.

The fact that God is holy and righteous and demands death as the payment for sin is one of these foundational themes. And along with this, the Bible clearly states that blood must be shed for sin.

 Read Leviticus 17:11.

God promised that if they came by faith, offering to Him the blood of animals, He would accept them and forgive their sins.

 Read Hebrews 9:22: *"And almost all things are by the law purged with blood; and* **without shedding of blood is no remission."** ²

These are just two examples of this foundational principle that runs throughout the Bible. The blood sacrifice for sin was part of God's gracious plan to deliver man from sin and Satan and death. ³

C. Both Cain and Abel came to offer sacrifices to God.

 Theme: Man can come to God only according to God's will and plan.

READ Genesis 4:3-5.

Both Cain and Abel believed in the existence of God, and both came to offer sacrifices to Him.

- Consider:

Cain and Abel remind us of two different classes of people who attend church: those who come to worship God according to man's ideas and those who come in the way God has said.

- Consider:

Just believing in God and even offering to God what we think is very good will not make us acceptable to Him. The Bible says in James 2:19, "Thou believest that there is one God; thou doest well: the devils also believe, and tremble." ("Devils" here refers to demons—those spirit beings that participated with Satan [then called Lucifer] in his rebellion against God and who were cast out

---

²The boldfaced portion of the verse is the part you want to emphasize. Do not get off track into a discussion of the Law. ☐

³A student may ask why people who do not believe the Bible also perform blood sacrifices.

You might point them to the fact that man's sin affected every part of life. Many things that we see are vestiges of what God originally ordained—fragments of the truth, but twisted by sin and by Satan's lies. Satan wants men to think they are doing the right thing, so he uses what seem to be religious methods to make people think they are pleasing God.

Remind the students that, though God's plan is still the same, we no longer are to bring the blood of animals to Him. ☐

Lesson 13: God Rejected Cain but Accepted Abel

of Heaven with Satan.) But believing in God doesn't make Satan's demons acceptable to God. As we go on, we will see what happened to Cain and Abel.

D. Abel's offering was accepted by God.

 Theme: Man must have faith in order to please God.

 Theme: Man can come to God only according to God's will and plan.

 READ Genesis 4:4.

Abel brought one of his sheep as an offering to God.
- It was the firstborn lamb of its mother.
- Abel killed the sheep so its blood ran out, and he offered the sheep, along with the fat, to God.

Why did Abel bring this offering to God?
- Because he agreed with God that he was a sinner and that only God could save him from everlasting punishment.
- Because he believed the promises God had given his parents while they were still in the garden of Eden.

Hebrews 11:4

God had promised that He would send a great Deliverer.

God promised that the Deliverer would destroy Satan and save man from Satan's power.

Was God pleased with Abel's offering? Did God accept Abel?

Yes, He did. God was very pleased with his offering, and He accepted Abel.

- Explain:

Hebrews 10:4; 11:6

It is important to understand that the blood of animals could never pay for sin. God did not accept Abel's lamb as the payment for his sin. Sin must be paid for by the sinner being separated from God forever. But God forgave Abel's sin and accepted him because Abel trusted, not in himself, but in God who had promised to send the Deliverer. [4]

E. Cain's offering was rejected by God.

 Theme: Man must have faith in order to please God and be saved.

 Theme: Man can come to God only according to God's will and plan.

 READ Genesis 4:5.

As an offering to God, Cain brought the things which he had grown.
But God would not accept Cain or his offering.
Why not?
- Was it because the things Cain grew and brought to God were not good?
- Was it because God doesn't like things grown from the ground?
- No, these are not the reasons.

---

[4] It is important in every story that your students be taught grace. They must come to realize that man cannot contribute anything to his salvation.

Make certain that they understand that the blood of animals could not and did not pay for sin. Sin must be paid for by human life being given. Animal blood, or life, is not equal to human life (Hebrews 10:4,5). Be sure to make it absolutely clear that God will not overlook sin. Sin must be paid for in full. The soul that sins, it shall die (Ezekiel 18:4), that is, be separated forever from God. ☐

Lesson 13: God Rejected Cain but Accepted Abel

Teacher's Notes

Scripture Reference

⁵In addition to the reasons given in the lesson, here are some additional considerations for the teacher. (Since these run ahead chronologically in detail and theme, they are not intended to be included in the lesson.)

Since there were acknowledged clean and unclean animals even in Noah's day, it is likely that, according to God's directive, animals were already classed as clean and unclean in Cain and Abel's time.

Surely it was no coincidence that Abel chose a lamb, a clean animal, and the most perfect type of the spotless Son of God (Isaiah 53:7; John 1:29; I Peter 1:19,20). The Lord Jesus and His sacrifice as a spotless lamb originated in the mind of the eternal God before the foundation of the earth, not in the mind of Abel (Revelation 13:8). ☐

⁶It is important that we emphasize faith as the reason for Abel's offering and unbelief as the reason for Cain's actions. If we emphasize obedience instead of faith, the minds of the people will be turned to doing rather than believing. According to Hebrews 11, God accepted Abel and his offering because Abel believed God. Faith was the great difference between Cain and Abel.

The foundational truth of believing God should be clearly laid so that when we come to the Gospel, the students will know that it is only through faith that we are accepted by God. Nevertheless, the balance should also be kept between faith and works. Because Abel believed God, he offered a lamb. Because Noah believed God, he built an ark. Because Abraham believed God, he went to the place of God's choice.

Keep in mind Hebrews 11 and use it to interpret the actions of the Old Testament characters. You will not be teaching from it, but using it only sparingly, as in this lesson, to support what you are presenting from the Old Testament. ☐

- Did God reject Cain's offering because Cain was a worse sinner than Abel?
- No, that wasn't the reason why God would not accept him.
- Both Cain and Abel were born sinners.

It is important that we are clear in our own minds **why** God rejected Cain and his offering but accepted Abel and his offering.⁵

- Explain:

The book of Hebrews gives us some clear insights. In Hebrews 11, God says that without faith it is impossible to please Him. He also tells us that Abel was a man of faith; Cain was not.

Hebrews 11:4,6

Then, in the book of Romans, God tells us that faith is always based on the Word of God. Romans 10:17 says, "...faith cometh by hearing, and hearing by the word of God." To approach God in any way except the way God has told us is presumption and sin. God will reject the man who tries to come to Him in his own way. Everything which originates with man is unacceptable to God.

Psalm 3:8

John 14:6

Acts 4:12

On this basis, we can be sure that Abel's faith was dependent on a clear directive given by God. It must have been; otherwise, it would not have been acceptable to God.

Another indication that Abel was following God's command is emphasized through Abel's action in bringing to God the fat of the lamb. Later in Scripture, God commands Israel, that is, the Hebrew people, to bring the fat to Him. To suggest that bringing the fat of animals to God originated with Abel is contrary to the whole emphasis of Scripture. God doesn't accept anything which originates with man.

Leviticus 3:16

Suggested Visual:

CHRONOLOGICAL PICTURE NO. 8, "CAIN AND ABEL BRING OFFERINGS TO GOD"

God rejected Cain and his offering because:
- Cain didn't come to God admitting he was a sinner.
- He came to God in his own way, according to his own ideas, and not in the way which God had commanded.
- Cain did not believe God.
- He did not trust in the way which God had told them to come.
- That is why God rejected him.⁶
- Compare:

Psalm 66:18

Hebrews 11:4

Do you remember how God rejected the clothes which Adam and Eve made for themselves? Why did God refuse to accept the clothing they made? Because God wanted to show them that they couldn't make themselves acceptable to God by anything they could do. It had to be done in God's way. The animals had to die, and their blood had to be shed so that Adam and Eve could have clothes that were acceptable to God.

222

Lesson 13: God Rejected Cain but Accepted Abel

Likewise with Cain and Abel. God would not accept them unless they trusted in Him and came to Him in the way He had said. God would only accept them if they brought a sheep and killed it, shedding its blood. Abel believed God and came God's way, so God accepted him. Cain came trusting in his own way, so God refused him.

God has not changed; He is still the same today. Although He does not command us now to sacrifice sheep, He still does stipulate the only way anyone can come to Him. We too must come God's way; otherwise, He will reject us as He rejected Cain. **7**

- Illustrate:

DISPLAY BRANCH BROKEN OFF FROM TREE.

Take a look at this branch broken off from a tree. It died after a while because it was separated from the life it received from the tree. What if you tried to join this dead branch back onto the tree so that once again it would be able to receive the life from the tree? If you tied the branch back onto the tree, would it come back to life again? Would the leaves turn green once again and begin to grow? Do you think that you would be able to join the branch back on the tree so it would have life again? No, you cannot join a dead branch back onto the tree so that it will live once again. It was separated from the tree, and you cannot put it back.

Suggested Visual:

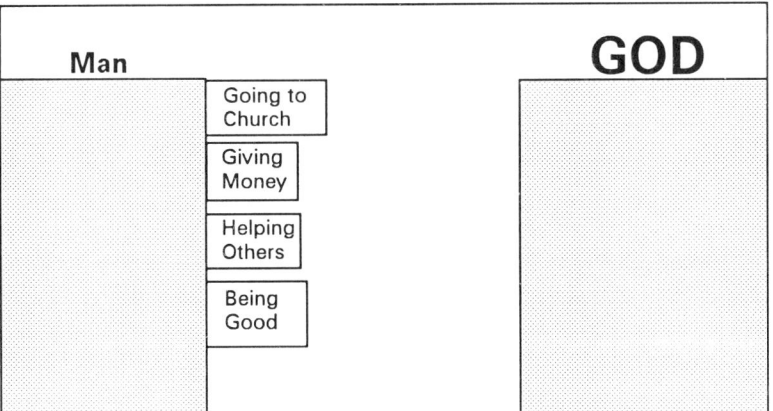

POINT TO THE VISUAL AS YOU GIVE THE FOLLOWING COMMENTARY:

- Comment:

It seems like many people spend a good part of their lives trying to find a way to "reattach" themselves to the source of spiritual life. Their efforts might include activities that seem very religious: going to church, giving money to the church, doing all sorts of "good deeds," being a "good person," or any number of things. Can you think of some examples of this type of self-effort to come to God?

Since we are all born sinners, we were all "detached" from our source of life, who is God. But there is absolutely nothing that we can do on our own that will restore us to God. Sin has broken us off from God, just like the limb was broken off from the tree.

- Compare:

That is how it was with Adam, Eve, Cain, and Abel. Because Adam and Eve disobeyed God, they were separated from God. Therefore,

---

Scripture Reference

Isaiah 59:2; 64:6

Romans 3:23

Teacher's Notes

7Someone may ask, "What is God's way?" Of course, the answer is Jesus Christ; but some of your students may need more understanding before you can present the Gospel.

You might want to say, "God has certainly made a way, and that's what this Bible study is all about. He was going to send a Deliverer, just as He promised. If you'd like, I'll be glad to talk more with you about this after class."

We need to be continually sensitive to the Holy Spirit. The student who asks may truly have a heart prepared to put His trust in Jesus Christ as his Saviour. Or he may just be "thinking out loud" about what he has heard but have little understanding or conviction of sin.

God promises us wisdom if we ask Him (James 1:5), and we can trust Him to give what He has promised. ☐

Teacher's Notes

Lesson 13: God Rejected Cain but Accepted Abel

Scripture Reference

Cain and Abel were born outside of the garden and were also separated from God. They could not bring themselves back into fellowship with God.

Adam and Eve made themselves clothes to try to make themselves acceptable to God, but He rejected their clothes. Cain came to God in his own way, and God rejected him and his offering. Only God was able to make a way so they could come back to Him and be His friends once again.

We, too, are all the descendants of Adam. We were all born sinners, separated from God because of our father Adam. We cannot make ourselves God's friends. Only God could make a way for us to come back to Him.

Acts 17:26

Romans 5:12

F. God reasoned with angry Cain.

 Theme: God communicates with man.

 Theme: God is loving, merciful, and gracious.

 READ Genesis 4:6,7.

Even though Cain refused to believe God and deliberately went his own way, God reasoned with him.

Because of God's love and mercy, He talked to Cain and tried to get him to come to God in the right way.

Proverbs 1:23

God wanted Cain to know that he, too, would be accepted if he came as his brother came, believing God's Word, offering the blood, and trusting in God and His promise of the Deliverer.

G. Cain refused to listen to God, and he killed Abel.

 Theme: Man is a sinner. He needs God and is helpless to save himself.

 READ Genesis 4:8.

Cain was very angry.

He would not listen to God. He was listening to Satan, just as his mother and father had done in the garden.

Suggested Visual:

CHRONOLOGICAL PICTURE NO. 9, "CAIN KILLS ABEL"

- Compare:

Many people today are just like Cain; they refuse to listen to God, and they end up hurting others. Sometimes their rebellion against God leads to violent crimes like Cain's murder of his brother Abel.

Sometimes the result is less violent—it may only show in bitter attitudes or selfish actions. But the result is always tragic and hurtful to others.

 Theme: Satan fights against God and His will. He is a liar and a deceiver. He hates man.

Who was leading Cain? To whom was Cain listening? Who do you think put it into Cain's mind to kill his brother?

Satan![8]

- Consider:

  Remember that we talked about Satan's deceitfulness? He wants us to think that we would never be like Cain; we would never hurt or kill someone. But look how quickly Cain's anger flared! And look at the trail of sin and violence that has followed his rebellion!

  One of the things that many people fail to look at is that the way of sin is death, whether it be a violent murder, or a slow process of simply living apart from God, and finally dying and going to an eternity spent away from God's presence in the Lake of Fire.

  Originally, Satan murdered Cain's mother and father. He said to them, "You won't die. You will be all right. Don't listen to God. God is only trying to keep back some good fruit from you." But Satan knew that, if Adam and Eve ate the fruit of the tree of the knowledge of good and evil, they would die. He lied to them when he said, "You will not die." Satan wanted Adam and Eve to die, and he wanted Cain to kill Abel. Satan is a murderer.

  Satan hates all people and will lie and deceive with the purpose of leading all of us to the place of everlasting punishment where he is going.

  In John 8:44, the Bible calls Satan a "murderer."

  Even right now, Satan is still telling people not to believe God; not to believe God's Word, the Bible.

H. God's judgment on Cain.

 Theme: God is everywhere all the time; He knows everything.

 Theme: God communicates with man.

 READ Genesis 4:9.

Although God asked this question, He already knew that Cain had killed Abel.

- God saw him do it.
- God is everywhere and knows everything.

 Theme: God is supreme and sovereign.

 Theme: God is holy and righteous. He demands death as the payment for sin.

Scripture Reference

Proverbs 14:12

Revelation 20:10,15

Proverbs 15:3

Teacher's Notes

[8] Even though Satan is not mentioned in these verses, we know that he was involved. I John 3:12 says that Cain *"was of that wicked one, and slew his brother."* ☐

Lesson 13: God Rejected Cain but Accepted Abel

Teacher's Notes		Scripture Reference
	READ Genesis 4:10-15.	
	God is the avenger of all sin.	
	- All sin against other people is also sin against God.	
	- God is the Creator of all people; therefore He punishes anyone who says or does anything harmful to another person.	Ezekiel 18:4
	- Compare:	
	Would you stand by and not do anything while someone attacked your wife, your child, or someone you loved?	
	God is the Creator of all people. He gave Adam life, and He gave life to each one of us. Even though we are all born into this world separated from God, we still belong to Him. God is concerned about what happens to us, even though we are sinners. Just as we have concern for even our wayward family members, so God also has concern for us. And we rightfully belong to Him, because He made us.	
	What if someone came and stole your stereo equipment; would the stereo be the property of the thief, or would it still be yours? Of course, it would still belong to you. What if the person who stole the stereo ruined it? Still, it would belong to you, even though it had been ruined.	
	All people rightfully belong to God even though Satan stole Adam and all of us from God.	
	God will punish those who hurt others because everyone rightfully belongs to Him. An offense is not just against an individual; it is against God, because He is the Giver of life to all people.	
	- This doesn't mean that God will immediately avenge all evil, but the payment for all sin must be paid to God.	
9 We must be careful how we teach repentance. Many people teach that repentance means to leave, or promise to leave, all sin. But this is incorrect.	The wages of sin is death.	Romans 6:23a
	No other payment is acceptable.	
	- Giving money to a charity will not pay for our sins.	
Repentance is a change of mind, a change of attitude toward God, oneself, and one's own sin. Repentance is the sinner acknowledging before God, "God, You are right. I am wrong. Everything you commanded is good and righteous and holy. I have failed. I have no hope in myself." That is true repentance.	- Giving money to a church will not pay for our sin or satisfy God.	
	All sin will finally be punished by God, for He is the rightful owner of every person.	
	READ Genesis 4:16.	
	Cain still would not listen to God.	
	- He went away from God, following Satan's ways.	
	Cain would not repent; He refused to change his attitude toward God and toward his sin. **9**	
Be sure to emphasize faith, rather than following or doing. If we stress obedience, we will have followers and doers rather than believers.	**I. Cain's descendants were materialistically minded.**	
	Theme: Man is a sinner. He needs God and is helpless to save himself.	
God doesn't ask a sinner to promise to leave his sin and "never do it again" before He will save him. God doesn't strike a bargain with the sinner. He does not say, "You do this, and I will do that." God does not require reformation before salvation. ☐	Cain's descendants followed his example.	Genesis 4:17-24
	- They lived without thinking about God.	
	Instead, they filled their lives with material and physical things.	
	They built towns, raised cattle, and made tools and musical instruments.	

Lesson 13: God Rejected Cain but Accepted Abel

There is nothing wrong with these things in themselves; what was wrong was that they concerned themselves with these things and excluded God.

They filled their minds and time doing the things they wanted to do.

They had no interest or time for God and the things He wanted them to know.

- They were under the control of Satan.
- Consider:

See what a terrible effect disobedience to God had already brought into the world! Because Adam and Eve sinned, all of their descendants were born sinners, separated from God and without oneness of mind with God. Their first son, Cain, murdered their second son, Abel. Cain turned away from God and would not listen to His words. As a result, Cain's children and their children also went their own way instead of God's way. They lived according to their own sinful ways because they didn't know God nor did they seek Him and His truth. They were guided by Satan and his lies.

If parents turn away from God's truth and refuse to listen to God, probably their children will not listen to the Word of God either. We are responsible, not only for ourselves, but for our children, too. We should listen to God's Word and also make sure that our children are exposed to the Word of God.

J. God gave Seth to replace Abel.

 Theme: God is faithful; He never changes.

 READ Genesis 4:25.

POINT TO SETH ON THE CHRONOLOGICAL CHART.

God gave Adam and Eve another child in place of Abel who was killed by Cain.

In the garden, God had promised that He would send a Deliverer who would overcome Satan.

- This one would have come through the line of Abel who had trusted in God.
- But Satan guided Cain to kill Abel.

Satan tried in every way to hinder God's plan to send the Deliverer.

- Consider:

Did this mean the end of God's plan and promise to send the Deliverer? No! God always does what He promises. He doesn't give up or change because of the things Satan does.

In place of Abel, God gave Seth to Adam and Eve.

 Theme: Man must have faith in order to please God and be saved.

Seth was also born separated from God, but he trusted in God just as Abel did.

God planned that the Deliverer would come into the world through the line of Seth.

227

Lesson 13: God Rejected Cain but Accepted Abel

Teacher's Notes

Scripture Reference

QUESTIONS:

1. Why did God accept Abel and his offering? *Abel believed God:*

   a. Abel agreed with God that he was a sinner and that only God could save him from punishment.

   b. Abel believed God. He was trusting God to send a Deliverer, just as He had promised to Adam and Eve while they were still in the Garden of Eden.

   c. Abel brought a sheep, killed it, and let its blood run out, just as God had told them to do.

2. Why did God reject Cain and his offering? *Cain did not believe God:*

   a. Cain did not agree with God that he was a sinner and that only God could save him from punishment.

   b. Cain did not believe God. He did not trust in God's promise to send a Deliverer who would destroy Satan and save man.

   c. Cain didn't bring the offering which God said they must bring.

3. Why did God reason with Cain? *Because God loved Cain and wanted him to agree that he was a sinner and that he should bring the correct sacrifice.*

4. Did Cain believe and agree with God? *No.*

5. What did Cain do? *He was angry, and he killed Abel.*

6. How did God know what Cain had done? *God sees and knows everything.*

7. Why will God punish people for saying and doing evil things to others? *Because all people rightfully belong to God. When people hurt others, they are also sinning against God.*

8. Does God forget about sin against others if the person makes it right with the one whom he wronged? *No, God's punishment for all sin is separation from Him forever in the place of everlasting punishment which He prepared for Satan and the evil spirits who followed him.*

9. Did Cain finally change his mind? *No! He went away from God.*

10. What was the result? *Cain's descendants followed his example. They all lived and died separated from God.*

11. Do you know of anything you can do to make payment for the sins you have committed? *No. There is nothing man can do to make payment for his sins.*

12. What were the things for which Cain and his descendants lived? *For money and the material things of life.*

13. Why did God give Seth to Adam and Eve.?

    a. God gave him to replace Abel.

    b. God gave him so the Deliverer would be born through his family line.

THE FOLLOWING IS AN OPTIONAL QUESTION:

14. What lessons can we learn from these stories of ancient men? *Answers will vary, but some of the key areas are:*

    a. Men who refuse to believe and obey God often have children and successive generations who refuse to believe and obey God.

Lesson 13: God Rejected Cain but Accepted Abel

b. Men who refuse to believe and obey God involve themselves with worldly things and soon forget God altogether.

c. Men who believe God and obey Him often have children and successive generations who believe and follow God.

d. God severely judges those who refuse to believe Him.

e. God is gracious to those who believe Him.

Scripture Reference

Psalm 104:6-9
Matthew 24:37-39
Hebrews 11:7

LESSON 14

God Judged the Whole World and Delivered Noah and All in the Ark

LESSON PREPARATION
This section is for you, the teacher.

The passages in the Scripture Reference column are for your own study in preparing for this lesson. Since they may contain concepts that run ahead of the lesson, they are not to be taught at this point.

Note: If you have not taught previously from this series of lessons, please read carefully the note to teachers in the front of this book.

SCRIPTURE: Genesis 6:3,5-22; 7:1-5,15-17,23

LESSON GOALS:

- To show that God does what He says; He will punish all sin.
- To show that God saves those who believe in Him and come to Him in His way.
- To show that there is only one way to come to God.
- To show that God is the only one who can save us.
- To show that God is faithful; He always keeps His promises.

THIS LESSON SHOULD HELP THE STUDENTS:

- To fear God.
- To see the deceitfulness of sin and the danger of following the crowd or persisting in being independent of God.
- To see the necessity of simple faith and obedience to God.

PERSPECTIVE FOR THE TEACHER:

What a timely passage of Scripture is covered in this lesson! It should be difficult to sit through this teaching and not see similarities between the men of Noah's day and our day. But that is exactly the problem: many people have heard about God's judgment in Noah's day, but their hearts become so hardened by sin that they can totally disregard what God has so clearly revealed.

The presentation of God's judgment of sin should cause men to fear God. Our society does not like to talk about fearing God. But God says that *"The fear of the Lord is the beginning of knowledge: but fools despise wisdom and instruction"* (Proverbs 1:7).

This is another Bible story, like the story of Adam and Eve, that people in our society have heard most of their lives. But, unfortunately, many people look at both of these stories as myths or folk tales and not as part of our history. Even sadder is the fact that many churchgoers look at these stories, perhaps "believing" them, but without really applying the truth to their lives.

Pray for your students as you teach this lesson. Some may be struggling with deep areas of sin. Pray that their hearts will be tender to God's message and not hardened like the people of Noah's day.

These passages from Genesis are for us today so that we may know God's character: His hatred of sin, His patience with men and His desire for all to be saved, His swift and sure judgment, and His gracious care and salvation for all who come to Him by faith.

Teacher's Notes

OVERVIEW

This lesson spans the time from Cain and Abel to Noah and the flood. It presents God's omniscience and wrath against sinners, but also His grace and patience in seeking to draw all men to repentance. God's sovereignty and omnipotence are shown in His control over all creation.

In God's instructions to Noah about how to build the ark, we see His precise communication regarding His one way of salvation. The ark is a picture of Christ which you will use later when you teach the New Testament.

The decadence of men in Noah's day is compared with the decadence of our own society, with a warning against hard-heartedness.

God's saving Noah and his family is presented as an act of grace—God's kindness to undeserving sinners.

The flood is historical fact—an act of God's sovereign power in judging unrepentant sinners.

Teacher's Notes

Lesson 14: God Judged the World and Delivered Noah

Scripture Reference

A NOTE ABOUT NON-BIBLICAL FLOOD STORIES:

Virtually every culture has a flood story. This is because there was a flood. But the stories other than the Genesis account are filled with mythical characters and often bizarre details that are far from the historical record. Why? Because every other story was passed down from generation to generation by word of mouth. Along the way, the people of these ungodly societies twisted, added to, and took from the truth. The influence of pagan thinking, worship of false gods and goddesses, and human forgetfulness of details all combined to produce stories that carry only a fragment of what really happened. If you have ever played a game of "gossip" (sitting in a circle whispering something from one person to another until it goes all around the circle), you know that the story that was introduced into the circle is scarcely related to the one that emerges after "making the rounds"! Compound this with the confusion of minds blinded by Satan, and you have the reason for the strange variations of the flood story.

But God saw it all and is able to tell us exactly what happened. He spoke to His prophets the true details of the flood. How fortunate we are to have the Bible and not to have to depend upon word of mouth for our knowledge of God![1]

For those who want more information about the flood from a geological standpoint, several books are available from Christian bookstores. One excellent source of materials is the Institute for Creation Research in El Cajon, California. (See addresses under Resource Material, Lesson 4.)

Noah's Ark and the Lost World, by John D. Morris, Ph.D., published by Master Books, El Cajon , CA 92022, is an excellent children's book. It can also be a help for adults who want some good background information from a scientific perspective without having to wade through scientific terminology.

[1]Remember, when you are teaching **anything** as it is written in God's Word, you are teaching **the truth.** Don't be concerned if you can't answer all of your students' questions. Use whatever Scripture and scripturally accurate reference material you can find to help in answering questions. But remember that some of the answers simply have not been revealed to us by the Lord. The scientific and archeological evidences that have been assembled confirm what is written in the Bible. But the external evidences are not complete. **The evidence that is complete is that God has said it in His Word.**

Encourage your students to read and to research answers for themselves, using the resources mentioned in this course and other biblically sound references. But, most of all, depend upon God's Word, taught in reliance upon God's Holy Spirit, to do God's work in hearts. ☐

VISUALS:

- Chronological Picture No. 10, "Noah's Ark"
- Chronological Chart
- Small visual, "Grace" (illustrated in lesson)

ON TEACHING THIS LESSON:

These lessons are designed to **teach unbelievers.** You are carefully laying a scriptural foundation on which the Gospel will later be presented. If your class contains believers, teach with the goal of giving them an understanding of the basis for their faith and **with the goal of enabling them to teach the same material to unbelievers.**

DON'T COMPLICATE THE MESSAGE!

As you teach, keep in mind that this is a directed study—not an exhaustive survey of the Bible and not an unlimited group discussion. Keep your lesson on track and moving ahead by limiting and directing any discussion.

Carefully follow the outline. Emphasize the doctrinal themes.

LESSON FORMAT: The **center column** on the following pages contains the lesson material to be taught to the students. The **bold outline headings** are only for reference and need not be spoken, as they are incorporated into the outlined material that follows. The material in the **side columns** is for the teacher's own reference and is not intended to be included in the lesson.

Lesson 14: God Judged the World and Delivered Noah

Scripture Reference | Teacher's Notes

TO BE TAUGHT TO THE STUDENTS
(Center Column Only)

LESSON OUTLINE:

REVIEW questions from Lesson 13.

A. Introduction

In our last lesson we saw the terrible results of sin, passed down from one generation to another.

We also saw God's gracious provision of a way for men to come to Him by faith.

The Bible is an amazing historical record.

Let's begin by taking a look at the chronological chart.

B. From Adam to Noah

From Adam to Noah there were ten generations of men who believed God and continued to look for the coming Deliverer promised in the Garden of Eden.

CHRONOLOGICAL CHART: Show the names of the generations of believers from Adam to Noah: Adam, Seth, Enos, Cainan, Mahalaleel, Jared, Enoch, Methuselah, Lamech, and Noah.

The portion of Bible history we will study today tells about God's grace to Noah and his three sons, Shem, Ham, and Japheth, and their families.

This story took place 1,500 years or more after the creation of Adam.[2]

Keep in mind as we read that this account in Genesis is mentioned again many times throughout the Bible, and it is always presented as historical fact.

C. Increased population

By the time of Noah, Shem, Ham, and Japheth, there was a large population living on the earth.[3]

But the vast majority were interested only in having what they thought was a good time.[4]

- They were obsessed with sex and marrying.
- They gave no thought as to how they should please God.

D. God the Holy Spirit was striving with the people.

 Theme: God communicates with man.

 Theme: God is loving, merciful, and gracious.

God saw and hated the sin of these people, but He also loved them and wanted them to repent.

- He wanted them to change their minds.
- He wanted them to admit they were wrong.
- He wanted them to believe in Him.

Ezekiel 18:32
II Peter 3:9

[2] This figure is taken from the numbers given in Genesis 5, assuming there are no gaps in these genealogies.

Some students may question this. You may suggest they do some study on their own in selected reference material. ☐

[3] Assuming current population growth figures, there would have been over three billion people living on the earth at this time. Source: *Biblical Cosmology and Modern Science*, Henry Morris, p. 78. ☐

[4] You are really teaching here from Genesis 6:1,2, but these verses are very difficult verses to interpret and could cause unnecessary discussion in your class. Therefore, it is best to avoid them. ☐

233

Lesson 14: God Judged the World and Delivered Noah

Teacher's Notes		Scripture Reference

God the Holy Spirit was constantly telling them to repent, but they would not.

 READ Genesis 6:3.

God warned them that He would not always continue to tell them His message.
- If they continued to resist Him, He would let them follow Satan, and He would punish them.
- God said He would give them 120 years.
- If they did not repent in 120 years, He would punish them.

There is a battle raging for men's minds:
- God the Holy Spirit speaks to us in our minds, striving for our attention.
    He speaks to us through God's Word and through other people.
    The voice of God the Spirit says to us, "Listen to God's way and trust in Him."
- But because Satan also speaks inside our minds, sometimes it seems as if a war is going on inside of us.
    The voices of Satan and his demons say, "Don't listen to God's message."
    Satan tries to tell us, "You can get along without God."

But if you refuse to listen to God and believe, the voice of God the Spirit which has been talking to you may leave.
- His voice may not always keep trying to make you believe God. — Romans 1:24
- If you refuse to agree with Him and believe His message, His voice may become quieter and quieter.
- He will let you go your own way.

When a person's heart no longer listens to God, the Bible calls this a hardened heart.
- This is terribly grievous to God, for He knows that when a person dies with a hardened heart, he will go to everlasting punishment to be separated from God forever. — Revelation 20:15
- God says in Ezekiel 33:11, "...I have no pleasure in the death of the wicked; but that the wicked turn from his way and live: turn ye, turn ye from your evil ways; for why will ye die...?"

E. Increased wickedness

 Theme: Man is a sinner. He needs God and is helpless to save himself.

 READ Genesis 6:5,11. **5**

The majority of the people followed the godless ways of Cain.
- They were becoming more and more sinful.
- They refused to believe God's message and to trust in Him and His mercy.

These people were born sinners because they were Adam's descendants.

Besides, they loved their sin and deliberately refused to agree with God.
- Compare:

Not only were the people of Noah's day the offspring of Adam, but all of us, too, are descendants of Adam. We were all born outside

5 Someone may ask why you are skipping over 6:4. You may remind him that we are studying the Bible to gain a foundation for God's message; we are not doing a verse-by-verse study. We are studying only those verses that pertain to the foundation.

This is an obscure passage — one that has been interpreted many ways. If someone persists, you might suggest to them that they could do some research on their own in a good Bible commentary. But we will not discuss it because it is not necessary to the themes and foundations we are studying. ☐

Lesson 14: God Judged the World and Delivered Noah

of the Garden of Eden, separated from God, and sinners because we are from Adam. All people sin because we were all born sinners, separated from God.

People also sin because they love their sin. No one can blame anyone else. We cannot blame Adam or God or Satan. We ourselves have chosen to sin.

As we read the Bible, we need to ask ourselves, "How does this passage apply to me? Am I thinking in the way that is talked about here? Am I doing any of the things mentioned here?"

The people of Noah's time had no room in their thoughts for God.

Romans 1:18-32

- They refused to acknowledge God even though they knew of His existence.
  - Signs of His handiwork were all around them in His creation, but they were not thankful to God nor did they believe Him.
- He also spoke to them through men called prophets.

Jude 14-16

  - One of Seth's descendants, Enoch, was one of God's prophets.
  - Now God was speaking through Noah. (II Peter 2:5 calls Noah "*a preacher of righteousness.*")
- Men had no excuse for their behavior.
  - They were simply rebelling against God.
  - They were giving in to their own evil desires.

Verse 5 tells us that *"every imagination of the thoughts of his [man's] heart was only evil continually."*

- Their minds were focused on material things and on their bodies and on their ambition for self-advancement.⁶
  - They were proud, self-centered, and boastful.
  - They wanted what other people had.
  - They were jealous of and hateful to other people.
  - They argued and fought all the time.
  - They were cruel, and many were even murderers.
  - They constantly tricked, lied, and deceived one another.
  - They were ruthless in their business practices.
  - They continually gossiped and said evil things about others behind their backs.
  - They were totally unrestrained in their sexual passions, and they even engaged in unnatural relationships.
- Compare:

  As we read today's newspaper or listen to the news on television or radio, we can easily become almost deaf or insensitive to the parade of sins being announced unashamedly. The moral and spiritual condition of mankind described in Genesis 6 should make us stop to think about the fact that man is now in a similar state of decline and wickedness.

F. God saw the unbelieving world and its sin.

 Theme: God is everywhere all the time; He knows everything.

 READ Genesis 6:5,12.

⁶You are paraphrasing Romans 1:18-32 here. If a student asks where you are getting all this information, you may refer him to this passage, or it could be read to the students. It is not included in the lesson because of time considerations.

Remember, however, to adhere to the themes of this lesson. Do not go into the surrounding context if you read from this passage in Romans. ☐

Teacher's Notes

Lesson 14: God Judged the World and Delivered Noah

Scripture Reference

God saw all their sin.
- They may have hidden their lies, adultery, stealing, and murder from others.
- But none of it was hidden from God; He saw it all.
  God always sees everything.
  No one can hide anything from Him.
  God is everywhere and sees everything at all times.
  He knows our thoughts and sees everything that is done in secret.
  He hears every word we speak and knows the motives of our hearts.

Hebrews 4:13

G. God decided to destroy the world.

 Theme: God is holy and righteous. He demands death as the payment for sin.

 READ Genesis 6:6,7. **7**

The people were so wicked that the Lord said He would destroy them and everything on the earth that He had made and given to them.
- Consider:

Do you think God really would destroy all who would not repent and trust in Him? Yes, God does what He says.

- Compare:

Back in the garden, God said to Adam and Eve, "If you disobey, you will die. You will be separated from Me." They disobeyed, and they died just as God had said. God made it clear to Cain and Abel that, if they wanted to approach Him and be accepted, they had to bring a sheep and shed its blood. God meant what He said. He rejected Cain because he came in his own way. Now, in Noah's time, God said He was going to destroy the earth and all life in it by sending a great flood. God was going to make it rain, even though it had never rained before. Does God keep His Word? Were these mere threats?

How many times have you threatened to do something when you were angry, and then forgotten it when you "cooled off"? Or how many times have you who are parents threatened to punish your children and then let them slip by without your making true your word? Is God like people? Does He merely make threats? No! God always does what He says.

H. God was gracious to Noah.

 Theme: God is loving, merciful, and gracious.

 Theme: Man is a sinner. He needs God and is helpless to save himself.

Because of God's love and mercy, there was one man and his family whom God was not going to destroy.

 READ Genesis 6:8-10.

Noah was born a sinner under Satan's control just like all of Adam's descendants.

7Someone may ask how God could "repent" if God never changes. You might answer that the word "repent" in the context here and in many places in the Old Testament can mean "feel sorry about" or "be grieved."

Mention to them that this interpretation is in keeping with the principles of understanding the Bible: We must always look at a passage in the light of the context, that is, the surrounding verses; and, even more important, in light of what is clearly known about God. The major truths, or doctrines, are clearly stated many, many times. Therefore, an isolated instance that seems to contradict what we have seen in many other passages should not be taken as a contradiction, but rather as an instance that needs special understanding or additional insight. The truth does not change. God has made very clear to us those things that are vital to our understanding of Him and His Word. If a particular passage is not clear, we can rest in the fact that it is not essential that we understand it; or, if it is critical that we know, we can trust Him, in His way and His time, to give us the insight we need.
☐

236

Lesson 14: God Judged the World and Delivered Noah

- Noah did not deserve to be saved by God.
- He, too, deserved to be punished.

 Theme: Man must have faith in order to please God.

 Theme: Man can come to God only according to God's will and plan.

But Noah came to God like Abel, Seth, and Enoch, bringing the blood of animals.[8]
- Noah listened to God's words to him.
- He repented, believed, and came to God in the way God told him.
- Noah trusted God to save him through the coming Deliverer.

Because of His grace, God forgave and accepted Noah.

The word "grace" has many depths of meaning, but here is a simple definition:

Suggested Visual:

> **GRACE**
> God's kindness
> to undeserving sinners

I. God gave instructions to Noah.

 Theme: God communicates with man.

Because the people were so evil and would not change their minds and come to God, He decided to destroy the whole earth.

But what about Noah and his family?

 READ Genesis 6:13-21.

God told Noah that He was going to send a great flood which would cover the whole earth.

God also told Noah to build a large boat so that all those who trusted in God could be saved.

 Theme: Man can come to God only according to God's will and plan.

- This boat had to be built just as God told Noah.
    Noah had to follow God's instructions.
    The ark had to be built according to God's plan.
    - Consider:
      God didn't just say, "Noah, I am going to judge the world. I am going to send a great flood. You had better do something about it. Now start building an ark." God instructed Noah how to build it.
    - Compare:
      It was just like the clothing of Adam and Eve. The clothing they made was not acceptable to God. Their clothing had to

[8]That Noah brought blood sacrifices to the Lord is inferred by 1) Genesis 8:20—he sacrificed burnt offerings and 2) Scripture has no other pattern for forgiveness for sin. Before Jesus Christ, all who believed brought animal sacrifices as an act of faith in God's promise to send a Saviour.
Leviticus 17:11 and Hebrews 9:22b clearly illustrate this principle. ☐

Lesson 14: God Judged the World and Delivered Noah

Teacher's Notes

[9] Some students may question how all the animals could possibly fit into the ark. In *The Genesis Record*, Henry Morris writes that "...the total volumetric capacity of the Ark was approximately 1,400,000 cubic feet, which is equal to the volumetric capacity of 522 standard livestock cars...over 125,000 sheep could have been carried in the ark....there might have to be a total of about seventy-two thousand animals on the Ark...and since the average size of land animals is surely less than that of a sheep...no more than 60 percent of its capacity would have to be used for animals....There were a few large animals...probably represented by young (therefore small) individuals...." (pp. 181,185).

What about dinosaurs?

Yes, dinosaurs really did exist, and God created them. They were no doubt on the ark—perhaps young animals. Dinosaurs are lizards; lizards continue to grow as they get older.

Dinosaurs probably died out after the flood because of the global change in climate. It is believed that prior to the flood, the earth was enveloped in a canopy of mist (there was no rain before the flood). This canopy caused what is referred to as a "greenhouse effect," keeping the temperature and humidity stable over the whole earth. But after the flood, the vapor canopy no longer existed and temperatures varied greatly over the globe. Many species of animals probably died out as their habitat decreased.

For an excellent treatment of the subject of dinosaurs, see the book, *"The Great Dinosaur Mystery,"* by Paul S. Taylor, Master Books, El Cajon, CA 92022, 1987. This is a children's book, but also addresses the basic questions asked by adults. ☐

[10] Be sure to clearly teach the concept of "one door," and "one ark." You will refer back to this later when you teach about Jesus Christ, who is the "one way" of salvation. ☐

be what God wanted. Cain and Abel's offerings also had to be according to the way God had said. The ark, too, had to be built according to God's plan.

 Theme: God is everywhere all the time; He knows everything.

- God knew exactly how the ark should be built, and He gave Noah careful instructions. [9]
- Consider:

We do not know exactly how the ark looked, but God did record specific dimensions that are meaningful to us today. Interestingly enough, the dimensions that God gave Noah for the ark were proportional to the huge, ocean-going carrier ships built in this century. God created the universe; God set up the laws that control flotation; God had no problem creating the perfect design for a huge ship! And, to our knowledge, no ships this large were built from the time of the ark until the twentieth century!

These are interesting details that remind us of God's great knowledge of all things and of the truth of the Bible.

- But there is one very important point we need to especially remember about the way God told Noah to build this boat.
- God told Noah to put only **one door** in the side of the ark. [10]

    There was to be only one way to get inside.

    Every person and every animal that was to be saved from God's judgment had to come into the ark by this door.

    There was only **one ark** in which people could be saved from God's wrath, and there was only **one door** to enter the ark.

J. Noah obeyed God.

 Theme: Man must have faith in order to please God and be saved.

 READ Genesis 6:22.

Noah believed God.

- He trusted in and depended on God to save him and his family from the flood which God said He would send.

    Remember, there had never been rain in the world.

    Until this time, the world was watered by mist which rose up from the ground.

    No one had ever seen rain.

- Nevertheless, Noah believed that God could not lie when He said He would send a flood.

Noah believed God, so He obeyed and built the ark just as God had said.

- Contrast:

Because we cannot see God, Heaven, or the place of punishment which God has prepared, some people will not believe. Nevertheless, all that the Bible says is true. Noah believed God, even though Noah had never seen rain.

Lesson 14: God Judged the World and Delivered Noah

Scripture Reference

I Peter 3:20

II Peter 2:5

Teacher's Notes

K. God told Noah to bring his family, the animals, and the birds into the ark.

 READ Genesis 7:1-5.

Noah warned the people of God's coming judgment.

The people in Noah's time did not accept God's words which Noah spoke to them.

- They wouldn't agree with the Holy Spirit when He spoke in their minds, reminding them of God's warnings.
- They refused to agree with God that they were wrong and that they deserved His punishment.
- They would not trust in His promise to send the Deliverer.
- They didn't believe that God would destroy the world with a great flood.

 Theme: God is loving, merciful, and gracious.

God had waited patiently for 120 years for them to change their minds, but He would wait no longer; it was time for God to punish them. [11]

 Theme: God communicates with man.

Before it started to rain, God told Noah to take his family and the chosen animals into the finished boat.

 Theme: Man must have faith in order to please God and be saved.

Noah believed that God was going to destroy the whole world.

He also believed that he and his family could only be saved by God, so he did what God said.

God didn't save Noah because of his good life.

God saved him because Noah agreed with and trusted in God.

L. They all entered by one door.

 Theme: Man can come to God only according to God's will and plan.

 READ Genesis 7:15,16.

Noah and his family all went into the ark through the one door which God had told Noah to make.

- This was the only way anyone could be saved from the flood and God's wrath against sin.
- All the animals also came into the boat by the only door.

M. God shut them in.

 Theme: God is supreme and sovereign.

 READ Genesis 7:16.

After they were all inside, God shut the door.

[11] The Bible tells us that before the flood, people lived for hundreds of years. Genesis 5 gives many examples of this. Scientists have suggested various theories for these long life spans, but we do not have a clearly-stated reason in God's Word; we simply know that this is factual information.

Interestingly, when the Sumerian king lists were unearthed and translated in recent years, the lists revealed that long life spans had been recorded for these kings. Though the lists also contained much obviously mythical information, there was a parallel to the facts of the Bible regarding the great age of men before the flood.

So, considering that men lived for hundreds of years, God's 120-year span of warning was well within the life span of the average man. People had no excuse to refuse to listen to God then (neither do people now!). ☐

239

Lesson 14: God Judged the World and Delivered Noah

- Consider:
- *"...the LORD shut him in" (v. 16)! Sometimes we read right through wonderful things in the Bible without even realizing what God has said! God Himself shut Noah, as well as his family and all the animals, inside the place of safety.*

God wasn't going to allow more time for the other people to change their minds and believe.

- When God shut the door, it was too late.

    Even if they cried or pleaded outside the door, they could not enter the ark.

    Noah could not let them in because God had shut them out. They had no way to be saved.

- Those inside the boat were safe because God had shut them in.
- Those outside of the boat now had no way to escape God's anger because God had shut them out.
- Compare:
- When God put Adam and Eve out of the garden, away from the tree of life, was there any way for them to get back in? No, none!
- When God decides it is time to punish the world, there is no escape from Him.

N. God destroyed all those outside the ark.

 Theme: God is holy and righteous. He demands death as the payment for sin.

 READ Genesis 7:17,23.

After God had shut the door of the ark, He sent the rain.

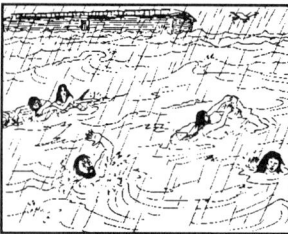

CHRONOLOGICAL PICTURE NO. 10, "NOAH'S ARK"

 Theme: God is all-powerful.

 Theme: God is supreme and sovereign.

- God has control over all the earth, the rain, wind, sun, moon, stars, and everything else.
- He made all these things, and He controls them all.

There was so much water that it covered the whole world — even the highest mountains.

Where did all the water come from?

- Do you remember what the world was like when God first made it?

    It was in darkness, and deep water was covering the whole earth.

Lesson 14: God Judged the World and Delivered Noah

On the first day, God created the light.

On the second day, He made the air and the blue sky, and He put much of the water which had been on the earth up above the sky, probably as a canopy of mist or vapor which encircled the earth.

- Now, when God's time to flood the earth had come, God made the water which He had placed up above the sky fall back onto the ground as rain.
- This was no ordinary rain; this was a **deluge!**
- The waters also came from underground sources.

    Originally, the rivers and streams on the earth were probably fed from subterranean reservoirs and rivers of water.

    God may have caused great earthquakes and volcanic eruptions to open the earth's crust so that these great fountains of water gushed out onto the earth's surface (Genesis 8:2).

 Theme: God is all-powerful.

God can do anything.

- Nothing is impossible to Him.
- He alone is almighty.

God made it rain for forty days and nights until the whole earth was covered with water, even the highest mountains and trees.

Everyone outside of the ark was destroyed by God.

- All of the other people had refused to believe, and God destroyed them all.
- Only Noah and his family had believed God and had entered the ark.

O. Conclusion

God is patient with men.

In Noah's day, God waited for 120 years for men to repent of their evil ways.

They had no excuse for their sin.

They simply refused to listen to God, though He warned them again and again through Noah.

Then, in a moment, in the midst of their sin and their godless living, they were swept away.

Every man, woman, and child outside of the ark died in the flood.

God is holy and righteous.

He is a God of love, but He is indeed a God of wrath against sin.

But Noah and his family believed God, and they weathered the storm safely inside the ark.

QUESTIONS:

1. What was the attitude of the majority of the people in the time when Noah lived? *They were obsessed with sex, marriage, and pleasing themselves. They were selfish and violent. They were not interested in knowing or pleasing God.*

2. Do we see many similarities in the world today to the times of Noah? Name some of these similarities. *Yes, there are many, such*

Lesson 14: God Judged the World and Delivered Noah

Teacher's Notes / **Scripture Reference**

as: refusal to acknowledge God, thinking only of self, and actively pursuing all kinds of evil—adultery, stealing, murder, etc.

3. Who was speaking to the people's minds, telling them to change their attitude and come to God in faith? *God the Holy Spirit.*

4. Who reminds people of God's Word and wants each one to seriously consider and believe what God has written in the Bible? *God the Holy Spirit.*

5. What did God say He was going to do because the people would not repent? *God said He would destroy all living things on earth.*

6. Did Noah deserve to be delivered from everlasting punishment by God? *No, Noah was also a sinner. He deserved to be killed like all the other people.*

7. Why then did God decide to save Noah? *Because Noah agreed with God that he was a sinner and trusted God to save him through the coming Deliverer.*

8. What did God tell Noah to do? *God told him to build an ark.*

9. Did God allow Noah to build the ark however he thought best? *No, it had to be built exactly as God commanded Noah.*

10. What one important thing should we remember about the ark? *The ark had only one door. There was only one way to enter the ark and be saved from the judgment of God.*

11. Did Noah build the ark just as God said? *Yes.*

12. What else did Noah do while he was building the ark? *He was telling the people God's message and warning them that God was going to make it rain and the whole world would be destroyed by a flood.*

13. Had the people ever seen rain before? *No, it had never rained before this time.*

14. Did the people accept what Noah said and change their attitude? *No, they refused to believe and agree with God.*

15. How long did God wait for the people in Noah's time to agree with Him and to believe His Word? *120 years.*

16. How did those saved from judgment get into the ark? *They all entered by the one and only door which God had told Noah to put in the side of the ark.*

17. Who shut the door? *God did.*

18. Why did God shut the door? *So that all those inside the ark would be safe and those outside the ark would not have the opportunity to enter and be saved.*

19. Can anyone escape God when He decides it is time to punish sin? *No.*

20. How did God cause the flood to cover all the high mountains and the earth? *God returned to the earth the water that He had placed above the sky on the second day when He was creating the earth, and He opened up the "springs of the great deep."*

21. Did anyone outside the ark escape death? *No, they all died.*

Lesson 14: God Judged the World and Delivered Noah

Scripture Reference

Teacher's Notes

OPTIONAL DISCUSSION QUESTION:

23. The Bible tells us that the people who predated Noah were skilled men—materialistic but very capable. By Noah's time, men had become so thoroughly sinful that their every thought was totally evil and godless. What does this tell you with regard to the theories of so-called "evolution" of man, which imply that man is continually improving? *Man did not and does not evolve. Man was created perfect by God, but he degenerated spiritually and morally because of his sin.*

Scripture Reference: Jeremiah 50:35-40

Teacher's Notes

LESSON 15

God Remembered Noah and All in the Ark; God Scattered the Rebels at the Tower of Babel

OVERVIEW

This lesson completes the story of God's salvation of Noah and his family and their resettlement of the earth after the flood.

It mentions the Table of Nations in Genesis 10 and then goes into the story of the builders of the tower of Babel.

Emphasis is on God's omniscience and His sovereign control over all history as shown in His scattering the rebellious builders of Babel and the resultant confusion of languages.

LESSON PREPARATION
This section is for you, the teacher.

The passages in the Scripture Reference column are for your own study in preparing for this lesson. Since they may contain concepts that run ahead of the lesson, they are not to be taught at this point.

Note: If you have not taught previously from this series of lessons, please read carefully the note to teachers in the front of this book.

SCRIPTURE: Genesis 8:1-4,14-17; 9:1,2,12-15; 11:1-9

LESSON GOALS:

- To show that God will not tolerate any attempt to take over His authority.
- To show how our differing language groups have developed as a result of God's intervention.
- To show God's sovereignty in all the affairs of men.

THIS LESSON SHOULD HELP THE STUDENTS:

- To understand that God will not condone pride and rebellion against Him.
- To understand that God is supreme and sovereign.
- To realize that every part of our history is rooted in God's acts and plans for men.
- To see that the Bible presents a factual history of man.

PERSPECTIVE FOR THE TEACHER:

Many times we have heard history presented something like this: "At its height, this empire stretched from 'here to there,' but because of 'such and such' a problem, the empire declined. Now all that can be seen are the ruins of what was once a great civilization." Genesis 11 gives us God's perspective on the rise and fall of a great city. Verse 4 reveals the driving force of these zealous builders: *"us"* and *"we."* And verses 7 and 8 give us God's conclusion to the project: *"...let us go down, and there confound their language, that they may not understand one another's speech. So the LORD scattered them abroad from thence upon the face of all the earth: and they left off to build the city."* This critical change in man's history was engineered and accomplished by the Lord! Wouldn't it be interesting to hear God's true account of every great building project and civilization and its eventual decline?

We need to remember the message of this passage as we study any history: God is the sovereign controller of the affairs of men. Any attempts to explain the flow of history must include our Creator and sovereign God. In recent years, His name has been "written out" of secular history books by those who follow humanistic thinking. But His name can never be erased from the truth!

It is interesting to note that God has left us not only His biblical record of the tower of Babel; He has also allowed us to uncover some of the remains of the city of Babylon itself. Though we do not know the exact spot of the original tower, many ruined towers are still visible in the area of Babylon; and there are probably more ruins in areas not yet excavated. Babylon was rebuilt sometime after its first builders had been scattered by God. But it eventually became so

245

Lesson 15: God Scattered the Rebels at the Tower of Babel

Teacher's Notes | Scripture Reference

thoroughly evil that God caused it to become a total ruin, with no inhabitants even to this day.

Babylon is a real place with a message for our times from our great and sovereign God. God will not allow men to exalt themselves and live in continued rebellion against Him. He judges sin and moves with power to achieve all that He has purposed to do.

VISUALS:

- Chronological Picture No. 12, "The Tower of Babel"
- Chronological Map 1
- Chronological Chart

ON TEACHING THIS LESSON:

These lessons are designed to **teach unbelievers.** You are carefully laying a scriptural foundation on which the Gospel will later be presented. If your class contains believers, teach with the goal of giving them an understanding of the basis for their faith and **with the goal of enabling them to teach the same material to unbelievers.**

DON'T COMPLICATE THE MESSAGE!

As you teach, keep in mind that this is a directed study—not an exhaustive survey of the Bible and not an unlimited group discussion. Keep your lesson on track and moving ahead by limiting and directing any discussion.

Carefully follow the outline. Emphasize the doctrinal themes.

LESSON FORMAT: The **center column** below contains the lesson material to be taught to the students. The **bold outline headings** are only for reference and need not be spoken, as they are incorporated into the outlined material that follows. The material in the **side columns** is for the teacher's own reference and is not intended to be included in the lesson.

TO BE TAUGHT TO THE STUDENTS
(Center Column Only)

LESSON OUTLINE:

REVIEW questions from Lesson 14.

A. Introduction

The Bible is an amazing book.

It has the answers to the most important questions of life.

And it also explains the history of mankind in depths unattainable by any other resource.

For instance: have you ever wondered why people around the world speak so many different languages?

The Bible has the answer.

We are going to look at that answer in a moment.

But first we are going to complete the record of Noah and his family.

Lesson 15: God Scattered the Rebels at the Tower of Babel

B. God remembered Noah and all those inside the ark.

 Theme: God is faithful; He never changes.

 Theme: God is supreme and sovereign.

READ Genesis 8:1-4,14-17.

Noah and his family and the animals in the ark were kept safe by God.

- Not one of them died.
- God remembered them, and He stopped the rain.
- He sent a strong wind to dry up the water, and the dry land again appeared.
- God controls the rain and the wind.

God never changes; He never forgets.

- He didn't forget Noah and the others in the ark.
- He does what He says.
- He said He would save them, and He did.
- He said He would destroy all outside of the ark, and He did.

ON MAP 1, POINT TO MT. ARARAT (located in what is now Turkey).

- Consider: [1]

You have undoubtedly heard of the many expeditions in the past several years which have attempted to find the ark on Mt. Ararat. This is an interesting possibility, and one day God may allow men to find the ark there in the ice. But the thing we need to remember is that regardless of whether or not the ark is found, the account of Noah and the ark and the flood is true.

Many scientists now see that the biblical record of the flood is the true scientific explanation for the great number of fossil remains of animals such as dinosaurs and other now-extinct animals.

The flood also accounts for many geological formations that were once thought of in terms of evolutionary processes. The more we learn about the Bible, the more we realize that God's Word is an amazing, accurate, scientific record of historical fact.

C. God gave His commands and promises to Noah.

 Theme: God communicates with man.

READ Genesis 9:1,2.

God gave Noah and his sons, Shem, Ham, and Japheth, control over the animals, birds, and fish just as He had given it to Adam in the beginning.

- The world and everything in it belongs to God.
- But He gave it to man to take care of for Him.

D. God gave the rainbow as His sign.

 Theme: God is faithful; He never changes.

---

[1] Some students will appreciate this type of information, and it will help them to be open to learn more. But others will only see it as a signal to debate.

You will not want to use this material if you think it will cause unnecessary discussion. By this time, you probably know your class well enough to know what is appropriate. ☐

Lesson 15: God Scattered the Rebels at the Tower of Babel

 READ Genesis 9:12-15.

- The rainbow was given as God's sign to show that He would never again destroy the earth by a flood.

 Read Psalm 104:6-9.

- Many thousands of years have passed since the flood.
- God has kept His word.
- When you see a rainbow, remember that God gave the rainbow as a sign that He will never again destroy the world by a flood.
- God can be trusted.

E. God's record of the nations

Genesis 10, often called the "Table of Nations," records the generations of the sons of Noah.

POINT TO THE "TABLE OF NATIONS" ON THE CHRONOLOGICAL CHART.

Though we won't take time to study this chapter, it is truly an amazing document—a carefully composed, objective record made by the God who knows everything and every person.

God's record stands in sharp contrast to the often mythical writings of ancient men from ungodly civilizations.

Just as all of us find our ancestry in Adam, so we also find our ancestry somewhere in Genesis 10.

F. The rebellious, proud attitude of the people

 Theme: Man is a sinner. He needs God and is helpless to save himself.

 READ Genesis 11:1-4.

Many years had passed since God saved Noah, his wife, their three sons, and their sons' wives from the great flood.

Once again, many people lived on the earth.

CHRONOLOGICAL PICTURE NO. 12, "THE TOWER OF BABEL"

The majority of the descendants of Noah soon forgot about God's terrible judgment on the earth by the flood.

They deliberately ignored God.

- They refused to consider His will for them.
- They did not want to know and believe on the Lord like Abel, Seth, and Noah.

Lesson 15: God Scattered the Rebels at the Tower of Babel

Scripture Reference

Psalm 19:1-3

Romans 1:18-32

Teacher's Notes

They were under Satan's control and like Satan in their thinking.
- They wanted to be great and exalt themselves.
- They were not interested in knowing, worshiping, or trusting God, nor in obeying His Word.

Among these people were our ancestors.
- They had heard about the flood, and they knew that God was their Creator.

  Every day and every night, they could see His mighty power revealed through all the things that He had made.

  God also continued to show His faithfulness to His promise never to destroy the earth again by a flood—by putting the rainbow in the sky.

  They didn't have any excuse for not believing God.

- But they would not give God the place of honor which He deserves or thank Him for life, health, sunshine, rain, and food. **2**
- They deliberately turned away from what they knew to be the truth about God, and their minds became more and more evil and foolish.

  They made images of people and worshiped them.

  They worshiped animals and birds.

  Finally, they worshiped snakes and other reptiles.

 Theme: Satan fights against God and His will. Satan is a liar and a deceiver. He hates man.

Satan was leading our ancestors in rebellion against God and His will.
- Satan wants people to worship false gods.
- Many primitive societies still worship the sun, moon, stars, birds, or animals.
- Consider:

How easy it is for us to look at the people who do these things and see their folly. But Satan is clever. He knows the weaknesses of each culture, and he knows what lies will be culturally "acceptable."

Even though we may not think we see many people obviously involved in idol worship, we do find that the horoscope is printed in our daily paper! We do see people going more and more deeply into debt and sacrificing all their time and energy and even relationships in order to keep up with the incredible pressures of our materialistic culture. We do see people centering their thoughts, time, and energies on exalting self. Where does God fit into all of this?

Worship has to do with the giving of our thoughts, our hearts, our resources—even our lives—to serve the object of our worship. Worship comes from the word "worth." God, and God alone, is worthy of our adoration and worship.

Satan doesn't care what we worship as long as we don't worship the only true and living God.

 Theme: God is supreme and sovereign.

2The comments about these people and their progressive turning away from God are based on Romans 1:18-32.

If your students ask how we know that this applies to this particular group of people, you might mention that this is the pattern of moral degradation described in God's Word. It is accurate, even in describing people today who turn away from God. The outward manifestations are perhaps more subtle, but the pattern is the same. (Ascribing significance to horoscopes and signs of the zodiac is one example of this kind of ungodly worship.) ☐

Lesson 15: God Scattered the Rebels at the Tower of Babel

Teacher's Notes		Scripture Reference

God is sovereign.
- He and He alone is God.
- In Isaiah 42:8 God says, *"I am the LORD: that is my name: and my glory will I not give to another, neither my praise to graven images [idols]."*

But the builders of Babel (also called Babylon) were not thinking about God.

POINT TO THE WORD "BABEL" ON THE CHRONOLOGICAL CHART.

[3]*The Bible Knowledge Commentary: Old Testament,* by John F. Walvoord and Roy B. Zuck, p. 44. Victor Books, 1986. ☐

- The *Bible Knowledge Commentary*[3] gives some interesting insights into the idolatrous, prideful thinking of the builders of these cities:

  "Written Babylonian accounts of the building of the city of Babylon refer to its construction in heaven by the gods as a celestial city, as an expression of pride....These accounts say it was made by the same process of brick-making described in verse 3 [Genesis 11], with every brick inscribed with the name of the Babylonian god Marduk. Also the ziggurat, the step-like tower believed to have been first erected in Babylon, was said to have its top in the heavens (cf. v. 4). This artificial mountain became the center of worship in the city, a miniature temple being at the top of the tower. The Babylonians took great pride in their building; they boasted of their city as not only impregnable, but also as the heavenly city, *babili* ('the gate of God')."

- Marduk, by the way, is another name for Baal, one of the false gods the people set up to worship instead of the one true God. The practices associated with Baal worship were evil, sensual, and cruel.

POINT ON MAP 1 TO THE AREA WHERE BABEL WAS SITUATED IN THE TIGRIS-EUPHRATES PLAIN.

- In the area of the Tigris-Euphrates plain, there are many visible remnants of later civilizations which still bear towers, or ziggurats, calling to mind the tower of Babel. Construction of these structures also reveals the burnt clay and bitumen (tar) mentioned in the Bible.

 Theme: God is supreme and sovereign.

The people gathered to build the tower of Babel because they did not want to be scattered over all the earth.

 READ Genesis 11:4.

[4]See if the students notice the "let us...let us make us a name..."

Also, see if they remember God's commandment to Noah and his sons after the flood. ☐

Whom were they thinking about?[4]

Themselves! These men were full of pride!

They should have been interested in exalting God's name, not their own!

But look again at the last part of this verse. What else was wrong?

Do you remember what command God gave to Adam and then repeated to Noah and his descendants?

 READ Genesis 1:28 and 9:1,2.

- God had told Adam and Noah that they were to multiply and to take control of all animals, birds, and fish in all parts of the world.

Lesson 15: God Scattered the Rebels at the Tower of Babel

- God didn't want people to live together in one place, doing only as they pleased.
- God knew that, if they all stayed together, they would quickly forget about God and His will.
- Man was created by God to do God's will on the earth.
    - God is the Creator and owner of us all, no matter where we live, what color we are, or what language we speak.

These people deliberately disobeyed the command given to Noah and Adam by God, their Creator.

- They did not want to be scattered into different parts of the world as God commanded.
- They congregated in one place, built a city, and began to erect a great, tall tower.

G. God saw them.

 Theme: God is everywhere all the time; He knows everything.

Was God interested in these rebellious people?
- Did God see them?
- Did He know their thoughts and what they planned?
- Did He care what they did?

 READ Genesis 11:5.

Yes, the Lord was interested in them even though they had forgotten Him.

God sees all people everywhere.

 Read Proverbs 15:3.

- He is interested in every person.
- He knows all about us, too.
    - Neither you nor I can keep any secret from Him.
    - He knows everything we have ever thought, said, or done.

He is our Creator.
- He owns every person.
- He even owns those who are separated from Him because of their sin.

H. God scattered them.

 Theme: God is supreme and sovereign.

Can anyone fight against God and win?
- When Satan was in Heaven, he tried to fight against God, but he lost.
- The other angels who followed Satan also lost in their fight against God.
- Adam and Eve, Cain, and the people at the time when Noah lived lost in their fight against God.

Psalm 139

Ezekiel 18:4

Lesson 15: God Scattered the Rebels at the Tower of Babel

- What do you think happened this time? Did Satan and the people win?

No one can fight against God and be the winner; He is greater than all.

Now we will read how the Lord took control of the situation.

 READ Genesis 11:6-9.

- Note:

  Do you remember that God said in the beginning, "...Let us make man in our image..." (Genesis 1:26)?

  Now again we see the Lord—God the Father, God the Son, and God the Holy Spirit—discussing what He was about to do.

- The Lord caused the people to speak different languages.
- Because men could no longer understand one another, they separated into their various families and moved away to different parts of the country.
- Over many years, they moved to other parts of the world on foot or by boats.

This was God's original plan—that man populate the whole earth, not just one region.

- Consider:

  Often we hear explanations of the history and development of nations and languages told only from the standpoint of man's limited understanding. If we really want to know the true origin and history of man, we need to look closely at the Bible. We need to realize that God alone can give us many of the details of the past. When we believe His Word, we have a framework on which to place archeological discoveries and other historical evidences. Apart from the Bible, we cannot possibly construct an accurate history. God created everything and has recorded accurately for us those foundations that man needs to know.

  This passage in Genesis tells us how the different nations and races began, including each of our particular ancestors. Our ancestors were at the tower of Babel. This is the beginning of the history of your family as part of a distinct nationality or language group.

  Our ancestors turned away from the truth of God which they knew and followed the ideas which Satan and his spirits gave to them. If you have studied ancient cultures, you know of the prevalence of idol worship and false gods. Both sophisticated and unsophisticated societies turned away from the true and living God to follow after human leaders, sinful desires, false gods, and idols.

There were a few people who continued to worship the true and living God, but the majority turned away from God.

I. Conclusion

The Bible gives us insight into history; but more than that, it shows us what God is like and how God deals with man.

You may already be noticing some patterns in these ancient stories that sound a lot like the pattern of life today—men and women are still rebelling against God.

But God hasn't changed either.

He cares about every individual.

Lesson 15: God Scattered the Rebels at the Tower of Babel

He knows exactly what is happening in each life.
He still judges sin.
And He is still calling people to believe in Him.

QUESTIONS:

1. Why could God give Noah and his sons control over all the animals, birds, and fish? *Because the world and everything in it belongs to God.*

2. What sign did God give to show He would never again destroy the earth by a flood? *The rainbow.*

3. Has God kept His promise? *Yes, God is true to His Word. He never lies. He never changes.*

4. Did the generation following the flood know the truth about God? *Yes.*

5. How did they know?

    a. *The truth about God the Creator and His judgment by the flood was told from one generation to the next.*

    b. *They could see that there was an almighty Creator by the things which God had made. The sun, moon, stars, and all the things on the earth were proof that God was their almighty Creator.*

    c. *The rainbow was God's sign in the sky.*

6. Did the descendants of Noah all worship God? Did they agree with what He said and trust in His promise to send the Deliverer? *No, only a few believed and worshiped God.*

7. What did the majority of the people do?

    a. *They deliberately turned away from what they knew was the truth and followed the lies of Satan.*

    b. *They worshiped idols made like people, birds, animals, and reptiles. They also worshiped the sun, moon, and stars.*

8. Who were these people? *They were the descendants of Adam and Noah's sons, Shem, Ham, and Japheth, so they were our ancestors.*

9. Why did they begin to build the tower of Babel?

    a. *So that they would not be scattered all over the world as God had commanded.*

    b. *So that they would be greatly exalted on the earth.*

10. Did God know what they were planning to do? *Yes.*

11. Does God know all the secrets which people have? *Yes, He knows them all.*

12. What did the Lord do? *He gave different languages to different families so they could no longer understand one another.*

13. What was the result? *The various families separated from one another and moved to different places.*

14. Where did our earliest ancestors get their religious beliefs? *From Satan and also from their own ideas when they deliberately turned from the truth about God.*

Lesson 15: God Scattered the Rebels at the Tower of Babel

THE FOLLOWING ARE OPTIONAL QUESTIONS

15. Name some attitudes prevalent among the people of Babel that are common to people today. *Pride and rebellion.*

16. What would you say are some of the things that men and women worship today?

Scripture Reference

Teacher's Notes

LESSON 16

God Chose, Called, and Guided Abram; Lot Chose the Fertile Plains of Sodom and Gomorrah

OVERVIEW

This lesson presents God's faithfulness and grace in calling Abram out of Ur into Canaan and Abram's response of faith. In Genesis 12 is the beginning of God's promises to Abram: that He would make of him a great nation, and that all families of the earth would be blessed in him (through the line of Abram would come the Deliverer).

Also presented: Lot's choice of what seemed to him the better land—the area of Sodom and Gomorrah.

LESSON PREPARATION

This section is for you, the teacher.

The passages in the Scripture Reference column are for your own study in preparing for this lesson. Since they may contain concepts that run ahead of the lesson, they are not to be taught at this point.

Note: If you have not taught previously from this series of lessons, please read carefully the note to teachers in the front of this book.

Hebrews 11:8-10

SCRIPTURE: Genesis 11:27-32; 12:1-5; 13:5-13

LESSON GOALS:

- To show that God is faithful to carry out His plans and to fulfill His promises.
- To show man's need to trust and obey God, regardless of what other men are doing.

THIS LESSON SHOULD HELP THE STUDENTS:

- To see the unity of the Bible.
- To see that God is not turned aside from His purposes by the actions of men, but that He is always faithful to carry out what He has promised to do.
- To anticipate the story of the Deliverer.

PERSPECTIVE FOR THE TEACHER:

A wonderful passage of Scripture says, *"Even as Abraham believed God, and it was accounted to him for righteousness. Know ye therefore that they which are of faith, the same are the children of Abraham. And the scripture, foreseeing that God would justify the heathen through faith, preached before the gospel unto Abraham, saying, In thee shall all nations be blessed. So then they which be of faith are blessed with faithful Abraham"* (Galatians 3:6-9).

The ways of our God are marvelous, indeed! This man Abraham is our "father" in faith! We should be greatly encouraged and comforted by the testimony of this man. He appears like a sunlit figure against a very dark, stormy sky as he moves away from his pagan heritage. Hebrews 11:8 tells us that he did not know where he was going. Yet he, like Noah, believed God and obeyed. Abraham is held up to us as an example of faith, yet he was also very human—riddled with failure and lapses in his faith.[1] But we see in Abraham a man who repented of his sin and always resumed his walk with God.

Our culture needs "heroes." We are sorely lacking in men with enough consistency in their lives to be considered even good examples. But God used Abraham's life over and over to exhibit His grace and to channel His blessing. Yet the main character of this story and of all the Bible is God! It is HIS GRACE we see in Abraham.

Abraham is not some shadowy figure of antiquity. Abraham is our father in the faith! Remember what Jesus said in Matthew 22:31,32: *". . . have ye not read that which was spoken unto you by God, saying, I am the God of Abraham,*

[1] These lessons do not cover the passages concerning Abraham's sins. The story of Hagar and Ishmael is not discussed; nor is circumcision. We are presenting only those events and details that are foundational for presenting the character of God and His provision for salvation by faith.

If a student wants to discuss other things, remind Him that we are only "hitting the high spots" in this course and dealing with foundational issues. You may be able to answer some of his questions after class. ☐

255

Teacher's Notes

Lesson 16: God Chose, Called, and Guided Abram

Scripture Reference

and the God of Isaac, and the God of Jacob? God is not the God of the dead, but of the living."

Think about that! We are teaching God's living Word. We need to ask our Lord for His Spirit's enabling to teach it as it is—alive and real—so our students may hear and believe.

VISUALS:

- Chronological Picture No. 14, "Leaving Haran"
- Chronological Map 1
- Chronological Chart

ON TEACHING THIS LESSON:

These lessons are designed to **teach unbelievers.** You are carefully laying a scriptural foundation on which the Gospel will later be presented. If your class contains believers, teach with the goal of giving them an understanding of the basis for their faith and **with the goal of enabling them to teach the same material to unbelievers.**

DON'T COMPLICATE THE MESSAGE!

As you teach, keep in mind that this is a directed study—not an exhaustive survey of the Bible and not an unlimited group discussion. Keep your lesson on track and moving ahead by limiting and directing any discussion.

Carefully follow the outline. Emphasize the doctrinal themes.

LESSON FORMAT: The **center column** below contains the lesson material to be taught to the students. The **bold outline headings** are only for reference and need not be spoken, as they are incorporated into the outlined material that follows. The material in the **side columns** is for the teacher's own reference and is not intended to be included in the lesson.

TO BE TAUGHT TO THE STUDENTS
(Center Column Only)

LESSON OUTLINE:

REVIEW questions from Lesson 15.

A. Introduction

How many of you know the name of your great-great-grandfather?

Not many of us know the names of our ancestors, but today we are going to talk about a man who lived about 4,000 years ago and is still remembered by his descendants.

Why is he remembered?

- He is remembered because of God's promises to him.
- He is remembered because he believed God.

B. Abram was a descendant of Shem.

Noah had three sons, Shem, Ham, and Japheth; Abram was a descendant of Shem.

Lesson 16: God Chose, Called, and Guided Abram

Abram, the son of Terah, lived close to where the people had begun to build the great tower of Babel.

POINT TO BABEL ON MAP 1.

 READ Genesis 11:27-30.

POINT TO ABRAHAM, SARAH, AND LOT ON THE CHRONOLOGICAL CHART.

Later on in their story, we will see Abram's and Sarai's names change.

Abram married Sarai, but Abram and Sarai didn't have any children.

- Note:

  In those days, the inability to have children was considered to be a disgrace. Couples who had no children were looked down upon by society. Male children were most desirable so that a man might have heirs to carry on his family name.

 READ Genesis 11:31,32.

Terah, Abram's father, moved from Ur and traveled up to Haran.
- Terah took Abram and Sarai with him.
- He also took his grandson, Lot, because Lot's father had died in Ur.

Terah planned to go into Canaan, but they only got as far as Haran, where Terah died.

ON MAP 1, POINT TO UR, HARAN, AND CANAAN AS YOU COME TO THEM IN THE TEXT.

C. God called and commanded Abram.

 Theme: God is faithful; He never changes.

 READ Genesis 12:1.[2]

 Theme: God communicates with man.

- God called Abram to leave his own country and go into the land of Canaan.
- God spoke directly to Abram and told him what he was to do; the Bible was not yet written in Abram's day.

  God doesn't speak to us now through a voice.

  He speaks to us through His written Word, the Bible.

  The only way we can know about God and His message for us is through the words of this book, the Bible.

Theme: Man is a sinner. He needs God and is helpless to save himself.

Where Abram lived in Mesopotamia the people worshiped idols.
- They did not trust, love, or obey God, their Creator.
- Joshua 24:2 tells us that Abram's father, Terah, was an idolater.

Was Abram also a sinner?

[2] Acts 7:2,3 says that God had called Abram to go into Canaan before he moved with his father to Haran. ☐

Lesson 16: God Chose, Called, and Guided Abram

Teacher's Notes | **Scripture Reference**

Yes, he, too, was a descendant of Adam.

But Abraham believed God.

- He came to God in God's revealed way.
- He trusted in God and His promises.

 Theme: God is supreme and sovereign.

God's plan for Abram could not be achieved while Abram was living among his idolatrous countrymen.

- He must leave his homeland.
- He must go to the country to which God promised He would guide him.

God had the right to tell Abram what to do.

- God is greater than all.
- He is supreme.

D. God's promises to Abram

 Theme: God is loving, merciful, and gracious.

 Theme: God is faithful; He never changes.

Our ancestors, the descendants of Noah, had deliberately turned away from God and the truth.

- They worshiped the things which God had created instead of God, their Creator. *(Romans 1:23-25)*
- They rebelled against Him by beginning to build the tower of Babel.

In spite of all their sinfulness, however, God did not abandon His plan to rescue mankind from Satan's power and everlasting punishment. *(Genesis 11:3,4)*

- No one and nothing can stop God from carrying out His plans.
- Consider:

Listen to what God said many years later through His prophet Isaiah to people who were still worshiping Babylon's false god, Marduk: "Remember this, and shew yourselves men: bring it again to mind, O ye transgressors. Remember the former things of old: for I am God, and there is none else; I am God, and there is none like me, Declaring the end from the beginning, and from ancient times the things that are not yet done, saying, My counsel shall stand, and I will do all my pleasure" (Isaiah 46:8-10).

> Whatever God promises to do, He does.
>
> Whatever God begins, He brings to a conclusion.
>
> Nothing can keep God from carrying out His plans and accomplishing His purposes.

- Calling Abram was God's next step in His plan to deliver men from their bondage to sin.

God is still the same today as He was in the days of Abram.

- He is still loving, merciful, and gracious.
- He has not forgotten His plan to save people from everlasting punishment.
- He wants everyone to be saved from Satan's power and from sin.

Let's read God's promises to Abram.

Lesson 16: God Chose, Called, and Guided Abram

 READ Genesis 12:2.

- Even though Abram and Sarai did not have any children, God promised Abram that he would become the father of a great nation.
- God also promised that He would protect and prosper Abram so that he would become an important man and that, through him, others would also receive great benefit and help.

 READ Genesis 12:3.

- God also promised that He would prosper those who helped Abram, but He would bring evil on anyone who treated Abram wrongly.
- Let's take a closer look at the end of verse 3: *"...in thee shall all families of the earth be blessed."*

    Galatians 3:8

    This is the greatest of all the promises given to Abram, because it is about the Deliverer.

    Do you remember our studying that, in the garden of Eden, God promised He would send a Deliverer into the world to crush the power of Satan?

    God now promised that one of Abram's descendants would be that Deliverer.

    All families of the earth would be blessed through Abram's descendant.

    - That promise includes you and your family and me and my family and all of the other families and all people in the world.
    - The Deliverer whom God promised to send was for all people in every part of the world.

E. Abram believed and obeyed God.

 Theme: Man must have faith in order to please God and be saved.

Abraham's environment and circumstances:
- Remember that Abram was living in a very idolatrous, sinful world and came from a family that did not worship God.
- Abram, like Noah, was surrounded by men and women who scorned God and followed after their own evil desires.
- Abram and Sarai were childless.

In spite of his environment and his circumstances, Abraham believed God's promises.
- Abram believed that God would send the Deliverer and that the Deliverer would be one of his descendants.
- Abram, like Noah, believed God's Word, and for that reason, he obeyed God.

 READ Genesis 12:4,5.

ON MAP 1, POINT TO UR, HARAN, AND CANAAN, SHOWING THE PROBABLE ROUTE OF ABRAM'S JOURNEY.

Teacher's Notes

Lesson 16: God Chose, Called, and Guided Abram

Scripture Reference

- Consider:

Let's keep in mind as we study the story of Abram that he was a real person in history, one who is mentioned many times throughout the Old and New Testament.

Archeological discoveries at Ur, Mari, Ebla and other ancient sites agree with the details in the Bible concerning life in Abram's time, that is, about 2,000 B.C. Recently, many new details have come to light about travel and trade, marriage and family, and even common names which agree with the biblical account.

Suggested Visual:

CHRONOLOGICAL PICTURE NO. 14, "LEAVING HARAN"

- Consider:

Abram was very rich and had many servants, cattle, sheep, and goats. He took all that he owned with him. It is impossible for us to appreciate everything that was involved in such a journey, but we need to think about the fact that Abram's decision to follow God was not a mere whim or desire for adventure. Abram made the decision to go because Abram believed God.

Can you imagine "pulling up stakes" and taking off across the land with all your family and possessions and heading for a strange country—all in obedience to the God whom your neighbors scoffed at? Remember, Abram was a man of wealth and standing. People were watching him.

The city Abram had left earlier, Ur of the Chaldees, was an urban center with houses and temples similar to those at Babel. The remains of the city of Ur can be seen in the country of Iraq today.

But now Abram had to travel and live in tents.

In spite of inconvenience and social pressures, Abram believed God and obeyed Him, trusting all his family and possessions and reputation into God's care. Abraham realized that God was totally worthy of his trust.

Lot, Abram's nephew, also went with Abram and Sarai.

Lot also believed God and trusted in His promises.

II Peter 2:7-9

 Theme: God is faithful; He never changes.

The Lord faithfully guided Abram to Canaan, the land that He had promised to give to him.

F. Trouble between Lot's and Abram's herdsmen

 READ Genesis 13:5-7.

Lot, Abram's nephew, was also rich like his uncle.

Lesson 16: God Chose, Called, and Guided Abram

Because they both had many sheep and cattle, it wasn't long before trouble developed between the men taking care of their herds and flocks.

G. Abram's solution

Abram had a solution which he proposed to Lot.

 READ Genesis 13:8,9.

H. Lot's choice

 READ Genesis 13:10,11.

Lot looked around to make his choice; he chose the grassy plain which he thought would be best for his animals.

- Even though Lot believed and trusted in God, he wasn't thinking of what was the best thing for him and his family and how this move would affect their knowledge of God or their ability to please Him.
- Lot was probably thinking only of how to make more money.
- Some terrible things happened to Lot because of this choice.
- Consider:

Remember Cain's foolish decision to ignore God? All of his descendants were drowned in the flood.

We need to be careful of the choices we make. In our society, we are continually pressured to make choices about things that really have no eternal value: How can we make more money? What shall we buy? Where will we go? What will we do tomorrow? What about vacation?

But the real issues of life are seldom mentioned: What about our relationship to God? What do our children know about God? What has God written for us in His Word? What about the penalty for our sins?

 Read Proverbs 14:12.

If a person chooses to turn away from learning what God has written for him in the Bible, that person will regret it forever. We do not want to face the fact that God has prepared a place of punishment for all who turn against Him. Satan does not want us to think about it! But the Lake of Fire is a real place where Satan and all his demons and everyone who refuses God will spend eternity. What good will it do us to own everything in the world if we die and go to Hell?

No one wants to talk about these things. We are continually urged to have more things and to think less about God. But God calls to us through His Word—pleads with us—to listen to Him and to believe Him.

II Peter 3:9

 Theme: Man is a sinner. He needs God and is helpless to save himself.

- Compare:
- *Abram stayed up in the rocky, less fertile hills and mountains.*

Lesson 16: God Chose, Called, and Guided Abram

- *Lot moved down to the fertile plain.*
- *In the eyes of men, it would seem that Abram was the "loser" in this division of territory.*
- *But God knows the truth which we cannot see on the surface of things.*

 READ Genesis 13:12,13.

Down on the plains, there were two cities, Sodom and Gomorrah.
- These cities were very wicked.
- The people who lived there didn't want to know about God or what He wanted them to do.
- They were only thinking of themselves and of the evil things they were doing.

God knew this and would have told Lot if he had asked.

But instead, Lot just chose what seemed to look the best to him, and in doing so he took a tragic step away from God and into a terribly dangerous place of great evil.

 Theme: God is everywhere all the time; He knows everything.

Even though the people of Sodom and Gomorrah weren't thinking about God, He saw all they did.
- He was their Creator.
- He rightfully owned them, even though they were following Satan.
- Consider:

Although people ignore God and refuse to listen to His message, He still knows all about them. They may choose to reject God and follow Satan, but they still rightfully belong to God. He will judge and punish them when He decides that He has given them enough time to change their minds and agree with Him.

I. Conclusion:

Lot made a choice based on selfish desires.

But Abram obeyed God because he believed that God would do all He had promised.

In our next lesson, we will consider further how God worked in these men's lives.

Let's think about our own lives and our choices, too, in light of what we're learning about God.

QUESTIONS:

1. Did God abandon His plan to send a Deliverer for mankind because they rebelled against God and built the tower of Babel? *No.*

2. What did God do to ensure that the Deliverer would be born into the world? *God chose and called Abram to be the ancestor of the Deliverer.*

3. What did God tell Abram to do? *God told him to leave his own country and go to the place to which God promised to lead him.*

Lesson 16: God Chose, Called, and Guided Abram

Scripture Reference

Teacher's Notes

4. How many children did Abram and Sarai have when God told Abram to go into a different country? *They didn't have any children.*

5. What did God promise Abram?

   a. God said that Abram's descendants would become a great nation.

   b. God promised that He would protect and prosper Abram so that he would become an important man, and through him others would receive great help and benefit.

   c. God said He would prosper those who helped Abram, but He would bring evil on anyone who treated Abram wrongly.

   d. God also said that all of the nations and tribes in the world would receive God's help through one certain descendant of Abram.

6. Who would this descendant of Abram be? *He would be the Deliverer, the one who would overcome Satan and make it possible for people to be in oneness with God.*

7. God spoke directly to Abram, but how does God speak to people today? *Through the Bible.*

8. Did God choose Abram because Abram wasn't a sinner? *No, all people are sinners.*

9. How did Abram come to God to worship Him? *He came the same way Abel, Seth, and Noah had come. They came the way God had told them.*

10. What did Abram do when God gave him the promises? *He believed God. He left his own country and went where God guided him.*

11. What similarities do you see in Abel, Seth, Enoch, Noah, and Abram? *They believed God and came to God in the way God asked them to come; they obeyed God.*

12. Why did Lot move away from Abram and live down on the plain near to Sodom and Gomorrah?

    a. Abram and Lot had so many animals that there wasn't sufficient grass and room for them to live together.

    b. Lot moved to the plain because it was well-watered and had much more grass for his animals.

13. What benefit will riches be to people if, when they die, they go to everlasting punishment? *Their riches will not be of any benefit to them at all.*

14. Who saw the wicked things the people of Sodom and Gomorrah did? *God did.*

15. Are any thoughts, words, or actions hidden from God? *No.*

| Scripture Reference | | Teacher's Notes |

LESSON 17

God Destroyed Sodom and Gomorrah; God Renewed His Promises to Abraham

OVERVIEW

This lesson focuses on two continuing stories:

God credited Abraham's faith to him as righteousness.

But God rescued Lot from Sodom and Gomorrah so God could destroy those two wicked cities.

Some points:

- God's communication with man, shown in His promises to Abraham
  Note: You will refer to these promises in later lessons, so be sure you teach them now.
- Man's need to come to God by faith, shown in Abraham's response
- God's concern for all men, but His certain judgment of sin, shown in the story of Sodom and Gomorrah.

LESSON PREPARATION

This section is for you, the teacher.

The passages in the Scripture Reference column are for your own study in preparing for this lesson. Since they may contain concepts that run ahead of the lesson, they are not to be taught at this point.

Note: If you have not taught previously from this series of lessons, please read carefully the note to teachers in the front of this book.

Hebrews 11:11,12

SCRIPTURE: Genesis 13:14-17; 15:5,6,13-16; 17:1-5,15-17; 18:20,21; 19:1-7,10-17,24-26.

LESSON GOALS:

- To show that God credited Abraham's faith to him as righteousness.
- To show that God judges sin.
- To show the results of wrong choices.
- To show God's concern for individuals.

THIS LESSON SHOULD HELP THE STUDENTS:

- To see that Abraham's faith was counted to him as righteousness.
- To realize that no one "gets away with" sin.
- To see the seriousness of sin and rebellion against God.
- To realize that God cares about them personally.
- To see that the Bible is true.

PERSPECTIVE FOR THE TEACHER:

To our society that disdains any standards of morality and righteousness, the story of Sodom and Gomorrah stands as a clear testimony of God's unwavering truth.

This passage of Scripture is particularly timely for us because of the kind of sin prevalent in these cities. Homosexuality (and every other kind of sexual sin) is flourishing in our day, but many excuse their sin as a "chosen lifestyle." Godless lifestyles have become popular and socially acceptable. But God has not changed. God never has and never will accept immoral behavior.

Many people in our society like to think that a "loving God" would never punish anyone. But God is righteous; and though He is indeed loving, He is also to be feared. God does punish all sin.

One of the great lessons of this story is that we need to be mindful of the choices we make. Abraham chose to believe God, and God is still pouring out blessing on the descendants of Abraham—those who, like Abraham, believe God. But Lot made a choice that unnecessarily placed him and his family in the middle of a perverted, godless environment. That choice cost him the lives of his wife and his sons-in-law and his testimony and that of his daughters. The story of Lot and his daughters in 19:30-38 (we will not teach this passage) shows that even though they escaped the cities, they still carried with them the taint of the sins that flourished there. The sons born to Lot's daughters became the

Lesson 17: God Destroyed Sodom and Gomorrah

Teacher's Notes • Scripture Reference

fathers of the Moabites and the Ammonites who were to be continual enemies of Abraham's descendants.

Sin leaves a horrible trail of pain, sorrow, wasted lives, destruction, and death. Perhaps someone who hears the story of Sodom and Gomorrah will believe and repent of his own life of sin. Pray for the Lord's enabling for you as a teacher and for His working in hearts as you teach this lesson.

VISUALS:

- Chronological Picture No. 16, "Lot and His Daughters Escape"
- Chronological Picture No. 17, "The Destruction of Sodom and Gomorrah"
- Chronological Map 1
- Small poster, "Abraham Believed God" (shown in lesson)

ON TEACHING THIS LESSON:

These lessons are designed to **teach unbelievers.** You are carefully laying a scriptural foundation on which the Gospel will later be presented. If your class contains believers, teach with the goal of giving them an understanding of the basis for their faith and **with the goal of enabling them to teach the same material to unbelievers.**

DON'T COMPLICATE THE MESSAGE!

As you teach, keep in mind that this is a directed study—not an exhaustive survey of the Bible and not an unlimited group discussion. Keep your lesson on track and moving ahead by limiting and directing any discussion.

Carefully follow the outline. Emphasize the doctrinal themes.

LESSON FORMAT: The **center column** below contains the lesson material to be taught to the students. The **bold outline headings** are only for reference and need not be spoken, as they are incorporated into the outlined material that follows. The material in the **side columns** is for the teacher's own reference and is not intended to be included in the lesson.

TO BE TAUGHT TO THE STUDENTS
(Center Column Only)

LESSON OUTLINE:

REVIEW questions from Lesson 16.

A. Introduction

This lesson addresses some very important issues.

What does God consider to be righteousness?

How can anyone be counted righteous in God's sight?

Does God care if people choose to live an immoral life?

Is homosexuality really a sin?

The Bible answers these questions very clearly.

This story reminds us of what happened in Noah's day.

And it makes us think about what is happening right now in our society.

Lesson 17: God Destroyed Sodom and Gomorrah

Scripture Reference | Teacher's Notes

B. God's promises renewed to Abram

 Theme: **God communicates with man.**

After Lot left Abram, the Lord spoke to Abram and promised once again to give him all of the land of Canaan.

 READ Genesis 13:14-17.

SHOW AREA OF CANAAN ON MAP 1.

- Compare:

  How many stars can you see in the sky on a dark, cloudless night?

  One night, God took Abram outside of his tent and told him to look up and see if he could count the stars.

God promised Abram, even before he had one child, that his descendants would be as many as the stars.

 READ Genesis 15:5,6.

 Theme: **Man must have faith in order to please God and be saved.**

Abram believed God.
- What God had promised would have seemed impossible.
- Abram and Sarai had been married for many years and were now old, but they had never been able to have a child.
- But Abram trusted in God to give him a child and to send the Deliverer as one of his descendants.

Therefore, because Abram believed God, God accepted him as if he had no sin.

- Abram was a sinner; but because of his trust in God, he was accepted by God as if he were perfectly right.

Romans 4:3

 READ Genesis 15:6.

What is righteousness?
- The root word is "right."
- God "*counted it to him*" or gave Abram credit for being right or acceptable to God.

But Abram was a sinner, a descendant of Adam, like us.

What did God find in Abram that would cause God to credit Abram with righteousness?

Why should God accept Abram, a sinner?

The only reason why God credited righteousness to Abram was that **Abram believed God.**

Suggested Visual:

> **Abraham BELIEVED GOD.**
> **GOD counted it to him for righteousness.**

267

Teacher's Notes

Lesson 17: God Destroyed Sodom and Gomorrah

Scripture Reference

You might say that, though Abram's bank account with God was in the red because of his sins, God put righteousness into Abram's account.

This righteousness, given to him as a gift from God, was the reason Abram was fully acceptable to God.

Why did God do this for him?

Because Abram **believed** God!

Abram knew that he could not save himself from his sins, but he **believed** that God was going to send a Deliverer who would be able to save him from Satan and sin and death.

Galatians 3:8

 Theme: God is everywhere all the time; He knows everything.

 READ Genesis 15:13-16.

God knew all that would happen to Abram's descendants before they were ever born.

- Compare:

  Do you know what will happen next week, next year, in ten years' time? What about in one or two hundred years' time? No one knows the answers to these questions except God. He alone knows all about your future.

 READ Genesis 17:1-5.

God again spoke to Abram when he was 99 years old.

- God changed Abram's name to Abraham because God promised he would become the father of many descendants.
- Abram means "exalted father;" Abraham means "father of a multitude of children."

C. God's promise that Abraham and Sarah would have a son

 Theme: God communicates with man.

 READ Genesis 17:15,16.

God also changed Sarai's name to Sarah because, even though she had never been able to have a child, God promised she would have a son.

- Sarai means "princess," but Sarah means "mother of nations."
- She would become the mother of millions of descendants.

 Theme: God is all-powerful.

 Theme: Man needs God.

 READ Genesis 17:17.

It seemed impossible that Abraham and Sarah would have a son.

- Abraham would be 100 years old.

Lesson 17: God Destroyed Sodom and Gomorrah

Scripture Reference	**Teacher's Notes**

- Sarah would be 90 years old.
- But the promise did not depend on their human frailty.

It was **God** who made the promise, and He is almighty.

D. God's attitude toward Sodom and Gomorrah [1]

Let's turn our attention now to Abraham's nephew, Lot.

🔑 Theme: Man is a sinner. He needs God and is helpless to save himself.

🔑 Theme: God is everywhere all the time; He knows everything.

📖 READ Genesis 18:20,21.

ON MAP 1, POINT TO THE PROBABLE LOCATION OF SODOM AND GOMORRAH.

You will remember that Lot had moved down near these two wicked cities.

Even though there were many people in the world at that time, God saw everything that the people of Sodom and Gomorrah did, and He heard everything that they said.

🔑 Theme: God is loving, merciful, and gracious.

🔑 Theme: God is supreme and sovereign.

🔑 Theme: God is holy and righteous. He demands death as the payment for sin.

God had been displeased with these wicked cities for a long time, even before Lot moved near them.

- For a long while, the Lord had been patient with their inhabitants, but now He decided that He could not tolerate their sinfulness any longer.
- They could not escape the judgment of God.
- Compare:

Do you remember how God patiently waited for the people to repent in the days when Noah lived? But the time came when God decided He had given the people sufficient time to repent. Not one of those who refused to agree with God escaped His punishment. He is sovereign and supreme. He doesn't ask anyone what He should do. When He decides to punish sinners, no one can stop Him.

- Consider:

II Peter 3:9

Because God doesn't immediately punish sin, it may seem like God overlooks sin. Nevertheless, He will eventually punish all sin. No one can escape from God, our almighty Creator. He sees and will punish the sin of every person.

---

[1] At this point, you may prefer to read all of Genesis 18 which gives good preparation for Genesis 19 and the destruction of Sodom and Gomorrah.

Point out that, on several occasions in the Bible, God appeared briefly to individuals in the form of a man. These appearances are called "theophanies."

God's grace and His knowledge of all things are demonstrated in chapter 18 in His knowledge of Sarah's response (v. 12-15) and in His conversations with Abraham.

Be careful to explain that God's comment to Abraham in 18:18 was for Abraham's benefit. God knew exactly what was happening in Sodom and Gomorrah. You might say God's words were a little like the words of a father who tells his young son, "I'll go take a look at your room and see if it's as big a mess as I've heard," when the father knows very well that it is!

But in this instance, God wanted to draw Abraham into the conversation that ensued so Abraham (and we) could see the depth of God's grace and His knowledge of all things. God said He would not destroy Sodom if He found ten righteous men there. (As it was, only three people fully heeded God's warning and escaped.)

If you use this chapter, you may also use Chronological Picture No. 15, "Abraham, Sarah, and Their Heavenly Visitors." ☐

E. God's angels came to Sodom.

 READ Genesis 19:1-3.

Where was Lot?
- Previously, Lot was living near the city.
- Now he had moved right in and was living with these wicked people.

Who were his visitors, and why did they come?
- They were two of God's good angels who had not followed Satan.
- God sent them to Sodom for a special purpose.

He sent these angels to warn Lot and his family of what was about to happen.

Theme: God is everywhere all the time; He knows everything.

God knew that Lot believed Him, even though Lot lived among the people of Sodom and Gomorrah. *(Genesis 19:18-20)*

God knows everything.

The Bible gives us more insight into the sin of Sodom.

 Read Ezekiel 16:49,50.

These people were proud, they were gluttons, and they didn't care about the needs of others.

F. The sinfulness of the Sodomites

Theme: Man is a sinner. He needs God and is helpless to save himself.

 READ Genesis 19:4-7.

- Consider:

  What a sickening passage. But God has put it here for us to read. Stop and think: is our society doing any better? The word "sodomy" is still in our language because the sin is still in our midst.

  God's only plan for sex was that it be the special bond between a man and his wife, and the means for them to have children. The unnatural, perverted, out-of-control, selfish passions that plagued Sodom are still raging today. Our whole society is threatened by a horrible disease because men and women have refused God's plan for their lives.

  Lot's earlier choice of the "best" land appears quite different now in light of this awful scene. If God had not sent His angels, what a horrible end Lot and his two daughters would have faced! But the Bible tells us that Lot believed God, and God rescued him. *(II Peter 2:6-9)*

G. Lot, his wife, and his daughters rescued out of Sodom

Theme: Man is a sinner. He needs God and is helpless to save himself.

Lesson 17: God Destroyed Sodom and Gomorrah

Scripture Reference

Teacher's Notes

 READ Genesis 19:10-17.

God did not save Lot and his wife and daughters because they were good.

- Lot was not living a wicked life like the people of Sodom, but he, too, was born a sinner.
- Lot, however, had agreed with God that he was a sinner, and he trusted in God's mercy.

 Theme: Man must have faith in order to please God and be saved.

- Lot believed the promises given to Adam and to his uncle Abraham about the coming Deliverer.

Theme: God is loving, merciful, and gracious.

God's angels led Lot out before the wicked cities were destroyed.

God always saves those who agree with Him and trust in Him.

Hebrews 11:4,7

II Peter 2:5

- Abel agreed with God and trusted in Him, and God accepted Abel.
- Noah agreed with God and trusted in Him, and God saved Noah from the flood.
- Lot agreed with God and trusted in Him, and God delivered him before Sodom was destroyed.

H. God destroyed Sodom and Gomorrah.

 Theme: God is holy and righteous. He demands death as the payment for sin.

 READ Genesis 19:24,25.

Suggested Visual:

CHRONOLOGICAL PICTURE NO. 17: "THE DESTRUCTION OF SODOM AND GOMORRAH"

- Commentary:

Once Lot was safely outside the city, God destroyed Sodom and Gomorrah. God hates sin. Just as He destroyed the world by a flood in the time of Noah, now He destroyed these wicked people by fire.

In II Peter 2:6 God calls the destruction of these cities an example of what is going to happen to ungodly people.

 Theme: God is faithful; He never changes.

God is still the same today.

- He has not changed.

271

Lesson 17: God Destroyed Sodom and Gomorrah

- He still sees and hates sin.
- No one can escape His judgment.

I. Lot's wife looked back.

 Theme: God is holy and righteous. He demands death as the payment for sin.

 READ Genesis 19:26.

When the angels took Lot, his wife, and his two daughters out of Sodom, they told them not to look behind but to run to the mountains. But Lot's wife disobeyed.

Suggested Visual:

CHRONOLOGICAL PICTURE NO. 16: "LOT AND HIS DAUGHTERS ESCAPE"

God knew what was in the heart of Lot's wife.
- Lot's wife was like Cain.
- She did not trust in God.

God knew why she looked back.
- She looked back because she liked the sinful ways of the people of Sodom.
- She didn't want to leave.

She was very foolish to ignore God's warning because, when she looked back, God turned her into a pillar of salt.

 Theme: God is faithful; He never changes.

- Consider:

  If we get angry at someone, we may threaten lots of things, but, after a while, we probably forget. But God doesn't threaten to punish and then forget. He is always the same. He remembers and keeps His promises to bless those who trust in Him and to punish those who disobey Him. God never forgets about sin until it is paid for in full. The punishment for sin is death, separation from God forever in the Lake of Fire.

J. Conclusion

- Consider:

  God is interested in all people. Even though there are now billions of people in the world, God still knows and is interested in every individual. Every living thing is important to God—even sparrows. Though there are millions of sparrows in the world, the Bible tells us (in Matthew 10:29) that God knows when one sparrow dies. In Psalm 50:11 God says, "I know all the fowls of the mountains: and the wild beasts of the field are mine."

Lesson 17: God Destroyed Sodom and Gomorrah

Scripture Reference

Teacher's Notes

But we are much more precious to God than the birds. Psalm 139:1-4 tells us: "O LORD, thou hast searched me, and known me. Thou knowest my downsitting and mine uprising, thou understandest my thought afar off. Thou compassest my path and my lying down, and art acquainted with all my ways. For there is not a word in my tongue, but, lo, O LORD, thou knowest it altogether."

Think of the vastness of God's knowledge! This great, all-knowing, all-powerful God CARES about everyone, even you and me! God knows that we are studying His Word right now, and He wants us to believe what He is teaching us.

John 3:18
Revelation 20:11-15

- *God wants us to listen and to believe because not only is God interested in every individual, but He will also judge every single person who refuses to believe His Word.*

Some people think that they are just too insignificant for God to bother with. That is not true. Remember what we just read from Psalms. Even the birds are important enough to God that He knows every one of them! And how much more God cares about people; He knows everything about us. He knows everything about YOU!

Ezekiel 18:4
II Peter 3:9

- *God cares about us and wants us to believe Him, but He is also righteous and true and will judge the person who refuses Him. No person escapes God's concern; no sin escapes God's righteous judgment.*

God is the same today as He was in the day of Abraham and Lot and Sodom and Gomorrah.

QUESTIONS:

1. What did God tell Abram after Lot left him?

    a. *God told Abram that He would give him all the land of Canaan.*

    b. *God promised that Abram's descendants would number more than the stars.*

    c. *God said that Abram's descendants would go to live in another country and that they would be ill-treated for four hundred years, but after that time, God would bring them back to the land of Canaan which God had promised to Abram.*

2. What new names did God give to Abram and Sarai? *Abraham and Sarah.*

3. Why couldn't Abraham and Sarah have a child unless God performed a miracle?

    a. *Sarah was unable to have a child.*

    b. *They were both too old. Abraham was now 100 years old, and Sarah was 90 years old.*

4. Who created the first man and woman and gives life to every baby? *God.*

5. Is there anything which God wants to do but cannot? *No, God can do everything He wants to do.*

6. Who knows the future of every person? *Only God.*

7. Did God know about all the wickedness of Sodom and Gomorrah? *Yes.*

Lesson 17: God Destroyed Sodom and Gomorrah

Teacher's Notes

Scripture Reference

8. If people ignore God, will He bypass them and not punish them? *No, God is interested in all people. He is the judge of every person.*

9. Why didn't God immediately punish the evil people of Sodom and Gomorrah, and why doesn't God immediately punish sinners now? *Because God is loving, merciful, gracious, and patient, He gives people time to change their minds and trust in Him.*

10. Does God merely threaten but never punish sinners? *No, even though God is patient, He will eventually punish sinners.*

11. Can anyone stop God from punishing people when He decides they have had sufficient time to repent (change their minds)? *No, God is supreme. No one is greater than He is.*

12. Why did the Lord send His angels to rescue Lot, his wife, and his family? *Because Lot agreed with God that he was a sinner and trusted in God's promises to send the Deliverer.*

13. Why did God turn Lot's wife into a pillar of salt? *Because she disobeyed the command of the Lord when He told them they must not look back at the burning cities.*

OPTIONAL DISCUSSION QUESTION:

14. Men and women today are telling us that sexual relationships outside of marriage are all right, because everyone is doing it. Do you think God agrees? *We know for certain that God does not agree, because God does not change.*

Scripture Reference

Hebrews 11:17-19

LESSON 18

God Gave Isaac; God Delivered Isaac from Death

Teacher's Notes

OVERVIEW

This lesson shows God's supreme faithfulness, grace, and sovereign power in giving Isaac and then providing a ram to die in Isaac's place.

Abraham's faith is presented as a correct response to God's faithfulness.

This story is a type of Christ, which you can later use in presenting the Gospel.

LESSON PREPARATION

This section is for you, the teacher.

The passages in the Scripture Reference column are for your own study in preparing for this lesson. Since they may contain concepts that run ahead of the lesson, they are not to be taught at this point.

Note: If you have not taught previously from this series of lessons, please read carefully the note to teachers in the front of this book.

SCRIPTURE: Genesis 21:1-3, 22:1-19

LESSON GOALS:

- To show that everyone and everything belongs to God.
- To show that nothing is too hard for God.
- To show that man cannot save himself.
- To show that God saves those who trust Him.

THIS LESSON SHOULD HELP THE STUDENTS:

- To see that they can come to God only by faith.
- To see God's sovereignty, omnipotence, faithfulness, immutability, and grace.
- To see that an ordinary man can have faith to do something terribly difficult if his faith is in God, who is completely trustworthy.
- To see God's claim on their lives because He owns everyone and everything.

PERSPECTIVE FOR THE TEACHER:

For most people, this story is impossible to even imagine. How could a holy, righteous God ask a man to kill his son? How could a man bind his own son, lay him on an altar, and reach for the knife to kill him? How could the son (who was apparently already a young man and possibly stronger than his aging father) allow his father to bind him, lay him on the altar, and make him the sacrifice?

To the unbeliever, these things must simply be presented as facts. Do not expect your students to understand this story; because the only way it can in any way be understood is as we view it by faith, looking back from the Cross. It is not a story of usual, predictable actions; it is a story of faith that gives us a glimpse of God sacrificing His own Son, Jesus Christ. Abraham's faith becomes a pattern for our faith, as we must trust God alone to provide the perfect sacrifice for our sins.

In this deeply moving account, Abraham, in a sense, has released the grip of every finger that might clutch the ownership and control of his possessions, his life, and the life of his only son. His trust in God is a childlike rest and freedom from doubt that allows him to hand everything over to God.

This is a story of Abraham's faith; but, in an even greater way, this is a story of **God's faithfulness.** Abraham realized what we all need to realize: God is supremely faithful. He always keeps His promises.

Lesson 18: God Gave Isaac; God Delivered Isaac from Death

Teacher's Notes

Scripture Reference

Hebrews 11:19 tells us that Abraham expected God to raise Isaac from the dead. He knew that God had promised to give descendants and to send a Deliverer through Isaac. So Abraham's actions reflect his trust in God to take care of the present dilemma and to do what He promised to do in the future.

But we know that when God's own Son was the sacrifice, God did not put another on the Cross in Jesus' place. God allowed His Son to take **our** place and be our sacrifice for sin! And the only way we can be partakers of that immeasurably gracious provision is to come as Abraham did, by **faith**!

We can meditate on these truths as we teach this great foundational story upon which we can later build the Gospel of Jesus Christ.

VISUALS:

- Chronological Picture No. 18, "Abraham Offers Isaac"
- Chronological Chart

ON TEACHING THIS LESSON:

These lessons are designed to **teach unbelievers.** You are carefully laying a scriptural foundation on which the Gospel will later be presented. If your class contains believers, teach with the goal of giving them an understanding of the basis for their faith and **with the goal of enabling them to teach the same material to unbelievers.**

DON'T COMPLICATE THE MESSAGE!

As you teach, keep in mind that this is a directed study—not an exhaustive survey of the Bible and not an unlimited group discussion. Keep your lesson on track and moving ahead by limiting and directing any discussion.

Carefully follow the outline. Emphasize the doctrinal themes.

LESSON FORMAT: The **center column** below contains the lesson material to be taught to the students. The **bold outline headings** are only for reference and need not be spoken, as they are incorporated into the outlined material that follows. The material in the **side columns** is for the teacher's own reference and is not intended to be included in the lesson.

TO BE TAUGHT TO THE STUDENTS
(Center Column Only)

LESSON OUTLINE:

REVIEW questions from Lesson 17.

A. Introduction

In our last lesson we read that Abraham believed God, and God credited Abraham's faith to him as righteousness.

- Today we are going to study the greatest test of Abraham's faith.
- But more important than Abraham's faith is the **faithful God** in whom he trusted.

God is the central focus of this story and of the whole Bible.

Lesson 18: God Gave Isaac; God Delivered Isaac from Death

Scripture Reference

Teacher's Notes

B. God fulfilled His promise and gave Abraham and Sarah a son.

 Theme: God is all-powerful.

Even though Abraham and Sarah were too old to have children, God had promised to give them a son.

- By this time, Abraham was 100 years old and Sarah was 90.

Genesis 18:12

- Sarah had laughed when God said she would have a child.
    - Sarah had never had a child.
    - She knew it was naturally impossible at her age.

Psalm 115:3

But nothing is impossible with God; He can do anything He wants to do.

Jeremiah 32:17
Luke 1:37

 Theme: God is faithful; He never changes.

Many years had passed since God first promised to give Abraham a son, but God hadn't forgotten His promise.

- He had not changed His mind.
- Sarah had a son just as God had promised.

Abraham and Sarah called their son Isaac.

READ Genesis 21:1-3.

POINT TO ISAAC ON THE CHRONOLOGICAL CHART.

 Theme: God is supreme and sovereign.

Acts 17:25

God could decide to give Abraham and Sarah a son because He is the Creator of all people and all things.

- God gives life to all people everywhere.
- He gave life to our ancestors.
- He gave life to each of us and to our children.

I Chronicles 29:11,12

This world and everyone in it belongs to God.

- Abraham and Sarah belonged to God.
- Their son Isaac belonged to God.

Psalm 24:1

C. God commanded Abraham to offer up Isaac.

 Theme: God communicates with man.

Many years passed by, and Isaac grew to be a young man.[1]
His father and mother loved him.

Abraham believed that all of God's promises concerning the coming Deliverer were to be fulfilled through Isaac and his descendants.

One day God told Abraham to do a most unexpected and difficult thing.

 Theme: God is supreme and sovereign.

 READ Genesis 22:1,2.

God was testing Abraham to see if he loved Isaac more than he loved God.

---

[1] The word used in this passage to describe Isaac as a "lad" is also translated in other places as "young man" (as in Abraham's servants, Genesis 22:3) or "servant."

The passage of time since Isaac's birth is not given, though several events have taken place in the intervening time. Obviously, Isaac was strong enough to carry the wood for the sacrifice.
☐

What authority did God have to tell Abraham to take Isaac and offer him as a sacrifice?
- Compare:

    Does your neighbor or anyone else have the right to tell you what to do with your children, your house, your car, or your possessions? No! Why not? Because they are yours. They belong to you. They don't belong to your neighbor.

    But didn't Isaac belong to Abraham? Wasn't Isaac Abraham's son? Didn't Abraham have authority over Isaac? Isaac was Abraham's son, but who gave Isaac his life? Who gave Isaac to Abraham and Sarah? God did! Isaac belonged to God.

God gives life to every person and every living thing.

God created everything.

Therefore, God has authority over all people and all things.

D. Abraham believed God.

 Theme: Man must have faith in order to please God and be saved.

Think about what was happening!
- What a surprise this must have been to Abraham!
- What an impossibly difficult test!
- Had God changed His mind about Isaac and His promises?
- How could God's promises be fulfilled through Isaac if Abraham killed him?
- Had God changed His mind?
- Had God decided that the Deliverer would not be one of Isaac's descendants?

How did Abraham respond?
- Even though Abraham was told to offer Isaac as a sacrifice, he did not doubt or question God.
- He accepted what God had said.

How could he respond like this?

He knew and believed God.
- He knew that God would not lie.
- He knew that God would not give him promises and then change His mind.
- He trusted God and believed that God would still keep His word.

Wasn't this an impossible thing for a man to do?
- Abraham was just a person like us.
- This test of his faith was terribly difficult — we might say, impossible.
- But Abraham had put his full trust in God.
- He had come to realize that **God never fails**!
- Compare:

    It is hard for us to imagine one who never fails to keep His word. Oh, our intentions are often very good, but we just don't follow through. We get busy, or tired, or distracted, and we fail to do the thing we promised.

    God is not like us. Abraham discovered just what each person needs to discover for himself: God never fails to do the things He

Lesson 18: God Gave Isaac; God Delivered Isaac from Death

has promised to do. We can fully trust Him. This is what God wants us to do—to BELIEVE Him.

Hebrews 11:19 says that Abraham believed that even if he did kill Isaac in obedience to God, God would raise Isaac from the dead.

- He knew it was impossible for man.
- But He trusted God to do this.
- Compare:

    Abraham was different from Adam and Eve. When they were in the garden, God had told Adam not to eat of the fruit of the tree of the knowledge of good and evil, for if he did, that day that he would surely die. But when Satan told Eve they wouldn't die, Adam and Eve believed Satan. They doubted the word of God, and they disobeyed Him. Adam and Eve did not believe God, but Abraham did. He believed that God would keep His word.

Because Abraham believed and trusted in God, he immediately made preparations to go to the place where God promised to lead him.

 READ Genesis 22:3-5.

E. Isaac questioned and Abraham answered.

 Theme: Man must have faith in order to please God.

 READ Genesis 22:6-7.

Consider Isaac's situation.
- He had undoubtedly witnessed many sacrifices.
- He could not understand why they had not taken a sheep with them to sacrifice.
- Abraham had not told Isaac what God had told him to do.

 READ Genesis 22:8.

Abraham trusted God.

Believing God is the most important thing that we can do.
- Just listening to a sermon or even hearing or reading the words of the Bible will not deliver us from Satan's control.
- We must accept God's words and trust in Him.
- Compare:

    If you were sick and went to the doctor and he prescribed medicine, would it be any benefit to you if he only told you about the medicine and how it could heal you? Would just listening to him tell about it heal you?

    Only listening to God's words will not help us. If we only listen but refuse to believe, then we are doing what Satan did when he spoke to Eve: We are calling God a liar. God will never accept those who refuse to believe Him. God accepts those who, like Abraham, believe all God says and trust only in Him.

F. Abraham bound Isaac.

 Theme: Man is a sinner. He needs God and is helpless to save himself.

Hebrews 11:17-19

Lesson 18: God Gave Isaac; God Delivered Isaac from Death

 Theme: God is holy and righteous. He demands death as the payment for sin.

 READ Genesis 22:9,10.

There was no escape for Isaac.

- He was bound and laid on the altar.
- Abraham had lifted up the knife to kill him.
- God had commanded Abraham to offer Isaac as a sacrifice, and there was no way for Isaac to escape once he was on the altar.
- Compare:

It was the same when God shut the door of the ark after Noah. Noah's family and all the animals and birds were safe inside, but there was no escape for the people outside the ark who didn't believe God and were shut out.

And there was no escape for the people in the wicked cities of Sodom and Gomorrah when God sent down fire on them. There was no escape for Lot's wife when she disobeyed God and looked back at the city of Sodom.

God saved Noah and his family from the flood. God saved Lot and his daughters from the fire which destroyed Sodom and Gomorrah. Only God could save Isaac from being killed.

Is there any way that we can save ourselves from death and everlasting punishment for our sins? No! We cannot save ourselves. God will punish all sin. No one can escape from God.

God and only God can make a way to escape. Do you know what God did? Let's read what the Bible says.

G. God provided a ram to take Isaac's place.

 Theme: God communicates with man.

 Theme: God is loving, merciful, and gracious.

 READ Genesis 22:10-12.

God saved Isaac; God told Abraham not to kill his son.

Isaac couldn't be saved, however, unless there was another suitable sacrifice to offer to God.

- Abraham and Isaac didn't have a suitable sacrifice with them.
- But God provided another offering instead of Isaac.
- Abraham could not provide the sacrifice.

God graciously provided a ram instead of Isaac.

 READ Genesis 22:13.

Lesson 18: God Gave Isaac; God Delivered Isaac from Death

Scripture Reference | Teacher's Notes

CHRONOLOGICAL PICTURE NO. 18, "ABRAHAM OFFERS ISAAC"

 Theme: God is holy and righteous. He demands death as the payment for sin.

 Theme: Man can come to God only according to God's will and plan.

God caused the ram to be caught by its horns in the bush.
- If it had been caught by any other part of its body, it would have injured itself by struggling and trying to get free.
- If it had been injured, it would not have been an acceptable offering to God.
    God would only accept a healthy, strong animal as a sacrifice.
    Because God is perfect, He will only accept whatever is perfect.

God provided an acceptable sacrifice in place of Isaac.

Exodus 12:5
Leviticus 22:17-22

 Theme: God is faithful; He never changes.

God is faithful.
- He kept His promise to Abraham.
- Through Isaac, God would give Abraham many descendants.

Abraham took Isaac off the altar and put the ram which God had provided on the altar so it could be killed instead of Isaac.
- Abraham killed the ram and burned it as an offering to God.
- The ram died instead of Isaac.
- The ram was his substitute.
- God saved Isaac by providing the ram to die in his place.

H. Abraham trusted God to send the Deliverer.

 Theme: Man must have faith in order to please God and be saved.

 READ Genesis 22:14-19.

Abraham called the place where God provided the ram "The Lord will provide."
- God provided a ram to die instead of Isaac.
- Abraham believed that God would also provide the Deliverer to rescue mankind from the power of Satan and from the punishment of sin.

Galatians 3:6-9

I. Conclusion

We cannot begin to imagine such a difficult test as Abraham faced.

Lesson 18: God Gave Isaac; God Delivered Isaac from Death

Teacher's Notes

Scripture Reference

But we can see that God rewarded Abraham's faith.

He provided a way for Isaac to be saved; He provided an acceptable sacrifice—a ram to die in his place.

The line of the promised Deliverer was preserved.

God can be completely trusted to fulfill His promises.

God is worthy of **our** trust!

QUESTIONS:

1. Why was God able to give Abraham and Sarah a son even though he was 100 years old and she was 90?

    a. Because God gives life to all people everywhere.

    b. God is omnipotent. He can do anything He wants to do.

2. What authority did God have to ask Abraham to offer Isaac as a sacrifice?

    a. God is the Creator of all things; therefore, He is the owner of all things.

    b. God gave life to Isaac.

3. Did Abraham think that God had changed His mind about Isaac being the father of a great nation and the forefather of the Deliverer? *No, Abraham believed and trusted in God because he was convinced that God always keeps His promises.*

4. What did Abraham think God might do? *Abraham thought that, if he did kill Isaac as God had commanded him, then God would raise Isaac from the dead.*

5. Once Abraham had bound Isaac and put him on the altar, was there any way Isaac could deliver himself from death? *No, Isaac could not deliver himself from death.*

6. Is there any way a person can save himself from the payment of death and everlasting punishment which he deserves because of his sins? *No, no one can save himself or herself from the punishment of God. No one can escape from God.*

7. Who spoke to Abraham and saved Isaac from death? *God did.*

8. Was there anyone else who could have saved Isaac from death except God? *No.*

9. Who provided a sacrifice to take Isaac's place? *God did.*

10. Why was the ram held in the bush by its horns? *Because God is perfect, He would only accept an offering if it was strong and healthy.*

11. Why did Abraham call the place where God provided the ram "The Lord will provide"? *Because Abraham believed that, just as the Lord provided the ram instead of Isaac, the Lord would one day provide the Deliverer who would overcome Satan and deliver mankind from Satan's power and everlasting punishment.*

Scripture Reference		Teacher's Notes

LESSON 19

Isaac's Sons, Esau and Jacob; Jacob's Son Joseph

OVERVIEW

This lesson bridges the span of Abraham's descendants from Isaac to Joseph, emphasizing God's faithfulness to sustain His promises to send a Deliverer. The lesson ends with Joseph in Egypt.

Some points:
- Esau: a man who did not value God's promises
- Jacob: a man who valued God's promises
- Jacob's dream: speaks of God's plan to send a Saviour to reconcile man with God
- Jacob and Esau's story: presented only briefly, emphasizing only those things which point to the coming Deliverer
- Joseph: Jacob's favorite son; his dream shows God's understanding of Joseph's future.

LESSON PREPARATION

This section is for you, the teacher.

The passages in the Scripture Reference column are for your own study in preparing for this lesson. Since they may contain concepts that run ahead of the lesson, they are not to be taught at this point.

Note: If you have not taught previously from this series of lessons, please read carefully the note to teachers in the front of this book.

SCRIPTURE: Genesis 25:19-21,24-27; 28:10-15; 29:1; 37:1-14, 18-20,24,28; 39:1

LESSON GOALS:

- To show the faithfulness of God to carry out His promise to bring a Deliverer.
- To show that God works through ordinary, sinful men to bring about His desired results.
- To show that there is only one way to God and that He alone provides that way.

THIS LESSON SHOULD HELP THE STUDENTS:

- To see God's faithfulness.
- To see the folly of choosing a worldly lifestyle.
- To realize that they are helpless to save themselves from the penalty of sin.
- To see that God is the only one who can make a way to save them from the penalty of their sins.

PERSPECTIVE FOR THE TEACHER:

Psalm 146:5 says, *"Happy is he that hath the God of Jacob for his help, whose hope is in the LORD his God."* The God of Jacob? When we read the Bible's complete account of Jacob, we see that Jacob was not always a man of faith. Yet Jacob the schemer became Jacob the man of faith. He is listed in the "hall of faith" in Hebrews 11:9,20,21, and he is the man whom God chose to be the father of the twelve tribes which became the nation Israel.

This lesson will not cover all the details of Jacob's and Esau's lives; rather, it will highlight those things which point the students to the coming Deliverer.

But as we who teach read for ourselves the whole story of Jacob, it may serve to remind us that God's ways are not man's ways. We might never have "chosen" a man like Jacob. In the same way, some of our students may not be particularly easy to teach; they may be, in fact, downright difficult! But we must remember that God knows the end from the beginning, and He has brought these students to us so that we can give them His Word.

How do we know? The student who seems the least likely to believe may astonish us with his response to God's Word! It is exciting to know God, and to know that His wisdom and knowledge and judgments are far beyond our understanding. We are His servants, and our job is to present the Word clearly to every student.

Scripture Reference sidebar: You may want to read the entire story of Jacob and Esau yourself so you will be prepared for any questions the students may ask. Genesis 25:19-34; 27:1-33:20; 35:1-29

Lesson 19: Isaac's Sons, Esau and Jacob; Jacob's Son Joseph

Teacher's Notes

Scripture Reference

One of the beautiful things about the story of Jacob is that God spoke personally to Jacob several times and gave His promises to him.

May we be faithful to teach in the power of God's Spirit so that we may love the unlovely and share the Word with complete faith in the one who can transform even the vilest sinner into His own dear child!

The "Jacob" that plagues our classes may turn out to be the "father" of a great "tribe" of believers!

VISUALS:

- Chronological Picture No. 20, "Jacob's Dream"
- Chronological Map 1
- Chronological Chart
- Small visuals showing the "ladder" from God to man (illustrated in lesson)

ON TEACHING THIS LESSON:

These lessons are designed to **teach unbelievers.** You are carefully laying a scriptural foundation on which the Gospel will later be presented. If your class contains believers, teach with the goal of giving them an understanding of the basis for their faith and **with the goal of enabling them to teach the same material to unbelievers.**

DON'T COMPLICATE THE MESSAGE!

As you teach, keep in mind that this is a directed study—not an exhaustive survey of the Bible and not an unlimited group discussion. Keep your lesson on track and moving ahead by limiting and directing any discussion.

Carefully follow the outline. Emphasize the doctrinal themes.

LESSON FORMAT: The **center column** below contains the lesson material to be taught to the students. The **bold outline headings** are only for reference and need not be spoken, as they are incorporated into the outlined material that follows. The material in the **side columns** is for the teacher's own reference and is not intended to be included in the lesson.

TO BE TAUGHT TO THE STUDENTS
(Center Column Only)

LESSON OUTLINE:

REVIEW questions from Lesson 18.

A. Introduction

Today's lesson will briefly touch on the most important events in the lives of Abraham's descendants as they are recorded in the last twenty-six chapters of Genesis.

Our story begins in Canaan, but it will close with Abraham's descendants living in Egypt.

Lesson 19: Isaac's Sons, Esau and Jacob; Jacob's Son Joseph

B. Isaac married Rebekah.

 READ Genesis 25:19,20.

Rebekah, Isaac's wife, was born in the land where Abraham had lived before the Lord led him to Canaan.

POINT TO MESOPOTAMIA ON MAP 1.

God had spared Isaac's life; God had promised Abraham that through Isaac would come many descendants, including the Deliverer.

C. Esau and Jacob were born.

 READ Genesis 25:21,24-26.

POINT TO JACOB AND ESAU ON THE CHRONOLOGICAL CHART.

D. Esau did not believe or value God's promises.

 Theme: Man is a sinner. He needs God and is helpless to save himself.

 READ Genesis 25:27a.

Esau was a skillful hunter; he spent his time tracking and killing wild animals out in the fields.

The promises concerning the Deliverer would have ordinarily been passed on to Esau.[1]

- He was Isaac's firstborn child.
- The Deliverer from God would then have been one of Esau's descendants.

But Esau was not interested in the promises of God.

- He did not trust in God like Abraham and Isaac did.
- Esau was like Cain.
    He did not see that he was a sinner.
    He did not see that he needed to be accepted by God.
- As we read about Esau, we will see that he went his own way and lived only for the things of this world.
- These were more important to him than the things which God wanted to give him and teach him.

Hebrews 12:16

E. Jacob cherished and believed God's promises.

 Theme: Man must have faith in order to please God and be saved.

 READ Genesis 25:27b.

Jacob lived quietly in his tent and kept sheep and cattle.

In contrast to Esau, Jacob was a believing man like Abraham and Isaac.

- Jacob admitted that he was a sinner and needed God to send the Deliverer.
- He was very interested in God's promises.

[1] The Bible and other writings from this period of time mention the rights of inheritance.

These rights were very important, as they usually bestowed on the older son the family leadership, any special privileges, and a greater (double) portion of the father's accumulated wealth. ☐

Lesson 19: Isaac's Sons, Esau and Jacob; Jacob's Son Joseph

- Consider:

  Each one of us needs to ask, "Am I turning away from God's truth and following my own way like Cain and Esau? Or, am I like Abel, Enoch, Noah, Abraham, Isaac, and Jacob who admitted their sin and trusted in God to provide the Deliverer?"

F. Jacob returned to the land of Abraham and Rebekah.

Because of the great differences between Esau and Jacob, problems between the two brothers increased to the point that Esau threatened to kill Jacob.

Therefore, Jacob left his father and mother's home and began the long trek back to Mesopotamia, the land from which his grandfather, Abraham, had come.

POINT TO MESOPOTAMIA ON MAP 1.

 READ Genesis 28:10.

G. Jacob's dream

 Theme: God communicates with man.

It was a long way from Canaan to Mesopotamia so, on his way, Jacob had to sleep out in the mountains.

 READ Genesis 28:11.

One night as Jacob slept, God gave him a dream.

- Occasionally during those times, God would speak to people through dreams.
- But now that His Word is completed, He speaks to us though the Bible.

 READ Genesis 28:12.

CHRONOLOGICAL PICTURE NO. 20, "JACOB'S DREAM"

Through this dream, God was showing Jacob that the coming Deliverer would bridge the gap between man and God.

- God is the only one who can make a way for us to come to Him.
- Even if a person were to do many, many good deeds to try to please God, his efforts would still not bridge the gap caused by sin.
- Compare:

  This reminds us that, in the beginning, Adam and Eve were in oneness with God. God walked with Adam and Eve. They were friends with God. But when they disobeyed God, they and all of their descendants, including you and me, were separated from God. The stairway, or the way to God, had been removed. There was no

John 14:6

I Timothy 2:5

Lesson 19: Isaac's Sons, Esau and Jacob; Jacob's Son Joseph

way that people could come back to God and be in fellowship with Him unless God made a way.

Suggested Visual:

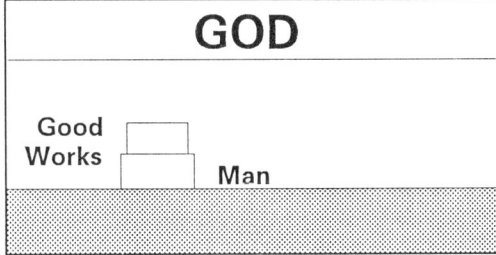

John 1:51
II Corinthians 5:19,21

But God promised the Deliverer who would destroy Satan and reconcile man to God. The Deliverer would be like the stairway which Jacob saw reaching from earth to Heaven. Through the Deliverer, people would once again be able to be in oneness with God.

Suggested Visual:

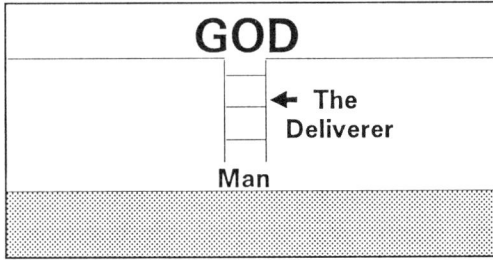

Even though all people have been separated from God because of Satan's lies and Adam's disobedience to God, God planned to send the Deliverer who would make it possible for God and man to be reconciled and reunited.

 Theme: God is loving, merciful, and gracious.

Jacob was a sinner, just like us.

- God graciously showed Jacob that there is only one way to God.
- God was also showing Jacob that blessings could only come from God Himself and that Jacob must put his trust in God—not in his own ability to manipulate the circumstances.

H. God passed on to Jacob the promises He had given to Abraham and Isaac.

 Theme: God is faithful; He never changes.

 READ Genesis 28:13-15.

God was continuing to work out His plan to send the Deliverer.

- Many years had passed since God gave the first promise of the Deliverer in the garden of Eden.
- Abraham, whom God had called to be the forefather of the Deliverer, was now dead.

Psalm 33:11

- But God had not forgotten His plan.

Lesson 19: Isaac's Sons, Esau and Jacob; Jacob's Son Joseph

God promised Jacob that the Deliverer would be one of his descendants. Jacob knew for certain that the promises given to his grandfather, Abraham, and his father, Isaac, now belonged to him.

 READ Genesis 29:1.

Many years later, Jacob returned to Canaan.

POINT TO CANAAN ON MAP 1.

In all, Jacob had twelve sons.

POINT TO THE TWELVE SONS OF JACOB (ISRAEL) ON THE CHRONOLOGICAL CHART.

God changed Jacob's name to Israel.
The land of Canaan, the Promised Land, is still called by his name.

Genesis 32:28

I. Joseph, Jacob's favorite son

 READ Genesis 37:1-3.

POINT TO JOSEPH ON THE CHRONOLOGICAL CHART.

When Joseph's brothers did wrong, Joseph told his father, Jacob.

J. Joseph's older brothers hated him.

 Theme: Man is a sinner. He needs God and is helpless to save himself.

 READ Genesis 37:4.

Because Joseph was his father's favorite son, all of his older brothers hated him.

- Consider:

    The reason why people get angry and hate one another is that everyone has been born separated from God and everyone's heart is evil. Do you have anger, hatred, and evil things in your heart and mind sometimes? All of us were born separated from God, and there is no way we can change ourselves. We do these sinful, evil things because we were born sinners just like our father, Adam.

K. Joseph's dreams

 Theme: God is everywhere all the time; He knows everything.

 READ Genesis 37:5-11.

God knew exactly what was going to happen to Joseph's family.
- Joseph could not see his future.
- He didn't know how his dreams would be fulfilled.
- But God made it clear that Joseph would become the leader and ruler over the family.

The future is all known to God.

Isaiah 46:10

Lesson 19: Isaac's Sons, Esau and Jacob; Jacob's Son Joseph

L. Joseph was sold into Egypt.

 READ Genesis 37:12-14,18-20,24,28; 39:1.

POINT TO CANAAN, MIDIAN, AND EGYPT ON MAP 1.

M. Conclusion

Joseph, the one whom God had promised would become a leader, was now a slave in Egypt, separated from his family and his homeland.

But God carries to completion every promise He makes.

God knows the future.

- He knew Joseph's future.
- He knows my future.
- He knows your future.

In our next lesson, we will continue the story of God's dealings in Joseph's life.

QUESTIONS:

1. What was the big difference between Esau and Jacob? *Esau did not value God's promises given to Abraham concerning the Deliverer. Esau did not admit he was a sinner and trust in God's mercy. Esau lived for the present and for material gain. Jacob admitted that he was a sinner and trusted in God. Jacob valued the promises concerning the Deliverer.*

2. Why didn't God forget His promises about the Deliverer given to Adam and Eve in the garden of Eden and to Abraham? *God didn't forget because He is unchanging and He always does what He says.*

3. What did Jacob see in the dream given to him by God? *He saw a stairway resting on the earth with its top reaching to Heaven. God's angels were walking up and down the ladder, and God stood above the ladder.*

4. What did this dream mean? *It meant that the Deliverer, who would be the descendant of Jacob, would be like the stairway connecting the earth to Heaven. Through the Deliverer, people could be brought back into oneness with God.*

5. God spoke to Jacob in a dream. How does God speak to people today? *God speaks to people today through His Word, the Bible.*

6. Who was Jacob's favorite son? *Joseph.*

7. How did Joseph's older brothers react to their father's love for Joseph? *They were jealous, and they hated Joseph.*

8. What did Joseph dream? *Read Genesis 37:7-9.*

9. What did these dreams mean? *They meant that Joseph would be given a position of authority over all his family.*

10. Who knew Joseph's future and showed it to him through his dreams? *God did.*

11. How much of our future does God know? *God knows it all.*

12. What did Joseph's older brothers do? *They sold Joseph to become a slave in Egypt.*

Scripture Reference

Psalm 105:16-23
Acts 7:9-15

Teacher's Notes

LESSON 20

God Promoted Joseph and Took Israel into Egypt

OVERVIEW

This lesson presents God's sovereign working in and through the life of Joseph to bring Israel into Egypt. God's faithfulness is highlighted through Joseph's trust in Him. God communicated with Joseph through dreams and brought to fulfillment all He had promised.

The bare essentials of Joseph's story are presented—just those details that define the main themes and carry the historical framework of Joseph's rise to rulership, his relationship with his brothers, and Israel's move to Egypt.

LESSON PREPARATION

This section is for you, the teacher.

The passages in the Scripture Reference column are for your own study in preparing for this lesson. Since they may contain concepts that run ahead of the lesson, they are not to be taught at this point.

Note: If you have not taught previously from this series of lessons, please read carefully the note to teachers in the front of this book.

SCRIPTURE: Genesis 39:20; 41:1-8,14-16,25-32,38-41; 42:1-3,6-8; 43:1,2; 45:3-9,25-28; 46:5-7

LESSON GOALS:

- To show that God is sovereign.
- To show that God fulfills His promises.
- To present Joseph as a man of faith.

THIS LESSON SHOULD HELP THE STUDENTS:

- To see that God's plans and promises are operative regardless of circumstances.
- To realize that God is in control.
- To see that God is faithful.

PERSPECTIVE FOR THE TEACHER:

We are barraged daily by "analyses" of the news. Yet do we ever hear that something happened because "God directed the heart of the king"?

The story of Joseph is God's accurate presentation and flawless analysis of the "news" of Egypt and Israel. God not only **knows all** that happens, but He also **understands all** that happens, because **He is in supreme control over all** that happens.

Our students need to see that God still moves in the affairs of men and nations. He has not changed; and though some people consider this story ancient, it is really fresh for our needs today. God still works through men of faith and still carries out His purposes—even through the lives of pagan rulers.

As Joseph held fast in his faith, God was redirecting the future of the entire nation of Israel. Joseph was unshakable because his faith was deeply rooted in the invisible, immovable, unchanging God!

In a day of terrifying headlines and massive political struggles, our students need to see that God is still in control; He is our only hope for stability and salvation!

Joseph's story is a beautiful "type" of Christ—His trust, betrayal, suffering, and exaltation. Later on, after the Gospel has been presented, you will be able to refer back to this lesson and draw parallels between Joseph's life and the life of our Lord Jesus Christ.

Lesson 20: God Promoted Joseph and Took Israel into Egypt

Teacher's Notes | Scripture Reference

VISUALS:

- Chronological Picture No. 22, "Joseph's Brothers Bow Before Him"
- Chronological Map 1

ON TEACHING THIS LESSON:

These lessons are designed to **teach unbelievers.** You are carefully laying a scriptural foundation on which the Gospel will later be presented. If your class contains believers, teach with the goal of giving them an understanding of the basis for their faith and **with the goal of enabling them to teach the same material to unbelievers.**

DON'T COMPLICATE THE MESSAGE!

As you teach, keep in mind that this is a directed study—not an exhaustive survey of the Bible and not an unlimited group discussion. Keep your lesson on track and moving ahead by limiting and directing any discussion.

Carefully follow the outline. Emphasize the doctrinal themes.

LESSON FORMAT: The **center column** below contains the lesson material to be taught to the students. The **bold outline headings** are only for reference and need not be spoken, as they are incorporated into the outlined material that follows. The material in the **side columns** is for the teacher's own reference and is not intended to be included in the lesson.

TO BE TAUGHT TO THE STUDENTS
(Center Column Only)

LESSON OUTLINE:

REVIEW questions from Lesson 19.

A. Introduction

In our last lesson we read how Joseph was sold to traders who took him to Egypt, where he was sold as a slave.

POINT TO EGYPT ON MAP 1.

For a short time everything went well for Joseph in the home where he worked, but when his master's wife made false accusations against him, Joseph was put into prison.

B. Joseph was put into prison.

 Theme: Man must have faith in order to please God and be saved.

 READ Genesis 39:20.

Joseph still trusted in God.

Lesson 20: God Promoted Joseph and Took Israel into Egypt

Scripture Reference

Teacher's Notes

- Even though Joseph was hated by his brothers and lied about by his master's wife, he still trusted in the only true and living God.
- He knew he was a sinner and could only be forgiven by God's mercy.
- He trusted in God's promises just like Abraham, Isaac, and Jacob.

Hebrews 11:6

No one can ever please God unless he believes what God says.

The greatest thing that you can do is to accept God's Word as the truth and to trust in all that He has written in the Bible.

 Theme: God is faithful; He never changes.

Acts 7:9,10

God did not fail Joseph even when he was in prison.

- God took care of him because He had a wonderful plan for Joseph's life.

Lamentations 3:22,23

- Now that Joseph was in prison, it looked impossible that he would ever become the leader and ruler of his family, but God never changes.

  He always does everything that He promises.

  He is not like people who change their minds, forget their promises, or tell lies.

C. Pharaoh's dreams

 Theme: God is everywhere all the time; He knows everything.

 READ Genesis 41:1-8.

- Consider:

  Although God spoke to people in the past through dreams and was planning to show Pharaoh through his dream what was about to happen in Egypt, that is not God's usual way of speaking to us now. Why is that? Does He no longer know what is going to happen? Of course He does. He has not changed. He still knows everything about the future. Since God doesn't usually speak to people today through dreams, how then does He tell us what He wants us to know about the future? He teaches us the things He wants us to know through His Word, the Bible.

Pharaoh, the king of Egypt, did not know or worship the true and living God.

The Egyptians worshiped the sun, moon, and stars, animals and creeping creatures, and the Nile River.

POINT TO THE NILE RIVER ON MAP 1.

But even though they did not worship God, God planned to use this king and his country to fulfill the purposes of God.

 Theme: God is supreme and sovereign.

 Read Proverbs 21:1.

God is ruler over all people and nations even though they may not know or worship Him.

Lesson 20: God Promoted Joseph and Took Israel into Egypt

- He can use anyone in whatever way He chooses to fulfill His purposes.
- God is sovereign.
- He is the supreme ruler of everything.
- Compare:

  Whenever we make something, it belongs to us; and we make the choices about how our belongings will be used.
  - *If you make a batch of cookies, they're yours to:*

    Keep

    Give

    Take to a bake sale.
  - *If you erect an apartment building, you decide whether to:*

    Rent it out

    Make it into condominiums

    Sell it to another owner.

  God is the Creator of all people.

  He is the giver and sustainer of life.
  - *He has made us, and we rightfully belong to Him.*
  - *God can do whatever He wishes with us.*
  - *And because God is righteous, everything that He ever does to people is right.*

  Psalm 24:1,2
  I Chronicles 29:11,12
  Acts 17:24,25

- God was working through the lives of an Egyptian pharaoh and an Israelite prisoner on behalf of **all** of His people.

  At this time, Joseph was in prison.
  - Even there in prison, Joseph believed that God's purposes were right for him.
  - Though he did not know at the time how God was going to work, Joseph trusted God and lived by faith, believing that God would do what was best.

  Hebrews 11:1,2

D. Joseph interpreted Pharaoh's dreams.

 Theme: **Man needs God and is helpless to save himself.**

 Theme: **God communicates with man.**

 READ **Genesis 41:14-16,25-32.**

Joseph was unable to interpret the dreams of the king, but he trusted in the Lord to give him the interpretation of Pharaoh's dreams.

God gave Joseph understanding so that the king would know what was about to take place in his country.

God never fails those who trust in Him.

Daniel 2:27,28

Psalm 22:4,5

E. Joseph was given the position second to Pharaoh.

 Theme: **God is faithful; He never changes.**

 READ **Genesis 41:38-41.**

Lesson 20: God Promoted Joseph and Took Israel into Egypt

Even though Joseph had been through difficult experiences, the Lord was still in control.
- The Lord had not forgotten Joseph.
- The dreams which God had given him as a youth were about to be fulfilled.

God always does what He plans.
- No one can stand against Him.
- When it was time for Him to do what He planned, He brought Joseph out of prison and gave him a high position, just like He had shown him through his dreams when he was a boy.

F. Joseph's brothers came to Egypt for food.

 READ Genesis 42:1-3,6-8.

 Theme: God is faithful; He never changes.

CHRONOLOGICAL PICTURE NO. 22, "JOSEPH'S BROTHERS BOW BEFORE HIM"

Again, God was bringing to pass the things that he had shown young Joseph in his dreams. His brothers did indeed bow down before him!

G. Joseph disclosed his true identity.

 Theme: God is supreme and sovereign.

 READ Genesis 43:1,2; 45:3-9.

Joseph wept when he disclosed his true identity to his brothers.

Rather than treating his brothers as their deeds deserved, Joseph explained to them that God was in control of the situation, and that He had used the brothers' horrible actions to work for good.

H. Israel went down to Egypt.

 Theme: God is everywhere all the time; He knows everything.

 READ Genesis 45:25-28; 46:5-7.

God knows what is going to happen; God always keeps His promises.
- Many years before, God had told Abraham that his descendants would go to another country.
- Even though many hundreds of years had passed, God did what He had promised.

Scripture Reference: Daniel 4:17; Genesis 37:5-9; Genesis 50:20; Genesis 15:13

Teacher's Notes

Teacher's Notes

Lesson 20: God Promoted Joseph and Took Israel into Egypt

Scripture Reference

- All that God says in His Word will happen just as God has said.

A very difficult series of events in Joseph's life actually was the unfolding of the fulfillment of God's promise.

The descendants of Jacob, or Israel, were now called the children of Israel, Israelites, or Israel.

I. Conclusion

Today, we are still hearing about Israel in the news.

And today, God still keeps His promises.

He is still the sovereign God.

And through the Bible, He is still calling men to believe Him.

QUESTIONS:

1. What happened to Joseph in Egypt? *The wife of Joseph's owner lied about him, and he was put into prison.*

2. Who took care of Joseph in prison? *God did.*

3. Why did God take care of Joseph?

    a. *Because, although Joseph was a sinner, he trusted in God and His mercy.*

    b. *Because Joseph believed God's promises regarding the Deliverer.*

    c. *Because God had a wonderful plan for Joseph's life.*

4. Who gave Joseph the understanding of Pharaoh's dreams? *God did.*

5. What did Pharaoh's dreams mean? *God was making known to the king that there would be seven years of very good harvest which would be followed by seven years of drought.*

6. Is God able to do whatever He wants to do even in places where the people do not know and worship Him? *Yes, God is able to do whatever He wants to do, for He is almighty.*

7. How did God fulfill the dreams which He had given to Joseph when he was a youth? *The Lord gave Joseph wisdom to interpret the king's dreams so that Joseph would be given the position next to the king.*

8. Why did Jacob take all of his family down to live in Egypt?

    a. *Because Jacob had heard that Joseph was down in Egypt.*

    b. *Because there was plenty of food in Egypt.*

    c. *Because the king invited Jacob to live in Egypt.*

    d. *Because God had planned for this to happen.*

9. What were Abraham, Isaac, and Jacob's descendants called? *The children of Israel, Israelites, or Israel.*

10. What motivated Joseph to act as he did? *His faith in God.*

Scripture Reference

Acts 7:17-35
Hebrews 11:23-26

LESSON 21

God Preserved Israel Enslaved in Egypt; God Chose, Protected, and Called Moses to Deliver Israel

LESSON PREPARATION

This section is for you, the teacher.

The passages in the Scripture Reference column are for your own study in preparing for this lesson. Since they may contain concepts that run ahead of the lesson, they are not to be taught at this point.

Note: If you have not taught previously from this series of lessons, please read carefully the note to teachers in the front of this book.

SCRIPTURE: Exodus 1:6-11; 2:1-22; 3:1-20; 4:13-20, 27-31

LESSON GOALS:

- To show that God is sovereign, omniscient, omnipotent, and holy.
- To show Satan's intense desire to thwart God's plan to deliver men from Satan's bondage.
- To show that no one can thwart the purposes of God; He is faithful to carry them out at His appointed time.
- To show that only God can deliver man from bondage to Satan. Man is helpless to save himself or to save others.

THIS LESSON SHOULD HELP THE STUDENTS:

- To see that God is faithful and sovereign and will carry out His purposes.
- To look to God alone for deliverance from Satan's bondage.
- To have an increased awe of God.
- To better understand God's character.

PERSPECTIVE FOR THE TEACHER:

Our society delights in assessing the weaknesses of men without giving any thought to the power and purpose of God. But the Bible gives us a true picture of God and of men—men who are weak in themselves, but who, by faith, can be mightily used by our gracious, almighty, sovereign Creator, God.

Many people in our culture have a vague knowledge of the story of Moses; they have heard bits and pieces but have never had any concept of the sovereign God who is really the main character in this wonderful true story.

Moses was very human, and God has graciously presented to us in His Word many examples of the human frailty of His chosen leader of Israel. Yet through this frail vessel, our almighty, gracious God worked deliverance for Israel. Ultimately, God provided salvation for all mankind through Israel's promised Deliverer, Jesus Christ.

The Bible is true. It is not only an exceedingly accurate history of man, it is also a living message from our God. We need to remind our students that this dramatic story is history.

As we teach this lesson, we are reminded by God's Word that "I Am" does not change. The God of the burning bush is the same God whom we worship and serve and whose Word we teach! Though He does not speak to us today from a burning bush, He does speak to us through His Word. And as we present

Teacher's Notes

OVERVIEW

This lesson shows God's sovereign, loving care in preserving Israel in slavery and in raising up Moses to deliver them.

Some themes:

- God's omniscience:
  He knew what Pharaoh would do.

- Satan's opposition:
  Satan wanted to cut off the line of the Deliverer.

- Man's inability to save himself:
  Moses tried to help Israel and failed.

- God's holiness and His communication with Moses:
  God spoke to Moses from the burning bush.
  God told Moses to say that "I AM" sent him.

Lesson 21: God Preserved Israel Enslaved in Egypt; God Called Moses

Teacher's Notes

Scripture Reference

His Word to our students, God Himself is communicating His message to those who are listening.

VISUALS:

- Chronological Picture No. 24, "Baby Moses Rescued"
- Chronological Picture No. 25, "The Burning Bush"
- Chronological Map 1
- Chronological Chart

ON TEACHING THIS LESSON:

These lessons are designed to **teach unbelievers.** You are carefully laying a scriptural foundation on which the Gospel will later be presented. If your class contains believers, teach with the goal of giving them an understanding of the basis for their faith and **with the goal of enabling them to teach the same material to unbelievers.**

DON'T COMPLICATE THE MESSAGE!

As you teach, keep in mind that this is a directed study—not an exhaustive survey of the Bible and not an unlimited group discussion. Keep your lesson on track and moving ahead by limiting and directing any discussion.

Carefully follow the outline. Emphasize the doctrinal themes.

LESSON FORMAT: The **center column** below contains the lesson material to be taught to the students. The **bold outline headings** are only for reference and need not be spoken, as they are incorporated into the outlined material that follows. The material in the **side columns** is for the teacher's own reference and is not intended to be included in the lesson.

TO BE TAUGHT TO THE STUDENTS
(Center Column Only)

LESSON OUTLINE:

REVIEW questions from Lesson 20.

A. Introduction

This study begins in the second book of the Bible—Exodus.
- Exodus means "going out."
- This book records how God took His people, the Israelites, out of Egypt.

As we study this amazing story, let's keep in mind these things:
- First, remember that the Bible is a true history.

   The events of Genesis and Exodus are mentioned many times throughout the Bible in both the Old and New Testaments.

   Many of the minute details of Genesis and Exodus have been confirmed by archeological discoveries.

- Second, keep your eyes on what God is doing.

   You will learn a great deal about God from this book.

Lesson 21: God Preserved Israel Enslaved in Egypt; God Called Moses

Just as our actions reveal our character, so God's actions reveal His character.

- Third, remember that God is the same today as He was at the time this story took place.

    He never changes.

    God is still holy, all-powerful, all-knowing, faithful, and sovereign.

B. Israel increased in number and in riches.

Joseph and all his generation died in Egypt.

- Joseph, his brothers, and their families continued to live in Egypt after their father's death even though the drought had ended.
- They did not return to the land which God had promised to give to Abraham, Isaac, and Jacob.
- The Bible says that Joseph and all that generation died in Egypt.

About 350 years passed between the time that Israel came down to live in Egypt and the time that their story picks up again here in the book of Exodus.

Israel had been living in Egypt all that time.

POINT TO EGYPT ON CHRONOLOGICAL MAP 1.

 READ Exodus 1:6,7.

The children of Israel prospered in Egypt.

- Their numbers increased rapidly.
- They also became very rich.

    They had many cows, goats, and sheep.

    There was plenty of grass for their animals.
- The king was very good to them.

But things were soon to change.

C. The new king's evil plans

> Theme: Satan fights against God and His will. Satan is a liar and a deceiver. He hates man.

 READ Exodus 1:8-11.

Who do you think was guiding Pharaoh in his evil plan?

Satan was; Satan hates God and man.

Why would Satan want to destroy the nation of Israel?

Satan knew that God had promised to send the Deliverer who would destroy Satan and deliver man from his power.

He also knew that God had promised that this Saviour would be born through the nation of Israel.

- Satan knew that the Deliverer would be a descendant of Abraham.
- Satan wanted to destroy the nation of Israel because they were the people God had chosen to fulfill His plan in the world.
- Satan didn't want anyone to be delivered from his power and from the righteous punishment of God.

Scripture Reference: Genesis 50:26; Genesis 12:3; 28:14

Teacher's Notes

Lesson 21: God Preserved Israel Enslaved in Egypt; God Called Moses

D. Moses' birth and his mother's plan

 Theme: Man must have faith in order to please God and be saved.

POINT TO THE NAME "MOSES" ON THE CHRONOLOGICAL CHART

 READ Exodus 2:1-4.

The parents of this child trusted in God to take care of their baby son.

E. Moses was adopted by Pharaoh's daughter.

 Theme: God is faithful; He never changes.

 READ Exodus 2:5.

Suggested Visual:

CHRONOLOGICAL PICTURE NO. 24, "BABY MOSES RESCUED"

 READ Exodus 2:6-10.

God used Moses' courageous sister and even Pharaoh's daughter to protect Moses!

Then God returned Moses to his own mother to nurse him until he was old enough to be sent back to Pharaoh's daughter.

God planned to use Moses to deliver the Israelites from slavery.

- God knew that Moses would be safer in Pharaoh's house than anywhere else.
- He also knew that Moses would learn many things there that would be important for him to know for his future work as the leader of his people.

   Acts 7:22

- Note:

  Egyptian writings of this time mention that the children of Egyptian leaders were given instruction in writing and literary skills as well as domestic and military leadership training. Moses may well have been instructed in these areas as he grew up in Pharaoh's household.

As in Joseph's story, we see God working through an adverse situation to accomplish His purposes and to bring about the best results for His people.

 Theme: God is supreme and sovereign.

God is greater than Satan; God is greater than everyone and everything.

Lesson 21: God Preserved Israel Enslaved in Egypt; God Called Moses

Romans 8:28

- No one and nothing can stop Him from doing whatever He plans.
- He continues to carry out His plans even in adverse situations and works through these situations to bring about good for those who trust Him.
- God has all wisdom.

  We can trust Him.

  He cared for His people Israel, even while they were in bondage; and He also cares for you.

Each of us needs to understand God's Word so we will know what God has done to deliver us all from the power of Satan and to bring us back to God.

F. Moses, when he reached manhood

 READ Exodus 2:11-22.

The Israelites were held captive by the evil pharaoh.

- They couldn't escape.
- Moses tried to help them, but he failed.
- No human being could release his people from the wicked ruler of Egypt.
- Only God could help them.

 Theme: Satan fights against God and His will. Satan is a liar and a deceiver. He hates man.

- Compare:

  Just as the Israelites were held captive by Pharaoh, so we, our forefathers, and all our children are born captives of Satan. We cannot deliver ourselves from him. No teacher or preacher can deliver us; no other human being can deliver us. Only God can deliver us from the bondage of Satan.

G. Moses saw the burning bush.

 Theme: God is all-powerful.

 READ Exodus 3:1-3.

Suggested Visual:

CHRONOLOGICAL PICTURE NO. 25, "THE BURNING BUSH"

This bush was an ordinary bush; the extraordinary thing was that the bush was burning and yet it was not being burned up.

Because God was in the bush, the bush wasn't consumed.

- God is almighty.

Lesson 21: God Preserved Israel Enslaved in Egypt; God Called Moses

- Nobody can do the things which God can do.

The burning bush was to remind Moses of the terrible conditions of his people Israel.

- They, like the burning bush, were in danger of being totally destroyed.
- But, just as God was in the bush and kept it from being consumed, so He was with Israel, the descendants of Abraham.

Isaiah 12:6

- Satan and Pharaoh could not destroy the Israelites while God was with them.

H. God gave His message to Moses.

 Theme: God communicates with man.

 READ Exodus 3:4.

Moses didn't know that God was in the bush until God spoke to him from out of the middle of the fire.

 Theme: God is holy and righteous.

 READ Exodus 3:5,6.

God told Moses to take his shoes off as a sign of respect to God who is perfect and is the great Creator.

- To be barefoot was a sign of humility and submission.
- Slaves went barefoot.

 Theme: God is supreme and sovereign.

The Lord chooses whomever He pleases to do His will, and when the time comes for the Lord to fulfill His plans, no one can stop Him.

Psalm 115:3; 135:5,6

God told Moses that He had chosen him to lead the Israelites out of slavery in Egypt and take them back to the land which God had given to Abraham.

 READ Exodus 3:7-10.

Moses had failed when he had tried to help his people previously, so he knew that he was not able by his own strength to confront the king and deliver Israel from slavery.

 READ Exodus 3:11.

God told Moses that He would be with him, and He gave Moses a sign.

- God promised Moses that He would bring him back to this mountain where he was standing before the burning bush.
- This mountain was called Mount Sinai or Mount Horeb.

ON MAP 1, POINT TO THE PROBABLE LOCATION OF MOUNT SINAI.

 READ Exodus 3:12.

Lesson 21: God Preserved Israel Enslaved in Egypt; God Called Moses

I. "I AM"

 READ Exodus 3:13.

Moses was still not satisfied.

- His own people, the Israelites, had rejected him when he had tried to assist them previously.
- He wondered if they would believe him when he went back to them and told them that the God of Abraham, Isaac, and Jacob had sent him to deliver them from slavery.

Theme: God is supreme and sovereign.

 READ Exodus 3:14.

- Explain:

  During the times written about in the Bible, names had meanings. A person's name emphasized some personal characteristic or quality. For example, Moses' name meant "to draw out of" because he was taken out of the water when the king's daughter found him.

- Compare:

  Some of you may have read through books looking for a name for your baby. Many names have interesting meanings behind them.

  But how could God give Himself just one or two names? It was impossible because God is so great. He is the mighty Creator, the all-seeing one, the all-knowing one, the almighty one, the faithful and unchanging one, the mighty judge and avenger of all evil, the loving, kind, and gracious Saviour who alone can provide a way to save men from Satan and sin and death. He is all of these things and many more.

  What one name could God give to Himself that would tell the Israelites all the things there are to know about Him? It could not be done. Therefore, God told Moses to tell Israel that "I AM" had sent him.

  This name, "I AM," includes so much that we cannot understand it completely. It means that God is the self-existent one. Do you remember the first words in the Bible, "In the beginning God...."? God was already there in the beginning. He had no beginning and can have no end. He never was and never will be dependent on anyone. He created all things and gave life to everything and everyone. All are dependent on Him for everything. He has control over all the earth, the rain, winds, rivers, the moon, stars, and sun. All things are under His control. He is the great "I AM"; He is greater than all. [1]

Pharaoh, the Egyptians, and even Satan could not hold God's people when the Lord, "I AM," decided to deliver them.

 READ Exodus 3:15-18.

J. God knew what the king would do.

 Theme: God is everywhere all the time; He knows everything.

[1] For us who teach and for all believers, the response to I AM should be, "Yes, Lord! YOU ARE!"

Teacher's Notes

Lesson 21: God Preserved Israel Enslaved in Egypt; God Called Moses

Scripture Reference

 READ Exodus 3:19,20.

God knew exactly how the king of Egypt would react.

God knows our thoughts, words, and actions before we ever think, say, or do them.

He knows everything about us from birth to death and even after death.

Psalm 139

Hebrews 4:13

K. God gave Aaron to be Moses' assistant.

 Theme: God is loving, merciful, and gracious.

Moses had one more suggestion: He told the Lord to send someone else more suitable than himself.

 READ Exodus 4:13.

The Lord was angry with Moses for continuing to argue, but He promised to send Aaron, Moses' older brother, to assist him.

 READ Exodus 4:14-17.

L. Moses obeyed the Lord.

 READ Exodus 4:18.

The Lord assured Moses that the king and all others who had previously planned to harm him were now dead.

No doubt this encouraged Moses as he finally set out for Egypt.

 READ Exodus 4:19,20.

M. The Lord sent Aaron to meet Moses.

 Theme: God is faithful; He never changes.

The Lord kept His promise to Moses and sent Moses' older brother, Aaron, to meet him.

He was to accompany and assist Moses as he went to Pharaoh to demand the release of the Israelites.

POINT TO "AARON" ON THE CHRONOLOGICAL CHART.

 READ Exodus 4:27,28.

Moses and Aaron went back to Egypt.

They called together their own people, the Israelites, and told them what the Lord had said to Moses.

N. Israel believed that the Lord had sent Moses.

 Theme: Man must have faith in order to please God and be saved.

 READ Exodus 4:29-31.

304

Lesson 21: God Preserved Israel Enslaved in Egypt; God Called Moses

The Israelites believed God's Word given through Moses.

They were thankful that the Lord had heard their cries for deliverance.

- Consider:

  The Israelites were wise to listen to and believe in God's message through Moses. When we don't believe the Word of the Lord, we are calling Him a liar. The Lord is unable to help those who refuse to believe His Word.

O. Conclusion

What we have just studied is much more than a story about a man named Moses.

It is the true history of Israel.

It is also part of the background of God's plan to send a Deliverer for mankind.

It is God's story.

No one is greater than God.

He knew exactly what was happening to Israel.

And He was going to bring deliverance to them and, ultimately, through them, to you and me.

We will study more about God's deliverance of Israel in our next lesson.

QUESTIONS:

1. Why did the king of Egypt make the Israelites slaves? *Because they had become more in number than the Egyptians, the king was afraid that the Israelites might join with the Egyptians' enemies to fight against them and take control of Egypt.*

2. Who was guiding the king in his wicked plans? *Satan.*

3. Why would Satan wish to destroy the Israelites? *Satan knew that God had promised Abraham, Isaac, and Jacob that one of their descendants would be the Deliverer.*

4. Why did God protect and prosper Israel? *Because God is unchanging. He was faithful to His promise given to Abraham, Isaac, and Jacob.*

5. Why did the Lord allow Pharaoh's daughter to adopt Moses? *Because God planned to use Moses to deliver the Israelites from slavery.*

6. Can Satan, any spirit, a human being, or anything hinder God from doing what He plans? *No, God does everything He wants to do.*

7. Could the Israelites or Moses deliver them from Pharaoh? *No.*

8. Who is the only one who can deliver a person from Satan's control? *God.*

9. Why did God decide to save the Israelites from slavery?

    a. *Because the Lord saw their suffering and heard their cries.*

    b. *Because God loved them and planned to reveal His love and mercy to them.*

Teacher's Notes

Lesson 21: God Preserved Israel Enslaved in Egypt; God Called Moses

Scripture Reference

  c. *Because the Lord had promised Abraham that He would make Abraham's descendants into a great nation and that, through them, the Deliverer would come into the world.*

10. Why was the bush which Moses saw not being consumed although it was burning? *The bush was not consumed because the Almighty God was in the bush.*

11. What does the name of God, "I AM," mean? *It means that God is the self-existent one. He doesn't need anything or anyone. He was before the beginning of all things. Because He is the Creator of all things, everything is under His power, and He is totally independent of all things.*

12. Did God think that the king of Egypt would release the Israelites immediately when Moses told him what the Lord had said? *No, He knew that the king would not free the Israelites until he had to. God knows everything.*

13. Did the Israelites believe that the Lord had sent Moses? *Yes, they did.*

14. Is God pleased with and will He accept those who do not believe what He says? *No, God rejects and punishes all who treat Him as if He were a liar.*

Scripture Reference | Teacher's Notes

LESSON 22

God Sent Plagues on Egypt; God Passed Over Israel

OVERVIEW

This lesson presents God's sovereignty, omniscience, and omnipotence in bringing the plagues on Egypt. It shows His holiness and grace and mercy in His deliverance of Israel through the Passover.

Some points:

- God's sovereignty, omniscience, and omnipotence:
  He used Pharaoh's resistance to display God's sovereign power to deliver Israel.

- God's faithfulness:
  He preserved Israel and the line of the Deliverer.

- Man's inability to save himself:
  The Israelites could not save themselves; God had to make a way to save them.

- The Passover—a type of Jesus Christ:
  You will want to teach carefully the details of the Passover which are presented in this lesson so you can use them later in presenting the Gospel.

LESSON PREPARATION

This section is for you, the teacher.

The passages in the Scripture Reference column are for your own study in preparing for this lesson. Since they may contain concepts that run ahead of the lesson, they are not to be taught at this point.

Note: If you have not taught previously from this series of lessons, please read carefully the note to teachers in the front of this book.

SCRIPTURE: Exodus 5:1,2; 6:1-8; 7:4,5; 11:1,4-7; 12:1-7,12-14,22,28-36,46

LESSON GOALS:

- To show God's sovereignty, faithfulness, and omnipotence.
- To show that the penalty for sin is death.
- To show that God provides a way of escape for those who trust Him.
- To present the Passover so that it may be referred to later as a type of Christ.

THIS LESSON SHOULD HELP THE STUDENTS:

- To see God's sovereignty.
- To see the seriousness of sin.
- To see that God honors His promises and cares for those who believe Him.
- To see that they are helpless to save themselves from God's judgment.

PERSPECTIVE FOR THE TEACHER:

What a tremendous story this is! We live in a day when many "religious scholars" are repulsed by any emphasis on blood. God was not repulsed by it; rather, He tells us in this passage that only those protected by the blood of a lamb would be spared the loss of their firstborn. Not only was the lamb's blood spilled out, it was also applied to the top and the sides of the door frame of each house.

We who know the story of the Lamb of God realize the tremendous implications of this passage in Exodus. Indeed, we too are spared the wrath of God because, by faith, we have been placed under the protection of the shed blood of Jesus Christ. But many reject this simple but eternally profound truth. Like Pharaoh, who trusted in his own power and the power of his false gods, people refuse to humble themselves to believe God.

The simplicity of God's provision is still a stumbling block for men. We live in a time of constant urging to be the "greatest" and to "do it your way." Pharaoh realized too late that he was not the greatest, nor could he do it his way. Your students may very well be struggling with these very issues. They have been carefully taught by the god of this world to put self first and not to allow God or anyone to tell them what to do.

Pray for your students. God can use His Word to penetrate hard hearts. Your students have at least come to hear about God. There may be a

Lesson 22: God Sent Plagues on Egypt; God Passed Over Israel

tremendous battle raging inside them, as the enemy hates to have them hear and believe. Trust God to open their eyes and hearts to believe the truth.

VISUALS:

- Chronological Picture No. 27, "Passover Blood Applied to the Doorposts"
- Chronological Picture No. 28, "Pharaoh and His Dead Son"
- Chronological Chart

ON TEACHING THIS LESSON:

These lessons are designed to **teach unbelievers.** You are carefully laying a scriptural foundation on which you may later present the Gospel. If your class contains believers, teach with the goal of giving them an understanding of the basis for their faith and **with the goal of enabling them to teach the same material to unbelievers.**

DON'T COMPLICATE THE MESSAGE!

As you teach, keep in mind that this is a directed study—not an exhaustive survey of the Bible and not an unlimited group discussion. Keep your lesson on track and moving ahead by limiting and directing any discussion.

Carefully follow the outline. Emphasize the doctrinal themes.

LESSON FORMAT: The **center column** below contains the lesson material to be taught to the students. The **bold outline headings** are only for reference and need not be spoken, as they are incorporated into the outlined material that follows. The material in the **side columns** is for the teacher's own reference and is not intended to be included in the lesson.

TO BE TAUGHT TO THE STUDENTS
(Center Column Only)

LESSON OUTLINE:

REVIEW questions from Lesson 21.

A. Introduction

Today's lesson starts with the Israelites enslaved in Egypt by a powerful pharaoh.
- Probably none of us have been enslaved as the Israelites were.
- But we have been slaves of sin.

Let's take a look at how God worked deliverance for the Israelites.

B. Pharaoh refused to obey God's command given through Moses and Aaron.

 Theme: God communicates with man.

 Theme: Man is a sinner. He needs God and is helpless to save himself.

Lesson 22: God Sent Plagues on Egypt; God Passed Over Israel

 READ Exodus 5:1,2.

God used Moses and Aaron to speak to the king of Egypt, but Pharaoh refused to obey the Lord's command.

(Note: Pharaoh was the title given to all the rulers of Egypt during this period. We are not told in the Bible which pharaoh was in power when Moses became Israel's leader.)

- Pharaoh did not know the only true and living God and Creator of the whole earth.

The Egyptians did not worship God; they worshiped the things that God had made.

- They worshiped the Nile, the largest river in their country.
- They also worshiped the sun, moon, and many different kinds of animals.
- They had many, many gods.
- In addition, the Egyptians worshiped Pharaoh, their king, as a god.

Most of the people of the world had deliberately turned away from the true knowledge of God.

- They had become foolish in their understanding about Him.
- Because they didn't want to know God, He allowed them to worship false gods.

Because the majority of the people of the world had turned to worship idols and had lost the true understanding of God, God called Abraham and made him the father of the nation of Israel

- God did this so that, through Israel, He could preserve the true knowledge of God.
- Through them, God planned to make known the truth about Himself to all other people of the world.
- The truth about God is in this book, the Bible, which God gave through the Israelites.

God would have taught the king of Egypt that idols are false gods and that the God of Abraham and Israel is the only true and living God, but Pharaoh did not want to listen.

C. Through Pharaoh's rebellion, the Lord purposed to show Israel that He was their God.

 Theme: God communicates with man.

The generation of Israelites living in Egypt when Moses returned there had not seen any evidence of the Lord's greatness and power.

- They had only heard about the Lord and what He had done for Abraham, Isaac, Jacob, and Joseph.
- Now the Lord was going to use this evil Pharaoh and his rebellion to display God's power and wisdom to this generation of Israelites so that they would know that He was still the almighty and caring God of Israel.

 READ Exodus 6:1-8.

Lesson 22: God Sent Plagues on Egypt; God Passed Over Israel

Teacher's Notes

Scripture Reference

D. Through Pharaoh's rebellion, the Lord planned to show the Egyptians that He alone is the true and living God.

 Theme: God communicates with man.

God also planned to show the Egyptians that

- He alone is the true and living God with power over the whole earth.
- The gods whom they trusted and worshiped were unable to protect them from the God of Israel.
- Consider:

    Among the Egyptians were intelligent, highly-skilled people: capable writers, mathematicians, chemists, military and civilian leaders, architects, artists, craftsmen, etc. But spiritually, they were totally blind and foolish. Though they held Israel in slavery, the Egyptians themselves were the ones hopelessly enslaved—held captive and completely subservient to Satan.

    Soon they would know that the God of Israel was alive, powerful, and able to set His people free.

- Consider:

    It may be easy for us to see the folly in Egypt's worship. But remember, Satan had deceived them in a way that they would accept in their day and culture. He is still doing the same thing to people today.

 Theme: God is holy and righteous. He demands death as the payment for sin.

Because Pharaoh was determined to fight against God, God planned to use this wicked king to display His mighty power and terrible judgment on all those who rebel against Him.

 READ Exodus 7:4,5.

This should be a warning to all of us.

- We cannot ignore or fight against God and escape His punishment.
- No one who fights against God can win or escape punishment.

E. The Lord sent nine plagues on Egypt.

 Theme: God is all-powerful.

Because the king of Egypt refused to release the Israelites, the Lord began to show His great power.²

Because of time, we will not read all the details of what happened.

But if you want to take the time on your own, you will find the story in Exodus 7:14-10:29.

- First, the Lord turned the water in their river into blood.
- Next, He sent plagues of frogs, lice (gnats), and flies.
- Then God caused the Egyptians' horses, cattle, sheep, camels, and donkeys to become sick.
- Next, the Lord caused all the Egyptians to have terrible boils.

²We want to devote the class time to the major themes of this lesson, so we will not read the biblical account of the plagues. Be sure to state that this is a true story, as recorded for us in the Bible. ☐

Lesson 22: God Sent Plagues on Egypt; God Passed Over Israel

- This was followed by a terribly destructive hailstorm, a plague of locusts, and three days of thick darkness in all the places where the Egyptians were living.

Pharaoh and the Egyptian people could not save themselves from these terrible plagues sent by the Lord.

Neither could their false gods save them.

- Note:

    Interestingly, each of the plagues pointed to the falseness of a particular god of the Egyptians: for example, their frog god, their sun god, and their storm god.

 Theme: God is loving, merciful, and gracious.

But for the Lord's mercy and love to the Israelites, they, too, would have suffered the plagues.

The Lord protected the Israelites so that none of these terrible things happened to any of them, even though they were living nearby in the same country.

- The Lord didn't protect the Israelites because they were without sin or because they deserved His care.
- He protected them because of His love, mercy, and grace.

 Theme: God is faithful; He never changes.

- Another reason why God protected the Israelites was that God had not forgotten His promises to Abraham, Isaac, and Jacob.

    God chose Abraham and promised to bless him and to make his descendants into a great nation and promised that He would be their God.

    Although hundreds of years had passed and the Israelites were now slaves in Egypt, God still claimed the Israelites as His special people because they were the descendants which God had promised to Abraham.

 Theme: God is supreme and sovereign.

- God also protected Israel from the plagues so that the king of Egypt would realize that the God of Israel was the only true and living God in the whole earth.

    God is supreme and sovereign.

    He does whatever He chooses to do.

 Theme: Man is a sinner. He needs God and is helpless to save himself.

With each of the plagues, the pattern of response was the same:

- Each time the Lord sent a plague on Egypt, Pharaoh called for Moses and asked him to remove the plague.
- Pharaoh claimed that he would then let Israel go.
- When Pharaoh said that he would allow the Israelites to go free, the Lord removed the plague.
- But as soon as the Lord removed the plague, Pharaoh hardened his heart and would not let the Israelites leave Egypt.
- Every time Pharaoh did this, he became more hard-hearted and proud.

Lesson 22: God Sent Plagues on Egypt; God Passed Over Israel

F. The Lord's last judgment on the Egyptians

 Theme: God is supreme and sovereign.

 Theme: God is everywhere all the time; He knows everything.

Although the Lord had already sent nine terrible plagues on the rebellious Egyptians, the king of Egypt still refused to obey the Lord and let the Israelites go free.

God knew all along that Pharaoh would be stubborn and would refuse to release the Israelites.

- Even before He sent Moses back to Egypt, God had told Moses that this would happen.
- God is never surprised by what people do or by what happens.
- He always knows everything before it happens, and He always has His plan worked out so that He always wins, no matter what people say or do.
- This wicked king could not stop God from delivering the descendants of Abraham.

The Lord knew that, after this final plague, Pharaoh would release the Israelites.

READ Exodus 11:1,4-7.

G. The Lord's instructions to Moses

 Theme: God communicates with man.

God told Moses how the Israelites must prepare for the final and most terrible plague of all.

 Theme: Man is a sinner. He needs God and is helpless to save himself.

The Israelites were also sinners and deserved to die for their sins.

 Theme: God is loving, merciful, and gracious.

They also would have suffered through this last terrible judgment if it had not been for the Lord's mercy and grace.

 Theme: God is faithful; He never changes.

God remembered His promises to Abraham, Isaac, and Jacob.

- God had promised to take Abraham's descendants back to the land which God had given to them.   *Genesis 15:13-16*
- It was now God's chosen time to do this.

This is what the Lord told Moses that the Israelites must do in order to save their firstborn children from death.

Lesson 22: God Sent Plagues on Egypt; God Passed Over Israel

1. **They must choose a lamb without blemish.**

    Theme: God is holy and righteous.

    READ Exodus 12:1-5.

   - The head of each home had to choose a lamb or goat. The lamb or goat had to be without blemish.
   - Recall:

   Do you remember the ram that was to be offered instead of Isaac? It was caught by the horns in a thorny bush. Why was it caught by the horns? God is perfect, and everything that He says and does is perfect. He would never accept as an offering an animal that was sick or hurt.

2. **They must kill the lamb and catch its blood in a basin.**

    Theme: God is holy and righteous. He demands death as the payment for sin.

    READ Exodus 12:6.

   The lamb was to be kept until the day specified by the Lord, which was the fourteenth day of the month.

   They were to kill the lamb in the evening of that day.

   The lamb must die. Its blood, on which its life depended, must be allowed to flow out. This was to remind the Israelites that the punishment for sin is death.

   - Recall:

   Until Adam and Eve sinned, there was no death in the world. But when Adam and Eve were separated from God because of their disobedience, God said that their bodies must also die. All of Adam and Eve's descendants were born sinners, separated from God. That is why all people must also die physically, including you and me. If there were no sin in the world, there would be no physical death. If there were no sin, there would be no separation from God in the everlasting fire prepared for Satan and his followers.

   - Explain:

   When the Israelites killed the lambs and the blood flowed out, the people were reminded that the punishment for sin is death. Just as the ram died instead of Isaac, the perfect lambs which were chosen and killed by the Israelites died instead of their firstborn children.

3. **They must place the blood on both of the doorposts and above the door.**

    Theme: God is holy and righteous. He demands death as the payment for sin.

Suggested Visual:

CHRONOLOGICAL PICTURE NO. 27, "PASSOVER BLOOD APPLIED TO THE DOORPOSTS"

 READ Exodus 12:7.

God told the Israelites to catch the blood in a basin.

Then they were to take a small branch of a certain bush and dip it into the blood.

With this bush, they were to put the blood on both sides of the door and over the door of the house where they were going to be eating the lamb on that night.

It was the blood of the lamb on the doorpost that would save the firstborn from God's judgment.

4. They must stay inside the house on which they had placed the blood.

They must not go out of the house until the morning.

 READ Exodus 12:22.

- Explain:

   The Israelites were to stay inside their houses on which they had placed the blood. It was just as if they were to hide behind the death and blood of the lamb which God said they must kill in place of the firstborn.

5. They must not break any of the lamb's bones.

They were not to break the bones of the animal when they killed it or ate it.

 READ Exodus 12:46.

 Theme: Man can come to God only according to God's will and plan.

These were God's instructions for Israel.

They had to do everything exactly as the Lord had told Moses.

- Recall:

   God has always been the same. He will not let people save themselves in their own way. Do you remember that He refused to accept the clothing that Adam and Eve made for themselves in the garden of Eden? God also refused the offering that Cain brought because it was not according to His instructions. God told Noah

Lesson 22: God Sent Plagues on Egypt; God Passed Over Israel

to make the ark exactly as He had instructed him. In the same way, everything had to be done by the Israelites exactly as God had instructed Moses.

- Compare:

  God is still the same. He has not changed. We cannot come to God according to our own ideas or the ideas of any other person. We can only come to God according to His way. If we don't come the way He says, then He will never accept us.

H. The Lord's promise to the Israelites

 READ Exodus 12:12-14.

God promised the Israelites that, when He saw the blood on their houses, He would not allow the plague to enter and kill their firstborn.

I. Israel's faith and obedience

 Theme: Man must have faith in order to please God and be saved.

- Consider:

  How would you feel if this was going to happen here? You can well imagine the tremendous fear of God that swept through the Israelites. They knew God meant what He said. They believed and obeyed the Lord.

 READ Exodus 12:28.

 Theme: Man can come to God only according to God's will and plan.

- Consider:

  What do you think would have happened if an Israelite had said, "I'm not going to kill one of my good lambs. I have a sick one. That will do." Do you think God would have accepted the blood of a sick lamb?

  Or, what if another man reasoned, "It's a shame to kill this good lamb. I won't kill it. I will just tie it up at the door. God will see the living lamb, and He will not kill my child by the plague." Do you think God would have passed by the firstborn of that house?

  No! The lamb had to die. The blood must be shed. They must not forget that the punishment for sin is death. It all had to be done the way God had told Moses.

The Israelites were to trust in God who had told them that, when He saw the blood on the doorposts of their houses, their firstborn children and the firstborn of their livestock would not die.

J. All the Egyptians' firstborn died.

 Theme: Man is a sinner. He needs God and is helpless to save himself.

Lesson 22: God Sent Plagues on Egypt; God Passed Over Israel

 Theme: God is holy and righteous. He demands death as the payment for sin.

 READ Exodus 12:29,30.

Suggested Visual:

CHRONOLOGICAL PICTURE NO. 28, "PHARAOH AND HIS DEAD SON"

Every firstborn Egyptian child and the firstborn of all the Egyptians' livestock died.

- Consider:

  The punishment for sin is death. But we must remember that the punishment for sin is not only physical death but also everlasting separation from God in the lake of fire.

 Theme: God is faithful; He never changes.

The Lord passed through Egypt just as He said He would.

- He always does what He says. He doesn't merely threaten and then not carry out His threats.
- When God decides to punish sinners, there is no way to escape.

Because the Israelites had put the blood on their houses in obedience to the Lord, not one of their firstborn children or livestock died.

- God always does what He says.
- He said He would destroy the firstborn in the Egyptian homes, and He did.
- He said He would pass over every house where He saw the blood, and He did.
- The Lord can be trusted to do everything He says.
- Consider:

  Had Pharaoh been warned? Yes! He had! All of the other nine plagues that the Lord had promised to send had come, just as announced by Moses. Pharaoh's refusal to yield to God cost him and all Egypt not only their livestock and crops, but now also their firstborn sons! Because Pharaoh refused to believe God, he and all Egypt paid a horribly tragic price. But even more tragic is the eternal price they would pay for their unbelief: separation from God forever in the Lake of Fire.

K. Pharaoh told the Israelites to go.

 Theme: God is supreme and sovereign.

Hebrews 2:2,3

Deuteronomy 7:9,10

Lesson 22: God Sent Plagues on Egypt; God Passed Over Israel

 READ Exodus 12:31-36.

Pharaoh called Moses that very night and told him to take the Israelites out of Egypt.

Pharaoh thought that he could fight against God and that God couldn't make him give in, but no one can fight against the Lord and win.

L. Conclusion

We are fortunate to have this story.

We do not need to refuse God as Pharaoh did.

We can learn from this awful tragedy to believe God and to believe His Word.

God has not changed.

- He still requires that we believe Him.
- He still judges sin.
- And He still keeps His promises.

The Lord delivered His people just as He had promised He would.

God will punish those who fight against Him, but He will show His mercy and give His peace to those who trust Him.

QUESTIONS:

1. What did Pharaoh say when Moses told him that the Lord God of Israel commanded him to let Israel go? *Pharaoh said, "I don't know the Lord, and I will not let Israel go."*

2. Did the king's answer surprise the Lord? *No, the Lord knew that Pharaoh would not let the Israelites go immediately.*

3. Does anything which a person says, thinks, or does take the Lord by surprise? *No, He knows everything before it ever happens.*

4. How did God plan to use this wicked king? *God planned to use this proud king to show everyone that the God of Israel is the only true and living God and that He is almighty.*

5. How did the Lord show His power? *The Lord sent great and terrible plagues on the Egyptians.*

6. What were those plagues? *The Lord turned the river to blood. He sent frogs, gnats, and flies. He destroyed the Egyptians' horses, cattle, sheep, camels, and donkeys. He also sent boils, hailstorms, locusts, and total darkness.*

7. Why didn't these plagues also come on the Israelites?

   a. *Because of the Lord's love and grace.*

   b. *Because God had not forgotten His promises to Abraham, Isaac, and Jacob that He would make their descendants into a great nation and that He would be their God.*

   c. *So that the king of Egypt would realize that the God of Israel was the only true and living God in the whole earth and that He does whatever He chooses.*

8. Did the Israelites deserve to be protected like this? *No, they, too, were sinners and deserved God's judgment.*

Teacher's Notes

Lesson 22: God Sent Plagues on Egypt; God Passed Over Israel

Scripture Reference

9. What did Pharaoh do each time the Lord sent a plague? *Pharaoh claimed to have changed his mind and asked Moses to remove the plague.*

10. What did Pharaoh do when the Lord removed the plague? *Pharaoh changed his mind, hardened his heart, and refused to allow Israel to leave.*

11. Was the Lord surprised? *No, He knew what the king would do.*

12. Was the king of Egypt able to win against God? *No.*

13. Can anyone fight against God and win? *No.*

14. What was the last judgment which God sent on the Egyptians? *God sent a plague which killed the firstborn in every Egyptian family and the firstborn of all their livestock.*

15. What did God tell the Israelites to do so their firstborn children would not die?

    a. *They must choose a lamb without blemish.*

    b. *They must kill the lamb and catch its blood in a basin.*

    c. *They must place the blood on both doorposts and above the door.*

    d. *They must stay inside the house on which they had placed the blood.*

    e. *They must not break any of the lamb's bones.*

16. What would have happened if the Israelites had not done everything exactly as God instructed Moses? *Their firstborn children would also have been killed.*

17. Who is the only one who can tell us how we can come to God and be accepted by Him? *God.*

18. What happened in the Egyptian homes on that night when God said that He would kill the firstborn of every family? *God killed them just as He said He would.*

19. What was God's promise to the Israelites? *God promised them that, when He saw the blood on either side of and above their doors, He would pass over them.*

20. What happened to the Israelites? *All of their children were safe. None of them died.*

21. Why didn't the Israelite children die?

    a. *Because the Israelites did what God said and placed the blood on their houses.*

    b. *Because God is trustworthy, He kept His promise and passed over their houses.*

22. Does God always do what He says? *Yes, when He says He will punish sin, He always does it. When He makes a promise to those who trust in Him, He always keeps it.*

23. What did Pharaoh, the king, tell Moses after the Egyptians' firstborn children died? *Pharaoh told Moses to take all the Israelites out of Egypt.*

OPTIONAL DISCUSSION QUESTION:

24. What have you learned from this lesson?

Scripture Reference

Psalm 78:13-53; 105:40-45; 106:6-15

Teacher's Notes

LESSON 23

God Delivered Israel at the Red Sea and Provided Them with Food and Water in the Desert

LESSON PREPARATION

This section is for you, the teacher.

The passages in the Scripture Reference column are for your own study in preparing for this lesson. Since they may contain concepts that run ahead of the lesson, they are not to be taught at this point.

Note: If you have not taught previously from this series of lessons, please read carefully the note to teachers in the front of this book.

SCRIPTURE: Exodus 13:17,18,21; 14:5-7,10-16,19-31; 16:1-3,11-15,35; 17:1-6

LESSON GOALS:

- To show God's sovereignty and omnipotence.
- To show that man is helpless to save himself.
- To show that man can be saved only according to God's will and plan.
- To show God's faithfulness to carry out His promises.
- To show that God is gracious and cares for the needs of undeserving people.

THIS LESSON SHOULD HELP THE STUDENTS:

- To realize that miracles are consistent with the nature of God; what seems impossible to man is possible to God.
- To see that God is concerned about people and wants everyone to come to know Him.
- To consider their own inability to save themselves.

PERSPECTIVE FOR THE TEACHER:

Our society has trouble accepting miracles. Many modern scholars are trying to "write out" of history the miraculous deeds of God which He has so clearly recorded in the Bible. Even some who call themselves Christian educators are deceiving themselves and others by giving natural explanations to miraculous occurrences. Some men totally deny the truth of Bible accounts, calling them just stories or myths.

In order to fully accept a miracle, a man must believe that God is who He says He is. If God is the sovereign Creator of the universe, then the miracles of the Bible are in no way beyond His power to achieve. It is not just the miracles themselves that men are rejecting; they are really rejecting God. When we believe that the Bible is God's true Word, we accept what God says about Himself. He is the sovereign Creator, the all-powerful, all-knowing, one-and-only God.

Careful examination of the biblical record gives no alternative but to call these events true miracles. For example: anyone who thinks that natural laws allowed for the provision of two and a half million people for forty years in the Sinai Desert might want to take a short trip there today.[1] It would be hard to imagine the logistics of sustaining even a small community of people in the Sinai for a short time, let alone meeting the immediate needs of such a vast number of people and animals who had suddenly run out of water.

OVERVIEW

This lesson presents God's power, faithfulness, grace, and mercy as shown in His provision for His often unfaithful people, Israel. It stresses the inability of the Israelites to deliver themselves.

God preserved Israel

- because of His promises to Abraham
- because He was going to give His message to the world through Israel
- to display His power, so they and we might believe in Him
- because He loved them

Stress that this lesson is historical fact.

[1] Many have questioned the numbers used in the Old Testament, particularly the numbers pertaining to the Israelites. An interesting passage to consider is Exodus 38:25,26. If the weights listed in the passage are multiplied out, they match exactly the great number of people (603,550—the number of men over the age of 20). ☐

Teacher's Notes

Lesson 23: God Delivered and Provided for Israel

Scripture Reference

We cannot change hearts and minds, but we can expose our students to the truth of God's Word and pray that they will hear and believe.

VISUALS:

- Chronological Picture No. 29, "The Crossing of the Red Sea"
- Chronological Picture No. 30, "Manna in the Wilderness"
- Chronological Picture No. 31, "Moses Strikes the Rock for Water"
- Chronological Map 1

ON TEACHING THIS LESSON:

These lessons are designed to **teach unbelievers.** You are carefully laying a scriptural foundation on which the Gospel will later be presented. If your class contains believers, teach with the goal of giving them an understanding of the basis for their faith and **with the goal of enabling them to teach the same material to unbelievers.**

DON'T COMPLICATE THE MESSAGE!

As you teach, keep in mind that this is a directed study—not an exhaustive survey of the Bible and not an unlimited group discussion. Keep your lesson on track and moving ahead by limiting and directing any discussion.

Carefully follow the outline. Emphasize the doctrinal themes.

LESSON FORMAT: The **center column** below contains the lesson material to be taught to the students. The **bold outline headings** are only for reference and need not be spoken, as they are incorporated into the outlined material that follows. The material in the **side columns** is for the teacher's own reference and is not intended to be included in the lesson.

TO BE TAUGHT TO THE STUDENTS
(Center Column Only)

LESSON OUTLINE:

REVIEW questions from Lesson 22.

A. Introduction

How should we consider a miracle?

- Is it just something to doubt or wonder about?
- Is it just some kind of a strange event?

When God chose to supercede the physical laws He established, He recorded the event in His Word as a miracle.

God presents miracles as a part of history—the history of His dealings with the world and its people.

And through the record of His miracles, God shows us truths about Himself.

Let's see what we can learn about God from this passage we're about to study.

Lesson 23: God Delivered and Provided for Israel

| Scripture Reference | | Teacher's Notes |

B. God led the Israelites by a cloud.

 Theme: God is faithful; He never changes.

Genesis 15:16a

God delivered the Israelites from slavery in Egypt, and He began to lead them back to the land that He had promised to their forefather, Abraham.

 READ Exodus 13:17,18.

- Archeological note: **2**

  A few years ago, archeologists discovered the ruins of a line of Egyptian fortresses that guarded the road through Philistine country. Again, we are reminded of the extreme accuracy of every detail of Scripture. Just as God tells us, this would not have been the way for God's people to have made their escape from Egypt!

  [2] For further details about this discovery, as told by an Israeli archeologist, see *National Geographic Magazine,* December 1982, pp. 738-768. ☐

- Text note:

  The words that are translated in our Bibles as "Red Sea," are the Hebrew words which mean "Sea of Reeds." Many Bible scholars believe that, rather than what we call the Red Sea today, this passage refers to a large inland "sea" or lake which is north of the tip of the Red Sea. This lake does have reeds, which are not found at the northern end of the Red Sea. We do not know the exact location, but we do know that the details of the story told in the Bible are exactly true, and that there was a considerable depth of water, as we will see in the story. We can look at the general area on our maps today.

ON MAP 1, POINT TO THE AREA OF THE NORTHERN END OF THE RED SEA.

 READ Exodus 13:21.

The number of Israelites had grown tremendously.
- When the Israelites first went to Egypt, there were only seventy of them.
- Now, 430 years later, there were probably about two and a half million Israelites!

Exodus 12:41

 Theme: God is loving, merciful, and gracious.

God directed them where He wanted them to go by a cloud.
- He kept the cloud before them at all times.
- They would have gotten lost, and eventually they would have died in the desert if the Lord had not directed them.

He loved them, and so He took care of them.

God was protecting the Israelites so that the great Deliverer would be born into the world.
- The Israelites are the descendants of Abraham.
- The Lord had promised Abraham that one of his descendants would be the Saviour of the world.

Isaiah 41:8-10

 Theme: God communicates with man.

Isaiah 49:6
Romans 3:1,2

The Lord also protected Israel because He was entrusting His Word to them to give to the world.

Lesson 23: God Delivered and Provided for Israel

Teacher's Notes	**Scripture Reference**

The words of God that we have been reading were given to Israel so that we, too, could learn about God and come to know Him.

C. Pharaoh decided to recapture Israel.

 Theme: Satan fights against God and His will. Satan is a liar and a deceiver. He hates man.

Pharaoh was guided by Satan. **3**
- He was not going to give up and let the Israelites go.
- He planned to go after them and recapture them.

 READ Exodus 14:5-7.

D. The Israelites were afraid, and they blamed Moses.

 Theme: Man is a sinner. He needs God and is helpless to save himself.

 READ Exodus 14:10-12.

Even though they had seen all the great and mighty things the Lord had done in Egypt, they still did not trust in the Lord.

 Theme: Man must have faith in order to please God and be saved.

Moses, however, trusted in the Lord and told the Israelites to believe God.

 READ Exodus 14:13,14.

- Consider:

  Are we any different from the Israelites? Are we willing to believe God's Word and trust only in Him? **4**

  Satan does not want us to believe. We may live and work with people who are telling us not to believe. But are we willing to believe God?

 Theme: Man is a sinner. He needs God and is helpless to save himself.

Theme: God is loving, merciful, and gracious.

Even though the Israelites sinned and didn't trust in the Lord, He was merciful and planned to deliver them.

They couldn't deliver themselves.
- The sea was in front of them, mountains were around them, and their enemies were behind them.
- ONLY GOD COULD SAVE THEM.
- Recall:

  When God put Adam and Eve out of the garden, away from Him, there was no way back into the garden, and they could not make

---

3 Some students might ask about the reference in Exodus 14:8 which refers to God hardening Pharaoh's heart. They may wonder how Pharaoh could be responsible for his actions if God was hardening his heart.
You can help them understand by explaining that it was the sinfulness of Pharaoh's heart that made it harden in response to God's dealing with him. God was showing mercy to Pharaoh by giving him opportunities to respond to the less severe plagues, but after each plague was lifted, Pharaoh refused to submit to God. ☐

4 Don't require or wait for an answer to questions like these. If anyone wishes to express their thoughts, however, let them. ☐

Lesson 23: God Delivered and Provided for Israel

things right between them and God. Only God could provide a way so that they could be accepted once again by Him. It was God who provided a way for Abel to be accepted by God. Only God could save Noah and his family from the flood. When Isaac was bound and placed on the altar and his father had the knife raised above him, only God could save him. The parents of the firstborn children of Israel could not save their children from death unless God chose to provide a way. Likewise, Israel could not escape from the Egyptians unless God made a way for them.

It is the same with us. We cannot make a way to escape the wrath of God. We cannot make things right between us and God by the things we do. Only God can save us from everlasting punishment.

E. God opened the sea.

 Theme: God is all-powerful.

 READ Exodus 14:15,16.

Psalm 95:5; 104:5-9

God created the sea, so He has complete control over it.

- Recall:

    In the beginning, the whole earth was covered with water. Remember how the Lord caused the water to move back so there was dry ground. The Lord, who in the beginning caused the water to move back, had not changed. He commanded this sea to move back so His people could walk on dry land to the other side. God could do this, for He has control over the whole earth.

It was not difficult for God to open the sea so that the Israelites could walk through to the other side.

Jeremiah 32:17

- The Lord is almighty.
- Nothing is too hard for Him.

F. Israel was led by God through the sea.

 Theme: God is faithful; He never changes.

READ Exodus 14:19-22.

Suggested Visual:

CHRONOLOGICAL PICTURE NO. 29, "THE CROSSING OF THE RED SEA."

The Lord did not forsake His people.

- He promised to lead them safely out of Egypt and into the land He had promised to Abraham.
- The Lord led the Israelites into the path which He had made through the sea.

Lesson 23: God Delivered and Provided for Israel

- The Lord moved the cloud that was leading Israel and placed it between them and the Egyptians.

    Behind the Israelites, the cloud was bright and shining like the sun.

    It gave light so the Israelites could see where they were going.

    Before the Egyptians, however, the cloud was black. There was only darkness in front of them.

Nevertheless, the Egyptians continued to follow because the Lord planned to destroy them.

 READ Exodus 14:23-25.

G. God drowned the Egyptian armies in the sea.

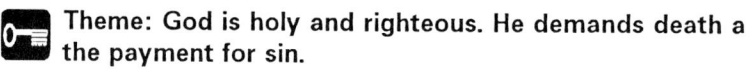 Theme: God is holy and righteous. He demands death as the payment for sin.

 Theme: God is supreme and sovereign.

 READ Exodus 14:26-29.

The Egyptian armies were drowned by God in the sea.

No one can fight against God and succeed.

- He punishes all those who fight against Him.
- But He is the merciful Saviour of all those who believe His Word and come to Him in the way He says. *(I Timothy 4:10)*

 Theme: God is loving, merciful, and gracious.

 Theme: God is faithful; He never changes.

 READ Exodus 14:30.

The Lord protected all of the Israelites.

- Not one of them was drowned, and the Egyptians did not catch any of them.
- The Lord saved them because of His love for them and because He had promised to save them. *(Psalm 105:42,43)*

 Theme: Man must have faith in order to please God and be saved.

 READ Exodus 14:31.

When Israel saw the great things which the Lord did, they believed in Him.

- Consider:

    Some people say they will only believe if they can see God do some great and wonderful thing. But God has not promised that He will do spectacular miracles so that we will believe. God has given us His Word, and He tells us to believe that and to trust in Him. If

Lesson 23: God Delivered and Provided for Israel

we refuse to believe what He has written in His Word, then we will die without God and go to everlasting punishment

H. Israel complained.

 Theme: Man is a sinner. He needs God and is helpless to save himself.

 READ Exodus 16:1-3.

Psalm 78:11

Even though the Lord had delivered the Israelites from the Egyptians by opening the Red Sea and leading them safely through, they had not learned trust in Him.

- They murmured and grumbled and blamed Moses and Aaron.
- Instead of complaining, they should have trusted in the Lord to give them food.

They could not get food anywhere. **5**

- Moses couldn't provide food for them.
- Not only were there no "supermarkets;" neither was anything growing there.
- It was a barren desert.

God wanted the Israelites to know that He alone could help them in this situation.

In the same way, God wants each sinner to realize that God alone can save him from the punishment for sin.

I. God promised them food.

 Theme: God is all-powerful.

 READ Exodus 16:11,12.

Although the Israelites and Moses couldn't provide food, the Lord could; nothing is impossible to God.

 Theme: God is loving, merciful, and gracious.

They didn't deserve anything from the Lord, but in His grace, He promised to give them food.

- No one deserves God's grace and mercy.
- We all deserve everlasting punishment.

J. God gave them food.

 Theme: God is loving, merciful, and gracious.

 READ Exodus 16:13-15.

5 Take the time to explain what the area of the Sinai Desert is like. Use your map and show pictures if you have them.

It is important that your students realize the impossibility of the Israelites or Moses providing food for themselves. Emphasize that only God could save the Israelites. Through these stories, we want to teach our hearers that "...Salvation is of the LORD" (Jonah 2:9). Our main objective in teaching the Old Testament is to show man's helplessness and God's salvation so that, when we present the Gospel, our students will turn to Christ alone. ☐

Lesson 23: God Delivered and Provided for Israel

Teacher's Notes

Scripture Reference

Suggested Visual:

CHRONOLOGICAL PICTURE NO. 30, "MANNA IN THE WILDERNESS"

God helps the helpless; He delivers those who have no way of escape.

- Recall:

When Adam and Eve sinned against God and were therefore separated from Him, God promised to send a Saviour to deliver them. They tried to make clothing from leaves, but God provided them with the skins of animals. God, in His mercy and grace, accepted Abel's offering. God saved Noah and his family from the flood. God called Abraham out of idolatry, protected Jacob's family from starvation through Joseph, called Moses to deliver the Israelites from slavery in Egypt, and opened up the sea for them. Now He promised to give the Israelites food. None of these people deserved the things that God did for them. He did it all because He is merciful and gracious.

 Theme: God is faithful; He never changes.

 READ Exodus 16:35.

The Lord faithfully provided manna for the Israelites from this time forward and throughout the time they were in the wilderness.

- He never failed them.
- God is faithful.
- He can be trusted to do everything He has said in His Word.

K. Israel murmured once again.

 Theme: Man is a sinner. He needs God and is helpless to save himself.

Although the Israelites were thankful for the Lord's provision of food, they soon forgot about His great power, and they began to complain again.

- (Does that sound familiar to you?)
- Listen to what happened this time.

 READ Exodus 17:1-4.

- Consider:

How long can a man live without water? Only a few days. The Israelites were afraid they were all going to die there in the desert. Can you imagine the burden Moses felt? He had no way of supplying water for these people. Only God could help them.

We know that God can do all things. But where could God get water in that dry, barren place? There was no oasis just ahead.

Lesson 23: God Delivered and Provided for Israel

	Teacher's Notes

Why should God provide for these people? The people did not deserve God's help. [6]

[6] Give you students time to answer. Their answers will reveal their understanding about God's nature and character. Some may still think that the people deserved God's help. Be sure to emphasize that God's provision comes out of His love and grace and faithfulness; not because man is deserving. ☐

L. God told Moses what to do.

 Theme: God is loving, merciful, and gracious.

God didn't let the Israelites die of thirst.

He gave them water because He is loving, merciful, and gracious.

 Theme: God communicates with man.

 READ Exodus 17:5,6a.

Suggested Visual:

CHRONOLOGICAL PICTURE NO. 31, "MOSES STRIKES THE ROCK FOR WATER"

God told Moses to strike the rock with his rod.

God promised that He would give water out of the rock.

- Consider:

  How much more sense it would have made to us if God had told them to dig a hole in the sand or make a well. Then we could have "explained" how He provided the water. But this was a true miracle of God. God and only God can bring water out of a rock in the middle of the desert. He wanted the Israelites (and us) to know that only God was able to save them from death.

 Theme: Man can come to God only according to God's will and plan.

Moses had to do it God's way.

Every time they had an impossible situation, God told them exactly what they must do.

- Compare:
- *God is the same today.*

  He does not leave it up to us to work out a way to escape from our sin, Satan's power, and everlasting punishment. God is the Saviour of all those who will turn from trusting in themselves and trust only in Him. He alone makes a way for sinners to escape.

M. God provided them with water.

 Theme: God is all-powerful.

Teacher's Notes

Lesson 23: God Delivered and Provided for Israel

Scripture Reference

 READ Exodus 17:6b.

In obedience to the Lord, Moses struck the rock.
Immediately, a great stream of water flowed out.
There was sufficient for all of the Israelites and their animals.
- Consider:

We do not know the exact number of Israelites at this time—only the men over twenty were counted in the census recorded in the Bible—but we can estimate from this census that there were perhaps two and a half million people. There was enough water for all of them and their animals! Psalm 105:41 says, "He opened the rock, and the waters gushed out; they ran in the dry places like a river."

Only Almighty God could give water from a rock in the wilderness—enough water for this vast community of people. Remember, God made everything; He spoke and it was created. Nothing is too hard for God.

 Theme: God is loving, merciful, and gracious.

God gave the Israelites food and water even though they didn't deserve anything from God.
- They didn't work for this food and water.
- God didn't ask for anything in return.
- He gave them food and water because He is loving and merciful.

No person merits God's love and mercy.
- We cannot gain acceptance with God by the things that we do.
- God's forgiveness to sinners is a gift.

Ephesians 2:8,9

Titus 3:5

Romans 6:23b

 Theme: God is faithful; He never changes.

God faithfully protected the Israelites and provided all they needed.
- God had promised that He would bless Abraham's descendants.
- God always does whatever He says.

Psalm 105:42

N. Conclusion

The story of God's provision for the Israelites is retold many times in the Old Testament and referred to in the New Testament.
These are historical events.
Yes, they are miracles, and they are **God's** miracles.
- They show us His faithfulness to keep His promises
- They show us His great love for His people.
- They show us His sovereign power over all creation.

God is beyond our understanding—so are His miracles.
But we can believe that these things really happened, because God said so in His Word.

QUESTIONS:

1. How did the Lord show the Israelites where to go? *God led them by a cloud during the day, and the cloud became a pillar of fire at night.*

Lesson 23: God Delivered and Provided for Israel

Scripture Reference

Teacher's Notes

2. To which land were the Israelites heading? *To Canaan, the land God gave to Abraham, Isaac, and Jacob.*

3. Why did God protect Israel?

   a. *Because He is loving and merciful.*

   b. *Because one of their descendants was to be the great Deliverer of sinners.*

   c. *Because of His promises to Abraham, Isaac, and Jacob.*

   d. *Because He was giving His Word to Israel to give to the world.*

4. What did the Israelites do when they saw Pharaoh's armies coming behind them? *They blamed Moses and said he should have left them in Egypt.*

5. Was there any way the Israelites could save themselves? *No.*

6. What should they have done? *They should have called on the Lord and trusted Him to rescue them.*

7. Why wasn't it difficult for God to open up the sea?

   a. *Because He created the sea.*

   b. *Because in the beginning, God had power over the water and the whole earth. He had not changed. He commanded this sea to move back so His people could walk to the other side on dry land.*

   c. *Because God is almighty. Nothing is too hard for Him.*

8. What did God do to protect the Israelites from the Egyptians when they were walking through the sea? *God placed the cloud behind the Israelites so it was between them and the Egyptians. The cloud shone brightly to show the way to the Israelites, but it was a dark, black cloud in front of the Egyptians.*

9. Why couldn't the Egyptians escape from God? *Because the Lord is greater than all. No one can fight against Him and win. He is almighty.*

10. Can anyone make a way to deliver himself from God's punishment for his sins and make himself acceptable to God? *No.*

11. What new problem did the Israelites face as they began their journey through the wilderness? *They didn't have any food.*

12. Did they remember all the great things God had done, and did they trust in Him? *No, they complained and blamed Moses and Aaron.*

13. Did Israel deserve to be given food by God? *No.*

14. Is there any person who merits God's love or deserves to be rescued from everlasting punishment? *No, we all deserve to be punished by God.*

15. What was the food which the Lord gave to the Israelites? *The Lord first gave them quail, and then He provided manna every morning.*

16. Why couldn't the Israelites get water? *Because they were in the wilderness.*

17. What did God tell Moses that he must do to provide water? *He had to hit the rock with his rod.*

18. When God delivered the Israelites, did He allow them to do things the way they wanted to do them? *No, it had to be done God's way.*

Scripture Reference

Isaiah 59:1,2
Romans 6:23
Hebrews 12:25-29
II Peter 3:3-12

LESSON 24

Preparation for the Giving of the Ten Commandments

LESSON PREPARATION
This section is for you, the teacher.

The passages in the Scripture Reference column are for your own study in preparing for this lesson. Since they may contain concepts that run ahead of the lesson, they are not to be taught at this point.

Note: If you have not taught previously from this series of lessons, please read carefully the note to teachers in the front of this book.

SCRIPTURE: Exodus 19:1-13,16-20; 20:1,2

LESSON GOALS:

- To show God's holiness, sovereignty, righteousness, and wrath against sin.
- To show man's absolute inability to keep the law.
- To show that man cannot be saved by anything he does.
- To show that only God can make a way for man to be saved.

THIS LESSON SHOULD HELP THE STUDENTS:

- To see the fallacy of the popular belief that the way to be saved is by keeping the Ten Commandments.
- To see that they are truly deserving of death and eternal punishment because they have broken God's law.

PERSPECTIVE FOR THE TEACHER:

Jesus Christ told his disciples that the Holy Spirit would convict the world of *"sin,...righteousness, and...judgment"* (John 16:8). But, strangely, much of the preaching of our day is built around, "Smile! God loves you!"

The truth of God's holiness, righteousness, and wrath is not a popular theme. Many today who even profess to be Christians do not seem to realize that God is, indeed, the same God we see in this passage in Exodus.

Much emphasis has been placed on God's love; little emphasis on the fact that we receive that love only as objects of His grace. And God's amazing grace has at times been presented without stressing the fact that grace is God's undeserved kindness toward otherwise hopelessly lost sinners.

God still hates sin, enough so that He will punish forever in the Lake of Fire all who refuse His plan of salvation.

We must not assume that our students understand the words "holy" and "righteous." They may have heard those words for years in religious ceremonies without ever realizing that God is not only pure and sinless, He is also a God of wrath who hates and punishes all sin.

As we teach this lesson, we can know that God's Word is powerful to penetrate man's false ideas and Satan's deception. Our students, like the people of Israel, need to know that sinners cannot stand in the presence of a holy, righteous God.

Teacher's Notes

OVERVIEW

This lesson sets the stage for the presentation of the Ten Commandments. It emphasizes God's righteousness and holiness along with His terrible wrath and certain judgment against all sin.

Some points:

God's covenant depended upon Israel's obedience, but the people did not realize that they were unable to obey fully.

The boundaries set for the people and animals around Mount Sinai emphasize the holiness of God, the sinfulness of man, the impossibility of sinful man coming near to God, and the certainty of judgment on all who dare to come into God's presence while still in their sin.

The Ten Commandments emphasize that God demands perfect obedience from every person. There is nothing of grace revealed in the Law. The purpose of the Law is to show people the impossibility of being saved by their own good works. This is God's way of preparing sinners to receive the gift of salvation through Christ's death on their behalf (Romans 3:19,20; Galatians 3:24).

Some of man's incorrect views of "salvation by works" are presented and shown to be false. ☐

Teacher's Notes

Lesson 24: Preparation for the Giving of the Ten Commandments

Scripture Reference

VISUALS:

- Chronological Picture No. 32, "God's Holy Mountain"
- Chronological Map 1
- Visuals on good works (illustrated in lesson)

ON TEACHING THIS LESSON:

These lessons are designed to **teach unbelievers.** You are carefully laying a scriptural foundation on which the Gospel will later be presented. If your class contains believers, teach with the goal of giving them an understanding of the basis for their faith and **with the goal of enabling them to teach the same material to unbelievers.**

DON'T COMPLICATE THE MESSAGE!

As you teach, keep in mind that this is a directed study—not an exhaustive survey of the Bible and not an unlimited group discussion. Keep your lesson on track and moving ahead by limiting and directing any discussion.

Carefully follow the outline. Emphasize the doctrinal themes.

LESSON FORMAT: The **center column** below contains the lesson material to be taught to the students. The **bold outline headings** are only for reference and need not be spoken, as they are incorporated into the outlined material that follows. The material in the **side columns** is for the teacher's own reference and is not intended to be included in the lesson.

TO BE TAUGHT TO THE STUDENTS
(Center Column Only)

LESSON OUTLINE:

REVIEW questions from Lesson 23.

A. Introduction

How do you view the Ten Commandments? **1**

Are they a set of rules to live by?

Are they a code of good conduct?

We're going to see what God says about His Ten Commandments.

But, first of all, we'll take a look at how He prepared His people Israel for receiving these laws.

That should be good preparation for us, too.

B. God brought Israel to Mount Sinai.

 Theme: God is supreme and sovereign.

 READ Exodus 19:1,2.

The Israelites didn't decide when they would travel or where they would go.

---

1 Don't slow down enough in your presentation for discussion on these questions. They are posed to make your students think. Since your students' answers would probably be countered by the lesson, you don't want to embarrass them. But, if a student does volunteer a wrong answer, don't immediately tell him his error. Let the Word do its work in hearts as you teach the lesson. ☐

Lesson 24: Preparation for the Giving of the Ten Commandments

Scripture Reference | **Teacher's Notes**

- God made these decisions for them.
- He wanted them to accept Him as their ruler, protector, and provider.

 Theme: God is faithful; He never changes.

 READ Exodus 19:3,4.

ON MAP 1, POINT TO THE AREA OF THE SINAI PENINSULA AND THE POSSIBLE LOCATION OF MOUNT SINAI.

- Note:

  Many scholars believe that the mountain called Jebel Musa is the Mount Sinai of the Bible as it fits the description in Exodus. Precise identification has not been possible, but we do know that this is the area spoken of in the Bible.

Exodus 3:1,2

Mount Sinai (also called Mount Horeb) was the place where Moses saw the burning bush.

At that time, the Lord had promised Moses that He would bring him and the Israelites back to this mountain.

 READ Exodus 3:12.

God is trustworthy.

- He protected Moses, delivered Israel, and brought them to Mount Sinai, just as He had promised.
- God does not make idle promises; neither does He work only through simple, predictable, "natural" means.
- Humanly speaking, every one of these things was impossible.
- But all things are possible for God.
- Even His choice of Moses as leader was totally against Moses' wishes.
- But God enabled Moses, overcame Pharaoh, and even sustained the grumbling multitudes of Israel.

God is all-powerful; God is faithful; God is sovereign.

You can trust God completely to do everything He promises.

C. The Lord's promise to Israel

 Theme: God communicates with man.

 READ Exodus 19:5,6.

The Lord told Moses His message for Israel.

God planned to make an agreement with Israel.

Theme: Man can come to God only according to God's will and plan.

This is the agreement:[2]

- The Lord promised to bless the Israelites if they obeyed Him perfectly.
- If they did everything that He told them, then He would accept them and give them all the good things they needed.

[2] This is the second time that God's acceptance has been linked with obedience. The first was when Adam was in the garden. The second is this promise by God to bless Israel on the basis of obedience to the Law. If they obeyed and kept their side of the covenant (perfect obedience), then they would be a peculiar treasure to God and be separated to His service as a kingdom of priests (Deuteronomy 26:16-19, 28:1-68).

We need to emphasize that the Law promises blessing on the basis of obedience but a curse to those who depart in heart or action from any of its holy demands (Galatians 3:10). Do not mix Law and Grace. The Law demands but gives no assistance to do what it demands. The purpose for this emphasis is to slowly bring your students to the point where they see the absolute impossibility of being accepted or blessed by God on the basis of obedience to the Law. ☐

Lesson 24: Preparation for the Giving of the Ten Commandments

D. Israel's promise to the Lord

 Theme: Man is a sinner. He needs God and is helpless to save himself.

 READ Exodus 19:7,8.

Israel promised to obey the Lord in everything.
- They had forgotten how they had doubted God at the Red Sea when the Egyptian armies were behind them.
- They had forgotten how they had complained when they didn't have food and water.
- They were self-confident.
- They thought that they could obey God well enough so that He would give them everything they needed.
- They didn't yet realize that their hearts were full of sin and that they could not please God by their own efforts.
- They were like Cain who thought that he could please God by the things which he gave to God.

The people of Israel did not realize that, under this agreement, God would no longer be able to bless them or give them the good things which they needed.
- The agreement was that, **if they obeyed God perfectly, then He would accept them and bless them, but if they disobeyed, then they would be cursed and punished by God.**

Suggested Visual:

> **THE LAW**
> **Demands**
> **PERFECT Obedience**

- The Lord knew that, in a very short time, the nation of Israel would disobey Him, and under the agreement of the Law, He would have to punish them for their sins.

Why then did the Lord make an agreement with the Israelites when He knew that they were not capable of keeping their side of the bargain?

The Lord did it because He wanted to prove to them that they were sinners and were unable to please Him.

The Lord wanted to teach them that they could not become His friends and earn His acceptance and gifts by their own efforts.
- Illustration:

    A man was swimming across a river, but he became tired and was caught in the swift-flowing current. A group of people were on the bank of the river watching. None of them were capable of helping the man who was going to drown, except for one strong man who was an excellent swimmer.

    The people on the bank kept urging this man to go to the assistance of the man in the river. But he didn't. He stood watching while

Scripture Reference

Romans 3:19,20

Galatians 3:10,23,24

the struggling man became weaker and weaker. Finally, when the drowning man became so tired that he gave up his struggle, the strong swimmer dived in and rescued him.

When the people criticized the man for waiting so long before he helped the drowning man, he answered, "The drowning man would never have allowed me to help him while he had any strength of his own. I could only help him when he gave up trying to help himself."

God gave the Law to Israel to show them that they were unable to please God and make themselves acceptable to Him.

When they gave up and trusted in Him, then He was willing to save them from everlasting punishment.

This is God's way with all people. God will only deliver those who agree with Him that they are sinners under the control of Satan, sin, and death.

This is what God wants us, also, to learn about ourselves.

- We are helpless sinners.
- We cannot deliver ourselves from sin, Satan, or death.

E. The preparation for the Lord's presence on the mountain

 Theme: God is holy and righteous. He demands death as the payment for sin.

 READ Exodus 19:9-11.

The Lord planned to display His great glory, power, and holiness before Israel so they would realize that He is a holy God who hates sin and will not accept those who disobey His Word.

 READ Exodus 19:12,13.

God told them to set a boundary around the mountain.

- They had to be sure that they didn't come near to or touch the mountain.
- If an Israelite or animal were even to touch the mountain when God came down on it, they were to be killed.

The punishment for all sin is death.

- This is because God is absolutely holy and man is sinful.
- God will not accept anyone or anything that is not perfect.
- He puts all sinners away from Himself.
- They cannot come near to God.
- Recall:

  Adam and Eve were separated from God because of their sin. Because they sinned, they were put out of the garden, away from God.

- God hates disobedience to His commands and will not keep company with sinners.

F. God spoke from Mount Sinai to Israel.

 Theme: God is all-powerful.

Teacher's Notes

Lesson 24: Preparation for the Giving of the Ten Commandments

Scripture Reference

 Theme: God is holy and righteous. He demands death as the payment for sin.

Suggested Visual:

Notice the piles of boundary stones at the base of the mountain. These were placed there to warn the people that they must not go up to the mountain where God was. God told them they would die if they passed the boundary.

CHRONOLOGICAL PICTURE NO. 32, "GOD'S HOLY MOUNTAIN"

 READ Exodus 19:16-20.

It is not surprising that the people were frightened when God spoke to them.

How would you feel if God were to show Himself like this to you?

The lightning, fire, thick cloud, and earthquake were to show the Israelites that God is almighty and a God of wrath who hates and punishes all sin.

- Recall:

  God had already shown the world His mighty power and His hatred and punishment of sin when He destroyed the whole world in Noah's time. He also rained fire and brimstone upon the wicked cities of Sodom and Gomorrah. He showed His power and His hatred and punishment of sin when He sent many terrible plagues on the Egyptians and drowned their armies in the sea.

- God hates and punishes all sin.

Hebrews 12:18-21,29

G. God spoke and gave His commandments to Israel.

 Theme: God communicates with man.

After Moses had returned to the bottom of Mount Sinai, God spoke to the Israelites from the mountain.

 READ Exodus 20:1,2.

- Consider:

  The mountain was still shaking and billowing smoke. Lightning flashed, thunder rumbled, trumpet blasts pierced the air. No wonder the people trembled with fear and kept away from the mountain! Then the Lord spoke to them and gave them His commandments.

 Theme: God is holy and righteous. He demands death as the payment for sin.

The punishment for disobedience to even one of these commandments is everlasting separation from God in the Lake of Fire, which God prepared for Satan and the angels who followed him in rebellion against the Lord.

Matthew 25:41

Revelation 20:15

Lesson 24: Preparation for the Giving of the Ten Commandments

Scripture Reference		Teacher's Notes

 Read James 2:10.³

Theme: **Man is a sinner. He needs God and is helpless to save himself.**

³This passage in James is very appropriate for this lesson. But do not go into the surrounding verses in James, as you will be running ahead of the chronological order and confusing the issues you are trying to teach. ☐

Why did God give His commandments?

God knew that the Israelites wouldn't be able to obey His commandments perfectly all of the time.

- But He wanted them to realize that they couldn't obey God perfectly and that they could never be accepted by God through their own efforts.
- But God did not give His Law just to prove that the Israelites were sinful and incapable of pleasing God.
- He gave His Law so **all** people would know how sinful they are and that it is impossible for anyone to make himself acceptable to God by the things which he does.
- God also gave His Law so that all people would trust only in His mercy to save them from His punishment for sin.
- Compare:
- The commands of God are like a mirror.
- Just as we cannot see our dirty faces until we look into a mirror, so we cannot see our sinful hearts until the Law shows them to us.
- The Law of God is like an X-ray machine.
- It shows us what we are on the inside, that is, how God sees us.

But what if we cannot obey all of God's commandments?

Will God accept us if we just do our best and obey as many as we can?

- Consider:

We often hear that if we do good works, we can hope that God will weigh them in a balance against our sins. This thought comforts people and often motivates them to do good deeds. They rationalize that their good works will certainly "outweigh" the bad things they have done.

Suggested Visual:

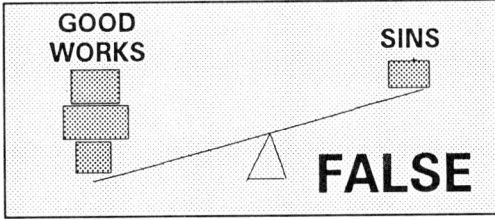

This may be a comforting thought and a motivation to do good works, but it is also Satan's lie! Satan does not want us to know or believe the truth. He wants us to believe that we can "work our way to Heaven."

How many times have you heard it said, "That person has done so many good things! I know he will go to Heaven!" Nothing could be further from the truth. God has one standard, and that standard is perfection.

Even if a person were able to do multitudes of good works and even if he obeyed God's commandments most of the time but failed

James 1:22-25

337

Lesson 24: Preparation for the Giving of the Ten Commandments

to obey just one time, that person would still have broken the whole law and would be guilty of sin.

Suggested Visual:

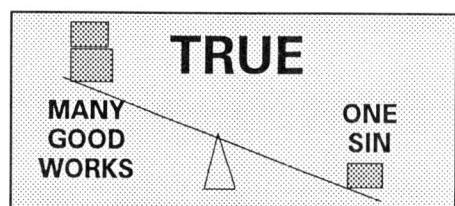

 Read again James 2:10.

God punishes sinners even if they only disobey one of His commandments one time.

- How many times did Adam and Eve disobey God before they were separated from God and put out of the garden?
- Adam and Eve only sinned once, and they received the punishment of death.
- God demands that we obey all of His commands all of the time.
- If we disobey one of His commands even only once, then He will not accept us.
- Compare:

   Is a chain still strong if one of its links is broken?

   Would you go near a vicious dog tied with a chain which had one broken link? But what if I said to you, "What are you afraid of? The chain has nine strong links. Only one link is broken"? Would you be willing to go near that vicious dog if you knew that nine of the links were strong and only one was broken? No, of course not! The chain is only strong if all of the links are unbroken. If one link is broken, then the whole chain is weak and useless.

   That is just like God's laws. If we break even one, it is as if we have broken them all. God says that if we disobey just one of His laws, then we have sinned and will be punished.

God wants all people to realize that they can never be good enough to please Him and so escape His punishment.

Suggested Visual:

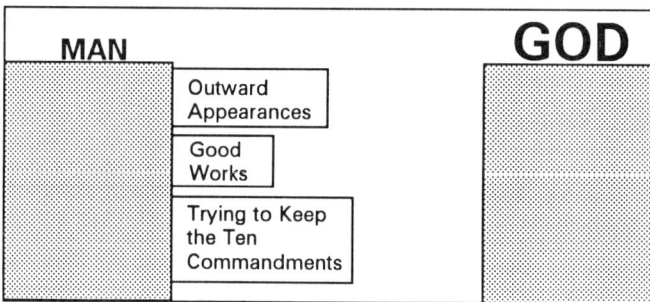

It is impossible for anyone to perfectly keep God's commandments as God demands because we were all born sinners and separated from God.

 Read Romans 3:10-12.

Read Romans 3:19,20.

We cannot know, love, and obey God in such a way that He will be pleased with us and accept us.

God gave the law to show us how very sinful we are.

- Explain:

No preacher, teacher, or missionary is exempt from these truths. All have broken God's laws and deserve to go to everlasting punishment. All are born sinners and cannot please God by their good works. God will never accept anyone because of the good things that they do.

As we read God's commandments, He wants each of us to admit that we have done things that He hates, that we are unable to obey His commands perfectly, and that we cannot save ourselves.

We cannot please God by what we do. We cannot remove our own sins from before God's eyes. All of our sin must be paid for. The punishment for sin is death, that is, everlasting separation from God in the Lake of Fire.

H. Conclusion

What do you think now about the Ten Commandments?

God's Word can really change our thinking.

In our next lesson, we'll consider each of the commandments.

It's possible you may have some more changes in your thinking after our next lesson, too!

QUESTIONS:

1. What did God promise Moses when Moses saw the burning bush at Mount Sinai? *God promised that He would bring Moses back safely to the same mountain.*

2. Did God do what He promised? *Yes, God always does what He says.*

3. Why did God plan to give His commandments to Israel? *God planned to give them His commandments to prove to them that they were sinners and that they were incapable of pleasing Him or being accepted by Him through their own efforts.*

4. What was Israel's attitude? *They had forgotten the numerous times when they had doubted God and sinned against Him. They were proud and self-confident.*

5. Why did God tell Moses to put a boundary around the mountain? *To emphasize that sinners cannot approach a holy God. God hates sin.*

6. Why were the people so frightened? *Because the mountain was shaking violently, and there was fire, smoke, and lightning.*

7. What did all of this show the Israelites? *It showed them that God is almighty. He is pure, and He hates and punishes sin.*

8. Who was God's messenger to Israel? *Moses.*

Lesson 24: Preparation for the Giving of the Ten Commandments

Teacher's Notes

Scripture Reference

9. How do we hear God's words today? *We hear God's message from the Bible.*

10. Today, has God changed His attitude toward sin? *No!*

11. What is God's punishment for disobeying even one of His commandments? *Everlasting separation from God and punishment in the Lake of Fire which God prepared for Satan and his angels.*

12. Did God think that the Israelites would be able to obey His ten commands? *No, God knew that no one would be able to obey them.*

13. Why is it impossible for any person to perfectly obey God's laws? *We were all born sinners and separated from God, so we are not capable of pleasing God.*

14. Will God accept us if we just do our best and obey as many of His commandments as we can? *No.*

LESSON 25: God Gave the Ten Commandments

LESSON PREPARATION

This section is for you, the teacher.

The passages in the Scripture Reference column are for your own study in preparing for this lesson. Since they may contain concepts that run ahead of the lesson, they are not to be taught at this point.

Note: If you have not taught previously from this series of lessons, please read carefully the note to teachers in the front of this book.

SCRIPTURE: Exodus 20:3-17

LESSON GOALS:

- To show God's sovereignty, holiness, and righteousness.
- To show man's absolute inability to keep the Law.
- To show that only God in His mercy can make a way for man to be saved.

THIS LESSON SHOULD HELP THE STUDENTS:

- To see the fallacy of the popular belief that the way to be saved is to obey the Ten Commandments.
- To see that they have broken God's laws and are truly deserving of death.
- To see that they cannot save themselves.

PERSPECTIVE FOR THE TEACHER:

Our society's view of the Ten Commandments reflects a progressive turning away from the truth of the Bible.

By rejecting God's Word and refusing to acknowledge that He is the sovereign Creator, by denying their accountability to God and ignoring what His Word says about the consequences and punishment of sin, men find it easy to rush headlong into the utter depths of sin. Our society has gone into a massive downward slide along the route of Romans 1:21-32.

But many people still have a vestige of conscience and realize that they need some kind of "religious" standard. They do not want to acknowledge God as their sovereign Creator, nor do they want to believe that He is holy and righteous—a God of wrath. Instead, they want just enough religion to make them feel better.

The Ten Commandments, therefore, are considered as a set of rules for good conduct—a sort of salve for the conscience. Sadly, many churches have had a large part in teaching this deception. (No doubt many have participated and believed in this kind of teaching simply because they did not have a thorough knowledge of the Bible.)

But the Bible shows us that the Ten Commandments are exactly the opposite of this sin-distorted view. They are instead impossibly difficult laws set forth by the holy, righteous, sovereign, Creator God to show sinful man his absolute inability to completely obey God or to save himself from eternal punishment.

Teacher's Notes

OVERVIEW

God's sovereignty is stressed in this lesson. Each commandment is set forth by Him and is therefore the righteous standard. God's holiness is contrasted against man's sinfulness and inability to keep God's perfect law.

Each commandment is read and explained and then applied to today's lifestyles to show that all people have broken God's laws.

The study of the Ten Commandments is done to bring conviction of sin—to give the students opportunity to see their inability to save themselves by their own good works and to see their need for a Saviour.

Lesson 25: God Gave the Ten Commandments

Teacher's Notes

Scripture Reference

PRESENTING THE TEN COMMANDMENTS:

1. Read each commandment and give a simple explanation. Don't be in a hurry with this lesson. Remember that *"by the law is the knowledge of sin"* (Romans 3:20).

2. Emphasize that the commands of God must be obeyed in the heart and mind and not just outwardly.

3. The main theme in each of the commandments is that God is supreme and sovereign. We must emphasize that right is right and wrong is wrong, simply because God, the sovereign and supreme ruler, has set the standard. God's will cannot and should not be questioned.

ON TEACHING THIS LESSON:

These lessons are designed to **teach unbelievers.** You are carefully laying a scriptural foundation on which the Gospel will later be presented. If your class contains believers, teach with the goal of giving them an understanding of the basis for their faith and **with the goal of enabling them to teach the same material to unbelievers.**

DON'T COMPLICATE THE MESSAGE!

As you teach, keep in mind that this is a directed study—not an exhaustive survey of the Bible and not an unlimited group discussion. Keep your lesson on track and moving ahead by limiting and directing any discussion.

Carefully follow the outline. Emphasize the doctrinal themes.

LESSON FORMAT: The **center column** below contains the lesson material to be taught to the students. The **bold outline headings** are only for reference and need not be spoken, as they are incorporated into the outlined material that follows. The material in the **side columns** is for the teacher's own reference and is not intended to be included in the lesson.

TO BE TAUGHT TO THE STUDENTS
(Center Column Only)

LESSON OUTLINE:

REVIEW questions from Lesson 24.

A. Introduction

The Israelites, like us, were born sinners, unable to please God.

It is amazing that, as sinful as we are, we still think that we are able to obey God.

- Israel was sure they could keep their part of God's covenant with them.

- We are the same today—how often have you heard someone say, "Oh, I just live by the Ten Commandments"?

Yet, another evidence that we are sinners is that we hate to be told what to do—we like to be the ones in charge.

Lesson 25: God Gave the Ten Commandments

But the Ten Commandments were given to us by our sovereign Creator who knew
- That we could not keep His laws.
- That we needed His sovereign standard of righteousness.
- And that by considering His righteous standard we could then see our own sinfulness.

Let's look now in God's Word at His Ten Commandments.

B. The first commandment

 Theme: God is supreme and sovereign.

 Theme: God is holy and righteous. He demands death as the payment for sin.

 READ Exodus 20:3.

In the first commandment, God said that He and only He should be everyone's God.

This means that people should worship only Him.
- The word "worship" comes from the word "worth."
- Only God is worthy of adoration and complete allegiance.

He must be the absolute and only leader—above all others in people's lives.
- God will not allow anyone or anything else to share His place as God.
- People must not depend on anyone or anything except Him for everything they need in this life or for life after death.
- They must not worship anyone or anything else.
- They must give God the highest place in their thoughts and give Him praise and thanks for everything.

[Scripture Reference: Matthew 22:36-38]

Isaiah 45:5 says, *"I am the LORD, and there is none else, there is no God beside me...."*

Nothing and no one else should take God's place in our lives.
- If a person puts anyone else in God's place, that is rebellion and sin.
- Even if we say with our lips that God is our ruler, yet we do not give Him the first place in our hearts all of the time, we have still broken this commandment.

 Theme: Man is a sinner. He needs God and is helpless to save himself.

- Consider:

Adam deliberately turned away from giving God first place in his life. Adam went his own way instead of God's way. All the descendants of Adam have gone their own way. No one has allowed God to rule every part of his life.[1]

Our own ancestors disobeyed this first command of God. They put the idols and spirits in God's place, and Satan took God's place in their lives.

---

[1] But God promises that **all** will bow to Him: Isaiah 45:23,24; Philippians 2:9-11.

Teacher's Notes

Lesson 25: God Gave the Ten Commandments

Scripture Reference

- Consider:

Today, many people are putting themselves in God's place—even to the point of calling this act of rebellion against God their religion. This religion (called "humanism") teaches the exaltation of man to the place which belongs only God, giving man the idea that he can have the position of ruler and controller of his own destiny, giving man the credit for all achievements.

Satan is the father of lies, and this lie is highly appealing to the ego of man. Satan appeals to man's weaknesses, knowing all the while that this very sin is like the one which caused Satan and his followers to be removed forever from their positions of service before God in Heaven. He knows, too, that he and all his followers will spend eternity in the Lake of Fire.

Maybe you wouldn't call yourself a humanist; you just want to make your own decisions. If you have even leaned on your ideas and desires instead of looking to God, you have broken the first commandment.

[2] Deuteronomy 8:17-20 is a good passage for those who think they are "self-made" men. ☐

Have you ever given people (yourself or others) full credit for something without giving any thought to God's part in what was done? If you have, you have broken this commandment. [2]

Have you ever looked for advice in a horoscope or ascribed any significance to the signs of the zodiac? If so, you have broken this commandment.

Have sports or family or home or money or possessions or work or position or social status or appearances or recreation or retirement or anything else ever become more important to you than God? If your answer is "yes," you have broken this commandment.

[3] Take time to enlarge on this. Make sure your students clearly understand that to agree that God is truly God means to listen to, obey, exalt, and worship Him and Him alone in every situation and not attribute His power or authority or give His glory to anyone else. Be careful that you do not teach as though this is something they must try to do in order to be saved. Show them rather that this is something which none of us have done and that we are not capable of doing what God commands. ☐

None of us has continually put God first in everything. [3]

The punishment for disobeying this first command is separation from God.

We are all guilty of breaking it.

C. The second commandment

 Theme: God is supreme and sovereign.

 READ Exodus 20:4-6.

God gave this second commandment to the Israelites so they would always remember that He is supreme and sovereign—greater than all the things He has created.

- Consider:

God is spirit, He does not have a material body, He had no beginning and will have no end, He is everywhere all the time, He knows everything, He is all-powerful, He is absolutely holy and perfect. He is supreme—greater than all. No part of God's creation, no man-made idol is worthy of worship—only God is to be worshiped.

No one knows what God looks like, so God said that we should never try to make anything which we think resembles Him. The only way anyone can know what God is like is to let Him teach them through this book, the Bible. Anything different from what the Bible says is a lie of Satan.

How important it is for us to know what the Bible says about God! Though we do not see Him now with our eyes, we can learn about Him through His Word. God wants us to know Him! That is why He has given us the Bible. The things we learn from the Bible about God are true. Because the Bible says that God is sovereign, holy, righteous, loving, gracious, merciful, unchanging, all-powerful, all-knowing, and everywhere all the time, we can know for sure that God is exactly like this. Because the Bible teaches us that God demands the death penalty for all sin, we can know for sure that this is the truth.

 Theme: Man is a sinner. He needs God and is helpless to save himself.

All over the world, Satan has led people away from the true knowledge of God. They no longer know the true and living God. Satan has given other things in the place of God. People have followed their own ideas and other people's thoughts of what they think God must be like.

Perhaps you might be thinking that today this commandment which talks about idols pertains only to foreign cultures. But a closer look reveals that right here in our culture, people are worshiping man-made representations of things they think will bring them favor with God. In their minds, they assign to these man-made things powers that really belong only to God. **4**

Romans 1:18-23

All who worship man-made things that they think represent God have broken this command of God and are condemned.

Again, in Isaiah, God tells us, "I am the LORD: that is my name: and my glory will I not give to another, neither my praise to graven images" (Isaiah 42:8).

D. The third commandment

 Theme: God is supreme and sovereign.

READ Exodus 20:7.

In the third commandment, God told the Israelites that they must always respect God, acknowledging that He is their Creator and rightful ruler, and never speak or use His name in a careless way.
- God is the almighty Creator and ruler of everyone and everything.
- Everyone should fear God and realize that He has the power to take our lives and to destroy us all in everlasting punishment.

 Theme: Man is a sinner. He needs God and is helpless to save himself.

- Consider:

It is wrong to say evil things about people or to refuse to give them the respect they deserve. A child should show respect for his or her parents. A wife and husband should show respect for one another. A young person should show respect for his or her elders.

Careless, disrespectful words have become socially acceptable in our society. We hear them spoken even against our leaders. The

4This can go by without further comment, unless a student asks what you are talking about.

If that happens, you might tell him that some people begin to worship things like the beads they use to help them recite prayers, the statues they pray to, etc.

If possible, try to keep any discussion from being an outright attack on the Roman Catholic religion. You are trying to make people think, not to insult them.

Issues like this are best addressed if you know your class and if you are prepared ahead by prayer. ☐

Teacher's Notes

Lesson 25: God Gave the Ten Commandments

Scripture Reference

concept of respect for human leadership—parents, teachers, government officials—has been all but forgotten as people use their "free speech" to say whatever they please without regard for others.

To insult a human being is bad, but how much more evil it is when we have shown disrespect for the true and living God or used the name of God in an incorrect way.

All who have not given God the respect He deserves are condemned.

E. The fourth commandment

 Theme: God is supreme and sovereign.

 READ Exodus 20:8-11.

In the fourth commandment, God told them to keep the seventh day as a special day of rest in honor of Him, the one who created all things in six days. **5**

- Do you remember what God did on the seventh day, the day after He finished creating the world?
- God rested because He had finished everything that He had planned to make.
- Consider:

The Lord told Israel that they should rest every seventh day so they would remember that God alone is the Creator of all the earth and everything in it. God is the only rightful owner of this world. Satan and His demons have taken over this world for their own, but it does not rightfully belong to them.

God gives life to all things. He gives the rain and the sunshine on the earth so everything will grow. He alone is the Creator, owner, and provider of all things. Satan is in control of most of the people in this world, but the world still belongs to God.

Psalm 24:1,2 says, "The earth is the LORD's, and the fulness thereof; the world, and they that dwell therein. For he hath founded it upon the seas, and established it upon the floods."

Psalm 33:8,9, says, "Let all the earth fear the LORD: let all the inhabitants of the world stand in awe of him. For he spake, and it was done; he commanded, and it stood fast."

 Theme: Man is a sinner. He needs God and is helpless to save himself.

All who have looked to and depended on anyone but God as the Creator and giver of all things have disobeyed God's command.

This terrible sin against the true Creator will be punished by God.

F. The fifth commandment

 Theme: God is supreme and sovereign.

 READ Exodus 20:12.

In the fifth commandment, God said that children must respect and obey their parents.

Ephesians 6:1-4

---

5 If any of your students are Seventh Day Adventists, then you may need to explain that God is not commanding us today to rest on the seventh day, just as He is not commanding us to offer sacrifices of sheep or other animals.

(Note, for your own reference: the fourth commandment is the only one of the Ten Commandments not given again in the New Testament. Also note Colossians 2:16,17. The commandments were only a shadow of what was to come. They have been completely carried out and all their requirements met in the person of Jesus Christ.)

Nevertheless, God does expect us to recognize that He alone is Creator of all things and that there is no other God.

Try to avoid making the Sabbath question a point of controversy or becoming the main subject. Make it very clear to those who do emphasize the Sabbath and make it an issue that, even if they do keep the Sabbath but fail to obey perfectly all of the other nine commandments every moment of their lives, their Sabbath observance will be useless in the sight of God (James 2:9-11). ☐

Lesson 25: God Gave the Ten Commandments

If they do not, they are sinning against their Creator.
Anyone who disobeys this command is sinning against God.

 Theme: Man is a sinner. He needs God and is helpless to save himself.

None of us have obeyed our parents completely.
- Some examples:
  Talking back
  Ignoring them when they speak
  Arguing with them
  Disobeying them
  Crying to get our way
  Pouting
  Giving them the silent treatment
  Criticizing them
  Thinking (but not saying) "You don't understand anything!"

We have all broken this commandment as well as all the others.
- Remember, even if we obeyed nine of the commandments and disobeyed one, we will still be condemned by God.
- Furthermore, God expects us to obey these commandments from the time we are born until we die.
- One act of disobedience will be punished by everlasting separation from God.

G. The sixth commandment

 Theme: God is supreme and sovereign.

 READ Exodus 20:13.

In the sixth commandment, God told them that to murder someone is sin against God.
- He is the Creator of all people.
- He gives life to every person.
- No one has the right to take another person's life unless God says so in His Word.[6]

 Theme: Man is a sinner. He needs God and is helpless to save himself.

God also makes it very clear in His Word that, if a person hates someone, he has committed murder in his heart.
God says that, if a person wishes to kill someone, he is already a murderer and is condemned by God.
In Matthew 5:21-22 we read, *"Ye have heard that it was said by them of old time, Thou shalt not kill; and whosoever shall kill shall be in danger of the judgment: But I say unto you, That whosoever is angry with his brother without a cause shall be in danger of the judgment...whosoever shall say, Thou fool, shall be in danger of hell fire."*

---

[6] God does give governments the authority to take the life of a murderer. (Romans 13:1-5).

Do not allow debate over this issue. If someone asks about the death penalty, tell them that this is not an issue that we are going to cover in depth. Tell them that you realize that this is a sensitive issue, and God's Word is the best place for them to study to find clear answers. However, it takes understanding of many passages before a person can make a clear conclusion, and we are not going to take the time during these lessons to research this issue. ☐

Lesson 25: God Gave the Ten Commandments

- If we curse a person, we have committed murder.
- God judges us, not just by what we do, but by what we really want to do.
- God knows our motives because God knows our hearts.

 Read Hebrews 4:12,13.

H. The seventh commandment

 Theme: God is supreme and sovereign.

 READ Exodus 20:14.

In the seventh commandment, God says that it is sin to have any sexual relationship with anyone except one's own wife or husband.

The punishment for all sexual sin is everlasting separation from God.
- Consider:

After God created Adam, He gave Eve to him to be his wife. God said that, because they were married, they were no longer two people before Him. They were now just like one person. Husband and wife belong to one another, and they must live only with one another.

Many people today will tell you that this commandment is old-fashioned and out-of-date. But God does not change. Sin is still sin. God has not changed His mind about adultery.

Adultery and all types of sexual sins are also committed in the mind.

 Read Matthew 5:27,28. **7**

⁷Don't get into a discussion of the context surrounding this verse. If you need to, remind your students that you are just emphasizing the main points and building foundations; you will not have time to go into other passages now. ☐

 Theme: Man is a sinner. He needs God and is helpless to save himself.

God says that if we look at someone other than our own husband or wife and want to have any type of sexual relationship with that person, then we have already broken this commandment.
- When we do this, we have sinned against God.
- He knows every one of our thoughts.
- Every sin will be judged, even if it was only committed in the mind.

I. The eighth commandment

 Theme: God is supreme and sovereign.

 READ Exodus 20:15.

In the eighth commandment, God said they must never take anything belonging to someone else.
- God is the one who gives each person the right to own and to keep his own property.
- Acts 17:25 says that God " *giveth to all life, and breath, and all things.*"
- If a person takes something which belongs to someone else, then he has sinned against God.

Lesson 25: God Gave the Ten Commandments

- Consider:

  Even if a thief gives back the thing he stole or compensates the person for the thing which he stole, that will still not satisfy God for the sin of stealing. The punishment for stealing is everlasting separation from God. God will not accept any payment except death. God will not forgive sin unless the full punishment of death is paid.

   Theme: Man is a sinner. He needs God and is helpless to save himself.

Even if a person desires or plans to steal something but doesn't do it because he is afraid of being caught, he is still guilty of stealing before God.

God will never forgive sin until it is paid for in full.

God will punish all sinners for the evil things which they planned to do even though they were not able to or simply did not do them.

Luke 12:2
I Corinthians 4:5
Hebrews 4:12,13

J. The ninth commandment

 Theme: God is supreme and sovereign.

 READ Exodus 20:16.

In the ninth commandment, God said that they must always tell the truth about everything.

God never lies, and He commands us not to lie.

- Consider:

  Satan is the greatest liar. He lied to Adam and Eve in the garden. He lied to our forefathers and is still telling lies to people all over the world. Satan is the father of all those who persist in telling lies.

John 8:44

 Theme: Man is a sinner. He needs God and is helpless to save himself.

- Consider:

  Some people make false accusations against other people. The motive behind these lies may be jealousy or anger or hatred; the lies are intended to cause the other person harm.

  Some people start rumors and make up stories. Others carry them on and add to them. Many people like to gossip. What may begin as a true incident is distorted or expanded to include things that are not true. All of this is lying and is sin against God.

  Some people do wrong things and then lie to cover up what they have done. Even when they are brought to court, they still lie.

  Many people have escaped punishment here on earth because they have lied and people didn't know that they were lying. But we can't hide lies from God. God always speaks the truth, and He knows the truth about everyone and everything.

  But you might say, "What about white lies?" There are no such things. A lie is a lie. God hates lying and will punish all liars.

Lesson 25: God Gave the Ten Commandments

K. The tenth commandment

 Theme: God is supreme and sovereign.

 READ Exodus 20:17.

God's tenth commandment said that they must not covet, that is, want what other people have.
- This was also Satan's sin.
- He was proud and envious of God's position.
-

 Theme: Man is a sinner. He needs God and is helpless to save himself.

- Consider:

    Many people are greedy and jealous of others' possessions. They dislike those who have more things than they have, and they covet other people's property. They are never satisfied with what they have. In their minds, they are angry because they don't have what someone else has.

    Instead of being satisfied, many people have the urge to continually "upgrade." They base their ambitions upon what they think others already possess.

    For many, this is a subtle sin. "Keeping up with the Joneses" is really just another form of coveting.

    Today, advertising goads people on to coveting. Day in and day out, we are faced with pressure to want more and to buy more, so we can be like the image portrayed on the television or the printed page. Why are so many people deeply in debt with credit cards? Coveting has become a mark of prestige and social status in our culture.

But God has not changed His mind about coveting.

He will punish all coveting because it is sin.

L. Conclusion

 Theme: God is holy and righteous. He demands death as the payment for sin.

These are the Ten Commandments which God gave to the Israelites.

God's commandments are the same for all people, everywhere.

Remember, if we try to repay people for the wrongs we have done them or if we bring an offering to church to pay for the sin of adultery or even if we serve a prison sentence for stealing, that does not mean our sin debt to God is paid.

The payment for sin is death, everlasting separation from God in the place of punishment which He prepared for Satan and his angels.

All sin will be punished by God.

God hasn't changed His mind about sin.

Has studying His Word changed your mind about sin?

What do you think now about the Ten Commandments?[8]

---

[8] Don't force any answers here from your students. The question is mainly intended to make them think. But any discussion that comes at this point will help you get some idea of what your students have learned from this lesson. ☐

Lesson 25: God Gave the Ten Commandments

Scripture Reference

Teacher's Notes

QUESTIONS:

1. Does God care if people worship or serve anything or anyone else besides Him? *Yes, that is sin against God. God will not share His position as God and supreme ruler with anyone or anything else.*

2. Is it all right to make an image of something or worship anything else we have made or which God has created? *No, this, too, is sin against God. We do not know what God looks like, so we must not try to make anything which we think looks like Him or worship any creation of his or anything we have made.*

3. Does God care what we think about Him and what we say about Him? *Yes, God will punish all those who do not always honor Him in their thoughts and by their words. It is sin to use God's name in vain.*

4. Why did God command the Israelites to rest on the seventh day of the week?

    a. *Because God created all things in six days and rested on the seventh day.*

    b. *Because God wants us to always remember that He is the Creator and everything that we have comes from Him. We must not give Satan or anyone else the praise for all the things in the world.*

5. Does God care if children disobey or are disrespectful to their parents? *Yes, God will punish all those who do not obey and respect their parents.*

6. Why does God punish all murderers? *Because God gives life to all people, He is the only one who has the authority to take a person's life.*

7. What does God say about a person who hates someone else? *God says that person is a murderer.*

8. What is God's attitude toward adultery? *God condemns all sexual relationships except between a man and his wife.*

9. Why will God punish all who steal? *Because God gives people the right to own things.*

10. Are people guilty of stealing if they plan to steal but then become afraid and do not do it? *Yes, they are guilty because God saw that they had planned in their hearts to steal.*

11. What is God's command about telling lies? *God said that lying to anyone is sin against God because He always speaks the truth and hates lies.*

12. Does God care if we are envious of other people and want what they have? *Yes, that is also sin against God. That was Satan's sin. He was envious of God and wanted His position.*

13. Can anyone obey the Ten Commandments? *(This will give the students opportunity to discuss their responses to the question you asked them at the beginning of this lesson. It will also give the teacher the opportunity to see if anyone still thinks he can keep God's commandments.)*

Scripture Reference		Teacher's Notes

LESSON 26: The Tabernacle

LESSON PREPARATION

This section is for you, the teacher.

The passages in the Scripture Reference column are for your own study in preparing for this lesson. Since they may contain concepts that run ahead of the lesson, they are not to be taught at this point.

Note: If you have not taught previously from this series of lessons, please read carefully the note to teachers in the front of this book.

Leviticus 16
Hebrews 8; 9; 10:1-25

SCRIPTURE: Exodus 24:12-18; 25:1-11,17-22; 26:31-33; 27:1,2; 28:1; 39:42,43; 40:17,34,35; Leviticus 1:1-5; 16:2,3

LESSON GOALS:

- To explain the purpose and basic structure of the tabernacle.[1]
- To present the pattern of the tabernacle in such a way that, in a later lesson, it will be seen to clearly picture Christ.
- To show that God made a way for sinners to come to Him for mercy.

THIS LESSON SHOULD HELP THE STUDENTS:

- To see that God has made a way for sinners to come to Him.
- To see the importance of the types and patterns prescribed by God; to see that man's own way is unacceptable.

PERSPECTIVE FOR THE TEACHER:

The tabernacle is a beautiful picture of our merciful God dwelling in the midst of His sinful people, making a way for them to come to Him to find the mercy and grace they needed. Like the body of our Lord, the outside of the tent, which was only skins, was not distinguished in appearance. But inside dwelled the glory of God!

We have the privilege of bringing our students an even greater message, for Jesus Himself came and dwelled among us, offering **Himself** for our sins, making the way open for **all** to come to God. In Christ, we are given not a system of sacrifices offered by one priest after another, but **one sacrifice for sins forever**, offered once for all by our Great High Priest, Jesus Christ, the righteous one.

The tabernacle stood in full view of all. Mercy was available to all who would come by faith. Jesus Christ died for all. Through Him we can *"come boldly unto the throne of grace"* and *"obtain mercy, and find grace to help in time of need"* (Hebrews 4:16).

But the greatest wonder is that now our God dwells **in those who believe**. What greater message of mercy and grace could be offered?

As we teach the story of God's tabernacle, God's Spirit will be preparing hearts to receive the ultimate message of the finished work of Jesus Christ.

VISUALS:

For this lesson, it would be helpful to have a simple model of the tabernacle. You may be able to purchase through a Christian bookstore a paper model

OVERVIEW

This lesson presents the basic plan of the tabernacle. Included are only those things which will point the student to understanding the Gospel when it is presented in later lessons.

Mercy is defined in this lesson as God's provision for sinners to escape the punishment they deserve for their sins. Emphasis is given to the fact that man can only come to God according to God's will and plan.

---

[1] The tabernacle is an extremely interesting and meaningful subject, especially for the believer. Many books are available for deeper study. Since the purpose of these lessons is to lead the unsaved to know Christ, it is best to keep this lesson on the tabernacle as simple as possible, covering only those things necessary for presenting the Gospel. The laver, the table of shewbread, the candlestick, and the altar of incense all relate to the believer and are covered in *"Building on Firm Foundations,"* Volume 4, by Trevor McIlwain, pp. 187-195, New Tribes Mission, Sanford, FL. If you have students who want further study, this could be done at another time. ☐

Lesson 26: The Tabernacle

Teacher's Notes | **Scripture Reference**

which you can construct. You need to make only the pieces of tabernacle furniture about which you are going to teach in this lesson. They are the outer fence, the brazen altar, the holy place, the holy of holies, the veil, the ark, and the mercy seat. If you do not have a three-dimensional model, use a picture and a diagram of the layout of the tabernacle. Point out the location of the pieces of furniture within the tabernacle as you mention them. If possible, use both a model and a diagram or picture.

- Chronological Picture No. 34, "The Tabernacle"
- Chronological Picture No. 35, "The Components of the Tabernacle"
- Chronological Picture No. 36, "The Sin Offering"
- Chronological Chart
- Small poster, "Mercy" (illustrated in lesson)

ON TEACHING THIS LESSON:

These lessons are designed to **teach unbelievers.** You are carefully laying a scriptural foundation on which the Gospel may later be presented. If your class contains believers, teach with the goal of giving them an understanding of the basis for their faith and **with the goal of enabling them to teach the same material to unbelievers.**

DON'T COMPLICATE THE MESSAGE!

As you teach, keep in mind that this is a directed study—not an exhaustive survey of the Bible and not an unlimited group discussion. Keep your lesson on track and moving ahead by limiting and directing any discussion.

Carefully follow the outline. Emphasize the doctrinal themes.

LESSON FORMAT: The **center column** below contains the lesson material to be taught to the students. The **bold outline headings** are only for reference and need not be spoken, as they are incorporated into the outlined material that follows. The material in the **side columns** is for the teacher's own reference and is not intended to be included in the lesson.

TO BE TAUGHT TO THE STUDENTS
(Center Column Only)

LESSON OUTLINE:

REVIEW questions from Lesson 25.

A. Introduction

What is mercy?

Who needs it?

Could the Israelites keep their promises to God?

Can you keep your promises?

Today's lesson is about God's holiness and His mercy.

B. Moses was once again called by God up into the mountain.

 Theme: God communicates with man.

Lesson 26: The Tabernacle

Scripture Reference

God spoke to the Israelites from Mount Sinai and told them His Ten Commandments.

The Lord did not want the Israelites to forget His commandments, so He told Moses to come up into the mountain once again.

- The Lord Himself planned to write His commandments on two pieces of stone so Moses could teach them to the Israelites.
- They had heard His Law, but God intended to give them a permanent, written record of His holy standard.

 READ Exodus 24:12.

C. Joshua went with Moses up into the mountain.

Moses obeyed the Lord and went up into the mountain.

 READ Exodus 24:13-18.

A young man named Joshua accompanied Moses.

Joshua was Moses' assistant.

POINT TO JOSHUA ON THE CHRONOLOGICAL CHART.

D. God commanded Moses to build the tabernacle.

 Theme: God communicates with man.

While Moses was on the mountain, the Lord gave him the Ten Commandments written on two tablets of stone.

The Lord also explained to Moses other rules and customs that He commanded the Israelites to follow.

- God was their king.
- He told them everything that He wanted them to do.

The Lord also wanted Moses and the people to do something very important.

- Explain.

The Lord had given Israel His Ten Commandments. The Lord had agreed with Israel that, if they obeyed His laws, then He would be with them, protect them, and give them all that they needed. But, if they disobeyed His laws, then the punishment was death.

The Lord knew that the Israelites were sinners and would not be able to always obey His commands. God knew that they would disobey Him and that, unless they had some way of escape, He would have to punish all of them. [2]

 Theme: God is loving, merciful, and gracious.

However, because the Lord loved them, He did not want to destroy them. Therefore, He told them to build a special place where He would live with them.

The people would learn how to approach their holy God without being destroyed.

 READ Exodus 25:1-8.

Teacher's Notes

[2] The story of the golden calf (Exodus 32) is not covered in these lessons. But you may want to mention to your students that the Bible records that, even while God was giving to Moses the instructions for the Tabernacle, the people of Israel were already breaking His commands. ☐

Lesson 26: The Tabernacle

Teacher's Notes

Scripture Reference

- Note:

  This didn't mean that God would no longer be everywhere. Even when He came to live in the tabernacle, God would continue to be everywhere.

  This special place was built so man could learn how God must be approached.

E. **The tabernacle had to be built exactly as God commanded Moses.**

 Theme: Man can come to God only according to God's will and plan.

 READ Exodus 25:9.

The Hebrew word used for tabernacle means tent, dwelling place, or home.

Everything in this place had to be built exactly as the Lord told Moses when he was up in the mountain.

- It all had to be done God's way.
- Remember that Cain refused to come to God in the way God had said, and so God would not accept him.
- But Noah believed God and built the ark exactly as the Lord told him. God accepted and saved Noah and his family.
- We cannot tell God how we will come to Him.
- We must come to God in the way He teaches us through the Bible.

Because the Israelites were walking back to the land from which their forefathers had come, the tabernacle had to be lightweight and portable.

- Therefore, the Lord told them to build most of the tabernacle with materials made from animal skins and goat hair.
- Their tents were also made of these types of materials.

F. **The holy of holies**

 Theme: God is holy and righteous. He demands death as the payment for sin.

Suggested Visual:

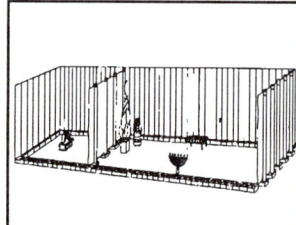

CHRONOLOGICAL PICTURE NO. 35, "THE COMPONENTS OF THE TABERNACLE"

³If possible, use both Chronological Picture 32 and a model to show the students the layout of the holy place and the holy of holies, and each special part, as you teach. ☐

God told Moses that the tabernacle must have two rooms.³

- The first room, which was entered from the outside, was called the **holy place**, or the separate place.

    God is holy, perfect, righteous—set apart from sinners.

356

Lesson 26: The Tabernacle

It was a room set apart by God to be used only for Him.

It was only to be used by God's chosen priests when they were serving God.

We will study more about the priests in a little while.

- The second room, the inner room, was even more important.

This was called the **most holy place** or the holy of holies, that is, the most separate room in God's house.

This room was set apart just for God except for once a year when the high priest, whom we will study about shortly, was allowed to enter.

God's presence would be in this inside room.

This was the special room in the tabernacle where God promised to live in the center of the Israelites' camp.

G. The ark and the mercy seat

 READ Exodus 25:10,11.

The Lord also directed Moses to make a box which was to be placed inside the second room, the most holy place where God was to live.

- The Lord told Moses that this box, called the **ark of the covenant**, must be made from the wood of a particular tree which was chosen by God.

- After they made the ark of the covenant, they were to cover it with gold.

 READ Exodus 25:17.

Moses was told to make a lid of pure gold and place it on top of the ark in the inner room.

- The lid was called the **mercy seat**.
- The mercy seat was the most important part of the whole tabernacle.

This was the place where God promised to live with the sinful Israelites and show them mercy.

Mercy is God's provision for sinners to escape the punishment they deserve for their sins.

Suggested Visual:

> **MERCY**
> God's provision for sinners to escape the punishment they deserve for their sins

The Lord told Moses that he was to make two gold **cherubim** at either end of the mercy seat.

 READ Exodus 25:18.

- Recall:

Do you remember when we last heard about cherubim? God put cherubim outside the garden of Eden so that Adam and Eve would not be able to return to the tree of life. The cherubim outside of the garden of Eden were real live cherubim, but these which Moses were to make were obviously just made from gold.

 READ Exodus 25:19,20.

- The two **cherubim** were to be placed facing one another at either end of the mercy seat.

- The cherubim's wings were to be made so they would stretch out toward one another over the lid, which was called the mercy seat.

- Their faces were to be looking down at the cover of the box.

 READ Exodus 25:21,22.

The ark was to be placed in the inner room just inside the curtain.

- The Lord told Moses to place the two tablets of stone inside the ark of the covenant, under the mercy seat. These were the two tablets upon which God wrote the Ten Commandments.

God promised that, when everything was finished just as He had commanded, He would come into the inner room.

His presence would be evidenced by a very bright light between the cherubim.

This bright light is referred to as the Shekinah glory — the radiance, glory, or presence of God, living with His people Israel.

H. The veil

 Theme: Man is a sinner. He needs God and is helpless to save himself.

 Theme: God is holy and righteous. He demands death as the payment for sin.

 READ Exodus 26:31-33.

God told Moses that he was to hang a beautiful, thick **curtain** as a divider between the two rooms.

This curtain was to remind the Israelites that they were separated from God because of sin.

I. The tabernacle coverings and the brazen altar

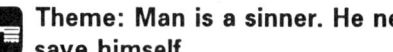 Theme: Man is a sinner. He needs God and is helpless to save himself.

 Theme: God is holy and righteous. He demands death as the payment for sin.

God also told Moses to make a fence of cloth curtains held upright between posts and to place it around the two-roomed structure.

Lesson 26: The Tabernacle

Scripture Reference

Teacher's Notes

Suggested Visuals:

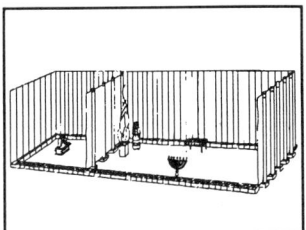

CHRONOLOGICAL PICTURE NO. 35, "THE COMPONENTS OF THE TABERNACLE"

CHRONOLOGICAL PICTURE NO. 34, "THE TABERNACLE"

Exodus 26:14

The two-roomed tabernacle was covered over with dyed animal skins and a final covering of animal hides to form the roof of the tent. **4**

Just inside the entrance of the curtain fence, they were to place an altar which God said was to be made of wood covered with brass.

 READ Exodus 27:1,2.

4 Show the rooms and their curtains in Picture 35, and then show the position of these rooms in Picture 34. ☐

Suggested Visual:

CHRONOLOGICAL PICTURE NO. 36, "THE SIN OFFERING"

When a person wanted to approach God, his first step was to bring a burnt offering to the Lord.

He was to bring it to the **brazen altar**, just inside the gate.

- Note: "Brazen" means made of brass.

He was to place his hand on the head of the animal and then kill it.

- By doing this, he was admitting to God that he was a sinner and deserved to die.
- By placing his hands on the animal, he was identifying himself with this animal that was to die in his place.
- But he was asking God to accept the animal's death instead of his.

 READ Leviticus 1:1-5.

- God allowed sheep, goats, bulls, and birds as sacrifices.
- The animals were to be perfect males.

359

Lesson 26: The Tabernacle

Teacher's Notes		Scripture Reference

- The animal's blood must be shed.
- Remember what we read before:

 Read Leviticus 17:11.

Hebrews 9:22 says, *"...without shedding of blood is no remission."*

But could the blood of animals pay for sin?

No! The blood of animals was only a reminder, or illustration, or pattern, of the punishment demanded for sin.

Hebrews 10:4

Separation of the sinner from God is the only just payment for sin.

Obviously, God doesn't ask us to bring animal sacrifices to Him today, but that was the provision He made for the Israelites.

God was going to make a better way to take care of sins.

Hebrews 9:23,24

J. Aaron and his sons were made priests.

 Theme: Man is a sinner. He needs God and is helpless to save himself.

The Lord appointed Aaron to be the high priest.

His sons were also to be priests.

 READ Exodus 28:1.

Only Aaron, the high priest, was allowed to go into the inner room, the most holy place where God was.[5]

- If anyone else had gone behind the curtain and entered the inner room, he would have been killed.
- Aaron could only go into the most holy place once each year, on the Day of Atonement, which means the "day of covering."
- The only way he could enter was to come with the blood of an animal which had been sacrificed.

[5]Note also Numbers 3:38: only the priests could enter the sanctuary and only the high priest could enter the most holy place, and he only on the day of atonement (Leviticus 16:2, Hebrews 9:7). □

 READ Leviticus 16:2,3.

 Theme: God is holy and righteous. He demands death as the payment for sin.

Before Aaron entered the holy of holies, he had to kill an animal and catch its blood in a basin.

Then, after he passed behind the heavy curtain which hung between the two rooms, Aaron was to sprinkle the blood on the mercy seat, the pure gold cover of the ark of the covenant.

 Theme: Man can come to God only according to God's will and plan.

If everything was done the way the Lord had told Moses, then God promised to forgive the sins of Israel for the past year.

Could the blood of animals pay for their sins?

No! The blood of the animals could not pay for their sins.

- The punishment for sin is death, and that includes the separation of the sinner from God forever.

Leviticus 16:34

Hebrews 10:1-4

Revelation 20:10,15

Lesson 26: The Tabernacle

- Sin must be paid for in full.

Nevertheless, God promised to hold off the judgment they deserved and forgive their sins for the past year, if they came to Him in the way He had told them.

They must come to him believing Him and bringing a blood sacrifice for their sins.

God will only accept those who come to Him in the way He says in the Bible.[6]

K. The tabernacle was finished and erected, and God came to live in it as His house.

 Theme: Man can come to God only according to God's will and plan.

God had told Moses that the Israelites were to build the tabernacle so that He could live with them.

The Israelites built the tabernacle for the Lord and erected it exactly as He had instructed Moses.

Suggested Visual:

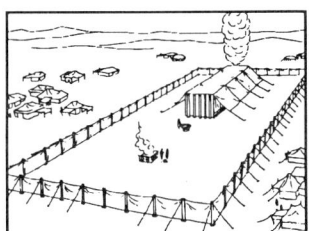

CHRONOLOGICAL PICTURE NO. 34, "THE TABERNACLE"

 READ Exodus 39:42,43; 40:17.

If they had not made it exactly as God told them, God would not have come to live with them.

But because Moses and the Israelites did everything the way God instructed them, God came to live in the center of the Israelites' camp in the most holy place of the tabernacle.

 READ Exodus 40:34,35.

The Israelites could now come to God in the way that He had taught them.

Each year, Aaron, the high priest, could enter the most holy place and sprinkle the blood on the mercy seat under the cherubim.

Why did the high priest have to repeat this every year?

Because the blood of animals cannot pay for sin.

Hebrews 10:4 says, *"...it is not possible that the blood of bulls and of goats should take away sins."*

In His mercy, God was simply holding off for another year the punishment the Israelites deserved.

L. Conclusion

The Israelites, like us, were sinners.

---

[6] It may occur to your students that there is an apparent contradiction here, for, on one hand, we are saying that God demands full payment for sin but then, on the other hand, we are saying that God forgave the sins of the believing Israelites who came to Him according to the way in which He stipulated.

We are teaching here the doctrine of atonement. During the Old Testament, the sinner who came in God's way was fully forgiven and released from the judgment due to his sins, but God did this only because He intended to deal with that sin righteously and completely through the sacrificial blood and death of the Lord Jesus Christ on the Cross. When the Lord Jesus died, God laid on Him the sins of the Old Testament believers which, in the forbearance of God, He had left unpunished (Romans 3:25, Hebrews 9:15).

Do not feel pressured to jump ahead and explain how this seeming contradiction was dealt with at the Cross. But be alert to talk with and share the Gospel with those who realize their sinfulnes and helplessness to save themselves from God's judgment. ☐

Teacher's Notes

Lesson 26: The Tabernacle

Scripture Reference

They needed God's mercy.

And God made a way for them to come to Him.

We cannot decide how we will come to God. He is perfect, and He will only accept us if we come to Him in the way He tells us in His Word.

QUESTIONS:

1. On what did God write His Ten Commandments? *On two tablets of stone.*

2. What did God tell Moses that he and the Israelites must build? *The tabernacle, a place where God would live among them.*

3. Why did God tell the Israelites to build this place? *God knew that the Israelites would disobey the Ten Commandments which He had given them. Unless they had some place where they could go to God and receive His forgiveness and mercy, they would all be punished by death.*

4. How were they to make everything? *They were to make everything exactly as God instructed Moses up in the mountain.*

5. In which room was the bright light, or Shekinah glory, which showed that God was there? *In the inner room, called the most holy place, or the holy of holies.*

6. Who was the only one who could go once each year behind the large, heavy curtain into the inner room? *The high priest.*

7. What must he take with him? *The blood of an animal which had been killed.*

8. What was the high priest to do with the blood? *He was to sprinkle it on the mercy seat.*

9. What did God promise He would do if the high priest did this? *God promised that He would hold off His judgment on the Israelites for one more year.*

10. Did the blood of animals satisfy God as a payment for sin? *No, the blood of animals could never pay for sin.*

11. What is the only payment for sin? *Sinners must die. They are separated from God and destined to be punished by Him forever.*

12. Would God have come to live in the tabernacle if they had not done everything exactly as God had instructed Moses? *No.*

13. Can sinners come to God in whatever way they wish? *No, if we don't come to God in the way that He says, we will not be accepted.*

14. How can we know the way to God? *Only through the Bible, the Word of God.*

Scripture Reference

John
3:14;
6:40;
8:28;
12:32

Hebrews
11:6

LESSON 27

Israel's Unbelief; God's Judgments and Deliverances

LESSON PREPARATION
This section is for you, the teacher.

The passages in the Scripture Reference column are for your own study in preparing for this lesson. Since they may contain concepts that run ahead of the lesson, they are not to be taught at this point.

Note: If you have not taught previously from this series of lessons, please read carefully the note to teachers in the front of this book.

SCRIPTURE: Numbers 13:1-3,25-33; 14:1-4,26-32; 20:1,2,7-12; 21:4-9

LESSON GOALS:

- To show the results of unbelief.
- To show God's mercy and grace.
- To prepare a foundation for presenting the story of Christ's death on the Cross for sinners.

THIS LESSON SHOULD HELP THE STUDENTS:

- To see that all are sinners.
- To realize how important it is to listen to God and to believe Him.

PERSPECTIVE FOR THE TEACHER:

In our society, we are barraged by discouraging news. Our students may come to us with problems that seem insurmountable. Family problems, health problems, cult involvement, drugs, alcohol, immorality, confusion, depression — and the list goes on.

As teachers, we need to be like Caleb and Joshua, continually presenting the message that our God is able. Our students need to see in our lives a positive testimony of faith. They need to see that we trust God to work through our problems and to meet our needs. They need to see that, yes, there are "giants" in the land in which we live, too, but we trust God to lead us and to give us victory for His glory.

We do not want to give the message that everything will be easy or that we "deserve" good things from God. What we do want is to live lives that bring glory to God and make our students thirsty to know this wonderful God who gives us hope and makes our lives refreshing in a sad, confusing world.

This can happen only as we allow God to control us through the power of His Spirit. It is not that we want to impress our students with our faith; instead we want our students to be impressed with the **great God** in whom we have faith!

VISUALS:

- Chronological Picture No. 37, "The Serpent on the Pole"
- Chronological Picture No. 38, "Joshua and Caleb"
- Chronological Map 1
- Chronological Chart

Teacher's Notes

OVERVIEW

This lesson presents God's judgment, grace, mercy, and faithfulness to unfaithful Israel, as shown through the report of the men who spied on the promised land and through the continued unbelief of the people. The story of the brazen serpent is presented so it can later be used as a type of Christ in presenting the Gospel.

This lesson stresses the fact that man is a sinner; he needs God and is helpless to save himself; he must come to God by faith.

As in every lesson, the focus is on God — His character and actions.

Teacher's Notes

Lesson 27: Israel's Unbelief; God's Judgments and Deliverances

Scripture Reference

ON TEACHING THIS LESSON:

These lessons are designed to **teach unbelievers.** You are carefully laying a scriptural foundation on which the Gospel will later be presented. If your class contains believers, teach with the goal of giving them an understanding of the basis for their faith and **with the goal of enabling them to teach the same material to unbelievers.**

DON'T COMPLICATE THE MESSAGE!

As you teach, keep in mind that this is a directed study—not an exhaustive survey of the Bible and not an unlimited group discussion. Keep your lesson on track and moving ahead by limiting and directing any discussion.

Carefully follow the outline. Emphasize the doctrinal themes.

LESSON FORMAT: The **center column** below contains the lesson material to be taught to the students. The **bold outline headings** are only for reference and need not be spoken, as they are incorporated into the outlined material that follows. The material in the **side columns** is for the teacher's own reference and is not intended to be included in the lesson.

TO BE TAUGHT TO THE STUDENTS
(Center Column Only)

LESSON OUTLINE:

REVIEW questions from Lesson 26.

A. Introduction

The Israelites had trembled in fear when God spoke to them from Mount Sinai.

Now God was graciously dwelling in their midst, offering them the mercy they needed and continuing to faithfully provide manna and water for them in the desert.

B. Spying out the promised land

God lifted up the cloud from Mount Sinai where He had given the Israelites His Ten Commandments and the instructions for the tabernacle.

The Israelites followed the cloud when it moved, and the Lord led them right to the edge of the land which He had promised to give to them.

Because the people who lived in the land of Canaan were very wicked and worshiped idols, the Lord planned to have them destroyed and to give their land to the Israelites.

- Recall:

    God cares about all people. II Peter 3:9 says that God is "...not willing that any should perish, but that all should come to repentance."

    We need to remember God's character when thinking about His judgment. He is holy and righteous and judges all sin. But He is also loving, merciful, and gracious.

Lesson 27: Israel's Unbelief; God's Judgments and Deliverances

What God planned to do to the Canaanites was in keeping with His character, just as were His judgments of Sodom and Gomorrah and of the whole world at the time of the flood.

Kadesh-barnea:
Numbers 13:26
Deuteronomy 1:19-25

POINT TO KADESH-BARNEA ON MAP 1.

 Theme: God communicates with man.

When the Israelites arrived at the border of the land which God had promised to Abraham and his descendants, the Lord told Moses to choose one man from each of the twelve tribes.

- These twelve men were to go and spy out the land before the Israelites entered.

 READ Numbers 13:1,2.

- Moses obeyed the Lord and sent the twelve men to look at the land and the people who were living there.

 READ Numbers 13:3.

C. Ten of the spies did not believe God.

 Theme: Man is a sinner. He needs God and is helpless to save himself.

When these twelve men returned, they went to Moses.

This is what they told the Israelites.

 READ Numbers 13:25-33.

- These men were telling the truth.
- The land was owned by strong people, and some of them were huge.

But ten of the men had forgotten all the great and mighty things that the Lord had done for them.

- They had forgotten that nothing is impossible to God.
- They forgot all the miracles that He had done in Egypt and how He had delivered them from slavery.
- They didn't believe that God was strong enough to overcome the people of Canaan and give them the land.

D. Caleb and Joshua believed God.

 Theme: Man must have faith in order to please God and be saved.

But Caleb and Joshua believed God.

- They, also, had seen the strong walls surrounding the cities in Canaan.
- They, also, had seen the size of the people.
- But they had not forgotten that God is almighty and that He can do anything that He wants to do.

Lesson 27: Israel's Unbelief; God's Judgments and Deliverances

- They remembered the mighty things that God had already done, and they believed that He would drive out the people of Canaan and give the land to the Israelites just as He had promised.

 READ Numbers 13:30.

E. **The Israelites did not believe God.**

 Theme: Man is a sinner. He needs God and is helpless to save himself.

Whom do you think the Israelites followed?

 Theme: God is everywhere all the time; He knows everything.

 READ Numbers 14:1-4.

Suggested Visual:

CHRONOLOGICAL PICTURE NO. 38, "JOSHUA AND CALEB"

The Lord heard everything the Israelites said.

He knew that they did not believe Him.

They were acting as if God were a liar.

- God had promised to give them the land, but they refused to believe Him.
- Compare:

  If someone tells you something and you don't believe him, isn't that calling him a liar? Yes, it is. If we hear God's Word but don't believe it, then we, too, are treating God as if He were a liar.

F. **God told them that they would all die in the wilderness.**

 Theme: God is holy and righteous. He demands death as the payment for sin.

The Lord was very angry with the Israelites.

 READ Numbers 14:26-32.

God told the Israelites that all of them who were twenty years old and older who did not believe God would die in the wilderness.

But Joshua and Caleb would not die, because they believed God.

God said that, after forty years, when they had all died, then He would take their children and Joshua and Caleb into the land and give it to them.

Lesson 27: Israel's Unbelief; God's Judgments and Deliverances

 Theme: Man must have faith in order to please God and be saved.

It is a very evil thing not to believe God.
- Recall:

    Satan told Eve that she would not die if she ate the fruit of the tree of the knowledge of good and evil. Satan called God a liar, and Eve believed him. Cain also did not believe God, and he came to God in his own way. God rejected him and his offering. When Noah told the people that a great flood was going to be sent by God, they refused to believe God. They would not enter the ark, and they were all destroyed. The Egyptians also did not believe that the God of Israel was the almighty and only true God. They trusted in their idols to deliver them. But God destroyed their land, killed their firstborn, and drowned their armies in the sea.

God will punish everyone who refuses to believe Him.
- God wanted to bring Israel right into the promised land of Canaan.
- But because of their unbelief, God made them wander in the wilderness.
- Just as He had said, all the unbelieving adults would die in the desert.

G. Israel blamed Moses and Aaron because they didn't have any water.

As the people wandered, they again complained.

 Theme: Man is a sinner. He needs God and is helpless to save himself.

 READ Numbers 20:1,2.

The Israelites blamed Moses and Aaron, his brother, because they didn't have any water.
Why didn't the Israelites ask the Lord for water?
- The Lord had given them water from the rock when they needed it before.
- The reason they didn't ask the Lord is because they did not trust in Him even though He had done so much for them.
- Compare:

    There are many people today who are like the Israelites. Every day and night, the Lord shows us that He is the almighty God. He shows us who He is by the things that He has made. He made the sun, the moon, and the stars. He sends the rain and the wind. He makes everything grow. All things are under His control. He has given all of these things so that we will believe in Him. He has given us our very lives. God has also given us His Word so that we can know the truth. In spite of all these things which God does every day, the majority of people are like the Israelites. They will not believe God.

- Consider:

    Some people say that they don't believe in God because of some tragedy or disappointment that has happened to them or to a loved one. After having studied the Bible this far, we know that it is not

Teacher's Notes

Lesson 27: Israel's Unbelief; God's Judgments and Deliverances

Scripture Reference

God's "fault" that men suffer. It is the result of man's sinfulness. We suffer because of our own sins, because of the sins of generations of other sinners, and because all of creation around us is suffering from man's sin. Sickness, disease, bad weather, hard work, etc. all came as a result of man's sin against God.

Knowing the things we have learned in the Bible should make us want to examine our own concept of God. Do you believe God? Do you believe His Word? **¹**

[1] These are rhetorical questions; just go on with the lesson without waiting for answers.

Do not use these questions with a small group—individuals may feel pressured to answer. ☐

H. God commanded Moses to speak to the rock.

 Theme: God communicates with man.

 Theme: Man can come to God only according to God's will and plan.

 READ Numbers 20:7,8.

The Lord commanded Moses to speak to the rock.
- Previously, when they had needed water, the Lord had told Moses to strike the rock.
- This time, the Lord told him to just speak to the rock.
- Each time, God told them exactly the way it should be done.

Exodus 17:5,6

I. Moses disobeyed.

 Theme: Man is a sinner. He needs God and is helpless to save himself.

Listen to what happened.

 READ Numbers 20:9-11.

Moses and Aaron flared with anger.
- They did not trust and depend on the Lord in this situation as they had when faced with other problems.
- Moses disobeyed the Lord and struck the rock.

J. The Lord's punishment on Moses and Aaron

 Theme: God is supreme and sovereign.

Moses and Aaron reacted in anger instead of trusting the Lord and obeying Him.

Through their words and actions they dishonored the Lord, for they failed to demonstrate His patience, grace, and mercy to undeserving Israel.

God wanted to show the people that He was faithful to provide water for them, just as He had promised.

God keeps His promises because He is perfect and holy.

But instead of showing God's faithfulness and holiness to the people by obeying His perfect instructions, Moses and Aaron showed the people their own anger.

Lesson 27: Israel's Unbelief; God's Judgments and Deliverances

For this reason, God told Moses and Aaron that they would not be allowed to enter the land of Canaan.

 READ Numbers 20:12.

K. Israel murmured once again.

 Theme: Man is a sinner. He needs God and is helpless to save himself.

The Lord had already given the Israelites water, but they still did not trust and depend on Him.

They soon forgot what He had done for them and began to complain again.

 READ Numbers 21:4,5.

L. God sent fiery serpents.

 Theme: God is holy and righteous. He demands death as the payment for sin.

The Lord punished the Israelites so that many of them died.

 READ Numbers 21:6.

The Israelites died because they were bitten by the snakes.

- This was God's judgment on them because of their sin.
- Compare:

The Israelites were bitten by the snakes, and they died. In a similar way, all people have been "bitten" by Satan and sin, and all died to God. I don't mean to say that Satan is a snake. He is not. I am only speaking figuratively when I say that Satan and sin bit us. Through Satan and sin, Adam and Eve died to God. They were separated from Him. It is also through Satan and sin that we were born sinners, dead to God and separated from God.

Hebrews 2:14,15

The Israelites could not escape the poisonous snakes sent by the Lord.

 Theme: God is supreme and sovereign.

- Recall:

When God decides to punish sinners, there is no place where they can hide from Him. In the days of Noah, was there any place where the people could escape judgment after God shut the door of the ark and sent the flood? Could the people of Sodom and Gomorrah escape the judgment of God when He sent fire and brimstone on them? Did Lot's wife escape God's judgment when she disobeyed the Lord and looked back? When God decides that it is the time to punish people, there is no place where they can go to escape.

Revelation 6:15-17

 Theme: Man must have faith in order to please God and be saved.

When God sent the poisonous snakes among them, the Israelites quickly changed their attitude toward God and acknowledged their sin.

369

Teacher's Notes

Lesson 27: Israel's Unbelief; God's Judgments and Deliverances

Scripture Reference

 READ Numbers 21:7.

They realized now that only the Lord could save them from His punishment, and so they asked Moses to ask the Lord for His help.

 Theme: Man is a sinner. He needs God and is helpless to save himself.

They could not help themselves, and Moses could not save them from the snakes. Only the Lord could save them.

M. The brazen serpent

 Theme: God is loving, merciful, and gracious.

Because the Lord is merciful, He decided to forgive and save them. They didn't deserve God's help, but He saves all those who trust in Him.

Psalm 145:18,19

Romans 10:13

 Theme: God communicates with man.

The Lord told Moses what he must do and what the Israelites must do if they were to be saved from death.

 READ Numbers 21:8.

 Theme: Man can come to God only according to God's will and plan.

The Lord didn't tell them to find their own way to be healed.
- God told Moses what to do.
- Moses had to do what God said, and the people had to look at the serpent just as God had instructed Moses.
- It had to be done God's way.

 READ Numbers 21:9.

Suggested Visual:

CHRONOLOGICAL PICTURE NO. 37, "THE SERPENT ON THE POLE"

²Emphasize that the Lord saved those who trusted in Him and looked at the brazen serpent. This story is referred to by Jesus Christ as a type of His death on the Cross (John 3:14,15). Be sure you teach it clearly so you can use it later when you are teaching the Gospel. ☐

 Theme: Man must have faith in order to please God and be saved.

- Emphasize:

  What did the Lord say they had to do in order to be healed from the snake bites? ² *They just had to look at the bronze serpent. Did*

370

Lesson 27: Israel's Unbelief; God's Judgments and Deliverances

the serpent on the pole have power in it to heal them? No! The power of God healed every Israelite who showed he or she trusted in God by looking at the serpent on the pole.

The Lord healed them because they believed in Him.

- Consider:

Do you think people would have been healed if they had prayed but not looked? No! What if they did not look at the brazen serpent but offered God a gift instead? Would they have been healed? No! They had to look at the brazen serpent, just as the Lord said.

 Theme: God is faithful; He never changes.

Do you think some did look, but the Lord did not heal them? No! God always keeps His promises. All who looked were immediately healed by the Lord. God can be trusted to do everything He says.

- Archeological Note:

A bronze serpent was found in an excavation at Timna, Israel. This serpent dates back to the time of Moses. [3] *Other bronze serpents have also been found in Israel and the area nearby. We do not know the particular background of the serpents that have been found, but it is another verification of Bible history. The original bronze serpent made by Moses was destroyed by King Hezekiah because the Israelites had been worshiping it.*

II Kings 18:4

N. Conclusion

The events we have just read about in the Bible happened some 3,400 years ago. Yet they are fresh for today.

God put these accounts in the Bible for us.

Even though we may never have been out in the desert in need of water, we can certainly identify with the **attitudes** of the Israelites. Human nature hasn't changed.

And neither has God.

We, like the Israelites, need to listen to God and believe Him.

[3]The January, 1976, *National Geographic Magazine,* p. 30, has a photo of a bronze serpent. ☐

QUESTIONS:

1. Why didn't the ten spies think that Israel would be able to enter Canaan?

    a. *Because they saw the giants and the walled cities.*

    b. *Because they did not believe God's promise that He would give them the land.*

2. Why did Joshua and Caleb think that Israel could enter Canaan? *Because they believed God's promise that He would give them the land.*

3. What are we calling God if we do not believe His Word and trust in Him? *We are calling God a liar.*

4. Will God accept anyone who does not believe what He says? *No, all who do not believe God will go to everlasting punishment.*

5. What was God's punishment on the Israelites because they did not believe His promise to give them the land? *God said all who*

Teacher's Notes — *Lesson 27: Israel's Unbelief; God's Judgments and Deliverances* — **Scripture Reference**

did not believe Him would die in the wilderness. They would not enter Canaan.

6. Who did God say would enter into the promised land?

    a. Caleb and Joshua, because they had believed God.

    b. The children of the Israelites.

7. What should the Israelites have done when they needed water? *They should have trusted in the Lord.*

8. Why did the Lord say that Moses and Aaron would not enter the promised land?

    a. Because they did not trust and obey Him and thereby honor Him as holy and perfect before the people. Instead they showed their own anger.

    b. Because Moses struck the rock instead of speaking to it as God had instructed him.

9. What did the Lord do to punish the Israelites for their unbelief? *The Lord sent poisonous snakes which bit and killed many people.*

10. Who, like a snake, has "bitten" all people and brought death into the world? *Satan.*

11. How did Satan bring death to all people? *Satan led Adam and Eve to sin against God so that they, and all of us, would die.*

12. What did God tell Moses to do to save the Israelites from death? *The Lord told Moses to make a serpent out of brass and put it on a pole.*

13. What did those who had been bitten by a snake have to do in order to be healed? *They had to look at the snake on the pole.*

14. Did the snake of brass have magical power to heal those who looked? *No.*

15. Who healed those who looked? *The Lord did.*

16. Did they deserve to be healed? *No, they were sinners and deserved to die.*

17. Why did the Lord heal all who looked?

    a. Because He is loving, merciful, and gracious.

    b. Because they believed His promise and looked at the brazen serpent just as He commanded.

18. Did anyone who looked at the snake on the pole die? *No, God always does what He promises.*

Scripture Reference

Psalm 106:34-45

Teacher's Notes

LESSON 28
Israel in the Promised Land Under Judges and Kings

LESSON PREPARATION
This section is for you, the teacher.

The passages in the Scripture Reference column are for your own study in preparing for this lesson. Since they may contain concepts that run ahead of the lesson, they are not to be taught at this point.

Note: If you have not taught previously from this series of lessons, please read carefully the note to teachers in the front of this book.

SCRIPTURE: Joshua 1:1,2; 11:23; Judges 2:7-19; II Samuel 5:4; 7:1-3,12-17; I Chronicles 22:5,6; 29:26-28; II Chronicles 2:1; 5:1

LESSON GOALS:

- To show the terrible sin of the Israelites and their godless neighbors.
- To show God's faithfulness to keep His promises to ungrateful, disobedient people.
- To introduce David as part of the line of the Deliverer.
- To show God's desire for all to be saved.

THIS LESSON SHOULD HELP THE STUDENTS:

- To see the historical progression of the Old Testament.
- To see God's desire for them to be saved.

PERSPECTIVE FOR THE TEACHER:

Many stories in the Old Testament are not mentioned in these lessons. Instead, we are presenting the basic structure upon which the Gospel can be built. Some have said there is a "scarlet thread" running through the Bible. Along this "thread" is the story of the eternal Lord and Saviour who promised to make a way for fallen man to be delivered from sin and Satan and eternal punishment.

The goal of these lessons is to lead the student to a saving knowledge of Jesus Christ. When that new birth takes place, the Holy Spirit puts a hunger in that new heart to read and study the Word. Hopefully, the student will then study the other phases in the series *Building on Firm Foundations* and explore for himself the riches of the whole Bible.

Your students may want to discuss many intermediate portions of Scripture, which is good. But for the purpose of this study, it would be well to continue on to the story of Jesus Christ's coming to earth.

We need to be in prayer that our students will have hearts prepared to receive the Gospel when it is presented to them from God's Word.

VISUALS:

- Chronological Picture No. 40, "Idol Worship"
- Chronological Picture No. 42, "Writer of the Psalms"
- Chronological Picture No. 43, "Solomon's Temple"
- Chronological Chart

OVERVIEW

This lesson spans the period from Joshua through the judges and the kings of Israel, without going into any detail except for a brief sketch of David, his plan for the temple, and the completion of the temple under Solomon.

You will use the Chronological Chart to illustrate the time that is being spanned in this lesson.

Again, the emphasis is upon God's judgment, mercy, grace, and faithfulness to His people Israel and His promise to send a Deliverer for the whole world.

Lesson 28: Israel in the Promised Land Under Judges and Kings

Teacher's Notes

Scripture Reference

- Chronological Maps 1 and 2
- You may want to have available some photos of Jerusalem and its walls and also photos of archeological discoveries from the period of the kings, such as Hezekiah's tunnel.

ON TEACHING THIS LESSON:

These lessons are designed to **teach unbelievers.** You are carefully laying a scriptural foundation on which the Gospel will later be presented. If your class contains believers, teach with the goal of giving them an understanding of the basis for their faith and **with the goal of enabling them to teach the same material to unbelievers.**

DON'T COMPLICATE THE MESSAGE!

As you teach, keep in mind that this is a directed study—not an exhaustive survey of the Bible and not an unlimited group discussion. Keep your lesson on track and moving ahead by limiting and directing any discussion.

Carefully follow the outline. Emphasize the doctrinal themes.

LESSON FORMAT: The **center column** below contains the lesson material to be taught to the students. The **bold outline headings** are only for reference and need not be spoken, as they are incorporated into the outlined material that follows. The material in the **side columns** is for the teacher's own reference and is not intended to be included in the lesson.

TO BE TAUGHT TO THE STUDENTS
(Center Column Only)

LESSON OUTLINE:

REVIEW questions from Lesson 27.

A. Introduction

The Israelites had wandered around in the wilderness for forty years, and all the generation who refused to believe that the Lord could give them the promised land had died.

This was God's punishment on them because they refused to believe His words.

- Compare:

Just as the Israelites were given God's words by Moses, so we are given God's words as we study together. We have the Bible readily available to us; we can read and study it on our own if we wish. Do you think God holds us responsible for what we know about Him? God gives us His Word so that we might believe Him. If we refuse to believe God, we, like the Israelites, will die in our sins.

Hebrews 3:17-4:2

B. Joshua led Israel into Canaan.

Just as God said they would, Moses and Aaron also died before Israel entered the promised land.[1]

So God appointed Joshua to be the new leader of Israel.

[1] From this point on, just a few strategic Old Testament highlights have been chosen for inclusion in the teaching. The purpose of these lessons is not to do an exhaustive study of the Bible but to build a foundation that leads the student to an understanding of his need for salvation, based on a true knowledge of God. Depending upon your class, you may want to include more of the Old Testament stories. But if you are teaching unbelievers, the stories chosen in the lessons are appropriate. ☐

Lesson 28: Israel in the Promised Land Under Judges and Kings

 READ Joshua 1:1,2.

The children of those who didn't believe God were now adults.

It was now the Lord's time to take them into Canaan.

POINT TO CANAAN ON MAP 1.

 Theme: God is faithful; He never changes.

Joshua led the Israelites into Canaan, and God gave them the land that He had promised to Abraham and his descendants.

- Recall:

  Although Satan and the king of Egypt had tried to stop the Israelites from leaving Egypt and although the Israelites had doubted God many times, the Lord still did what He had promised. He made a way for them through the Red Sea. He led them, protected them, and gave them water and food for forty years while they wandered in the wilderness. The Lord did not fail to do any of the things He had promised them.

 READ Joshua 11:23.

Before his death, Joshua said to the Israelites, "...*not one thing hath failed of all the good things which the LORD your God spake concerning you; all are come to pass unto you, and not one thing hath failed thereof*" (Joshua 23:14).

C. Israel turned to idols after Joshua's death.

 Theme: Man is a sinner. He needs God and is helpless to save himself.

 Theme: Satan fights against God and His will. Satan is a liar and a deceiver. He hates man.

While Joshua was alive, the Israelites remembered the Lord.

But after Joshua and the generation who had seen the Lord's miracles in the wilderness had died, the Israelites forgot the Lord.

- They followed the ways of the nations that did not know the true and living God and did not have His Word.
- They made idols and worshiped them instead of the Lord.

God had wanted to drive out the idolatrous Canaanites from the promised land and give Canaan to the Israelites.

- But Israel refused to believe and to obey God.
- So God allowed some of the Canaanite people to remain.
- Israel had settled among these idolatrous people.
- Instead of trusting God in the promised land, they adopted the evil practices of the Canaanites.

 READ Judges 2:7-13.

Joshua 23:16

Lesson 28: Israel in the Promised Land Under Judges and Kings

Suggested Visual:

CHRONOLOGICAL PICTURE NO. 40, "IDOL WORSHIP"

The Canaanites worshiped false gods named Baal and Ashtaroth.

- Satan had deceived these people into thinking that they were worshiping real and living gods.
- They did not realize that what they were really worshiping was Satan and his demons.
- Consider:

When people worship anything other than the true and living God spoken about in the Bible, they are really worshiping Satan. Satan disguises himself. He hides behind idols and other things which people worship, just as he disguised himself by using the serpent when he tempted Eve. Satan hates God and doesn't want anyone to worship God. Satan hates every person. He doesn't want anyone to trust in God and be delivered from death.

 Theme: God is holy and righteous. He demands death as the payment for sin.

 Theme: God is faithful; He never changes.

The Lord punished Israel because they forgot Him and worshiped idols.

- God allowed surrounding nations that hated Israel to overcome them and make them their servants.

 READ Judges 2:14,15.

- The Lord had warned the Israelites that this would happen to them if they did not obey and worship Him only.
- God does not change.
- No matter how many years pass, God remembers His promises, including His promises to punish those who do not believe.

D. The times of the judges

 Theme: God is loving, merciful, and gracious.

When Israel repented, that is, agreed with God about their sin and called to the Lord for help, He chose a man or woman to lead and deliver them from their enemies.

CHRONOLOGICAL CHART: POINT TO THE WORD "JUDGES" AND THE VARIOUS NAMES.

Scripture Reference

Numbers 33:51-53,55,56
Deuteronomy 4:25,26; 8:19; 30:15-20
Joshua 23:9-13; 24:19, 20

Lesson 28: Israel in the Promised Land Under Judges and Kings

These people who were chosen by God to lead Israel were called **judges**.

 Theme: **Man is a sinner. He needs God and is helpless to save himself.**

But over and over again, the Israelites forgot the Lord.

Therefore, the Lord allowed them to be conquered repeatedly by their enemies.

 READ Judges 2:16-19.

 Theme: **God is faithful; He never changes.**

Even though the Israelites were disobedient to God and He had to punish them, His love and care for them did not change.

- Recall:

  In the garden of Eden, the Lord had promised that He would send a Saviour who would destroy Satan and deliver the world from Satan's power. God also gave this promise of a Deliverer to Abraham, Isaac, and Jacob. The Lord assured them that the Saviour would be one of their descendants. God protected Israel, the descendants of Abraham, Isaac, and Jacob, for it was through Israel that God planned to fulfill all His promises of the Deliverer.

Furthermore, God wanted the world to know about Him.

We can only come to know God through the Bible.

It was through Israel that God gave much of the Bible.

- God used chosen Israelites to record His message in the Bible.
- Consider:

  God preserved Israel so that His Word and the story of the Deliverer could be taught to you and to me. Do you remember that when we first began to study, we talked about the fact that all but one of the men whom God used to write His Bible were Jews? It is through the Jewish or Israelite people that we have a Bible. And God was going to do just as He had promised. He was going to send the Saviour through the line of the Israelites so that all people might have a way to be saved. God wanted us to hear His Word so that we, too, could come to God and be saved.

E. **The times of the kings**

Of all the nations of the world, Israel was most fortunate, for their ruler and king was God Himself.

But Israel rejected God and asked for a king like the nations around them.

God granted their request.

Many kings ruled over Israel.

CHRONOLOGICAL CHART: POINT TO THE WORD "KINGS" AND SHOW THE MANY KINGS WHO RULED. **2**

- A few of these kings believed God and trusted in Him, but the majority of them did not.

Scripture Reference:
Isaiah 41:8-10; 44:1-8

Romans 3:1,2

I Samuel 8:4-7

Teacher's Notes:

2 Do not name all the kings, but show them to give a sense of the span of time. ☐

Lesson 28: Israel in the Promised Land Under Judges and Kings

Teacher's Notes | **Scripture Reference**

- They worshiped idols and led the people of Israel to sin against the commandments of God.
- Archeological Note:

  Over the years, archeologists have discovered many, many things that support the details of the reigns of the kings. Locations of towns and cities have been confirmed. Cult objects, idols, altars and other things from this period have been unearthed. The names of several of the kings have been found inscribed on monuments and tombs. Trade records verify names of rulers and towns. Records of wars list specific battles mentioned in the Bible.

  What has been found confirms the biblical record. Nothing found has gone against the biblical record. The Bible is a true history. We can believe every word of it because it is God's Word.

  A few examples of the archeologists' findings:

  Sennacherib's prism, which mentions King Hezekiah (c. 700 B.C.)
  King Hezekiah's tunnel (c. 700 B.C.)
  Jasper seal inscribed "Shema, servant of Jeroboam" (c. 750 B.C.)
  Ivory inscribed with the name of King Hazael (c. 800 B.C.)
  The Moabite Stone, which mentions King Omri (c. 800 B.C.)[3]

F. David, the great king of Israel

David was the greatest and best-known king of Israel.

 Theme: Man must have faith in order to please God and be saved.

 READ II Samuel 5:4.

Unlike many of the other kings who ruled over Israel, David truly believed in the Lord and wanted to obey Him in everything.

- Consider:

  David, like all of us, was born a sinner and was separated from God. But David knew that he was a sinner and that the wages of sin is death. He knew his only hope was in God's mercy and forgiveness. In obedience to God, David offered blood sacrifices for his sins. Because David trusted in the Lord, he was accepted and forgiven just like Abel, Enoch, Noah, Abraham, Isaac, Jacob, Moses, Joshua, and many others.

David was also one of God's prophets.

- God chose David to write many things that are in the Bible.
- David wrote many of the Psalms, which are songs of praise to God for His love and mercy.[4]

Suggested Visual:

SHOW CHRONOLOGICAL PICTURE NO. 42, "WRITER OF THE PSALMS"

---

[3] In case a student asks, these people and events may be found in the Bible as follows:

King Hezekiah and Sennacherib—II Kings 18,19; Isaiah 36,37

King Hezekiah's tunnel—II Kings 20:20

Shema, servant of Jeroboam (probably Jeroboam II)—II Kings 14:23-29 (Jeroboam II is mentioned, Shema is not, though "Shema" is a biblical name, mentioned in other passages.)

King Hazael—II Kings 8:8-15; 12:17,18

King Omri—I Kings 16:21-30

The list given here is very limited. You may want to encourage interested students to research other examples on their own, using Bible handbooks and Bible encyclopedias. ☐

[4] Have your students turn to the book of Psalms. Point out some of David's writings. ☐

Lesson 28: Israel in the Promised Land Under Judges and Kings

Scripture Reference

I Samuel 16:11; 17:15, 34, 35
Psalms 23, 65

Teacher's Notes

- Note:

  Before he became king, David was a shepherd. Some of the Psalms use imagery taken from David's knowledge of shepherds and sheep. God used this imagery to explain to us that our position as sinners is like needy, straying sheep. We need a wise, strong, kind shepherd to keep us from destruction and to guide us into right paths. The Lord is the only one who can do these things for us and be our Good Shepherd.

G. David planned to build the temple.

- Background:
  - *As king of Israel, David acquired a great deal of wealth. He built himself a beautiful palace of timber, stone, gold, and silver. One day, David was thinking about his beautiful dwelling, and he realized that the Lord's house was still the same one which had been made in the wilderness from animal skins and curtains of cloth. It was the tabernacle that the Israelites had made for the Lord when they were at Mount Sinai.*
  - *Therefore, David planned to build for the Lord a permanent and beautiful dwelling place made of stone, timber, silver, and gold.*

David wanted the Lord to have a permanent place where the people could come to worship Him and offer their sacrifices.

 Theme: God communicates with man.

The Lord was very pleased with David for wanting to do this.

God sent His prophet Nathan to speak to David.

 READ II Samuel 7:1-3.

H. God's promise to David.

The Lord told David that not he but his son would build this new place where Israel could bring their sacrifices and worship God.

 READ II Samuel 7:12-17.

 Theme: God is faithful; He never changes.

God gave David the same promise that He had given to Abraham, Isaac, and Jacob.

- The Lord promised David that the great Saviour of man and conqueror of Satan would be from his family.
- This great descendant of David would rule as king forever and ever.
- God never forgot His promise to send a Deliverer.

I. Solomon built the temple.

David prepared the materials for the house of the Lord which was to be built in Jerusalem.

- Note:

  Jerusalem is still a city in the news today. [5] *Like most ancient cities, it was surrounded by great stone walls to protect the people from their enemies. Archeologists have unearthed many ancient sites in the city and many levels of rebuilding of the wall. Visitors to*

[5] If possible, show a picture of Jerusalem and a picture of the city's stone walls. ☐

Lesson 28: Israel in the Promised Land Under Judges and Kings

Teacher's Notes

Scripture Reference

Jerusalem today can see many archeological sites, some dating back to the times of the kings of Israel.

POINT TO JERUSALEM ON MAP 2.

Before David died, he gave his son Solomon the responsibility of building the house of the Lord.

 READ I Chronicles 22:5,6.

Solomon became king over all Israel after his father, David, died.

 READ I Chronicles 29:26-28.

Solomon built the house of the Lord in Jerusalem.

 READ II Chronicles 2:1; 5:1.

Suggested Visual:

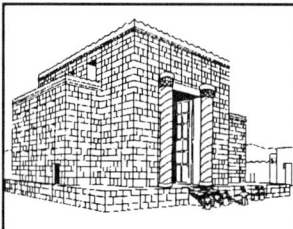

CHRONOLOGICAL PICTURE NO. 43, "SOLOMON'S TEMPLE"

Now there was no further need for the tabernacle which the Israelites had constructed in the wilderness using animal skins and cloth.

This new house of God was called the temple.

The temple of the Lord had the same two inner rooms and the same furniture as the tabernacle:

- The thick curtain was hung in front of the most holy place, the inner room where God was to dwell.⁶
- This curtain was there as a "DO NOT ENTER" sign for everyone except the high priest.
- It was a symbol of the separation between holy God and sinful man.

When the temple was dedicated and sacrifices offered to the Lord, the Lord came and entered the most holy place of the temple, just as He had entered the tabernacle.

II Chronicles 7:1-3

As the Lord came down and entered the temple, the people saw the brilliant light, the Shekinah glory, and worshiped God.

 Theme: Man is a sinner. He needs God and is helpless to save himself.

 Theme: Man can come to God only according to God's will and plan.

 Theme: God is holy and righteous. He demands death as the payment for sin.

⁶Be sure to teach this.
You will mention the curtain when you teach the death of Christ. ☐

Lesson 28: Israel in the Promised Land Under Judges and Kings

Scripture Reference

Teacher's Notes

Leviticus 16:2,3,34

- Recall:

  The high priest was only allowed to enter this inner room once a year on behalf of the people. The Israelites could not come to God themselves. The only way they could be accepted was to depend on the high priest and the animal blood he offered for them.

  Every year, the high priest took the blood of animals into the most holy place in the temple and sprinkled the blood on the mercy seat, the pure gold cover of the ark of the covenant.

  The Israelites were never to forget that they were sinners, that God is perfect, and that the punishment for sin is death. Because the blood of animals could not pay for their sin, the blood had to be placed before God every year.

Hebrews 10:4

  Every year, God forgave their sins and held off His judgment, waiting for the time when a perfect and complete payment for sin would be made.

J. Many kings ruled over Israel after Solomon died.

 Theme: Man is a sinner. He needs God and is helpless to save himself.

I Kings 11:9-13,31-37

After Solomon's death, the nation of Israel argued over who should be king, and they split into two kingdoms.

The ten northern tribes were called Israel, and the two southern tribes were called Judah.

POINT TO ISRAEL AND JUDAH ON MAP 2.

K. Conclusion

We have just covered a major span of Israel's history.

POINT TO THE PERIOD FROM JOSHUA TO THE KINGS ON THE CHRONOLOGICAL CHART.

In time, I hope that you will take the time to read the entire Bible for yourself, as the stories of each event and individual are full of valuable lessons and insights for us today.

But at this point, we are moving rapidly through the Old Testament so we can gain a good overview of God's message for us.

Next week we will take a look at some of God's prophets who spoke His messages to Israel and surrounding nations.

And we will consider Israel's response to God's stern warnings.

As we consider what we are learning, we need to think of **our own response** to God's Word.

God's Word is written for us **so that we may know Him**.

QUESTIONS:

1. Who was the leader of Israel after Moses died? *Joshua.*

2. Did God give Abraham's descendants the land which He had promised them? *Yes, God kept His promise and gave them the land.*

3. What did the Israelites do after Joshua died? *They turned away from the Lord and worshiped idols, like the people near them who didn't know the true and living God and did not have His Word.*

Lesson 28: Israel in the Promised Land Under Judges and Kings

4. Who deceives people so they worship idols and other created things? *Satan.*

5. If we worship anyone or anything other than the true and living God, whom are we really worshiping? *We are worshiping Satan and his spirits.*

6. Why does Satan lead people to worship idols and other things?

   a. *Because Satan hates God and doesn't want anyone to worship God.*

   b. *Because Satan hates all people and doesn't want them to trust in God and be delivered from death.*

   c. *Because Satan uses many things to disguise himself and to deceive people.*

7. How did God punish the Israelites for worshiping idols? *God allowed their enemies to conquer them.*

8. What did God do when the Israelites admitted they were wrong and asked God to deliver them? *God used Israelite men and women called judges to help them to fight and overcome their enemies.*

9. How was David different from many of the kings who ruled over Israel?

   a. *David believed and obeyed God.*

   b. *David agreed with God that he was a sinner, and he brought the blood of animals, trusting in God to forgive his sins and accept him.*

10. What important promise did God make to David? *God promised David that one of his descendants would be the Deliverer.*

11. After David had finished his own house, what did he decide to build? *David decided to build a temple for the Lord in Jerusalem.*

12. Did David build this temple for the Lord? *No, his son Solomon built it.*

13. In what way was this new stone building like the tabernacle the wilderness?

    a. *The temple still had the two inner rooms and the same furniture.*

    b. *The heavy, large curtain still hung across the entrance to the most holy place as a "DO NOT ENTER" sign for everyone except the high priest.*

14. When was the high priest permitted to enter this inner room? *Only once a year.*

15. What did the high priest do in the inner room? *The high priest sprinkled the blood of animals on the mercy seat, the golden lid of the box under the cherubim.*

16. Did the blood of animals pay for the sin of the Israelites?

    a. *No, sin must be paid for by the death of the sinner.*

    b. *The blood of animals was only a temporary offering, holding off punishment until a complete payment for sin would be made.*

17. What did God do because the high priest sprinkled the animals' blood on the mercy seat?

    a. *God forgave the sins of Israel committed during the past year.*

    b. *God held off His punishment until a complete payment for sin would be made.*

18. What happened after King Solomon died? *The ten northern tribes split away from the two southern tribes.*

Scripture Reference

Teacher's Notes

LESSON 29

God Sent His Messengers, the Prophets, to Israel; Israel Refused to Respond to Their Warnings

OVERVIEW

This lesson completes the Old Testament preparation for presenting the Saviour. It gives an overview of the messages of God's prophets to Israel and Judah, warning them that if they did not repent, they would be carried into captivity by their neighbors, Assyria and Babylon. And it shows the fulfilment of that promised judgment, as Israel and Judah refused to repent and were taken captive. It presents the return of some of the exiles, and sets the stage for the coming of Jesus Christ.

God's sovereignty and love and His communication with men are shown in His giving the Greek language, the Roman road system, and the dispersion of the Jewish people to distant lands to build synagogues—all a part of His preparation for the spread of His Gospel to the whole world.

LESSON PREPARATION
This section is for you, the teacher.

The passages in the Scripture Reference column are for your own study in preparing for this lesson. Since they may contain concepts that run ahead of the lesson, they are not to be taught at this point.

Note: If you have not taught previously from this series of lessons, please read carefully the note to teachers in the front of this book.

SCRIPTURE: Isaiah 10:5,6; Jeremiah 6:13,14; 20:5; II Kings 17:1-8; 25:1-12

LESSON GOALS:

- To show that God sent prophets to tell men the truth about God and their need to repent and come to God His way so they could be saved.
- To show God's faithfulness to keep His promises and to carry out His plans.
- To show the historical background and religious practices at the time immediately preceding the coming of Christ.

THIS LESSON SHOULD HELP THE STUDENTS:

- To see that God has given His message to men because He loves us and wants us to be saved.
- To see the horrible consequences of refusing to listen to God and continuing on in sin and rebellion against Him.
- To anticipate the story of the coming of Jesus Christ.

PERSPECTIVE FOR THE TEACHER:

One cannot read through the prophets without seeing that we have a God of wrath who hates and judges sin. But judgment is not the only message of the prophets. The message of judgment is intended to cause men to believe God and to repent of their horrible sin. In Ezekiel 33:11 God says, *"...I have no pleasure in the death of the wicked; but that the wicked turn from his way and live: turn ye, turn ye from your evil ways; for why will ye die, O house of Israel?"*

The message of the prophets is enough to give us chills as we consider the moral and spiritual condition of our own society. We have so much knowledge of God and His Word available to us, yet we are becoming an increasingly godless society. Self, money, things, pleasure, and even Satan are the focus of people's lives. We know that God will not let all this continue. In His time, He will bring swift, sure judgment on our society, just as He did upon Israel and her godless neighbors. How horrible it will be for those who have known so much about God but have still rejected Him and taught others to do the same!

II Timothy 3
II Peter 3

These lessons are exceedingly timely for our culture. The clock is ticking away toward that day when the Church will be removed from this earth. We do not know God's timing, but we do know that He has given us a job to do. Acts 1:7,8 is for us, just as it was for Jesus' first disciples: *"And he said unto them, It is not for you to know the times or the seasons, which the Father hath*

Teacher's Notes

Lesson 29: God's Prophets; Israel's Lack of Response

Scripture Reference

put in his own power. But ye shall receive power, after that the Holy Ghost is come upon you: and ye shall be witnesses unto me both in Jerusalem, and in all Judaea, and in Samaria, and unto the uttermost part of the earth." If we belong to Christ, we have His Spirit; and we have been given His precious Gospel to share with others, until all may have opportunity to hear.

This is the last lesson from the Old Testament. We need to be in prayer for our students that their hearts will be prepared to receive the story of God's coming to earth as a man. We will present His story, not as isolated incidents, but as what it is — the great plan of the eternal, sovereign, almighty Creator God to redeem a people for Himself.

"...Behold the Lamb of God, which taketh away the sin of the world" (John 1:29).

VISUALS:

- Chronological Picture No. 46, "Rejection of the Prophets"
- Chronological Picture No. 47, "Destruction of Jerusalem"
- Chronological Picture No. 48, "Restoration of the Temple"
- Chronological Picture No. 49, "Roman Rule"
- Chronological Map 2
- Chronological Chart

ON TEACHING THIS LESSON:

These lessons are designed to **teach unbelievers.** You are carefully laying a scriptural foundation on which the Gospel will later be presented. If your class contains believers, teach with the goal of giving them an understanding of the basis for their faith and **with the goal of enabling them to teach the same material to unbelievers.**

DON'T COMPLICATE THE MESSAGE!

As you teach, keep in mind that this is a directed study — not an exhaustive survey of the Bible and not an unlimited group discussion. Keep your lesson on track and moving ahead by limiting and directing any discussion.

Carefully follow the outline. Emphasize the doctrinal themes.

LESSON FORMAT: The **center column** below contains the lesson material to be taught to the students. The **bold outline headings** are only for reference and need not be spoken, as they are incorporated into the outlined material that follows. The material in the **side columns** is for the teacher's own reference and is not intended to be included in the lesson.

TO BE TAUGHT TO THE STUDENTS
(Center Column Only)

LESSON OUTLINE:

REVIEW questions from Lesson 28.

A. Introduction

Have you ever tried to tell someone something they didn't want to hear?

Lesson 29: God's Prophets; Israel's Lack of Response

| Scripture Reference | | Teacher's Notes |

It's not easy, is it!

Harder still, have you ever warned someone you love of something you saw that was going to cause them ruin if they didn't heed your warning?[1]

B. God spoke to man from the beginning.

 Theme: God is loving, merciful, and gracious.

 Theme: God communicates with man.

[1]Don't get into a discussion here, but give your students a moment to think about this and make a few comments. It is important that their minds be alert to hear what you are about to teach from the Word. ☐

Isaiah 45:12,18, 21,22
John 3:16
II Peter 3:9

God is the Creator of all people in the world.

God loves all mankind and wants all people everywhere to be delivered from the power of Satan, sin, and death.

Therefore, from the very beginning of the world, God has spoken to people so they would know His will.

- Recall:

God spoke to Adam and Eve and to Cain and to Noah. God gave His message to Noah so that he could tell the people of his day that God commanded them to repent and to believe only in Him. God also spoke to Abraham, Isaac, Jacob, and Joseph. God gave His message to Moses, and Moses gave it to Pharaoh and the Israelites. God continued to speak to Moses as He led the Israelites toward the land He had promised to give them. God spoke to the nation of Israel and gave them His commandments from the top of Mount Sinai.

God spoke through His messengers to Israel and Judah to teach the Israelites His ways and to warn them of His judgment on sin.

God also sent some of His messengers to other nations near the land of Israel.

C. The message of the prophets.

 Theme: God communicates with man.

God's messengers were called prophets.

Let's look on the chart at the names of some of God's prophets.

POINT TO THE PROPHETS ON THE CHRONOLOGICAL CHART.

Isaiah, Jeremiah, Ezekiel, and Daniel were some of the well-known messengers of the Lord.

You will find these and the names of some of the other prophets used as titles to the Old Testament books which God had these men write.[2]

 Theme: God is supreme and sovereign.

 Theme: Man must have faith in order to please God and be saved.

[2]Have the students look at the table of contents in their Bibles. Show them the names of these books as well as the other writings of the prophets.

You might want to tell them that the longer books are called the "major prophets" and the shorter books are called the "minor prophets," a distinction based only on the length of the books. ☐

God's prophets told the people to repent, to destroy their idols, and to trust only in the Lord.

- Remember that "repentance" means a change of mind.

I Kings 18:21

- To repent is to agree with God about our own sin.

Many of the Israelites who worshiped in the temple also worshiped idols.

Teacher's Notes

Lesson 29: God's Prophets; Israel's Lack of Response

Scripture Reference

- God told them that He would never agree to that.
- They must choose whom they were going to serve.
- Those who worship God must do so from their hearts, and their worship must be according to God's Word.

John 4:24

- He is the only true God.

God will not accept worship from anyone who worships anything or anyone else.

 Theme: God is faithful; He never changes.

 Theme: God is holy and righteous. He demands death as the payment for sin.

God's prophets also reminded the Israelites of God's laws given to them through Moses.

³For a description of the spiritual and moral condition of the people and their deserved judgment, note Jeremiah 5. ☐

- The Israelites had disobeyed these laws.³
- The prophets told the people that the Lord said they must repent or He would punish them.
   - He would send their enemies to fight against them.
   - Their enemies would conquer them and lead them away captive to foreign lands.
   - The Israelites would then be slaves of their enemies who spoke languages which the Israelites did not know.
- Isaiah the prophet warned Israel (the northern ten tribes) that the Lord would send the Assyrians to fight against them and capture them if they didn't repent.

POINT TO ASSYRIA AND ISRAEL ON MAP 2.

 READ Isaiah 10:5,6.

- Jeremiah warned the people of Jerusalem and Judah that the Lord would send the Babylonians to destroy them.

POINT TO BABYLON AND JUDAH ON MAP 2.

 READ Jeremiah 20:5.

God has not changed.
- He is the only true and living God.
- He is our Creator and will punish all those who worship or serve anyone or anything besides Him.

D. God had not forgotten His promise to send the Deliverer.

 Theme: God is faithful; He never changes.

Even though thousands of years had passed since God gave the first promise of the Deliverer in the garden of Eden, the Lord had not forgotten His promise to send the Saviour who would destroy Satan, deliver man, and make it possible for man to once again be the friend of God.

- Recall:

  God repeated the same promise to Abraham, Isaac, and Jacob. He promised them that the Deliverer would be one of their descendants. All through the years, God repeatedly reminded Israel of

Lesson 29: God's Prophets; Israel's Lack of Response

the promised Saviour. The Lord promised David that the coming Deliverer would be of his family line.

 Theme: God is everywhere all the time; He knows everything.

 Theme: God communicates with man.

Hundreds of years before the great Deliverer came, God foretold many more things about Him.
- He told His chosen messengers, the prophets, what would happen to the Deliverer.
- They wrote these things down in their books which are now recorded in the Bible.
- In the coming lessons we will look at some of these prophecies and see how God fulfilled them.

He knows everything before it ever happens.

 Theme: God is loving, merciful, and gracious.

God did not abandon His plan to send the Saviour even though the vast majority of people were not interested in His will for them nor in His promises.

God loved the world and did not want anyone to go to everlasting punishment.

Ezekiel 18:32
John 3:16
II Peter 3:9

E. Israel's attitude toward God, His prophets, and their message

 Theme: Man is a sinner. He needs God and is helpless to save himself.

There were always some Israelites who believed God and believed the messages of His prophets.

But the majority of the Israelites refused to obey the words of God.

They persecuted and killed God's messengers.

Suggested Visual:

CHRONOLOGICAL PICTURE NO. 46, "REJECTION OF THE PROPHETS"

- They continued to worship idols.
- They followed the wicked ways of the surrounding nations.
- Many continued to go to the temple to worship the Lord, to perform all the ceremonies, and to offer sacrifices, but they did not obey God in their everyday living.

387

Teacher's Notes

Lesson 29: God's Prophets; Israel's Lack of Response

Scripture Reference

- They said many good things to God, but He did not accept what they said because He could see that they did not mean them in their hearts.
- Isaiah 29:13 says, *"...this people draw near me with their mouth, and with their lips do honour me, but have removed their heart far from me...."*
- Consider:

  Maybe someone has made you bitter against God and against the church. You say to yourself, "I would never want to be like that person. If that's religion, you can forget it."

  God detests that kind of religion, too. Don't let a false worshiper keep you from believing God and coming to know Him as He is.

  God does not lie. He is always faithful and true. He never changes. He is loving and kind and merciful.

  He is also holy and righteous and punishes all sin.

  God will take care of the sins of false worshipers. Let Him take care of those who are offending you and interfering with your understanding of Him.

  He wants us to admit our own sins and to trust Him.

 Theme: God is everywhere all the time; He knows everything.

We cannot fool God.
- Man can only see the outside of us and can only hear our words.
- God looks into our thoughts and our hearts.

He knows what we are really like inside.
- He says that we are all sinners.
- None of us pleases God by what we do.

Most of the priests and leaders were evil men.
- They did not trust in the Lord.
- They did not obey His commands.

I Samuel 16:7
Isaiah 64:6
Romans 3:23
Ephesians 2:8,9
Titus 3:5

 Theme: Satan fights against God and His will. Satan is a liar and a deceiver. He hates man.

But besides the prophets sent by God, there were also false prophets who spoke lies to Israel.
- They claimed to be the messengers of God, but they were the servants of Satan.
- They spoke lies to the people.
- They told the people that everything would be all right and that God would not punish them.

📖 READ Jeremiah 6:13,14.

- Compare:

  Satan is still the same today. Satan speaks through people who may tell you that God's Word is not true, or they may say that God

Lesson 29: God's Prophets; Israel's Lack of Response

will not punish sin. Many are preaching that there is no eternal punishment, that God would never send anyone to Hell. They may tell you that things are going to be fine. Everybody is going to make peace with each other, and we will just all be one happy family.

Some are suggesting that God exists so He can give people material and physical benefits. They say that if you give a lot of money to the church, God has to give you lots of wealth in return. Some are telling people to demand things from God, because God owes it to people to give them what they ask.

- Consider:

Isaiah 57:20,21

God does not owe people anything. God is sovereign. He is still the holy, righteous, sovereign God who will not tolerate sin in His presence and who will judge all sin. Those who refuse to believe Him and to come to Him in His way will be punished forever in the Lake of Fire. God says that there is no peace for the wicked. Anyone who tells you that the Bible has changed or that the Bible is not true is a false prophet. Do not listen to anyone who is teaching anything contrary to what God has said in the Bible. Everyone must make a choice to either believe the words of men or the Word of God.

F. God's judgment on Israel and Judah

 Theme: God is loving, merciful, and gracious.

II Peter 3:9

God is patient.

He does not immediately punish sinners.

- Compare:

He warned the people in Noah's time for 120 years before the flood destroyed them.

For many hundreds of years, He sent His messengers to Israel. They warned Israel of God's anger and His coming punishment on them if they did not repent.

 Theme: God is faithful; He never changes.

Israel did not believe that God would allow their enemies to take their land and make them captives.

Because Israel would not believe and repent, God allowed their enemies to fight against them and conquer them.

The Assyrians conquered the northern ten tribes and took them away as captives.

POINT TO ASSYRIA AND NORTHERN ISRAEL ON MAP 2.

 READ II Kings 17:1-8.

The Assyrians then brought people from other countries to live in the northern part of Israel.

- These people worshiped idols.
- They did not know the true and living God of Israel.

Many of the people from the ten tribes of Israel who were not taken to Assyria intermarried with these people who had come from other countries.

- The descendants of these mixed marriages were called Samaritans.

Teacher's Notes

Lesson 29: God's Prophets; Israel's Lack of Response

Scripture Reference

- The Samaritans continued to worship the Lord, but they worshiped Him according to their own ways and not according to the way God had told Moses.
- Furthermore, they refused to go to God's temple in Jerusalem.
- For these reasons God refused to accept their worship.

John 4:20-22

Judah, which included the two southern tribes of Israel and the people of Jerusalem, also refused to repent, so God allowed the Babylonians to take them away into their country.

POINT TO BABYLON, JUDAH, AND JERUSALEM ON MAP 2.

II Chronicles 36:15-21

- The Babylonians smashed down the stone walls of Jerusalem.
- They also tore down and burned the temple of God which Solomon the king had built.

Jeremiah 52:1-30

 READ II Kings 25:1-12.

Suggested Visual:

CHRONOLOGICAL PICTURE NO. 47, "DESTRUCTION OF JERUSALEM"

God did what He had warned the Israelites He would do if they did not repent.
- The people would not believe His Word, so He punished them.
- All unbelievers will be punished by God forever.

G. The return of the exiles from Babylon

 Theme: God is loving, merciful, and gracious.

 Theme: God is faithful; He never changes.

After many years, the people of Judah who were in Babylon repented and asked the Lord to take them back to their own land.

The Lord heard their cries for His help, and He brought many of them back to Jerusalem.
- They rebuilt Jerusalem and the stone walls around the city. **4**
- They also rebuilt the temple.

4For your own reference, Ezra and Nehemiah give these stories. ☐

Suggested Visual:

CHRONOLOGICAL PICTURE NO. 48, "RESTORATION OF THE TEMPLE"

390

Lesson 29: God's Prophets; Israel's Lack of Response

The Israelites who returned to their land were also given another name.
- They were called Jews, the name still used for the descendants of these people today.
- The name Jew is probably derived from the word Judah.

The Jews continued to worship the Lord, although the majority did not do it from their hearts.
- They went to the temple with their sacrifices.
- But they did not really believe they were sinners who needed God's mercy.

H. The Greeks and the Romans

The Lord punished them once again by allowing other nations to conquer them.

The Greeks took control of the Jews' country and taught them to speak the Greek language.[5]

POINT TO GREECE ON MAP 2.

 Theme: **God is supreme and sovereign.**

 Theme: **God communicates with man.**

God, in His sovereignty, was going to use the Greek language to spread His Word over much of the civilized world.
- Expand:

  At that time, the Bible was not yet completed. Only the part we know as the Old Testament had been written. Some of these books were being translated into Greek from the Hebrew language in which they were originally written. People in places far from Israel were being prepared, through reading God's Word, for the coming Deliverer.

  Later, in the first century A.D., when God gave to men the rest of His Word, the New Testament, He caused it to be written down in the Greek language, which was by then spoken by many people in distant countries.

After a time, the Romans overcame the Greeks, and they took control of Jerusalem and the land of Israel.[6]

POINT TO ROME ON MAP 2.

Suggested Visual:

CHRONOLOGICAL PICTURE NO. 49, "ROMAN RULE"

The Romans ruled over the Jews and made them pay taxes.
- If anyone disobeyed, he was strictly punished.
- The Romans killed many Jews with sword and spear; others they crucified.

---

[5] Greece flourished around 400 B.C. Palestine (Israel) came under the rule of Alexander the Great in about 330 B.C. ☐

[6] In 63 B.C., Palestine (Israel) became subject to Roman rulership. Rome continued to rule Palestine until Rome fell in 476 A.D. ☐

Lesson 29: God's Prophets; Israel's Lack of Response

Teacher's Notes

Scripture Reference

The Roman Emperor, Caesar, appointed men to rule for him over the countries which he had conquered.
- The Romans worshiped many false gods; they also worshiped Caesar.
- Nevertheless, the Romans permitted the Jews to continue worshiping the Lord by going to the temple.

Again, in God's sovereignty, Roman rule had its benefits.
- God allowed the Romans to build many excellent roads linking their vast empire.
- God was preparing a way for His Word to be carried to distant lands.

 Theme: God is loving, merciful, and gracious.

God cares about the people of all nations and wants them to know Him.

Isaiah 45:22
John 3:16
II Peter 3:9

I. Synagogues built for the teaching of the Law

During these times, the Jews built meeting houses, called synagogues, where they could read and teach the Old Testament Scriptures.
- Because of persecution and captivity, the Jewish people were now scattered to many countries.
- Synagogues were built, not only in most of the cities and towns in Israel, but also in many cities in Asia Minor, Greece, Persia, and North Africa.

SHOW THESE AREAS ON MAP 2.

- On the last day of the week, the Jews met in their synagogues, and the Jewish religious teachers and leaders read and explained the writings of Moses and the prophets.
- But in many cases, their explanations were not according to what God had spoken and written in the Bible.
- The majority of the Jews went to the temple and the synagogues, but they did not truly trust in the Lord or obey His Word.
- They were only meeting as part of their cultural duties and habits; they were not worshiping God from the heart.

J. The godly Jewish believers

 Theme: Man must have faith in order to please God and be saved.

 Theme: Man can come to God only according to God's will and plan.

However, there were always a small number who believed God's Word given through His messengers.
- They trusted in the Lord and tried to follow His commands.
- They were accepted by the Lord because of their faith in Him.
- Compare:

  They were like Abel, Noah, Abraham, and many more who realized they were sinners and trusted in the Lord for His mercy and forgiveness.

- They were waiting for the coming Saviour whom God had promised would save them from Satan and the punishment for their sins.[7]

[7]It is clear from what Zacharias said that the Old Testament saints at this time were aware of the redemptive purpose of the coming Saviour (Luke 1:76-79). ☐

Lesson 29: God's Prophets; Israel's Lack of Response

- Thousands of years had passed since God had first promised to send the Deliverer, but they knew that He would come at the exact time which God had planned.
- Consider:
  Whom are we like? Are we like the Israelites who refused to believe God, or are we like those few who wisely believed His words and trusted only in Him?

K. Conclusion

Israel's unbelief and rejection of God's promises brought deep grief and sadness to the Lord.

In Psalm 81:13,14,16, God says, *"Oh that my people had hearkened unto me, and Israel had walked in my ways! I should soon have subdued their enemies...."* God said He would have *"...fed them ...with the finest of the wheat: and with honey out of the rock...."*

God was, indeed, saddened by Israel; but He had never changed His plans or forgotten His promises.

Now He was extending His grace and mercy to the whole world.

He had established a common language, an excellent road system, and meeting places in distant countries.

He was making a way for all to hear about the long-promised Saviour.

QUESTIONS:

1. Why did God call men to be His messengers? *Because God loves all people, He wants them to know the truth and to be delivered from the power of Satan, sin, and death.*

2. What did God's prophets say to Israel at this time? *They told them to repent, to destroy their idols, and to trust only in the Lord.*

3. What did the Lord say He would do if they refused to repent? *The Lord said that He would allow the Assyrians to capture Israel and the Babylonians to destroy Jerusalem.*

4. Has God changed? *No, God is still the same. He will punish all those who worship or serve anyone or anything besides Him, the only true and living God.*

5. Although thousands of years had gone by, had God forgotten His promise to send the Deliverer? *No, God had not forgotten.*

6. To whom did God give much more information about the coming Deliverer? *God gave it to His prophets.*

7. Where are these things written? *They are written in the Bible.*

8. What was the attitude of the majority of the Israelites to God and His prophets?

    a. *They persecuted and killed God's prophets.*

    b. *They continued to worship idols.*

    c. *They followed the wicked ways of the surrounding nations.*

9. Did the Israelites continue to go to the temple, offer sacrifices, and worship God? *Yes, they did.*

10. Was God pleased with them? Did He accept their worship and their sacrifices? *No.*

Lesson 29: God's Prophets; Israel's Lack of Response

Teacher's Notes

Scripture Reference

11. Why didn't God accept the worship and sacrifices of many of the Israelites? *Because they were worshiping God with their lips, but in their hearts, they were unrepentant and they didn't trust in God.*

12. Who sees into our thoughts and knows our hearts? *God.*

13. What does God say about us all? *God says that we are all sinners and cannot please Him.*

14. Did God accept any Israelites? *Yes, God accepted those who agreed with Him that they were sinners and trusted in Him for His mercy and forgiveness.*

15. For whom were these believing Israelites waiting? *They were waiting for the Deliverer who God had promised would save them from Satan and the punishment of their sins.*

16. What did the Lord allow to happen to the northern ten tribes of Israel? *The Lord allowed the Assyrians to take them as captives.*

17. What did the Lord allow to happen to Jerusalem and the two southern tribes? *The Lord allowed the Babylonians to destroy Jerusalem and take the two tribes captive.*

18. Did any of the Israelites return to their own land? *Yes, when they repented, the Lord brought many of them back to Jerusalem.*

19. What did they do when they returned to Jerusalem? *They rebuilt the city and its stone walls, and they rebuilt the temple of the Lord in Jerusalem.*

20. What new name were the Israelites given? *They were now called Jews.*

21. What other people conquered the Jews? *The Greeks and the Romans.*

22. Whom did the Romans worship? *They worshiped many false gods and also their king, Caesar.*

23. What were synagogues? *They were buildings which the Jews erected in all their towns as places to teach the Old Testament Scriptures. The Jews met in the synagogues on the last day of each week.*

24. Were there any Jews who were true believers like Abraham, Isaac, Jacob, Moses, and David? *Yes, some realized they were sinners and trusted in God. They came to God in the way He had told Moses, bringing animals and blood sacrifices. They were waiting for God to send the Deliverer.*

LESSON 30

God Foretold the Birth of John and Jesus

LESSON PREPARATION

This section is for you, the teacher.

The passages in the Scripture Reference column are for your own study in preparing for this lesson. Since they may contain concepts that run ahead of the lesson, they are not to be taught at this point.

Note: If you have not taught previously from this series of lessons, please read carefully the note to teachers in the front of this book.

SCRIPTURE: Luke 1:5-17,24-38

LESSON GOALS:

- To show that Jesus is God the Son.
- To show that Jesus is the Son of God.
- To show that Jesus is the promised Deliverer.

THIS LESSON SHOULD HELP THE STUDENTS:

- To realize that God was fulfilling His promises about the Deliverer.
- To see that the Lord Himself was going to be the Deliverer.
- To see that nothing is too hard for God.

PERSPECTIVE FOR THE TEACHER:

The fact of the virgin birth of Jesus Christ has been viciously rejected by many "scholars" in recent years. No wonder! To accept the fact of the virgin birth, one must see God as holy and all-powerful.

We live in a world that exalts man—and also exalts man's fleshly lusts. Most people do not like to think about holiness because it convicts them of their own sin. And because men desire to exalt themselves, they refuse to acknowledge their Creator, the almighty God.

But we have the privilege of teaching God's truth. The virgin birth of Jesus Christ is one of the central truths of our faith. God proclaims His holiness from Genesis to Revelation. None of Adam's sinful descendants could be our Saviour. Only the holy Son of the holy God could be the spotless Lamb who died in our place.

We have had the privilege of building a foundation of truth through the Old Testament. Now what a privilege we have to present this wonderful Deliverer, Jesus Christ, the Son of God—God the Son!

VISUALS:

- Chronological Picture No. 50, "Zacharias in the Temple"
- Chronological Picture No. 51, "Gabriel Appears to Mary"
- Graphics, "ADAM—Sinner" (also used in Lesson 11) and "GOD—Holy." These may be done ahead of class as small posters, since you will use these illustrations again in later lessons. They are very simple, so you may prefer to write them on a board as you teach the lesson.

Scripture Reference

Teacher's Notes

OVERVIEW

This lesson announces the birth of John and the birth of Jesus. God's faithfulness and immutability are shown in His fulfillment of prophecy. His sovereignty, holiness, and omnipotence are shown in His giving John and in His sending Jesus Christ, the promised Deliverer.

Jesus Christ is presented as the Son of God and God the Son. He is shown to be the sinless Son of the holy God, born without a human father. He is the King of the line of David.

Mary is presented as an ordinary young woman, a believer in God—a sinner who needed a Saviour. She was chosen by God to be the mother of Jesus.

Teacher's Notes

Lesson 30: God Foretold the Birth of John and Jesus

Scripture Reference

ON TEACHING THIS LESSON:

These lessons are designed to **teach unbelievers.** You are carefully laying a scriptural foundation on which the Gospel will later be presented. If your class contains believers, teach with the goal of giving them an understanding of the basis for their faith and **with the goal of enabling them to teach the same material to unbelievers.**

DON'T COMPLICATE THE MESSAGE!

As you teach, keep in mind that this is a directed study—not an exhaustive survey of the Bible and not an unlimited group discussion. Keep your lesson on track and moving ahead by limiting and directing any discussion.

Carefully follow the outline. Emphasize the doctrinal themes.

LESSON FORMAT: The **center column** below contains the lesson material to be taught to the students. The **bold outline headings** are only for reference and need not be spoken, as they are incorporated into the outlined material that follows. The material in the **side columns** is for the teacher's own reference and is not intended to be included in the lesson.

TO BE TAUGHT TO THE STUDENTS
(Center Column Only)

LESSON OUTLINE:

REVIEW questions from Lesson 29.

A. Introduction

The last prophet to speak for God had been a man called Malachi.

POINT TO MALACHI ON THE CHRONOLOGICAL CHART.

Let's turn in our Bibles to the Book of Malachi, the last book of the Old Testament. When you locate it, keep your place in Malachi, because we will be reading from there later.

- Malachi reminded the Jews that God's promised Deliverer would come to save them.
- He also told them that, before the Deliverer came, God would send another prophet.
- This prophet's work would be to teach the people so that they would be ready for the coming Saviour.

Malachi 3:1; 4:5,6

After Malachi, however, four hundred years passed during which God did not speak through any prophet.

But, just as we studied in our last lesson, God was still at work during this time which is often referred to as "the silent years."

POINT TO "THE SILENT YEARS" ON THE CHRONOLOGICAL CHART.

Quietly, unnoticed by most men, God was making vast preparation for the fulfillment of His great promises to send a Saviour for the whole world.[1]

The time had come.

God was ready to do what He had first promised in the garden.

Genesis 3:15

[1] He made the Greek language common to many parts of the world.

He linked distant cities with Roman roads.

He dispersed His people to many different countries where they built synagogues and taught from His Word. ☐

Lesson 30: God Foretold the Birth of John and Jesus

We are now going to begin our study in the New Testament with a story of an elderly Jewish couple who believed God and were awaiting the fulfillment of His promises.

B. God promised that Zacharias and Elizabeth would have a son.

 Theme: Man must have faith in order to please God and be saved.

 Theme: Man can come to God only according to God's will and plan.

 READ Luke 1:5,6.

Zacharias and his wife, Elizabeth, were Jews who trusted in God and believed His Word.

- They offered sacrifices at the temple, just as God had commanded Moses.
- Because they trusted in God and came to Him the way He had told them, God accepted them just as He had accepted Abel and all others who had trusted in Him from the beginning of the world.

 READ Luke 1:7.

Both Zacharias and Elizabeth were now old, but they had never been able to have any children.

 READ Luke 1:8-10.

Zacharias was one of the priests in the temple in Jerusalem.

 Theme: God communicates with man.

CHRONOLOGICAL CHART: POINT TO THE NAME "JOHN."

Listen to what happened to Zacharias while he was doing his work as a priest in the temple.

 READ Luke 1:11-14.

Suggested Visual:

CHRONOLOGICAL PICTURE NO. 50, "ZACHARIAS IN THE TEMPLE"

God's angel promised Zacharias a son and told him he must name his son John.

Teacher's Notes

Lesson 30: God Foretold the Birth of John and Jesus

Scripture Reference

C. John was given the work of preparing the way for the Deliverer.

 Theme: **God is everywhere all the time; He knows everything.**

 Theme: **God is faithful; He never changes.**

 READ Luke 1:15-17.

The Lord knew all about Zacharias' son even before Elizabeth became pregnant.

- Everything is known to God before it ever happens.
- God knew all about us, too, before our parents knew we would be born!

Psalm 139:13-16

God had foretold about Zacharias' son, John, through the prophet Malachi.

Not only did God foretell many things through His prophets, but everything that He promised, He also fulfilled.

 Read Malachi 3:1.

Four hundred years before John was born, God told Malachi to write this about God's messenger, John!

 Theme: **Jesus Christ is God.**

Zacharias' son would be the prophet who would prepare the people to receive the coming Deliverer.

The angel said that Zacharias' son, John, would go ahead of the Deliverer to prepare the way for Him.

The angel called the coming Deliverer "the Lord."

The coming Deliverer, the Saviour of men, was to be God Himself!

 READ Luke 1:24,25.

Elizabeth knew that God was the one who had made it possible for her to conceive.

- She was very thankful and happy.
- In those days, the Jewish people looked down on couples who weren't able to have any children.
- Now Zacharias and Elizabeth were going to have a son in their old age!

D. God promised Mary a son.

 Theme: **God is faithful; He never changes.**

It was now God's time to fulfill all of His promises regarding the Deliverer.

Listen to what God says.

 Theme: **God communicates with man.**

Lesson 30: God Foretold the Birth of John and Jesus

 READ Luke 1:26-31.

Suggested Visual:

CHRONOLOGICAL PICTURE NO. 51, "GABRIEL APPEARS TO MARY"

God sent an angel to tell a virgin named Mary that God had chosen her to be the mother of the Deliverer.

Mary was just an ordinary young woman who, although she was a sinner, trusted in God to send the Deliverer. [2]

 Theme: God is supreme and sovereign.

God chose Mary to be the mother of the Deliverer because God does whatever He wants to do.

God is sovereign.

He doesn't ask anyone or have to answer to anyone for what He does.

 Theme: God is faithful; He never changes.

 Theme: God is loving, merciful, and gracious.

Mary's son was to be the promised Deliverer.

His name was to be Jesus, which means Saviour, or Deliverer.

God had never forgotten His promise to send the Deliverer.

God loved the whole world, and He wanted sinners to be delivered from the punishment they deserve.

CHRONOLOGICAL CHART: DISPLAY THE NAME "JESUS."

E. Mary's son would be both man and the Son of God.

 Theme: Jesus Christ is God.

 Theme: Jesus Christ is man.

The angel Gabriel also told Mary some amazing things about her future son.

 READ Luke 1:32.

Mary's son was not only to be truly her son, but He would also be the Son of the Highest, that is, the Son of God.

Six hundred years earlier, God had announced these things to His prophet Isaiah.

 Read Isaiah 9:6,7.

Scripture Reference

Psalm 115:3; 135:5,6
Isaiah 45:21,22

John 3:16

Teacher's Notes

[2] You may have students in your class who have been taught that Mary was sinless. Do not make an issue of their previous teaching. Simply tell them that Mary herself calls God her Saviour (Luke 1:47), indicating that she, too, needed the Lord to save her from her sins. The Bible says that *"all have sinned"* (Romans 3:23). □

Lesson 30: God Foretold the Birth of John and Jesus

Teacher's Notes

[3] As mentioned previously, you may have students who do not believe in the fact of the Trinity. Do not debate with them. Do not try to explain the Trinity. Simply tell them that we are presenting what the Bible says, and that the fact of the Trinity runs throughout the Bible.

If they are interested in studying what the Bible has to say, offer to set up an appointment to talk with them outside of class time. Be sure that you are prepared for your meeting by studying and getting whatever help you need so you can clearly point out the fact of the Trinity in Scripture.

Pray for them. But do not debate with them. If, in class, they persist in debating, you may have to ask them to step out of the class. ☐

Scripture Reference

As the Son of God, Jesus had many names.

Jesus was His name as a man — His human name.

- Explain:

When we began studying the Bible together, we learned about the Trinity. [3] *We learned that, although there is only one God, God is three persons who are equal in every way. These three, who are the one God, are God the Father, God the Son, and God the Holy Spirit.*

God the Father, God the Son, and God the Holy Spirit never had a body as we humans do. God is Spirit and doesn't have a human body. But the Saviour had to be a human being just as we are — except that He must be sinless.

So that God's plan about the Deliverer could be fulfilled, God the Son had to be born as a human being.

God chose Mary to be the mother of the Deliverer. The Deliverer, who was God the Son, had to come down from Heaven to be born on the earth as the child of Mary. Mary's son would be both God and man in one body.

This son, Jesus, would be fully God and fully man!

 Theme: God is faithful; He never changes.

Furthermore, the angel told Mary that because the Deliverer would be a direct descendant of David the king, He was to be king over Israel.

- He was to be king forever.

 READ Luke 1:32b,33.

- God was going to do what He had promised King David.

God keeps His promises.

F. Jesus, the Deliverer, would not have a human father.

 READ Luke 1:34.

Mary could not understand how she could have a child who wouldn't have a human father.

 READ Luke 1:35.

The angel said that God the Holy Spirit would perform this miracle.

 Theme: Jesus Christ is holy and righteous.

 Theme: Jesus Christ is God.

Because Jesus would be born without a human father, He would be born sinless.

No descendant of Adam is holy and righteous.

- Every person in the world inherited Adam's sin.
- We are all sinners because the sin of Adam was passed down to us.

Suggested Visual:

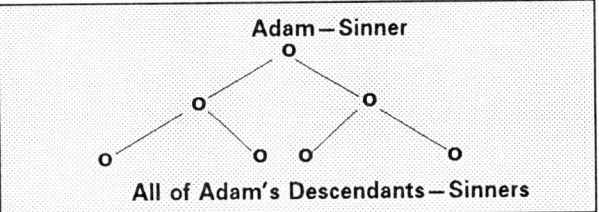

But Jesus' Father was God.
- God is perfect and holy, without sin.
- Jesus would not inherit Adam's sinfulness!
- Jesus was the perfect Son of God, holy and sinless!

Suggested Visual:

> **GOD—Holy**
> JESUS, Son of God—Holy, Without Sin

 Theme: God is all-powerful.

 READ Luke 1:36,37.

- Consider:

  It was impossible for a virgin to have a child, just as it was impossible for Elizabeth, the mother of John, to have a child in her old age. Nevertheless, with God all things are possible. God can do anything!

  God created the first man, Adam, out of the dust of the ground, and God gives life to every person. It was not difficult for God to give this child to Mary without the baby having a human father. And neither was it hard for God to give Elizabeth a child in her old age. God can do anything!

 Theme: Man must have faith in order to please God and to be saved.

 READ Luke 1:38.

Mary trusted in the Lord and accepted that it was God's will for her to be the mother of the Saviour.

G. Conclusion

Who was this Saviour to be?

Jesus
- The one announced in the Garden of Eden
- Descendant of David
- The Deliverer
- The Saviour
- The holy Son of God

Lesson 30: God Foretold the Birth of John and Jesus

- God the Son
- God in a human body — the holy, sinless Son of the holy, sinless God.

In our next lesson we will see God continue to bring to pass the things He had foretold.

QUESTIONS:

1. What name was Zacharias to give to his son? *John.*

2. What was John's work to be? *John's work would be to prepare the Jews to receive and trust in the Deliverer.*

3. Of whom was Mary's son to be a descendant? *Of David the king.*

4. Why did the Saviour have to be born of the line of David? *Because God had promised David that the Deliverer would be one of his descendants.*

5. Why did the Saviour have to be born of a virgin? *So that He would not inherit Adam's sin as we did.*

6. What was Mary's child to be called? *Jesus.*

7. What does the name Jesus mean? *Jesus means Saviour or Deliverer.*

8. Was Jesus to be more than just man? *Yes, Jesus was to be God the Son whom God planned should come down from Heaven to be born as a human baby.*

9. How could Jesus be given life without a human father? *God is all-powerful. He can do anything He wishes to do.*

10. Was Jesus to be the promised Saviour? *Yes, Jesus was to be the Deliverer whom God first promised in the Garden of Eden.*

11. Who is the author of the New Testament? *God.*

Scripture Reference		Teacher's Notes

LESSON 31
God Began to Fulfill His Promises Concerning John and Jesus

LESSON PREPARATION
This section is for you, the teacher.

The passages in the Scripture Reference column are for your own study in preparing for this lesson. Since they may contain concepts that run ahead of the lesson, they are not to be taught at this point.

Note: If you have not taught previously from this series of lessons, please read carefully the note to teachers in the front of this book.

SCRIPTURE: Matthew 1:1,2; Luke 1:57,67-80

LESSON GOALS:

- To show that God keeps His promises.
- To show that Jesus Christ is the only Saviour.

THIS LESSON SHOULD HELP THE STUDENTS:

- To see that there is only one Saviour for the whole world.

PERSPECTIVE FOR THE TEACHER:

In our time, many false prophets have been given extensive coverage by the news media. People like to talk about the prophecies made by these impostors and speculate on whether or not the things predicted will really happen. Then the same people like to look back and laugh when the things prophesied fail to come true.

It is very natural for people to form ideas based on what they see in men and transfer these ideas to their view of God and His Word. Even though they are hearing the Word spoken, they may not really be understanding and believing in their hearts. As we teach, we need to emphasize that God's promises **always** come true. We need to emphasize that **everything** in His Word is true.

Pray that the Holy Spirit will work in the hearts of your students to cause them to hear and understand and believe!

VISUALS:

- **PROPHECY CHART**

    Before class, prepare a chart listing Old Testament prophecies concerning Christ. You will use this chart in this lesson and many of the lessons ahead. For your convenience, the chart is printed at the end of this lesson. If your class is small, you may be able to use the chart at this size. (You may want to cut it out and put it on cardboard.) Or, if your class is large, you may want to enlarge the chart in sections on a copier and put it on a piece of posterboard. Or, you may prefer to make your own chart to suit your class' needs. You will want to make the chart large enough to be clearly visible to all your students.

    Leave the chart covered, and uncover each prophecy as you reach it in the lesson. If you begin by uncovering the entire chart, some students may want to discuss material that you have not yet reached.

    As you study the fulfillment of each prophecy, write the verse reference in the appropriate space. This way, your students will see how God gradually fulfilled all these Old Testament prophecies through the life of

OVERVIEW

This lesson shows that God fulfilled His promise and gave John. Through Zacharias' prophecy, we are told that his son would prepare the way for the Deliverer. Also through his prophecy, we are given many insights into the Deliverer, Jesus Christ:

- He would be the One through whom God would fulfill His promise to Abraham.
- He would be God Himself.
- He would explain how men could be saved.
- He alone would be the Saviour for the whole world; there would be only one Saviour for all men.

The prophecy chart is put into use in this lesson.

Jesus is announced as God's Anointed One — Prophet, Priest, and King.

Lesson 31: God's Promises Fulfilled in John and Jesus

Teacher's Notes

Scripture Reference

Jesus Christ. If possible, leave the chart on the wall as a constant reminder to your students of God's faithfulness.

- Visual about Jesus Christ (illustrated in lesson)

ON TEACHING THIS LESSON:

These lessons are designed to **teach unbelievers.** You are carefully laying a scriptural foundation on which the Gospel will later be presented. If your class contains believers, teach with the goal of giving them an understanding of the basis for their faith and **with the goal of enabling them to teach the same material to unbelievers.**

DON'T COMPLICATE THE MESSAGE!

As you teach, keep in mind that this is a directed study—not an exhaustive survey of the Bible and not an unlimited group discussion. Keep your lesson on track and moving ahead by limiting and directing any discussion.

Carefully follow the outline. Emphasize the doctrinal themes.

LESSON FORMAT: The **center column** below contains the lesson material to be taught to the students. The **bold outline headings** are only for reference and need not be spoken, as they are incorporated into the outlined material that follows. The material in the **side columns** is for the teacher's own reference and is not intended to be included in the lesson.

TO BE TAUGHT TO THE STUDENTS
(Center Column Only)

LESSON OUTLINE:

REVIEW questions from Lesson 30.

A. Introduction

When God makes a promise, He will fulfill it.

- No matter how difficult, no matter how impossible it may seem
- No matter if it takes thousands of years to bring it to pass
- God will fulfill every promise, down to the very last detail.

B. John was born.

 Theme: God is faithful; He never changes.

 READ Luke 1:57.

God did what He had promised Zacharias.

Zacharias and his wife, Elizabeth, had a son, and they named him John, just as the angel had instructed.

Can you remember some other promises God made and fulfilled?¹

---

¹Give your students time to answer. See if they can remember some of the promises which God made and fulfilled.

Here are a few:

- His warnings to Adam and Eve
- His warnings to the people in Noah's day
- His promises to Abraham to give him descendants
- His promises to Joseph through dreams that Joseph would be a ruler
- His promise to Moses to bring the Israelites out of Egypt and to bring them back to Mount Sinai
- His promise to the Israelites to preserve them through the final plague if they carried out His instructions concerning the Passover
- His promise to bring Israel back to the promised land
- His warnings to Israel and Judah that they would be taken captive if they did not repent of their sins ☐

Lesson 31: God's Promises Fulfilled in John and Jesus

C. Zacharias believed that God's promises concerning the Deliverer would soon be fulfilled.

 Theme: Man must have faith in order to please God and be saved.

 READ Luke 1:67-79.

Zacharias knew that, very soon, God's promised Saviour was coming to deliver mankind from Satan, sin, and death.

- Zacharias believed the promises which God had given to the prophets.
- God the Holy Spirit used Zacharias' knowledge of the Old Testament to bring this message that these promises were, indeed, about to be fulfilled!
- Consider:

  Each one of us must be delivered from Satan, from the sinful things that control our lives, and from death and separation from God. That is why God planned to send the Saviour into the world.

 Theme: God is faithful; He never changes.

 READ again Luke 1:72-75.

Abraham was the father of the nation of Israel.

Do you remember that, before Abraham went to live in Canaan, God had promised him that one of his descendants would be the Saviour?

Read Genesis 12:3, *"And I will bless them that bless thee, and curse him that curseth thee:* **and in thee shall all families of the earth be blessed."** [2]

Even though thousands of years had passed since God made that promise to Abraham, God had not forgotten.

God always does exactly what He says.

D. John was to prepare Israel to believe on the Deliverer.

 Theme: Man must have faith in order to please God and be saved.

 Theme: God communicates with man.

 READ again Luke 1:76.

God the Holy Spirit gave this message to Zacharias, and Zacharias believed Him.

- Through the Holy Spirit, Zacharias was speaking about his son, John.
- John was going to be the prophet who would prepare the way for the coming Saviour.
- He would announce to Israel that the Saviour would soon come to them.

[2] You are discussing only the boldfaced portion of this verse. Do not get sidetracked into discussion about the rest of the verse. ☐

Lesson 31: God's Promises Fulfilled in John and Jesus

Teacher's Notes		Scripture Reference

 Theme: Jesus Christ is God.

The Deliverer, the Saviour, for whom John was to prepare the way, was to be the Lord Himself.

- No ordinary man could deliver us from Satan, sin, and death.
- The Lord is the great Deliverer of all who trust in Him.
- Recall: **3**

[3] Reviews like this are important. Students need to keep in mind the continuity of Biblical themes—they need to be reminded that God does not change. He is still the same God today as He was in the Old Testament and always will be.

Hopefully, one day, as believers, they will trust in God's unchanging character and attributes and be reminded by His Holy Spirit of these very passages of Scripture as they face the pressures and circumstances of their own lives. ☐

Who delivered Noah and his family from the flood? Who delivered Isaac from death and provided a ram to die in his place? Who delivered Lot from the destruction of Sodom and Gomorrah? Who delivered Joseph from prison in Egypt? Who delivered the Israelites from slavery in Egypt? Who saved the Israelites from Pharaoh's army at the Red Sea? Who delivered the Israelites from death by providing them with water and food in the desert? The Lord alone is the great Deliverer.

There is no other Saviour but the Lord.

Isaiah 45:22

Acts 4:12

 Read Isaiah 43:11.

- Consider:

People today like to think that they are the ones who are strong and important. They like to boast that they are the most popular or the smartest or the most talented or the greatest or the richest or the strongest.

Satan wants us to think about all these things because He doesn't want us to listen to and believe God!

Even if a man were known all over the world and had great intelligence and talent and had won many awards and had a great deal of money and even ruled as president or king, he still could not deliver himself from the penalty of his sins! Only God can do that. He is the only Deliverer, the only Saviour of men!

Jeremiah 9:23,24

 Theme: God is loving, merciful, and gracious.

 Theme: God is holy and righteous. He demands death as the payment for sin.

 READ again Luke 1:77.

Zacharias said that, when the Saviour came, He would show His people how their sins could be forgiven.

God cannot and will not forgive sins unless the full price for sin is paid.

- The punishment for sin is separation from God forever.
- How then could sin be paid for? **4**
- How can sinners be forgiven and saved from everlasting punishment?

[4] Do not be in a hurry to give the Gospel, but be alert to your students and be ready to explain the Gospel fully to anyone who seems to have a prepared heart. ☐

Zacharias said that the Saviour would make all of that clear and plain.

 READ again Luke 1:78,79.

The Deliverer would come like the sun rising in the morning.

Lesson 31: God's Promises Fulfilled in John and Jesus

Scripture Reference

Teacher's Notes

- Compare:

  How would you feel if you went for a walk in the woods and got lost? When the sun went down, you would be not only lost, but you wouldn't even be able to see where you were. You would be very eager for the sun to rise in the morning so you could find your way back.

  In a similar way, Adam and Eve's sin put all of us into darkness. They had been very safe in the garden of Eden because they depended on God for everything and He gave them all they needed. But when they sinned, their sin separated them from God. They were cast out of the garden. Now they were in the dark, so to speak, in constant danger of Satan's attack.

  All of their children and all of their descendants, including you and me, were born in the darkness of sin.

But God was making a way out of that darkness!

- Zacharias said that the Deliverer would come into this world to be the light to all people.
- The Deliverer would come just as the sun rises after a dark night and gives light to all people everywhere.

 Theme: Jesus Christ is the only Saviour.

- Compare:

  How many suns give light to this earth? Only one. The same sun gives light all over the world.

  How many Deliverers did God promise to send into the world?

  Only one.

Isaiah 43:10,11; 44:6; 45:5,6,21, 22
John 3:16
Acts 4:12
Romans 3:22,23, 29,30
I Timothy 2:5
Revelation 5:9

God did not promise to send different Deliverers, one for us and another for people in other parts of the world.

- God only promised one Deliverer who would make it possible for us to come to God.⁵
- He would bring "light" to the whole world, like the rising sun!

 READ Luke 1:80.

John lived in the desert until it was God's time for him to begin giving God's message to Israel to prepare them to trust in the coming Deliverer.

 Theme: Man must have faith in order to please God and be saved.

Theme: Man can come to God only according to God's will and plan.

John believed God.

He knew that he was a sinner, but he came to God with the animal and blood sacrifices.

- He trusted in God to save him from the everlasting punishment.
- John trusted in the coming Deliverer.
- John was going to be the final prophet to announce to Israel the coming of Jesus Christ.

⁵This is important. Many people think that it is insulting to suggest that Jesus Christ is the only way to God. They argue that there are many ways and it doesn't matter as long as you are "religious."

Don't make an issue of it at this point. Just tell them that the Bible says that God promised only one Deliverer for the whole world. Tell them that we will talk more about this in later lessons. ☐

Lesson 31: God's Promises Fulfilled in John and Jesus

E. God fulfilled His promises concerning Jesus, the Deliverer.

 Theme: God is faithful; He never changes.

 READ Matthew 1:1,2.

Jesus, the coming Deliverer, was to be a descendant of Abraham, Isaac, Jacob, and David.

God had promised them that the Deliverer would be from their family.

For hundreds of years, God had given His prophets messages about this coming Saviour.

POINT TO THE PROPHECY CHART, UNCOVERING ONLY THE TITLE.

We are going to use this chart to record the fulfillment of some of these things which God said would happen to the Deliverer.

God planned everything that would happen to the Saviour even before He came into the world.

- Explain:

   As we look at these Old Testament prophecies concerning the Deliverer, we will see that many of them are situated in the context of another subject. Very often, prophecies referred to an event that would take place immediately as well as to an event that was to take place hundreds of years later. The first fulfillment often came to pass in the lifetime of the prophet, showing the people of his day that the prophet was truly of God because what he had said came true, just as he had prophesied.

   The prophets themselves did not know exactly how these prophecies would be fulfilled. They simply spoke and wrote down the messages God gave them.

   I Peter 1:10-12

   But looking back, we can see that particular details of these prophecies had their exact fulfillment in Jesus Christ.

 Read Isaiah 9:7.

POINT TO THE PROPHECY CHART. Uncover the first prophecy, "Will be David's descendant," and write Matthew 1:1 opposite Isaiah 9:7. Read the prophecy and the fulfillment.

This is the fulfillment of God's promise to David and the fulfillment of the words God spoke to Isaiah.

 Theme: Jesus Christ is the only Saviour.

Jesus was also to be called the Christ.
- "Christ" is a Greek word meaning "Anointed One" — one set apart by God for special duties.
- "Christ" is also the Greek translation of the Hebrew word "Messiah."
- He was God's Anointed One, set apart for three special duties, or high offices.
- He was to be God's **Prophet, Priest,** and **King**.

Lesson 31: God's Promises Fulfilled in John and Jesus

Suggested Visual:

> **JESUS CHRIST**
> God's Anointed One
>
> **PROPHET
> PRIEST
> KING**
>
> **DELIVERER of SINNERS**

As God's **Prophet,** Jesus was going to be sent into the world to tell God's way for all people to be delivered from Satan, sin, and everlasting punishment.

God was also sending Jesus to be the final, great **High Priest.**

Remember that the high priest took the blood of animals into the inner room of the temple once a year so the sins of the people could be forgiven.

Furthermore, Jesus was to become the ruling **King,** the descendant of King David.

Only Jesus was promised by God to be the Christ, the Anointed One.

- No one else can rightfully claim this position.
- Jesus Christ was promised by God to be the only Deliverer of sinners.
- God was going to send only one Saviour for the whole world.

F. Conclusion

God keeps His promises.
He alone is God.
He alone can deliver men from their sins.

QUESTIONS:

1. What work did God plan for John to do? *God planned for John to go ahead of the Deliverer to prepare the people to receive and trust in Him.*

2. What did Zacharias say the coming Saviour would do? *Zacharias said that the Deliverer would:*

   a. *Fulfill all God's promises to Abraham, Isaac, and Jacob as well as those made through the prophets.*

   b. *Teach His people the way of deliverance from Satan, sin, and everlasting punishment of sin.*

   c. *Be like the rising sun. He would give light to those who were in darkness. This meant that the Saviour would guide people in the way of deliverance from fear and death.*

3. How did Zacharias know what the Saviour would do? *Zacharias read and believed what God had said through the prophets.*

4. Are there many different saviours for people in different parts of the world? *No. God sent one Saviour for the whole world.*

5. What does Jesus' name "the Christ" mean? *It means "Anointed One."*

Teacher's Notes

Lesson 31: God's Promises Fulfilled in John and Jesus

Scripture Reference

6. Jesus was set apart by God for what three special duties? *Jesus was being sent by God to be His greatest prophet, the final, great High Priest, and King forever.*

7. What great Jewish king was a forefather of Jesus? *David.*

8. What does the word *Messiah* mean? *It means the same as the word "Christ." "Messiah" is the Hebrew word; "Christ" is the Greek word.*

WHAT GOD SAID WOULD HAPPEN TO THE DELIVERER:

Isaiah 9:7	David's descendant	
Isaiah 7:14	Born of a virgin	
Micah 5:2	Born in Bethlehem	
Hosea 11:1	Flee into Egypt	
Isaiah 11:2	Some of His characteristics	
Isaiah 53:4,5	Suffer for others	
Psalm 41:9	Betrayed by a friend	
Zec. 11:12,13	Sold for 30 pieces of silver	
Psalm 27:12	Accused by false witnesses	
Isaiah 50:6	Smitten and spat upon	
Isaiah 53:7	Silent when accused	
Isaiah 53:3	Rejected by Jews	
Psalm 69:4	Hated without a cause	
Psalm 22:16	His hands and feet pierced	
Psalm 22:18	His clothing gambled for	
Isaiah 53:12	Die with the wicked	
Psalm 22:6-8	Mocked and insulted	
Isaiah 53:9	Buried with the rich	
Psalm 16:10	Rise again	
Psalm 68:18	Go back to Heaven	

Scripture Reference

LESSON 32

God Fulfilled His Promises by Giving Jesus, the Deliverer

Teacher's Notes

OVERVIEW

This lesson presents the birth of Jesus Christ, emphasizing the fulfillment of prophecy and the deity of Christ—the Son of God and God the Son.

The story of Jesus' birth is presented through Matthew 1 and 2, referencing the associated Old Testament prophecies. Jesus' boyhood and maturation into manhood are presented from Luke 2.

Be sure to take the time to show the prophecies and their fulfillment and to emphasize that Jesus is the Son of God, the only sinless man. All others are descendants of Adam and therefore are sinners. Jesus alone is holy and sinless.

LESSON PREPARATION
This section is for you, the teacher.

The passages in the Scripture Reference column are for your own study in preparing for this lesson. Since they may contain concepts that run ahead of the lesson, they are not to be taught at this point.

Note: If you have not taught previously from this series of lessons, please read carefully the note to teachers in the front of this book.

SCRIPTURE: Matthew 1:18-25; 2:1-15,19-23; Luke 2:40,52

LESSON GOALS:

- To show that God keeps His promises.
- To show that Jesus Christ is the only Saviour.
- To show that Jesus Christ is the Son of God.
- To show that Jesus Christ is God.
- To show that Jesus Christ is holy and righteous.
- To show that Jesus Christ is man.

THIS LESSON SHOULD HELP THE STUDENTS:

- To see the amazing fulfillment of God's promises.
- To learn who Jesus is.

PERSPECTIVE FOR THE TEACHER:

The story of the birth of Jesus Christ, often called the "Christmas Story," is familiar to many people in our society. The beloved scene of the little baby in the manger is all some people really know of this event.

We are presenting more than a story of a sweet baby in a manger; we are also presenting the coming of **the Lord Himself, the mighty God, the promised Deliverer, the Saviour of sinners!**

The story of the baby Jesus lifts men, women, and children emotionally. But the full story of the baby Jesus who is the Saviour of the world is the story that offers forgiveness and eternal life to all who will believe.

As we who teach study His Word, may our own hearts be stirred afresh with the mighty truths of our blessed Saviour and Lord. As our hearts are filled with wonder and awe, may we be enabled, by His Spirit, to present His story with love and power.

VISUALS:

- Chronological Picture No. 53, "An Angel Speaks to Joseph"
- Chronological Picture No. 54, "Jesus Is Born"
- Chronological Picture No. 57, "The Wise Men"
- Chronological Picture No. 58, "The Flight to Egypt"
- Graphics from Lesson 30, "ADAM—Sinner" and "GOD—Holy"
- Chronological Maps 2 and 3
- Prophecy Chart

Lesson 32: God Fulfilled His Promises by Giving Jesus, the Deliverer

Teacher's Notes

Scripture Reference

ON TEACHING THIS LESSON:

These lessons are designed to **teach unbelievers.** You are carefully laying a scriptural foundation on which the Gospel will later be presented. If your class contains believers, teach with the goal of giving them an understanding of the basis for their faith and **with the goal of enabling them to teach the same material to unbelievers.**

DON'T COMPLICATE THE MESSAGE!

As you teach, keep in mind that this is a directed study—not an exhaustive survey of the Bible and not an unlimited group discussion. Keep your lesson on track and moving ahead by limiting and directing any discussion.

Carefully follow the outline. Emphasize the doctrinal themes.

LESSON FORMAT: The **center column** below contains the lesson material to be taught to the students. The **bold outline headings** are only for reference and need not be spoken, as they are incorporated into the outlined material that follows. The material in the **side columns** is for the teacher's own reference and is not intended to be included in the lesson.

TO BE TAUGHT TO THE STUDENTS
(Center Column Only)

LESSON OUTLINE:

REVIEW questions from Lesson 31.

A. Introduction

The Deliverer—

The Saviour—

Jesus Christ—

Someone has said that history is "His story."

Did you ever consider that every time we write the date, we are making note of the birth of Jesus Christ?

- [This year], A.D. means [this year], *anno Domini,* "the year of our Lord."
- We date all history B.C. (before Christ) and A.D.

Jesus Christ is the center of history.

B. Joseph's problem

Mary, who was to be Jesus' mother, had already been promised to be married to a man called Joseph.

Now Joseph discovered that Mary was pregnant, and Joseph knew that he was not the father of this baby.

- According to Jewish law, Joseph could have made a public announcement, and Mary could have been killed for being pregnant with a child that was not Joseph's.

Deuteronomy 22:20,21

- But Joseph loved Mary, so he decided to break off their engagement quietly.

READ Matthew 1:18,19.

Lesson 32: God Fulfilled His Promises by Giving Jesus, the Deliverer

C. God's angel explained to Joseph.

Had Mary been with a man? No.

How then had she become pregnant?

- The baby within her had been given by God the Holy Spirit.
- Her baby was the Son of God who had come down from Heaven to become a human being so He could be the Deliverer of sinners.

 Theme: God communicates with man.

God wasn't going to allow Joseph to separate from Mary.

- Joseph was a good man who trusted in God.
- He, too, was a sinner, but he came to God in the way God had said to come.
- God wanted Joseph to take Mary as his wife so Jesus would also have a good earthly father.
- For this reason, God sent His angel to tell Joseph the truth about Mary.

Suggested Visual:

CHRONOLOGICAL PICTURE NO. 53, "AN ANGEL SPEAKS TO JOSEPH"

 Theme: God is loving, merciful, and gracious.

 Theme: Man is a sinner. He needs God and is helpless to save himself.

 READ Matthew 1:20,21.

Jesus was to be born into this world to save sinners from God's punishment for their sins.

He came to save all those who agree with God that they are sinners needing a Saviour.

 READ Matthew 1:22,23.

 Theme: God is faithful; He never changes.

The prophets had said that the promised Saviour would be born of a virgin.

 Read Isaiah 7:14.

POINT TO THE PROPHECY CHART. Uncover "Born of a virgin," and write Matthew 1:18-25 opposite Isaiah 7:14. Read the prophecy and the fulfillment of God's promise.

Lesson 32: God Fulfilled His Promises by Giving Jesus, the Deliverer

- God remembered His promise.
- Jesus was to be born of a virgin.

 Theme: Jesus Christ is God.

Because Jesus was to be God as well as man, He was to have many names.

- One of His names was to be Emmanuel, meaning "God with us."
- This means that He would be God Himself, come to earth to be born as a child and live with people here in this world.

Jesus is the only Saviour.

And He is also God! **1**

Remember that we learned that God is a Trinity of three persons.

- Jesus Christ is **God the Son**.
- Imagine! God Himself was coming to earth as a little baby!

D. Joseph's response

 Theme: Man must have faith in order to please God and be saved.

 READ Matthew 1:24,25.

Joseph believed God and took Mary home as his wife.

- We read these words, but it is hard for us to imagine the difficulty this couple faced.
- Yet they trusted God.

E. The wise men looked for Jesus.

 Theme: God is faithful; He never changes.

 READ Matthew 2:1,2.

POINT TO BETHLEHEM ON MAP 3.

Jesus was born in Bethlehem just as the prophets of God had said many years earlier.

Suggested Visual:

CHRONOLOGICAL PICTURE NO. 54, "JESUS IS BORN"

Jesus was born to be the Saviour of sinners, to free them from the control of Satan, sin, and death.

 Read Micah 5:2.

Teacher's Notes

1 Many of the cults do not believe that Jesus is God. **Do not allow yourself to be drawn into an argument with a student.** Simply state that this is what the Bible teaches. If a student persists in expressing his views, you might suggest that he could arrange another time to discuss the matter, but in class we will limit the discussion to what is written in God's Word. ☐

Lesson 32: God Fulfilled His Promises by Giving Jesus, the Deliverer

POINT TO THE PROPHECY CHART. Uncover "Born in Bethlehem," and write Matthew 2:1 opposite Micah 5:2. Read the prophecy and the fulfillment.

God the Father, the Son, the Holy Spirit, are eternal.
This Saviour, God the Son, born in Bethlehem, was truly God.
The Eternal God had come in a human body to live with men.

F. King Herod's fear

 Theme: **Man is a sinner. He needs God and is helpless to save himself.**

 READ Matthew 2:3,4.

Herod, just like the Egyptian pharaoh during the time of Moses, did not want anyone to rule over him.

Herod was afraid that he would lose his position as king when this baby grew up to be a man.

 READ Matthew 2:5,6.

The chief priests and scribes read from the prophet Micah's writings of the place where the Deliverer would be born, just as we have read.

 Theme: **Jesus Christ is God.**

 READ Matthew 2:7-11.

Suggested Visual:

CHRONOLOGICAL PICTURE NO. 57, "THE WISE MEN"

- Consider:

Was it right for the wise men to worship Jesus? [2] *God had written in the Law which He gave to Moses that only God should be worshiped. Do you think that God was angry with these men for worshiping Jesus? No, Jesus is God, so it was right for them to worship Him. Jesus is both God and man.*

Exodus 20:3
Deuteronomy 5:7

G. God's warning to the wise men and to Joseph

 Theme: **God is faithful; He never changes.**

 Theme: **God communicates with man.**

 READ Matthew 2:12-15.

[2] Someone may ask why the picture does not show the manger. The Bible tells us that the wise men came to "the house," and it also says that Jesus was now a young child, not a newborn baby. ☐

Teacher's Notes

Lesson 32: God Fulfilled His Promises by Giving Jesus, the Deliverer

Scripture Reference

God directed Joseph to take Jesus to Egypt, where He would be safe from Herod's evil plan to destroy Him.

Neither Herod nor any other power in Heaven or on earth could stop God from carrying out **His plan** to save people from their sins.

Suggested Visual:

CHRONOLOGICAL PICTURE NO. 58, "THE FLIGHT TO EGYPT"

POINT TO BETHLEHEM ON MAP 3 AND TO EGYPT ON MAP 2.

Jesus was taken to Egypt just as the prophets had said long before.

 Read Hosea 11:1.

POINT TO THE PROPHECY CHART. Uncover "Flee into Egypt," and write Matthew 2:14 opposite Hosea 11:1. Read the prophecy and its fulfillment.

 Theme: God is everywhere all the time; He knows everything.

God knew what Herod was planning to do.

H. Joseph, Mary, and Jesus returned to Nazareth.

 Theme: God is faithful; He never changes.

 Theme: God communicates with man.

 READ Matthew 2:19-22.

When Herod was dead, the Lord sent one of His angels to tell Joseph to take Mary and Jesus out of Egypt back into the land of Israel.

 READ Matthew 2:23.

God's words given through His prophets were fulfilled.

The Deliverer lived in the town of Nazareth.³

POINT TO NAZARETH ON MAP 3.

I. Jesus, a boy in Nazareth

 Theme: Jesus Christ is holy and righteous.

 Theme: Man is a sinner. He needs God and is helpless to save himself.

---

³Though there are no specific Old Testament prophecies concerning Nazareth, it was a town which was scorned by the Jews because a garrison of Roman soldiers was stationed there. In John 1:46, we read, *"...Can there any good thing come out of Nazareth?...."* Old Testament prophecies do record that the Deliverer was to be scorned, despised, and rejected (Psalm 22:6 and Isaiah 53:3). So prophecy was fulfilled in a way that communicated well with the people of that day. (References: *The Bible Knowledge Commentary: New Testament,* by John F. Walvoord, and Roy B. Zuck. SP Publications, Wheaton, IL, 1985, p. 23; and *Believers Bible Commentary,* by William MacDonald. A & O Press, Wichita, KS, 1989, p. 24.) □

Lesson 32: God Fulfilled His Promises by Giving Jesus, the Deliverer

 READ Luke 2:40.

Jesus grew from a baby into a strong boy.

His Father, God, protected and guided Him in everything that He thought, said, and did.

He obeyed every command of God.

- He never sinned because He was not born a sinner.
- He was not separated from God, like all of the descendants of Adam.

Every other person who has ever lived has disobeyed God's commands, but Jesus perfectly obeyed every command of God.

Suggested Visuals:

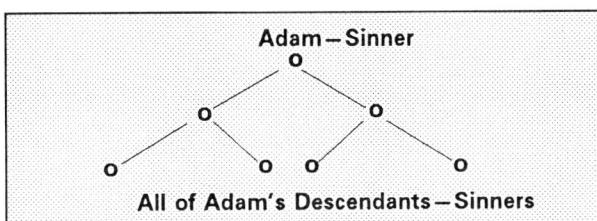

Only God is completely holy and righteous, and Jesus Christ is God!

J. Jesus grew into manhood.

 Theme: Jesus Christ is man.

 READ Luke 2:52.

Even though Jesus was God, He was also a real human being.

- He grew into manhood in a human body.

A while ago we learned that the Deliverer had to be both God and man in one body.

- God was Jesus' Father.
- And Jesus was, indeed, God.
- But Jesus was born into this world as a man, in a human body, so He could be the Deliverer, the Saviour, for human beings!

Jesus grew to be a wise man.

God was pleased with Him, and people liked Him.

His character as a man was the character of God:

- He was sinless and holy.
- He always kept His word.
- He was faithful in everything He did.
- He was completely righteous.
- His knowledge was perfect.
- He was merciful and gracious, completely loving and kind.

No wonder Jesus was a man who found favor with God and men.

Lesson 32: God Fulfilled His Promises by Giving Jesus, the Deliverer

Teacher's Notes

 Theme: God is faithful; He never changes.

 Read Isaiah 11:2.

God's prophet, Isaiah, said that the Deliverer would be wise and have great knowledge because He would be in oneness with God the Holy Spirit.

This prediction given by God was completely, beautifully fulfilled in Jesus Christ, God the Son.

- Nothing that God says is ever forgotten.
- Everything happens just as He says.

POINT TO THE PROPHECY CHART. Uncover "Some of His characteristics," and write Luke 2:52 opposite Isaiah 11:2. Read the prophecy and its fulfillment.

K. Conclusion

The baby in the manger was the Son of God.

And as a man, He was to be the Deliverer, the Saviour of men.

God Himself had come to earth as a man.

The promised Deliverer, the Saviour of men, had come at last.

QUESTIONS:

1. What does the name Emmanuel mean? *It means "God with us." Jesus was God, come to earth to live with human beings.*

2. In what country was Jesus born? *In the land of Israel.*

3. In what town in Israel did the prophets say Jesus would be born? *Bethlehem.*

4. Was it right for the wise men to worship Jesus? *Yes, because Jesus was God the Son.*

5. To which country did God tell Joseph to take Jesus in order to escape from Herod? *Egypt.*

6. To which town in Israel did Joseph take Mary and Jesus after they left Egypt? *Nazareth.*

7. Why was Jesus born into the world? *To be the Deliverer of sinners—to save people from the control of Satan, sin, and death.*

8. Although Jesus looked like other children, what great difference was there? *Jesus was God as well as a human being.*

9. Did Jesus ever do anything wrong? *No, Jesus was born sinless, and He never thought, said, or did anything which displeased His Father.*

10. Was anyone else sinless like Jesus? *No, everyone else inherited Adam's sin and disobeys God's laws.*

Scripture Reference

 **LESSON 33**

God Sent John to Teach and Baptize; John Baptized Jesus

Teacher's Notes

OVERVIEW

This lesson presents Jesus Christ as the Lamb of God.

Through the ministry of John the Baptist, it also shows the need for an attitude of repentance, as negatively portrayed by the proud, unrepentant Jewish leaders.

Some points:

- Explanation of repentance—a change of attitude toward God and toward one's sin
- Explanation of John's baptism—a baptism of repentance
- Emphasis of John's lifestyle—though he believed and obeyed God, he was poor in material wealth (refuting the currently popular teaching that God has to give material blessings to those who believe in Him)
- Validation of Jesus' deity as God spoke from Heaven

LESSON PREPARATION

This section is for you, the teacher.

The passages in the Scripture Reference column are for your own study in preparing for this lesson. Since they may contain concepts that run ahead of the lesson, they are not to be taught at this point.

Note: If you have not taught previously from this series of lessons, please read carefully the note to teachers in the front of this book.

SCRIPTURE: Matthew 3:1-9,13-17; John 1:24-27; 29-37

LESSON GOALS:

- To show the need for repentance.
- To show the dangers of refusing to repent.
- To show that Jesus Christ is God.
- To show that Jesus Christ is the Lamb of God and the promised Deliverer.

THIS LESSON SHOULD HELP THE STUDENTS:

- To see the need to repent.
- To see that they are helpless to save themselves.
- To see that Jesus is the promised Deliverer.

PERSPECTIVE FOR THE TEACHER:

If ever a society needed to repent, it is our society today. This lesson defines repentance as a change in attitude toward God, about ourselves, and about sin. The prevailing attitude in our culture is to take care of self and forget God and what He says about sin.

Humility, the opposite of pride, is seldom seen. Not often do we hear anyone say, "God is right! I am a sinner!" But those rare words are among the most important that man can speak.

Pray that the Holy Spirit will convict the hearts of your students. This lesson should tie together many of the Old Testament truths they have heard about the sacrifice and the coming Deliverer.

Who but God Himself could be both the almighty, sovereign, supreme Lord and the humble, obedient Lamb of God who takes away the sin of the world!

VISUALS:

- Chronological Picture No. 60, "John the Baptist Tells the People that Jesus is the Lamb of God"
- Chronological Map 3
- Visual showing the separation between God and man (illustrated in lesson)

Lesson 33: God Sent John to Teach and Baptize; John Baptized Jesus

ON TEACHING THIS LESSON:

These lessons are designed to **teach unbelievers.** You are carefully laying a scriptural foundation on which the Gospel will later be presented. If your class contains believers, teach with the goal of giving them an understanding of the basis for their faith and **with the goal of enabling them to teach the same material to unbelievers.**

DON'T COMPLICATE THE MESSAGE!

As you teach, keep in mind that this is a directed study—not an exhaustive survey of the Bible and not an unlimited group discussion. Keep your lesson on track and moving ahead by limiting and directing any discussion.

Carefully follow the outline. Emphasize the doctrinal themes.

LESSON FORMAT: The **center column** below contains the lesson material to be taught to the students. The **bold outline headings** are only for reference and need not be spoken, as they are incorporated into the outlined material that follows. The material in the **side columns** is for the teacher's own reference and is not intended to be included in the lesson.

TO BE TAUGHT TO THE STUDENTS
(Center Column Only)

LESSON OUTLINE:

REVIEW questions from Lesson 32.

A. Introduction

How do you get someone's attention?

One of the best ways is to mention something that is personally important to them.

That's exactly what God the Holy Spirit did through John the Baptist.

He sent John to announce the coming of the Saviour.

And He made sure that John gave a message that would command the people's attention.

B. John was God's messenger to Israel.

 Theme: **God communicates with man.**

John, who had been chosen by God to be the prophet to prepare the Jews to receive the Deliverer, was now an adult.

It was now God's time for John to begin teaching the people.

 Theme: **Man is a sinner. He needs God and is helpless to save himself.**

 READ Matthew 3:1,2.

POINT TO THE AREA OF JUDAEA ON MAP 3.

John taught the people that they must **repent**.

Lesson 33: God Sent John to Teach and Baptize; John Baptized Jesus

- John meant that the people must change their attitude toward God, about themselves, and about sin.
- He told them to change their minds in preparation for the coming of the promised Saviour.

Here are the things they needed to understand and agree with:

- That God is the only true God and that they should serve and worship Him completely.
- That they had sinned against God by disobeying His laws and that they were unable to make themselves acceptable to Him.
- That all sin is against God and that God hates sin and will always punish it by separating the sinner from Himself in the everlasting fire.

These are the same things which God wants every one of us to understand about ourselves and to agree with.

- Recall:

    Remember when we studied the Ten Commandments? How many of us have been able to keep these commandments perfectly?

    That's right! None of us have.

    What does God call it when we break a commandment?

    Yes, He calls it sin. How many times do you need to sin in order to break all of the commandments?

 Read James 2:10.

What if you only told one lie? Would that count as sin? Of course it would. All sin separates us from God.

And because God is holy and righteous, He hates our sin. The punishment for sin is death and eternal separation from God.

 Theme: God is faithful; He never changes.

John was the one who the prophet Isaiah said would precede the promised Deliverer.

 Read Isaiah 40:3.

 READ Matthew 3:3.

C. John was a poor man.

John was God's prophet, but this did not mean that John was rich.

- John was very poor.
- He just ate the things he found in the wilderness, and his clothing was that of a very poor man.

 READ Matthew 3:4.

- Consider:

    Some people say that if you put your faith in God, then He has to give you all the money and possessions you want. They say that wealth and possessions are a sign of God's blessing. They will even say that if you are not getting all the money and things you want, you probably don't have enough faith.

Lesson 33: God Sent John to Teach and Baptize; John Baptized Jesus

But God does not promise that a person will become rich if he believes Him and obeys His Word. Many of God's greatest prophets and people who believed were very poor. Later you will see that even Jesus, God's Son, was a very poor man when He was here in the world.

D. Many people believed God's message through John.

 Theme: Man must have faith in order to please God and be saved.

 READ Matthew 3:5,6.

POINT TO THE JORDAN RIVER ON MAP 3.

Many of the Jews believed God's Word which John told them and went to him to be baptized.

- When a person was baptized, it was a sign to everyone that the person agreed with God that he deserved death for his sins, but he was trusting in God to send the Deliverer to save him.

- Note:

Baptism implies identification. The word "baptize" comes from the Greek word "baptizo." One of the ways this word was used was to describe the process of dying cloth. When a piece of cloth was plunged into a vat of dye, it would take on the color of the dye.

Just as the cloth was identified with the dye so that it took on that color, so also the Jews identified with John's message of repentance. Their baptism was an outward act which illustrated inner repentance and belief in John's message. They were identifying with the truth God was giving them through John.

Baptism will not make us acceptable to God. [1] *Baptism on the outside will not wash away our sins before the eyes of God. Being baptized cannot pay God for our sins. The payment for sin is death. Baptism is just a sign to show to others that a person agrees with God's message and that he is trusting only in God to save him.*

E. John's words to the proud and unrepentant

 Theme: Man is a sinner. He needs God and is helpless to save himself.

 READ Matthew 3:7.

Most of the leaders of the temple were proud.

Let's take a look at these leaders and consider what the Bible tells us about their attitudes.

- **Scribes**

All that Moses and the prophets had written was now on scrolls. The men who copied the words of God onto these scrolls were called scribes. They were also called "lawyers" and "teachers of the Law," because they were the men who were supposed to know and be able to explain the real meaning of the words of God.

Many scribes were very proud because of their learning. They thought they were pleasing to God just because they could remember and explain the meaning of many parts of God's Word. They didn't

---

[1] Baptism for the believer is symbolic of completely identifying with Christ's death, burial, and resurrection. (See Romans 6:3,4.)

Many people believe that baptism saves or that baptism is necessary for salvation. At this stage of the teaching, avoid discussions on this topic. Stress the points in the lesson—that John's baptism was a baptism of repentance, but it did not save people from their sins. ☐

Lesson 33: God Sent John to Teach and Baptize; John Baptized Jesus

realize that it is more important to God that we believe His Word and obey it.

- **Pharisees**

  Some of the other leaders of the Jews were called Pharisees. The Pharisees tried to please God and be accepted by Him by obeying many different rules which they themselves had written. The Pharisees added to God's Word.

  They did not think that they were sinners like other people. They kept themselves separate from anyone who was not a Pharisee. They were proud and thought that they were good enough to be accepted by God because of all the things that they were doing.

- **Sadducees**

  There were other Jewish leaders who were called Sadducees. The Sadducees also went to the temple and claimed to worship God. However, they did not believe many things which God had written in His Word. The Sadducees took away from God's Word some of the truths which were in it.

  For example, the Sadducees did not believe in the existence of angels, nor did they believe in the resurrection of the dead. They rejected everything except the first five books, from Genesis to Deuteronomy.

  They were interested in keeping in good standing with the Roman government and making sure that they kept their own position as leaders of the Jews. They did not really trust in God from their hearts.

Many of these religious leaders would not admit that they were sinners.

- They thought that they were good enough for God to accept them.
- Because the Pharisees and Sadducees were so proud, John's words to them were very strong.
- Explain:

  When we talk about being proud of ourselves, we are talking about an attitude that says, "I think my way is best, no matter what God says."

  Pride means selfishness, self-centeredness, and boastfulness. Many people think that they are always right. Even when they know they are wrong, they hate to admit it. They want everyone to think they are great when they really are sinful, like everyone else.

  If we find ourselves disagreeing with what God says in His Word, or thinking, "This doesn't apply to me," we are probably thinking that way because we are proud.

God's words are very strong to those who are proud and resist Him and refuse to listen to His message.

Proverbs 3:34

James 4:6 says, *"...God resisteth the proud...."*

God sets Himself to fight against people who are proud and who will not agree with Him.

But He promises to help and deliver those who agree that they are sinners and who acknowledge that only He can help them.

 READ Matthew 3:8.

John told the Pharisees and the Sadducees that, if they really accepted God's thoughts about them, as spoken through John, then they must show it by their actions.

Teacher's Notes

Lesson 33: God Sent John to Teach and Baptize; John Baptized Jesus

Scripture Reference

 READ Matthew 3:9.

Many of the Jews were proud that Abraham was the father of their nation.

They thought that God would accept them because they were the descendants of Abraham.

- Compare:
- *Some people think that they are automatically accepted by God because their parents' faith.*
- *Or a person may think that because he was raised in a church and has gone through all of the church ceremonies, God will accept him.*

Suggested Visual:

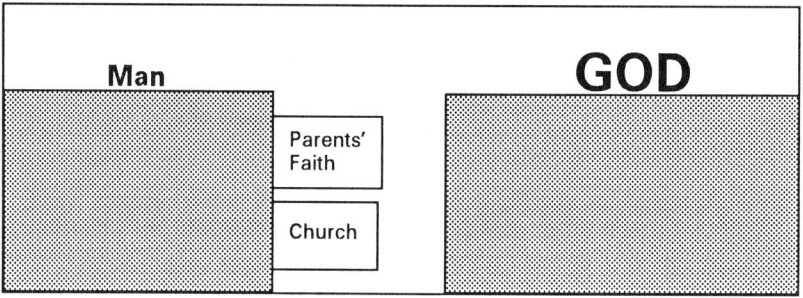

No one is accepted by God because of his parents or his church background. God judges everyone individually, not by his family, and not by his works nor his church affiliation.

John told the Pharisees and Sadducees not to be proud nor to trust in the fact that they were Abraham's children.

- God can do anything He wants to do.
- He could even make children for Abraham out of the stones if He wanted.
- He was telling them bluntly that in themselves they had nothing about which to boast.

F. What John said about the Deliverer

 Theme: Jesus Christ is God.

 READ John 1:24-27.

John was God's prophet sent to prepare the people to receive and trust in the Deliverer.

- John was just a man.
- But the coming Saviour was the Son of God.
- Explain:

  Back in John's time, men of high rank had servants to do all of their work. The important man would not put his own shoes on or take them off. That was the work of the servants. John said that he wasn't even worthy to be the servant who would take off the Deliverer's shoes. The Deliverer was the Son of God. He was the Creator of the world—the one who had given John his life.

Colossians 1:16

Lesson 33: God Sent John to Teach and Baptize; John Baptized Jesus

G. John baptized Jesus.

In Luke 3:23 the Bible says that Jesus was now about thirty years old.

 READ Matthew 3:13-16.

Although Jesus came to be baptized, it was not because He was a sinner and needed a Saviour like all the others who were baptized by John.

- Jesus was born perfect.
- He lived in full agreement with God.

Jesus came to be baptized because this was God's command to all Jews who accepted John as God's prophet.

- If Jesus wasn't baptized, people would think that He did not obey God's commands.
- Or people might have concluded that Jesus did not believe that John had been commanded by God to baptize.

The Holy Spirit came to be with Jesus to enable Him to do everything that God the Father had planned for Jesus to do.

Jesus was also Almighty God, but when He became a man, He chose to depend on God the Holy Spirit for power to do the work of the Deliverer here on earth.

H. What God said about Jesus

 Theme: Jesus Christ is God.

 READ Matthew 3:17.

God the Father called Jesus His Son.

- Jesus was a man.
- But He was also God the Son who had come down from Heaven.

 Theme: Jesus Christ is holy and righteous.

God was fully satisfied with Jesus.

- Jesus was the only man who did everything that pleased God.
- God knew that Jesus was absolutely without sin.
- Jesus was completely holy and righteous, perfect in God's sight.

I. Jesus, the Lamb of God

 Theme: Jesus Christ is the only Saviour.

 READ John 1:29.

When John saw Jesus, he said that Jesus was the Lamb who was given and sent by God.

Lesson 33: God Sent John to Teach and Baptize; John Baptized Jesus

Suggested Visual:

CHRONOLOGICAL PICTURE NO. 60, "JOHN THE BAPTIST TELLS THE PEOPLE THAT JESUS IS THE LAMB OF GOD"

Later, we will see exactly what John meant when he called Jesus the Lamb of God.

J. John knew that Jesus was the promised Deliverer.

 READ John 1:30-37.

John did not know who the Deliverer would be, but when he saw this sign from God, he was sure that Jesus was the Son of God, the Saviour of the world.

 Theme: Man must have faith in order to please God and be saved.

K. Conclusion

What about us?

Do we need signs like this one which God gave to John to prove that Jesus was the Son of God and the promised Deliverer?

- No, we do not need miraculous signs.
- We have the Word of God, the Bible.

Are we like the religious leaders who thought their good works and their religious background were enough to make them acceptable to God?

- Every one of us needs a Saviour.
- And God has given only one: Jesus Christ, the Lamb of God.
- He is the only Saviour for the whole world, and the only Saviour for you and for me.

QUESTIONS:

1. What did John tell the people? *John told the people to repent and be baptized.*

2. What does it mean to repent? *Repentance is a change of mind about ourselves, our sin, and God. It means we agree with God that we are sinners, that we have disobeyed His laws, and that we are unable to make ourselves acceptable to God.*

3. Whom was John getting the people ready to receive? *The promised Deliverer, the Saviour of men.*

Lesson 33: God Sent John to Teach and Baptize; John Baptized Jesus

4. Who were the scribes?

   a. *They were the Jewish religious leaders who made the hand-written copies of the Old Testament.*

   b. *They were very proud of their learning.*

   c. *They didn't realize that it is not only important to know God's Word but also to believe and obey it.*

5. Who were the Pharisees?

   a. *They were some of the religious leaders of the Jews.*

   b. *They tried to obey many rules of their own which they thought would make them acceptable to God.*

   c. *The Pharisees were proud and thought that God accepted them because of their own goodness.*

6. Who were the Sadducees?

   a. *They, like the Pharisees, were religious leaders of the Jews.*

   b. *They did not accept that all of the Old Testament was the Word of God.*

   c. *The Sadducees were more interested in retaining their acceptance with the Roman rulers and their position as rulers over the Jews than they were in pleasing God.*

7. Why didn't the priests and other religious leaders accept John's teaching?

   a. *They thought they were acceptable to God because of the things which they did.*

   b. *They thought God would accept them because they were the descendants of Abraham.*

8. Do we have to be baptized to be saved from the control and the punishment of our sin? *No, baptism can do nothing to deliver us from sin's control or make us acceptable to God. Baptism was the way God said that the people were to show they truly agreed with Him.*

9. Who was always helping Jesus in everything He did here on earth? *God the Spirit was guiding and helping Jesus in everything that He did.*

10. What did God the Father say when Jesus was baptized?

    a. *God the Father said He was completely pleased with Jesus.*

    b. *God the Father commanded the disciples to listen to Jesus.*

    c. *He called Jesus His Son.*

11. Did anyone else ever please God like Jesus? *No, no other human being ever pleased God in every way as Jesus did.*

Scripture Reference

 **LESSON 34**

Jesus, When Tempted, Resisted and Rebuked Satan

Teacher's Notes

OVERVIEW

Through the story of Jesus' temptation by Satan in the wilderness, this lesson presents Jesus as the sinless Son of God who fully obeyed God and resisted Satan. It also presents Jesus as God the Son who will one day cast Satan and his demons into the Lake of Fire.

Emphasized are the sovereignty of God and the deity of Jesus Christ.

LESSON PREPARATION

This section is for you, the teacher.

The passages in the Scripture Reference column are for your own study in preparing for this lesson. Since they may contain concepts that run ahead of the lesson, they are not to be taught at this point.

Note: If you have not taught previously from this series of lessons, please read carefully the note to teachers in the front of this book.

SCRIPTURE: Matthew 4:1-11

LESSON GOALS:

- To show that Jesus Christ as a man always obeyed God.
- To show that Satan is a liar and deceiver.
- To show that Jesus Christ is God; therefore, Jesus is stronger than Satan.

THIS LESSON SHOULD HELP THE STUDENTS:

- To see that Jesus Christ as a man faced Satan's temptation but never gave in. Jesus always obeyed God.
- To see the importance of knowing God's Word.

PERSPECTIVE FOR THE TEACHER:

Many people in our society today, having no understanding of saving faith, view what they call religion as a "crutch"—sort of a prop for people who can't stand alone. They do not realize that man cannot stand alone; all men need a Saviour.

The story of Jesus' encounter with Satan in the wilderness is a clear portrayal of our Lord and Saviour, the **only** one who has ever FULLY obeyed the Father and resisted the Devil.

This passage of Scripture is filled with insights for believers, but our purpose as we teach unbelievers is to show Christ's absolute supremacy over Satan. We want them to see, too, that Jesus as a man faced Satan's temptation; but, unlike us, Jesus always won the battle. This Saviour of ours is not a crutch; instead, He is the victor—the righteous and only Saviour of unrighteous, helpless sinners.

Yes, Jesus was gentle and meek; but He was also all-wise, all-powerful, holy Creator God. He will one day throw Satan and all who have followed him into the Lake of Fire.

Matthew 25:41
Revelation 1:18; 20:10

We want our students to know that Satan is a real enemy who holds men, women, and children captive. He is a liar and deceiver who twists the words of God. We also want our students to know that Jesus is the **only one** who can release them from Satan's power. We want them to see that Jesus defeated the enemy by correctly using God's Word!

We need to study this lesson prayerfully and ask God to enable us to teach in the power of His Spirit. What a wonderful Saviour we have!

Lesson 34: Jesus, When Tempted, Resisted and Rebuked Satan

Teacher's Notes

Scripture Reference

VISUALS:

- Chronological Picture No. 61, "Jesus in the Desert"
- You will use the visuals from Lessons 30 and 32, "ADAM—Sinner" and "GOD—Holy."
- Visuals showing the so-called forces of good and evil and the real struggle showing God's power over Satan (illustrated in lesson)

ON TEACHING THIS LESSON:

These lessons are designed to **teach unbelievers**. You are carefully laying a scriptural foundation on which the Gospel will later be presented. If your class contains believers, teach with the goal of giving them an understanding of the basis for their faith and **with the goal of enabling them to teach the same material to unbelievers.**

DON'T COMPLICATE THE MESSAGE!

As you teach, keep in mind that this is a directed study—not an exhaustive survey of the Bible and not an unlimited group discussion. Keep your lesson on track and moving ahead by limiting and directing any discussion.

Carefully follow the outline. Emphasize the doctrinal themes.

LESSON FORMAT: The **center column** below contains the lesson material to be taught to the students. The **bold outline headings** are only for reference and need not be spoken, as they are incorporated into the outlined material that follows. The material in the **side columns** is for the teacher's own reference and is not intended to be included in the lesson.

TO BE TAUGHT TO THE STUDENTS
(Center Column Only)

LESSON OUTLINE:

REVIEW questions from Lesson 33.

A. Introduction

When was the last time you failed to resist a temptation?[1]

Some temptations are quite obvious.

Others are much more subtle.

Sometimes we can be quite strong against temptation.

But what about when we're tired?

Did you know that, as a man, Jesus faced temptation, too?

B. Satan tempted Jesus.

> **Theme:** Satan fights against God and His will. Satan is a liar and a deceiver. He hates man.

[1] This is not intended to evoke a discussion but to make the students think. ☐

432

Lesson 34: Jesus, When Tempted, Resisted and Rebuked Satan

Scripture Reference

Teacher's Notes

 READ Matthew 4:1.

Ezekiel 28:15,17
Isaiah 14:13,14
John 8:44

God created Lucifer perfect.
- But Lucifer (now known as Satan) made a choice to rebel against God in the very beginning.
- Since then, Satan, also known as the Devil, has been continually evil.

Satan tempted Adam to rebel against God.

Now he was trying to tempt Jesus to rebel against God.

Suggested Visual:

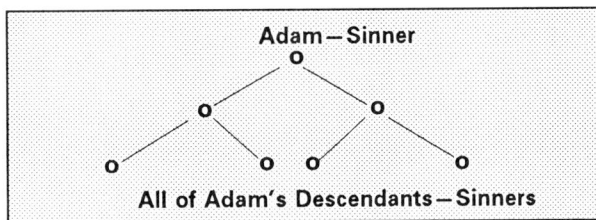

Satan wanted to bring Jesus under his control so Jesus would not be able to be our Deliverer.

C. The first temptation

 Theme: Jesus Christ is man.

 READ Matthew 4:2.

Although Jesus is God, He was also a real man.

He became hungry just as we do.

Suggested Visual:

CHRONOLOGICAL PICTURE NO. 61, "JESUS IN THE DESERT"

 Theme: Satan fights against God and His will. Satan is a liar and a deceiver. He hates man.

 Theme: Jesus Christ is God.

 Theme: Jesus Christ is holy and righteous.

433

Teacher's Notes

Lesson 34: Jesus, When Tempted, Resisted and Rebuked Satan

Scripture Reference

 READ Matthew 4:3.

Satan was trying to make Jesus prove that He was the Son of God.
- Satan asked Jesus to do something which God the Father had not told Him to do.
- Jesus came down to earth from Heaven to do only what His Father wanted Him to do.

Jesus was the Son of God.
- He could have turned stones into bread, but Jesus would not obey Satan.
- He would not do anything that Satan told Him to do.

Luke 22:42
John 8:28,29
Hebrews 10:7

 Theme: Man is a sinner. He needs God and is helpless to save himself.

 READ Matthew 4:4.

We need food to keep our bodies alive, but God says that there is something much more important than food.

We need God's Word to show us the truth and the way to everlasting life.
- Explain:

  Our bodies need food; obviously, without it we will die. But what benefit will it be if we have healthy bodies but die without God and suffer everlasting punishment? We not only need to eat food so our bodies will live, but we also need to hear and believe God's Word so that we will be able to live forever with God.

D. **The second temptation**

 Theme: Satan fights against God and His will. Satan is a liar and a deceiver. He hates man.

 READ Matthew 4:5,6.

Satan was quoting portions of Psalm 91:11,12.
- Satan knows the words of God in the Bible, but he uses them in the wrong way.
- Satan twists God's words in order to trick people.
- Recall:

  Remember how he tricked Eve? Satan asked her, "Did God say that you aren't allowed to eat any of the fruit from the trees in the garden?"

Satan knew what God had really said to Adam, but he changed it just a little.

Satan is a liar and a deceiver.
- Consider:

  Beware: Satan still uses this approach. He tries to make people think they should demand that God perform miracles to prove Himself to them. Satan tries to draw their attention to the spectacular and the miraculous and at the same time tries to keep them from giving attention to what God really says in His Word.

 Theme: God is faithful; He never changes.

Genesis 3:1

John 8:44

434

Lesson 34: Jesus, When Tempted, Resisted and Rebuked Satan

Satan told Jesus to throw Himself down from the temple to test God who had promised to take care of His Son.

- Jesus did not have to test His Father to see if He would take care of Him.

 READ Matthew 4:7.

- God the Father had promised to take care of His Son, so Jesus simply trusted His Father's words.

 Theme: Man must have faith in order to please God and be saved.

- Consider:

Down through the ages, God has proven Himself completely faithful. We, too, can trust Him completely. We should depend on the Lord to do everything that He has written in the Bible.

E. The third temptation

 Theme: Satan fights against God and His will. Satan is a liar and a deceiver. He hates man.

 READ Matthew 4:8,9.

John 12:31

II Corinthians 4:4

Ephesians 2:2

Satan could offer Jesus control over the people in this world because, when Adam rebelled against God and followed Satan, Satan became the god of this world.

Satan had gained influence over the minds of the people of the world so he could lead them to do the evil things he had planned.

 READ Matthew 4:10.

Satan tried to get Jesus to worship him.

- Recall:

Isaiah 14:13,14

In the beginning, Satan tried to take God's position as the ruler of the whole universe. Satan failed, but many angels followed him. Then Satan took control of the human race so that they would worship and serve him. Satan knew that Jesus was God's Son, so Satan tried to take God's place by asking Jesus to worship him.

Matthew 12:30a

Ephesians 2:1-3

All who have not been delivered by God from Satan's control are serving Satan instead of God.

Jesus defeated Satan by telling him what God really says in the Bible.

Jesus did not change God's words as Satan did.

 Theme: Jesus Christ is holy and righteous.

Jesus did not obey Satan as Adam did in the garden of Eden.
Jesus knew, loved, and obeyed God, His Father.

John 8:29

F. Jesus is God

 Theme: Jesus Christ is God.

435

Teacher's Notes

Lesson 34: Jesus, When Tempted, Resisted and Rebuked Satan

Scripture Reference

 Theme: God is supreme and sovereign.

Furthermore, Jesus is far greater than Satan: Jesus is also God.

- In the beginning, He created Satan as Lucifer, an important and beautiful angel who should have served God.
- Jesus will one day throw Satan into the Lake of Fire which God prepared for him and all his followers.
- Consider:

  You may have seen movies or videos that present the struggle between the so-called forces of good and evil.

  Often this struggle is presented as if there were two equal forces battling against one another—sort of a "horizontal" battle.

Suggested Visual:

Man's idea of the battle

But God's Word tells us that God is supreme; He is the sovereign Creator. Jesus is God the Son—the supreme owner and Creator of all things. In His body of flesh, He suffered, just like we do. But He never sinned.

Satan, that rebellious, created spirit being, could not make Jesus sin. Satan is a strong enemy, but he is no match for Almighty God. The battle is not at all like men show it. God is not a "force"; He is a Spirit. When Jesus came, He was God in a human body. God is totally superior to Satan in every way.

Suggested Visual:

The truth from God's Word

G. Satan left Jesus for a short time.

 Theme: Satan fights against God and His will. Satan is a liar and a deceiver. He hates man.

 Theme: Jesus Christ is holy and righteous.

 READ Matthew 4:11.

Satan knew he was defeated, so he left Jesus for a while.

- But Satan came back many, many times and tried in every way he could to get Jesus to disobey God.
- He tempted Jesus with every temptation people have ever faced.

Luke 12:4,5

Colossians 1:16

Revelation 1:18

Revelation 20:10

Hebrews 4:15

Lesson 34: Jesus, When Tempted, Resisted and Rebuked Satan

Scripture Reference

John 8:29

But Jesus did not do anything Satan said to do.
Jesus always did everything that pleased God, His Father.
God sent angels to take care of Jesus after Satan had left Him.

H. Conclusion

Jesus is the only one who has ever fully obeyed God and resisted the Devil.

Jesus Christ was fully man; He is also God.

He is the **only** one who can deliver us from sin, Satan, and death.

Teacher's Notes

QUESTIONS:

1. Why did Satan tempt Jesus?

    a. *Because Satan wanted Jesus to sin so that Jesus wouldn't be able to deliver us.*

    b. *Because Satan wanted Jesus to be under his control.*

    c. *Because Satan wants to take the position of God.*

2. Why didn't Jesus turn the stones into bread even though He was hungry? *Because His Father didn't tell Him to. Jesus would only do whatever His Father commanded Him to do.*

3. What is more important than food? *Knowing and believing what God says in the Bible.*

4. Does Satan know and use God's Word? *Yes, Satan knows God's words, but he twists them around to suit his own purposes.*

5. Why could Satan offer Jesus the position of ruler over all people in every part of the earth? *Because, when Adam obeyed Satan, he became ruler over Adam and all of the human race.*

6. How did Jesus fight against Satan? *Jesus used the words of God, written in the Old Testament.*

7. Who is greater, Jesus or Satan? *Jesus is greater. He created Lucifer, who is now called Satan, and will one day throw Satan into the everlasting fire.*

Scripture Reference

Teacher's Notes

Jesus Began His Ministry

OVERVIEW

This lesson presents Jesus Christ as God come to earth— with authority to speak and interpret God's Word, with power to deliver from Satan and sin and death and to heal with love and compassion.

LESSON PREPARATION
This section is for you, the teacher.

The passages in the Scripture Reference column are for your own study in preparing for this lesson. Since they may contain concepts that run ahead of the lesson, they are not to be taught at this point.

Note: If you have not taught previously from this series of lessons, please read carefully the note to teachers in the front of this book.

Isaiah 42:1-9; 61:1

SCRIPTURE: Mark 1:14-28,34-42

LESSON GOALS:

- To show that the only way to be saved is to trust God to save us through Jesus Christ, the Deliverer.
- To show that Jesus Christ is God.

THIS LESSON SHOULD HELP THE STUDENTS:

- To realize that only through Jesus Christ can they be saved.
- To see, by the things Jesus did and by what the Bible says, that Jesus Christ is God.

PERSPECTIVE FOR THE TEACHER:

Today's society cries out continually for something new, something better, a fresh approach. Advertisements tell us that a product is "new and improved," a "fresh idea," etc. But instead of remaining fresh, these things quickly become old and stale and worn out. Our human nature is never satisfied.

Now let's take a look at Jesus Christ, *"...the same yesterday, and today, and forever"* (Hebrews 13:8)!

Can you imagine the newness, improvement, and freshness He offered to the people of Israel? Enemies had plundered and murdered or carried off their ancestors into exile. Now as Jews living back in the "promised land" of Israel, the people were under a difficult system of Roman rulership. They were also suffering under the burden of their own Jewish law, which had been expanded to include hundreds of commands written by men, not God. Mercy had little place in their religious thinking. Satan had blinded the minds of their leaders, and few of the people had their hope set on God to deliver them.

Then John announced the coming of their Messiah. What a stir that must have brought! Surely, many were anticipating an earthly king who would deliver them from Roman rule. But then came Jesus!

A king? This man certainly didn't look like the king they were expecting. He was a poor man—a carpenter's son, they thought.

But when He began to speak, they heard the true law of God spoken with authority! None of their religious leaders could compare with this young man who spoke with power and love. Even the demons fled before Him! Jesus healed the sick and touched the untouchable. Truth, healing, and compassion flowed from this remarkable Messiah who was not just a king, but the King of kings Himself!

New, better, fresh—Jesus was and is! Our society, like Israel, is desperately sick and needy. We, like they, have had the truth available to us for a long time.

Lesson 35: Jesus Began His Ministry

When the Israelites rejected Christ, God gave the Gospel to the Gentiles. Today, all around the world, countless thousands who had never heard God's Word are eagerly receiving the Gospel—while many here who have Bibles let them collect dust.

The message of Jesus Christ is new life to all who believe. Jesus says that *"...whosoever drinketh of the water that I shall give him shall never thirst; but the water that I shall give him shall be in him a well of water springing up into everlasting life"* (John 4:14). What could be fresher! So as we teach, may we teach this message for what it is: the greatest, most wonderful, freshest news in the whole universe!

May we never, never teach the story of Jesus Christ as "a bunch of old stories we've heard a lot of times before." But may we teach it as it is: the Word of God, *"...quick [living], and powerful, and sharper than any twoedged sword, piercing even to the diving asunder of soul and spirit ...[discerning] the thoughts and intents of the heart"* (Hebrews 4:12).

VISUALS:

- Chronological Picture No. 62, "Jesus Teaching in the Synagogue"
- Chronological Map 3

ON TEACHING THIS LESSON:

These lessons are designed to **teach unbelievers.** You are carefully laying a scriptural foundation on which the Gospel will later be presented. If your class contains believers, teach with the goal of giving them an understanding of the basis for their faith and **with the goal of enabling them to teach the same material to unbelievers.**

DON'T COMPLICATE THE MESSAGE!

As you teach, keep in mind that this is a directed study—not an exhaustive survey of the Bible and not an unlimited group discussion. Keep your lesson on track and moving ahead by limiting and directing any discussion.

Carefully follow the outline. Emphasize the doctrinal themes.

LESSON FORMAT: The **center column** below contains the lesson material to be taught to the students. The **bold outline headings** are only for reference and need not be spoken, as they are incorporated into the outlined material that follows. The material in the **side columns** is for the teacher's own reference and is not intended to be included in the lesson.

TO BE TAUGHT TO THE STUDENTS
(Center Column Only)

LESSON OUTLINE:

REVIEW questions from Lesson 34.

A. Introduction

If John the Baptist were to come to our area today and preach a message of repentance, do you think anyone would listen?

Lesson 35: Jesus Began His Ministry

- Would you and I listen?
- Who needs repentance?[1]

[1] Again, these questions are not to begin a discussion but to cause your students to think.

Do not use these questions with a small group—individuals may feel pressured to answer. ☐

B. John the Baptist

John faithfully taught God's message to prepare the people to trust in Jesus the Deliverer.

Some of the people changed their minds about themselves and their sin.

- They knew that they needed a Saviour to save them from the punishment for their sins.
- They were looking and waiting for the Deliverer to begin His work.

Others, like the Pharisees, trusted in themselves and thought that they were good enough for God.

- Compare:

  We might compare them with people today who say they are religious and even come to church, but who are trusting in their own good works to save them from everlasting punishment. They really don't believe God when He says in His Word that there is nothing we can do to make ourselves acceptable to Him.

Matthew 14:1-12
Mark 6:14-29

King Herod, who was living a very sinful life, did not like some of the things which John said.

So Herod put John in prison and finally killed him.

C. Jesus' message

 Theme: God communicates with man.

 Theme: Man must have faith in order to please God and be saved.

 READ Mark 1:14,15.

Before he was killed, John had finished his work of preparing the way for the Lord.

It was now time for Jesus to begin teaching.

As we mentioned, Jesus was now about thirty years old.

He began to teach the people by commanding them

- To change their attitude
- To agree with God that they were helpless sinners
- To believe the good news that He had come to tell them.

If we don't believe God, we cannot please Him, and we will not be accepted by Him.

Hebrews 11:6 says that *"without faith it is impossible to please him."*

- Recall:

  Why was Abel accepted by God? Was it because Abel wasn't a sinner? No, it was because Abel believed God's Word and trusted in Him.

  When the Lord told Noah to build the ark because God was going to destroy the earth, Noah believed God, and the Lord saved him and his family.

441

Teacher's Notes

Lesson 35: Jesus Began His Ministry

Scripture Reference

God told Abraham to leave his own country and to go to a country that the Lord promised to show him. Abraham believed the Lord, and the Lord led him to the land of Canaan.

Moses trusted in the Lord and told the Israelites to put the blood on the doorposts of their houses. The Lord protected them from the angel of death.

Joshua and Caleb believed that God would give the land of Canaan to them even though there were giants in the land. They were the only two of that generation of Israelites who entered the promised land.

If you want to be accepted by God, you must believe Him and trust in what He has told us in the Bible.

 Theme: God is loving, merciful, and gracious.

The word "Gospel" means "good news."

Jesus told the people that they must agree with God and believe the Good News, because God's rule on earth was soon to begin.

- Satan had become the ruler of this world when Adam disobeyed God and followed Satan.

John 12:31

II Corinthians 4:4

Ephesians 2:2

- Because God is loving, merciful, and gracious to sinners, He sent Jesus into the world to overcome Satan and to deliver people from Satan's control.

- All of us, when we were born into this world, were born under the control of Satan (in Satan's kingdom).

- Jesus said that the only way for anyone to escape Satan's control is to agree with God and believe His Good News.

This is God's good news to each one of us: by believing God and trusting in the Saviour, we can escape Satan's control and come into friendship and oneness with God.

D. Jesus called men to assist Him in His work.

 READ Mark 1:16-20.

Jesus began to call men to follow Him.

- He was going to teach them.

- He was going to send them out to tell others the message of God's coming rule on the earth.

- When He said He would make them fishers of men, Jesus was talking about teaching them to bring men to God by telling them the Good News!

E. Jesus taught with authority.

 READ Mark 1:21.

442

Lesson 35: Jesus Began His Ministry

Suggested Graphic:

CHRONOLOGICAL PICTURE NO. 62, "JESUS TEACHING IN THE SYNAGOGUE"

POINT TO CAPERNAUM ON MAP 3.

As we mentioned in an earlier lesson, the Jews met in places called synagogues in towns throughout Israel and even in surrounding countries.

- There in the synagogues, the writings of Moses and the prophets were read and taught to the people.
- Jews living outside of Jerusalem went to the temple there only for important feasts, as God had instructed them through Moses.

 Theme: **Jesus Christ is God.**

 Theme: **God communicates with man.**

 READ Mark 1:22.

The people who heard Jesus speak were surprised by the authoritative way in which Jesus explained the meaning of God's Word.

Jesus taught very differently from the way the scribes taught.

- The scribes were the men who wrote copies of the Old Testament.
- They were also the teachers of God's Word.
- But the majority of them did not really have faith in God and believe His Word.
- They were trusting instead in their own good works and their own supposed knowledge of His Word to save them.
- They knew a lot about God's Word, but they didn't really know God.
- And because they were relying on their own knowledge and didn't really know God, they did not clearly understand His Word; therefore, they could only tell the people what they thought God's Word meant.

But Jesus is God.

- He knew His Father, and He clearly understood God's Word.
- When Jesus taught, He told the people exactly what God was saying to them through the writings of Moses and the prophets.

F. Jesus cast out evil spirits.

Theme: **Satan fights against God and His will. Satan is a liar and a deceiver. He hates man.**

Teacher's Notes

Lesson 35: Jesus Began His Ministry

Scripture Reference

 READ Mark 1:23,24.

Demons are angels who long ago rebelled against God and followed Satan.
- They like to live in and control people who are the children of Satan.

Luke 11:24-26

 Theme: Jesus Christ is God.

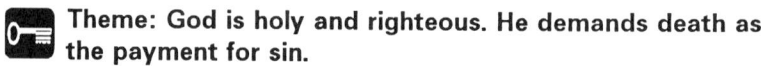 **Theme: God is holy and righteous. He demands death as the payment for sin.**

- Satan and the demons know that Jesus is God, their Creator.
- They also know that He is holy.
- They know He is perfect and hates all sin.
- This demon knew that someday he would be thrown into the Lake of Fire, and he knew that Jesus had the power to throw him into the fire right then!

Colossians 1:16
Luke 8:28
Revelation 1:18; 20:10

 READ Mark 1:25,26.

Jesus commanded the demon to be quiet.
- He did not want the demons to be the ones to tell people about Him.
- Satan is a liar; Jesus came to speak the truth.
- Jesus Himself would tell the people God's truth and show them His power by the miracles He did.

 READ Mark 1:27,28.

Again, the people were seeing that Jesus had tremendous power and authority.

G. Jesus healed many sick people, and He cast out demons.

 Theme: Jesus Christ is God.

 Theme: God is supreme and sovereign.

 Theme: God is all-powerful.

 READ Mark 1:34-39.

Because Jesus is God, all things are under His power.
God is the greatest power in Heaven and on earth.

 Theme: God is loving, merciful, and gracious.

Jesus felt compassion for these sick and demon-possessed people.
He knew that all of these sad things are in the world because of man's sin and the rule of Satan.
- Consider:

   The Lord is also concerned for you and for me. He has not changed. He is still the same today. He knows whether or not we are still

Lesson 35: Jesus Began His Ministry

under the power of death. The Lord desires to rescue everyone from Satan's control.

H. Jesus healed a leper.

 Theme: Man must have faith in order to please God and be saved.

 READ Mark 1:40.

- Explain:

  The word used in the Bible for leprosy includes several skin diseases. Some of these diseases would cause death of the nerves in the body extremeties, resulting in infection that would decay the flesh, causing the sick person to lose parts of his body, such as fingers, hands, or even part of his face. Back during that time, there wasn't any medicine to heal leprosy.

This man knew he couldn't heal himself, and he knew that men couldn't help him.

But Jesus was different.

- Yes, Jesus was a man, but He had the power of God, because He was God!
- The man who had leprosy realized that Jesus could help him even though no one else could.

He did the only thing he could do.

He came to Jesus asking for His mercy and His help.

 Theme: Man is a sinner. He needs God and is helpless to save himself.

- Compare:

  The sickness of leprosy is like the sin in our lives. There is no way that we can rid ourselves of sin. God hates sin. Only Jesus, the Saviour, can help us. That is why He came into the world.

  And that is why we are studying God's message: so each one of us will understand clearly what Jesus did to deliver us from Satan, sin, and death.

 Theme: Jesus Christ is God.

 Theme: God is all-powerful.

 READ Mark 1:41,42.

 Theme: God is loving, merciful, and gracious.

Lepers were outcasts in Bible times, and no one would even come near them.

But Jesus **touched** this man **because He loved him**.

- Jesus reached out His hand, touched the man and spoke, and the leprosy was gone.
- He could have merely spoken and the man would have been healed.

- No one else would dare to touch a leper.
- But Jesus did, because He wanted to show God's great love for this man.

I. Conclusion

We should all be able to identify with that leper:

- Because of our sins, we are "unclean" in the eyes of God.
- There is nothing we can do by ourselves to remove the guilt and penalty for sin.
- No one else can really help us.
- Sadly, those people who are aware of our sinfulness may not want to help us; they may have rejected us, just like the leper was rejected.
- We may feel that if anyone knew what we are really like inside they would never want to associate with us, either.
- We may even think that God looks at us that way, too.

But God knows every horrible detail of our lives and still wants to be our Saviour.

He not only **cares** and is **willing** to reach out to us, but He alone has the **power to save us**.

QUESTIONS:

1. Why didn't the Pharisees and other religious leaders accept John's teaching? *Because they were proud and thought that they were good enough for God to accept them.*

2. What did Jesus tell the people that they must do? *Jesus said that they must change their attitude, agreeing with God that they were helpless sinners, and believe the Good News which Jesus had come to tell them.*

3. What is the only way a person can please God? *By believing His Word.*

4. What was the occupation of some of the men whom Jesus called to follow Him? *Some of them were fishermen.*

5. What was the difference between the way Jesus taught and the way the scribes taught? *Jesus taught as one who was sure of what God meant in His Word. But the scribes just gave their opinion as to what they thought God meant or what others said God meant.*

6. What were demons originally? *They were the angels of God until they followed Satan in rebellion against God.*

7. Why were the demons afraid of Jesus? *They knew that He was their Creator and their judge and that, one day, He would throw them into the everlasting fire to be punished.*

8. How does leprosy remind you of sin? *Just as no ordinary person was able to cure leprosy, so no one but God can deliver us from the power of sin.*

| Scripture Reference | | Teacher's Notes |

LESSON 36

You Must Be Born Again

OVERVIEW

This lesson presents Jesus' conversation with Nicodemus concerning the new birth. Emphasis is on the work of the Holy Spirit through the Word of God.

Jesus is presented as the only way for men to be saved. He is the way of salvation for all men everywhere.

LESSON PREPARATION

This section is for you, the teacher.

The passages in the Scripture Reference column are for your own study in preparing for this lesson. Since they may contain concepts that run ahead of the lesson, they are not to be taught at this point.

Note: If you have not taught previously from this series of lessons, please read carefully the note to teachers in the front of this book.

SCRIPTURE: John 3:1-7,14-20

LESSON GOALS:

- To show that in order to be saved, a person must be born again.

THIS LESSON SHOULD HELP THE STUDENTS:

- To realize that there is nothing they can do to save themselves; they must be born again, as Jesus said.

PERSPECTIVE FOR THE TEACHER:

We can identify with Nicodemus. He couldn't understand Jesus Christ in light of what he had learned in the society of his day, even though he was a religious person. Neither can we understand in our own frame of thinking, no matter how "religious" we might be.

Don't get tangled in trying to explain the message of John 3. State it with simplicity, just as our Lord gave it to us. Quite possibly, God has used this beautiful message more than any other in His Word to reach and transform hopeless sinners into His own dear children.

Don't expect instant results, but do expect the Word to do God's work! Nicodemus came because the Holy Spirit drew him to our wonderful Saviour. The Holy Spirit is still at work; be ready with a clear, gracious answer when a student asks you how he or she can be saved!

VISUALS:

- Chronological Picture No. 37, "The Serpent on the Pole"
- Chronological Picture No. 63, "Nicodemus' Night Visit"
- The graphic, "Two Categories of People" (illustrated in the lesson), may be made as a small poster; or you may want to just write on a board as you teach.

Teacher's Notes

Lesson 36: You Must Be Born Again

Scripture Reference

ON TEACHING THIS LESSON:

These lessons are designed to **teach unbelievers.** You are carefully laying a scriptural foundation on which the Gospel will later be presented. If your class contains believers, teach with the goal of giving them an understanding of the basis for their faith and **with the goal of enabling them to teach the same material to unbelievers.**

DON'T COMPLICATE THE MESSAGE!

As you teach, keep in mind that this is a directed study—not an exhaustive survey of the Bible and not an unlimited group discussion. Keep your lesson on track and moving ahead by limiting and directing any discussion.

Carefully follow the outline. Emphasize the doctrinal themes.

LESSON FORMAT: The **center column** below contains the lesson material to be taught to the students. The **bold outline headings** are only for reference and need not be spoken, as they are incorporated into the outlined material that follows. The material in the **side columns** is for the teacher's own reference and is not intended to be included in the lesson.

TO BE TAUGHT TO THE STUDENTS
(Center Column Only)

LESSON OUTLINE:

REVIEW questions from Lesson 35.

A. Introduction

How many times have you made New Year's resolutions—and failed to keep them?

How many times have you tried to make a fresh start in your life—and failed?

Are you still trying—and failing?

Do you know that God doesn't expect you to change your own life?

As a matter of fact, He says you **can't** do it yourself.[1]

[1] These first questions would not be appropriate for a very small group, as people would feel pressured to answer. ☐

We're about to read one of the best known and most loved passages of Scripture.

Like all of the Bible, this was given by God so that we might learn.

II Timothy 3:16

This message is for you, and it is for me and for everyone in the whole world.

Please listen carefully.

B. Nicodemus came to Jesus.

 READ John 3:1,2.

Suggested Visual:

CHRONOLOGICAL PICTURE NO. 63, "NICODEMUS' NIGHT VISIT"

Nicodemus was sure that Jesus had been sent by God.

He knew that the great miracles which Jesus had done could only be accomplished by the power of God.

- Most of the other Pharisees hated Jesus and were saying that He did His miracles by the power of Satan.
- Nicodemus probably came to speak to Jesus at night so that the other Jewish leaders would not see him.

C. The new birth

 Theme: Man is a sinner. He needs God and is helpless to save himself.

 READ John 3:3.

The Jews, and especially the Pharisees, were very proud that they were the descendants of Abraham.

- They thought that they were in God's family because they were Abraham's children.
- The Pharisees did not realize that every person born into this world has been born under Satan's rule (into Satan's kingdom) and is therefore Satan's child.
- Recall:

When God created Adam and Eve, He made them in His own image. God gave them minds so they could know and understand Him. God made them so they could love Him. God also gave them the ability to obey His will, to do what He wanted them to do. But, when Adam and Eve sinned, they died to God. They were separated from Him. They were no longer in oneness (in fellowship) with God. They were no longer His friends as they were when He created them.

They still had minds, but, because of their sin, they were unable to know God and understand His words. Neither were they able to love or obey Him. Therefore, they were no longer able to please God. Their minds, hearts, and wills were now under the control of Satan.

Cain and Abel, and all people born into the world since that time, have been born unable to know, understand, love, or obey God. No person born into this world can please God. Every person in every place, regardless of nationality, color, or language, has been born under Satan's authority.

Jesus told Nicodemus that the only way a person can escape Satan's power and rule and be able to know, love, and obey God is to be born again.

Lesson 36: You Must Be Born Again

Teacher's Notes

Scripture Reference

- Jesus was telling Nicodemus that he must receive a new mind and heart which would be able to know and understand God, as Adam and Eve could when God created them.
- We, too, must be made new so that we can love and obey God.
- Note:

  Sometimes people use the words "born again" to describe things other than what Jesus was telling Nicodemus. **2**

  But when we talk about being born again, we are referring to what God tells us in the Bible.

How is it possible for a person to be born again?

How can someone be changed so that he can be under the rule of God and no longer under the rule of Satan?

Can we change ourselves?

No, we cannot.

 Theme: God is all-powerful.

Was it something you did that caused you to be born into this world under Satan's authority?

No, of course not; Adam sinned, and everyone who was born after Adam inherited his sin.

- We didn't do anything to cause ourselves to be born under Satan's control.
- Neither can we do anything to escape Satan and change our lives so we will be pleasing to God.
- Our good works can't bring us out of Satan's kingdom and into God's kingdom.
- When we were born into this world, we were all born separated from, or dead to, God.
- It is impossible for us to bring ourselves back into oneness with God.

Only God can do that.

- He is almighty.
- Nothing is impossible to Him.
- By His power, He causes people to be born again — a new birth into God's family.

 READ John 3:4.

Nicodemus was very surprised when Jesus said that a person must be born again before he can understand or come under the rule of God (enter God's kingdom).

Until he talked with Jesus, Nicodemus probably felt that his first birth was quite sufficient to put him in a right relationship with God.

- He was a descendant of Abraham.
- He was a Pharisee.
- He was a ruler of the Jews.

Nicodemus thought that Jesus meant that people's bodies have to be born a second time as a baby.

 Theme: God communicates with man.

 Theme: Man must have faith in order to please God and be saved.

2Example: A person may say, "I went jogging this morning, and I feel like I've been born again." □

John 1:13
I Peter 1:23
I John 2:29; 3:9; 4:7; 5:1,4,18

450

Lesson 36: You Must Be Born Again

Scripture Reference

Ephesians 5:26
John 15:3
Psalm 119:9

Teacher's Notes

 READ John 3:5.

The water of which Jesus spoke is not baptism.³

- Baptism cannot make us children of God nor can it wash away our sin.

 Read I Peter 1:23.

- When Jesus said that every person who comes under God's rule must first be born by water, Jesus meant that the only way a person can receive a new mind, be able to love and obey God, and be given new life is by hearing, understanding, and believing the Word of God.
- They will be changed by the Holy Spirit so that they can
    Know God
    Understand His words
    Be able to love Him
    Be able to live under His rule or authority
    And enter the kingdom of God.

Theme: Man can come to God only according to God's will and plan.

 READ John 3:6,7.

Jesus told Nicodemus not to be surprised that he must be born again. God says that there are only two categories of people in the world as far as He is concerned—

- Not rich and poor
- Not good and bad
- Not young and old.

Here are the two categories:

Suggested Visual:

TWO CATEGORIES OF PEOPLE:	
BORN ONCE	**BORN TWICE**
Those who have been born only once and are still under Satan's rule	Those who have been born a second time and are now under God's rule

- All those born only once are in Satan's family.
- All those who have been born a second time are in God's family.

D. Jesus must be lifted up.

 Theme: Jesus Christ is the only Saviour.

Nicodemus still could not understand how he could be born into God's family.

 READ John 3:14,15.

Jesus explained to Nicodemus by reminding him of what happened to his Jewish forefathers in the wilderness.

³Some students may think or have been previously taught that it is baptism that saves a person, or that faith coupled with baptism saves a person. Some passages in Scripture, taken out of the context of the rest of the Word, could be interpreted that way.

Encourage your students to read the Word, especially the verses used in this lesson and the ones listed in the side column opposite this note. Remember that an unsaved person cannot understand the Word, but God's Spirit will use the Word to bring conviction and salvation.

Do not argue with them, but let the Word do its work. They may not immediately agree with what they are hearing and reading, but just go on with the lesson, trusting the Holy Spirit to work in hearts. ☐

Teacher's Notes

Lesson 36: You Must Be Born Again

Scripture Reference

Suggested Visual:

CHRONOLOGICAL PICTURE NO. 37, "THE SERPENT ON THE POLE"

- Recall:

  The Israelites had sinned against God, so God sent poisonous snakes to bite them, and they began to die. When they repented, that is, changed their attitude and admitted their sin, God told Moses to make a brass snake and put it on a pole. God promised that whoever was bitten and looked at the brass snake would be healed.

  Numbers 21:8,9

- Compare:

  Nicodemus had been trying to observe God's laws. He hadn't realized that, in his own efforts, he was totally unacceptable to God. He needed to do what the Israelites had done and simply put his faith in the Lord.

- Compare:

  Our situation, too, is like that of the Israelites in the wilderness. Satan, who is called the old serpent, guided Adam away from God. When Adam sinned against God, he died. Now all of Adam's descendants are separated from God and are dying because they are sinners. The payment for sin is death. The Israelites could not save themselves from the snakes, and we cannot save ourselves from death. God delivered the Israelites, and only God can deliver us.

  Revelation 12:9; 20:2
  Romans 5:12; 6:23

Jesus said there is only one way we can be delivered from Satan, sin, and death and be born again into God's family.

  John 14:6

- Jesus said that He must be lifted up, just as the brass snake was in the wilderness, so that whoever trusts in Him will be born into the family of God and come once again under His authority.

  John 12:32,33

- All those who put their trust in Jesus will be given eternal life by God.

 Theme: God is loving, merciful, and gracious.

 READ John 3:16.

Jesus said, "For God so loved the world, that he gave his only begotten Son...."

Because God doesn't want any human being to go with Satan to everlasting destruction, God sent Jesus, the Saviour, into the world.

 Theme: Jesus Christ is God.

Whom did God give to be the Saviour?

- "his only begotten Son"

- Jesus was God's only Son.

- There is none other like Him.

452

Lesson 36: You Must Be Born Again

 Theme: Man must have faith in order to please God and be saved.

What did Jesus say a sinner has to do to be delivered from Satan's power?
"that whosoever believeth in him"

- When a man, woman, or child believes God's words and trusts in Jesus as his Saviour, God gives that person a new life.
- That person will no longer be Satan's child or under his rule.
- That person will become a child of God.
- That is why Jesus told people to change their minds and believe God's good news.

E. The way of life and death

 Theme: God is loving, merciful, and gracious.

Jesus said that all who believe on Him *"should not perish."*

Those who trust in the Saviour whom God sent will not go to everlasting punishment for their sins.

 Theme: God is faithful; He never changes.

What will all who believe on Jesus as their Saviour receive?
They will *"have everlasting life."*

 READ John 3:17.

This is God's promise.

- Can God be trusted?
- Yes! We have read how He has always done exactly what He has promised.
- We've read through thousands of years of God's good promises, and not one of them has failed.

 Theme: Jesus Christ is the only Saviour.

 READ John 3:18.

I John 5:10-13

No one needs to wait until he dies to know if he will be accepted or rejected by God.

Those who refuse the Saviour are condemned and rejected by God right now.

 Read John 5:24.

- Those who agree with God and trust in the Saviour, Jesus Christ, are not condemned.

Acts 4:12

- There is only one Saviour who has been given by God for sinners, and that Saviour is Jesus.

 Theme: Man is a sinner. He needs God and is helpless to save himself.

 READ John 3:19,20.

Teacher's Notes

Lesson 36: You Must Be Born Again

Scripture Reference

The reason people do not agree with God's Word and trust in Him is that they love their own sinful ways.
- They don't want to admit that they are wrong.
- They don't want God to change them.
- They try to keep away from God's truth so that their sinfulness will not be uncovered.
- God already knows everything about everyone, so it is foolish to think that sins are hidden.

 Read John 8:12.

Zacharias said that the Deliverer would *"...give light to them that sit in darkness and in the shadow of death..."* (Luke 1:79).

Jesus came to bring light and life to all who would believe in Him.

F. Conclusion

POINT TO THE VISUAL "TWO CATEGORIES."

Every one of us needs to consider which category we are in.⁴

The Bible tells us that God desires for every person to be part of His family.

That's why He sent His Son, Jesus Christ.

II Peter 3:9

⁴Do not pressure your students with this consideration. Allow the Holy Spirit to do the work in their hearts.

Be available to talk with your students after class, so that you may fully explain the Gospel to any who have prepared hearts. □

QUESTIONS:

1. Why did Nicodemus believe that Jesus was sent by God? *Because of the miracles which Jesus had done.*

2. In what were the Pharisees and others trusting to get them to Heaven?
   a. *Their own goodness.*
   b. *That they were the descendants of Abraham.*

3. What did Jesus mean when He said that we must be born of water? *Jesus meant that we must be born again by hearing, understanding, and believing God's Word.*

4. Who uses God's Word to cause us to be born into God's family? *God the Holy Spirit.*

5. How does the brass serpent which Moses put on the pole remind us of Jesus the Deliverer?
   a. *Just as the snake was put on a pole and lifted up, so Jesus had to be lifted up.*
   b. *Whoever looked at the snake was healed of the snakebite. Likewise, whoever trusts in Jesus, the Deliverer, will be saved from the power of Satan, sin, and death.*

6. Why did God send Jesus to this world? *To deliver the world from everlasting punishment for sin.*

7. Why don't people want to listen to God's Word? *Because they love their sinful ways. They want to please themselves.*

| Scripture Reference | | Teacher's Notes |

Jesus Evidenced His Divinity, but the Religious Leaders Rejected Him; Jesus Chose Twelve Disciples

OVERVIEW

This lesson presents Jesus' miracles of physical healing, a sign of His Deity.

It also presents the fact that many of the religious leaders rejected Him.

His choice of disciples shows His selection of ordinary men.

Some points:

- Jesus has power to forgive sins.
- Jesus came to save sinners.
- Men are helpless to save themselves.
- God sees through and deals with hypocrisy.
- The evil spirits knew who Jesus was, but He wouldn't let them speak; He would tell people Himself the true message.
- He knew men's hearts; He knew that Judas would betray Him.

LESSON PREPARATION

This section is for you, the teacher.

The passages in the Scripture Reference column are for your own study in preparing for this lesson. Since they may contain concepts that run ahead of the lesson, they are not to be taught at this point.

Note: If you have not taught previously from this series of lessons, please read carefully the note to teachers in the front of this book.

SCRIPTURE: Mark 2:1-17; 3:1-19

LESSON GOALS:

- To show that Jesus Christ is God.
- To show that people cannot save themselves.
- To show that only Jesus can save.
- To define religious hypocrisy.

THIS LESSON SHOULD HELP THE STUDENTS:

- To see that the Bible gives clear evidence that Jesus is God.
- To see the foolishness of self-effort.
- To see that Jesus came to save sinners.

PERSPECTIVE FOR THE TEACHER:

Most of the religious leaders of Jesus' day did not care about God; they used God's Word and His name only as a way to try to enlist their own followers. Although they made a pretense of being religious, in their hearts they did not submit to God nor did they believe Him; they rejected the only one who could save them from their sins.

Today we also have men like this—men who have built a great following after themselves, but men who have rejected God. Though their message may seem very religious and appealing, at the heart is not the truth but a lie. Some, like the Pharisees, tell people that they will go to Heaven if they **do** the right things. Others tell people that everyone is going to Heaven, no matter what they do, or they say that God is love and we just need to love everyone.

Years ago, a Christian magazine ran a simple but powerful cover which looked like an old-fashioned grocery label. The label read something like, "100% Pure Grace, Nothing Added. Accept No Substitutes." God has given us the only way to be saved. We must not add to it or look for any other way.

By studying the Bible we can know for sure what God has said. Interestingly, those who are leading people away from God can usually be identified by the fact that they twist, misuse, ignore, reject, or add to His Word. Satan did that in the garden to Eve, in the desert with Jesus, and he is still trying to do that to us today. Jesus defeated Satan by correctly using God's Word; we need to learn to do the same.

As teachers we are responsible to study God's Word. No one can know everything, but God the Holy Spirit lives inside each believer and helps us as we study.[1]

[1]Remember, it is all right to tell a student that you don't know an answer but that you will study and try to find an answer for them. If you need help, ask your pastor or a godly elder for assistance. It is much better to make your student wait for a scriptural answer than to give them an immediate reply that is incorrect

In the same way, if we as teachers realize that we have answered incorrectly or taught incorrectly, we should be willing to admit our error and make the truth clear. ☐

Teacher's Notes

Lesson 37: Jesus' Miracles; His Rejection by Religious Leaders

Scripture Reference

VISUALS:

- Chronological Picture No. 65, "Jesus Heals the Paralytic"
- Chronological Picture No. 66, "Jesus and the Twelve Disciples"
- Chronological Map 3

SOME NOTES ABOUT MIRACLES:

As we teach this lesson, may we keep in mind the purpose for Jesus' miracles. To those who truly were awaiting the Messiah, the Bible tells us that **Jesus' miracles were a validation of His deity.** (See John 10:38-42; 14:11; 20:30,31.)

If a student should ask, "Does God heal people today?" the answer is, "Yes, He certainly does." Encourage him that God knows what is the very best and He is able to heal though sometimes He chooses not to. We can trust Him to do what is absolutely perfect.

Some people today think that God **has to heal** when they ask Him; but miracles are God's prerogative, not ours. We do not want to make demands, but rather requests of our sovereign, all-wise God. A good passage to study is II Corinthians 12:1-10. His power is in no way diminished; Jesus Christ is the same today as then (Hebrews 13:8). But sometimes God has a higher purpose for our lives than physical healing. He has promised to give what is good, and He alone knows what is best for us. We need to weigh His promises in light of the whole content of His Word and rest in His infinite wisdom.

Let us remember that physical healing is only a reminder of the greater healing that Jesus performed on the Cross—the healing of sin-sick souls. No matter how sick or how healthy we are in this life, our bodies still die eventually because of sin. But through faith in Christ, we have eternal life and one day we will have perfect bodies like His own! *"For our conversation [citizenship] is in heaven; from whence also we look for the Saviour, the Lord Jesus Christ: Who shall change our vile body, that it may be fashioned like unto his glorious body, according to the working whereby he is able even to subdue all things unto himself"* (Philippians 3:20,21).

ON TEACHING THIS LESSON:

These lessons are designed to **teach unbelievers.** You are carefully laying a scriptural foundation on which the Gospel will later be presented. If your class contains believers, teach with the goal of giving them an understanding of the basis for their faith and **with the goal of enabling them to teach the same material to unbelievers.**

DON'T COMPLICATE THE MESSAGE!

As you teach, keep in mind that this is a directed study—not an exhaustive survey of the Bible and not an unlimited group discussion. Keep your lesson on track and moving ahead by limiting and directing any discussion.

Carefully follow the outline. Emphasize the doctrinal themes.

LESSON FORMAT: The **center column** on the following pages contains the lesson material to be taught to the students. The **bold outline headings** are only for reference and need not be spoken, as they are incorporated into the outlined material that follows. The material in the **side columns** is for the teacher's own reference and is not intended to be included in the lesson.

Lesson 37: Jesus' Miracles; His Rejection by Religious Leaders

Scripture Reference

Teacher's Notes

TO BE TAUGHT TO THE STUDENTS
(Center Column Only)

LESSON OUTLINE:

REVIEW questions from Lesson 36.

A. Introduction

What if we had lived during the time Jesus lived on earth as a man?
Would you and I be in the crowds that thronged around Him?
Yes, I think we would. We are here right now, wanting to learn together about Him.
People came to see Jesus for various reasons.
- Some were curious.
- Some wanted to be healed.
- Some thought He was going to be the king who would deliver them from Roman rule.
- Some wanted to hear Him because He spoke God's Word with power.
- But others hoped He would say or do something they could find fault with.
- They wanted to charge Him with a crime, not because He was guilty but because they were jealous of His ministry with the people.
- They didn't want the truth; they only wanted to be looked upon as important themselves.

If you and I were there in the crowd, what would we be thinking?

B. Jesus taught God's Word.

 Theme: God communicates with man.

 READ Mark 2:1,2.

POINT TO CAPERNAUM ON MAP 3.

Many people wanted to hear what Jesus was teaching.
- He taught them the Word of God.
- Jesus taught people the same message that we're studying today.

C. The sick man was brought to Jesus.

 Theme: Man is a sinner. He needs God and is helpless to save himself.

 READ Mark 2:3.

This man couldn't do anything to heal himself; he was paralyzed.
- No doctor could heal him.
- His friends couldn't make him better.

457

Lesson 37: Jesus' Miracles; His Rejection by Religious Leaders

Teacher's Notes

- Compare:

  This reminds us of the helplessness of all people. No one is able to deliver himself from Satan's rule, the sin which controls his life, and the punishment for his sin. Good deeds or a good life cannot save us. We cannot deliver ourselves. Not even a pastor or Bible study teacher or Christian friend can deliver us. No religion or church can save us. Baptism cannot save us. Who can?

 Theme: Man must have faith in order to please God and be saved.

 READ Mark 2:4.

These men took their sick friend to the only one who could help him.

- Note:

  The Jews built their houses with flat roofs. The roofs were made by laying beams across from wall to wall and covering them with a matting of reeds or thornbushes. Thick clay or earth was put over the mats. There was usually an outside stairway leading to the roof.

- These men took their sick friend up onto the roof of the house.
- They broke a hole through the roof and let him down on his sleeping mat right in front of Jesus.

Suggested Visual:

CHRONOLOGICAL PICTURE NO. 65, "JESUS HEALS THE PARALYTIC"

D. Jesus forgave the sick man's sin.

 Theme: Jesus Christ is God.

 READ Mark 2:5.

Jesus saw that they truly believed in Him, and He forgave the man's sins.

 READ Mark 2:6,7.

These men were right when they said that only God can forgive sins, but they were wrong when they said that Jesus had sinned.

- Because He is God, Jesus had authority to forgive people their sins.
- The scribes did not believe that Jesus was God the Son who had come down from Heaven to be the Deliverer.
- They thought that Jesus was just an ordinary man.
- Consider:

  Can a pastor or priest or any other man have God's authority to hear and forgive us our sins? No! Only God Himself can forgive sins. [2]

[2] By now your students should know that you are not "aiming" at other religions; you are simply teaching what the Bible says. ☐

Scripture Reference

I Timothy 2:5

I John 1:9; 2:1,2

Lesson 37: Jesus' Miracles; His Rejection by Religious Leaders

E. Jesus healed the sick man.

 Theme: Jesus Christ is God.

 Theme: God is everywhere all the time; He knows everything.

 READ Mark 2:8.

Even though these men didn't say anything, Jesus knew what they were thinking.

 Theme: Jesus Christ is God.

 Theme: God is all-powerful.

 READ Mark 2:9-12.

Jesus demonstrated His power as God by completely healing the sick man.
- The people were amazed and praised God.
- They had never seen anything like that before.

F. Jesus called Levi.

 Theme: Man is a sinner. He needs God and is helpless to save himself.

 READ Mark 2:13,14.

Jesus called Levi to follow Him as one of His disciples or learners.

Levi was also called Matthew.

When Jesus called Matthew to follow Him, Matthew was working for the Romans, collecting taxes from his own people, the Jews.
- Because tax collectors worked for the Romans, they were usually hated and despised by the Jews.
- Furthermore, the tax collectors had a reputation for exacting extra taxes from the people and keeping the money for themselves.

 Theme: Man must have faith in order to please God and be saved.

Matthew repented of his sin.
- He changed his mind about himself, his sin, and God's Word.
- He agreed with God.
- He trusted in Jesus as the Saviour whom God had sent into the world.

Many years later, the Lord used Matthew to wrote one of the books of the Bible.
- The Holy Spirit told Matthew what he should write.

- Matthew is the first book of the New Testament and is full of quotes from the Old Testament, which was very familiar to the Jewish people.

G. Jesus came to call sinners.

 Theme: Man is a sinner. He needs God and is helpless to save himself.

 READ Mark 2:15,16.

The scribes and Pharisees were proud.
- They believed that they were far better than others because they fasted, prayed, and did many other things to try to please God.
- The scribes and Pharisees would not eat a meal with people like tax collectors who openly sinned.

 READ Mark 2:17.

Jesus told the scribes and Pharisees that healthy people do not need a doctor, but sick people do.

 Theme: Jesus Christ is the only Saviour.

 Theme: Man is a sinner. He needs God and is helpless to save himself.

Jesus did not come to help people who think they are sinless or good enough for God to accept them.

Instead, He came to be the Deliverer of those who would admit that they are helpless sinners who can only be saved by the mercy of God.

H. The Pharisees' evil plan

 Theme: Man is a sinner. He needs God and is helpless to save himself.

 READ Mark 3:1,2.

The Pharisees and the other Jewish leaders rejected the message of God through John, and they also rejected the teaching of Jesus, the Saviour.

They were constantly watching Jesus, hoping that He would do something against their rules so they could arrest Him and condemn Him to death.

Jesus obeyed all of the laws of God, but the religious leaders had added their own rules to God's Word in an attempt to please God and be made acceptable to Him.
- One of the rules the religious leaders added was that it was wrong to heal on the Sabbath day.
- They considered that healing a person on the Sabbath was like working on the Sabbath.
- Jesus refused to follow this and the other rules which the leaders of the Jews had added to God's Word.

Lesson 37: Jesus' Miracles; His Rejection by Religious Leaders

Scripture Reference

Teacher's Notes

The Jewish leaders hated Jesus because He claimed to be God's Son, the promised Deliverer.

They also hated Him because Jesus told them that they were sinners. Jesus knew that the leaders were not honestly seeking to worship God.

- They acted religious on the outside, but on the inside, they were very selfish and evil.
- The Bible calls someone who acts like this a hypocrite.

    If a person tries to appear very religious when he really doesn't care about God, that is called hypocrisy.

    Jesus knew men's hearts, and He made it clear to the Jewish people that their leaders were hypocrites.

Matthew 6:2,5,16; 23:1-39

Crowds of people followed Jesus.

- This made the Jewish leaders hate Him even more.
- They were jealous of Him.
- Consider:

Some people today are like the Jewish leaders in Jesus' time. They claim to be very religious, but inside they really don't care about God at all. These people claim to be Christians, but they have not believed God. They are still under Satan's rule.

As we mentioned before, people like this turn others away from Christ. Some people say they would never want to become a Christian because they have seen someone who claims to be a Christian yet is really a hypocrite. We should not let other people's hypocrisy keep us away from learning about the Lord. We need to look at the Bible to see what is true and not be embittered by hypocrites. God knows each person's heart, and He will deal with those who are hypocrites. Each one of us is personally responsible to learn about Jesus Christ and to believe that He is the Saviour, the only one who can free us from Satan and sin and death.

I. Jesus healed the man's hand.

 READ Mark 3:3-4.

Jesus was angry with these Jewish leaders because they had set their minds and hearts against the things which God was trying to teach them.

- Recall:

This is what the pharaoh of Egypt did when God sent Moses to tell him to let the Israelites leave Egypt. Pharaoh set his mind and heart against God and was determined to do what he wanted to do. God destroyed that evil man and ruined his country.

- It is a very dangerous thing for people to set their minds against God and His message.
- God will eventually destroy everyone who refuses to obey Him.
- No one who fights against God will win.

 READ Mark 3:5.

 Theme: Jesus Christ is God.

 Theme: God is all-powerful.

461

Jesus completely healed this man's hand.
- No one could do that except God.
- Jesus is God, and God is all-powerful.

How did Jesus heal this man?
- What did He do?
- He just spoke, and the man's hand was healed.
- Recall:

  In the beginning when God created the world, He did it all just by speaking. Jesus is God. He created all things by simply commanding them to happen. In the same way, He commanded this man's hand to be healed, and it was completely well.

  Colossians 1:16

J. The Pharisees and the Herodians plotted Jesus' death.

 Theme: Man is a sinner. He needs God and is helpless to save himself.

 READ Mark 3:6.

The Herodians were the followers of King Herod.
- They did not want any other king.
- (This King Herod was the son of the Herod who tried to kill the Lord Jesus when He was a baby.)

K. Jesus taught the crowds and healed the sick.

 READ Mark 3:7,8.

Great crowds of people from nearby areas came to hear Jesus teach and to be healed of their sicknesses.

POINT OUT JERUSALEM, IDUMAEA, THE JORDAN RIVER, AND TYRE AND SIDON AND THE SEA OF GALILEE ON MAP 3.

 Theme: Jesus Christ is God.

 Theme: God is supreme and sovereign.

 Theme: God is all-powerful.

 READ Mark 3:9,10.

Jesus taught the people on the shore of the lake called the Sea of Galilee.

There were so many people wanting to get near Jesus that He told the disciples to have a boat ready in case the people crowded Him.

There has never been anyone like Jesus.
- He is greater than all.
- Even those who touched Him, believing that they would be healed, were healed immediately, regardless of the sickness that they had.

Mark 5:25-29

Lesson 37: Jesus' Miracles; His Rejection by Religious Leaders

L. The evil spirits knew Jesus.

 Theme: Jesus Christ is God.

 READ Mark 3:11.

The Jewish leaders did not believe that Jesus was really the Son of God, but the evil spirits knew that He was.

They had known Him and served Him in Heaven before they followed Satan.

 Theme: Man must have faith in order to please God and be saved.

 READ Mark 3:12.

Jesus told the evil spirits to be quiet.
- He did not want people to believe on Him because of what the demons said.
- Jesus wanted the people to realize, through His teaching, that they were sinners and needed Him as their Saviour.
- Consider:

  God does not need to show us miracles to make us believe Him. He expects us to believe because of what He has written in the Bible.

M. Jesus chose the twelve disciples.

 Theme: Man must have faith in order to please God and be saved.

ON THE CHRONOLOGICAL CHART, POINT TO "THE TWELVE APOSTLES."

 READ Mark 3:13-19.

Suggested Visual:

CHRONOLOGICAL PICTURE NO. 66, "JESUS AND THE TWELVE DISCIPLES"

Jesus had many disciples, or learners, who followed Him to learn the message of God.

From Jesus' large group of followers, He now chose twelve men to become His special disciples to help Him in His work of teaching, healing, and casting out demons.
- Jesus planned to train these men to become His apostles, or special representatives.

- (Sometimes the Bible refers to these men as "the twelve," other times as the disciples or apostles.)
- You may remember reading that Jesus called Levi (Matthew) from his tax collecting booth, and Levi followed him.
- Most of these twelve disciples whom Jesus picked were not highly educated.
- Neither were they rich men.
- Some of them were fishermen before they began to follow Jesus as His disciples.
- But they saw the value of believing and learning from this Saviour, Jesus Christ, whom God had sent into the world.

All of them believed Him, that is, except one—Judas Iscariot.

- Judas **said** that he agreed with God and truly believed on Jesus, but he spoke only with his lips.
- He was a hypocrite; his mind and heart did not agree with God.
- He did not truly trust in Jesus to be his Deliverer from the control of Satan, sin, and death.

 Theme: God is everywhere all the time; He knows everything.

The other eleven disciples didn't know that Judas was not a true believer, but Jesus knew what he was really like.

Jesus knew that Judas would one day betray Him to His enemies.

N. Conclusion

Jesus knew men's hearts.

He healed men's bodies.

He had power over demons.

Jesus Christ was truly God.

But the religious leaders rejected Him.

Jesus chose ordinary men to be His followers and disciples.

He wanted the whole world to know that He had come to save men, women, and children from Satan's power and from the penalty of their sins.

And He knew that one of His own disciples would, in time, betray Him to death.

QUESTIONS:

1. Why did Jesus have the authority to forgive the paralyzed man's sins? *Because Jesus is God.*

2. Why could Jesus heal the sick? *Because Jesus is God.*

3. What was Levi's other name? *Matthew.*

4. What was Matthew's work when Jesus called him? *He was collecting taxes from the Jews for the Romans.*

Lesson 37: Jesus' Miracles; His Rejection by Religious Leaders

5. Whom did Jesus come to call and save? *Those who agree with God that they are sinners and admit that they can only be saved by the mercy of God.*

6. Will those who trust in their own goodness go to Heaven? *No, God will never accept anyone because of his own good works.*

7. Why did the scribes and Pharisees closely watch Jesus? *Because they hated Him and they wanted to find some reason for which they could accuse Him and have Him killed.*

8. Why did they hate Him so much?

    a. *Because Jesus claimed to be the Son of God and the promised Deliverer.*

    b. *Because Jesus told them how evil they were and revealed their hypocrisy before the people.*

    c. *Because they were jealous that the crowds followed Jesus.*

9. Why did Jesus tell the demons to be quiet and not tell the people who He was? *Because Jesus did not want Satan and his demon spirits giving evidence of the truth on His behalf.*

10. Although Jesus had many disciples, how many did He choose to be His constant companions? *Twelve men.*

11. Were these twelve men well-educated or wealthy? *No, the majority of them were neither well-educated nor wealthy.*

12. Sometimes people can deceive each other, but no one can deceive God. Why? *God knows everything, even what is going on in our minds and hearts.*

| Scripture Reference | | Teacher's Notes |

Jesus Calmed the Storm and Delivered the Demon-Possessed Man of Gadara

OVERVIEW

This lesson presents Jesus as Almighty God, able to calm the storm with a word, able to completely make whole a man who was hopelessly demon possessed.

It also stresses man's absolute inability to free himself from Satan and sin.

LESSON PREPARATION

This section is for you, the teacher.

The passages in the Scripture Reference column are for your own study in preparing for this lesson. Since they may contain concepts that run ahead of the lesson, they are not to be taught at this point.

Note: If you have not taught previously from this series of lessons, please read carefully the note to teachers in the front of this book.

SCRIPTURE: Mark 4:35-41; 5:1-20

LESSON GOALS:

- To show that Jesus is God.
- To show that no one can deliver himself from sin, Satan, and death.
- To show that Jesus Christ is stronger than Satan and can deliver men from Satan's power.

THIS LESSON SHOULD HELP THE STUDENTS:

- To see that because Jesus is God, He has power over all things.
- To see that Jesus cares about people in hopeless situations.
- To see that Jesus alone can save them.

PERSPECTIVE FOR THE TEACHER:

Many people today are much the same as the man of Gadara—totally incapacitated by Satan. Our rehabilitation centers and prisons are full of men and women who have given up on ever living a normal life. Social agencies spend millions of dollars, often dealing with the same people year after year with little or no change wrought in lives. Grim, nameless statistics list increasing numbers of suicides.

But Jesus Christ is the same yesterday and today and forever! He is still transforming hopeless, useless, destructive, antisocial, suicidal outcasts into His own dear children. These are not people who have simply been taught new ways of thinking but men and women who have been reborn to a living hope in Christ. They are useful, productive, caring individuals with a firm, biblical understanding of their eternal destiny and a burning desire to spend the rest of their lives here telling others about this wonderful one who saved them!

Is it worthwhile to teach this lesson about a "wild man who lived out in the caves"? Think about it. Some of your students or members of their families may be deeply involved in drugs or even contemplating suicide. Society has no lasting help or solutions for people like this. All men can offer is a "repair job" on the old, ruined man. Jesus Christ offers new life and the power to live it for His glory!

He is stronger than the Enemy, and He cares enough to deliver the most wretched man from Satan's grasp. Our Lord still delights to deliver men and women and make them new and complete in Christ. What a mighty God we serve!

Teacher's Notes

Lesson 38: Jesus Calmed the Storm and Delivered the Man of Gadara

Scripture Reference

VISUALS:

- Chronological Picture No. 68, "Jesus Calms the Storm"
- Chronological Picture No. 69, "Jesus Heals a Demon-possessed Man"
- Chronological Map 3

ON TEACHING THIS LESSON:

These lessons are designed to **teach unbelievers.** You are carefully laying a scriptural foundation on which the Gospel will later be presented. If your class contains believers, teach with the goal of giving them an understanding of the basis for their faith and **with the goal of enabling them to teach the same material to unbelievers.**

DON'T COMPLICATE THE MESSAGE!

As you teach, keep in mind that this is a directed study—not an exhaustive survey of the Bible and not an unlimited group discussion. Keep your lesson on track and moving ahead by limiting and directing any discussion.

Carefully follow the outline. Emphasize the doctrinal themes.

LESSON FORMAT: The **center column** below contains the lesson material to be taught to the students. The **bold outline headings** are only for reference and need not be spoken, as they are incorporated into the outlined material that follows. The material in the **side columns** is for the teacher's own reference and is not intended to be included in the lesson.

TO BE TAUGHT TO THE STUDENTS
(Center Column Only)

LESSON OUTLINE:

REVIEW questions from Lesson 37.

A. Introduction

When was the last time you realized you were in a situation you couldn't handle on your own?[1]

Where do you go for help when you can't handle the problem?

What about the Lord?

How strong is the Lord?

Is anything too hard for Him?

Jeremiah 32:27

B. The storm

Having told the crowds to go home because it was now evening, Jesus and His twelve disciples got into a boat and started for the other side of the lake (the Sea of Galilee).

POINT TO THE SEA OF GALILEE ON MAP 3.

Listen to what happened.

---

[1] Again, these questions are intended to make the students think. Go ahead with the lesson without waiting for answers.

Do not use these questions with a small group—individuals may feel pressured to answer. ☐

Lesson 38: Jesus Calmed the Storm and Delivered the Man of Gadara

 READ Mark 4:35-37.

This was a bad storm.

The winds were howling, and huge waves were crashing over the boat so that it was filling up with water.

- Consider:

  Have you ever been out in a boat when a storm came up? If you have, you can probably identify with the way the disciples must have felt.

C. The disciples woke Jesus.

 Theme: Jesus Christ is man.

 READ Mark 4:38.

Jesus was asleep in the back of the boat.

- Even though Jesus was God, He was also a real man.
- He got tired and wanted to sleep, just as we do.

The disciples couldn't understand how Jesus could continue sleeping and not be worried, so they woke Jesus.

- The disciples should never have asked Jesus if He cared what was happening to them.
- They should have known that Jesus cared about their safety.

D. Jesus calmed the storm.

 Theme: Jesus Christ is God.

 Theme: God is supreme and sovereign.

 Theme: God is all-powerful.

- Consider:

  What do you think Jesus could do about their problem? Jesus had healed the sick and cast out demons, but what could He do about the howling winds and the roaring sea?

 READ Mark 4:39.

Suggested Visual:

CHRONOLOGICAL PICTURE NO. 68, "JESUS CALMS THE STORM"

Jesus is also God.

- He created the sea and the wind.

Lesson 38: Jesus Calmed the Storm and Delivered the Man of Gadara

- Recall:

  In the beginning, who told the water to move back so there would be dry land on the earth? Who opened up the Red Sea so the Israelites were able to escape from the Egyptians? It was God. All things, including all oceans and seas, are under God's control because He is the Maker of all things.

  Jesus Christ is God the Son.

- Colossians 1:16 says that *"by him were all things created."*
- Compare:

  The things you make are yours, and you can do what you want with them.

  The sea on which Jesus and His disciples were sailing rightfully belonged to Jesus. He made all things in the beginning. Jesus created the sea and the wind and the lightning and the clouds.

The storm had to stop when Jesus commanded it to stop because He is the maker and rightful owner of all things.

 Theme: God is everywhere all the time; He knows everything.

 READ Mark 4:40.

Jesus asked the disciples why they didn't trust Him and His Father, God.

The disciples had forgotten that God sees everything, at all times, whether good or bad.

Theme: Jesus Christ is God.

 READ Mark 4:41.

They had seen Jesus heal diseases and cast out demons, but they had never seen Him do anything like this.

E. **The demon-possessed man**

 Theme: Man is a sinner. He needs God and is helpless to save himself.

 Theme: Satan fights against God and His will. Satan is a liar and a deceiver. He hates man.

 READ Mark 5:1-4.

This man could not release himself from the power and control of these evil spirits.

People had tried to restrain him, but the demons in him were so strong that they even broke iron chains.

The man was living in caves which were used as tombs.

- He was helpless.
- There was no hope for him.

Scripture Reference

Psalm 24:1,2
Colossians 1:16

Lesson 38: Jesus Calmed the Storm and Delivered the Man of Gadara

- Consider:

    We may feel sorry for a person like this and think it is good that we are not like him, but every person born into this world is under Satan's control and is just as hopeless and helpless as this man was. Satan doesn't often make people do the things that this man did, but Satan holds all people under his control until Jesus sets them free.

Satan and his demons only want to destroy people.

Even when Satan and his demons treat people seemingly well, they are still only waiting for an opportunity to destroy them.

But look what they did to this man.

READ Mark 5:5.

Satan and his demons had so tormented this man that he was continually trying to take his own life.

- Consider:

    Many people today try to take their own lives. Satan and his demons put this thought into their minds. Satan tricks them into thinking that their only choice is to kill themselves. This is a lie. Remember? Satan is a liar and a murderer. He hates God, and he hates people.

    Satan makes people feel that they are condemned to continue doing the very thing that is ruining their bodies and their lives. Many people are hopelessly enslaved to drugs and alcohol and other addictions. They want to stop their addictive behavior, but Satan won't let them.

    They may have tried many avenues of help without finding any lasting relief. Some people are very much like the man of Gadara—they can no longer function in society, and society has no answers for them.

    Are these really hopeless cases?

    Satan would like them and the rest of the world to think so.

Satan, the liar, is intent on drawing people into eternal separation from God.

He will do whatever he can to keep them from believing God's truth.

Why? Because God's truth is the good news of everlasting life.

Read John 3:16.

God wants to give new life—a new birth from above, just like Jesus explained to Nicodemus.

- Consider:

    You may say, "Well, that's okay for Nicodemus; but what about a man like this fellow from Gadara or an addict today? Aren't they still hopeless?

    If they are trying to help themselves or if they are looking to men to help them, the answer is, "Yes, they are hopeless."

Men cannot deliver themselves from the control of Satan.

Jesus can.

Let's read what He did.

Teacher's Notes

Lesson 38: Jesus Calmed the Storm and Delivered the Man of Gadara

Scripture Reference

F. The demons knew Jesus.

 Theme: Jesus Christ is God.

 Theme: God is supreme and sovereign.

 READ Mark 5:6,7.

The demons knew that Jesus was their Creator, the Son of God.

The demons feared that Jesus might punish them immediately by sending them to the Lake of Fire.

God is the supreme ruler over Satan and all of the spirits.

- He can do with them whatever He pleases.
- He will throw them all into the Lake of Fire when the time comes which He has planned.

Colossians 1:16

G. Jesus commanded the demons to come out.

 READ Mark 5:8,9.

There are many, many spirits, or demons, in the world.

Satan is their master.

 Theme: Jesus Christ is God.

 Theme: God is supreme and sovereign.

 Theme: God is all-powerful.

 READ Mark 5:10.

The demons knew that they could not stand against Jesus who is God and their Creator.

- Jesus has all power over Satan and his demons.
- Satan and all of his demons cannot stand against Jesus.
- They know that one day they will finally be brought under His authority.
- Compare:

How foolish then if any of us think that we can stand against God and His right to rule our lives! How foolish it is for any of us to remain under Satan's control when we know that he and his followers will one day be thrown into the Lake of Fire! All authority and power in the world belongs to God!

Revelation 20:10

H. The demons entered the pigs.

 READ Mark 5:11-14.

Lesson 38: Jesus Calmed the Storm and Delivered the Man of Gadara

Suggested Visual:

CHRONOLOGICAL PICTURE NO. 69, "JESUS HEALS A DEMON-POSSESSED MAN"

The pigs drowned, but the demons did not, because they don't have bodies as people or animals do.

Jesus did not send these evil spirits into everlasting punishment at that time.
- He gave them permission to go into the pigs.
- It wasn't God's time to finally punish them for their rebellion and sin.
- Nevertheless, God has set a future time when Satan and all of the evil spirits will be finally dealt with.

I. A liberated man

 Theme: God is loving, merciful, and gracious.

 Theme: God is all-powerful.

 READ Mark 5:15.

This man was set free from the control of Satan and his demons by the power of the Lord Jesus.
- He no longer had to do the things that the demons told him to do.
- He was now under the authority of God.

J. Foolish people

 Theme: Man must have faith in order to please God and be saved.

 READ Mark 5:16,17.

These people were very foolish.
- Jesus, the Son of God and the Saviour, had come to teach them.
- They did not want Him to stay.

Why did they want Jesus to leave?
- They were more concerned about the loss of their pigs than they were about coming to know the truth and being liberated from Satan, sin, and the power of death.
- Compare:

There are still people like this in the world. They refuse to listen to God's words because they are more interested in the things of this world. They are not interested in what will happen to them

Teacher's Notes

Lesson 38: Jesus Calmed the Storm and Delivered the Man of Gadara

Scripture Reference

after death. They live only for the present. But the things of this life are only for a short time. They will all soon be gone.

When we die, we cannot take any of our things with us. The things that God teaches us in the Bible, however, will teach us the way to receive everlasting life.

K. A man with a message

 Theme: God communicates with man.

 READ Mark 5:18-20.

- Consider:

Imagine! This is the same man who had been uncontrollable, naked, and self-destructive. He had been unable to live at home or to do any work. He had been an outcast; he had been out of his mind; even chains could not hold him. Now this same man was dressed and in his right mind, able to go home and be useful. He had something worth living for!

He had a wonderful true story to tell others. Jesus wanted him to go home and tell his family what had happened. They would see, more than anyone else, the change in his life. Can you imagine how they must have felt when they saw him? Nothing is too hard for God. He is still the same today.

- Compare:

Everyone is born under Satan's control, though few people are controlled by spirits like this man.

I, too, used to be under Satan's rulership—on my way to everlasting punishment. But then I heard the words of God and agreed with Him. I knew I was a sinner because I had disobeyed His laws. God taught me from the Bible that I could not make myself acceptable to Him and that I could not escape punishment.

I learned that God sent Jesus, His Son, to be the Deliverer of sinners. I trusted in Jesus Christ as my Saviour. [2]

²The story has not yet reached the Gospel—the death, burial, and resurrection of the Lord Jesus. So if you give a testimony like this, do not go any further. Continue to build toward the full revelation of Christ's work on the Cross by which He broke the power of Satan, sin, and death and made it possible for people to be reconciled to God. ☐

L. Conclusion

 Read John 8:36.

Nothing is too hard for God.

He set free the man of Gadara; He can set anyone free.

QUESTIONS:

1. Why did Jesus get tired, hungry, and experience all the other things we do? *Because, although Jesus was God the Son, He was also a real man with a body like ours.*

2. Who was watching over the disciples during the storm? *God was.*

3. Why could Jesus command that the sea and wind be quiet? *Because Jesus is God and had created the sea.*

Lesson 38: Jesus Calmed the Storm and Delivered the Man of Gadara

Scripture Reference

Teacher's Notes

4. Could the demon-possessed man deliver himself from the power of the demons, or could any other ordinary person deliver him? *No! He was helpless.*

5. Can you deliver yourself or can any ordinary person deliver you from the power of Satan? *No! We are helpless.*

6. From this story, how can we tell that demons hate people? *Because the demons tormented this man and caused him to spend his life crying, cutting himself with stones, and living in caves where people were buried.*

7. Who controls all of the spirits who live here on earth? *Satan does.*

8. Who is greater than Satan and his demons? *God is.*

9. Did the demons drown in the sea? *No, demons are spirits.*

10. Who completely changed this man's life? *Jesus, the Deliverer, did.*

11. Who is the only one who can deliver all people from the power of Satan, sin, and death? *Jesus, who is God.*

Scripture Reference

Teacher's Notes

Lesson 39: Jesus Fed Five Thousand People

OVERVIEW

This lesson presents Jesus Christ as the Bread of Life who satisfies our need for salvation from sin and gives eternal life. The lesson emphasizes Jesus' deity by showing His omnipotence and omniscience.

It also shows man's inability to save himself and his need to trust only in the work of Jesus Christ as his Saviour.

LESSON PREPARATION

This section is for you, the teacher.

The passages in the Scripture Reference column are for your own study in preparing for this lesson. Since they may contain concepts that run ahead of the lesson, they are not to be taught at this point.

Note: If you have not taught previously from this series of lessons, please read carefully the note to teachers in the front of this book.

SCRIPTURE: John 6:1-35

LESSON GOALS:

- To show that Jesus Christ is God.
- To show that Jesus Christ is the only Saviour.
- To show that man is helpless to save himself; he must come to God by faith.

THIS LESSON SHOULD HELP THE STUDENTS:

- To see that the things Jesus did truly were miracles.
- To see that life consists of more than food and material benefits.
- To see that only Jesus Christ can save them.

PERSPECTIVE FOR THE TEACHER:

If you want to attract a crowd today, put up a sign that says "FREE." Businesses vie with one another to see which one can appear to give away the most in order to win the customers' favor. If it says "sale," many people will actually waste more in travel time and gasoline than the few cents they actually save on the sale.

We are a strange people—no different in heart than the men, women, and children of Jesus' day. People run to sales but refuse the free gift of eternal life in Jesus Christ. Somehow, fleshly appetites are enormous, but spiritual appetites are all too often poor or totally lacking.

When Jesus Christ came to offer His free gift of life, He did not dress it up with worldly advertising. Instead, He spoke the truth in love. He met people's physical needs with compassion and offered to meet their greatest need also, the need for salvation.

As we teach, let us remember His pattern and offer His message freely. Some people simply will not receive the gift of life, even though it is offered to them by the Lord Jesus Himself. *"But as many as received him, to them gave he power to become the sons of God, even to them that believe on his name"* (John 1:12).

VISUALS:

- Chronological Picture No. 71 "Jesus Feeds 5,000"
- Chronological Map 3

477

Teacher's Notes

Lesson 39: Jesus Fed Five Thousand People

Scripture Reference

ON TEACHING THIS LESSON:

These lessons are designed to **teach unbelievers.** You are carefully laying a scriptural foundation on which the Gospel will later be presented. If your class contains believers, teach with the goal of giving them an understanding of the basis for their faith and **with the goal of enabling them to teach the same material to unbelievers.**

DON'T COMPLICATE THE MESSAGE!

As you teach, keep in mind that this is a directed study—not an exhaustive survey of the Bible and not an unlimited group discussion. Keep your lesson on track and moving ahead by limiting and directing any discussion.

Carefully follow the outline. Emphasize the doctrinal themes.

LESSON FORMAT: The **center column** below contains the lesson material to be taught to the students. The **bold outline headings** are only for reference and need not be spoken, as they are incorporated into the outlined material that follows. The material in the **side columns** is for the teacher's own reference and is not intended to be included in the lesson.

TO BE TAUGHT TO THE STUDENTS
(Center Column Only)

LESSON OUTLINE:

REVIEW questions from Lesson 38.

A. Introduction

How long can you keep a loaf of bread at your house?

Before too many days, someone will either eat the last piece or else it will spoil.

We know it won't last long, but we still keep buying it, because we need to eat.

It's easy to recognize the importance of our physical needs.

But what about our spiritual needs?

B. Multitudes followed Jesus.

 Theme: Man is a sinner. He needs God and is helpless to save himself.

 READ John 6:1,2.

POINT TO THE SEA OF GALILEE ON MAP 3.

Why did these people follow Jesus?

- Did they see themselves as sinners needing a Saviour?
- No, they followed Him because they were looking for material benefits from Him.

    They did not care about spiritual things.

    They wanted things for their physical benefit.

478

Lesson 39: Jesus Fed Five Thousand People

Scripture Reference		Teacher's Notes
	- Consider:	
	It will not help a person if he follows the teachings of the Bible in order to receive earthly benefits or wealth. Jesus did not come into the world to give earthly riches.	
	Believing the Bible and trusting in Jesus as the Saviour won't assure us of better conditions. God does not promise anyone these things.	
I Timothy 1:15 John 12:27; 18:36,37	But here is the real reason why Jesus came. God sent Jesus to be the Deliverer from Satan, sin, and everlasting death. READ John 6:3,4.	
Exodus 12:1-28 Deuteronomy 16:1-8	- Recall: *At the Feast of the Passover, the Jews remembered the last night that their forefathers spent in Egypt. Do you remember that the angel of death passed over their houses because each family had killed a lamb and put the blood on the doorposts of the house? God told them that, every year, they were to kill and eat a lamb in remembrance of His deliverance of their forefathers. The Jewish people travelled great distances to participate in the annual observance of the Passover Feast which was held in Jerusalem.*	
	- Consider: *Perhaps as many as 1,400 years had passed since the Israelites left Egypt that first Passover night. Why were so many Jews still celebrating the Passover? Were they all true believers in God, awaiting His Deliverer?*	
	No, they were not. Some did it just because it was a custom; others celebrated the Passover because they wanted to obey God's law outwardly even though inside they didn't really care about God and believe Him.	
	But there were a few who observed the Passover because God had commanded them to and they believed God and trusted that He was going to send the Deliverer.	
	God had done as He promised. Jesus, the Deliverer, had come at last!	

C. Five loaves and two small fish

 READ John 6:5-7.

Jesus had already decided what He was going to do.

He asked Philip this question only in order to get Philip's response.
- Philip had seen the other miracles which Jesus had done.
- Can you remember some of Jesus' miracles?¹
- How should Philip have responded?
- Philip should have trusted in Jesus.

 READ John 6:8,9.

D. Jesus fed the five thousand.

 Theme: Jesus Christ is God.

¹Give your students opportunity to answer.

Some examples of Jesus' miracles already mentioned in the lessons:
- General categories:
  Healed the sick
  Cast out demons
- Specific miracles:
  Healed a leper
  Healed the paralytic
  Healed a man's hand
  Calmed the storm
  Healed the demon-possessed man of Gadara. ☐

Teacher's Notes • Lesson 39: *Jesus Fed Five Thousand People* • Scripture Reference

 Theme: God is all-powerful.

READ John 6:10-13.

Suggested Visual:

CHRONOLOGICAL PICTURE NO. 71, "JESUS FEEDS 5,000"

As Jesus broke the loaves and fish, they multiplied and multiplied in His hands.

- Compare:

  Can you feed your whole family and all your relatives on one sandwich?

  No! No one except God who is almighty could do that.

- Jesus was able to do this **because He is Almighty God.**

E. The people's plan

 Theme: Man is a sinner. He needs God and is helpless to save himself.

 READ John 6:14.

The people seemed ready to agree that Jesus must be the Saviour whom God had promised to send into the world.

However, they still didn't see the **need** for Him to be their Saviour from Satan's power, sin, and death.

They just wanted Jesus to be their king so He would heal their sicknesses, give them food, and deliver them from the control of the Romans.

READ John 6:15.

F. Jesus walked on the water.

 Theme: Jesus Christ is God.

 Theme: God is supreme and sovereign.

 Theme: God is all-powerful.

 READ John 6:16-21.

Man has been able to do a lot of things, but he can't walk on water.[2]
Jesus created the sea, so it wasn't difficult for Him to walk on it.

[2] Someone may mention the fact that Peter walked on the water. Yes, he did, but it was only because Jesus performed a miracle to enable Peter to do this. It was Jesus' power, not Peter's natural ability. □

Colossians 1:16

Lesson 39: Jesus Fed Five Thousand People

Scripture Reference | Teacher's Notes

G. The people looked for Jesus.

 Theme: **Jesus Christ is God.**

 Theme: **God is everywhere all the time; He knows everything.**

 READ John 6:22-26.

Jesus knew the minds of these people. He knew the real reason why they were looking for Him.

- Consider:

God knows every one of our thoughts. He knows if we don't really agree with Him and are unwilling to obey His Word. God knows why we are listening to His message. He also knows if we agree with Him and realize our need for Him to be our Saviour.

H. Jesus, the Bread of Life.

 Theme: **God communicates with man.**

 READ John 6:27.

- Explain:

Jesus wasn't saying that it is wrong to work for our food. But He was telling these people that they must not work just to get food for the body so they could live here in this world. They should also do all they could to make sure they would live forever with God when they left this world.

Jesus was telling them to give thought and effort to obtain everlasting, spiritual food. This everlasting, spiritual food is the truth which Jesus was teaching them.

Life continues on even after our bodies die. We will live forever in Heaven or in the place of everlasting punishment. What good will a healthy body or riches be to us if, when we die, we go to Hell?

 Theme: **Man must have faith in order to please God and be saved.**

 READ John 6:28,29.

- Recall:

What did the people who were bitten by the snakes in the wilderness have to do to be saved from death? They just had to look at the brass serpent put on the pole by Moses.

- Compare:

When you're a passenger in an airplane, what do you have to do to reach your destination? You just sit there and trust the airplane and its pilot to take you where you want to go.

This is the kind of trust God wants us to have in the Saviour, Jesus Christ. He alone can deliver us from death and make us acceptable to God.

Luke 12:15-23

Daniel 12:2
Matthew 25:46
John 5:29

Numbers 21:4-9

Lesson 39: Jesus Fed Five Thousand People

We cannot do anything to please God or make Him accept us.

God just requires us to turn from trusting in all other things and trust only in Jesus as our Saviour.

 READ John 6:30,31.

The people still didn't believe Jesus; they wanted to see another miracle.

They were just looking at the great things Jesus did, instead of listening to the truth He was teaching.

- They reminded Jesus of the manna which their forefathers ate in the wilderness for forty years.
- They attributed the giving of the manna to Moses, not God.
- They said that, if Jesus was really the Son of God, He should give a sign as great as Moses had given.

 Theme: God is faithful; He never changes.

 READ John 6:32,33.

Jesus told them that it was His Father, not Moses, who gave the manna to their forefathers.

Then Jesus told them that, just as His Father had given the manna from Heaven so the Israelites would not die in the wilderness, now God had given the true bread from Heaven.

- Jesus was speaking about Himself.
- Jesus is the bread which God gave so the world would not die and be separated from God forever.

 READ John 6:34.

But the people were still thinking of food for their bodies.

They wanted Jesus to keep giving them food, just as He had fed them with the bread and fish.

- Recall:

  Do you remember how Nicodemus could not understand when Jesus said, "You must be born again"? Nicodemus thought that Jesus was saying that we have to be born as a baby once again. These people, like Nicodemus, thought that Jesus was speaking about natural, earthly things.

 Theme: Jesus Christ is the only Saviour.

 Theme: God is loving, merciful, and gracious.

 READ John 6:35.

- Compare:

  God gave the Israelites manna from Heaven and water from the rock to save them from physical death in the wilderness.

  God sent Jesus from Heaven into the world to save sinners from eternal death.

  If a person refuses to eat food, he will die physically.

Lesson 39: Jesus Fed Five Thousand People

But anyone who refuses to trust in Jesus as his Saviour will remain dead to God, separated from Him, forever.

- Recall:

Do you remember that, when Adam and Eve sinned, they were immediately separated from God? Although they had been created in the image of God with the ability to know, love, and obey Him, they were no longer able to respond to God. They were under Satan's control. Because they were now sinners, they were no longer in fellowship with God. And as Adam's descendants, all of us are born sinners, separated from God.

- Compare:

A good meal can make you feel quite satisfied for a few hours. But then you get hungry again. The people ate what Jesus gave them, but then they wanted more the next day.

But Jesus says that those who trust in Him will find true life—life that satisfies completely.

How can Jesus do this for us?

He can satisfy us because He alone can bring us back into a relationship with God. He came to give us new life—life that is everlasting, life that satisfies.

Jesus fully satisfies those who depend on Him.

A beautiful passage in Psalms 107:9 says, *"...he satisfieth the longing soul, and filleth the hungry soul with goodness."*

Jesus Christ is the only one whom sinners need to make them acceptable to God and to give them eternal life.

 Theme: Man must have faith in order to please God and be saved.

All who trust in Jesus as their Saviour will not need to trust in any good deeds they might do or in anyone or in anything else.

I. Conclusion

All of us know that it takes work to keep food on the table.

Most of us are willing to make the effort, because we get hungry and so do our families.

But no matter how well you eat, it will only satisfy for this life.

What about your spiritual appetite?

Are you hungry for the food that the Lord wants to give—food that is eternal?

You can't work for it; you can only receive it by trusting God to give what is needed.

Only God can supply it, and that's what He has done in Jesus Christ.

QUESTIONS:

1. Why were many of the people following Jesus? *Because Jesus had given them food.*

2. What were the Jews remembering when they ate the feast of the Passover? *They were remembering the time when their forefathers*

Teacher's Notes

Lesson 39: Jesus Fed Five Thousand People

Scripture Reference

were in Egypt and the angel of death passed over their firstborn because God saw the blood which they had placed on the doorposts of their houses.

3. How many loaves and how many fish did Jesus have when He started to feed the five thousand people? *Five loaves and two fish.*

4. Why was Jesus able to do such great miracles? *Because Jesus is God.*

5. Why didn't Jesus let the people make Him their king? *Because He knew the hearts of the people. They didn't want Jesus because He could deliver them from Satan, sin, and death. They just wanted Him to be their king so He would give them material things and deliver them from the Romans who controlled their country.*

6. How was Jesus like the manna which God gave to the Israelites in the wilderness?

    a. *The manna was given from Heaven by God. Jesus was sent from Heaven to be the Deliverer.*

    b. *The Israelites would have died if God had not given them the manna. If God had not sent Jesus to be our Deliverer, we would all go to everlasting punishment.*

    c. *All those who ate the manna were saved from physical death. All those who trust only in Jesus are saved from everlasting death, separation from God in the everlasting fire.*

Scripture Reference

Matthew 6:1-18; 23:1-39
Romans 2:17-29; 3:1-31

The Way of the Scribes and Pharisees Is Not God's Way

LESSON PREPARATION

This section is for you, the teacher.

The passages in the Scripture Reference column are for your own study in preparing for this lesson. Since they may contain concepts that run ahead of the lesson, they are not to be taught at this point.

Note: If you have not taught previously from this series of lessons, please read carefully the note to teachers in the front of this book.

SCRIPTURE: Mark 7:1-9,14-23; Luke 18:9-14

LESSON GOALS:

- To show that man is a sinner. He needs God and is helpless to save himself.
- To show that man can come to God only according to God's will and plan.

THIS LESSON SHOULD HELP THE STUDENTS:

- To see that they cannot hide their sinfulness from God.
- To see that their good works cannot save them.
- To see that only God can save them.

PERSPECTIVE FOR THE TEACHER:

Jesus Christ came to set men free—a freedom that the Law could not give. The Law was given to show men their sinfulness. Christ fulfilled the whole Law. He indwells the believer and gives freedom and power to do what is right, not under duty of law but in the joy of the Lord.

Even though the Law cannot free men from sin, it is still the Law that most people attempt to follow. The flesh wants to "do" and to "earn" rather than to receive by faith through grace. Even little children quickly learn to conform to a system of "laws" without any real change of heart.

As we teach, we need to be continually asking God to help us to present the message of His **grace**, that wonderful, unmerited favor He bestows on undeserving sinners. We are saved by His grace, and we grow by His grace.

Think about it. Is there something commendable about us apart from Him? No! Our students need to know that we are not trusting in our good works to make us acceptable to God. They need to see that we, too, are only sinners, saved by grace. There is nothing about our "outside" that made us acceptable to God. We are His only because of His mercy and grace to accept us through Jesus Christ. God had to clean us up on the inside in order to make us acceptable to Him. We came to Him just like the tax collector, a sinner who believed God and trusted Him for forgiveness and new life.

VISUALS:

- Chronological Picture No. 72, "Traditions of the Pharisees"
- Visuals showing the separation between man and God (illustrated in lesson)

Teacher's Notes

OVERVIEW

This lesson, which presents the hypocrisy of the Pharisees and scribes, shows the futility of surface religion apart from repentance and faith in God. Man's good works cannot save him; he must come to God by faith, trusting in Jesus Christ to be his Saviour.

Also, the lesson contrasts the Pharisees to the repentant tax collector, who was accepted by God because he saw himself as a sinner and came to God by faith.

Teacher's Notes

Lesson 40: The Way of the Scribes and Pharisees Is Not God's Way

Scripture Reference

ON TEACHING THIS LESSON:

These lessons are designed to **teach unbelievers.** You are carefully laying a scriptural foundation on which the Gospel will later be presented. If your class contains believers, teach with the goal of giving them an understanding of the basis for their faith and **with the goal of enabling them to teach the same material to unbelievers.**

DON'T COMPLICATE THE MESSAGE!

As you teach, keep in mind that this is a directed study—not an exhaustive survey of the Bible and not an unlimited group discussion. Keep your lesson on track and moving ahead by limiting and directing any discussion.

Carefully follow the outline. Emphasize the doctrinal themes.

LESSON FORMAT: The **center column** below contains the lesson material to be taught to the students. The **bold outline headings** are only for reference and need not be spoken, as they are incorporated into the outlined material that follows. The material in the **side columns** is for the teacher's own reference and is not intended to be included in the lesson.

TO BE TAUGHT TO THE STUDENTS
(Center Column Only)

LESSON OUTLINE:

REVIEW questions from Lesson 39.

A. Introduction

Have you ever bought a used car—you know, one of those that looks nice and clean?

You may have discovered (too late) that the only part of that car that was in good condition was the paint job!

Had you known what was really inside, you never would have bought it.

We can't always look inside things, but God sees **everything.**

I Samuel 16:7

Hebrews 4:13

B. The rules of the Pharisees

🔑 Theme: Man is a sinner. He needs God and is helpless to save himself.

🔑 Theme: Man can come to God only according to God's will and plan.

📖 READ Mark 7:1-5.

486

Lesson 40: The Way of the Scribes and Pharisees Is Not God's Way

Scripture Reference

Teacher's Notes

Suggested Visual:

CHRONOLOGICAL PICTURE NO. 72, "TRADITIONS OF THE PHARISEES"

- Note:

    A typical Pharisee wore on his forehead a little leather box containing Scripture verses. He had another box attached to his arm by a leather thong. God had given the Israelites instructions to bind His laws on their hands and to put His laws between their eyes; they had taken God literally and were wanting everyone to see their observance of His Law. When the typical Pharisee gave money to the poor, he made sure that everyone was aware that he was going to give, so they could watch him deposit his gift in the treasury. He liked to pray in public so everyone could see his piety and devotion.

    The things he was doing—observing the Law, giving, praying— were not in themselves offensive to the Lord. It was the attitude of his heart that was wrong. He was not doing these things because he believed and trusted in God to save him from his sins. Instead, he thought he was good enough to please God, and he wanted people to see just how good he was.

Deuteronomy 6:8
Matthew 6:2,5; 23:1-28

The Pharisees disapproved of Jesus' disciples because they did not do many things which the Pharisees said were necessary for a person to be accepted by God.

- The scribes and Pharisees had added many rules to God's words.
- They taught that a person must follow these rules in order to be accepted by God.
- These Jewish leaders were very proud that they followed these rules (though they often broke the rules themselves).
- Note:

    The Pharisees had added literally hundreds of laws to the original laws given to Moses by God.[1] No one was able to keep all these laws; but the Pharisees lorded it over the people and condemned them whenever they broke a law, even though the Pharisees were committing the same offenses themselves. They had no compassion on sinners; they only made burdens heavier and more unbearable by adding to the load of guilt and condemnation.

They were hypocrites.

- They prided themselves on doing all the outward things, such as washing their hands, pots, and tables before they ate.
- But they did not realize or care that God saw all the evil in their hearts.
- Compare:

    There are people like this today, who make quite a show of their religion, criticizing those who aren't like them; yet in their own hearts, they themselves are still under Satan's rule.

[1] The Pharisees added laws which they thought would keep people from breaking God's original laws. For example, they had thirty-nine "principal species of prohibited acts on the sabbath." (*The Illustrated Bible Dictionary*, Vol. 3, p.1210.) ☐

487

Lesson 40: The Way of the Scribes and Pharisees Is Not God's Way

C. Jesus' condemnation of the Pharisees

 Theme: Man is a sinner. He needs God and is helpless to save himself.

 READ Mark 7:6.

Jesus quoted what the prophet Isaiah had spoken about the Jews.

Isaiah 29:13

- They said many good things about God with their lips.
- But in their hearts, they did not love God nor believe and obey His Word.

 Theme: Man can come to God only according to God's will and plan.

 READ Mark 7:7-9.

God did not accept the worship of the Jews who did not mean it with their hearts.

- God rejected them.
- They did not come to God agreeing with Him that they were sinners and trusting in His promises regarding the Deliverer.
- Compare:

  There are still those who teach their own ideas instead of God's Word.

  Many religions today teach rules that are not found in the Bible.

  People are taught that if they follow these rules and do the things these religions teach, they will be accepted by God.

Suggested Visual:

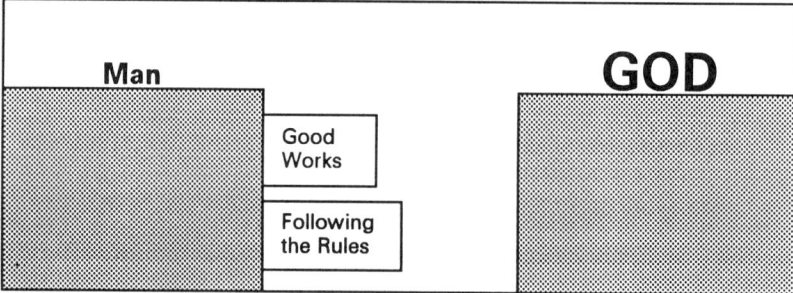

- God says that such teaching is useless.
- Those people say they are following and worshiping God, but they are not.
- Those who trust in keeping rules will not be accepted by God.

It is very wrong to add to or take away anything from God's Word.

D. Not what we eat but what we are

 Theme: Man is a sinner. He needs God and is helpless to save himself.

The scribes and Pharisees also put great emphasis on not eating certain food.

They thought that this, too, would help them to be accepted by God.

Lesson 40: The Way of the Scribes and Pharisees Is Not God's Way

 READ Mark 7:14-19.

Jesus made it very clear that it isn't what we eat that makes us unacceptable to God, but the sinful things that God sees in our hearts.
- Consider:

  How can what a person eats or refuses to eat change what is in his heart?

  What we eat or don't eat will never change our sinful hearts, and it will never make us acceptable to God.

 Theme: God is everywhere all the time; He knows everything.

 READ Mark 7:20-23.

God sees all of these wicked things in our hearts.
- They are the things which make us unacceptable to God.
- Even if we do not actually do these things, God says that many evil things, which He hates, are still in our hearts; and therefore, He cannot accept us.
- Consider:

  Take a close look at this list in Mark 7:21-23.

  If we are honest with ourselves, we will probably find something on the list that describes some of the things that go on in our hearts. Maybe we've not stolen anything, but have we ever had pride in our hearts and forgotten to give God the credit for what He actually gave us the strength to accomplish?

  A verse to consider is Deuteronomy 8:18, "But thou shalt remember the LORD thy God: for it is he that giveth thee power to get wealth...."

  We need to keep in mind James 2:10 which says that if we've broken just one of God's commandments, we're guilty of breaking them all.

E. **The proud Pharisee**

 Theme: Man is a sinner. He needs God and is helpless to save himself.

 Theme: Man can come to God only according to God's will and plan.

 READ Luke 18:9-12.

Jesus was telling a parable.

A parable is a story about things in this world, but it teaches us something about God and our relationship with Him.

The Pharisee went up to the temple to talk to God.
- He was a proud man, and he was trusting in his own goodness and the things which he did.
- He thought that he was good enough for God to accept him because of what he did.

Lesson 40: The Way of the Scribes and Pharisees Is Not God's Way

Teacher's Notes | **Scripture Reference**

- Compare:

  This Pharisee was like Cain. Cain came to God in his own way, trusting in the things which he himself had grown from the ground.

  Just as God rejected Cain, God also rejected this Pharisee.

- Compare:

  Is the Pharisee's position before God any different from the person today who relies on his own good works to save him? No. Both are separated from God by their sins.

  Satan knows that men and women today are still able to be controlled through their pride, like this Pharisee was. The Pharisee believed that in himself he had sufficient goodness to please God.

  How many people today are relying on their good works to save them? If you were to ask a number people why God should accept them into His Heaven, many would probably tell you that they are hoping to be accepted because of the good things they've done. [2]

  - They have lived a good life.
  - They have belonged to a church.
  - They were baptized.
  - They have worked hard in a benevolent organization.
  - They have given to charity.
  - They have been a good provider for their family
  - They have done many good works to provide for the less fortunate.

  Or, they might tell you that God should accept them because of what they don't do.

  - They don't drink.
  - They don't smoke.
  - They don't lie or steal.

  After all, they're better than the man who does these things, aren't they? Or are they?

God says all have sinned.

All are separated from Him, and there is nothing anyone can do by his own efforts to reunite himself with God.

Suggested Visual:

[2] As you mention each of these things, you may want to write them on a visual like the one shown below. ☐

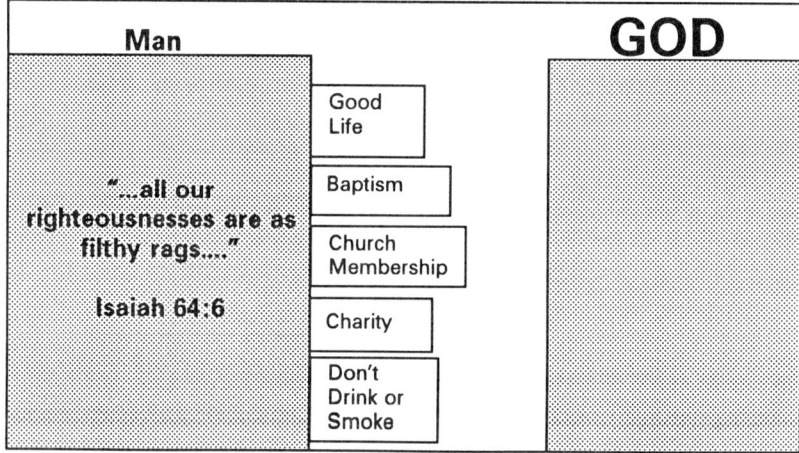

God says in Isaiah 64:6 that "...we are all as an unclean thing, and all our righteousnesses are as filthy rags...."

Lesson 40: The Way of the Scribes and Pharisees Is Not God's Way

F. The repentant publican

 Theme: **Man is a sinner. He needs God and is helpless to save himself.**

 Theme: **Man must have faith in order to please God and be saved.**

 READ Luke 18:13.

- Recall:

  Do you remember someone else we read about who was a tax collector (also called a publican)? Yes, it was Levi, called Matthew. Do you remember what the people thought of tax collectors? They hated them because most tax collectors took extra money from the people and kept it—they were actually stealing from the people.

This tax collector did not try to hide his sinfulness from God.

- He saw himself as God saw him.
- He agreed with God about his own sinfulness.
- He knew that, if God did not send a Saviour, he would spend all eternity being punished by God for his sins.

But this man trusted in the Lord as his Saviour.

- God had mercy on him.
- He forgave him and accepted him.
- Compare:

  He was like Abel who agreed with God and trusted only in God to be his Deliverer.

G. Jesus' verdict

 Theme: **Man can come to God only according to God's will and plan.**

 READ Luke 18:14.

The Pharisee would not admit that he was a guilty and helpless sinner who needed God's mercy, so his sins were not forgiven by God.

God rejected him just as He had rejected unbelieving, rebellious Cain.

 Theme: **Man must have faith in order to please God and be saved.**

 Theme: **God is loving, merciful, and gracious.**

The tax collector (publican) was different.

- He believed God's Word and admitted that he was a helpless sinner who could only be saved from God's judgment by the mercy of God.
- This tax collector deserved to be separated from God forever.
- But because of God's love, mercy, and grace, He accepted the tax collector just as He had accepted Abel who trusted in God's Word.

Lesson 40: The Way of the Scribes and Pharisees Is Not God's Way

Teacher's Notes		Scripture Reference
	H. Conclusion	
	Even though a man may not be well liked, and even though he has not done anything that men would call good, God still will accept that man if he comes to Him by faith, trusting in Jesus Christ as his Saviour. ³	Romans 5:8
³We are not promoting unrighteous living or denying the duty of the believer to walk in obedience to God.	God will accept that man on the basis of his faith in Jesus Christ as his Saviour.	Romans 3:19-28
We are teaching here that the only way for a man to be saved is by the grace of God through faith in the saving work of Jesus Christ. ▫	- That is the **only** way God will accept anyone. - He will reject anyone who comes to Him any other way. There is simply nothing we can do to save ourselves.	

QUESTIONS:

1. Why were the Pharisees angry with Jesus' disciples? *Because they did not follow all the rules which the Pharisees claimed were necessary to please God.*

2. What did the prophet Isaiah say about people like the Pharisees? *Isaiah said that they say good things about God with their lips, but in their hearts, they do not really believe God's Word, love God, or want to obey Him.*

3. Is it right for anyone to add his own ideas and rules to the Bible? *No, we must never add to or take anything away from what God has said in the Bible.*

4. Does what we eat or wear make us acceptable or unacceptable to God? *No! It isn't what goes into our stomachs or what clothes we wear that makes us acceptable or unacceptable to God.*

5. Man judges by what we do outwardly, but where does God look? *God looks inside our hearts.*

6. What are the sinful things which God sees in every person's heart? *Mark 7:21,22.*

7. Why did God accept the tax collector and refuse the Pharisee? *Because the tax collector agreed with God that he was a sinner and needed God's mercy. The Pharisee was proud and thought that his own goodness would make him acceptable to God.*

LESSON 41

Jesus Is the Christ, the Son of God; Jesus Was Transfigured

OVERVIEW

This lesson presents the deity of Christ as expressed in Peter's confession, the transfiguration, and God's words from the cloud.

It also points to Jesus' death, which was soon to occur in fulfillment of prophecy.

LESSON PREPARATION

This section is for you, the teacher.

The passages in the Scripture Reference column are for your own study in preparing for this lesson. Since they may contain concepts that run ahead of the lesson, they are not to be taught at this point.

Note: If you have not taught previously from this series of lessons, please read carefully the note to teachers in the front of this book.

SCRIPTURE: Mark 8:27-31; 9:2-8

LESSON GOALS:

- To show that Jesus is the Christ, the Son of God.
- To show that God always keeps His promises.
- To show that God offers eternal life to all who believe in Jesus Christ.

THIS LESSON SHOULD HELP THE STUDENTS:

- To see that Jesus was not just a man; He was also God the Son.
- To see the Old Testament promises of God being fulfilled.

PERSPECTIVE FOR THE TEACHER:

We often speak of our "secular" society, referring to the fact that people are geared to what is temporary, not eternal. People live as if there were no eternity, just "here and now."

Yet even among those who scoff at God's truth about eternal concerns, there is a tremendous fascination with such things as reincarnation and so-called "out of the body experiences." Satan, the ancient liar, continues to twist truth and package the resulting lie so that men will want the lie instead of God's Word.

The amazing account of Jesus' transfiguration is God's truth. Moses and Elijah's appearance with Christ on the mountain gives us a beautiful glimpse of the fact of eternal life. These men had long since passed from earthly life, but they were in no sense dead, because they had believed in God's provision of a Saviour.

Men and women today have been seduced by Satan to believe that they will reappear in other forms—animal or human. This idea of reincarnation is one of Satan's cruel tricks to fool people into feeling a false sense of hope for eternity.**1**

Unsaved people who have been clinically dead and revived describe "out of the body experiences" in which they see themselves going into life after death with no hint of judgment for sin. These mental experiences may be real in the mind of the unbeliever, but the source of these thoughts is none other than the Enemy of men's souls. The truth is that, apart from faith in Jesus Christ, eternity holds only separation from God forever and eternal punishment in the Lake of Fire.

Eternity is a reality, both for the believer and the unbeliever. Daniel 12:2, Matthew 25:46, John 5:28,29, and Acts 24:15 speak clearly of this.

1 If any of your students mention the idea of reincarnation, be sure to tell them that this is not found in the Bible; rather, the idea of reincarnation is one of Satan's lies. Do not argue with them; just state the truth: for the unbeliever there is nothing beyond death besides judgment and Hell. (See Hebrews 9:27)

Lesson 41: Jesus Is the Christ; Jesus Was Transfigured

Teacher's Notes

Scripture Reference

We have the opportunity to give our students a true sense of eternity as God has shown us in His Word. This passage of Scripture gives us a glimpse of "glory" that should fill our hearts with wonder and hope and joy in Jesus Christ. May we teach in this attitude and pray that our students may believe that God has given us eternal life in His Son, Jesus Christ, our Lord!

VISUALS:

- Chronological Picture No. 75, "The Transfiguration"
- Prophecy Chart

ON TEACHING THIS LESSON:

These lessons are designed to **teach unbelievers.** You are carefully laying a scriptural foundation on which the Gospel will later be presented. If your class contains believers, teach with the goal of giving them an understanding of the basis for their faith and **with the goal of enabling them to teach the same material to unbelievers.**

DON'T COMPLICATE THE MESSAGE!

As you teach, keep in mind that this is a directed study—not an exhaustive survey of the Bible and not an unlimited group discussion. Keep your lesson on track and moving ahead by limiting and directing any discussion.

Carefully follow the outline. Emphasize the doctrinal themes.

LESSON FORMAT: The **center column** below contains the lesson material to be taught to the students. The **bold outline headings** are only for reference and need not be spoken, as they are incorporated into the outlined material that follows. The material in the **side columns** is for the teacher's own reference and is not intended to be included in the lesson.

TO BE TAUGHT TO THE STUDENTS
(Center Column Only)

LESSON OUTLINE:

REVIEW questions from Lesson 40.

A. Introduction

Children enjoy make-believe stories.

Adults enjoy make-believe, too.

But when we consider eternity, we need to have the truth, not make-believe.

All over the world, people follow beliefs, stories, and ideas that originated not as truth but as lies of Satan, designed to draw men, women, and children away from the truth of God.

But when we read the Bible, we are reading the truth, given to us by God Himself, who is eternal and who does not lie.

494

Lesson 41: Jesus Is the Christ; Jesus Was Transfigured

Scripture Reference

Teacher's Notes

B. Who people said Jesus was

 Theme: Man must have faith in order to please God and be saved.

 READ Mark 8:27,28.

Mark 6:14-29

Because King Herod had imprisoned and killed John the Baptist, some people thought that Jesus was John come back to life from the dead.

Others thought that Jesus was Elijah.

II Kings 2:11

Malachi 4:5,6

- Elijah was a prophet who had been taken to Heaven by God about 850 years before Jesus came into the world.
- Some people thought that Jesus was Elijah come back down to the earth.

 Theme: Jesus Christ is the only Saviour.

Jesus had clearly presented to the people who He was.

- He had told the people that He was the Son of God, the Deliverer whom God had promised from the beginning of the world.
- He had shown them His power by the great miracles which He had done.

But the great majority of the Jews still did not believe on Him.

- Consider:

  It is very important who you believe Jesus was. [2] *Do you think that He was just another good man? Was He just a good teacher who did some miracles? Was He just another prophet as some of the Jews said He was?*

  Was He a liar, or did He speak the truth?

John 1:1,14; 8:58; 10:30; 14:7,9

Jesus did not leave us the option to believe only part of what He said about Himself. If anything He said was not true, then He could not be God the Son, because God is holy and perfect. If He spoke the truth, then we must believe Him and trust in what He said.

Jesus said that He was God.

[2] Be sure that you have your students' attention as you make these comments. This is extremely important, because many people have been deceived by lies that say that Jesus was just a good man or a good teacher. Because of the claims He makes directly about Himself and the claims made about Him by others in His Word, He **cannot** be any less than God. ☐

C. Who Peter believed Jesus to be

 Theme: Man must have faith in order to please God and be saved.

 Theme: Jesus Christ is the only Saviour.

 READ Mark 8:29.

Jesus knew that His disciples would never be accepted by God His Father if they did not believe that He was the Saviour whom God had promised to send into the world.

Peter knew and believed

- That Jesus was the one whom God had promised in the garden when Adam and Eve sinned.
- That Jesus was the one whom God had promised to send as the descendant of Abraham and David.

Lesson 41: Jesus Is the Christ; Jesus Was Transfigured

- That Jesus was the one whom God, through the prophets, had promised would come into the world.
- That Jesus was the Christ, that is, God's great Prophet, God's great High Priest, and God's great King.

    Jesus, the Christ, was God's messenger or **prophet** to the whole world—He only spoke the truth.

    Jesus, the Christ, was also the great **High Priest**—He came from God to take away the sins of the world.

    And Jesus, the Christ, was the great **King**—He was sent by God to be the final ruler of the whole world.

 READ Mark 8:30.

Jesus wanted people to listen to Him and really believe His words in their hearts.

- He didn't want people following Him just because the disciples said He was the Christ.
- Compare:

    God doesn't want you to believe in Jesus just because a teacher or pastor or someone else tells you what he believes about Jesus. You must not depend on me or anyone else, but you must believe the Word of God. If you only follow people and do not believe the Word of God, you will not be accepted by God. Your faith needs to be in God and in His Word.

D. Jesus foretold His death and resurrection.

 Theme: Jesus Christ is God.

 Theme: God is everywhere all the time; He knows everything.

 READ Mark 8:31.

Jesus knew He must die.

- Jesus knew that Satan would use the Jewish leaders to kill Him because they did not believe that He was God's Son, the Deliverer.
- Jesus also knew that, although He would die and be buried, He would come out of the grave after three days and three nights.
- Compare:

    Can you tell what is going to happen to you tomorrow? Are you going to get sick, or will you be healthy? Where will you be one year from now? How long will your life on earth be? We cannot know the answers to any of these questions.

- *We do not know our future, but Jesus knew His complete future.*

God knows everything.

- Jesus was not just a man like us.
- Jesus was also God the Son.

 Theme: God is faithful; He never changes.

Hundreds of years earlier, the prophets had foretold many exact details of what would happen to Jesus.

Lesson 41: Jesus Is the Christ; Jesus Was Transfigured

POINT TO THE PROPHECY CHART (NOT TO ANY SPECIFIC PROPHECY, AS THIS IS A GENERAL COMMENT).

- He would suffer many things.
- He would be rejected by the Jewish leaders.
- He would be killed.
- But He would be raised from the dead.

I Peter 1:10,11

Jesus knew and believed what was written in the Old Testament about Him.

- He knew that He was the Deliverer whom God had promised, and He knew that all that had been said about Him would come to pass.
- God's Word is always fulfilled.

E. Jesus was transfigured.

 Theme: Jesus Christ is man.

 READ Mark 9:2,3.

Jesus had a human body just as we do.

He was a real man, but He was also true God.

- As people looked at Him, He looked like any other man.
- But what He did and said showed that He was different.

Suggested Visual:

CHRONOLOGICAL PICTURE NO. 75, "THE TRANSFIGURATION"

 Theme: Jesus Christ is God.

This is the only time while Jesus was on earth that the "God part" of Jesus showed through His human body.

- His human body usually hid the "God part."

Isaiah 53:1,2

- So when people looked at Him, He just looked like an ordinary man.
- Recall:

Do you remember the tabernacle which God told Moses and the Israelites to build for Him when they were at Mount Sinai in the wilderness? The outside of this building was covered with the skins of animals. When the people looked at it, they saw only the old, dried-up skins, but inside the inner room, underneath the skins, was the very bright light which showed that God was there.

Exodus 36:14-19; 40:34,35

- Compare:

That is how it was with Jesus. His human body just looked like that of an ordinary man, but inside, He was also the great, almighty, all-knowing God who created the heavens and the earth.

Lesson 41: Jesus Is the Christ; Jesus Was Transfigured

Matthew, who was one of Jesus' disciples, says in the book he wrote in the Bible that, up there on the mountain, Jesus' face began to shine like the sun.	Matthew 17:2

F. Moses and Elijah talked with Jesus.

 READ Mark 9:4.

Elijah was a Jewish prophet.
- But Elijah did not die like other men.
- As we mentioned earlier, was taken to Heaven by God about 850 years before Jesus came to earth.

    II Kings 2:11

The Bible tells us in Deuteronomy that Moses died and was buried by God.
- Moses' death took place approximately 1,400 years before Jesus came to earth.
- God did not take him to Heaven in the same way as He took Elijah.
- Moses left his body when he died, and his body was buried.
- Consider:

    Deuteronomy 34:5,6

Elijah and Moses had been with God for hundreds of years. When they were alive on the earth, they had believed God's Word and they had trusted in God and the coming Deliverer. Because of this, when they left this world, they were not separated from God in Hell.

God accepted them along with Abel, Seth, Enoch, Abraham, Sarah, Isaac, Jacob, Joseph, Moses, Joshua, and David, and everyone else who had agreed with God that they were helpless sinners and trusted in God to send a Saviour.

God now allowed Elijah and Moses to come back to earth to talk to Jesus.

Heaven is a real place, but it is not in this world.
- Heaven is God's home.
- Everyone who agrees with God and trusts in Jesus, the Saviour whom God sent, will go to live with God in Heaven when they die.

II Chronicles 6:30

John 3:16; 14:1-6

 Theme: God is faithful; He never changes.

When Moses and Elijah, God's prophets, were alive on the earth, they knew that the promised Deliverer had to be born and die.

Luke 24:27

Luke, who also wrote about Jesus' life here on earth, said that there on the mountain Moses and Elijah talked to Jesus about His death, which was to take place in Jerusalem.

Hebrews 11:24-28,32-40

 Read Luke 9:30,31.

Even though these men left the world many, many years before Jesus was born, they knew that God's promises about the Deliverer would all happen exactly in the way which God had promised.

God never forgets His promises, even though thousands of years may pass before they are fulfilled.

Isaiah 46:10

G. What God the Father said about Jesus

 Theme: God communicates with man.

Lesson 41: Jesus Is the Christ; Jesus Was Transfigured

 Theme: Jesus Christ is God.

 READ Mark 9:5-8.

This was God the Father speaking.

He told the disciples that Jesus was who He claimed to be, that is, the much loved Son of God.

- Because Jesus was the Son of God, God told the disciples that they must listen to and obey whatever Jesus said.
- There has never been and there will never be anyone else like Jesus, the Son of God.

H. Conclusion

God does not speak to us by a voice from Heaven now, because all that He wants to say to us has been written in this book, the Bible.

All of the words of Jesus that God wants us to know and obey have been written in the Bible, and God expects us to listen to them and put our trust in them.

Years after Jesus' transfiguration, Peter wrote the following:

 Read II Peter 1:16-21.

The Bible is true.

God's prophets spoke God's truth.

Jesus spoke the truth.

His words were given to lead us to God and to eternal life.

QUESTIONS:

1. Is it important who we believe Jesus really is? *Yes. If we do not believe that Jesus is the Deliverer whom God sent into the world, then we will be separated from God and go to everlasting punishment.*

2. Who did Peter believe Jesus to be? *Peter believed that Jesus was the Christ, the Deliverer whom God had sent into the world.*

3. What did Jesus tell His disciples was going to happen to Him? *Jesus said that He would be rejected by the rulers of the Jews and be killed, but that He would rise from the dead after three days.*

4. When people saw Jesus, did He look just like an ordinary man? *Yes, He was no different from any other man in appearance.*

5. Even though Jesus looked like other men, what was different about Him? *Jesus was God as well as man.*

6. What happened to Jesus on the mountain? *The "God part" of Jesus began to shine out through His human body.*

7. Who was Elijah? *Elijah was one of God's prophets, who, like Enoch, was taken to Heaven without dying.*

8. What were Jesus, Moses, and Elijah talking about up on the mountain? *They were talking about the soon-coming death of Jesus in Jerusalem.*

Lesson 41: Jesus Is the Christ; Jesus Was Transfigured

Teacher's Notes

Scripture Reference

9. What did God the Father say to Peter and the others? *God told them that Jesus was His Son with whom He was fully satisfied and that they were to listen to and believe Him.*

10. How can we know the words of Jesus so that we, too, can believe? *All of the words of Jesus which God wants us to know and trust in are written in the Word of God, the Bible.*

Scripture Reference | Teacher's Notes

LESSON 42

Jesus Is the Only Doorway to Eternal Life

OVERVIEW

This lesson presents Jesus Christ as the only Saviour, the only door to God and to eternal life.

Jesus, the only Saviour, is compared to the ark and its one door through which Noah and his family and all the animals passed, the only way they could be saved from destruction in the flood.

Some of Satan's lies are discussed and shown to be false.

God's Word is presented as the source of truth.

LESSON PREPARATION

This section is for you, the teacher.

The passages in the Scripture Reference column are for your own study in preparing for this lesson. Since they may contain concepts that run ahead of the lesson, they are not to be taught at this point.

Note: If you have not taught previously from this series of lessons, please read carefully the note to teachers in the front of this book.

SCRIPTURE: John 10:7-11, 14:6

LESSON GOALS:

- To show that Jesus Christ is the only way to God.

THIS LESSON SHOULD HELP THE STUDENTS:

- To see that there is no other way to come to God.
- To see that Satan is a liar and a deceiver.

PERSPECTIVE FOR THE TEACHER:

Have you heard statements like these? "There are many different ways to God." "It is up to each person to choose his own path to God." "Everyone must depend upon a higher power. It is up to the individual how he seeks and chooses that higher power." "We need to understand different cultures and realize that there are different religions in different countries. God will accept anyone if they are sincere." No matter how educated and refined these comments may seem, they are all of one source and nature. These are Satan's lies.

God knew what manner of deception Satan would offer each generation. In the Bible, God has given us clear, direct answers for these lies.

Jesus said, "...I am the way, the truth, and the life: no man cometh unto the Father, but by me" (John 14:6). What could be more clear?[1]

What a gracious Heavenly Father we have. He has made sure that we have the answers we need for life. We do not need to flounder in Satan's deceit. We have a firm foundation of truth in Jesus Christ, and we do not need to be swayed.

Neither do we need to apologize for the truth. Satan would like to make us believe that we are impolite if we tell the truth as it is written in God's Word. After all, we might offend someone. Yes, the truth does offend those who refuse to believe. But to those who believe, God gives forgiveness, sonship, and eternal life.

We can teach the truth in love and know that God will not change. He will do all that He has promised. In glory, we will be glad that we have stood firm in our belief and taught others to do the same.

[1]As you prepare to teach this lesson, consider the fact that some of your students still may not believe that Jesus is the only way to God. Whenever someone disagrees with what you are teaching, make sure that you do not argue with him; rather, show him that the difference is between what he thinks and what God's Word says. ☐

VISUALS:

- Chronological Picture No. 73, "A Jewish Sheep Pen"
- Prophecy Chart

501

Teacher's Notes

Lesson 42: Jesus Is the Only Doorway to Eternal Life

Scripture Reference

ON TEACHING THIS LESSON:

These lessons are designed to **teach unbelievers.** You are carefully laying a scriptural foundation on which the Gospel will later be presented. If your class contains believers, teach with the goal of giving them an understanding of the basis for their faith and **with the goal of enabling them to teach the same material to unbelievers.**

DON'T COMPLICATE THE MESSAGE!

As you teach, keep in mind that this is a directed study—not an exhaustive survey of the Bible and not an unlimited group discussion. Keep your lesson on track and moving ahead by limiting and directing any discussion.

Carefully follow the outline. Emphasize the doctrinal themes.

LESSON FORMAT: The **center column** below contains the lesson material to be taught to the students. The **bold outline headings** are only for reference and need not be spoken, as they are incorporated into the outlined material that follows. The material in the **side columns** is for the teacher's own reference and is not intended to be included in the lesson.

TO BE TAUGHT TO THE STUDENTS
(Center Column Only)

LESSON OUTLINE:

REVIEW questions from Lesson 41.

A. Introduction

Safety.

Security.

Do those words mean anything to you?

These words were important to the people of Jesus' time, too.

Many of the people whom we have read about in the Old Testament were shepherds.

In the days when Jesus lived here on earth, shepherding was still common work among the Jews.

So when Jesus spoke of sheep and shepherds, the people were able to identify with what He was telling them.

Though we may not be familiar with sheep, the message of this story applies to every one of us.

B. The door of the sheep

- Background:

Much of the land of Israel is dry and barren, and sometimes it was very hard to find grass for the sheep. Often, the shepherds had to leave their homes and lead their sheep a long way in search of food. Many times, the shepherds would be so far from their homes at nightfall that they had to sleep out in the fields or mountains with their sheep. It was dangerous to sleep out in the open because there were robbers who would try to steal the sheep, and there were wild animals which would kill them. So, before the night came, the shepherds would find a cave where the sheep would be safe, or

Lesson 42: *Jesus Is the Only Doorway to Eternal Life*

they would make places where they could put their sheep for the night. The places which the shepherds built were usually enclosures with walls of thornbushes and stones.

Suggested Visual:

CHRONOLOGICAL PICTURE NO. 73, "A JEWISH SHEEP PEN"

- Explain:

This is a picture of a Jewish sheep pen, called a sheepfold. Pens built like this can still be found in the area of Israel today.

When night came, the shepherds would put their sheep in this protected area and then lie down at the entrance. Anyone who went into the sheepfold had to go past the shepherd. He was like the door or the gate into the sheep enclosure. There was only one door into the sheepfold, and that was where the shepherd was lying.

 Theme: Jesus Christ is the only Saviour.

 READ John 10:7.

Jesus meant that He was the way into the place of safety and security.

Hebrews 2:14,15
I Peter 5:8

- Outside, in this world, are Satan, his evil spirits, sin, and death.
- They are like the robbers and the wild animals which killed and ate the sheep.

 Theme: Satan fights against God and His will. Satan is a liar and a deceiver. He hates man.

- Consider:

To those "outside the sheepfold," Satan gives the message that it is much safer out in his territory. After all, wouldn't a person have to give up a lot of life's pleasures to step inside that door?

And what would other people think if someone began to believe Christ instead of following the crowd? That could make life really difficult. That person might get a lot of pressure and even lose some of his friends.

These are some of the thoughts Satan puts into people's minds as they contemplate putting their faith in Jesus Christ as their Saviour.

Satan is a liar and a deceiver. As we have read in God's Word, Satan tells only part of the truth, and he appeals to our sinful desires.

Think about it:

What if a person had every selfish pleasure this life could offer him, but one day he died and went to Hell. (Satan doesn't mention that part.)

And what if a person were able to keep all his friends with him and keep on the good side of all of them. One day, that person and, eventually, all of his friends might end up in the lonely separation and eternal fire of punishment.

But if a man cares about his own life and cares about his friends, he will believe in the only one who can save him, Jesus Christ. And perhaps some of his friends will see that he has a new life and decide to learn about Jesus, too. (Satan doesn't tell people that part either.)

Is Satan's territory better?

Proverbs 14:12 says, "There is a way which seemeth right unto a man, but the end thereof are the ways of death."

In John 8:44, Jesus called Satan a liar and a murderer.

Satan has been deceiving and destroying people for thousands of years.

- We are born under his control, because we are born into Adam's race of sinners.
- Satan's only purpose is to destroy us so we will be separated from God forever.
- Remember, he is a deceiver—he does everything he can to make his way look best.
- But it is the way of death, separation, and eternal punishment.

 Theme: Jesus Christ is the only Saviour.

There is only one door or gate into the sheepfold, the place of safety, security, and life.

- Jesus is God, and He is the Saviour.
- Jesus is the only door to eternal life.
- There is no other way.

 Theme: Jesus Christ is God.

 Theme: God is loving, merciful, and gracious.

- Compare:

Just as a shepherd loved and cared for his sheep, the Lord Jesus loves and cares for all people.

He wants to be our Deliverer from Satan, sin, and death—separation from God.

C. False saviours

 READ John 10:8.

Before Jesus was born, other men had come to the Jews, each one claiming to be the Deliverer sent from God

Jesus said that these people were like the robbers who came at night to steal and kill the sheep.

II Corinthians 11:13-15

Satan uses many tricks to try to make us think that the way he teaches is the right way.

- The ways of Satan may look good.

Proverbs 16:25

Lesson 42: Jesus Is the Only Doorway to Eternal Life

Scripture Reference

Teacher's Notes

- But the end of all his ways is death, everlasting separation from God in the fire where God will throw Satan and all his followers.

How can we know what is really true?

Romans 10:17

The only way that we can really know the truth is to know what the Bible says.

John 8:32,36 says, *"And ye shall know the truth, and the truth shall make you free...If the Son therefore shall make you free, ye shall be free indeed."*

Jeremiah 29:13 says, *"And ye shall seek me, and find me, when ye shall search for me with all your heart.*

Are you confused over what is true?

Ask God to show you the truth in His Word.

John 17:3

That is why we are studying together — so that we can know Him and know Jesus Christ, whom He sent to be our Saviour.

D. Jesus, the only door

 Theme: **Jesus Christ is the only Saviour.**

 Theme: **Man can come to God only according to God's will and plan.**

 READ John 10:9.

There was only one door into the sheepfold.

Likewise, Jesus is the only doorway into eternal life.

- Consider:

  Some people may say to you that what the Bible teaches is all right for Christians, but there are other religions that also lead people to God. **2** *That is a lie of Satan. There are not many ways or many doors to acceptance and oneness with God. There are not many ways to eternal life. There is only one door to God and to eternal life.*

  Jesus is that door. He came to be the Saviour of all people, in every place, no matter what language they speak or how they live.

- Recall:

  God told Noah to build the ark because God was going to punish the whole world. God commanded Noah to build only one boat and to put only one door in it. Only those who came through that one door into the ark Noah built were saved from God's judgment.

 Theme: **Man must have faith in order to please God and be saved.**

- *Noah believed God, and he entered by the door into the ark.*
- *Because Noah trusted in God and His words, he entered by the door and was saved from the punishment of God.*

The way to enter the door to everlasting life is to agree with God and His Word and trust only in Jesus who is the Saviour.

- Jesus is the doorway to God.
- There is no other way to God.

2Do not debate over this. Simply state what the Bible says.

Through the Word, God the Holy Spirit works in hearts.
☐

Lesson 42: Jesus Is the Only Doorway to Eternal Life

 Theme: Jesus Christ is God.

 Theme: God is loving, merciful, and gracious.

READ John 10:10.

Jesus said that He is not like Satan, who only wants to destroy people.

Jesus came into the world to give life with God forever to all who believe on Him.

- Consider:

  One of Satan's lies is that his way is the best, the most interesting and fun way to live. He gives people just enough pleasure to make them think that his way is better than the way offered by Jesus Christ. What a terrible lie! The Bible makes it very clear that all who refuse to believe Jesus' offer of life will be separated from God and punished forever in the Lake of Fire.

Jesus said clearly here in this verse that He gives us life and gives it in the fullest way.

- His promises are true.
- The life Jesus gives is the best way, and it is never disappointing in the end.
- He came to give new life, eternal life to those who will believe in Him.
- We read in an earlier lesson that the life given by Jesus is life that truly satisfies.

Read John 6:35.

E. Jesus, the Good Shepherd

 Theme: Jesus Christ is God.

 Theme: God is loving, merciful, and gracious.

READ John 10:11.

Jesus had already told His disciples that the leaders of the Jews would not believe that He was the Son of God and the Saviour sent by God.

Therefore, the Jewish leaders would kill Him.

Jesus said that He was like a shepherd who loved his sheep so much that he would die for them in order to save them from the robbers or the wild animals who planned to kill them.

 Theme: God is faithful; He never changes.

Isaiah the prophet said that Jesus would suffer and die for others.

God did everything that He promised through His prophet Isaiah.

Read Isaiah 53:4,5.

Scripture Reference

Proverbs 14:12

Revelation 20:15

Lesson 42: Jesus Is the Only Doorway to Eternal Life

Scripture Reference | **Teacher's Notes**

POINT TO THE PROPHECY CHART. Write John 10:11 opposite Isaiah 53:4,5. Read the prophecy and its fulfillment.

F. Jesus, the way, the truth, the life

 Theme: Jesus Christ is the only Saviour

 READ John 14:6.

Jesus is the only way to God and everlasting life.

Jesus is the one who came to tell us everything that God wants to say to us.

- All that Jesus said is the truth.
- He cannot tell a lie.

Jesus is the Saviour of all who believe.

He is the only one who can save us from everlasting death — separation from God — and give us everlasting life.

G. Conclusion

One God.

One Saviour.

For the whole world.

For you.

For me.

There is no other way to be saved..

Isaiah 43:11
John 3:16
Acts 4:12
I Timothy 2:5,6

QUESTIONS:

1. How did the shepherds in Jesus' day make themselves like a door to the sheep? *At nighttime, the shepherds would lie across the entrance to the enclosure where they put their sheep to protect them.*

2. Why did Jesus call Himself the door of the sheep? *Because He is the door through whom we must enter into eternal life.*

3. How does the one door into Noah's ark remind us of Jesus?

    a. Just as there was only one door into the ark, so Jesus is the only way to eternal life.

    b. Just as only those who entered into the ark by the door were saved from God's judgment, so only those who put their faith in Jesus will be saved from the everlasting fire.

4. Of whom do the thieves and robbers who killed the sheep remind us? *Of Satan, the evil spirits, and people who say that there are ways to be accepted by God other than Jesus, the Deliverer.*

5. What did Jesus say He would do for His sheep? *He said that He would give His life for them.*

6. What did Jesus promise to give to His sheep? *Everlasting life.*

7. Who are Jesus' sheep? *All those who have agreed with God that they are helpless sinners and have put their trust only in Jesus as their Saviour.*

Lesson 42: Jesus Is the Only Doorway to Eternal Life

8. Is there another way to God for people in other countries? *No. Jesus is the only Saviour for all people everywhere.*

Scripture Reference

Teacher's Notes

LESSON 43

Jesus Raised Lazarus from the Dead

OVERVIEW

This lesson presents Jesus Christ as the resurrection and the life, the Saviour who came to give eternal life to all who believe.

Through the story of Jesus raising Lazarus from the dead, we see:

- Jesus' compassion and ability to identify with the sorrows of men
- The attitudes of Mary and Martha who believed in Jesus
- The attitudes of the Jewish leaders who hated Jesus.

LESSON PREPARATION

This section is for you, the teacher.

The passages in the Scripture Reference column are for your own study in preparing for this lesson. Since they may contain concepts that run ahead of the lesson, they are not to be taught at this point.

Note: If you have not taught previously from this series of lessons, please read carefully the note to teachers in the front of this book.

SCRIPTURE: John 11:1-48

LESSON GOALS:

- To show that Jesus is God and that He has power to give men life.
- To show that all people will have to spend eternity either in Heaven or in the Lake of Fire.

THIS LESSON SHOULD HELP THE STUDENTS:

- To see that they must choose to believe God.
- To see that, apart from Jesus Christ, they cannot escape separation from God and eternal punishment.
- To see that Jesus loves and cares for them and feels sad over sin and death.

PERSPECTIVE FOR THE TEACHER:

Some interesting facts come to light as we study this passage of Scripture. Lazarus actually died and was buried. Jesus actually raised Lazarus back to life. Some people put their faith in Jesus because of this. Other people were jealous of Jesus and hated Him enough to want to put Him to death.

As we think about these things, we are reminded that Jesus' disciples saw these things taking place. They believed (except Judas) and were willing to give their own lives to take the Gospel to others after Jesus went back to Heaven. If the disciples had not believed what is written here, they would not have been willing to die for Jesus' sake. They knew He was who He claimed to be: the resurrection and the life. They not only saw Him raise Lazarus, but they also saw Jesus Himself die and rise again from the dead.

These facts alone should be enough to make people believe in Jesus Christ. But like the people of Jesus' time, many today will not believe, even though the Bible record is clear and readily available. Jesus commented about the Jewish people, *"...If they hear not Moses and the prophets, neither will they be persuaded, though one rose from the dead"* (Luke 16:31).

Even astounding facts which are clearly verified will not move a stubborn heart. Only the Holy Spirit can give sight to blinded minds.

Present these wonderful true stories clearly and with the enthusiasm and conviction that God gives through His Spirit. Pray for your students that the Holy Spirit may work in their minds and hearts and that they may believe.

Teacher's Notes

Lesson 43: Jesus Raised Lazarus from the Dead

Scripture Reference

VISUALS:

- Chronological Picture No. 74, "Resurrection of Lazarus"
- Chronological Map 3

ON TEACHING THIS LESSON:

These lessons are designed to **teach unbelievers.** You are carefully laying a scriptural foundation on which the Gospel will later be presented. If your class contains believers, teach with the goal of giving them an understanding of the basis for their faith and **with the goal of enabling them to teach the same material to unbelievers.**

DON'T COMPLICATE THE MESSAGE!

As you teach, keep in mind that this is a directed study—not an exhaustive survey of the Bible and not an unlimited group discussion. Keep your lesson on track and moving ahead by limiting and directing any discussion.

Carefully follow the outline. Emphasize the doctrinal themes.

LESSON FORMAT: The **center column** below contains the lesson material to be taught to the students. The **bold outline headings** are only for reference and need not be spoken, as they are incorporated into the outlined material that follows. The material in the **side columns** is for the teacher's own reference and is not intended to be included in the lesson.

TO BE TAUGHT TO THE STUDENTS
(Center Column Only)

LESSON OUTLINE:

REVIEW questions from Lesson 42.

A. Introduction

Our lesson today concerns something which people try to avoid talking about.

- It's strange how most people avoid mentioning it, because it's common to all of us.
- We talk about our health.
- We even talk about our age.
- Many spend enormous amounts of money trying to get well and stay well, trying to look young and stay young—trying to avoid getting old.
- But few people want to talk about death.

Jesus talked about it.

And what He had to say should change forever our thoughts about life **and** about death!

Lesson 43: Jesus Raised Lazarus from the Dead

B. Jesus waited until Lazarus died.

 Theme: Jesus Christ is God.

 Theme: God is everywhere all the time; He knows everything.

 READ John 11:1-6.

POINT TO BETHANY, JERUSALEM, AND TO THE AREA EAST OF THE JORDAN ON MAP 3.

Jesus was on the other side of the Jordan River.

Even though He was a long way from where Lazarus was, Jesus still knew all that was going to happen to Lazarus.

- Jesus is God.
- There isn't anything that He doesn't know.
- Jesus knew that Lazarus was going to die.

Jesus had all power available to Him.

- He could have healed Lazarus without even going to where he was.
- Or Jesus could have gone immediately to Lazarus to heal him.

Instead, Jesus waited two days because He knew that this situation was going to be another opportunity for Him to show His mighty power as the Son of God.

 Theme: God is loving, merciful, and gracious.

It may seem as though Jesus didn't love Martha, Mary, and Lazarus, but that is not true.

He loved them and was concerned for them, but He had a good reason for allowing Lazarus to die.

Jesus truly loves every person and wants everyone of us to trust in Him as our Saviour.

Through Lazarus' death, Jesus was going to show His power to give life to those who believe.

C. Jesus went to raise Lazarus from the dead.

 READ John 11:7-16.

The disciples did not understand what Jesus meant.

- They thought that Jesus was going to allow the Jewish leaders to kill Him so He could be with Lazarus.
- That is not what Jesus meant.

D. Jesus is the resurrection and the life.

 Theme: Man must have faith in order to please God and be saved.

 READ John 11:17-22.

Lesson 43: Jesus Raised Lazarus from the Dead

Teacher's Notes

Scripture Reference

Martha believed that Jesus had the power to heal her brother and that God, His Father, would do whatever Jesus asked Him to do.

 READ John 11:23,24.

- Explain:

- *Jesus meant for Martha to understand that He intended to bring her brother back to life right away, but she thought that Jesus was referring to the time at the end of the world when all people will be brought back to life.*

- *God had taught the Jews, through His prophets, that all people will be made alive in the body again. God gives life to every person, even before each one is born, and He will also give life to all the dead when the time comes for everyone to stand before God and be judged.* [1]

[1] The judgment for unbelievers (Revelation 20:15) is different from the judgment for believers (I Corinthians 3:11-15). Do not, however, get sidetracked on this issue. ☐

The only way anyone can escape the punishment for sins is through Jesus, the Deliverer.

 Theme: Jesus Christ is God.

 Theme: God is supreme and sovereign.

 Theme: God is all-powerful.

 READ John 11:25.

"Jesus said unto her, I am the resurrection, and the life...."

- Jesus wanted Martha to understand that Lazarus did not have to remain dead until the day of God's judgment of all people.

- He is the giver of life and therefore has the power to restore life to the dead.

He is the only one who can give life to the dead.

- No other person can give life to the dead.

- Satan cannot give life to those who are dead.

- Only God can give life, for He is the almighty Creator who gave life to everyone and everything.

- Consider:

Some people today believe in reincarnation. [2] *They think that someone who dies comes back to live on earth again as another person or as an animal or other creature. This is a lie of Satan. He wants people to think that they don't need to be delivered from their sins. He wants them to believe that there is no Hell and no judgment. If he can get people to believe that there is another life for them right here on earth, then they will think that they don't need Jesus Christ and they don't need to be saved from God's righteous punishment for their sins. Satan is a deceiver, and the lie of reincarnation is another of his attempts to keep men away from God and eternal life.*

No matter how cleverly this lie of reincarnation is presented to you, don't believe it! The Bible clearly tells us in Hebrews 9:27 that "it is appointed unto men once to die, but after this the judgment."

[2] The lie of reincarnation is very prevalent; take time to address it, especially in light of the Scripture being studied.

Don't argue the point, just state it clearly. If a student persists, remind him gently that the difference is between what he thinks and what God's Word says. ☐

Daniel 12:2
Matthew 25:46
John 5:28,29
Acts 24:15
Revelation 20:12-15

Psalm 24:1
Acts 17:25
Colossians 1:16

Lesson 43: Jesus Raised Lazarus from the Dead

Scripture Reference

Teacher's Notes

 Theme: Man must have faith in order to please God and be saved.

John 3:16; 5:24

 READ John 11:25,26.

Jesus said that, although those who trust in Him as their Saviour die physically, they never die to God.
- They are never separated from God to be punished for their sins.
- They only leave this world to go to live with God in Heaven.

READ John 11:27.

Martha was not like most of the people.
- They only followed Jesus because they wanted healing or food for their bodies or political freedom.
- They were not interested in knowing Him as their Saviour from sin and everlasting punishment.

Martha truly believed and trusted in Jesus as the promised Deliverer who had come from God.

E. Jesus went to the tomb of Lazarus.

 Theme: Jesus Christ is God.

 Theme: God is loving, merciful, and gracious.

 READ John 11:28-38.

Jesus knew that He was going to bring Lazarus back to life again, but He wept because He felt the grief of the people who were grieving over Lazarus.

II Corinthians 1:3
Hebrews 4:15

- Recall:

  Do you remember that we studied about the fact that God made man in God's image? He gave man emotions because God has emotions. He feels sadness.

  Jesus Christ is God, and He feels sorrow and grief. He is able to identify with us when we grieve.

  Jesus cried—not because He had no hope of seeing Lazarus alive again in this world but because He identified with the grief of the people and He grieved for all men because of the horrible results of sin. This was the very reason He came into the world: to deliver men, women, and children from death and to give them eternal life.

- Consider:

  Some people think that emotions always have a bad connotation. But God gave us emotions. He Himself feels grief, compassion, love, anger because of injustice, and joy over what is true and right.

God is deeply grieved for all people because there is sin in the world.
- Because there is sin, there is sickness and death.

Romans 5:12
- Sin and death came into the world because of Adam's disobedience to God.
- All people are now sinners, and we die because we are all the descendants of Adam.

Lesson 43: Jesus Raised Lazarus from the Dead

Teacher's Notes

Scripture Reference

- Consider:

  Does God care when you are sick or when someone dies? Yes, He does care. God loves you, and He wants you to believe His words and trust in Jesus as your Saviour. He wants you to be with Him forever and ever. Because God doesn't want any of us to go to the place of everlasting separation and punishment, He sent Jesus into the world to deliver each of us from our sins and Satan and death.

John 3:16

II Peter 3:9

F. Jesus raised Lazarus from the dead.

 Theme: Jesus Christ is God.

 Theme: God is supreme and sovereign.

 Theme: God is all-powerful.

 READ John 11:39-44.

Suggested Visual:

CHRONOLOGICAL PICTURE NO. 74, "RESURRECTION OF LAZARUS"

Jesus is God.
- There has never been any other man like Him.
- He is almighty.
- In the beginning, He, with God the Father and God the Holy Spirit, created all things.
- They created all things just by speaking.

Now, Jesus stood at the entrance to the tomb and spoke.
- He commanded Lazarus to come back to life.
- Whatever Jesus says always happens.

Colossians 1:16

G. Some believed, and others refused to believe.

 Theme: Man is a sinner. He needs God and is helpless to save himself.

 READ John 11:45-48.

Many Jews believed in the Lord Jesus when they saw His power demonstrated in the raising of Lazarus from the dead.

But the priests and the Pharisees were only interested in keeping their position of power and their wealth.

They were afraid that the people might make Jesus their king.
- These Jewish leaders knew that the Romans who controlled the Jews and their land would never agree to Jesus being king.

Lesson 43: Jesus Raised Lazarus from the Dead

- The Romans would be angry and blame the Jewish leaders for allowing the people to make Jesus their king, and they would replace the Jewish leaders with Roman leaders.

Because the scribes, priests, and Pharisees wanted to keep their place of authority, they planned to kill Jesus.

Satan was leading these men.

- Satan does not want anyone to believe on Jesus and be saved from his power.
- He is still trying today to keep people deceived so they won't believe in Jesus as their Saviour.

H. Conclusion

Of Satan, Jesus said, *"...He was a murderer from the beginning, and abode not in the truth, because there is no truth in him..."* (John 8:44).

But of Himself, Jesus said, *"...I am the resurrection, and the life: he that believeth in me, though he were dead, yet shall he live"* (John 11:25).

Jesus has the words of life.

"For God so loved the world, that he gave his only begotten Son, that whosoever believeth in him should not perish, but have everlasting life" (John 3:16).

QUESTIONS:

1. Who has the power to give and to take life? *God does.*

2. Will all people be raised from the dead and judged by God? *Yes, all people, whether they believe God's words or not, will one day be raised from the dead and judged by God.*

3. Why didn't Lazarus have to wait until the final day to be raised? *Because Jesus was there, and He is God. He created all things, so He is able to give life to the dead.*

4. What did Jesus mean when He said that those who believe in Him will never die? *Jesus meant that they will never be separated from God in the fire of everlasting punishment.*

5. Did Jesus know before He got to Bethany that Lazarus had died? *Yes, He is God. He knows everything.*

6. Why did Jesus plan to raise Lazarus back to life? *To demonstrate His power so that people would see how great and mighty God really is.*

7. Why did Jesus cry? *Because He was sad to see the problems which sin and death have caused all people, and He identified with the grief of the people.*

8. Why weren't the priests and Pharisees happy to see Jesus performing these great miracles? *They were afraid the people might make Jesus king and that the Romans would blame the Jewish leaders and remove them from their position of power and wealth.*

9. Who was leading these men? *Satan.*

10. Why does Satan want to make people believe in reincarnation? *He wants them to think that they will not have to suffer judgment for their sins and eternal separation from God in the Lake of Fire.*

Scripture Reference | Teacher's Notes

LESSON 44

Jesus Loved the Children and Taught the Rich Young Ruler

OVERVIEW

This lesson shows that we must come to the Lord as a child does, simply trusting Him. We have nothing good in ourselves to offer to God.

It also shows the danger of material wealth — God has commanded us to love Him above all else.

LESSON PREPARATION

This section is for you, the teacher.

The passages in the Scripture Reference column are for your own study in preparing for this lesson. Since they may contain concepts that run ahead of the lesson, they are not to be taught at this point.

Note: If you have not taught previously from this series of lessons, please read carefully the note to teachers in the front of this book.

SCRIPTURE: Mark 10:13-24

LESSON GOALS:

- To show that we must come to God with childlike trust.
- To show that we cannot be good enough to earn acceptance by God.
- To show the foolishness of trusting in riches.

THIS LESSON SHOULD HELP THE STUDENTS:

- To see that Jesus loves them.
- To see that they need to be saved.

PERSPECTIVE FOR THE TEACHER:

The rich young man in this story inquired of Jesus much like people in our day inquire of Him. With regard to material wealth, the young man had all he needed and more; yet he knew he was not right with God, so he came to ask Jesus what he should do to inherit eternal life. Jesus knew that this young man loved his riches more than he loved God, and when He asked him to sell all he had and give the money to the poor, the man could not bear to do it.

In our society, many people seek religious activity because, though they have plenty of material possessions, they do not have peace with God through Jesus Christ. Like this young man, they seek Jesus and find that He reaches out to them in love and understanding, but they are not willing to release their attachment to things of this world. They do not come to God trusting in what He did for them in Christ; rather, they prefer to trust in their own riches to see them through this life. Good works and token religion salve their consciences against the eternal consequences of refusal to believe.

What a contrast we see between the rich young man who trusts in riches and works to save him, and a little child who comes to Jesus Christ, believing in Him and Him alone.

We need to pray that our students will be tender to the Spirit's working in their hearts to draw them to put their faith completely in Jesus Christ. May we as teachers put Him first and allow His Spirit to control our lives so that our students may see not us, but **Christ** in us!

VISUALS:

- Chronological Picture No. 76, "Jesus and the Children"
- Chronological Picture No. 77, "The Rich Young Man"

NOTE:
If you find that you are going to be pressed for time at the end of this course, this lesson (Lesson 44) could be deleted. You want to be sure to have adequate time to clearly present the Gospel (Lessons 48-50). ☐

Lesson 44: Jesus Loved Children and Taught the Rich Young Ruler

ON TEACHING THIS LESSON:

These lessons are designed to **teach unbelievers.** You are carefully laying a scriptural foundation on which the Gospel will later be presented. If your class contains believers, teach with the goal of giving them an understanding of the basis for their faith and **with the goal of enabling them to teach the same material to unbelievers.**

DON'T COMPLICATE THE MESSAGE!

As you teach, keep in mind that this is a directed study—not an exhaustive survey of the Bible and not an unlimited group discussion. Keep your lesson on track and moving ahead by limiting and directing any discussion.

Carefully follow the outline. Emphasize the doctrinal themes.

LESSON FORMAT: The **center column** below contains the lesson material to be taught to the students. The **bold outline headings** are only for reference and need not be spoken, as they are incorporated into the outlined material that follows. The material in the **side columns** is for the teacher's own reference and is not intended to be included in the lesson.

TO BE TAUGHT TO THE STUDENTS
(Center Column Only)

LESSON OUTLINE:

REVIEW questions from Lesson 43.

A. Introduction

A well-dressed young businessman entered the waiting room of a prestigious corporate office. He presented his card to the receptionist who graciously offered him coffee and asked him to have a seat while she checked to see if the president would speak with him.

After a while, he was ushered into the president's office and allowed to discuss business with him. The president was cordial and listened to the young man, but after a short time the visit was politely terminated.

As the young man walked out the door of the president's office, he was almost knocked over by a little boy coming in. The little fellow stopped briefly to apologize and then ran on into his dad's office where he was immediately received by his father's welcoming hug.

As the young businessman sadly exited the waiting room, the secretary put her head into the president's office and said with a grin, "I see that your next client made it in okay!"

"He's the kind I want," said the president, still hugging his son. "He came to see **me**. The other guy just wanted to impress me with what he thought he could do."

B. Jesus loved the children.

 READ Mark 10:13.

The disciples did not think that Jesus would want to take the time to show love and care for little children.

Lesson 44: Jesus Loved Children and Taught the Rich Young Ruler

 Theme: God is loving, merciful, and gracious.

 Theme: Man must have faith in order to please God and be saved.

📖 READ Mark 10:14.

Suggested Visual:

CHRONOLOGICAL PICTURE NO. 76, "JESUS AND THE CHILDREN"

Jesus loves children.

He wants them to believe His Word and trust in Him, too.

- All of us are born sinners and are under the power of Satan and death.
- The only way any of us, young or old, can be rescued is by putting our trust in Jesus as our Saviour.

 READ Mark 10:15,16.

Those who are unwilling to come to God and trust in Him like a little child will not enter Heaven.

- Consider:

A little baby just rests in your arms. He's not afraid of being dropped. He trusts you to hold him and take care of him.

When you were a baby, you didn't even ask your parents questions. You just believed whatever they told you. You didn't try to figure things out for yourself.

But, as you grew older, you became more independent. Certainly, we should become responsible as adults.

But God did not design us to be independent of Him. *He made man in His image, to know, love, and obey Him.*

As sinners, we cannot do that. We are separated from God by our sins. We are naturally independent and self-centered.

Somehow, we think that if there is any change to take place in our lives, it is up to us to do all the work.

That is not the message of the Gospel.

Jesus Christ came to save sinners.

He said that we must be born again. Just as it is impossible for anyone to bring about his own physical birth, so it is impossible for us to bring about our own spiritual birth.

 Read John 1:12,13.

Lesson 44: Jesus Loved Children and Taught the Rich Young Ruler

God alone is able to give us new life; He alone can save us from the penalty of our sins. That is why He sent His Son Jesus Christ into the world.

 Read John 3:16.

Because we are so independent and want to be in control of everything that happens to us, we may find it very difficult to accept the simplicity of the Gospel. That is why Jesus said we must come to Him in childlike dependence.

Many people will go to Hell because they simply will not trust God and His Word.

But when anyone humbles himself and believes God's Word like a little child, God saves that person from the control of Satan, sin, and death.

C. The rich young man's question

 Theme: Man can come to God only according to God's will and plan.

 READ Mark 10:17.

Suggested Visual:

CHRONOLOGICAL PICTURE NO. 77, "THE RICH YOUNG MAN"

This young man thought that he could please God and gain entrance to God's kingdom by his own goodness and obedience to God's laws.

- He thought that, by doing good things, he could be good enough to deserve eternal life.
- This is why he asked Jesus what he had to do to earn everlasting life.
- Recall:

This young man was like Cain. Cain thought that, by bringing the things which he had grown to God, he could obtain God's favor. But did God accept Cain because of the things which he brought? No!

D. Only God is good

 Theme: God is holy and righteous.

 READ Mark 10:18.

This young man did not understand that no man had ever been good enough to please God.

- He didn't realize that God is the only one who is good.

Lesson 44: Jesus Loved Children and Taught the Rich Young Ruler

- He thought that he was good, and he thought that Jesus was just another good man like himself.
- Even though he did not realize that Jesus was God, he called Jesus good.
- When Jesus answered him, He wasn't denying that He Himself was good or that He was God.
- But Jesus wanted the young man to realize that no ordinary man is good.

If this young man believed that Jesus was good, then he should also have realized that Jesus was God, for the only one who is good is God.

E. The way of the Law

 Theme: Man is a sinner. He needs God and is helpless to save himself.

 READ Mark 10:19,20.

This young man did not realize
- That he was born a sinner
- That he was born under Satan's control
- Therefore, he could never perfectly obey God's laws and so please God.

Isaiah 64:6
Romans 3:11-20

God says that there is not one person on earth who is good and does what is right in His sight.

No one, except Jesus, has perfectly obeyed God's laws.

This man thought he had kept the Ten Commandments perfectly because he had obeyed them outwardly.

But even if he did obey the laws of God outwardly, he had not obeyed them in his heart.

Matthew 5:17-28

Jesus had already taught the the meaning of the Law by explaining that
- If a person hates another in his heart, he has committed murder.
- If a man looks at a woman and desires her, he has committed adultery in God's sight.

I Samuel 16:7
Hebrews 4:12,13

God doesn't judge a person according to his outward acts alone.

In Hebrews 4:12, we are told that God knows a person's inner thoughts, attitudes, and desires.
- If a person plans to take something which belongs to someone else, he has stolen.
- If an adult or a child outwardly submits to someone's authority but is angry in his heart or obeys grudgingly, he has sinned before God.

Romans 3:19-23

God did not give His laws to Israel because He thought that they could obey them.

Rather, God gave the Ten Commandments to prove to them and to us that all have sinned and come short of God's standard of goodness.
- Illustrate:

  This is just a story to illustrate what the Bible teaches about this subject.

Teacher's Notes

Lesson 44: Jesus Loved Children and Taught the Rich Young Ruler

Scripture Reference

The people in a little town decided to hold a special contest to see if anyone could jump across the narrow spot in the stream that flowed alongside the town.

Many people trained for weeks. The children practiced their running jumps at school. Some of them were very good jumpers. A few of the adults were very serious about training and worked out every day developing their jumping muscles under the guidance of a trainer. Even some of the elderly people thought they might like to try. They enjoyed getting together and cheering each other as they practiced their jumps.

When the big day came, a starting place was marked on one side of the stream and a landing place was marked on the other side.

All those who had trained, young and old, came. Many other people also decided at the last minute to try the jump just for fun.

But the stream was quite wide, even at the narrowest place. One after another, the jumpers made their running start, jumped, and fell in the water, far short of the other side. Young and old, trained and untrained, those who were trying hard and those who just did it for the fun of it—all of them missed the mark on the other side.

- Compare:

This is how it is with God's laws. Even those who try very hard are not able to obey them perfectly as God demands. We have all failed to reach God's standard of goodness and perfection.

You may think that you are a good person and that you do not deserve to go to Hell.

Nevertheless, you, too, have failed to do what God requires.

It is impossible for us to please God by our own efforts because we are born descendants of Adam and are separated from God.

- God looks at our hearts and sees the wickedness.
- We can never earn God's favor by our own efforts.

F. The danger of being rich

 Theme: God is loving, merciful, and gracious.

 READ Mark 10:21a.

"Then Jesus beholding him loved him...."

Jesus loved this young man even though the man was proud and did not see himself as a sinner as God saw him.

God loves each of us, even though He knows that we are sinners.

He does not want us to be separated from Him forever.

 Theme: Man is a sinner. He needs God and is helpless to save himself.

 READ Mark 10:21.

Jesus told this wealthy man to sell all of his possessions and give the proceeds to the poor.

- Jesus knew that the man was covetous and loved his riches more than he loved his fellowman.

Lesson 44: Jesus Loved Children and Taught the Rich Young Ruler

Scripture Reference

Teacher's Notes

- Jesus was trying to show him that he had broken God's law which says that we must love our neighbor as much as we love ourselves.
- Jesus wanted him to admit that he was a sinner and needed a Saviour.

Jesus also told him that he should leave his home and follow Jesus, because Jesus is God.

- Jesus knew that this man loved his wealth more than he loved God.

Matthew 22:37,38

- The first great commandment of God says that we must love God with all our heart, with all our soul, and with all our mind, and that we must not put anything or anyone in the place of God.

Jesus was trying to help this young man realize that he had put his wealth in the place of God.

- He had broken God's laws, and therefore, he was a condemned sinner in the sight of God.
- Jesus wanted him to realize that he could not be accepted by God for the things he did. He was already dead to God and rejected by Him.

 Theme: God is holy and righteous. He demands death as the payment for sin.

No one has given God the place in his life which God should have.

The payment for this is death, separation from God in the place of punishment.

- God will not overlook the payment for our sin.
- He will never forgive us unless the full payment for sin has been made.

Is there any way that our sin can be paid for so that we can be saved from the everlasting fire?

Yes, there is! That is what Jesus came to do!

 Theme: Man is a sinner. He needs God and is helpless to save himself.

 READ Mark 10:22-24.

This rich young ruler had made his choice.

- He chose his riches, which he could only enjoy in this life, and he turned away from life forever with God.
- He was sad because, although he wanted eternal life, he loved his money more than he loved God or people.
- He did not want to do what Jesus told him.

Maybe you are like this young man and think that the most important thing in life is to get rich.

When you die, however, you will not be able to take any of your wealth with you.

The rich and the poor are the same in the sight of God.

The important thing to God is not our material possessions, but whether we are ready to listen to His words and believe Him.

Lesson 44: Jesus Loved Children and Taught the Rich Young Ruler

G. Conclusion

Do your remember our reading from God's Word how Jesus had fed five thousand men with five loaves and two small fish?

Following this, the people came looking for Jesus, hoping to get some more food.

Do you remember what Jesus said to them?

 Read John 6:27-29.

QUESTIONS:

1. Did Jesus care for children? *Yes, Jesus loves all children.*

2. Do children need to be rescued from the power of Satan, sin, and death? *Yes, they, too, need to understand and trust in Jesus as their Deliverer, just as adults do.*

3. What did Jesus mean when He said that we must become as little children if we are to enter His kingdom? *Children find it easier to simply believe than adults. We must trust in Jesus, the Deliverer, just as a little child trusts in his parents.*

4. How did the young man who came to Jesus think he would please God and get into Heaven? *By obeying God's commandments.*

5. Was Jesus saying that He isn't good and that He is not God when He said to the rich young man, "Why do you call me good? No one is good—except God alone"? *No! Jesus is God and is therefore good like God the Father and God the Holy Spirit.*

6. What did Jesus want this young man to understand? *Jesus wanted him to understand that all people have disobeyed God's laws and that only God is good.*

7. Why did this young man go away sad? *Because he did not want to do what Jesus had told him. He loved his money more than he loved God or other people.*

8. Did Jesus say it is sinful to be rich? *No, it is not sinful to be rich, but it is sinful to love riches more than we love God or other people.*

9. What is far more important than working for the riches of this world? *Making certain that we have our trust in Jesus, the Deliverer.*

LESSON 45: The Foolishness of Trusting in Riches

LESSON PREPARATION

This section is for you, the teacher.

The passages in the Scripture Reference column are for your own study in preparing for this lesson. Since they may contain concepts that run ahead of the lesson, they are not to be taught at this point.

Note: If you have not taught previously from this series of lessons, please read carefully the note to teachers in the front of this book.

SCRIPTURE: Luke 12:15-21; 16:19-31

LESSON GOALS:

- To show the foolishness of trusting in riches.
- To show that when man dies, he spends eternity in either Heaven or Hell.

THIS LESSON SHOULD HELP THE STUDENTS:

- To see how short this life is.
- To see the importance of trusting God to save them.

PERSPECTIVE FOR THE TEACHER:

We live in a day of the "here and now." Few people want to think about the consequences tomorrow of what they do today. Credit buying with high interest payments is just one example of this nearsighted thinking which can bring ruin and sorrow here in this life.

But eternally important consequences hinge upon our response to God's provision for our salvation.

Jesus knew men's hearts. Even two thousand years ago, men were living for their "today" and not for eternity. The parable of the rich man and the story of Lazarus and the rich man give us a unique opportunity to view today from the perspective of eternity. How we need to take a long, careful look at these solemn stories, graciously given by God to warn us of eternal, unending punishment for all who refuse God's provision of salvation through Jesus Christ.

Pray that God will put in your students' minds and hearts an eternal perspective. Salvation is not just an escape for today; it is God's provision of eternal life instead of the eternal punishment justly deserved by every person because of sin.

VISUALS:

- Chronological Picture No. 78, "The Rich Fool"
- Chronological Picture No. 79, "The Rich Man in Hell"
- A simple time line is illustrated in this lesson; you may want to draw it as you teach. Or, if you prefer, it could be prepared ahead.

Teacher's Notes

OVERVIEW

This lesson presents the foolishness of trusting in riches as shown in the parable of the rich fool. The true story of the rich man and Lazarus presents the fact of eternal punishment and separation from God for the unbeliever and the fact of eternal happiness in God's presence for the believer.

Teacher's Notes

Lesson 45: *The Foolishness of Trusting in Riches*

Scripture Reference

ON TEACHING THIS LESSON:

These lessons are designed to **teach unbelievers.** You are carefully laying a scriptural foundation on which the Gospel will later be presented. If your class contains believers, teach with the goal of giving them an understanding of the basis for their faith and **with the goal of enabling them to teach the same material to unbelievers.**

DON'T COMPLICATE THE MESSAGE!

As you teach, keep in mind that this is a directed study—not an exhaustive survey of the Bible and not an unlimited group discussion. Keep your lesson on track and moving ahead by limiting and directing any discussion.

Carefully follow the outline. Emphasize the doctrinal themes.

LESSON FORMAT: The **center column** below contains the lesson material to be taught to the students. The **bold outline headings** are only for reference and need not be spoken, as they are incorporated into the outlined material that follows. The material in the **side columns** is for the teacher's own reference and is not intended to be included in the lesson.

TO BE TAUGHT TO THE STUDENTS
(Center Column Only)

LESSON OUTLINE:

REVIEW questions from Lesson 44.

A. Introduction

Are you confronted with a lot of problems?

How about a million dollars?

Would that take care of everything?

Sometimes we might think that it would, but let's take a look at things in light of eternity.

B. The foolishness of living only for the things of this life

 Theme: **Man must have faith in order to please God and be saved.**

 READ Luke 12:15.

Many people want the things of this world more than anything else.
- They are jealous of what other people have.
- They think that they would be happy and satisfied if they were rich.

Jesus told these people a parable.
- As we mentioned before, a parable is a story about things in this world, but it teaches us something about God and our relationship with Him.
- Jesus told this parable because He wanted the people to realize that our relationship with God is far more important than the riches of this world.

Lesson 45: The Foolishness of Trusting in Riches

Scripture Reference

Teacher's Notes

- Even if a man had all the wealth in the world, it wouldn't be of any benefit to him if he were to go to Hell.
- Believing God and having everlasting life is of far more value than being comfortable and secure in this life.

 READ Luke 12:16-19.

Suggested Visual:

CHRONOLOGICAL PICTURE NO. 78, "THE RICH FOOL"

This farmer thought that he had all that he needed.
- He thought that he had nothing to worry about because he was a very rich man.
- He thought that he could ignore God and live his life the way he wanted.

Ezekiel 18:4

This man did not take into account that God is the one who gives life and the one who takes life.

 Theme: God is supreme and sovereign.

Although he did not acknowledge God's authority over him, God had not forgotten him.
- The rich man made his plans as to what he would do, but God had different plans for him—that very night.
- This is what Jesus said that God had planned.

 READ Luke 12:20.

When God decides that it is the time for a person to die, he will die.

No one can do anything to keep that person from dying.

 Theme: Man must have faith in order to please God and be saved.

God called this rich man a fool because he made plans without recognizing God and lived only for the riches of this world.

 READ Luke 12:21.

The things that God gives to those who trust in Him are far better than the riches of this world.
- The things of this world only last for a short time, and we never know when we may have to leave them all behind.
- But the things that God gives those who trust in Him will last forever.
- God is warning us to be wise and to invest our time and energy in learning about Him and trusting Him to show us what is really needed in our lives.

Lesson 45: *The Foolishness of Trusting in Riches*

Teacher's Notes

Scripture Reference

C. The rich man and Lazarus

 READ Luke 16:19-21.

Unlike the story we just read, this is not a parable.

- This really happened.
- At some time prior to when Jesus told this story, these two men actually lived on this earth.

When we look at these two men, it would certainly seem that the rich man was better off than Lazarus.

- The rich man seemed to have everything he needed and more.
- But Lazarus was sick, he didn't have enough food, and the dogs even came and licked his sores.

Listen to what Jesus said happened to these two men.

 READ Luke 16:22.

Think about it:

- Did the rich man's wealth keep him from dying?
- Were his riches any benefit to him after he died?
- Where did Lazarus go when he died?
- He went to the place where Abraham was.
- What about the rich man?
- Did he go where Lazarus went?
- Jesus said that the rich man's body was buried.
- Where did he go when he left his body?

When people die, they either go directly to be with God or immediately to the place of punishment.

Luke 23:43

II Corinthians 5:8

Abraham had been buried hundreds of years before these other men died, but he was still living with God.

You will live forever with God in Heaven, or you will be forever in the place of fire and punishment for sin.[1]

[1] We have not previously and will not now take the time to teach the unsaved the difference between Hades and the Lake of Fire. Although Hades, to which the rich man went, is not the final destination of the unsaved, those who are there have already entered into everlasting suffering.

After the Great White Throne judgment, those who occupy Hades will be cast into the Lake of Fire which was prepared for Satan and his angels (Revelation 20:10,12-15). ☐

Let's see where Jesus said that the rich man went after he died.

D. The rich man's cry for help

 Theme: Jesus Christ is God.

 Theme: God is everywhere all the time; He knows everything.

 READ Luke 16:23.

Lesson 45: The Foolishness of Trusting in Riches

Suggested Visual:

CHRONOLOGICAL PICTURE NO. 79, "THE RICH MAN IN HELL"

Psalm 139:7,8

Jesus knew where Lazarus and the rich man went after they died. He is God, and so He knows where every person is, even after he has died.

Lazarus went to the place of happiness and acceptance with God, but the rich man went to the place of fire and everlasting punishment.

Think about it.

- Right now, perhaps two thousand years later, the rich man is still in Hell, and he will suffer for all eternity.
- Lazarus is still with God and will be with Him for all eternity.

 Theme: God is holy and righteous. He demands death as the payment for sin.

 READ Luke 16:24.

There is great suffering in Hell.

All who refuse to believe what God says in His Word go there and suffer.

God hates sin.

- God is not merely threatening about the punishment for sin.
- All sin must be paid for in full.

E. **Abraham's answer**

 Theme: Man must have faith in order to please God and be saved.

 READ Luke 16:25.

- Consider:

Did Lazarus go to the place of happiness and acceptance with God because he was poor on this earth? Did the rich man go to the place of punishment because he was wealthy? Does God reject the rich and accept the poor? No! That is not what made the difference between the two men.

The rich man went to Hell because he did not agree with God that he was a sinner and he did not trust in God and His promises to send a Deliverer to rescue him from the power of Satan, sin, and death. The rich man didn't take time to think of God or to believe His Word. He just lived his life on this earth to enjoy his riches. He lived for himself and did not care about God (or people).

Lesson 45: The Foolishness of Trusting in Riches

Teacher's Notes

2If someone asks about "purgatory," tell him that the Bible does not mention purgatory. (Purgatory is man's false idea of a place where a person can have another opportunity after he dies to get things right with God).

When you point out a false teaching like this, do not attack the religion that teaches it; simply state the fact that the particular teaching does not line up with what the Bible says.

If a student is offended, be gracious to him and suggest he study the Word himself so he can see that what the Bible really teaches. ☐

3You may have a student who asks about a loved one who has already died without trusting the Lord as his Saviour. This is an extremely emotional issue—one that must be handled with a great deal of wisdom and compassion.

There is no easy answer; the facts are not comforting. But pray that the Lord will use this very sad and difficult situation to cause the one left behind, not to be bitter, but to seek the Lord and to put his or her trust in Him.

You might consider answering something like this:

"I really sympathize with you. I am so sorry you have lost your loved one. Many of us have relatives who may have died without putting their trust in Jesus Christ. Satan would like those of us who are left behind to think that it would be better to join our loved ones in Hell than to put our trust in Jesus Christ.

"Don't be deceived. Hell is not a place of fellowship.

"If you were in the position of the rich man, would you want your loved ones there? We must also think about those of our family and friends who are still alive. They are watching our response to God.

"God calls to us who are still alive to be born again through Jesus Christ into God's family. He feels our grief, and He loves us." ☐

But Lazarus was different. Lazarus agreed with God that he was a sinner, and he trusted in God and His promises to send the Saviour, just as Abraham did when he was alive.

 READ Luke 16:26.

Once a person dies and goes to Hell, there is no way he can be delivered.

- There is no way of escape.
- He will be there forever and ever.

If you refuse to listen to God's Word and die unacceptable to Him, then you, too, will go to Hell.

Those who die separated from God by their sin remain separated from God forever. **2**

F. The rich man's appeal on behalf of his brothers

 READ Luke 16:27,28.

Even though he was in terrible suffering, the rich man still remembered his brothers and his relatives.

- People in Hell still remember this world.
- They remember what they did when they were alive, and they remember the relatives and friends that they have left behind.

Think about it

- Why did the rich man want Abraham to send Lazarus back to the home of the rich man's five brothers?
- What did he want Lazarus to say to his brothers?

The rich man wanted Abraham to allow Lazarus to come back to earth to warn the man's relatives so they wouldn't also go to the same terrible place of punishment where he was. **3**

G. Abraham's answer

Was Lazarus allowed to return to this world?

No! God will not allow the dead to return.

 Theme: God communicates with man.

How did Abraham answer the rich man?

 READ Luke 16:29.

Abraham told the rich man that his brothers should take notice of the things which Moses and all of the prophets wrote in the Bible.

- No one needs to go to Hell.
- If we listen to God's Word, He will teach the way to everlasting life through the Lord Jesus.

H. The rich man's argument and Abraham's verdict

 Theme: Man is a sinner. He needs God and is helpless to save himself.

Lesson 45: The Foolishness of Trusting in Riches

 Theme: Man must have faith in order to please God and be saved.

 READ Luke 16:30,31.

If people refuse to believe God's written Word, they will not believe even if God did send someone back from the dead to warn them.

Even though the leaders of the Jews saw Jesus raise Lazarus from the dead, they still would not believe.

I. Conclusion

The Enemy has really deceived people about living for today.

Money, things, even health seem more important than God to many people.

Before we close, let's draw a time line.

Suggested Visual:

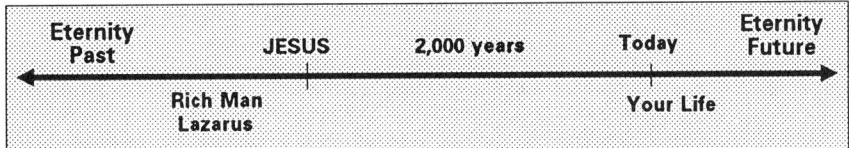

The line in the middle represents time.

You'll notice that it stretches endlessly in both directions.

Around two thousand years have passed since Jesus told the story of the rich man and Lazarus.

Both of these men are still in the same state as when Jesus told the story:

- Lazarus is with God.
- The rich man is in Hell.

There is no changing places; their future was decided while they still lived on earth.

- Lazarus believed God.
- The rich man didn't, at least not while he was on the earth.

But once he was in torment, he cried out to Abraham to send Lazarus to warn the rich man's relatives against the punishment that they too were going to face.

- But there was nothing Abraham or Lazarus could do.
- Abraham said that the rich man's relatives had the testimony of Moses and the prophets.

What about us?

Look at where we are on this time line.

How long do you think your life will be?

- Fifty, sixty, seventy, eighty years?
- How long a span would that be on this chart?
- How long is it compared to eternity?

Think about it.

Eternity is a **long** time.

Whether or not you believe God's Word and trust in His provision for your sins will determine where you spend **all eternity**.

Lesson 45: The Foolishness of Trusting in Riches

Jesus said it clearly:

 Read Mark 8:36.

QUESTIONS:

1. What is much more important than being rich? *Understanding and believing God's words about Jesus, the Deliverer.*

2. Who decides when we will die? *God.*

3. Is the story of the rich man and Lazarus a parable? *No, it really happened.*

4. Where do people go when they die? *Either to Heaven or to a place of punishment.*

5. Will anyone ever be released from the place of punishment? *No, once a person goes to the place of punishment, he will never escape.*

6. What did the rich man ask Abraham to do?

    a. *He asked Abraham to send Lazarus with even one drop of water to cool his tongue.*

    b. *He asked Abraham to send Lazarus back to earth to warn his brothers so they wouldn't end up in the place of punishment.*

7. What did Abraham tell the rich man that his brothers should do? *Abraham said that they should believe the writings of Moses and the prophets, that is, the Old Testament.*

8. How can we find the way to God and to everlasting life? *Through God's Word, the Bible.*

Scripture Reference

LESSON 46

Jesus Rode into Jerusalem; Judas Planned to Betray Jesus; Jesus Instituted the Lord's Supper

LESSON PREPARATION

This section is for you, the teacher.

The passages in the Scripture Reference column are for your own study in preparing for this lesson. Since they may contain concepts that run ahead of the lesson, they are not to be taught at this point.

Note: If you have not taught previously from this series of lessons, please read carefully the note to teachers in the front of this book.

SCRIPTURE: Mark 11:1-10; 14:1,2,10-26

LESSON GOALS:

- To show that Jesus Christ is the Deliverer, the only one who can save us from our sins.
- To show the fulfillment of prophecy regarding Jesus' betrayal.
- To present the institution of the Lord's Supper.

THIS LESSON SHOULD HELP THE STUDENTS:

- To consider their own sinfulness.
- To see the horribleness of the sin of Judas' betrayal of Jesus.
- To see the fulfillment of prophecy.

PERSPECTIVE FOR THE TEACHER:

This passage of Scripture presents contrasts of devotion.

The Jewish people were delighted to think that, at last, they were going to have deliverance from foreign rule. They were devoted to Jesus for what He could give them as an earthly king. Many welcomed Him as their deliverer from the Romans; but few saw Him as their Deliverer from Satan and sin and death.

Judas was devoted to personal gain, so much so that he willingly sold the Son of God for thirty pieces of silver.

Jesus Christ was devoted to God the Father and to saving a world of sinners—so much so that He willingly gave His own life as a ransom.

Judas did not believe God, even though he walked, talked, and worked at His side for three years. Judas refused the offer of eternal life because his heart was set on personal, earthly riches.

What a heart-searching message this story is for our materialistic society! Who can put a "value" on forgiveness and eternal life? Jesus paid the ultimate price in His own body and blood, broken and poured out for sinners.

VISUALS:

- Chronological Picture No. 81, "The Triumphal Entry"
- Chronological Picture No. 82, "The Lord's Supper"
- Prophecy Chart
- Chronological Map 3

Teacher's Notes

OVERVIEW

In this lesson, Jesus is shown to be the Passover Lamb who died to save all men.

In the Lord's Supper, the bread represents His body, broken for men. The cup represents His blood, shed for the sins of all men.

This lesson shows that most of the people welcomed Jesus as an earthly king, not as their Saviour.

Judas' betrayal of Jesus is shown as the plot of Satan, who intended to keep Jesus from delivering men.

The details of Jesus' life are shown as the fulfillment of prophecy.

Teacher's Notes

Lesson 46: Triumphal Entry; Betrayal; The Lord's Supper

Scripture Reference

ON TEACHING THIS LESSON:

These lessons are designed to **teach unbelievers.** You are carefully laying a scriptural foundation on which the Gospel will later be presented. If your class contains believers, teach with the goal of giving them an understanding of the basis for their faith and **with the goal of enabling them to teach the same material to unbelievers.**

DON'T COMPLICATE THE MESSAGE!

As you teach, keep in mind that this is a directed study—not an exhaustive survey of the Bible and not an unlimited group discussion. Keep your lesson on track and moving ahead by limiting and directing any discussion.

Carefully follow the outline. Emphasize the doctrinal themes.

LESSON FORMAT: The **center column** below contains the lesson material to be taught to the students. The **bold outline headings** are only for reference and need not be spoken, as they are incorporated into the outlined material that follows. The material in the **side columns** is for the teacher's own reference and is not intended to be included in the lesson.

TO BE TAUGHT TO THE STUDENTS
(Center Column Only)

LESSON OUTLINE:

REVIEW questions from Lesson 45.

A. Introduction

Crowds of people followed Jesus everywhere He went.
- Some wanted healing for physical problems.
- Others wanted political freedom from the Romans.
- Very few were thinking about their spiritual needs.
- Very few were willing to admit that their greatest need was to be saved from Satan and sin and death.

What do you expect to find in Jesus?[1]

Think about it as we study our lesson.

B. Jesus sent His disciples to get a young donkey for Him to ride.

As Jesus and His disciples walked toward Jerusalem, they came to the little town of Bethany, just outside of the city of Jerusalem.

POINT TO BETHANY AND JERUSALEM ON MAP 3.

Bethany was the home of Mary and Martha and Lazarus.
Only a short time before, Jesus had raised Lazarus from the dead.

 READ Mark 11:1-6.

C. The people welcomed Jesus as the Deliverer.

 Theme: God is faithful; He never changes.

---

[1] This is another of those questions designed to make the students think. Don't wait for their answers; just go on with the lesson.

534

Lesson 46: Triumphal Entry; Betrayal; The Lord's Supper

 READ Mark 11:7-10.

Jesus sat on the young donkey and rode into Jerusalem just as God had said that He would.

 Read Zechariah 9:9.

Suggested Visual:

CHRONOLOGICAL PICTURE NO. 81, "THE TRIUMPHAL ENTRY"

The crowds welcomed Jesus as the promised Deliverer from God.
- They praised Him as the one whom all the prophets of God had promised that God would send to be their king.
- But, unfortunately, most of the people did not trust in Jesus to save them from Satan's power, their sins, and God's punishment.
- They only wanted Jesus to be their king so He would deliver them from their enemies, particularly from the Romans who ruled their country.

D. **The Jewish leaders' plan**

 Theme: Man is a sinner. He needs God and is helpless to save himself.

 READ Mark 14:1,2.

The Jewish leaders were determined to kill Jesus, but they were frightened of the crowds.

Jesus was very popular because of all the great miracles He had done.

E. **Judas planned to betray Jesus.**

 Theme: Man is a sinner. He needs God and is helpless to save himself.

 READ Mark 14:10.

Judas was one of the twelve men whom Jesus had chosen to be His closest companions, but Judas was not concerned about his own sinfulness before God.
- He did not trust in Jesus as the Saviour of sinners.
- Judas followed Jesus for his own personal gain.
- Note:

  John 12:6 tells us that Judas was a thief. As keeper of the money bag, he helped himself to what was in it.

When it seemed that he wasn't going to receive any personal benefits from following Jesus, he was willing to sell Jesus to His enemies.

Lesson 46: Triumphal Entry; Betrayal; The Lord's Supper

 Theme: God is everywhere all the time; He knows everything.

What God said in His Word came true.
- God said that a friend of Jesus would sell Him to His enemies.
- Judas had been a close companion of Jesus for three years.

 READ Psalm 41:9.

POINT TO THE PROPHECY CHART. Uncover "Betrayed by a friend" and write Mark 14:10,11 opposite Psalm 41:9. Read the prophecy and its fulfillment.

 Theme: Satan fights against God and His will. Satan is a liar and a deceiver. He hates man.

Satan was guiding Judas to betray Jesus.
- Satan hates Jesus because Jesus is God and He speaks the truth.
- Satan thought that, if he could get the Jewish leaders to kill Jesus, he would hinder God's plan to destroy Satan and deliver sinners.
-

 Theme: God is everywhere all the time; He knows everything.

Judas went to the enemies of Jesus and told them that he was willing to betray Jesus for money.
What do you think the Jewish leaders thought of that?

 READ Mark 14:11.

Matthew tells us that the Jewish leaders promised to pay Judas thirty pieces of silver.
- Note:
  Thirty pieces of silver was the price of a common slave.
Over five hundred years earlier, God had told His prophet Zechariah that this was exactly what was going to happen to the Deliverer.

 READ Zechariah 11:12,13.

POINT TO THE PROPHECY CHART. Uncover "Sold for 30 pieces of silver" and write Matthew 26:14,15 opposite Zechariah 11:12,13. Read the prophecy and its fulfillment.

The Word of God is absolutely amazing.
Not one detail of prophecy goes unfulfilled.

F. Preparation for the Passover Feast

 READ Mark 14:12.

Who remembers what particular event the Jews were remembering when they ate the Feast of the Passover?

Exodus 12:21-27

 Theme: Jesus is God.

Lesson 46: Triumphal Entry; Betrayal; The Lord's Supper

Scripture Reference | Teacher's Notes

 Theme: God is everywhere all the time; He knows everything.

 READ Mark 14:13-15.

Jesus knew that the disciples would meet a man carrying a water jar.

- This was an unusual thing to see because the work of getting and carrying water was usually left to women.
- The Lord knows everything before it happens.
- Consider:

   He knew, five hundred years before it happened, that Jesus would be sold for thirty pieces of silver.

   He knows even the small and insignificant things; the Bible tells us that God sees and knows even when one little sparrow falls to the ground and dies.

   God is infinitely wise, and yet He sees and cares about the smallest details of life.

Matthew 10:29

 READ Mark 14:16.

G. Jesus knew His betrayer.

 Theme: Jesus Christ is God.

 Theme: God is everywhere all the time; He knows everything.

 READ Mark 14:17,18.

Suggested Visual:

CHRONOLOGICAL PICTURE NO. 82, "THE LORD'S SUPPER"

Jesus knew, without anyone telling Him, that Judas was going to betray Him.

Yet Jesus loved him and was very sad to think Judas would do this to Him.

Psalm 41:9; 55:12-13

READ Mark 14:19,20.

- Note:

   When the Jews ate together like this, they broke pieces of bread from the loaves on the table, and then they dipped the pieces into a large bowl in the center of the table. This bowl usually contained mashed fruit.

Teacher's Notes

Lesson 46: Triumphal Entry; Betrayal; The Lord's Supper

Scripture Reference

Jesus was acting as the host at this meal. In the Mideast, it is a particularly evil thing to accept hospitality from a person and then injure him in any way.

Jesus said that the one who was going to betray Him was one of his twelve companions who was sharing the meal with Him.

- Jesus and the one who was going to betray Him were dipping pieces of bread into the same dish.
- Even though they were sharing this meal together, very soon afterward, this companion of Jesus was going to sell Him to His enemies.

When Jesus said that it would be one of the twelve, He was probably trying to make Judas realize what a horrible thing he was planning to do.

Jesus was giving Judas an opportunity to change his mind.

 Theme: Jesus Christ is God.

 Theme: Jesus Christ is man.

 READ Mark 14:21.

Jesus often called Himself "the Son of man," for although He was the Son of God, He was also a real man.

Jesus knew that He had to die, just as God had foretold through the prophets in the Old Testament.

I Peter 1:10,11

But even though Jesus had to die, it did not excuse Judas. **2**

God did not make him betray Jesus.

Judas would be punished forever for his sins: his selfishness, his part in the murder of an innocent man—the Son of God, and, most of all, for his refusal to trust Jesus Christ as His Saviour.

His horrible deed was evidence that he did not believe.

H. The meaning of the bread and the wine

 Theme: Jesus Christ is the only Saviour.

 READ Mark 14:22.

Jesus broke the bread and then explained that, just as He had broken the bread, so His body would soon be broken by evil men.

 READ Mark 14:23,24.

Jesus said that the wine which He poured out for them to drink was a picture, or illustration, of His blood which, when He died, would flow out of His body.

Jesus said that, when He died, He would be giving His life in the place of sinners. **3**

 READ Mark 14:25,26.

I. Conclusion

It's impossible for us to imagine the deep love of Jesus.

He had never sinned.

---

2 Ungodly men have written books and scripts to the effect that Judas was a "victim" in this horrible crime—that it was not really Judas' fault; God just chose him to do the evil deed.

If one of your students brings up these ideas, tell them that this is entirely against the character of God.

Read to them II Peter 3:9.

You might also read to them John 12:4-6, which sheds more light on Judas' character.

A student may want to debate the issue of God's sovereign will and man's free choice. Avoid getting into this type of discussion. Tell the student that God's wisdom is perfect and that we are studying those things He has given us to consider. Some things are too great for us to understand, and we can leave them in the hands of God.

If a student wants to do deeper study on his own, he is welcome to do so. But he should make the center of his study the Bible itself. ☐

3 Through these words, you are virtually giving the Gospel. Be sensitive to share further with any of the students who seem to have hearts prepared to hear the Gospel explained more fully. ☐

Lesson 46: Triumphal Entry; Betrayal; The Lord's Supper

Yet He was going to die for sinners.

Everyone at that table needed what He was going to do.

Everyone in the world, past, present, and future, needed what He was going to do.

Everyone of us, you and me included, needed what He was going to do in our place.

QUESTIONS:

1. Why didn't Jesus accept the offer of the people for Him to be their king? *Because they just wanted Jesus to deliver them from their enemies and the control of the Romans. They didn't want Jesus to save them from the power of Satan, sin, and death.*

2. Why didn't the priests and Jewish leaders arrest and kill Jesus immediately? *They knew that Jesus was very popular, and they thought that, if they arrested Him, the people might turn on them and kill them.*

3. Had Judas ever realized his sinfulness, repented, and trusted in Jesus? *No, he did not really mean in his heart what he said with his lips.*

4. For how much had the prophets said the Deliverer would be sold? *Thirty pieces of silver.*

5. For how much was Jesus sold? *Thirty pieces of silver, just as the prophets had foretold.*

6. How did Jesus know what Judas planned to do? *Jesus is God. He knows everything.*

7. Who did the prophets say would betray the Deliverer? *A friend and close companion.*

8. To what did Jesus liken the broken bread? *His own body, which was soon to be broken by His enemies.*

9. To what did Jesus liken the poured-out wine? *His own blood, which His enemies would soon cause to flow out of His body.*

10. For whom did Jesus say His blood would flow out? *For sinners.*

Scripture Reference

Teacher's Notes

Jesus Was Arrested by His Enemies

OVERVIEW

This lesson presents Jesus' arrest, one of His false trials, and the cruel punishment He suffered prior to His crucifixion. In His suffering, He is shown to be sinless, holy, and uncomplaining as He willingly takes our punishment.

Fulfillment of prophecy is stressed throughout this lesson.

LESSON PREPARATION

This section is for you, the teacher.

The passages in the Scripture Reference column are for your own study in preparing for this lesson. Since they may contain concepts that run ahead of the lesson, they are not to be taught at this point.

Note: If you have not taught previously from this series of lessons, please read carefully the note to teachers in the front of this book.

Isaiah 53
Psalm 22

SCRIPTURE: Mark 14:32-65; 15:1-19

LESSON GOALS:

- To show that Jesus Christ is God.
- To show that what happened to Jesus was the fulfillment of prophecy.
- To show the terrible suffering Jesus willingly underwent for us at the hands of sinners.

THIS LESSON SHOULD HELP THE STUDENTS:

- To realize that Jesus Christ suffered as a man.
- To see the terrible injustice done to Jesus.
- To see how Jesus reacted when He was mistreated.

PERSPECTIVE FOR THE TEACHER:

"That's not fair! I don't deserve that kind of treatment!" How many times have we heard (or thought!) something similar to this?

One look at Jesus before His accusers should silence us and move our hearts deeply with stinging remorse for ever having complained. He, the altogether righteous, holy, loving God, willingly took the false accusations, derision, and most cruel punishment ever given; and He did it all for us guilty sinners who really deserved to die. I Peter 2:23,24 says, *"Who, when he was reviled, reviled not again; when he suffered, he threatened not; but committed himself to him that judgeth righteously: Who his own self bare our sins in his own body on the tree, that we, being dead to sins, should live unto righteousness: by whose stripes ye were healed."*

May our hearts be filled with tender love for our Saviour as we present Him in His time of horrible trial.

VISUALS:

- Chronological Picture No. 83, "Jesus Praying"
- Chronological Picture No. 84, "Jesus Arrested"
- Chronological Picture No. 85, "Jesus Before Pilate"
- Chronological Picture No. 86, "The Soldiers Mock Jesus"
- Prophecy Chart
- Chronological Map 3

Lesson 47: Jesus Was Arrested by His Enemies

ON TEACHING THIS LESSON:

These lessons are designed to **teach unbelievers.** You are carefully laying a scriptural foundation on which the Gospel will later be presented. If your class contains believers, teach with the goal of giving them an understanding of the basis for their faith and **with the goal of enabling them to teach the same material to unbelievers.**

DON'T COMPLICATE THE MESSAGE!

As you teach, keep in mind that this is a directed study—not an exhaustive survey of the Bible and not an unlimited group discussion. Keep your lesson on track and moving ahead by limiting and directing any discussion.

Carefully follow the outline. Emphasize the doctrinal themes.

LESSON FORMAT: The **center column** below contains the lesson material to be taught to the students. The **bold outline headings** are only for reference and need not be spoken, as they are incorporated into the outlined material that follows. The material in the **side columns** is for the teacher's own reference and is not intended to be included in the lesson.

TO BE TAUGHT TO THE STUDENTS
(Center Column Only)

LESSON OUTLINE:

REVIEW questions from Lesson 46.

A. Introduction

Every now and then we hear of someone being arrested for a crime he didn't commit.

Our hearts really go out to anyone in this position.

Have you ever been accused of something you didn't do?

How did you feel about it?

But let's turn the situation around.

Has someone ever taken the blame for something **you** did?

Has anyone ever taken punishment for what you've done wrong?

Think about this as we look at this account of Jesus' arrest.

B. Jesus in Gethsemane

 Theme: Jesus Christ is man.

 READ Mark 14:32-36.

Lesson 47: Jesus Was Arrested by His Enemies

Suggested Visual:

CHRONOLOGICAL PICTURE NO. 83, "JESUS PRAYING"

Even though Jesus was God, He was also a man.
- It was very difficult for Him to face the terrible things He knew He had to suffer.
- He knew that in order to be our Saviour, He would have to go through more terrible suffering than anyone had ever endured.

As we study further, we will see what it was that brought the most grief to Jesus.

 READ Mark 14:37-42.

C. Jesus was betrayed and arrested.

 Theme: Satan fights against God and His will. Satan is a liar and a deceiver. He hates man.

 READ Mark 14:43-46.

Suggested Visual:

CHRONOLOGICAL PICTURE NO. 84, "JESUS ARRESTED"

They probably didn't realize it, but Judas and all the men who came to arrest Jesus were being guided by Satan.
- Compare:
  People today may not think of it either, but if they oppose or ignore God's Word and refuse to trust Jesus as the Saviour sent from God, they are also being led by Satan.

 READ Mark 14:47-49.

Jesus knew that everything which had been foretold about Him in the Old Testament would happen just as God had said.

D. The disciples all fled.

 READ Mark 14:50-52.

Scripture Reference: Mark 15:34

Teacher's Notes

Teacher's Notes

Lesson 47: Jesus Was Arrested by His Enemies

Scripture Reference

The disciples all ran away and left Jesus, just as He had predicted they would.
- They were afraid, disappointed, and confused.
- They believed that Jesus was the Saviour sent from God, but they couldn't understand how He could be the Saviour if He was going to be killed by His enemies.
- They didn't understand how His death could deliver them from Satan, sin, and death.

Zechariah 13:7
Mark 14:27

E. Jesus was tried by the Jewish leaders.

 READ Mark 14:53,54.

Peter followed at a distance.

He was afraid that he, too, might be arrested and killed.

 Theme: Jesus Christ is holy and righteous.

 Theme: Man is a sinner. He needs God and is helpless to save himself.

 READ Mark 14:55.

Jesus stood before the Sanhedrin, the high court of the Jewish people.[1]
- Jesus hadn't done anything wrong.
- Therefore, they couldn't find any lawful reason to condemn Him.
- They didn't have any reason to hate Jesus except that they loved their own sinful ways and did not want to obey God's words which Jesus had told them.

[1] Note: This is one of six false trials suffered by Jesus. Three of the trials were before the religious leaders; three were before Roman officials. All of these trials were illegal because of the way they were conducted and/or the use of false witnesses. ☐

 Theme: God is everywhere all the time; He knows everything.

 READ Mark 14:56-59.

God's prophets had said that false witnesses would tell lies about the Deliverer.

 Read Psalm 27:12.

POINT TO THE PROPHECY CHART. Uncover "Accused by false witnesses," and write Mark 14:56,57 opposite Psalm 27:12. Read the prophecy and its fulfillment.

God had caused David to write this prophecy nearly one thousand years earlier.

Now, as Jesus stood before the Sanhedrin, the exact words David wrote were being fulfilled.

 Theme: Jesus Christ is God.

 Theme: God is everywhere all the time; He knows everything.

Lesson 47: Jesus Was Arrested by His Enemies

Scripture Reference

I Peter 2:23

Teacher's Notes

READ Mark 14:60-62.

When they told lies about Him, Jesus was quiet and wouldn't answer.

- Jesus was trusting in God, His Father, to do what He had planned for Him.
- He knew that everything that would happen to Him was according to His Father's plan so that we could be delivered from the power of Satan, sin, and death.

But when they asked Him if He really was the Christ (meaning the promised Deliverer) and the Son of God, Jesus answered very plainly that He was.

- Recall:

  Do you remember the name God gave when Moses asked Him what he should tell the people when they asked who sent him?

  In Exodus 3:14 God said, "...I AM THAT I AM...say unto the children of Israel, I AM hath sent me...."

- Consider:

  In the account of Jesus' arrest given in John 18, the men said they were looking for Jesus of Nazareth. John 18:6 says, "As soon then as he had said unto them, I am he, they went backward, and fell to the ground."

  The Jewish leaders were well aware of God's name, "I AM."

  And they were also well aware that Jesus was telling them that He was God.

 Theme: Jesus Christ is God.

 Theme: Jesus Christ is the only Saviour.

When Jesus came the first time to this world, He came to be the Saviour.

The next time Jesus comes to this world, it will be as the almighty Son of God and judge of all people.

- When He returns to this earth, everyone will see Him sitting alongside of His Father.
- Everyone will see that He is really God because He will show everyone that He is equal to God, His Father.

 READ Mark 14:63,64.

When the Jews wanted to show that they were very angry or distressed, it was their custom to rip their clothes.

The high priest was very angry because, by His answer, Jesus had said that He was equal to God.

 Theme: God is everywhere all the time; He knows everything.

 READ Mark 14:65.

This is exactly what God's prophets had said would happen to the Saviour.

Teacher's Notes

Lesson 47: Jesus Was Arrested by His Enemies

Scripture Reference

 Read Isaiah 50:6.

POINT TO THE PROPHECY CHART. Uncover "Smitten and spat upon," and write Mark 14:65 opposite Isaiah 50:6. Read the prophecy and its fulfillment. Point out that this is the fulfillment of God's Word.

Isaiah wrote this almost seven hundred years before Jesus suffered these things.

And Jesus bore his sufferings willingly, just as Isaiah had predicted.

F. Jesus was tried by Pilate.

 READ Mark 15:1.

The Romans who ruled Israel would not allow the Jews to kill anyone unless they gave permission.

Caesar, the Roman emperor, had appointed Pilate to be the governor of Samaria and Judaea.

So the Jewish leaders took Jesus to Pilate, hoping that, on the basis of the false charges they had prepared, Pilate would sentence Jesus to death.

POINT TO JUDAEA AND SAMARIA ON MAP 3.

Suggested Visual:

CHRONOLOGICAL PICTURE NO. 85, "JESUS BEFORE PILATE"

 READ Mark 15:2.

Jesus was a descendant of King David and should have been King over the Jews.

Theme: **God is faithful; He never changes.**

 READ Mark 15:3-5.

The prophet Isaiah had said that the Saviour would be silent when He was falsely accused.

Everything God says is always fulfilled in every detail.

 Read Isaiah 53:7.

POINT TO THE PROPHECY CHART. Uncover "Silent when accused," and write Mark 15:3-5 opposite Isaiah 53:7. Read the prophecy and its fulfillment. Point out that this is the fulfillment of God's Word.

Lesson 47: Jesus Was Arrested by His Enemies

G. Barabbas or Jesus?

 Theme: **Jesus Christ is holy and righteous.**

 Theme: **Man is a sinner. He needs God and is helpless to save himself.**

 READ Mark 15:6-11.

It was a custom at the Passover that Pilate, the governor, would release one prisoner for whom the Jews asked.
- Pilate knew that Jesus hadn't done anything wrong.
- He knew that the Jewish leaders wanted to kill Jesus only because they were jealous of His popularity.
- Pilate hoped that the Jews would choose to let Jesus go free rather than Barabbas who was a murderer.

H. The Jewish leaders wanted Jesus to be crucified.

 Theme: **Man is a sinner. He needs God and is helpless to save himself.**

 READ Mark 15:12-14.

Crucifixion was used by the Romans for the very worst of criminals. Today it might be compared to the gas chamber or the electric chair. But crucifixion was even worse because the person who was crucified usually did not die immediately; He endured hours and sometimes days of intense physical agony before dying.

 Theme: **God is everywhere all the time; He knows everything.**

One by one, the Old Testament prophecies about the Deliverer were being fulfilled in Jesus Christ.
- God had said through His prophet Isaiah that the Jews would hate the Deliverer even though there was no reason for them to do so.
- He said that they would reject Him.
- Everything that God said through His prophets about the coming Deliverer was fulfilled through what happened to Jesus.

 Read Isaiah 53:3.

 READ Mark 15:10.

POINT TO THE PROPHECY CHART. Uncover "Will be rejected by Jews," and write Mark 15:9-14 opposite Isaiah 53:3. Uncover "Hated without a cause," and write Mark 15:10 opposite Psalm 69:4. Read the prophecies and their fulfillment. Point out that these are the fulfillment of God's Word.

Teacher's Notes

Lesson 47: Jesus Was Arrested by His Enemies

Scripture Reference

I. Jesus was whipped and mocked.

 Theme: Man is a sinner. He needs God and is helpless to save himself.

 READ Mark 15:15.

Records from this period tell us about scourging.
- The whip consisted of many lashes of leather.
- Pieces of sharp metal and bone were tied onto the lashes so they would cut the back of the prisoner when he was beaten.
- So he couldn't escape, the prisoner was tied down with arms extended.
- Repeated blows of the lash laid open the skin, cutting flesh, muscle, and nerves, often putting the victim into severe shock.
- Some prisoners died from the scourging itself.

 READ Mark 15:16-19.

Suggested Visual:

CHRONOLOGICAL PICTURE NO. 86, "THE SOLDIERS MOCK JESUS"

After the terrible scourging, the soldiers mocked Jesus.
- They dressed Him in a purple robe. (This was the color which kings wore during that time.)

 Theme: Jesus Christ is the only Saviour.

- They made a crown of twigs which had large, sharp thorns and put the crown on Jesus' head.
- Note:

When Adam and Eve sinned, God cursed the earth and said that thorns would grow. Jesus came to suffer and die to deliver us from God's curse. God allowed Jesus' enemies to place these thorns on Jesus' head as a sign that He was going to die for the sins of the world.

Genesis 3:17,18

J. Conclusion

We feel deep sadness and even indignation when we think of someone suffering for something that they didn't even do.

But what about Jesus?

He was suffering for you and for me — for the things **we've** done.

He was suffering verbal abuse, disgrace, and physical harm; but He wasn't even complaining.

He did it for me — for my sins.

Lesson 47: Jesus Was Arrested by His Enemies

Scripture Reference

He did it for you—for your sins.

Think about it.²

Teacher's Notes

²Be ready at any point to share the Gospel more fully with any of your students who inquire. ☐

QUESTIONS:

1. Jesus was God. Why then was it hard for Him to face the terrible suffering that was before Him? *Because, although Jesus was God, He was also man, and the suffering which was before Him was more terrible than anyone had ever suffered.*

2. Who was leading Judas and the Jewish leaders to arrest and kill Jesus? *Satan.*

3. Who are being guided by Satan even now? *All those who refuse to believe God's Word, agree with Him, and trust in Jesus, the Saviour.*

4. Had Jesus done anything wrong? Did He deserve to die? *No! Jesus was perfect. He did not deserve to die.*

5. What did the prophets say about the witnesses who would speak against Jesus? *The prophets said that the witnesses would tell lies about Jesus.*

6. What did Jesus say when they lied about Him? *He didn't answer.*

7. What did Jesus answer when He was asked if He was the Sent One of God and the Son of God? *He said that He was and that, sometime in the future, the Jewish leaders would see Jesus sitting at God's right hand and coming back to earth again, showing everyone that He was equal to God.*

8. Why did the high priest and the Jewish leaders say that Jesus must be killed? *They said He had blasphemed, that is, He had spoken against God, because, although Jesus, according to them, was only a man, He had claimed to be God.*

9. What things did they do to Jesus which were written beforehand by the prophets? *They punched Him and spat on Him.*

10. What other things did they do to Jesus before they crucified Him?

    a. *They put a purple robe on Him.*

    b. *They put a crown of thorns on His head.*

    c. *They hit Him on the head with a stick.*

    d. *They mocked Him by pretending to worship Him.*

11. Of what does the crown of thorns remind us? *It reminds us of the curse which God put on the earth because of Adam's sin.*

| Scripture Reference | | Teacher's Notes |

LESSON 48: Jesus Was Crucified and Buried

OVERVIEW

This lesson presents the death of Jesus Christ as the only payment for sin. It emphasizes the detailed fulfillment of Old Testament prophecy.

The fact that Jesus paid for sin by death is brought out in the following points:
- Sin must be paid for.
- Jesus was sinless.
- Jesus was separated from God for our sins.
- Jesus did all that was necessary for our deliverance from Satan, sin, and death.

LESSON PREPARATION

This section is for you, the teacher.

The passages in the Scripture Reference column are for your own study in preparing for this lesson. Since they may contain concepts that run ahead of the lesson, they are not to be taught at this point.

Note: If you have not taught previously from this series of lessons, please read carefully the note to teachers in the front of this book.

Hebrews 9, 10

SCRIPTURE: Mark 15:20-46

LESSON GOALS:

- To present the death of the Lord Jesus as the only acceptable payment for sin.

THIS LESSON SHOULD HELP THE STUDENTS:

- To see that Jesus Christ died for their sins and that they can be saved only by believing in Him.

PERSPECTIVE FOR THE TEACHER:

Of all the facts of history, this is the greatest: Jesus Christ died for sinners, was buried, and rose again. All the previous lessons, like all the Scriptures, point to this one event.

Two thousand years later, we have the privilege of telling men and women, boys and girls that their own sins were indeed fully paid for by Jesus Christ on the Cross.

There is no other message than this to save sinners. Nothing can be added. Nothing can be taken away. This is the truth.

Pray for your students that they may hear and believe.

VISUALS:

- Chronological Picture No. 18, "Abraham Offers Isaac"
- Chronological Picture No. 37, "The Serpent on the Pole"
- Chronological Picture No. 60, "John the Baptist Tells the People that Jesus Is the Lamb of God"
- Chronological Picture No. 87, "The Crucifixion"
- Prophecy Chart
- Chronological Map 3
- Visuals showing the separation between God and man and that Jesus Christ paid completely for man's sins so that man could again come to God (illustrated in lesson)

551

Teacher's Notes

Lesson 48: Jesus Was Crucified and Buried

Scripture Reference

ON TEACHING THIS LESSON:

These lessons are designed to **teach unbelievers.** You are carefully laying a scriptural foundation on which you are presenting the Gospel. If your class contains believers, teach with the goal of giving them an understanding of the basis for their faith and **with the goal of enabling them to teach the same material to unbelievers.**

DON'T COMPLICATE THE MESSAGE!

As you teach, keep in mind that this is a directed study—not an exhaustive survey of the Bible and not an unlimited group discussion. Keep your lesson on track and moving ahead by limiting and directing any discussion.

Carefully follow the outline. Emphasize the doctrinal themes.

LESSON FORMAT: The **center column** below contains the lesson material to be taught to the students. The **bold outline headings** are only for reference and need not be spoken, as they are incorporated into the outlined material that follows. The material in the **side columns** is for the teacher's own reference and is not intended to be included in the lesson.

TO BE TAUGHT TO THE STUDENTS
(Center Column Only)

LESSON OUTLINE:

REVIEW questions from Lesson 47.

A. Introduction

Of all the events of history, the one we are going to study today is the most important.

Nothing else has ever or will ever affect the lives of men and women as this one event.

No one else but God knows what you are thinking at this moment.

This lesson is for you.

This lesson is for me.

This lesson is for the whole world.

Listen very carefully.

We are going to study now what Jesus did for us so that we can be fully accepted by God and never go to everlasting punishment.

B. Jesus was crucified.

 Theme: Man is a sinner. He needs God and is helpless to save himself.

 READ Mark 15:20-22.

Golgotha was just outside the walls of Jerusalem.

POINT TO JERUSALEM ON MAP 3.

 READ Mark 15:23.

Hebrews 13:11,12

552

Lesson 48: Jesus Was Crucified and Buried

This drink was prepared by women of Jerusalem as an act of mercy to help deaden the pain of those who were being crucified.

- Note:

  Myrrh was a sap from a low, scrubby tree.

 Theme: Jesus Christ is the only Saviour.

 READ Mark 15:24.

Nails were driven through Jesus' hands and feet into the wooden Cross.

The Cross was then placed in an upright position.

- Recall:

  Do you remember that Jesus told Nicodemus that, as Moses in the wilderness lifted up the serpent on a pole, even so Jesus, the Deliverer, had to be lifted up so that sinners could be saved from punishment? Jesus was nailed to the Cross and lifted up just as He said He would be.

Numbers 21:4-9
John 3:14

Suggested Visuals:

CHRONOLOGICAL PICTURE NO. 37, "THE SERPENT ON THE POLE"

CHRONOLOGICAL PICTURE NO. 87, "THE CRUCIFIXION"

Point to the details shown in Chronological Picture No. 87, "The Crucifixion," as you teach through the remainder of this lesson.

 Theme: God is everywhere all the time; He knows everything.

Nearly a thousand years before, God had guided King David to write that the Deliverer's hands and feet would be pierced.

- Note:

  As far as we know, crucifixion was not even practiced in David's time, which makes his prophecy even more amazing.

David also said that the Deliverer's clothes would become the prize in a gambling game.

Lesson 48: Jesus Was Crucified and Buried

Teacher's Notes		Scripture Reference
	Read Psalm 22:16. POINT TO THE PROPHECY CHART. Uncover "His hands and feet pierced," and write Mark 15:24 opposite Psalm 22:16. Uncover "His clothing gambled for," and write Mark 15:24 opposite Psalm 22:18. Read the prophecies and their fulfillment. Point out that these are the fulfillment of God's Word. - Archeological Notes: *Crucifixion was mentioned in early writings, but until 1968, no remains of a person crucified with nails had been found. Then in that year a tomb was discovered, dating to the first century A.D. In the tomb were the bones of a man who had died from crucifixion. The following is a quote from Dr. N. Haas of the Hebrew University and the Hadassah Medical School:*[1]	
[1] As quoted by Josh McDowell in *He Walked Among Us*. Here's Life Publishers, San Bernadino, CA, 1989, p. 223. ☐	"*Both the heel bones were found transfixed by a large iron nail. The shins were found intentionally broken. Death caused by crucifixion.*"	Genesis 3:15
	READ Mark 15:25,26. Usually a sign was put above the criminal to indicate what crime he had been found guilty of committing. But Jesus had committed no crime. Pilate could find nothing with which to charge Him. But he said that this nameplate had to be placed above Jesus' head. - Pilate did not believe that Jesus was the King of the Jews. - Pilate may have done it to mock the Jews and their desire to be liberated from the control of the Romans and to have their own king. The Jews did not want Pilate to put this title above Jesus' head where everyone could read it. - Consider: *The sign on the Cross would normally have listed the crime for which the person had been condemned. Jesus had not sinned—his sign or title read, "King of the Jews."* *But think about it. Jesus was dying for sins: my sins, your sins, and the sins of the whole world. You and I are the ones who deserved to be on that Cross. He was taking our punishment.* *Quietly, before God, think of what your sign would read. What are the sins that you know separate you from God?*[2]	Colossians 2:14 Matthew 27:24 Luke 23:4,13-15 John 19:6
[2] You are not asking the students to confess their sins to you. You are suggesting that, before God, they consider their sins and believe that Jesus Christ died for those very sins for their sakes. You may want to wait quietly for a moment and give your students time to think about this. Don't force this, just pause for a moment and allow the Holy Spirit to work as He wills. ☐	*Jesus was taking on Himself all the shame and the full punishment for every one of those sins as well as all the sins that we can't even remember committing. He was paying the full price for us: He was paying the death penalty—for me, for you.* READ Mark 15:27,28. Through Isaiah the prophet, God said that the Deliverer would die in the company of evil men. Read Isaiah 53:12.	

Lesson 48: Jesus Was Crucified and Buried

POINT TO THE PROPHECY CHART. Uncover "Will die with the wicked," and write Mark 15:27 opposite Isaiah 53:12. Read the prophecy and its fulfillment. Point out that this is the fulfillment of God's Word.

C. Jesus was mocked while He was on the Cross.

 Theme: Man is a sinner. He needs God and is helpless to save himself.

 Theme: God is everywhere all the time; He knows everything.

 READ Mark 15:29-32.

 Read John 2:18-21.

Even though they crucified Him, He planned to rise up again three days later.
- The Jews didn't understand that Jesus meant His body.
- They thought that He was talking about the temple in Jerusalem.

King David had written that the Deliverer's enemies would mock Him and laugh at His sufferings.

God knew exactly what was going to happen to His Son long before He came into the world.

 Read Psalm 22:6-8.

POINT TO THE PROPHECY CHART. Uncover "Mocked and insulted," and write Mark 15:29-32 opposite Psalm 22:6-8. Read the prophecy and its fulfillment. Point out that this is the fulfillment of God's Word.

D. Jesus paid for sin by death.

 Theme: Jesus Christ is the only Saviour.

We mentioned earlier that what we are studying today is the most important event in all history.

This is the event of which God's prophets spoke.

Jesus is the one of whom they spoke and wrote; He is the Deliverer — His very name means "God saves."

We said when we began that the Bible is God's letter to us.
- This is the heart of the letter.
- This is God's message to each one of us.
- This is the reason for the visit of God the Son to this earth.

Here is what God has done so that we can be **delivered forever** from Satan and sin and death:

1. Sin must be paid for.

 Theme: God is holy and righteous. He demands death as the payment for sin.

Teacher's Notes

Lesson 48: Jesus Was Crucified and Buried

Scripture Reference

God could never forgive us for our sin and accept us unless the punishment for our sin was completely paid.

- What is the punishment for sin? Death.
- This means not only physical death but separation from God in Hell.

Romans 6:23a

Therefore, the only way Jesus could deliver us was for Him to take our place before God and be punished for our sins.

2. Jesus was sinless.

 Theme: Jesus Christ is holy and righteous.

Jesus did not have any of His own sins for which He must die.

- Jesus was perfect.
- When Jesus was baptized by John, God the Father said from Heaven that Jesus was His well-beloved Son with whom He was fully pleased.

Matthew 3:17

Suggested Visual:

CHRONOLOGICAL PICTURE NO. 60, "JOHN THE BAPTIST TELLS THE PEOPLE THAT JESUS IS THE LAMB OF GOD"

Because Jesus was sinless, He was able to offer Himself to God as the offering for our sins.

II Corinthians 5:21

- Recall:

From the time that man sinned, God said that, whenever a person offered a lamb or other animals to God, the animal had to be without fault. It must not be sick or injured.

Suggested Visual:

CHRONOLOGICAL PICTURE NO. 18, "ABRAHAM OFFERS ISAAC"

Do you remember that, when Isaac lay bound on the altar and Abraham was just about to kill him, God told Abraham not to do it. Then Abraham looked up and saw a ram caught in a bush. Do you remember which part of the ram was caught in the bush? Yes, the ram was caught by its horns. God put the ram there so it could die in the place of Isaac. But why did God make sure that the ram was caught by the horns? Because if the ram had been injured, it

Genesis 22:13

Lesson 48: Jesus Was Crucified and Buried

Scripture Reference

Exodus 12:5

would not have been a suitable offering instead of Isaac. It would not have been acceptable to God.

God is perfect; therefore, any offering made to Him had to be without fault.

Because Jesus was without fault before God, He was able to offer Himself to God in our place.

Just as the ram died in place of Isaac, so Jesus came into the world to take our place before God and to die instead of us.

3. Jesus was separated from God for our sins.

 Theme: God is holy and righteous. He demands death as the payment for sin.

Consider Jesus' sufferings:
- He had been betrayed by His own disciple, falsely arrested, falsely accused, tried without a just cause—rejected by the very people who should have received Him as their King and Lord.
- He was mercilessly beaten, scourged, and crucified.
- Now He hung there on the Cross, exhausted, bleeding, in agony.

But **none of these things** moved Him so deeply as what He now faced to complete the punishment due for **OUR** sins.

 READ Mark 15:33.

Why was the light of the sun blotted out?

Why was there darkness for three hours?

It was because **God turned His back on Jesus.**

God turned away from Jesus and left His beloved Son, Jesus, completely alone.

 READ Mark 15:34.

Why did God do such a terrible thing to Jesus?
- Jesus had always obeyed God.
- Jesus had never done anything wrong.
- He had obeyed all of the laws of God.

Why did God leave Him like this?

Because God was punishing Jesus for my sins, for your sins, and for the sins of the whole world.

During this time on the Cross, Jesus was separated from God, His Father, as the punishment for our sins.

Jesus suffered the complete punishment for our sins so that God could freely (without any cost to us) forgive and accept as His children all those who agree with God and trust only in Jesus.

- Recall:

    In the beginning, God told Adam that, if he ate of the tree of the knowledge of good and evil, he would die. Adam would be separated from God who had given him life. This meant that Adam's body would die, and after death, he would be separated

Teacher's Notes

Lesson 48: Jesus Was Crucified and Buried

from God in the place of terrible punishment which God prepared for Satan and his angels. Sin must be paid for by separation from God.

Suggested Visual:

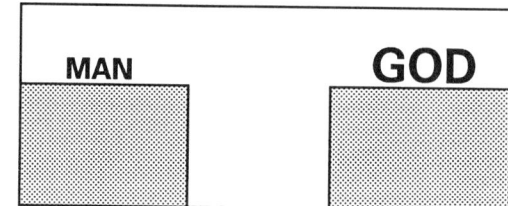

- Compare:

This is why Jesus had to be separated from God. It was the only way He could pay for our sins.

 READ Mark 15:34 again, then Mark 15:35,36.

The people around the Cross misunderstood what Jesus had said.

 READ Mark 15:37.

Jesus died and gave His life for us.

4. Jesus did all that was necessary for our deliverance from Satan, sin, and death.

 Theme: Jesus Christ is the only Saviour.

Mark tells us that Jesus cried with a loud voice and gave up His spirit, but Mark doesn't tell us what Jesus said.

But John, another of Jesus' disciples, wrote what He said.

 Read John 19:30.

"...It is finished...."

- Consider:
- What do you think Jesus meant?

   Did He mean that He was finished?

   No, He had said that He would rise again after three days.

- What then was finished?

The work that He came into the world to do was completely finished.

- Jesus came into the world to deliver sinners from Satan, sin, and death.
- He finished this work by being separated from God and by giving His blood and His life as the full payment for our sins.

 Theme: Man must have faith in order to please God and be saved.

Jesus paid to God all that was necessary for our sins.

All those who agree with God and trust in Jesus and His death for them are forgiven by God of all their sins.

God gives them the gift of everlasting life.

Lesson 48: Jesus Was Crucified and Buried

There is no longer any need for anyone to be separated from God. Jesus Christ did for us what we could not do ourselves to bring us to God.

Suggested Visual:

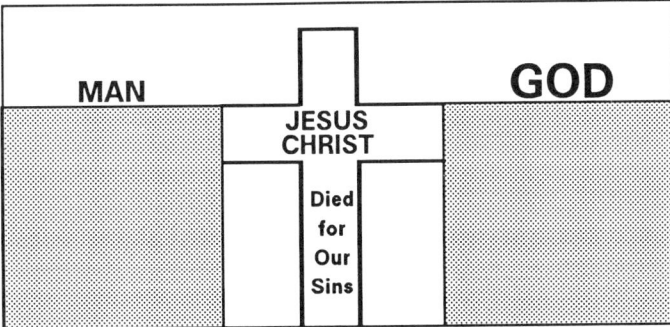

The work Jesus did for us by dying on the Cross for our sins is the only work that God will ever accept as payment for our sins.

Jesus was separated from God for our sakes so that through Him, we can again be in fellowship with God.

When be put our trust in what Jesus did for us on the Cross, we are reunited with God through Jesus Christ.

- Recall:

In the garden of Eden, God promised that He would send a Deliverer, and God kept His promise. Jesus finished the work which His Father had given Him to do for us.

Adam's sin separated all men from God.

But the death of Jesus Christ on the Cross reunites with God forever all those who put their faith in Christ.

Genesis 3:15

Romans 5:12-21

E. **The veil in the temple was ripped.**

 Theme: God is faithful; He never changes.

 READ Mark 15:38.

- Recall:

This thick curtain, or veil, had hung in front of the inner room in the tabernacle the Israelites built as God's house in the wilderness.

When the temple was built, this great curtain was hung in front of the inner room in the temple.

God had told the Jews to put this curtain in front of the inner room so they would never forget that, because of sin, they were shut out of God's presence.

Behind this curtain shone the Shekinah glory to show that God was there living with them.

Leviticus 16:12-16

This was the place where the high priest came every year to sprinkle the blood of animals.

Who do you think ripped this curtain from the top down to the bottom?

God Himself did!

But why did He do that?

Teacher's Notes

Lesson 48: Jesus Was Crucified and Buried

Scripture Reference

- God did it to show that He was fully satisfied with the payment that Jesus made to Him for sinners.
- There was no longer a need for animal sacrifices to be made.
- Compare:
- The high priest had entered the inner room every year to sprinkle the blood of animals before God.
- But the blood of animals never pleased God.
- The blood of animals could never pay for sin.
- But God forgave the sins of all who trusted in Him before Jesus died because He knew that His own Son would come and give His blood as a complete payment for all sin.

Hebrews 9:1-28; 10:1-18

When Jesus died, God ripped the curtain to show everyone that He was completely satisfied and that there was no more need to offer the blood of animals.

The way back to God was open because Jesus gave His blood as the complete payment for sin.

God has promised that all who agree with Him and trust only in Jesus and His payment for their sins will be fully accepted by God, and they will never go to Hell.

 Read John 3:16.

F. The centurion and the women at the Cross

 READ Mark 15:39.

A centurion was in charge of one hundred soldiers.

 READ Mark 15:40,41.

These were women who trusted in God's Word and had accepted that Jesus was the promised Saviour.

G. Jesus was buried.

 Theme: God is faithful; He never changes.

 READ Mark 15:42-46.

Even as Jesus was buried, prophecy was being fulfilled.
- Joseph of Arimathea was a rich man.
- Jesus was buried in the burial cave which belonged to Joseph.

 Read Isaiah 53:9.

POINT TO THE PROPHECY CHART. Uncover "Buried with the rich," and write Mark 15:43-46 opposite Isaiah 53:9. Read the prophecy and its fulfillment. Point out that this is the fulfillment of God's Word.

H. Conclusion

Consider Jesus Christ:
- He lived on earth without ever sinning.
- He completely fulfilled all of God's righteous laws.

Lesson 48: Jesus Was Crucified and Buried

Scripture Reference

- He endured the horrible punishment you and I deserve.
- On the Cross He was separated from God because **we** deserve to be separated from God forever.

It is finished—He died in our place.

- The full payment has been made.
- Nothing more needs to be done or can be done to pay for our sins.
- The veil was torn.
- The way is open to God through Jesus Christ.[3]

QUESTIONS:

1. Where was Jesus crucified? *On a hill outside of Jerusalem.*

2. Why was Jesus crucified? *To die for our sins and the sins of the whole world.*

3. What did David write would happen to the hands and feet of the promised Deliverer? *They would be pierced. Nails were driven through His hands and feet.*

4. Why did it become very dark for three hours while Jesus was on the Cross? *It was God's sign that Jesus was taking the punishment for sin by being separated from God.*

5. What did Jesus mean when He said, "It is finished"? *Jesus meant that He had completed the work given to Him by His Father which was to bear the complete punishment for sinners to be delivered from the power of Satan, sin, and death.*

6. If Jesus didn't have any sin, why was He crucified? *He was dying for our sins.*

7. Why did God rip the curtain in the temple from top to bottom?

   a. *To show that He was fully satisfied with the payment which Jesus had made.*

   b. *To show that there was no more need for the high priest to take the blood of animals into the inner room of the temple.*

Teacher's Notes

[3] Be ready to personally talk with any of your students who seek further explanation or who express a desire to be saved or who want to give testimony to their faith in what Jesus has done for them.

Don't try to force their testimony; simply answer their questions and ask them what they believe. ☐

Teacher's Notes

OVERVIEW

This lesson presents the meaning of Christ's death in the light of five Old Testament passages. Man is shown as totally unable to save himself. Jesus Christ is presented as the only Saviour, the Saviour of all who acknowledge their sin and put their trust in His death for them.

Lesson 49: The Meaning of Christ's Death from the Old Testament

Scripture Reference

LESSON 49

The Meaning of Christ's Death from the Old Testament

LESSON PREPARATION
This section is for you, the teacher.

The passages in the Scripture Reference column are for your own study in preparing for this lesson. Since they may contain concepts that run ahead of the lesson, they are not to be taught at this point.

Note: If you have not taught previously from this series of lessons, please read carefully the note to teachers in the front of this book.

SCRIPTURE: Genesis 3:7,21; 4:1-5; 6:5,7-9,13,16; Exodus 12:5-7,27

LESSON GOALS:

- To present the meaning of the death of Jesus Christ in the light of Old Testament passages.
- To show that man is helpless to save himself.
- To show that salvation is by faith.

THIS LESSON SHOULD HELP THE STUDENTS:

- To better understand the meaning of Christ's death.
- To see their need to personally put their trust in the death of Jesus Christ as the only acceptable payment for their sins.

PERSPECTIVE FOR THE TEACHER:

Our society is in a headlong rush to find meaning and purpose in life. The usual begining and end of these pursuits is self: self-seeking, self-fulfillment, self-expression; possessions, position, recreation. Though there are pleasures in each of these things, there is no lasting fulfillment. People spend their lives looking for meaning without really understanding the basic issues.

How deeply this must grieve our God! From beginning to end in His Word He has clearly stated what we need to know: who He is, who we are, and that we are sinners, separated from Him, in desperate need of a Saviour—Jesus Christ—who has already paid the complete price to restore us to a right relationship with God.

Many people who **have** heard the Gospel have never seen Christ in the light of the whole Word of God. They have the answer to their need, but they have not fully understood their need, for they have not seen that God is holy and altogether righteous. They see salvation as a free gift, but they relate it to the receiver rather than the giver.

This is often the way people are taught initially, and they never seem to go beyond that stage. It is like an artist who paints with only one color when the whole palette is available, or like a musician who plays one note and never sounds a chord. The full meaning is missing.

This lesson gives us the opportunity to present the death of our Lord Jesus Christ in light of the Old Testament foundations which were laid by our Lord Himself. Our God delights to teach men to know Him. As you present this lesson, be in prayer for your students, remembering that the Holy Spirit is able to take these tremendous truths and give understanding to your students. *"And this is life eternal, that they might know thee the only true God, and Jesus Christ, whom thou hast sent"* (John 17:3).

Lesson 49: The Meaning of Christ's Death from the Old Testament

Scripture Reference

Teacher's Notes

VISUALS:

- Chronological Picture No. 6, "Fig Leaf Coverings"
- Chronological Picture No. 7, "Adam and Eve Driven from the Garden"
- Chronological Picture No. 8, "Cain and Abel Bring Offerings to God"
- Chronological Picture No. 10, "Noah's Ark"
- Chronological Picture No. 27, "Passover Blood Applied to the Doorposts"
- Chronological Picture No. 34, "The Tabernacle"
- Chronological Picture No. 35, "Components of the Tabernacle"
- Visuals, "To Be Accepted by God," and "Jesus—One Sacrifice for Sins Forever," (illustrated in the lesson) which may be done ahead or as the lesson is taught.

ON TEACHING THIS LESSON:

These lessons are designed to **teach unbelievers.** You are carefully laying a scriptural foundation on which you are presenting the Gospel. If your class contains believers, teach with the goal of giving them an understanding of the basis for their faith and **with the goal of enabling them to teach the same material to unbelievers.**

DON'T COMPLICATE THE MESSAGE!

As you teach, keep in mind that this is a directed study—not an exhaustive survey of the Bible and not an unlimited group discussion. Keep your lesson on track and moving ahead by limiting and directing any discussion.

Carefully follow the outline. Emphasize the doctrinal themes.

LESSON FORMAT: The **center column** below contains the lesson material to be taught to the students. The **bold outline headings** are only for reference and need not be spoken, as they are incorporated into the outlined material that follows. The material in the **side columns** is for the teacher's own reference and is not intended to be included in the lesson.

TO BE TAUGHT TO THE STUDENTS
(Center Column Only)

LESSON OUTLINE:

Review questions from Lesson 48.

A. Introduction

Have you ever thought of the Old Testament as a signpost?

God knows that everyone has been lost.

But He has made sure that the way back to Himself is well-marked.

The Old Testament is like God's signpost because a great many of the historical incidents recorded in the Old Testament pointed forward to the birth, death, burial, and resurrection of the Lord Jesus.

In our lesson today we will review some of these past events and see how they pointed forward to the Lord Jesus and His death for us on the Cross.

Lesson 49: The Meaning of Christ's Death from the Old Testament

B. God killed animals and made clothes from the skins for Adam and Eve.

 Theme: Man is a sinner. He needs God and is helpless to save himself.

 Theme: God is holy and righteous. He demands death as the payment for sin.

Do you remember what Adam and Eve did when they sinned and became aware they were naked?

They made coverings of leaves.

Suggested Visual:

CHRONOLOGICAL PICTURE NO. 6, "FIG LEAF COVERINGS"

 READ Genesis 3:7.

Did God accept the clothing they made?

No, God refused to accept what they made because He wanted to teach them that they couldn't do anything to make themselves acceptable to Him.

- Compare:

    This, too, is what God wants each one of us to realize.

    There is nothing we can do to make ourselves acceptable to God.

    Going to church, providing for our families, doing good deeds, giving to the needy, taking care of the environment—all of these are things we should do.

    But none of these things will make us acceptable to God.

Are you trying to do something to make yourself right before God?

If you are, you need to realize that what you are doing is no more acceptable to God than the clothes Adam and Eve made.

No matter how hard we try, we can never make ourselves fit for Heaven by the things we do.

 Theme: God is loving, merciful, and gracious.

 Theme: Jesus Christ is the only Saviour.

 READ Genesis 3:21.

God refused to accept the clothing Adam and Eve made.

Lesson 49: The Meaning of Christ's Death from the Old Testament

Suggested Visual:

CHRONOLOGICAL PICTURE NO. 7, "ADAM AND EVE DRIVEN FROM THE GARDEN"

Instead, He Himself killed animals and made clothes for them.

- Compare:

   Similarly, God refuses to accept anything we do to make ourselves pleasing to Him.

   But because He loved us, He sent His Son the Lord Jesus to die for us so we could be made acceptable to Him.

 Theme: Man must have faith in order to please God and be saved.

How then must a person respond to God in order to be accepted by Him?

Suggested Visual: ¹

> **TO BE ACCEPTED BY GOD, A PERSON MUST:**
>
> **Admit that he is a sinner and refuse to trust any longer in what he can do.**
>
> **Put his faith in the Lord Jesus Christ as his Saviour, believing that when Jesus died on the Cross and shed His blood, He made full payment with His life for our sins.**

If you put your faith only in Him, then, just as God put the clothes He had made on Adam and Eve, He will forgive your sins and accept you as perfectly right before Him.

God will accept you, not because you are sinless, but because the Lord Jesus who died in your place is sinless.

All who trust in Him alone are forever accepted by God because they are clothed, or covered, with the righteousness of the Lord Jesus.

C. God accepted Abel's offering but rejected Cain's.

 Theme: God is holy and righteous. He demands death as the payment for sin.

The next story we need to consider is the one about Cain and Abel, Adam and Eve's first two sons, who both brought offerings to the Lord.

Scripture Reference: Isaiah 61:10

Teacher's Notes:

¹Keep this graphic simple—just the words. You have been teaching salvation by God's grace through faith in Jesus Christ. Don't complicate it or pollute it with many "steps" or "things to do." ☐

Teacher's Notes

Lesson 49: The Meaning of Christ's Death from the Old Testament

Scripture Reference

Suggested Visual:

CHRONOLOGICAL PICTURE NO. 8. "CAIN AND ABEL BRING OFFERINGS TO GOD"

Whose offering did God accept? Abel's.

 READ Genesis 4:1-5.

Why did God reject Cain and the things he brought?

 Theme: Man must have faith in order to please God and be saved.

 Theme: Jesus Christ is the only Saviour.

God rejected Cain because he came to God in his own way, according to his own ideas, and not in the way God had commanded.

God had made it clear from the beginning that, whenever anyone came to worship Him, he must bring an animal, kill it, and allow its blood to run out.

God said to do this because He knew that one day His own Son would give His blood to pay for the sins of the world.

Abel was a sinner too, but he was accepted by God because he trusted in God to save him and brought the blood sacrifice God required.

The lamb that Abel killed and offered to God reminds us of the Lord Jesus.

Do you remember what John the Baptist said about the Lord when John saw Him walking toward him on the banks of the Jordan river?

 Read John 1:29.

God accepted Abel because he trusted in Him and brought the right offering.

In the same way, God will accept all those who put their faith in the Lord Jesus and His blood that He shed for the sins of everyone in the whole world.

D. God saved Noah and all in the ark.

 Theme: God is holy and righteous. He demands death as the payment for sin.

 Theme: Man must have faith in order to please God and be saved.

Lesson 49: The Meaning of Christ's Death from the Old Testament

Do you remember reading in the Bible about the way people were living in Noah's time, before the flood?

 READ Genesis 6:5.

Finally, because the people refused to listen to God's warning given through Noah, God said He was going to destroy the world by a flood.

 READ Genesis 6:7.

But did God intend to destroy Noah who, like Abel, knew he was a sinner and trusted in God to send a Deliverer?

 READ Genesis 6:8,9,13,14.

Do you remember how many doors God told Noah to make in the ark?

 Read Genesis 6:16.

Suggested Visual:

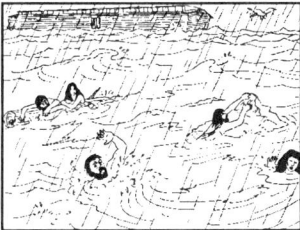

CHRONOLOGICAL PICTURE NO. 10, "NOAH'S ARK"

There was only one way they could enter the ark and be saved from God's judgment.
- Before the flood came, the animals and Noah and his family all entered by the one door, and God shut them in.
- Inside the ark, they were safe from God's punishment on the sinful world.

Theme: Jesus is the only Saviour.

Everyone outside died in the flood because they refused to believe God and enter the ark by the one door.
- That door reminds us of the Lord Jesus who is the only way to eternal life.
- When anyone believes that Jesus died for his sins and puts his trust only in Him, God forgives his sins and gives him eternal life.

Don't be foolish like the people in Noah's day who refused to enter the ark and be saved.

 Read John 14:6.

E. When God saw the blood, He passed over the Israelite homes.

Another incident recorded in the Old Testament that pointed forward to the Lord Jesus and His death for sinners is when God punished the Egyptians by killing the firstborn child in every family.

Teacher's Notes

Lesson 49: The Meaning of Christ's Death from the Old Testament

Scripture Reference

 Theme: God is loving, merciful, and gracious.

The Israelites would have lost their firstborn, too, but God made a way for them to escape.

1. A lamb without blemish

 Theme: God communicates with man.

- God commanded the Israelites to choose a lamb that was in perfect physical condition.

 READ Exodus 12:5.

 Theme: Jesus Christ is holy and righteous.

- These perfect lambs of the Israelites remind us of the Lord Jesus:
   He was born without sin.
   He lived a sinless life.
- Because Jesus was sinless, He could be accepted by God as the payment for our sin.
- Note:

    To hasten the death of a crucifixion victim, the guards would break the leg bones. This made it impossible for the person to use his legs to push up to help him breathe.

    But John 19:32,33 says that when the soldiers came to break the bones of Jesus and the two men who were crucified with him, Jesus was already dead. They did not break his bones.

    Do you remember that this was one of the requirements of the Passover lamb? The Israelites must not break its bones. Thus Jesus fulfilled every requirement of the perfect sacrifice for sin.

2. The lamb had to die.

 Theme: God is holy and righteous. He demands death as the payment for sin.

 Theme: Jesus Christ is the only Saviour.

- The Israelites had to keep the lamb until the time God had said they should kill it.

 READ Exodus 12:6.

- Compare:

    The lamb had to die and its blood had to be shed if the firstborn child was to be saved from death.

    In the same way, it was necessary for the Lord Jesus to give His blood as the payment for our sins.

    There was no other way we could be saved from God's judgment on our sins.

Lesson 49: The Meaning of Christ's Death from the Old Testament

3. The lamb's blood had to be placed on the top and sides of the door frame.

 Theme: Man must have faith in order to please God and be saved.

- Even though the Israelites killed the lamb and caught its blood in the basin as God had commanded them, the firstborn child **would still have died** unless they did the next thing God commanded them.

 READ Exodus 12:7.

Suggested Visual:

CHRONOLOGICAL PICTURE NO. 27, "PASSOVER BLOOD APPLIED TO THE DOORPOSTS"

- This teaches us that merely knowing that we are sinners and that the Lord Jesus died for our sins will not save us from God's terrible judgment.
- Compare:

   The Israelites had to put the blood of the lamb on the door frames of their houses to show God they were trusting in the blood to protect them from the angel of death.

   In the same way, we have to trust personally in the Lord Jesus and His death as the payment for our sins to God.

- We must believe that what the Lord Jesus did on the Cross was for us as individuals.

   Jesus died for me personally.

   Jesus died for **you** personally.

- **Only** in Jesus can we find forgiveness of our sins.

4. None of the Israelites' firstborn died.

 Theme: God is faithful; He never changes.

- Did the angel of death kill any firstborn child inside a house where the blood had been applied?

 READ Exodus 12:27.

- God always does what He says.
- Compare:

   He said He would pass over every house where He saw the blood, and He did.

Lesson 49: The Meaning of Christ's Death from the Old Testament

In the same way, you can be absolutely certain that, if you trust in the Lord Jesus and His death for you, you will never be punished for your sins.

- Because Jesus' blood paid for all your sins, you can be certain that God will never demand a second payment.
- All who trust only in Christ have everlasting life.

 Read John 3:16-18,36.

F. God covered the sins of Israel when the blood was placed on the mercy seat.

 Theme: God is holy and righteous. He demands death as the payment for sin.

 Theme: God is loving, merciful, and gracious.

- Recall:

After God delivered the Israelites from the Egyptians, He led them through the Red Sea and into the wilderness until they came to Mount Sinai.

Here at this mountain God gave them His commandments which showed them they were helpless sinners under the condemnation of death.

But because God is also loving, merciful, and gracious, He instructed Moses to have a tabernacle built where He would meet with His people and forgive their sins.

Suggested Visuals:

CHRONOLOGICAL PICTURE NO. 34, "THE TABERNACLE"

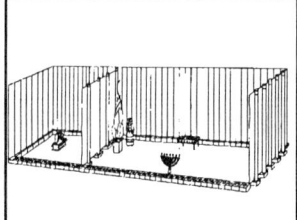

CHRONOLOGICAL PICTURE NO. 35, "COMPONENTS OF THE TABERNACLE"

POINT TO THE INNER ROOM, THE HOLY OF HOLIES.

As you continue to teach the lesson, point to the various details of the tabernacle.

Lesson 49: The Meaning of Christ's Death from the Old Testament

Scripture Reference

Hebrews 9:7; 10:2-4

Once a year the high priest was to enter the inner room of the tabernacle and sprinkle the blood of a lamb on the mercy seat between the two cherubim.

Year after year animals were sacrificed and their blood sprinkled on the mercy seat in the tabernacle, and later in the temple in Jerusalem.

But the blood of animals could never pay for sin.

Hebrews 10:1-10

These offerings only pointed forward to the Lord Jesus who was yet to come to provide the one complete sacrifice for sin by the giving of His own perfect life.

- Do you remember what God did in the temple when Jesus died?

 Read Mark 15:37,38.

- This is the curtain that hung in front of the place in the temple where the lamb's blood had been sprinkled year after year to cover the sins of Israel.
- Why did God tear it in two?²
- God wanted everyone to know that Jesus had paid the full price for sin.
    - There was no longer any need to offer the blood of animals.
    - The payment Jesus made was once for all.

 Theme: Man must have faith if he is to please God and be saved.

- How foolish the Jews were who refused to accept that Jesus was the Deliverer sent from God.
- How foolish they were not to believe that His blood had fully paid for all sin.
    - They probably sewed up the curtain in front of the holy of holies and continued to offer the blood of animals.
    - How foolish it would have been for them to do that when the price for the forgiveness of all sins had been paid by Jesus once for all.
- Compare:

    But aren't people today just as foolish when they try to save themselves by the things they do instead of simply trusting in what Jesus has already done?

- What are you going to do?
- Are you going to trust in what you do or in what Jesus has done for you on the Cross?

Suggested Visual:

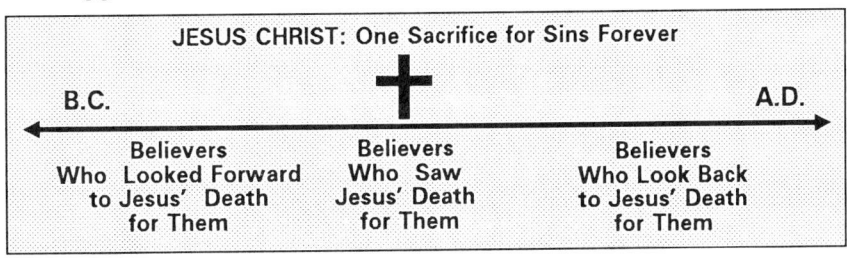

Teacher's Notes

²Give the students time to answer this question if they can.

Lesson 49: The Meaning of Christ's Death from the Old Testament

Teacher's Notes

Scripture Reference

- Jesus Christ made the full payment for all.

The sins of all who believed in the coming Deliverer in Old Testament times, men like Abraham, Moses, and David, were fully forgiven because Jesus died for them on the Cross also.

All who lived in Jesus' time and trusted in Him — people such as Matthew, Mark, Luke, and John — were also forgiven by God and accepted by Him because of the righteousness of the Lord Jesus.

And since that time, millions of people from countries all over the world have looked back to what the Lord Jesus did when He died for them, and they have trusted in Him as their Saviour.

G. Conclusion

- Testimony:[3]

I am one who has agreed with God that I am a sinner and have trusted in the Lord Jesus and His death for me. I know I have eternal life because Jesus paid for all my sin. But it was not only for me that Jesus died; it was for you too. So, if you trust only in Him and accept His death as the payment for your sin, God will forgive you and give you everlasting life, just as He did me.

[3] This is a sample of a very simple testimony; it must, however, be **your** testimony — not just something read to the students. They need to know that **you** believe what you are saying.

Some students may express their desire to put their trust in Jesus Christ and His death for them. Explain to those who seem ready that Jesus not only died but was raised from the dead on their behalf. ☐

QUESTIONS:

1. Why can the Old Testament be likened to a signpost? *Because a great many of the historical incidents recorded in the Old Testament pointed forward to the birth, death, burial, and resurrection of the Lord Jesus.*

2. Do you remember what Adam and Eve did when they sinned and realized they were naked? *They made themselves coverings of leaves. Read Genesis 3:7.*

3. What did God do when He saw the clothing Adam and Eve had made? *He refused to accept what they had made, and He Himself killed animals, made clothes from their skins, and put them on Adam and Eve.*

4. How does this incident remind you of what God has done for us? *Just as God provided clothes for Adam and Eve, so He sent His Son, the Lord Jesus, to die for us so we could be made acceptable to God in the righteousness of the Lord Jesus.*

5. How then can you be made acceptable to God?

    a. *Admit that I am a helpless sinner and refuse to trust any longer in what I can do to make myself good enough for God.*

    b. *Put my faith in the Lord Jesus and His blood which He gave as the full payment to God for my sins.*

6. Why did God reject Cain and the things he brought? *Because he came to God in his own way, according to his own ideas, and not in the way God had commanded.*

7. What did John the Baptist say about the Lord when He saw Him walking towards him on the banks of the Jordan river? *Read John 1:29.*

8. How many doors did God tell Noah to make in the ark? *Read Genesis 6:16.*

Lesson 49: The Meaning of Christ's Death from the Old Testament

9. How does the one door into the ark point forward to the Lord Jesus? *Just as the one door into the ark was the only way to escape death, so the Lord Jesus is the only door to everlasting life.*

10. What sort of lamb did God command the Israelites to choose so their firstborn child would be saved from death? *A lamb that was in perfect physical condition.*

11. How does the perfect lamb remind us of the Lord Jesus? *He was born without any sin and lived a sinless life, so He could be accepted by God as the payment for our sin.*

12. Could the firstborn children of the Israelites have been saved if the lambs were not killed? *No.*

13. Was there any way we could have been saved from God's punishment for our sins if Jesus had not died for us? *No. It was necessary for the Lord Jesus to give His blood as the payment for our sins.*

14. After an Israelite had killed a perfect lamb and caught its blood in a basin, was there anything else he had to do to ensure that his firstborn child would not die? *Yes. He had to wipe the blood on the top and sides of the door frames of his house.*

15. What does this remind us that we, too, must do if we are to be saved from the punishment we deserve for our sins? *We must believe that what the Lord Jesus did on the Cross was for us individually, and we must trust only in Him for the forgiveness of our sins.*

16. Did the angel of death kill any firstborn child that stayed inside a house where the blood had been applied? *No.*

17. Why is it now totally unnecessary to offer any sacrifice for sin? *Because Jesus paid the full price for sin.*

Teacher's Notes

Lesson 50: Jesus' Resurrection and Ascension

Scripture Reference

OVERVIEW

This lesson covers the events of the empty tomb, Jesus' appearances to His disciples, His instructions to His followers, His ascension into Heaven, and His promised return.

Emphasis is placed on the necessity of putting one's faith in Jesus Christ as Saviour.

He will return, not to save but to judge unbelievers.

Jesus Was Raised from the Dead, Appeared to His Disciples, Returned to Heaven, and Promised to Come Again

LESSON PREPARATION
This section is for you, the teacher.

The passages in the Scripture Reference column are for your own study in preparing for this lesson. Since they may contain concepts that run ahead of the lesson, they are not to be taught at this point.

Note: If you have not taught previously from this series of lessons, please read carefully the note to teachers in the front of this book.

SCRIPTURE: Mark 14:61,62; Luke 24:1-32,35-48; Acts 1:9-11

LESSON GOALS:

- To present Jesus' resurrection, His ascension, and His promise to come again.

THIS LESSON SHOULD HELP THE STUDENT:

- To see that Jesus Christ died for their sins and that they can be saved only by believing in Him.

PERSPECTIVE FOR THE TEACHER:

He is risen! Jesus Christ triumphed over sin, Satan, and death! Can there be a more joyful message?

This Lamb, unlike the millions slaughtered before His coming, died, was buried, and **rose again**—the complete and only payment for sins.

Though He took upon Himself the punishment for every sin of mankind, death could not hold Him. Nor shall death hold those who believe in Him, for He purchased eternal, unending life for all who put their trust in Him.

We live in a day of self-seeking—seeking after pleasure, prestige, self-fulfillment, wealth, etc. People seek after things that will pass away; people seek after things that will pamper bodies of flesh—the very things that are destined to die because of sin.

How much better it is for us to seek after the things of Jesus Christ—eternal riches, purchased for us by His own shed blood. How much better it is for us to spend our short lives in these dying bodies telling others, men, women, and children, about this wonderful, eternal Saviour and Lord, Jesus Christ!

We are part of the story of Jesus Christ; we are part of His Bride, His Church; we are the ones to whom He has committed His Gospel; we have been commissioned to share the truth of Jesus Christ with others, that together we may share eternity in His Presence. What a privilege we have to tell others of this wonderful Jesus who suffered, bled, died, was buried, and rose again on our behalf—this Jesus who is **coming again!**

May we teach this lesson in full conviction that the truth of the Gospel is more important than anything else in the whole world! **He is risen, and He is coming again!**

VISUALS:

- Chronological Picture No. 88, "The Resurrection"

Lesson 50: Jesus' Resurrection and Ascension

Scripture Reference

- Chronological Picture No. 90, "The Ascension"
- Prophecy Chart
- If possible, find a photo of a first-century tomb with the circular stone door. (You might look in a Bible handbook or Bible encyclopedia.)

Teacher's Notes

ON TEACHING THIS LESSON:

These lessons are designed to **teach unbelievers.** You are carefully laying a scriptural foundation on which you are presenting the Gospel. If your class contains believers, teach with the goal of giving them an understanding of the basis for their faith and **with the goal of enabling them to teach the same material to unbelievers.**

DON'T COMPLICATE THE MESSAGE!

As you teach, keep in mind that this is a directed study—not an exhaustive survey of the Bible and not an unlimited group discussion. Keep your lesson on track and moving ahead by limiting and directing any discussion.

Carefully follow the outline. Emphasize the doctrinal themes.

LESSON FORMAT: The **center column** below contains the lesson material to be taught to the students. The **bold outline headings** are only for reference and need not be spoken, as they are incorporated into the outlined material that follows. The material in the **side columns** is for the teacher's own reference and is not intended to be included in the lesson.

TO BE TAUGHT TO THE STUDENTS
(Center Column Only)

LESSON OUTLINE:

REVIEW questions from Lesson 49.

A. Introduction

When we began to study the Bible, we talked about the fact that the Bible is a true history.

Of all history, Jesus Christ is the central figure.

His story is true.

We are not studying about another religious leader; we are studying the true story of God the Son, the Almighty God who came to earth to be our Saviour.

B. The women came to the tomb.

Jesus was dead and buried in the tomb for three days and three nights.[1]

At the end of this time, on the morning of the first day of the week, some of the women who had believed in Jesus, and had been present when Jesus was buried, returned to the burial cave.

 READ Luke 24:1.

It was the custom of the Jews to put fragrant spices on the bodies of the dead before they were buried.

[1] A student may ask how the three days and three nights are calculated. You might tell him that though we will not take the time to study it, the Jewish way of telling time makes this statement more understandable. He may want to look this up on his own in a good Bible commentary. ☐

Teacher's Notes

Lesson 50: Jesus' Resurrection and Ascension

Scripture Reference

But Jesus had been hurriedly buried.
- The Jewish people were in the midst of their Passover commemoration.
- They hadn't had time to put the ointments on His body.
- The next day was their Sabbath when they weren't allowed to do any work.
- So they waited until the first day of the week to come and anoint His body with the spices.

These women came early on Sunday morning to anoint the body of Jesus.
They expected to find His body still in the tomb.

 Theme: God is all-powerful.

But what a shock they received!

 READ Luke 24:2.

The women didn't know that God had sent His angel to roll the heavy stone away from the entrance to the grave where the body of Jesus had been buried.

Matthew 28:1-4

- Archeological Note:

  Still visible today in the area of Jerusalem are tombs which date back to the time of Jesus. Some of these tombs, cut into caves in the rock, have a great circular rock door, set in a groove so the rock can be rolled across the entrance, just as described in this passage of the Bible.

If you have a picture of an actual first-century Jerusalem tomb, show this to the students, reminding them that archeological discoveries agree in minute detail with God's Word.

C. The angels' message

 READ Luke 24:3,4.

Suggested Visual:

CHRONOLOGICAL PICTURE NO. 88, "THE RESURRECTION"

The body of Jesus was not in the tomb!
And, to add to their shock, they were greeted by two angels!
Listen to what the angels told them.

 Theme: Jesus Christ is God.

 Theme: God is faithful; He never changes.

 READ Luke 24:5-7.

Lesson 50: Jesus' Resurrection and Ascension

Scripture Reference

Teacher's Notes

Jesus had risen from the dead, just as He said He would!

Jesus is God.

- He came down to earth and became a man to deliver us from Satan, sin, and death.
- Jesus knew before He left Heaven that He must give His life for our deliverance.
- He also knew that He would rise again and that never again would He die.

 Read Psalm 16:10.

POINT TO THE PROPHECY CHART. Uncover "Will rise again," and write Luke 24:6 opposite Psalm 16:10. Read the prophecy and its fulfillment. Point out that this is the fulfillment of God's Word.

 READ Luke 24:8-12.

All of His followers should have been waiting for Him and expecting Him to rise from the dead because He had told them many times before He died that He would rise on the third day.

- Either they didn't understand or remember what He had said, or else they just didn't believe that it was possible that He would come out of the grave alive.
- But regardless of how impossible it may seem, God always does what He promises.

D. Jesus is the Son of God.

 Theme: Jesus Christ is God.

Romans 1:4; 10:9

We are sure that Jesus is the Son of God and the promised Deliverer because God raised Jesus from the dead.

- The Jewish leaders crucified Jesus because He claimed to be the Son of God and the Deliverer.
- But God raised Jesus from the dead so that everyone would know that Jesus was who He claimed to be.

E. God is satisfied with Jesus' payment.

 Theme: God is holy and righteous. He demands death as the payment for sin.

 Theme: God is faithful; He never changes.

We know that God was fully satisfied with the payment which Jesus made for our sins.

- Recall:

  Do you remember that just before Jesus died, He called out, "It is finished?"

  God then ripped the curtain in the temple from the top to the bottom.

  God did this to show that the way back to Him was now open, for the complete payment for sin had been made by Jesus' blood.

There is something else that assures us that God was completely satisfied with the payment for our sins which Jesus made with His blood.

- God raised Jesus up from the dead.
- God would not have raised Jesus if God had not been fully satisfied with the payment which Jesus had made.
- Compare:

If a man is put into prison by a judge, he must stay there until he is released. If he breaks out of prison, then the police will recapture him and put him back. But if the man stays in prison and finishes the time to which he was sentenced by the judge, he has no need to be afraid when he is released. The police may see him after he has been released, but they will not arrest him and put him back in prison. He has been released because he has taken the full punishment for his crime.

Jesus didn't have any sin of His own, but He accepted the responsibility of paying the complete price for our sins. The complete price for our sins had to be paid if we were to be accepted by God. Jesus took our place before God, the Judge, and God punished Jesus instead of us.

Now, how do we know that Jesus paid the full price for our sins and that God the Judge is completely satisfied? *(Romans 4:25)*

- God showed us that there is no more to pay by releasing Jesus from death and raising Him back to life.
- If God, the Judge, had not been satisfied, He would not have released Jesus from death.

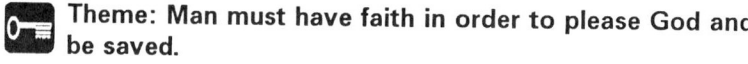

Theme: Man must have faith in order to please God and be saved.

So how can you be delivered from Satan, sin, and everlasting separation from God?

You must put your complete trust in the Lord Jesus, believing that He gave His blood as the full payment for your sins and rose again from the dead to give you eternal life.

F. Jesus appeared to some of His followers.

Theme: Man must have faith in order to please God and be saved.

READ Luke 24:13-24.

Even though Jesus was there with them, they did not recognize Him.

The Bible does not tell us why they didn't; we could only guess.

G. Using the words of the prophets in the Old Testament, Jesus taught about Himself.

Then Jesus taught them, just as we have been doing, referring to the Old Testament prophecies about Himself.

READ Luke 24:25-27.

Lesson 50: Jesus' Resurrection and Ascension

Even after that, they still didn't realize that it was Jesus talking to them.

H. Jesus' followers recognize the risen Christ.

 READ Luke 24:28-32.

Many times before they had sat together and watched their Teacher and Lord break the bread!

Now, as He again broke the bread, they suddenly realized that it was Jesus!

Later, when the disciples were gathered together, He appeared to them again.

 READ Luke 24:35-44.

I. Jesus' last words to His disciples

 Theme: God is loving, merciful, and gracious.

 Theme: Jesus Christ is the only Saviour.

 READ Luke 24:45-48.

This was Jesus' command, not only to His original disciples, but also to all those who believe in Him and accept His payment for them.

- Jesus died for all people, so God wants everyone to know that they can be delivered from Satan, sin, and death.
- God doesn't want anyone to suffer everlasting punishment.

II Peter 3:9

 Read John 3:16.

This is why we have studied the Bible together—so we can hear and understand and believe this wonderful Good News and be able to share it with others.

- This is God's message for you and for me.
- He wants us to believe what He has done for us in Jesus Christ so we will be accepted by Him and be able to live with Him forever.

J. We must believe the Word of God.

 Theme: Man must have faith in order to please God and be saved.

- Testimony:

  I have not seen Jesus with my eyes, but I believe that Jesus came into the world and that He died for our sins and rose again on the third day. I know this and believe it because God has written it in the Bible. I have agreed with God that I am a helpless sinner, and I have trusted in Jesus. His payment for me by His death is the only thing that I trust in for my acceptance before God.

It is important that you believe this message which God has written in His Word.

- Recall:

  Do you remember that, before Jesus died, He told about a rich man and a poor man called Lazarus? Jesus said that both of these men died. Lazarus was accepted by God, but God sent the rich man into everlasting punishment.

Jesus said that the rich man was in terrible suffering and that he asked Abraham to send Lazarus back to earth to warn his brothers so that they would not go to everlasting punishment. But Abraham told the rich man that his brothers had the writings of God's prophets and that they are responsible to believe them.

- Compare:

That is also what God expects of us.

Although we haven't seen Jesus with our eyes, we have the message of the Bible.

God says that we must believe this Good News that Jesus is the Deliverer who died for our sins, was buried, and rose again from the dead.

- By believing, we, too, can know that our sins are forgiven by God and that God will accept us.
- If you agree with what God has written in His Word and trust only in Jesus and His payment for your sins, then God forgives all of your sin, and He accepts you and gives you the gift of everlasting life.

K. Jesus ascended into Heaven.

Theme: God is faithful; He never changes.

After Jesus commanded His disciples to take this Good News to every person, He left them and returned to His Father in Heaven.

 READ Acts 1:9.

Suggested Visual:

CHRONOLOGICAL PICTURE NO. 90, "THE ASCENSION"

 Read Psalm 68:18.

POINT TO THE PROPHECY CHART. Uncover "Will go back to Heaven" and write Acts 1:9 opposite Psalm 68:18. Read the reference and the fulfillment. Point out that this is the fulfillment of God's Word.

L. Jesus will come again.

 READ Acts 1:10.

These were two of God's angels.

Lesson 50: Jesus' Resurrection and Ascension

 Theme: Jesus Christ is God.

 Theme: God is holy and righteous. He demands death as the payment for sin.

 READ Acts 1:11.

Jesus is coming back to this earth again, but when He comes, it will not be to deliver sinners from Satan, sin, and death — Jesus has completed that work.

God now commands everyone to repent, that is, agree with God that they are helpless sinners deserving His punishment, and to trust only in the payment which Jesus has made for them.

Acts 17:30,31

The next time Jesus comes, it will be as the great almighty judge of the whole earth.

This is what He told the leaders of the Jews before they had Him crucified.

 READ Mark 14:61,62.

When Jesus comes again as the almighty judge, all those who have not repented and trusted in Jesus and His payment for them will be thrown, along with Satan and all his angels, into the everlasting fire.

 Read Revelation 20:15.

M. Conclusion

God's message to us is very clear.

All of Jesus' disciples (with the exception of Judas, who betrayed Him for thirty pieces of silver) believed in Jesus.

They knew He was the one whom God had promised to send.

They saw His miracles; they saw Him die; they saw Him alive again; they saw Him go up into the clouds.

The disciples went out and told others about Jesus, and many thousands believed their message.

But others opposed them just as Jesus had been opposed.

Historians have recorded that all of Jesus' disciples died after being punished by men for their faith in Christ.

Some of the disciples were tortured; some were crucified; one died in prison.

Would these men have given their lives for a lie? No.

They died for what they had seen to be true.

We can rest our faith firmly in God's Word, because it is true.

Read John 3:16 again.

Teacher's Notes

Lesson 50: Jesus' Resurrection and Ascension

Scripture Reference

QUESTIONS:

1. What did the women find on the morning of the first day of the week when they went to the cave where Jesus was buried? *The stone had been rolled away from the door of the tomb.*

2. What had happened prior to the arrival of the women at the tomb? *There had been a great earthquake, and God had sent His angel to roll away the stone from the door.*

3. What did the women see when they entered the tomb?

    a. *They saw that the body of Jesus was gone.*
    b. *They saw two angels of God.*

4. What does the resurrection of Jesus show us? *That Jesus was the Son of God and the Deliverer just as He claimed to be. If He were not the Son of God and the Deliverer, then God would not have raised Him from the dead.*

5. How can we be forgiven by God and receive the gift of everlasting life which Jesus bought for us with His blood? *By agreeing with God that we are helpless sinners and trusting only in Jesus who died as the payment for our sins and rose from the dead to give us eternal life.*

6. What did Mary Magdalene and other believers tell the disciples? *They told them that they had seen Jesus, for He had risen from the dead and had appeared to them.*

7. Did the disciples believe Mary Magdalene and the other believers who had seen Jesus? *No.*

8. Should they have been surprised to hear that Jesus had risen from the dead? *No, Jesus had told them this many times before He was crucified.*

9. Why did Jesus tell His disciples to go into all the world? *So all people could hear and believe in Jesus and His death, burial, and resurrection for them.*

10. Will Jesus ever return to this earth? *Yes, Jesus will come back again.*

11. When Jesus comes back to this world again, what will He do? *He will judge all those who refused to trust in Him as their Saviour, and He will throw them, along with Satan and all his angels, into the Lake of Fire to be punished forever and ever.*